FINANCIAL REPORTING AND ANALYSIS

CFA Institute

WILEY

ISBN 978-1-937537-62-3 (paper)
ISBN 978-1-937537-83-8 (ebk)

10 9 8 7 6 5 4 3 2 1

Please visit our website at
www.WileyGlobalFinance.com.

CONTENTS

Financial Reporting and Analysis

◙ indicates an optional segment

◙ indicates an optional segment

Contents

◙ indicates an optional segment

Contents

◙ indicates an optional segment

◙ indicates an optional segment

◙ indicates an optional segment

◙ indicates an optional segment

How to Use the CFA Program Curriculum

Congratulations on your decision to enter the Chartered Financial Analyst (CFA®) Program. This exciting and rewarding program of study reflects your desire to become a serious investment professional. You are embarking on a program noted for its high ethical standards and the breadth of knowledge, skills, and abilities it develops. Your commitment to the CFA Program should be educationally and professionally rewarding.

The credential you seek is respected around the world as a mark of accomplishment and dedication. Each level of the program represents a distinct achievement in professional development. Successful completion of the program is rewarded with membership in a prestigious global community of investment professionals. CFA charterholders are dedicated to life-long learning and maintaining currency with the ever-changing dynamics of a challenging profession. The CFA Program represents the first step towards a career-long commitment to professional education.

The CFA examination measures your mastery of the core skills required to succeed as an investment professional. These core skills are the basis for the Candidate Body of Knowledge (CBOK™). The CBOK consists of four components:

■ A broad topic outline that lists the major top-level topic areas (CBOK Topic Outline)

■ Topic area weights that indicate the relative exam weightings of the top-level topic areas

■ Learning outcome statements (LOS) that advise candidates about the specific knowledge, skills, and abilities they should acquire from readings covering a topic area (LOS are provided in candidate study sessions and at the beginning of each reading)

■ The CFA Program curriculum, readings, and end-of-reading questions, which candidates receive upon exam registration

Therefore, the key to your success on the CFA exam is studying and understanding the CBOK™. The following sections provide background on the CBOK, the organization of the curriculum, and tips for developing an effective study program.

CURRICULUM DEVELOPMENT PROCESS

The CFA Program is grounded in the practice of the investment profession. Using the Global Body of Investment Knowledge (GBIK) collaborative website, CFA Institute performs a continuous practice analysis with investment professionals around the world to determine the knowledge, skills, and abilities (competencies) that are relevant to the profession. Regional expert panels and targeted surveys are conducted annually to verify and reinforce the continuous feedback from the GBIK collaborative website. The practice analysis process ultimately defines the CBOK. The CBOK contains the competencies that are generally accepted and applied by investment professionals. These competencies are used in practice in a generalist context and are expected to be demonstrated by a recently qualified CFA charterholder.

A committee consisting of practicing charterholders, in conjunction with CFA Institute staff, designs the CFA Program curriculum in order to deliver the CBOK to candidates. The examinations, also written by practicing charterholders, are designed to allow you to demonstrate your mastery of the CBOK as set forth in the CFA Program curriculum. As you structure your personal study program, you should emphasize mastery of the CBOK and the practical application of that knowledge. For more information on the practice analysis, CBOK, and development of the CFA Program curriculum, please visit www.cfainstitute.org.

ORGANIZATION OF THE CURRICULUM

The Level I CFA Program curriculum is organized into 10 topic areas. Each topic area begins with a brief statement of the material and the depth of knowledge expected.

Each topic area is then divided into one or more study sessions. These study sessions—18 sessions in the Level I curriculum—should form the basic structure of your reading and preparation.

Each study session includes a statement of its structure and objective, and is further divided into specific reading assignments. An outline illustrating the organization of these 18 study sessions can be found at the front of each volume.

The reading assignments are the basis for all examination questions, and are selected or developed specifically to teach the knowledge, skills, and abilities reflected in the CBOK. These readings are drawn from CFA Institute-commissioned content, textbook chapters, professional journal articles, research analyst reports, and cases. All readings include problems and solutions to help you understand and master the topic areas.

Reading-specific Learning Outcome Statements (LOS) are listed at the beginning of each reading. These LOS indicate what you should be able to accomplish after studying the reading. The LOS, the reading, and the end-of-reading questions are dependent on each other, with the reading and questions providing context for understanding the scope of the LOS.

You should use the LOS to guide and focus your study, as each examination question is based on an assigned reading and one or more LOS. The readings provide context for the LOS and enable you to apply a principle or concept in a variety of scenarios. The candidate is responsible for the entirety of all of the required material in a study session, the assigned readings as well as the end-of-reading questions and problems.

We encourage you to review the material on LOS (www.cfainstitute.org/programs/ cfaprogram/courseofstudy/Pages/study_sessions.aspx), including the descriptions of LOS "command words" (www.cfainstitute.org/programs/Documents/cfa_and_cipm_ los_command_words.pdf).

FEATURES OF THE CURRICULUM

OPTIONAL
SEGMENT

Required vs. Optional Segments   You should read all of an assigned reading. In some cases, however, we have reprinted an entire chapter or article and marked certain parts of the reading as "optional." The CFA examination is based only on the required segments, and the optional segments are included only when they might help you to better understand the required segments (by seeing the required material in its full context). When an optional segment begins, you will see text and a dashed vertical bar in the outside margin that will continue until the optional segment ends, accompanied by another icon. *Unless the material is specifically marked as optional, you should assume it is required.* You should rely on the required segments and the reading-specific LOS in preparing for the examination.

Problems/Solutions   *All questions and problems in the readings as well as their solutions (which are provided directly following the problems) are part of the curriculum and are required material for the exam.* When appropriate, we have included problems within and after the readings to demonstrate practical application and reinforce your understanding of the concepts presented. The questions and problems are designed to help you learn these concepts and may serve as a basis for exam questions. Many of these questions are adapted from past CFA examinations.

Margins   The wide margins in each volume provide space for your note-taking.

Six-Volume Structure   For portability of the curriculum, the material is spread over six volumes.

Glossary and Index   For your convenience, we have printed a comprehensive glossary in each volume. Throughout the curriculum, a **bolded** word in a reading denotes a term defined in the glossary. Each volume also contains an index specific to that volume; a combined index can be found on the CFA Institute website with the Level I study sessions.

Source Material   The authorship, publisher, and copyright owners are given for each reading for your reference. We recommend that you use this CFA Institute curriculum rather than the original source materials because the curriculum may include only selected pages from outside readings, updated sections within the readings, and contains problems and solutions tailored to the CFA Program.

LOS Self-Check   We have inserted checkboxes next to each LOS that you can use to track your progress in mastering the concepts in each reading.

DESIGNING YOUR PERSONAL STUDY PROGRAM

Create a Schedule   An orderly, systematic approach to examination preparation is critical. You should dedicate a consistent block of time every week to reading and studying. Complete all reading assignments and the associated problems and solutions in each study session. Review the LOS both before and after you study each reading to ensure that you have mastered the applicable content and can demonstrate the knowledge, skill, or ability described by the LOS and the assigned reading. Use the LOS self-check to track your progress and highlight areas of weakness for later review.

As you prepare for your exam, we will e-mail you important exam updates, testing policies, and study tips. Be sure to read these carefully. Curriculum errata are periodically updated and posted on the study session page at www.cfainstitute.org. You may also sign up for an RSS feed to alert you to the latest errata update.

Successful candidates report an average of over 300 hours preparing for each exam. Your preparation time will vary based on your prior education and experience. For each level of the curriculum, there are 18 study sessions, so a good plan is to devote 15–20 hours per week, for 18 weeks, to studying the material. Use the final four to six weeks before the exam to review what you've learned and practice with sample and mock exams. This recommendation, however, may underestimate the hours needed for appropriate examination preparation depending on your individual circumstances, relevant experience, and academic background. You will undoubtedly adjust your study time to conform to your own strengths and weaknesses, and your educational and professional background.

You will probably spend more time on some study sessions than on others, but on average you should plan on devoting 15-20 hours per study session. You should allow ample time for both in-depth study of all topic areas and additional concentration on those topic areas for which you feel least prepared.

CFA Institute Question Bank   The CFA Institute topic-based question bank is intended to assess your mastery of individual topic areas as you progress through your studies. After each test, you will receive immediate feedback noting the correct responses and indicating the relevant assigned reading so you can identify areas of weakness for further study. The topic tests reflect the question formats and level of difficulty of the actual CFA examinations. For more information on the topic tests, please visit www.cfainstitute.org.

CFA Institute Mock Examinations   In response to candidate requests, CFA Institute has developed mock examinations that mimic the actual CFA examinations not only in question format and level of difficulty, but also in length and topic weight. The three-hour mock exams simulate the morning and afternoon sessions of the actual CFA exam, and are intended to be taken after you complete your study of the full curriculum so you can test your understanding of the curriculum and your readiness for the exam. You will receive feedback at the end of the mock exam, noting the correct responses and indicating the relevant assigned readings so you can assess areas of weakness for further study during your review period. We recommend that you take mock exams during the final stages of your preparation for the actual CFA examination. For more information on the mock examinations, please visit www.cfainstitute.org.

Preparatory Providers   After you enroll in the CFA Program, you may receive numerous solicitations for preparatory courses and review materials. When considering a prep course, make sure the provider is in compliance with the CFA Institute Prep Provider Guidelines Program (www.cfainstitute.org/partners/examprep/Pages/cfa_prep_provider_guidelines.aspx). Just remember, there are no shortcuts to success on the CFA examinations; reading and studying the CFA curriculum is the key to success on the examination. The CFA examinations reference only the CFA Institute assigned curriculum—no preparatory course or review course materials are consulted or referenced.

SUMMARY

Every question on the CFA examination is based on the content contained in the required readings and on one or more LOS. Frequently, an examination question is based on a specific example highlighted within a reading or on a specific end-of-reading question and/or problem and its solution. To make effective use of the CFA Program curriculum, please remember these key points:

1   All pages printed in the curriculum are required reading for the examination except for occasional sections marked as optional. You may read optional pages as background, but you will not be tested on them.

2   All questions, problems, and their solutions—printed at the end of readings—are part of the curriculum and are required study material for the examination.

3   You should make appropriate use of the online sample/mock examinations and other resources available at www.cfainstitute.org.

4 You should schedule and commit sufficient study time to cover the 18 study sessions, review the materials, and take sample/mock examinations.

5 **Note:** Some of the concepts in the study sessions may be superseded by updated rulings and/or pronouncements issued after a reading was published. Candidates are expected to be familiar with the overall analytical framework contained in the assigned readings. Candidates are not responsible for changes that occur after the material was written.

FEEDBACK

At CFA Institute, we are committed to delivering a comprehensive and rigorous curriculum for the development of competent, ethically grounded investment professionals. We rely on candidate and member feedback as we work to incorporate content, design, and packaging improvements. You can be assured that we will continue to listen to your suggestions. Please send any comments or feedback to info@cfainstitute.org. Ongoing improvements in the curriculum will help you prepare for success on the upcoming examinations, and for a lifetime of learning as a serious investment professional.

Financial Reporting and Analysis

STUDY SESSIONS

TOPIC LEVEL LEARNING OUTCOME

The candidate should be able to demonstrate a thorough knowledge of financial reporting procedures and the standards that govern financial reporting disclosure. Emphasis is on basic financial statements and how alternative accounting methods affect those statements and the analysis of financial statements.

Note: In 2009, the U.S. Financial Accounting Standards Board (FASB) released the FASB Accounting Standards Codification™. The Codification is the single source of authoritative nongovernmental U.S. generally accepted accounting principles (U.S. GAAP) effective for period endings after 15 September 2009. The Codification supersedes all previous U.S. GAAP standards. We have attempted to update the readings to reference or cross-reference the Codification as appropriate. Candidates are responsible for the content of accounting standards as addressed in the readings, not for the actual reference numbers.

Financial Reporting and Analysis

An Introduction

The readings in this study session describe the general principles of financial reporting, underscoring the critical role of the analysis of financial reports in investment decision making.

The first reading introduces the range of information that an analyst may use in analyzing the financial performance of a company, including the principal financial statements (the income statement, balance sheet, cash flow statement, and statement of changes in owners' equity), notes to those statements, and management's discussion and analysis of results. A general framework for addressing most financial statement analysis tasks is also presented.

A company's financial statements are the end-products of a process for recording the business transactions of the company. The second reading illustrates this process, introducing such basic concepts as the accounting equation and accounting accruals.

The presentation of financial information to the public by a company must conform to applicable financial reporting standards based on factors such as the jurisdiction in which the information is released. The final reading in this study session explores the roles of financial reporting standard-setting bodies and regulatory authorities. The International Accounting Standards Board's conceptual framework and the movement towards global convergence of financial reporting standards are also described.

Note: New rulings and/or pronouncements issued after the publication of the readings in financial reporting and analysis may cause some of the information in these readings to become dated. Candidates are expected to be familiar with the overall analytical framework contained in the study session readings, as well as the implications of alternative accounting methods for financial analysis and valuation, as provided in the assigned readings. Candidates are not responsible for changes that occur after the material was written.

Candidates should be aware that certain ratios may be defined and calculated differently. Such differences are part of the nature of practical financial analysis. For examination purposes, when alternative ratio definitions exist and no specific definition is given in the question, candidates should use the ratio definitions emphasized in the CFA Institute copyrighted readings.

READING ASSIGNMENTS

Reading 22   Financial Statement Analysis: An Introduction
by Elaine Henry, CFA, and Thomas R. Robinson, CFA

(continued)

Financial Statement Analysis: An Introduction

by Elaine Henry, CFA, and Thomas R. Robinson, CFA

LEARNING OUTCOMES

Mastery	The candidate should be able to:
☐	**a.** describe the roles of financial reporting and financial statement analysis;
☐	**b.** describe the roles of the key financial statements (statement of financial position, statement of comprehensive income, statement of changes in equity, and statement of cash flows) in evaluating a company's performance and financial position;
☐	**c.** describe the importance of financial statement notes and supplementary information —including disclosures of accounting policies, methods, and estimates— and management's commentary;
☐	**d.** describe the objective of audits of financial statements, the types of audit reports, and the importance of effective internal controls;
☐	**e.** identify and describe information sources that analysts use in financial statement analysis besides annual financial statements and supplementary information;
☐	**f.** describe the steps in the financial statement analysis framework.

Note: New rulings and/or pronouncements issued after the publication of the readings in financial reporting and analysis may cause some of the information in these readings to become dated. Candidates are expected to be familiar with the overall analytical framework contained in the study sessions readings, as well as the implications of alternative accounting methods for financial analysis and valuation, as provided in the assigned readings. Candidates are not responsible for changes that occur after the material was written.

1   INTRODUCTION

Financial analysis is the process of examining a company's performance in the context of its industry and economic environment in order to arrive at a decision or recommendation. Often, the decisions and recommendations addressed by financial analysts pertain to providing capital to companies—specifically, whether to invest in the company's debt or equity securities and at what price. An investor in debt securities is concerned about the company's ability to pay interest and to repay the principal lent. An investor in equity securities is an owner with a residual interest in the company and is concerned about the company's ability to pay dividends and the likelihood that its share price will increase. Overall, a central focus of financial analysis is evaluating the company's ability to earn a return on its capital that is at least equal to the cost of that capital, to profitably grow its operations, and to generate enough cash to meet obligations and pursue opportunities. Fundamental financial analysis starts with the information found in a company's financial reports. These financial reports include audited financial statements, additional disclosures required by regulatory authorities, and any accompanying (unaudited) commentary by management. Basic financial statement analysis—as presented in this reading—provides a foundation that enables the analyst to better understand information gathered from research beyond the financial reports.

This reading is organized as follows: Section 2 discusses the scope of financial statement analysis. Section 3 describes the sources of information used in financial statement analysis, including the primary financial statements (balance sheet, statement of comprehensive income, statement of changes in equity, and cash flow statement). Section 4 provides a framework for guiding the financial statement analysis process. A summary of the key points and practice problems in the CFA Institute multiple-choice format conclude the reading.

2   SCOPE OF FINANCIAL STATEMENT ANALYSIS

The role of financial reporting by companies is to provide information about a company's performance, financial position, and changes in financial position that is useful to a wide range of users in making economic decisions.[1] The role of financial statement analysis is to use financial reports prepared by companies, combined with other information, to evaluate the past, current, and potential performance and financial position of a company for the purpose of making investment, credit, and other economic decisions. (Managers within a company perform financial analysis to make operating, investing, and financing decisions but do not necessarily rely on analysis of related financial statements. They have access to additional financial information that can be reported in whatever format is most useful to their decision.)

---

1 The role of financial reporting is specified in International Accounting Standard (IAS) 1 *Presentation of Financial Statements*, paragraph 9, and paragraph 12 of the *Framework for the Preparation and Presentation of Financial Statements*. An updated framework is currently a joint project between the International Accounting Standards Board (IASB), which issues International Financial Reporting Standards (IFRS), and the Financial Accounting Standards Board (FASB). The FASB issues U.S. generally accepted accounting principles (U.S. GAAP) contained in the FASB Accounting Standards Codification™ (FASB ASC). The set of accounting standards that a company uses to prepare its financial reports depends on its jurisdiction. The IASB and FASB will be discussed further in a later reading.

In evaluating financial reports, analysts typically have a specific economic decision in mind. Examples of these decisions include the following:

- Evaluating an equity investment for inclusion in a portfolio.
- Evaluating a merger or acquisition candidate.
- Evaluating a subsidiary or operating division of a parent company.
- Deciding whether to make a venture capital or other private equity investment.
- Determining the creditworthiness of a company in order to decide whether to extend a loan to the company and if so, what terms to offer.
- Extending credit to a customer.
- Examining compliance with debt covenants or other contractual arrangements.
- Assigning a debt rating to a company or bond issue.
- Valuing a security for making an investment recommendation to others.
- Forecasting future net income and cash flow.

These decisions demonstrate certain themes in financial analysis. In general, analysts seek to examine the past and current performance and financial position of a company in order to form expectations about its future performance and financial position. Analysts are also concerned about factors that affect risks to a company's future performance and financial position. An examination of performance can include an assessment of a company's profitability (the ability to earn a profit from delivering goods and services) and its ability to generate positive cash flows (cash receipts in excess of cash disbursements). Profit and cash flow are not equivalent. Profit (or loss) represents the difference between the prices at which goods or services are provided to customers and the expenses incurred to provide those goods and services. In addition, profit (or loss) includes other income (such as investing income or income from the sale of items other than goods and services) minus the expenses incurred to earn that income. Overall, profit (or loss) equals income minus expenses, and its recognition is mostly independent from when cash is received or paid. Example 1 illustrates the distinction between profit and cash flow.

EXAMPLE 1

Profit versus Cash Flow

Sennett Designs (SD) sells furniture on a retail basis. SD began operations during December 2009 and sold furniture for €250,000 in cash. The furniture sold by SD was purchased on credit for €150,000 and delivered by the supplier during December. The credit terms granted by the supplier required SD to pay the €150,000 in January for the furniture it received during December. In addition to the purchase and sale of furniture, in December, SD paid €20,000 in cash for rent and salaries.

1 How much is SD's profit for December 2009 if no other transactions occurred?

2 How much is SD's cash flow for December 2009?

3 If SD purchases and sells exactly the same amount in January 2010 as it did in December and under the same terms (receiving cash for the sales and making purchases on credit that will be due in February), how much will the company's profit and cash flow be for the month of January?

Solution to 1:

SD's profit for December 2009 is the excess of the sales price (€250,000) over the cost of the goods that were sold (€150,000) and rent and salaries (€20,000), or €80,000.

Solution to 2:

The December 2009 cash flow is €230,000, the amount of cash received from the customer (€250,000) less the cash paid for rent and salaries (€20,000).

Solution to 3:

SD's profit for January 2010 will be identical to its profit in December: €80,000, calculated as the sales price (€250,000) minus the cost of the goods that were sold (€150,000) and minus rent and salaries (€20,000). SD's cash flow in January 2010 will also equal €80,000, calculated as the amount of cash received from the customer (€250,000) minus the cash paid for rent and salaries (€20,000) *and* minus the €150,000 that SD owes for the goods it had purchased on credit in the prior month.

Although profitability is important, so is a company's ability to generate positive cash flow. Cash flow is important because, ultimately, the company needs cash to pay employees, suppliers, and others in order to continue as a going concern. A company that generates positive cash flow from operations has more flexibility in funding needed for investments and taking advantage of attractive business opportunities than an otherwise comparable company without positive operating cash flow. Additionally, a company needs cash to pay returns (interest and dividends) to providers of debt and equity capital. Therefore, the expected magnitude of future cash flows is important in valuing corporate securities and in determining the company's ability to meet its obligations. The ability to meet short-term obligations is generally referred to as **liquidity**, and the ability to meet long-term obligations is generally referred to as **solvency**. Cash flow in any given period is not, however, a complete measure of performance for that period because, as shown in Example 1, a company may be obligated to make future cash payments as a result of a transaction that generates positive cash flow in the current period.

Profits may provide useful information about cash flows, past and future. If the transaction of Example 1 were repeated month after month, the long-term average monthly cash flow of SD would equal €80,000, its monthly profit. Analysts typically not only evaluate past profitability but also forecast future profitability.

Exhibit 1 shows how news coverage of corporate earnings announcements places corporate results in the context of analysts' expectations. Panel A shows the earnings announcement, and Panel B shows a sample of the news coverage of the announcement. Earnings are also frequently used by analysts in valuation. For example, an analyst may value shares of a company by comparing its price-to-earnings ratio (P/E) to the P/Es of peer companies and/or may use forecasted future earnings as direct or indirect inputs into discounted cash flow models of valuation.

Exhibit 1	An Earnings Release and News Media Comparison with Analysts' Expectations

Panel A: Excerpt from Apple Earnings Release

Apple Reports Second Quarter Results
Record March Quarter Revenue and Profit

Exhibit 1	(Continued)

iPhone Sales More Than Double

CUPERTINO, California—April 20, 2010—Apple® today announced financial results for its fiscal 2010 second quarter ended March 27, 2010. The Company posted revenue of $13.50 billion and net quarterly profit of $3.07 billion, or $3.33 per diluted share. These results compare to revenue of $9.08 billion and net quarterly profit of $1.62 billion, or $1.79 per diluted share, in the year-ago quarter. Gross margin was 41.7 percent, up from 39.9 percent in the year-ago quarter. International sales accounted for 58 percent of the quarter's revenue.

Apple sold 2.94 million Macintosh® computers during the quarter, representing a 33 percent unit increase over the year-ago quarter. The Company sold 8.75 million iPhones in the quarter, representing 131 percent unit growth over the year-ago quarter. Apple sold 10.89 million iPods during the quarter, representing a one percent unit decline from the year-ago quarter.

"We're thrilled to report our best non-holiday quarter ever, with revenues up 49 percent and profits up 90 percent," said Steve Jobs, Apple's CEO. "We've launched our revolutionary new iPad and users are loving it, and we have several more extraordinary products in the pipeline for this year."

"Looking ahead to the third fiscal quarter of 2010, we expect revenue in the range of about $13.0 billion to $13.4 billion and we expect diluted earnings per share in the range of about $2.28 to $2.39," said Peter Oppenheimer, Apple's CFO.

Source: www.apple.com/pr/library/2010/04/20results.html

Panel B: Excerpt Downloaded from FOXBusiness.com Report: Tuesday, 20 April 2010

"Apple Earnings Surge By 90% in Second Quarter" by Kathryn Glass

In what's beginning to become its trademark, Apple Inc. (AAPL: 238.7911, −9.5489, −3.85%) delivered much better-than-expected second-quarter earnings, but gave third-quarter guidance below expectations.

The personal-technology behemoth said it expects third-quarter earnings in the range of $2.28 to $2.39 per share on revenue between $13 billion and $13.4 billion. Analysts were expecting third-quarter earnings of $2.70 a share on revenue of $12.97 billion, according to a poll by Thomson Reuters.

Apple reported second quarter profit of $3.07 billion, or $3.33 per share, compared with year-ago profit of $1.62 billion, or $1.79 per share. Revenue rose to $13.5 billion, compared with revenue of $9.08 billion, one year ago. The tech giant said 58% of revenue came from international sales.

The results soared above expectations; analysts' second-quarter profit estimates were for $2.45 per share on revenue of $12.04 billion.

Analysts are also interested in the current financial position of a company. The financial position can be measured by comparing the resources controlled by the company (**assets**) in relation to the claims against those resources (**liabilities** and **equity**). An example of a resource is cash. In Example 1, if no other transactions occur, the company should have €230,000 more in cash at 31 December 2009 than at the start of the period. The cash can be used by the company to pay its obligation to the supplier (a claim against the company) and may also be used to make distributions to the owner (who has a residual claim against the company's assets, net of liabilities). Financial position is particularly important in credit analysis, as depicted in Exhibit 2. Panel A of the exhibit is an excerpt from an April 2010 announcement by a credit rating agency of an upgrade in the credit ratings of Teck Resources Ltd., a Canadian mining company. The rating agency explained that it upgraded the credit rating of the company (its "corporate credit rating") and the credit rating of the company's debt securities (the "issue-level rating") because the company had repaid its debt quickly ("accelerated debt repayment"). Panel B of the exhibit is an excerpt from the company's second quarter 2010 earnings announcement in which the company's CEO describes the company's repayment of debt. Panel C of the exhibit is an excerpt from the company's financial report illustrating the change in the company's financial position in June 2010 compared with December 2009. As shown, the amount of the company's debt liabilities relative to the amount of its equity declined substantially over the period.

Exhibit 2

Panel A: Excerpt from Announcement by Standard & Poor's Ratings Services: 16 April 2010

Teck Resources Ltd. Upgraded To 'BBB' From 'BB+' On Improved Financial Risk Profile; Removed From CreditWatch

> We are raising our long-term corporate credit rating on Vancouver-based mining company Teck Resources Ltd. to 'BBB' from 'BB+'.... We are also raising the issue-level rating on the company's notes outstanding to 'BBB' from 'BB+'.... We base the upgrade on Teck's materially improved financial risk profile following the accelerated debt repayment in the past year. The stable outlook reflects our opinion that Teck will maintain relatively stable credit metrics in the medium term, despite inherent volatility in the commodities market.

Source: Market News Publishing.

Panel B: Excerpt from Earnings Announcement by Teck Resources Limited: 28 July 2010

Teck Reports Second Quarter Results for 2010

> Vancouver, BC—Teck Resources Limited (TSX: TCK.A and TCK.B, NYSE: TCK) announced quarterly earnings of $260 million, or $0.44 per share, for the second quarter of 2010. Our operating profit before depreciation was approximately $1.0 billion and EBITDA was $844 million in the second quarter.
>
>   Don Lindsay, President and CEO said, "During the quarter we eliminated the outstanding balance of our term bank loan and have now repaid the US$9.8 billion bank debt related to the Fording

| Exhibit 2 | (Continued) |

acquisition in less than 18 months, just over two years ahead of schedule. In addition, all of our operations performed well, and we met or exceeded the guidance given in our previous quarterly report. Our second quarter benefitted from a substantial increase in coal sales to 6.4 million tonnes and the higher benchmark prices negotiated for the second quarter. In addition, in the quarter we re-established our investment grade credit ratings from all of the major rating agencies and declared a semi-annual dividend of $0.20 per share."

Source: Teck Resources Form 6-K, filed 11 August 2010.

Panel C: Financial Position of Teck Resources Limited: 28 July 2010 and 31 December 2009

(in millions of Canadian $)	28 July 2010	31 December 2009
ASSETS	$ 28,570	$ 29,873
LIABILITIES		
Debt	5,678	8,004
All other liabilities	7,273	7,288
Total liabilities	12,951	15,292
EQUITY	15,619	14,581
Debt divided by equity	0.36	0.55

In conducting a financial analysis of a company, the analyst will regularly refer to the company's financial statements, financial notes, and supplementary schedules and a variety of other information sources. The next section introduces the major financial statements and some commonly used information sources.

MAJOR FINANCIAL STATEMENTS AND OTHER INFORMATION SOURCES

3

In order to perform an equity or credit analysis of a company, an analyst collects a great deal of information. The nature of the information collected will vary on the basis of the individual decision to be made (or the specific purpose of the analysis) but will typically include information about the economy, industry, and company as well as information about comparable peer companies. Much of the information will likely come from outside the company, such as economic statistics, industry reports, trade publications, and databases containing information on competitors. The company itself provides some of the core information for analysis in its financial reports, press releases, investor conference calls, and webcasts.

Companies prepare financial reports at regular intervals (annually, semiannually, and/or quarterly depending on the applicable regulatory requirements). Financial reports include financial statements along with supplemental disclosures necessary to assess the company's financial position and periodic performance. Financial statements are the result of an accounting recordkeeping process that records economic activities of a company, following the applicable accounting standards and principles. These statements summarize the accounting information, mainly for users outside the company (such as investors, creditors, analysts, and others) because users of financial information inside a company have direct access to the underlying financial data that are summarized in the financial statements and to other information that is collected but not included in the financial reporting process. Financial statements are almost always audited by independent accountants who provide an opinion on whether the financial statements present fairly the company's performance and financial position in accordance with a specified, applicable set of accounting standards and principles.

3.1 Financial Statements and Supplementary Information

A complete set of financial statements include a statement of financial position (i.e., a balance sheet), a statement of comprehensive income (i.e., a single statement of comprehensive income or an income statement and a statement of comprehensive income), a statement of changes in equity, and a statement of cash flows.[2] The balance sheet portrays the company's financial position at a given point in time. The statement of comprehensive income and statement of cash flows present different aspects of a company's performance over a period of time. The statement of changes in equity provides additional information regarding the changes in a company's financial position. In addition, the accompanying notes or footnotes to the financial statements are required and considered an integral part of a complete set of financial statements.

Along with the required financial statements, a company typically provides additional information in its financial reports. In many jurisdictions, some or all of this additional information is mandated by regulators or accounting standards boards. The additional information provided may include a letter from the chairman of the company, a report from management discussing the results (typically called management discussion and analysis [MD&A] or management commentary), an external auditor's report providing assurances, a governance report describing the structure of the company's board of directors, and a corporate responsibility report. As part of his or her analysis, the financial analyst should read and assess this additional information along with the financial statements. The following sections describe and illustrate each financial statement and some of the additional information.

3.1.1 *Balance Sheet*

The **balance sheet** (also called the **statement of financial position** or **statement of financial condition**) presents a company's current financial position by disclosing the resources the company controls (assets) and its obligations to lenders and other creditors (liabilities) at a specific point in time. **Owners' equity** represents the excess of assets over liabilities. This amount is attributable to the company's owners or shareholders. Owners' equity is the owners' residual interest in (i.e., residual claim on) the company's assets after deducting its liabilities.

The relationship among the three parts of the balance sheet (assets, liabilities, and owners' equity) can be expressed in the following equation form: Assets = Liabilities + Owners' equity. This equation (sometimes called the accounting equation or the balance sheet equation) shows that the total amount of assets must equal or *balance* to the combined total amounts of liabilities and owners' equity. Alternatively, the equation may be rearranged as follows: Assets − Liabilities = Owners' equity. This

---

2 The names of the financial statements are those in IAS 1. Commonly used terms for these financial statements are indicated in parentheses. Later readings will elaborate on each of these financial statements.

formulation emphasizes the residual claim aspect of owners' equity. Depending on the form of the organization, owners' equity may be referred to as "partners' capital" or "shareholders' equity."

Exhibit 3 presents the balance sheet of the Volkswagen Group (FWB: VOW) from its Annual Report 2009.

Exhibit 3	Balance Sheet of the Volkswagen Group		
€ million	Note	31 Dec. 2009	31 Dec. 2008
Assets			
Noncurrent assets			
Intangible assets	12	12,907	12,291
Property, plant and equipment	13	24,444	23,121
Leasing and rental assets	14	10,288	9,889
Investment property	14	216	150
Equity-accounted investments	15	10,385	6,373
Other equity investments	15	543	583
Financial services receivables	16	33,174	31,855
Other receivables and financial assets	17	3,747	3,387
Noncurrent tax receivables	18	685	763
Deferred tax assets	18	3,013	3,344
		99,402	**91,756**
Current assets			
Inventories	19	14,124	17,816
Trade receivables	20	5,692	5,969
Financial services receivables	16	27,403	27,035
Other receivables and financial assets	17	5,927	10,068
Current tax receivables	18	762	1,024
Marketable securities	21	3,330	3,770
Cash and cash equivalents	22	20,539	9,474
Assets held for sale	23	—	1,007
		77,776	**76,163**
Total assets		**177,178**	**167,919**
Equity and liabilities			
Equity	24		
Subscribed capital		1,025	1,024
Capital reserves		5,356	5,351
Retained earnings		28,901	28,636
Equity attributable to shareholders of Volkswagen AG		35,281	35,011
Minority interests		2,149	2,377
		37,430	**37,388**
Noncurrent liabilities			
Noncurrent financial liabilities	25	36,993	33,257

(continued)

Exhibit 3	(Continued)		

€ million	Note	31 Dec. 2009	31 Dec. 2008
Other noncurrent liabilities	26	3,028	3,235
Deferred tax liabilities	27	2,224	3,654
Provisions for pensions	28	13,936	12,955
Provisions for taxes	27	3,946	3,555
Other noncurrent provisions	29	10,088	9,073
		70,215	**65,729**
Current liabilities			
Current financial liabilities	25	40,606	36,123
Trade payables	30	10,225	9,676
Current tax payables	27	73	59
Other current liabilities	26	8,237	8,545
Provisions for taxes	27	973	1,160
Other current provisions	29	9,420	8,473
Liabilities associated with assets held for sale	23	—	766
		69,534	**64,802**
Total equity and liabilities		**177,178**	**167,919**

Note: Numbers are as shown in the annual report and may not add because of rounding.

In Exhibit 3, the balance sheet is presented with the most recent year in the first column and the earlier year in the second column. Although this is a common presentation, analysts should be careful when reading financial statements. In some cases, the ordering may be reversed, with years listed from most distant to most recent.

At 31 December 2009, Volkswagen's total resources or assets were €177 billion. This number is the sum of non-current assets of €99 billion and current assets of €78 billion.[3] Total equity was €37 billion. Although Volkswagen does not give a total amount for all the balance sheet liabilities, it can be determined by adding the non-current and current liabilities, €70,215 million + €69,534 million = €139,749 million, or €140 billion.[4]

Referring back to the basic accounting equation, Assets = Liabilities + Equity, we have €177 billion = €140 billion + €37 billion. In other words, Volkswagen has assets of €177 billion, owes €140 billion, and thus has equity of €37 billion. Using the balance sheet and applying financial statement analysis, the analyst can answer such questions as

- Has the company's liquidity (ability to meet short-term obligations) improved?
- Is the company solvent (does it have sufficient resources to cover its obligations)?
- What is the company's financial position relative to the industry?

---

3 Current assets are defined, in general, as those that are cash or cash equivalents; are held for trading; or are expected to be converted to cash (realized), sold, or consumed within 12 months or the company's normal operating cycle. All other assets are classified as non-current.
4 Current liabilities are defined, in general, as those that are expected to be settled within 12 months or the company's normal operating cycle. All other liabilities are classified as non-current.

Volkswagen, a German-based automobile manufacturer, prepares its financial statements in accordance with International Financial Reporting Standards (IFRS). IFRS require companies to present classified balance sheets that show current and non-current assets and current and non-current liabilities as separate classifications. However, IFRS do not prescribe a particular ordering or format, and the order in which companies present their balance sheet items is largely a function of tradition. As shown, Volkswagen presents non-current assets before current assets, owners' equity before liabilities, and within liabilities, non-current liabilities before current liabilities. This method generally reflects a presentation from least liquid to most liquid. In other countries, the typical order of presentation may differ. For example, in the United States, Australia, and Canada, companies usually present their assets and liabilities from most liquid to least liquid. Cash is typically the first asset shown, and equity is presented after liabilities.

As a basis for comparison, Exhibit 4 presents the balance sheet of Wal-Mart Stores, Inc., or Walmart (NYSE: WMT) from its 2010 Annual Report.

Exhibit 4	Walmart Consolidated Balance Sheet		

| | | 31 January | |
(Amounts in millions except per share data)		2010	2009
ASSETS			
Current assets:			
Cash and cash equivalents		$7,907	$7,275
Receivables, net		4,144	3,905
Inventories		33,160	34,511
Prepaid expenses and other		2,980	3,063
Current assets of discontinued operations		140	195
Total current assets		**48,331**	**48,949**
Property and equipment:			
Land		22,591	19,852
Buildings and improvements		77,452	73,810
Fixtures and equipment		35,450	29,851
Transportation equipment		2,355	2,307
Property and equipment		137,848	125,820
Less accumulated depreciation		(38,304)	(32,964)
Property and equipment, net		**99,544**	**92,856**
Property under capital leases:			
Property under capital leases		5,669	5,341
Less accumulated amortization		(2,906)	(2,544)
Property under capital leases, net		**2,763**	**2,797**
Goodwill		**16,126**	**15,260**
Other assets and deferred charges		**3,942**	**3,567**
Total assets		**$170,706**	**$163,429**

LIABILITIES AND EQUITY

Current liabilities:

(continued)

| Exhibit 4 | (Continued) |

	31 January	
(Amounts in millions except per share data)	2010	2009
Short-term borrowings	$523	$1,506
Accounts payable	30,451	28,849
Accrued liabilities	18,734	18,112
Accrued income taxes	1,365	677
Long-term debt due within one year	4,050	5,848
Obligations under capital leases due within one year	346	315
Current liabilities of discontinued operations	92	83
Total current liabilities	55,561	55,390
Long-term debt	33,231	31,349
Long-term obligations under capital leases	3,170	3,200
Deferred income taxes and other	5,508	6,014
Redeemable non-controlling interest	307	397
Commitments and contingencies		
Equity:		
Preferred stock ($0.10 par value; 100 shares authorized, none issued)	—	—
Common stock ($0.10 par value; 11,000 shares authorized, 3,786 and 3,925 issued and outstanding at 31 January 2010 and 31 January 2009, respectively)	378	393
Capital in excess of par value	3,803	3,920
Retained earnings	66,638	63,660
Accumulated other comprehensive loss	(70)	(2,688)
Total Walmart shareholders' equity	70,749	65,285
Non-controlling interest	2,180	1,794
Total equity	72,929	67,079
Total liabilities and equity	**$170,706**	**$163,429**

Walmart has total assets of $170.7 billion. Liabilities and other non-equity claims total $97.8 billion, and equity is $72.9 billion. A later reading will cover the analysis of the balance sheet in more depth. The next section describes and illustrates the statement of comprehensive income.

3.1.2 *Statement of Comprehensive Income*

The statement of comprehensive income, under IFRS, can be presented as a single statement of comprehensive income or as two statements, an income statement and a statement of comprehensive income that begins with profit or loss from the income statement. The Volkswagen Group chose the latter form of presentation rather than a single statement.

3.1.2.1 Income Statement The income statement presents information on the financial results of a company's business activities over a period of time. The income statement communicates how much **revenue** and other income the company generated during a period and the expenses it incurred to generate that revenue and other income. Revenue typically refers to amounts charged for the delivery of goods or services in the ordinary activities of a business. Other income includes gains, which may or may not arise in the ordinary activities of the business. **Expenses** reflect outflows, depletions of assets, and incurrences of liabilities that decrease equity. Expenses typically include such items as cost of sales (cost of goods sold), administrative expenses, and income tax expenses and may be defined to include losses. Net income (revenue plus other income minus expenses) on the income statement is often referred to as the "bottom line" because of its proximity to the bottom of the income statement. Net income may also be referred to as "net earnings," "net profit," and "profit or loss." In the event that expenses exceed revenues and other income, the result is referred to as "net loss."

Income statements are reported on a consolidated basis, meaning that they include the income and expenses of subsidiary companies under the control of the parent (reporting) company. The income statement is sometimes referred to as a **statement of operations** or **profit and loss (P&L) statement**. The basic equation underlying the income statement is Revenue + Other income − Expenses = Income − Expenses = Net income.

In general terms, when one company (the parent) controls another company (the subsidiary), the parent presents its own financial statement information consolidated with that of the subsidiary. (When a parent company owns more than 50 percent of the voting shares of a subsidiary company, it is presumed to control the subsidiary and thus presents consolidated financial statements.) Each line item of the consolidated income statement includes the entire amount from the relevant line item on the subsidiary's income statement (after removing any intercompany transactions); however, if the parent does not own 100 percent of the subsidiary, it is necessary for the parent to present an allocation of net income to the minority interests. Minority interests, also called non-controlling interests, refer to owners of the remaining shares of the subsidiary that are not owned by the parent. The share of consolidated net income attributable to minority interests is shown at the bottom of the income statement along with the net income attributable to shareholders of the parent company. Exhibit 5 presents the income statement of the Volkswagen Group from its Annual Report 2009.

| Exhibit 5 | Income Statement of the Volkswagen Group for the Period 1 January to 31 December* |

€ million	Note	2009	2008
Sales revenue	1	**105,187**	**113,808**
Cost of sales	2	−91,608	−96,612
Gross profit		**13,579**	**17,196**
Distribution expenses	3	−10,537	−10,552
Administrative expenses	4	−2,739	−2,742
Other operating income	5	7,904	8,770
Other operating expenses	6	−6,352	−6,339
Operating profit		**1,855**	**6,333**
Share of profits and losses of equity-accounted investments	7	701	910
Finance costs	8	−2,268	−1,815
Other financial result	9	972	1,180
Financial result		**−595**	**275**
Profit before tax		**1,261**	**6,608**
Income tax income/expense	10	−349	−1,920
Current		−1,145	−2,338
Deferred		796	418

(continued)

Exhibit 5	(Continued)

€ million	Note	2009	2008
Profit after tax		**911**	**4,688**
Minority interests		−49	−65
Profit attributable to shareholders of Volkswagen AG		960	4,753
Basic earnings per ordinary share in €	11	2.38	11.92
Basic earnings per preferred share in €	11	2.44	11.98
Diluted earnings per ordinary share in €	11	2.38	11.88
Diluted earnings per preferred share in €	11	2.44	11.94

*The numbers are as shown in the annual report and may not add because of rounding.

Exhibit 5 shows that Volkswagen's sales revenue for the fiscal year ended 31 December 2009 was €105,187 million. Subtracting cost of sales from revenue gives gross profit of €13,579 million. After subtracting operating costs and expenses and adding other operating income, the company's operating profit totals €1,855 million. Operating profit represents the results of the company's usual business activities before deducting interest expense or taxes. Operating profit (also called operating income) is thus often referred to as earnings before interest and taxes (EBIT). Next, operating profit is increased by Volkswagen's share of the profits generated by certain of its investments (€701 million) and by profits from its other financial activities (€972 million) and decreased by finance costs (i.e., interest expense) of €2,268 million, resulting in profit before tax of €1,261 million. Total income tax expense for 2009 was €349 million, resulting in profit after tax (net income) of €911 million.

After allocating the losses attributable to minority interest ownership in Volkswagen subsidiary companies, the profit attributable to shareholders of Volkswagen for 2009 was €960 million. Allocating the losses attributable to minority interest ownership resulted in the allocation to shareholders of the parent company, Volkswagen AG, exceeding net income (profit after tax). Volkswagen's disclosures indicate that its minority interests relate primarily to Scania AB, a subsidiary in which Volkswagen owns about 72 percent of the voting rights (with the minority interests owning the remaining 28 percent).

Companies present both basic and diluted earnings per share on the face of the income statement. Earnings per share numbers represent net income attributable to the class of shareholders divided by the relevant number of shares of stock outstanding during the period. Basic earnings per share is calculated using the weighted-average number of common (ordinary) shares that were actually outstanding during the period and the profit or loss attributable to the common shareowners. Diluted earnings per share uses **diluted shares**—the number of shares that would hypothetically be outstanding if potentially dilutive claims on common shares (e.g., stock options or convertible bonds) were exercised or converted by their holders—and an appropriately adjusted profit or loss attributable to the common shareowners.

Volkswagen has two types of shareholders, ordinary and preferred, and presents earnings per share information for both, although there is no requirement to present earnings per share information for preferred shareowners. Volkswagen's basic earnings per ordinary share was €2.38. A note to the company's financial statements explains that this number was calculated as follows: €960 million profit attributable to shareholders of Volkswagen, of which €703 million is attributable to ordinary shareholders and €257 million is attributable to preferred shareholders. The €703 million attributable to ordinary shareholders divided by the weighted-average number of ordinary shares of 295 million shares equals basic earnings per share for 2009 of €2.38. Similar detail is provided in the notes for each of the earnings per share numbers.

An analyst examining the income statement might note that Volkswagen was profitable in both years. The company's profitability declined substantially in 2009, primarily because of lower sales and reduced gross profit. This was not unexpected given the global financial and economic crisis in that year. A better understanding of Volkswagen's profitability could likely be gained by examining income statements over a longer time period. The analyst might formulate questions related to profitability, such as the following:

- Is the change in revenue related to an increase in units sold, an increase in prices, or some combination?

- If the company has multiple business segments (for example, Volkswagen's segments include passenger cars, light commercial vehicles, and financial services, among others), how are the segments' revenue and profits changing?

- How does the company compare with other companies in the industry?

Answering such questions requires the analyst to gather, analyze, and interpret information from a number of sources, including, but not limited to, the income statement.

3.1.2.2 Other Comprehensive Income   Comprehensive income includes all items that impact owners' equity but are not the result of transactions with shareowners. Some of these items are included in the calculation of net income, and some are included in other comprehensive income (OCI). Under IFRS, when comprehensive income is presented in two statements, the statement of comprehensive income begins with the profit or loss from the income statement and then presents the components of other comprehensive income. Although U.S. generally accepted accounting principles (U.S. GAAP) indicate a preference for this type of presentation when a single statement of comprehensive income is not presented, they permit companies to present the components of other comprehensive income in the statement of changes in equity.[5]

Exhibit 6 presents the statement of comprehensive income of the Volkswagen Group from its Annual Report 2009.

Exhibit 6	Statement of Comprehensive Income of the Volkswagen Group for the Period 1 January to 31 December		
€ million		**2009**	**2008**
Profit after tax		**911**	**4,688**
Exchange differences on translating foreign operations:			
Fair value changes recognized in other comprehensive income		917	−1,445
Transferred to profit or loss		57	
Actuarial gains/losses		−860	190
Cash flow hedges:			

(continued)

---

5 See FASB ASC paragraphs 220-10-45-8 to 220-10-45-10. However, the IASB and the FASB have each issued a jointly developed proposal that would require entities to present a continuous statement of total comprehensive income. The continuous statement would include separate sections for profit or loss and other comprehensive income.

Exhibit 6	(Continued)		
€ million		**2009**	**2008**
Fair value changes recognized in other comprehensive income		683	1,054
Transferred to profit or loss		−908	−1,427
Available-for-sale financial assets (marketable securities):			
Fair value changes recognized in other comprehensive income		200	−330
Transferred to profit or loss		71	100
Deferred taxes		216	145
Share of profits and losses of equity-accounted investments recognized directly in equity, after tax		30	−188
Other comprehensive income		**406**	**−1,901**
Total comprehensive income		**1,317**	**2,787**
Of which attributable to			
Shareholders of Volkswagen AG		1,138	3,310
Minority interests		179	−523

Exhibit 6 shows that other comprehensive income, although smaller in absolute terms than profit after tax (net income), had a significant effect on total comprehensive income. In 2009, other comprehensive income represented approximately 31 percent of total comprehensive income and was approximately 45 percent of the size of profit after tax (net income). In 2008, other comprehensive income was negative (a loss) and was approximately 41 percent of the size of profit after tax (net income) in absolute terms. The statement of comprehensive income will be discussed in greater detail in a later reading. The next section briefly describes the statement of changes in equity.

3.1.3 *Statement of Changes in Equity*

The statement of changes in equity, variously called the "statement of changes in owners' equity" or "statement of changes in shareholders' equity," primarily serves to report changes in the owners' investment in the business over time. The basic components of owners' equity are paid-in capital and retained earnings. Retained earnings include the cumulative amount of the company's profits that have been retained in the company. In addition, non-controlling or minority interests and reserves that represent accumulated other comprehensive income items are included in equity. The latter items may be shown separately or included in retained earnings. Volkswagen includes reserves as components of retained earnings.

The statement of changes in equity is organized to present, for each component of equity, the beginning balance, any increases during the period, any decreases during the period, and the ending balance. For paid-in capital, an example of an increase is a new issuance of equity and an example of a decrease is a repurchase of previously issued stock. For retained earnings, income (both net income as reported on the income statement and other comprehensive income) is the most common increase and a dividend payment is the most common decrease.

Volkswagen's balance sheet in Exhibit 3 shows that equity at the end of 2009 totaled €37,430 million, compared with €37,388 million at the end of 2008. The company's statement of changes in equity presents additional detail on the change in each line item. Exhibit 7 presents an excerpt of the statement of changes in equity of the Volkswagen Group from its Annual Report 2009.

In Exhibit 7, the sum of the line items total comprehensive income (€1,102 million) and deferred taxes (€216 million) equals the amount of total comprehensive income reported in the statement of comprehensive income, except for a rounding difference. Using the balance at 31 December 2009, the sum of the columns accumulated profit through equity-accounted investment equals the amount of retained earnings on the balance sheet (€28,901 million in Exhibit 3), except for a rounding difference. Dividends (€779 million) are reported in this statement and reduce retained earnings. Explanatory notes on equity are included in the notes to the consolidated financial statements. The next section describes the cash flow statement.

3.1.4 Cash Flow Statement

Although the income statement and balance sheet provide measures of a company's success in terms of performance and financial position, cash flow is also vital to a company's long-term success. Disclosing the sources and uses of cash helps creditors, investors, and other statement users evaluate the company's liquidity, solvency, and financial flexibility. **Financial flexibility** is the ability of the company to react and adapt to financial adversities and opportunities. The cash flow statement classifies all cash flows of the company into three categories: operating, investing, and financing. Cash flows from **operating activities** are those cash flows not classified as investing or financing and generally involve the cash effects of transactions that enter into the determination of net income and, hence, comprise the day-to-day operations of the company. Cash flows from **investing activities** are those cash flows from activities associated with the acquisition and disposal of long-term assets, such as property and equipment. Cash flows from **financing activities** are those cash flows from activities related to obtaining or repaying capital to be used in the business. IFRS permit more flexibility than U.S. GAAP in classifying dividend and interest receipts and payments within these categories.

Exhibit 8 presents Volkswagen's statement of cash flows for the fiscal years ended 31 December 2009 and 2008.

Exhibit 8	Cash Flow Statement of the Volkswagen Group: 1 January to 31 December		
€ million		**2009**	**2008**
Cash and cash equivalents at beginning of period (excluding time deposit investments)		**9,443**	**9,914**
Profit before tax		1,261	6,608
Income taxes paid		−529	−2,075
Depreciation and amortization of property, plant and equipment, intangible assets and investment property		5,028	5,198
Amortization of capitalized development costs		1,586	1,392
Impairment losses on equity investments		16	32
Depreciation of leasing and rental assets		2,247	1,816
Gain/loss on disposal of noncurrent assets		−547	37
Share of profit or loss of equity-accounted investments		−298	−219
Other noncash expense/income		727	765

(continued)

Exhibit 7 Excerpt from Statement of Changes in Equity of the Volkswagen Group for the Period 1 January to 31 December 2009*

€ millions	Subscribed capital	Capital reserves	RETAINED EARNINGS						Equity-accounted investments	Equity attributable to shareholders of VW AG	Minority interests	Total equity
			Accumulated profit	Currency translation reserve	Reserve for actuarial gains/losses	Cash flow hedge reserve	Fair value reserve for securities				
Balance at 1 Jan. 2009	1,024	5,351	31,522	−2,721	−672	1,138	−192	−439	35,011	2,377	37,388
Capital increase	0	4							4		4
Dividend payment			−779						−779	−95	−874
Capital transactions involving change in ownership			−76						−76	−316	−392
Total comprehensive income			960	839	−851	−361	271	30	888	214	1,102
Deferred taxes					247	83	−80		250	−34	216
Other changes			−21		2				−18	4	−15
Balance at 31 Dec. 2009	1,025	5,356	31,607	−1,881	−1,274	860	−1	−409	35,281	2,149	37,430

28,902

*Numbers are as shown in the annual report and may not add and cross-add because of rounding.

Exhibit 8 (Continued)

€ million	2009	2008
Change in inventories	4,155	−3,056
Change in receivables (excluding financial services)	465	−1,333
Change in liabilities (excluding financial liabilities)	260	815
Change in provisions	1,660	509
Change in leasing and rental assets	−2,571	−2,734
Change in financial services receivables	−719	−5,053
Cash flows from operating activities	**12,741**	**2,702**
Investments in property, plant and equipment, intangible assets and investment property	−5,963	−6,896
Additions to capitalized development costs	−1,948	−2,216
Acquisition of equity investments	−3,989	−2,597
Disposal of equity investments	1,320	1
Proceeds from disposal of property, plant and equipment, intangible assets and investment property	153	95
Change in investments in securities	989	2,041
Change in loans and time deposit investments	−236	−1,611
Cash flows from investing activities	**−9,675**	**−11,183**
Capital contributions	4	218
Dividends paid	−874	−722
Capital transactions with minority interests	−392	−362
Other changes	23	−3
Proceeds from issue of bonds	15,593	7,671
Repayment of bonds	−10,202	−8,470
Change in other financial liabilities	1,405	9,806
Finance lease payments	−23	−15
Cash flows from financing activities	**5,536**	**8,123**
Effect of exchange rate changes on cash and cash equivalents	190	−113
Net change in cash and cash equivalents	**8,792**	**−471**
Cash and cash equivalents at end of period (excluding time deposit investments)	**18,235**	**9,443**
Cash and cash equivalents at end of period (excluding time deposit investments)	18,235	9,443
Securities and loans (including time deposit investments)	7,312	7,875
Gross liquidity	**25,547**	**17,318**
Total third-party borrowings	−77,599	−69,555
Net liquidity	**−52,052**	**−52,237**

The operating activities section of Volkswagen's cash flow statement begins with profit before tax,[6] €1,261 million, subtracts actual income tax payments, and then adjusts this amount for the effects of non-cash transactions, accruals and deferrals,

---

6 Other companies may choose to begin with net income.

and transactions of an investing and financing nature to arrive at the amount of cash generated from operating activities of €12,741 million. This approach to reporting cash flow from operating activities is termed the indirect method. The direct method of reporting cash flows from operating activities discloses major classes of gross cash receipts and gross cash payments. Examples of such classes are cash received from customers and cash paid to suppliers and employees.

The indirect method emphasizes the different perspectives of the income statement and cash flow statement. On the income statement, income is reported when earned, not necessarily when cash is received, and expenses are reported when incurred, not necessarily when paid. The cash flow statement presents another aspect of performance: the ability of a company to generate cash flow from running its business. Ideally, for an established company, the analyst would like to see that the primary source of cash flow is from operating activities as opposed to investing or financing activities.

The sum of the net cash flows from operating, investing, and financing activities and the effect of exchange rates on cash equals the net change in cash during the fiscal year. For Volkswagen, the sum of these four items was €8,792 million in 2009, which thus increased the company's cash, excluding amounts held in time deposit investments, from €9,443 million at the beginning of the period to €18,235 million at the end of the period. As disclosed in a note to the financial statements, the time deposit investments are €42 million and €2,304 million for the years 2008 and 2009, respectively. The note also disclosed that €11 million of cash and cash equivalents held for sale [sic] are included in the cash and cash equivalents as reported in cash flow statement but are not included in the cash and cash equivalents as reported in the balance sheet in 2008. When these amounts are included with the amounts shown on the cash flow statement, the total cash and cash equivalents for the years 2008 and 2009 are €9,474 (= 9443 + 42 − 11) million and €20,539 million. These are the same amounts reported as cash and cash equivalents on the balance sheets in Exhibit 3. The cash flow statement will be covered in more depth in a later reading.

3.1.5 *Financial Notes and Supplementary Schedules*

The notes (also sometimes referred to as footnotes) that accompany the four financial statements are required and are an integral part of the complete set of financial statements. The notes provide information that is essential to understanding the information provided in the primary statements. Volkswagen's 2009 financial statements, for example, include 91 pages of notes.

The notes disclose the basis of preparation for the financial statements. For example, Volkswagen discloses in its first note that its fiscal year corresponds to the calendar year, that its financial statements are prepared in accordance with IFRS as adopted by the European Union, that the statements are prepared in compliance with German law, that the statements are denominated in millions of euros unless otherwise specified, and that the figures have been rounded, which might give rise to minor discrepancies when figures are added. Volkswagen also discloses that its financial statements are on a consolidated basis—that is, including Volkswagen AG and all of the subsidiary companies it controls.

The notes also disclose information about the accounting policies, methods, and estimates used to prepare the financial statements. As will be discussed in later readings, both IFRS and U.S. GAAP allow some flexibility in choosing among alternative policies and methods when accounting for certain items. This flexibility aims to meet the divergent needs of many businesses for reporting a variety of economic transactions. In addition to differences in accounting policies and methods, differences arise as a result of estimates needed to record and measure transactions, events, and financial statement line items.

Overall, flexibility in accounting choices is necessary because, ideally, a company will select those policies, methods, and estimates that are allowable and most relevant and that fairly reflect the unique economic environment of the company's business and industry. Flexibility can, however, create challenges for the analyst because the use of different policies, methods, and estimates reduces comparability across different companies' financial statements. Comparability occurs when different companies' information is measured and reported in a similar manner over time. Comparability helps the analyst identify and analyze the real economic differences across companies, rather than differences that arise solely from different accounting choices. Because comparability of financial statements is a critical requirement for objective financial analysis, an analyst should be aware of the potential for differences in accounting choices even when comparing two companies that use the same set of accounting standards.

For example, if a company acquires a piece of equipment to use in its operations, accounting standards require that the cost of the equipment be reported as an expense by allocating its cost less any residual value in a systematic manner over the equipment's useful life. This allocation of the cost is known as **depreciation**. Accounting standards permit flexibility, however, in determining the manner in which each year's expense is determined. Two companies may acquire similar equipment but use different methods and assumptions to record the expense over time. An analyst's ability to compare the companies' performance is hindered by the difference. Analysts must understand reporting choices in order to make appropriate adjustments when comparing companies' financial positions and performance.

A company's significant accounting choices (policies, methods, and estimates) must be discussed in the notes to the financial statements. For example, a note containing a summary of significant accounting policies includes how the company recognizes its revenues and depreciates its non-current tangible assets. Analysts must understand the accounting choices a company makes and determine whether they are similar to those of other companies identified and used as benchmarks or comparables. If the policies of the companies being compared are different, the analyst who understands accounting and financial reporting can often make necessary adjustments so that the financial statement data used are more comparable.

For many companies, the financial notes and supplemental schedules provide explanatory information about every line item (or almost every line item) on the balance sheet and income statement, as illustrated by the note references in Volkswagen's balance sheet and income statement in Exhibits 3 and 5. In addition, note disclosures include information about the following (this is not an exhaustive list):

- financial instruments and risks arising from financial instruments,
- commitments and contingencies,
- legal proceedings,
- related-party transactions,
- subsequent events (i.e., events that occur after the balance sheet date),
- business acquisitions and disposals, and
- operating segments' performance.

Exhibit 9	Excerpt from Notes to the Consolidated Financial Statements of the Volkswagen Group for Fiscal Year Ended 31 December 2009: Selected Data on Operating Segments (€ millions)

2008	Passenger Cars and Light Commercial Vehicles	Scania	Volkswagen Financial Services	Total Segments
Sales revenue from external customers	98,710	3,865	10,193	112,768
Segment profit or loss	6,431	417	893	7,741
Segment assets	91,458	10,074	74,690	176,222

2009	Passenger Cars and Light Commercial Vehicles	Scania	Volkswagen Financial Services	Total Segments
Sales revenue from external customers	86,297	6,385	11,095	103,777
Segment profit or loss	2,020	236	606	2,862
Segment assets	87,786	9,512	76,431	173,729

An analyst uses a significant amount of judgment in deciding how to incorporate information from note disclosures into the analysis. For example, such information as financial instrument risk, contingencies, and legal proceedings can alert an analyst to risks that can affect a company's financial position and performance in the future and that require monitoring over time. As another example, information about a company's operating segments can be useful as a means of quickly understanding what a company does and how and where it earns money. The operating segment data shown in Exhibit 9 appear in the notes to the financial statements for Volkswagen. (The totals of the segment data do not equal the amounts reported in the company's financial statements because the financial statement data are adjusted for intersegment activities and unallocated items. The note provides a complete reconciliation of the segment data to the reported data.) From the data in Exhibit 9, an analyst can quickly see that most of the company's revenues and operating profits come from the sale of passenger cars and light commercial vehicles. Over 80 percent of the company's revenues was generated by this segment in both years. In 2008, this segment accounted for over 80 percent of the company's total segment operating profits, although the percentage declined to 70 percent in 2009 because of higher sales growth in the other two segments. Experience using the disclosures of a company and its competitors typically enhances an analyst's judgment about the relative importance of different disclosures and the ways in which they can be helpful.

3.1.6 Management Commentary or Management's Discussion and Analysis

Publicly held companies typically include a section in their annual reports where management discusses a variety of issues of concern, including the nature of the business, past results, and future outlook. This section is referred to by a variety of names, including management report(ing), management commentary, operating and financial review, and management's discussion and analysis. Inclusion of a management report is recommended by the International Organization of Securities Commissions and frequently required by regulatory authorities, such as the U.S. Securities and Exchange Commission (SEC) or the U.K. Financial Services Authority. In Germany, management reporting has been required since 1931 and is audited. The discussion by management is arguably one of the most useful parts of a company's annual report besides the financial statements themselves; however, other than excerpts from the financial statements, information included in the management commentary is typically unaudited. When using information from the management report, an analyst should be aware of whether the information is audited or unaudited.

To help improve the quality of the discussion by management, the International Accounting Standards Board (IASB) issued an exposure draft in June 2009 that proposed a framework for the preparation and presentation of management commentary. Per the exposure draft, that framework will provide guidance rather than set forth requirements in a standard. The exposure draft identifies five content elements of a "decision-useful management commentary." Those content elements include 1) the nature of the business; 2) management's objectives and strategies; 3) the company's significant resources, risks, and relationships; 4) results of operations; and 5) critical performance measures.

In the United States, the SEC requires listed companies to provide an MD&A and specifies the content.[7] Management must highlight any favorable or unfavorable trends and identify significant events and uncertainties that affect the company's liquidity, capital resources, and results of operations. The MD&A must also provide information about the effects of inflation, changing prices, or other material events and uncertainties that may cause the future operating results and financial condition to materially depart from the current reported financial information. In addition, the MD&A must provide information about off-balance-sheet obligations and about contractual commitments such as purchase obligations. Companies should also provide disclosure in the MD&A that discusses the critical accounting policies that require management to make subjective judgments and that have a significant impact on reported financial results.

The management commentary or MD&A is a good starting place for understanding information in the financial statements. In particular, the forward-looking disclosures in an MD&A, such as those about planned capital expenditures, new store openings, or divestitures, can be useful in projecting a company's future performance. However, the commentary is only one input for the analyst seeking an objective and independent perspective on a company's performance and prospects.

The management report in the Annual Report 2009 of Volkswagen Group includes much information of potential interest to an analyst. The 78-page management report contains sections titled Business Development; Shares and Bonds; Net Assets; Financial Position; Results of Operations; Volkswagen AG (condensed, according to German Commercial Code); Value-Enhancing Factors; Risk Report; and Report on Expected Developments.

3.1.7 *Auditor's Reports*

Financial statements presented in companies' annual reports are generally required to be audited (examined) by an independent accounting firm in accordance with specified auditing standards. The independent auditor then provides a written opinion on the financial statements. This opinion is referred to as the audit report. Audit reports take slightly different forms in different jurisdictions, but the basic components, including a specific statement of the auditor's opinion, are similar. Audits of financial statements may be required by contractual arrangement, law, or regulation.

International standards for auditing have been developed by the International Auditing and Assurance Standards Board of the International Federation of Accountants. These standards have been adopted by many countries and are referenced in audit reports issued in those countries. Other countries, such as the United States, specify

---

7 Relevant sections of SEC requirements are included for reference in the FASB ASC. The FASB ASC does not include sections of SEC requirements that deal with matters outside the basic financial statements, such as the MD&A.

their own auditing standards. With the enactment of the Sarbanes–Oxley Act of 2002 in the United States, auditing standards for public companies are promulgated by the Public Company Accounting Oversight Board.

Under international standards for auditing (ISAs), the objectives of an auditor in conducting an audit of financial statements are

A To obtain reasonable assurance about whether the financial statements as a whole are free from material misstatement, whether due to fraud or error, thereby enabling the auditor to express an opinion on whether the financial statements are prepared, in all material respects, in accordance with an applicable financial reporting framework; and

B To report on the financial statements, and communicate as required by the ISAs, in accordance with the auditor's findings.[8]

Publicly traded companies may also have requirements set by regulators or stock exchanges, such as appointing an independent audit committee within its board of directors to oversee the audit process. The audit process provides a basis for the independent auditor to express an audit opinion on whether the information presented in the audited financial statements present fairly the financial position, performance, and cash flows of the company in accordance with a specified set of accounting standards. Because audits are designed and conducted using audit sampling techniques and financial statement line items may be based on estimates and assumptions, independent auditors cannot express an opinion that provides absolute assurance about the accuracy or precision of the financial statements. Instead, the independent audit report provides *reasonable assurance* that the financial statements are *fairly presented*, meaning that there is a high probability that the audited financial statements are free from *material* error, fraud, or illegal acts that have a direct effect on the financial statements.

The standard independent audit report for a publicly traded company normally has several paragraphs under both the international and U.S. auditing standards. The first or "introductory" paragraph describes the financial statements that were audited and the responsibilities of both management and the independent auditor. The second or "scope" paragraph describes the nature of the audit process and provides the basis for the auditor's expression about reasonable assurance on the fairness of the financial statements. The third or "opinion" paragraph expresses the auditor's opinion on the fairness of the audited financial statements.

An *unqualified* audit opinion states that the financial statements give a "true and fair view" (international) or are "fairly presented" (international and U.S.) in accordance with applicable accounting standards. This is often referred to as a "clean" opinion and is the one that analysts would like to see in a financial report. There are several other types of opinions. A *qualified* audit opinion is one in which there is some scope limitation or exception to accounting standards. Exceptions are described in the audit report with additional explanatory paragraphs so that the analyst can determine the importance of the exception. An *adverse* audit opinion is issued when an auditor determines that the financial statements materially depart from accounting standards and are not fairly presented. An adverse opinion makes analysis of the financial statements easy: Do not bother analyzing these statements, because the company's financial statements cannot be relied on. Finally, a *disclaimer of opinion* occurs when, for some reason, such as a scope limitation, the auditors are unable to issue an opinion. Exhibit 10 presents

---

8 See the International Auditing and Assurance Standards Board (IAASB) *Handbook of International Quality Control, Auditing, Review, Other Assurance, and Related Services Pronouncements.*

the independent auditor's report for Volkswagen. Note that Volkswagen received an unqualified or clean audit opinion from PricewaterhouseCoopers for the company's fiscal year ended 31 December 2009.

Exhibit 10	Volkswagen's Independent Audit Report

Auditors' Report

On completion of our audit, we issued the following unqualified auditors' report dated February 17, 2010. This report was originally prepared in German. In case of ambiguities the German version takes precedence:

Auditors' Report

We have audited the consolidated financial statements prepared by VOLKSWAGEN AKTIENGESELLSCHAFT, Wolfsburg, comprising the income statement and statement of comprehensive income, the balance sheet, the statement of changes in equity, the cash flow statement and the notes to the consolidated financial statements, together with the group management report, which is combined with the management report of the Company for the business year from January 1 to December 31, 2009. The preparation of the consolidated financial statements and the combined management report in accordance with the IFRSs, as adopted by the EU, and the additional requirements of German commercial law pursuant to § (article) 315a Abs. (paragraph) 1 HGB ("Handelsgesetzbuch": German Commercial Code) are the responsibility of the Company's Board of Management. Our responsibility is to express an opinion on the consolidated financial statements and on the combined management report based on our audit.

We conducted our audit of the consolidated financial statements in accordance with § 317 HGB and German generally accepted standards for the audit of financial statements promulgated by the Institut der Wirtschaftsprüfer (Institute of Public Auditors in Germany) (IDW). Those standards require that we plan and perform the audit such that misstatements materially affecting the presentation of the net assets, financial position and results of operations in the consolidated financial statements in accordance with the applicable financial reporting framework and in the combined management report are detected with reasonable assurance. Knowledge of the business activities and the economic and legal environment of the Group and expectations as to possible misstatements are taken into account in the determination of audit procedures. The effectiveness of the accounting-related internal control system and the evidence supporting the disclosures in the consolidated financial statements and the combined management report are examined primarily on a test basis within the framework of the audit. The audit includes assessing the annual financial statements of those entities included in consolidation, the determination of the entities to be included in consolidation, the accounting and consolidation principles used and significant estimates made by the Company's Board of Management, as well as evaluating the overall presentation of the consolidated financial statements and the combined management report. We believe that our audit provides a reasonable basis for our opinion.

Our audit has not led to any reservations.

In our opinion, based on the findings of our audit, the consolidated financial statements comply with the IFRSs as adopted by the EU and the additional requirements of German commercial law pursuant to Article 315a paragraph 1 HGB and give a true and fair view of the net assets, financial position and results of operations of the Group in accordance with these requirements. The

(continued)

Exhibit 10	(Continued)

combined management report is consistent with the consolidated financial statements and as a whole provides a suitable view of the Group's position and suitably presents the opportunities and risks of future development.

Hanover, February 17, 2010

PricewaterhouseCoopers
Aktiengesellschaft
Wirtschaftsprüfungsgesellschaft

Harald Kayser
Wirtschaftsprüfer

ppa. Martin Schröder
Wirtschaftsprüfer

Source: Volkswagen's Annual Report 2009.

In the United States, under the Sarbanes–Oxley Act, the auditors must also express an opinion on the company's internal control systems. This information may be provided in a separate opinion or incorporated as a paragraph in the opinion related to the financial statements. The internal control system is the company's internal system that is designed, among other things, to ensure that the company's process for generating financial reports is sound. Although management has always been responsible for maintaining effective internal control, the Sarbanes–Oxley Act greatly increases management's responsibility for demonstrating that the company's internal controls are effective. Management of publicly traded companies in the United States are now required by securities regulators to explicitly accept responsibility for the effectiveness of internal control, evaluate the effectiveness of internal control using suitable control criteria, support the evaluation with sufficient competent evidence, and provide a report on internal control.

Although these reports and attestations provide some assurances to analysts, they are not infallible. The analyst must always use a degree of healthy skepticism when analyzing financial statements.

3.2 Other Sources of Information

The information described in Section 3.1 is generally provided to shareholders at least annually. In addition, companies also provide information on management and director compensation, company stock performance, and any potential conflicts of interest that may exist between management, the board, and shareholders. This information may appear in the company's annual report or other publicly available documents. Public companies often provide this information in proxy statements, which are statements distributed to shareholders about matters that are to be put to a vote at the company's annual (or special) meeting of shareholders.

Interim reports are also provided by the company either semiannually or quarterly, depending on the applicable regulatory requirements. Interim reports generally present the four basic financial statements and condensed notes but are not audited. These interim reports provide updated information on a company's performance and financial position since the last annual period.

Companies also provide relevant current information on their websites, in press releases, and in conference calls with analysts and investors. One type of press release, which analysts often consider to be particularly important, is the periodic earnings announcement. The earnings announcement often happens well before the company files its formal financial statements. Such earnings announcements are often followed by a conference call in which the company's senior executives describe the company's performance and answer questions posed by conference call participants. Following the earnings conference call, the investor relations portion of the company's website may post a recording of the call accompanied by slides and supplemental information discussed during the call.

When performing financial statement analysis, analysts should review all these company sources of information as well as information from external sources regarding the economy, the industry, the company, and peer (comparable) companies. Information on the economy, industry, and peer companies is useful in putting the company's financial performance and position in perspective and in assessing the company's future. In most cases, information from sources apart from the company is crucial to an analyst's effectiveness. For example, an analyst studying a consumer-oriented company will typically seek direct experience with the products (taste the food or drink, use the shampoo or soap, visit the stores or hotels). An analyst following a highly regulated industry will study the existing and expected relevant regulations. An analyst following a highly technical industry will gain relevant expertise personally or seek input from a technical specialist. In sum, thorough research goes beyond financial reports.

The next section presents a framework for using all this information in financial statement analysis.

FINANCIAL STATEMENT ANALYSIS FRAMEWORK

4

Analysts work in a variety of positions within the investment management industry. Some are equity analysts whose main objective is to evaluate potential investments in a company's equity securities (i.e., the shares or stock it issues) as a basis for deciding whether a prospective investment is attractive and what an appropriate purchase price might be. Others are credit analysts who evaluate the credit-worthiness of a company to decide whether (and with what terms) a loan should be made or what credit rating should be assigned. Analysts may also be involved in a variety of other tasks, such as evaluating the performance of a subsidiary company, evaluating a private equity investment, or finding stocks that are overvalued for purposes of taking a short position. This section presents a generic framework for financial statement analysis that can be used in these various tasks. The framework is summarized in Exhibit 11.[9]

---

9 Components of this framework have been adapted from van Greuning and Bratanovic (2003, p. 300) and from Benninga and Sarig (1997, pp. 134–156).

Exhibit 11	Financial Statement Analysis Framework	

Phase	Sources of Information	Output
1 Articulate the purpose and context of the analysis.	▪ The nature of the analyst's function, such as evaluating an equity or debt investment or issuing a credit rating. ▪ Communication with client or supervisor on needs and concerns. ▪ Institutional guidelines related to developing specific work product.	▪ Statement of the purpose or objective of analysis. ▪ A list (written or unwritten) of specific questions to be answered by the analysis. ▪ Nature and content of report to be provided. ▪ Timetable and budgeted resources for completion.
2 Collect input data.	▪ Financial statements, other financial data, questionnaires, and industry/economic data. ▪ Discussions with management, suppliers, customers, and competitors. ▪ Company site visits (e.g., to production facilities or retail stores).	▪ Organized financial statements. ▪ Financial data tables. ▪ Completed questionnaires, if applicable.
3 Process data.	▪ Data from the previous phase.	▪ Adjusted financial statements. ▪ Common-size statements. ▪ Ratios and graphs. ▪ Forecasts.
4 Analyze/interpret the processed data.	▪ Input data as well as processed data.	▪ Analytical results.
5 Develop and communicate conclusions and recommendations (e.g., with an analysis report).	▪ Analytical results and previous reports. ▪ Institutional guidelines for published reports.	▪ Analytical report answering questions posed in Phase 1. ▪ Recommendation regarding the purpose of the analysis, such as whether to make an investment or grant credit.
6 Follow-up.	▪ Information gathered by periodically repeating above steps as necessary to determine whether changes to holdings or recommendations are necessary.	▪ Updated reports and recommendations.

The following sections discuss the individual phases of financial statement analysis.

4.1 Articulate the Purpose and Context of Analysis

Prior to undertaking any analysis, it is essential to understand the purpose of the analysis. An understanding of the purpose is particularly important in financial statement analysis because of the numerous available techniques and the substantial amount of data.

Some analytical tasks are well defined, in which case articulating the purpose of the analysis requires little decision making by the analyst. For example, a periodic credit review of an investment-grade debt portfolio or an equity analyst's report on a particular company may be guided by institutional norms such that the purpose of the analysis is given. Furthermore, the format, procedures, and/or sources of information may also be given.

For other analytical tasks, articulating the purpose of the analysis requires the analyst to make decisions. The purpose of an analysis guides further decisions about the approach, the tools, the data sources, the format in which to report the results of the analysis, and the relative importance of different aspects of the analysis.

When facing a substantial amount of data, a less experienced analyst may be tempted to just start making calculations and generating financial ratios without considering what is relevant for the decision at hand. It is generally advisable to resist this temptation and thus avoid unnecessary or pointless efforts. Consider the questions: If you could have all the calculations and ratios completed instantly, what conclusion would you be able to draw? What question would you be able to answer? What decision would your answer support?

The analyst should also define the context at this stage. Who is the intended audience? What is the end product—for example, a final report explaining conclusions and recommendations? What is the time frame (i.e., when is the report due)? What resources and resource constraints are relevant to completion of the analysis? Again, the context may be predefined (i.e., standard and guided by institutional norms).

Having clarified the purpose and context of the financial statement analysis, the analyst should next compile the specific questions to be answered by the analysis. For example, if the purpose of the financial statement analysis (or, more likely, the particular stage of a larger analysis) is to compare the historical performance of three companies operating in a particular industry, specific questions would include the following: What has been the relative growth rate of the companies, and what has been the relative profitability of the companies?

4.2 Collect Data

Next, the analyst obtains the data required to answer the specific questions. A key part of this step is obtaining an understanding of the company's business, financial performance, and financial position (including trends over time and in comparison with peer companies). For historical analyses, financial statement data alone are adequate in some cases. For example, to screen a large number of alternative companies to find those with a minimum level of profitability, financial statement data alone would be adequate. But to address more in-depth questions, such as why and how one company performed better or worse than its competitors, additional information would be required. As another example, to compare the historical performance of two companies in a particular industry, the historical financial statements would be sufficient to determine which had faster-growing sales or earnings and which was more profitable; however, a broader comparison with overall industry growth and profitability would obviously require industry data.

Furthermore, information on the economy and industry is necessary to understand the environment in which the company operates. Analysts often take a top-down approach whereby they 1) gain an understanding of the macroeconomic environment, such as prospects for growth in the economy and inflation, 2) analyze the prospects of the industry in which the subject company operates based on the expected macroeconomic environment, and 3) determine the prospects for the company in the expected industry and macroeconomic environments. For example, an analyst may need to forecast future growth in earnings for a company. To project future growth, past company data provide one basis for statistical forecasting; however, an understanding of economic and industry conditions can improve the analyst's ability to forecast a company's earnings on the basis of forecasts of overall economic and industry activity.

4.3 Process Data

After obtaining the requisite financial statement and other information, the analyst processes these data using appropriate analytical tools. For example, processing the data may involve computing ratios or growth rates; preparing common-size financial statements; creating charts; performing statistical analyses, such as regressions or Monte Carlo simulations; performing equity valuation; performing sensitivity analyses; or using any other analytical tools or combination of tools that are available and appropriate for the task. A comprehensive financial analysis at this stage would include the following:

- Reading and evaluating financial statements for each company being analyzed. This includes reading the notes and understanding what accounting standards have been used (for example, IFRS or U.S. GAAP), what accounting choices have been made (for example, when to report revenue on the income statement), and what operating decisions have been made that affect reported financial statements (for example, leasing versus purchasing equipment).

- Making any needed adjustments to the financial statements to facilitate comparison when the unadjusted statements of the subject companies reflect differences in accounting standards, accounting choices, or operating decisions. Note that commonly used databases do not make such analyst adjustments.

- Preparing or collecting common-size financial statement data (which scale data to directly reflect percentages [e.g., of sales] or changes [e.g., from the prior year]) and financial ratios (which are measures of various aspects of corporate performance based on financial statement elements). On the basis of common-size financial statements and financial ratios, analysts can evaluate a company's relative profitability, liquidity, leverage, efficiency, and valuation in relation to past results and/or peers' results.

4.4 Analyze/Interpret the Processed Data

Once the data have been processed, the next step—critical to any analysis—is to interpret the output. The answer to a specific financial analysis question is seldom the numerical answer alone. Rather, the answer to the analytical question relies on the analyst's interpretation of the output and the use of this interpreted output to support a conclusion or recommendation. The answers to the specific analytical questions may themselves achieve the underlying purpose of the analysis, but usually, a conclusion or recommendation is required. For example, an equity analysis may require a buy, hold, or sell decision or a conclusion about the value of a share of stock. In support of the decision, the analysis would cite such information as target value, relative performance, expected future performance given a company's strategic position, quality of management, and whatever other information was important in reaching the decision.

4.5 Develop and Communicate Conclusions/ Recommendations

Communicating the conclusion or recommendation in an appropriate format is the next step. The appropriate format will vary by analytical task, by institution, and/ or by audience. For example, an equity analyst's report would typically include the following components:[10]

- summary and investment conclusion;
- earnings projections;
- valuation;
- business summary;
- risk, industry, and competitive analysis;
- historical performance; and
- forecasts.

The contents of reports may also be specified by regulatory agencies or professional standards. For example, the CFA Institute *Standards of Practice Handbook* (*Handbook*) dictates standards that must be followed in communicating recommendations. According to the *Handbook*:

> Standard V(B) states that members and candidates should communicate in a recommendation the factors that were instrumental in making the investment recommendation. A critical part of this requirement is to distinguish clearly between opinions and facts. In preparing a research report, the member or candidate must present the basic characteristics of the security(ies) being analyzed, which will allow the reader to evaluate the report and incorporate information the reader deems relevant to his or her investment decision making process.[11]

The *Handbook* requires that limitations to the analysis and any risks inherent to the investment be disclosed. Furthermore, the *Handbook* requires that any report include elements important to the analysis and conclusions so that readers can evaluate the conclusions themselves.

4.6 Follow-Up

The process does not end with the report. If an equity investment is made or a credit rating is assigned, periodic review is required to determine if the original conclusions and recommendations are still valid. In the case of a rejected investment, follow-up may not be necessary but may be useful in determining whether the analysis process is adequate or should be refined (for example, if a rejected investment turns out to be successful in the market, perhaps the rejection was due to inadequate analysis). Follow-up may involve repeating all the previous steps in the process on a periodic basis.

---

10 Pinto, Henry, Robinson, and Stowe (2010).
11 *Standards of Practice Handbook* (2010, p. 137).

SUMMARY

The information presented in financial and other reports, including the financial statements, notes, and management's commentary, help the financial analyst to assess a company's performance and financial position. An analyst may be called on to perform a financial analysis for a variety of reasons, including the valuation of equity securities, the assessment of credit risk, the performance of due diligence in an acquisition, and the evaluation of a subsidiary's performance relative to other business units. Major considerations in both equity analysis and credit analysis are evaluating a company's financial position, its ability to generate profits and cash flow, and its ability to generate future growth in profits and cash flow.

This reading has presented an overview of financial statement analysis. Among the major points covered are the following:

- The primary purpose of financial reports is to provide information and data about a company's financial position and performance, including profitability and cash flows. The information presented in financial reports—including the financial statements and notes—and other reports—including management's commentary or management's discussion and analysis—allows the financial analyst to assess a company's financial position and performance and trends in that performance.

- The basic financial statements are the statement of financial position (i.e., the balance sheet), the statement of comprehensive income (i.e., a single statement of comprehensive income or two statements consisting of an income statement and a statement of comprehensive income), the statement of changes in equity, and the statement of cash flows.

- The balance sheet discloses what resources a company controls (assets) and what it owes (liabilities) at a specific point in time. Owners' equity represents the net assets of the company; it is the owners' residual interest in or residual claim on the company's assets after deducting its liabilities. The relationship among the three parts of the balance sheet (assets, liabilities, and owners' equity) may be shown in equation form as follows: Assets = Liabilities + Owners' equity.

- The income statement presents information on the financial results of a company's business activities over a period of time. The income statement communicates how much revenue and other income the company generated during a period and what expenses, including losses, it incurred in connection with generating that revenue and other income. The basic equation underlying the income statement is Revenue + Other income − Expenses = Net income.

- The statement of comprehensive income includes all items that change owners' equity except transactions with owners. Some of these items are included as part of net income, and some are reported as other comprehensive income (OCI).

- The statement of changes in equity provides information about increases or decreases in the various components of owners' equity.

- Although the income statement and balance sheet provide measures of a company's success, cash and cash flow are also vital to a company's long-term success. Disclosing the sources and uses of cash helps creditors, investors, and other statement users evaluate the company's liquidity, solvency, and financial flexibility.

- The notes (also referred to as footnotes) that accompany the financial statements are an integral part of those statements and provide information that is essential to understanding the statements. Analysts should evaluate note disclosures regarding the use of alternative accounting methods, estimates, and assumptions.

- In addition to the financial statements, a company provides other sources of information that are useful to the financial analyst. As part of his or her analysis, the financial analyst should read and assess this additional information, particularly that presented in the management commentary (also called management report[ing], operating and financial review, and management's discussion and analysis [MD&A]).

- A publicly traded company must have an independent audit performed on its annual financial statements. The auditor's report expresses an opinion on the financial statements and provides some assurance about whether the financial statements fairly present a company's financial position, performance, and cash flows. In addition, for U.S. publicly traded companies, auditors must also express an opinion on the company's internal control systems.

- Information on the economy, industry, and peer companies is useful in putting the company's financial performance and position in perspective and in assessing the company's future. In most cases, information from sources apart from the company are crucial to an analyst's effectiveness.

- The financial statement analysis framework provides steps that can be followed in any financial statement analysis project. These steps are:
  - articulate the purpose and context of the analysis;
  - collect input data;
  - process data;
  - analyze/interpret the processed data;
  - develop and communicate conclusions and recommendations; and
  - follow up.

REFERENCES

Benninga, Simon Z., and Oded H. Sarig. 1997. *Corporate Finance: A Valuation Approach* (New York: McGraw-Hill Publishing).

International Auditing and Assurance Standards Board (IAASB).*Handbook of International Quality Control, Auditing, Review, Other Assurance, and Related Services Pronouncements*, Standard 200, available at www.ifac.org/IAASB.

Pinto, Jerald E., Elaine Henry, Thomas R. Robinson, and John D. Stowe. 2010. *Equity Asset Valuation*, 2nd edition. Hoboken, NJ: John Wiley & Sons.

van Greuning, Hennie, and Sonja Brajovic Bratanovic. 2003. *Analyzing and Managing Banking Risk: A Framework for Assessing Corporate Governance and Financial Risk*. Washington, DC: World Bank.

PRACTICE PROBLEMS

1   Providing information about the performance and financial position of companies so that users can make economic decisions *best* describes the role of:

   A   auditing.

   B   financial reporting.

   C   financial statement analysis.

2   A company's current financial position would *best* be evaluated using the:

   A   balance sheet.

   B   income statement.

   C   statement of cash flows.

3   A company's profitability for a period would *best* be evaluated using the:

   A   balance sheet.

   B   income statement.

   C   statement of cash flows.

4   Accounting policies, methods, and estimates used in preparing financial statements are *most likely* found in the:

   A   auditor's report.

   B   management commentary.

   C   notes to the financial statements.

5   Information about management and director compensation would *least likely* be found in the:

   A   auditor's report.

   B   proxy statement.

   C   notes to the financial statements.

6   Information about a company's objectives, strategies, and significant risks would *most likely* be found in the:

   A   auditor's report.

   B   management commentary.

   C   notes to the financial statements.

7   What type of audit opinion is preferred when analyzing financial statements?

   A   Qualified.

   B   Adverse.

   C   Unqualified.

8   Ratios are an input into which step in the financial statement analysis framework?

   A   Process data.

   B   Collect input data.

   C   Analyze/interpret the processed data.

SOLUTIONS

1 B is correct. This is the role of financial reporting. The role of financial statement analysis is to evaluate the financial reports.

2 A is correct. The balance sheet portrays the current financial position. The income statement and statement of cash flows present different aspects of performance.

3 B is correct. Profitability is the performance aspect measured by the income statement. The balance sheet portrays the current financial position. The statement of cash flows presents a different aspect of performance.

4 C is correct. The notes disclose choices in accounting policies, methods, and estimates.

5 A is correct. Information about management and director compensation is not found in the auditor's report. Disclosure of management compensation is required in the proxy statement, and some aspects of management compensation are disclosed in the notes to the financial statements.

6 B is correct. These are components of management commentary.

7 C is correct. An unqualified opinion is a "clean" opinion and indicates that the financial statements present the company's performance and financial position fairly in accordance with a specified set of accounting standards.

8 C is correct. Ratios are an output of the process data step but are an input into the analyze/interpret data step.

READING

23

Financial Reporting Mechanics

by Thomas R. Robinson, CFA, Jan Hendrik van Greuning, CFA,
Karen O'Connor Rubsam, CFA, Elaine Henry, CFA, and
Michael A. Broihahn, CFA

LEARNING OUTCOMES

Mastery	The candidate should be able to:
☐	a. explain the relationship of financial statement elements and accounts, and classify accounts into the financial statement elements;
☐	b. explain the accounting equation in its basic and expanded forms;
☐	c. describe the process of recording business transactions using an accounting system based on the accounting equation;
☐	d. describe the need for accruals and other adjustments in preparing financial statements;
☐	e. describe the relationships among the income statement, balance sheet, statement of cash flows, and statement of owners' equity;
☐	f. describe the flow of information in an accounting system;
☐	g. describe the use of the results of the accounting process in security analysis.

Note: New rulings and/ or pronouncements issued after the publication of the readings on financial reporting and analysis may cause some of the information in these readings to become dated. Candidates are expected to be familiar with the overall analytical framework contained in the study session readings, as well as the implications of alternative accounting methods for financial analysis and valuation, as provided in the assigned readings. Candidates are not responsible for changes that occur after the material was written.

1   INTRODUCTION

The financial statements of a company are end-products of a process for recording transactions of the company related to operations, financing, and investment. The structures of financial statements themselves reflect the system of recording and organizing transactions. To be an informed user of financial statements, the analyst must be knowledgeable about the principles of this system. This reading will supply that essential knowledge, taking the perspective of the user rather than the preparer. Learning the process from this perspective will enable an analyst to grasp the critical concepts without being overwhelmed by the detailed technical skills required by the accountants who prepare financial statements that are a major component of financial reports.

This reading is organized as follows: Section 2 describes the three groups into which business activities are classified for financial reporting purposes. Any transaction affects one or more of these groups. Section 3 describes how the elements of financial statements relate to accounts, the basic content unit of classifying transactions. The section is also an introduction to the linkages among the financial statements. Section 4 provides a step-by-step illustration of the accounting process. Section 5 explains the consequences of timing differences between the elements of a transaction. Section 6 provides an overview of how information flows through a business's accounting system. Section 7 introduces the use of financial reporting in security analysis. A summary of the key points and practice problems in the CFA Institute multiple-choice format conclude the reading.

2   THE CLASSIFICATION OF BUSINESS ACTIVITIES

Accountants give similar accounting treatment to similar types of business transactions. Therefore, a first step in understanding financial reporting mechanics is to understand how business activities are classified for financial reporting purposes.

Business activities may be classified into three groups for financial reporting purposes: operating, investing, and financing activities.

- **Operating activities** are those activities that are part of the day-to-day business functioning of an entity. Examples include the sale of meals by a restaurant, the sale of services by a consulting firm, the manufacture and sale of ovens by an oven-manufacturing company, and taking deposits and making loans by a bank.

- **Investing activities** are those activities associated with acquisition and disposal of long-term assets. Examples include the purchase of equipment or sale of surplus equipment (such as an oven) by a restaurant (contrast this to the sale of an oven by an oven manufacturer, which would be an operating activity), and the purchase or sale of an office building, a retail store, or a factory.

- **Financing activities** are those activities related to obtaining or repaying capital. The two primary sources for such funds are owners (shareholders) or creditors. Examples include issuing common shares, taking out a bank loan, and issuing bonds.

Understanding the nature of activities helps the analyst understand where the company is doing well and where it is not doing so well. Ideally, an analyst would prefer that most of a company's profits (and cash flow) come from its operating activities. Exhibit 1 provides examples of typical business activities and how these activities relate to the elements of financial statements described in the following section.

Exhibit 1	Typical Business Activities and Financial Statement Elements Affected

Operating activities	■ Sales of goods and services to customers: (R)
	■ Costs of providing the goods and services: (X)
	■ Income tax expense: (X)
	■ Holding short-term assets or incurring short-term liabilities directly related to operating activities: (A), (L)
Investing activities	■ Purchase or sale of assets, such as property, plant, and equipment: (A)
	■ Purchase or sale of other entities' equity and debt securities: (A)
Financing activities	■ Issuance or repurchase of the company's own preferred or common stock: (E)
	■ Issuance or repayment of debt: (L)
	■ Payment of distributions (i.e., dividends to preferred or common stockholders): (E)

Accounting elements: Assets (A), Liabilities (L), Owners' Equity (E), Revenue (R), and Expenses (X).

Not all transactions fit neatly in this framework for purposes of financial statement presentation. For example, interest received by a bank on one of its loans would be considered part of operating activities because a bank is in the business of lending money. In contrast, interest received on a bond investment by a restaurant may be more appropriately classified as an investing activity because the restaurant is not in the business of lending money.

The next section discusses how transactions resulting from these business activities are reflected in a company's financial records.

ACCOUNTS AND FINANCIAL STATEMENTS

3

Business activities resulting in transactions are reflected in the broad groupings of financial statement elements: Assets, Liabilities, Owners' Equity, Revenue, and Expenses.[1] In general terms, these elements can be defined as follows: **assets** are the economic resources of a company; **liabilities** are the creditors' claims on the resources

---

1 International Financial Reporting Standards use the term "income" to include revenue and gains. Gains are similar to revenue; however, they arise from secondary or peripheral activities rather than from a company's primary business activities. For example, for a restaurant, the sale of surplus restaurant equipment for more than its cost is referred to as a gain rather than revenue. Similarly, a loss is like an expense but arises from secondary activities. Gains and losses may be considered part of operations on the income statement (for example, a loss due to a decline in value of inventory) or may be part of nonoperating activities (for example, the sale of nontrading investments). Under U.S. GAAP, financial statement elements are defined to include assets, liabilities, owners' equity, revenue, expenses, gains, and losses. To illustrate business transactions in this reading, we will use the simple classification of revenues and expenses. All gains and revenue will be aggregated in revenue, and all losses and expenses will be aggregated in expenses.

of a company; **owners' equity** is the residual claim on those resources; **revenues** are inflows of economic resources to the company; and **expenses** are outflows of economic resources or increases in liabilities.[2]

Accounts provide individual records of increases and decreases in a *specific* asset, liability, component of owners' equity, revenue, or expense. The financial statements are constructed using these elements.

3.1 Financial Statement Elements and Accounts

Within the financial statement elements, accounts are subclassifications. **Accounts** are individual records of increases and decreases in a specific asset, liability, component of owners' equity, revenue, or expense. For financial statements, amounts recorded in every individual account are summarized and grouped appropriately within a financial statement element. Exhibit 2 provides a listing of common accounts. These accounts will be described throughout this reading or in following readings. Unlike the financial statement elements, there is no standard set of accounts applicable to all companies. Although almost every company has certain accounts, such as cash, each company specifies the accounts in its accounting system based on its particular needs and circumstances. For example, a company in the restaurant business may not be involved in trading securities and, therefore, may not need an account to record such an activity. Furthermore, each company names its accounts based on its business. A company in the restaurant business might have an asset account for each of its ovens, with the accounts named "Oven-1" and "Oven-2." In its financial statements, these accounts would likely be grouped within long-term assets as a single line item called "Property, plant, and equipment."

A company's challenge is to establish accounts and account groupings that provide meaningful summarization of voluminous data but retain enough detail to facilitate decision making and preparation of the financial statements. The actual accounts used in a company's accounting system will be set forth in a **chart of accounts**. Generally, the chart of accounts is far more detailed than the information presented in financial statements.

Certain accounts are used to offset other accounts. For example, a common asset account is accounts receivable, also known as "trade accounts receivable" or "trade receivables." A company uses this account to record the amounts it is owed by its customers. In other words, sales made on credit are reflected in accounts receivable. In connection with its receivables, a company often expects some amount of uncollectible accounts and, therefore, records an estimate of the amount that may not be collected. The estimated uncollectible amount is recorded in an account called **allowance for bad debts**. Because the effect of the allowance for bad debts account is to reduce the balance of the company's accounts receivable, it is known as a "contra asset account." Any account that is offset or deducted from another account is called a "**contra account**." Common contra asset accounts include allowance for bad debts (an offset to accounts receivable for the amount of accounts receivable that are estimated to be uncollectible), **accumulated depreciation** (an offset to property, plant, and equipment reflecting the amount of the cost of property, plant, and equipment that has been allocated to current and previous accounting periods), and **sales returns and allowances** (an offset to revenue reflecting any cash refunds, credits on account, and discounts from sales prices given to customers who purchased defective or unsatisfactory items).

---

2 The authoritative accounting standards provide significantly more detailed definitions of the accounting elements. Also note that "owners' equity" is a generic term and more specific titles are often used such as "shareholders' equity," "stockholders' equity," or "partners' capital." The broader terms "equity" and "capital" are also used on occasion.

Exhibit 2	**Common Accounts**

Assets	■ Cash and cash equivalents
	■ Accounts receivable, trade receivables
	■ Prepaid expenses
	■ Inventory
	■ Property, plant, and equipment
	■ Investment property
	■ Intangible assets (patents, trademarks, licenses, copyright, goodwill)
	■ Financial assets, trading securities, investment securities
	■ Investments accounted for by the equity method
	■ Current and deferred tax assets
	■ [for banks, Loans (receivable)]
Liabilities	■ Accounts payable, trade payables
	■ Provisions or accrued liabilities
	■ Financial liabilities
	■ Current and deferred tax liabilities
	■ Reserves
	■ Minority interest
	■ Unearned revenue
	■ Debt payable
	■ Bonds (payable)
	■ [for banks, Deposits]
Owners' Equity	■ Capital, such as common stock par value
	■ Additional paid-in capital
	■ Retained earnings
	■ Other comprehensive income
Revenue	■ Revenue, sales
	■ Gains
	■ Investment income (e.g., interest and dividends)
Expense	■ Cost of goods sold
	■ Selling, general, and administrative expenses "SG&A" (e.g., rent, utilities, salaries, advertising)
	■ Depreciation and amortization
	■ Interest expense
	■ Tax expense
	■ Losses

For presentation purposes, assets are sometimes categorized as "current" or "noncurrent." For example, Tesco (a large European retailer) presents the following major asset accounts in its 2006 financial reports:

Noncurrent assets:

■ Intangible assets including goodwill;

■ Property, plant, and equipment;

- Investment property;
- Investments in joint ventures and associates.

Current assets:

- Inventories;
- Trade and other receivables;
- Cash and cash equivalents.

Noncurrent assets are assets that are expected to benefit the company over an extended period of time (usually more than one year). For Tesco, these include the following: intangible assets, such as goodwill;[3] property, plant, and equipment used in operations (e.g., land and buildings); other property held for investment, and investments in the securities of other companies.

Current assets are those that are expected to be consumed or converted into cash in the near future, typically one year or less. **Inventory** is the unsold units of product on hand (sometimes referred to as inventory stock). **Trade receivables** (also referred to as **commercial receivables**, or simply **accounts receivable**) are amounts customers owe the company for products that have been sold as well as amounts that may be due from suppliers (such as for returns of merchandise). **Other receivables** represent amounts owed to the company from parties other than customers. **Cash** refers to cash on hand (e.g., petty cash and cash not yet deposited to the bank) and in the bank. **Cash equivalents** are very liquid short-term investments, usually maturing in 90 days or less. The presentation of assets as current or noncurrent will vary from industry to industry and from country to country. Some industries present current assets first, whereas others list noncurrent assets first. This is discussed further in later readings.

3.2 Accounting Equations

The five financial statement elements noted previously serve as the inputs for equations that underlie the financial statements. This section describes the equations for three of the financial statements: balance sheet, income statement, and statement of retained earnings. A statement of retained earnings can be viewed as a component of the statement of stockholders' equity, which shows *all* changes to owners' equity, both changes resulting from retained earnings and changes resulting from share issuance or repurchase. The fourth basic financial statement, the statement of cash flows, will be discussed in a later section.

The **balance sheet** presents a company's financial position at a *particular point in time*. It provides a listing of a company's assets and the claims on those assets (liabilities and equity claims). The equation that underlies the balance sheet is also known as the "basic accounting equation." A company's financial position is reflected using the following equation:

$$\text{Assets} = \text{Liabilities} + \text{Owners' equity} \tag{1a}$$

Presented in this form, it is clear that claims on assets are from two sources: liabilities or owners' equity. Owners' equity is the **residual claim** of the owners (i.e., the owners' remaining claim on the company's assets after the liabilities are deducted). The concept of the owners' residual claim is well illustrated by the slightly rearranged balance sheet equation, roughly equivalent to the structure commonly seen in the balance sheets of U.K. companies:

$$\text{Assets} - \text{Liabilities} = \text{Owners' equity} \tag{1b}$$

---

3 Goodwill is an intangible asset that represents the excess of the purchase price of an acquired company over the value of the net assets acquired.

Other terms are used to denote owners' equity, including shareholders' equity, stockholders' equity, net assets, equity, net worth, net book value, and partners' capital. The exact titles depend upon the type of entity, but the equation remains the same. Owners' equity at a given date can be further classified by its origin: capital contributed by owners, and earnings retained in the business up to that date:[4]

Owners' equity = Contributed capital + Retained earnings   (2)

The **income statement** presents the performance of a business for a *specific period of time*. The equation reflected in the income statement is the following:

Revenue – Expenses = Net income (loss)   (3)

Note that **net income** (loss) is the difference between two of the elements: revenue and expenses. When a company's revenue exceeds its expenses, it reports net income; when a company's revenues are less than its expenses, it reports a net loss. Other terms are used synonymously with revenue, including sales and turnover (in the United Kingdom). Other terms used synonymously with net income include net profit and net earnings.

Also, as noted earlier, revenue and expenses generally relate to providing goods or services in a company's primary business activities. In contrast, gains (losses) relate to increases (decreases) in resources that are not part of a company's primary business activities. Distinguishing a company's primary business activities from other business activities is important in financial analysis; however, for purposes of the accounting equation, gains are included in revenue and losses are included in expenses.

The balance sheet and income statement are two of the primary financial statements. Although these are the common terms for these statements, some variations in the names occur. A balance sheet can be referred to as a "statement of financial position" or some similar term that indicates it contains balances at a point in time. Income statements can be titled "statement of operations," "statement of income," "statement of profit and loss," or some other similar term showing that it reflects the company's operating activity for a period of time. A simplified balance sheet and income statement are shown in Exhibit 3.

Exhibit 3	Simplified Balance Sheet and Income Statement

ABC Company, Inc. Balance Sheet As of 31 December 20X1		ABC Company, Inc. Income Statement For the Year Ended 31 December 20X1	
Assets	2,000	Revenue	250
Liabilities	500	Expense	50
Owners' equity	1,500	Net income	200
	2,000		

---

4 This formula reflects the fundamental origins of owners' equity and reflects the basic principles of accounting. The presentation is somewhat simplified. In practice, the owners' equity section of a company's balance sheet may include other items, such as treasury stock (which arises when a company repurchases and holds its own stock) or other comprehensive income. **Comprehensive income** includes all income of the company. Some items of comprehensive income are not reported on the income statement. These items as a group are called **other comprehensive income**; such items arise, for example, when there are changes in the value of assets or liabilities that are not reflected in the income statement.

The balance sheet represents a company's financial position at a point in time, and the income statement represents a company's activity over a period of time. The two statements are linked together through the retained earnings component of owners' equity. Beginning retained earnings is the balance in this account at the beginning of the accounting period, and ending retained earnings is the balance at the end of the period. A company's ending retained earnings is composed of the beginning balance (if any), plus net income, less any distributions to owners (dividends). Accordingly, the equation underlying retained earnings is:

$$\text{Ending retained earnings} = \text{Beginning retained earnings} + \text{Net income} - \text{Dividends} \tag{4a}$$

Or, substituting Equation 3 for Net income, equivalently:

$$\text{Ending retained earnings} = \text{Beginning retained earnings} + \text{Revenues} - \text{Expenses} - \text{Dividends} \tag{4b}$$

As its name suggests, retained earnings represent the earnings (i.e., net income) that are retained by the company—in other words, the amount not distributed as dividends to owners. Retained earnings is a component of owners' equity and links the "as of" balance sheet equation with the "activity" equation of the income statement. To provide a combined representation of the balance sheet and income statement, we can substitute Equation 2 into Equation 1a. This becomes the expanded accounting equation:

$$\text{Assets} = \text{Liabilities} + \text{Contributed capital} + \text{Ending retained earnings} \tag{5a}$$

Or equivalently, substituting Equation 4b into Equation 5a, we can write:

$$\text{Assets} = \text{Liabilities} + \text{Contributed capital} + \text{Beginning retained earnings} + \text{Revenue} - \text{Expenses} - \text{Dividends} \tag{5b}$$

The last five items, beginning with contributed capital, are components of owners' equity.

The **statement of retained earnings** shows the linkage between the balance sheet and income statement. Exhibit 4 shows a simplified example of financial statements for a company that began the year with retained earnings of $250 and recognized $200 of net income during the period. The example assumes the company paid no dividends and, therefore, had ending retained earnings of $450.

Exhibit 4	Simplified Balance Sheet, Income Statement, and Statement of Retained Earnings

Point in Time: Beginning of Period Balance Sheet		Change over Time: Income Statement *and* Changes in Retained Earnings		Point in Time: End of Period Balance Sheet	
ABC Company, Inc. (Beginning) Balance Sheet As of 31 December 20X0		**ABC Company, Inc. Income Statement Year Ended 31 December 20X1**		**ABC Company, Inc. (Ending) Balance Sheet As of 31 December 20X1**	
Assets	2,000	Revenue	250	Assets	2,200
		Expense	50		
Liabilities	500	Net income	200	Liabilities	500
Contributed equity	1,250			Combined equity	1,250
Retained earnings	**250**			**Retained earnings**	**450**
Owners' equity	1,500			Owners' equity	1,700
	2,000				2,200

Exhibit 4	(Continued)

Point in Time: Beginning of Period Balance Sheet	Change over Time: Income Statement *and* Changes in Retained Earnings	Point in Time: End of Period Balance Sheet
	ABC Company, Inc. **Statement of Retained Earnings Year Ended 31 December 20X1**	
	Beginning retained earnings 250	
	Plus net income 200	
	Minus dividends 0	
	Ending retained earnings 450	

The basic accounting equation reflected in the balance sheet (Assets = Liabilities + Owners' equity) implies that every recorded transaction affects at least two accounts in order to keep the equation in balance, hence the term **double-entry accounting** that is sometimes used to describe the accounting process. For example, the use of cash to purchase equipment affects two accounts (both asset accounts): cash decreases and equipment increases. As another example, the use of cash to pay off a liability also affects two accounts (one asset account and one liability account): cash decreases and the liability decreases. With each transaction, the accounting equation remains in balance, which is a fundamental accounting concept. Example 1 presents a partial balance sheet for an actual company and an application of the accounting equation. Examples 2 and 3 provide further practice for applying the accounting equations.

EXAMPLE 1

Using Accounting Equations (1)

Canon is a manufacturer of copy machines and other electronic equipment. Abbreviated balance sheets as of 31 December 2004 and 2005 are presented below.

Canon and Subsidiaries Consolidated Balance Sheets (Millions of Yen)		
	31 Dec 2005	**31 Dec 2004**
Assets		
Total assets	¥4,043,553	¥3,587,021
Liabilities and stockholders' equity		
Total liabilities	1,238,535	1,190,331
Total stockholders' equity	?	2,396,690
Total liabilities and stockholders' equity	¥4,043,553	¥3,587,021

Using Equation 1a, address the following:

1 Determine the amount of stockholders' equity as of 31 December 2005.

2 A Calculate and contrast the absolute change in total assets in 2005 with the absolute change in total stockholders' equity in 2005.

B Based on your answer to 2A, state and justify the relative importance of growth in stockholders' equity and growth in liabilities in financing the growth of assets over the two years.

Solution to 1:

Total stockholders' equity is equal to assets minus liabilities; in other words, it is the residual claim to the company's assets after deducting liabilities. For 2005, the amount of Canon's total stockholders' equity was thus ¥4,043,553 million – ¥1,238,535 million = ¥2,805,018 million in 2005.

Solutions to 2:

A Total assets increased by ¥4,043,553 million – ¥3,587,021 million = ¥456,532 million. Total stockholders' equity increased by ¥2,805,018 million – ¥2,396,690 million = ¥408,328 million. Thus, in 2005, total assets grew by more than total stockholders' equity (¥456,532 million is larger than ¥408,328 million).

B Using the relationship Assets = Liabilities + Owners' equity, the solution to 2A implies that total liabilities increased by the difference between the increase in total assets and the increase in total stockholders' equity, that is, by ¥456,532 million – ¥408,328 million = ¥48,204 million. (If liabilities had not increased by ¥48,204 million, the accounting equation would not be in balance.) Contrasting the growth in total stockholders' equity (¥408,328 million) with the growth in total liabilities (¥48,204 million), we see that the growth in stockholders' equity was relatively much more important than the growth in liabilities in financing total asset growth in 2005.

EXAMPLE 2

Using Accounting Equations (2)

An analyst has collected the following information regarding a company in advance of its year-end earnings announcement (amounts in millions):

Estimated net income	$150
Beginning retained earnings	$2,000
Estimated distributions to owners	$50

The analyst's estimate of ending retained earnings (in millions) should be closest to:

A $2,000.

B $2,100.

C $2,150.

D $2,200.

Solution:

B is correct. Beginning retained earnings is increased by net income and reduced by distributions to owners: $2,000 + $150 − $50 = $2,100.

EXAMPLE 3

Using Accounting Equations (3)

An analyst has compiled the following information regarding RDZ, Inc.

Liabilities at year-end	€1,000
Contributed capital at year-end	€1,000
Beginning retained earnings	€500
Revenue during the year	€4,000
Expenses during the year	€3,800

There have been no distributions to owners. The analyst's estimate of total assets at year-end should be closest to:

A €2,000.

B €2,300.

C €2,500.

D €2,700.

Solution:

D is correct. Ending retained earnings is first determined by adding revenue minus expenses to beginning retained earnings to obtain €700. Total assets would be equal to the sum of liabilities, contributed capital, and ending retained earnings: €1,000 + €1,000 + €700 = €2,700.

Having described the components and linkages of financial statements in abstract terms, we now examine more concretely how business activities are recorded. The next section illustrates the accounting process with a simple step-by-step example.

THE ACCOUNTING PROCESS
4

The accounting process involves recording business transactions such that periodic financial statements can be prepared. This section illustrates how business transactions are recorded in a simplified accounting system.

4.1 An Illustration

Key concepts of the accounting process can be more easily explained using a simple illustration. We look at an illustration in which three friends decide to start a business, Investment Advisers, Ltd. (IAL). They plan to issue a monthly newsletter of securities trading advice and to sell investment books. Although they do not plan to manage any clients' funds, they will manage a trading portfolio of the owners' funds to demonstrate the success of the recommended strategies from the newsletter. Because this illustration is meant to present accounting concepts, any regulatory implications will not be addressed. Additionally, for this illustration, we will assume that the entity will not be subject to income taxes; any income or loss will be passed through to the owners and be subject to tax on their personal income tax returns.

As the business commences, various business activities occur. Exhibit 5 provides a listing of the business activities that have taken place in the early stages of operations. Note that these activities encompass the types of operating, investing, and financing business activities discussed above.

Exhibit 5		Business Activities for Investment Advisers, Ltd.
#	Date	Business Activity
1	31 December 2005	■ File documents with regulatory authorities to establish a separate legal entity. Initially capitalize the company through deposit of $150,000 from the three owners.
2	2 January 2006	■ Set up a $100,000 investment account and purchase a portfolio of equities and fixed-income securities.
3	2 January 2006	■ Pay $3,000 to landlord for office/warehouse. $2,000 represents a refundable deposit, and $1,000 represents the first month's rent.
4	3 January 2006	■ Purchase office equipment for $6,000. The equipment has an estimated life of two years with no salvage value.*
5	3 January 2006	■ Receive $1,200 cash for a one-year subscription to the monthly newsletter.
6	10 January 2006	■ Purchase and receive 500 books at a cost of $20 per book for a total of $10,000. Invoice terms are that payment from IAL is due in 30 days. No cash changes hands. These books are intended for resale.
7	10 January 2006	■ Spend $600 on newspaper and trade magazine advertising for the month.
8	15 January 2006	■ Borrow $12,000 from a bank for working capital. Interest is payable annually at 10 percent. The principal is due in two years.
9	15 January 2006	■ Ship first order to a customer consisting of five books at $25 per book. Invoice terms are that payment is due in 30 days. No cash changes hands.
10	15 January 2006	■ Sell for cash 10 books at $25 per book at an investment conference.
11	30 January 2006	■ Hire a part-time clerk. The clerk is hired through an agency that also handles all payroll taxes. The company is to pay $15 per hour to the agency. The clerk works six hours prior to 31 January, but no cash will be paid until February.
12	31 January 2006	■ Mail out the first month's newsletter to customer. This subscription had been sold on 3 January. See item 5.

Exhibit 5	(Continued)

13 31 January 2006
- Review of the investment portfolio shows that $100 of interest income was earned and the market value of the portfolio has increased by $2,000. The balance in the investment account is now $102,100. The securities are classified as "trading" securities.

*Salvage value (residual value) is the amount the company estimates that it can sell the asset for at the end of its useful life.

4.2 The Accounting Records

If the owners want to evaluate the business at the end of January 2006, Exhibit 5 does not provide a sufficiently meaningful report of what transpired or where the company currently stands. It is clear that a system is needed to track this information and to address three objectives:

- Identify those activities requiring further action (e.g., collection of outstanding receivable balances).
- Assess the profitability of the operations over the month.
- Evaluate the current financial position of the company (such as cash on hand).

An accounting system will translate the company's business activities into usable financial records. The basic system for recording transactions in this illustration is a spreadsheet with each of the different types of accounts represented by a column. The accounting equation provides a basis for setting up this system. Recall the accounting Equation 5b:

Assets = Liabilities + Contributed capital + Beginning retained earnings + Revenue − Expenses − Dividends

The specific accounts to be used for IAL's system include the following:

- Asset Accounts:

    Cash

    Investments

    Prepaid rent (cash paid for rent in advance of recognizing the expense)

    Rent deposit (cash deposited with the landlord, but returnable to the company)

    Office equipment

    Inventory

    Accounts receivable

- Liability Accounts:

    Unearned fees (fees that have not been earned yet, even though cash has been received)

    Accounts payable (amounts owed to suppliers)

    Bank debt

- Equity Accounts:

    Contributed capital

    Retained earnings

Income

Revenue

Expenses

Dividends

Exhibit 6 presents the spreadsheet representing IAL's accounting system for the first 10 transactions. Each event is entered on a new row of the spreadsheet as it occurs. To record events in the spreadsheet, the financial impact of each needs to be assessed and the activity expressed as an accounting transaction. In assessing the financial impact of each event and converting these events into accounting transactions, the following steps are taken:

1   Identify which accounts are affected, by what amount, and whether the accounts are increased or decreased.

2   Determine the element type for each account identified in Step 1 (e.g., cash is an asset) and where it fits in the basic accounting equation. Rely on the economic characteristics of the account and the basic definitions of the elements to make this determination.

3   Using the information from Steps 1 and 2, enter the amounts in the appropriate column of the spreadsheet.

4   Verify that the accounting equation is still in balance.

At any point in time, basic financial statements can be prepared based on the subtotals in each column.

The following discussion identifies the accounts affected and the related element (Steps 1 and 2) for the first 10 events listed in Exhibit 5. The accounting treatment shows the account affected in bold and the related element in brackets. The recording of these entries into a basic accounting system (Steps 3 and 4) is depicted on the spreadsheet in Exhibit 6.

Because this is a new business, the accounting equation begins at zero on both sides. There is a zero beginning balance in all accounts.

	31 December 2005	
#	**Business Activity**	**Accounting Treatment**
1	■ File documents with regulatory authorities to establish a separate legal entity. Initially capitalize the company through deposit of $150,000 from the three owners.	■ **Cash [A]** is increased by $150,000, and **contributed capital [E]*** is increased by $150,000.

Accounting elements: Assets (A), Liabilities (L), Equity (E), Revenue (R), and Expenses (X).
*The account title will vary depending upon the type of entity (incorporated or not) and jurisdiction. Alternative account titles are "common shares," "common stock," "members' capital," "partners' capital," etc.

This transaction affects two elements: assets and equity. Exhibit 6 demonstrates this effect on the accounting equation. The company's balance sheet at this point in time would be presented by subtotaling the columns in Exhibit 6:

Exhibit 6   Accounting System for Investment Advisers, Ltd.

#	Assets = Cash	Assets = Other Assets	Assets = Account	Liabilities + Amount	Liabilities + Account	Contributed Capital	Beginning Retained Earnings	Owners' Equity Revenue	Owners' Equity Expense	Owners' Equity Dividends
Beg. Balance	0	0		0		0	0	0	0	0
1 Capitalize	150,000					150,000				
2 Investments	(100,000)	100,000	Investments							
3 Pay landlord	(3,000)	1,000	Prepaid rent							
		2,000	Rent deposit							
4 Buy equipment	(6,000)	6,000	Office equipment							
5 Sell subscription	1,200			1,200	Unearned fees					
6 Buy books		10,000	Inventory	10,000	Accounts payable					
7 Advertise	(600)								(600)	
8 Borrow	12,000			12,000	Bank debt					
9 Sell books on account		125	Accounts receivable					125	(100)	
		(100)	Inventory							
10 Cash sale	250	(200)	Inventory					250	(200)	
Subtotal	**53,850**	**118,825**		**23,200**		**150,000**		**375**	**(900)**	

Investment Advisers, Ltd. Balance Sheet As of 31 December 2005	
Assets	
Cash	$150,000
Total assets	$150,000
Liabilities and owners' equity	
Contributed capital	$150,000
Total liabilities and owners' equity	$150,000

The company has assets (resources) of $150,000, and the owners' claim on the resources equals $150,000 (their contributed capital) as there are no liabilities at this point.

For this illustration, we present an unclassified balance sheet. An **unclassified balance sheet** is one that does not show subtotals for current assets and current liabilities. Assets are simply listed in order of liquidity (how quickly they are expected to be converted into cash). Similarly, liabilities are listed in the order in which they are expected to be satisfied (or paid off).

	2 January 2006	
#	**Business Activity**	**Accounting Treatment**
2	■ Set up a $100,000 investment account and purchase a portfolio of equities and fixed-income securities.	■ **Investments [A]** were increased by $100,000, and **cash [A]** was decreased by $100,000.

Accounting elements: Assets (A), Liabilities (L), Equity (E), Revenue (R), and Expenses (X).

This transaction affects two accounts, but only one element (assets) and one side of the accounting equation, as depicted in Exhibit 6. Cash is reduced when the securities are purchased. Another type of asset, investments, increases. We examine the other transaction from 2 January before taking another look at the company's balance sheet.

	2 January 2006	
#	**Business Activity**	**Accounting Treatment**
3	■ Pay $3,000 to landlord for office/warehouse. $2,000 represents a refundable deposit, and $1,000 represents the first month's rent.	■ **Cash [A]** was decreased by $3,000, **deposits [A]** were increased by $2,000, and **prepaid rent [A]** was increased by $1,000.

Accounting elements: Assets (A), Liabilities (L), Equity (E), Revenue (R), and Expenses (X).

Once again, this transaction affects only asset accounts. Note that the first month's rent is initially recorded as an asset, prepaid rent. As time passes, the company will incur rent expense, so a portion of this prepaid asset will be transferred to expenses and thus will appear on the income statement as an expense.[5] This will require a later adjustment in our accounting system. Note that the transactions so far have had no impact on the income statement. At this point in time, the company's balance sheet would be:

Investment Advisers, Ltd. Balance Sheet As of 2 January 2006	
Assets	
Cash	$ 47,000
Investments	100,000
Prepaid rent	1,000
Deposits	2,000
Total assets	$150,000
Liabilities and owners' equity	
Contributed capital	$150,000
Total liabilities and owners' equity	$150,000

Note that the items in the balance sheet have changed, but it remains in balance; the amount of total assets equals total liabilities plus owners' equity. The company still has $150,000 in resources, but the assets now comprise cash, investments, prepaid rent, and deposits. Each asset is listed separately because they are different in terms of their ability to be used by the company. Note also that the owners' equity claim on these assets remains $150,000 because the company still has no liabilities.

	3 January 2006	
#	**Business Activity**	**Accounting Treatment**
4	■ Purchase office equipment for $6,000 in cash. The equipment has an estimated life of two years with no salvage value.	■ **Cash [A]** was decreased by $6,000, and **office equipment [A]** was increased by $6,000.

Accounting elements: Assets (A), Liabilities (L), Equity (E), Revenue (R), and Expenses (X).

The company has once again exchanged one asset for another. Cash has decreased while office equipment has increased. Office equipment is a resource that will provide benefits over multiple future periods and, therefore, its cost must also be spread over

---

5 An argument can be made for treating this $1,000 as an immediate expense. We adopt the approach of recording a prepaid asset in order to illustrate accrual accounting. A situation in which a company prepays rent (or insurance or any similar expense) for a time span covering multiple accounting periods more clearly requires the use of accrual accounting.

multiple future periods. This will require adjustments to our accounting records as time passes. **Depreciation** is the term for the process of spreading this cost over multiple periods.

	3 January 2006	
#	**Business Activity**	**Accounting Treatment**
5	▪ Receive $1,200 cash for a one-year subscription to the monthly newsletter.	▪ **Cash [A]** was increased by $1,200, and **unearned fees [L]** was increased by $1,200.

Accounting elements: Assets (A), Liabilities (L), Equity (E), Revenue (R), and Expenses (X).

In this transaction, the company has received cash related to the sale of subscriptions. However, the company has not yet actually earned the subscription fees because it has an obligation to deliver newsletters in the future. So, this amount is recorded as a liability called **unearned fees** (or **unearned revenue**). In the future, as the company delivers the newsletters and thus fulfills its obligation, this amount will be transferred to revenue. If the company fails to deliver the newsletters, the fees will need to be returned to the customer. As of 3 January 2006, the company's balance sheet would appear as

Investment Advisers, Ltd. Balance Sheet As of 3 January 2006	
Assets	
Cash	$ 42,200
Investments	100,000
Prepaid rent	1,000
Deposits	2,000
Office equipment	6,000
Total assets	$151,200
Liabilities and owners' equity	
Liabilities	
Unearned fees	$ 1,200
Equity	
Contributed capital	150,000
Total liabilities and owners' equity	$151,200

The company now has $151,200 of resources, against which there is a claim by the subscription customer of $1,200 and a residual claim by the owners of $150,000. Again, the balance sheet remains in balance, with total assets equal to total liabilities plus equity.

	10 January 2006	
#	**Business Activity**	**Accounting Treatment**
6	▪ Purchase and receive 500 books at a cost of $20 per book for a total of $10,000. Invoice terms are that payment from IAL is due in 30 days. No cash changes hands. These books are intended for resale.	▪ **Inventory [A]** is increased by $10,000, and **accounts payable [L]** is increased by $10,000.

Accounting elements: Assets (A), Liabilities (L), Equity (E), Revenue (R), and Expenses (X).

The company has obtained an asset, inventory, which can be sold to customers at a later date. Rather than paying cash to the supplier currently, the company has incurred an obligation to do so in 30 days. This represents a liability to the supplier that is termed accounts payable.

	10 January 2006	
#	**Business Activity**	**Accounting Treatment**
7	▪ Spend $600 on newspaper and trade magazine advertising for the month.	▪ **Cash [A]** was decreased by $600, and **advertising expense [X]** was increased by $600.

Accounting elements: Assets (A), Liabilities (L), Equity (E), Revenue (R), and Expenses (X).

Unlike the previous expenditures, advertising is an expense, not an asset. Its benefits relate to the current period. Expenditures such as advertising are recorded as an expense when they are incurred. Contrast this expenditure with that for equipment, which is expected to be useful over multiple periods and thus is initially recorded as an asset, and then reflected as an expense over time. Also, contrast this treatment with that for rent expense, which was paid in advance and can be clearly allocated over time, and thus is initially recorded as a prepaid asset and then reflected as an expense over time. The advertising expenditure in this example relates to the current period. If the company had paid in advance for several years worth of advertising, then a portion would be capitalized (i.e., recorded as an asset), similar to the treatment of equipment or prepaid rent and expensed in future periods. We can now prepare a partial income statement for the company reflecting this expense:

Investment Advisers, Ltd. Income Statement For the Period 1 January through 10 January 2006		
Total revenue		$ 0
Expenses		
Advertising	600	
Total expense		600
Net income (loss)		$ (600)

Because the company has incurred a $600 expense but has not recorded any revenue (the subscription revenue has not been earned yet), an income statement for Transactions 1 through 7 would show net income of minus $600 (i.e., a net loss). To prepare a balance sheet for the company, we need to update the retained earnings account. Beginning retained earnings was $0 (zero). Adding the net loss of $600 (made up of $0 revenue minus $600 expense) and deducting any dividend ($0 in this illustration) gives ending retained earnings of minus $600. The ending retained earnings covering Transactions 1–7 is included in the interim balance sheet:

Investment Advisers, Ltd. Balance Sheet As of 10 January 2006	
Assets	
Cash	$ 41,600
Investments	100,000
Inventory	10,000
Prepaid rent	1,000
Deposits	2,000
Office equipment	6,000
Total assets	$160,600
Liabilities and owners' equity	
Liabilities	
Accounts payable	$ 10,000
Unearned fees	1,200
Total liabilities	11,200
Equity	
Contributed capital	150,000
Retained earnings	(600)
Total equity	149,400
Total liabilities and owners' equity	$160,600

As with all balance sheets, the amount of total assets equals total liabilities plus owners' equity—both are $160,600. The owners' claim on the business has been reduced to $149,400. This is due to the negative retained earnings (sometimes referred to as a retained "deficit"). As noted, the company has a net loss after the first seven transactions, a result of incurring $600 of advertising expenses but not yet producing any revenue.

15 January 2006		
#	**Business Activity**	**Accounting Treatment**
8	■ Borrow $12,000 from a bank for working capital. Interest is payable annually at 10 percent. The principal is due in two years.	■ **Cash [A]** is increased by $12,000, and **bank debt [L]** is increased by $12,000.

Accounting elements: Assets (A), Liabilities (L), Equity (E), Revenue (R), and Expenses (X).

Cash is increased, and a corresponding liability is recorded to reflect the amount owed to the bank. Initially, no entry is made for interest that is expected to be paid on the loan. In the future, interest will be recorded as time passes and interest accrues (accumulates) on the loan.

	15 January 2006	
#	**Business Activity**	**Accounting Treatment**
9	■ Ship first order to a customer consisting of five books at $25 per book. Invoice terms are that payment is due in 30 days. No cash changes hands.	■ **Accounts receivable [A]** increased by $125, and **revenue [R]** increased by $125. Additionally, **inventory [A]** decreased by $100, and **cost of goods sold [X]** increased by $100.

Accounting elements: Assets (A), Liabilities (L), Equity (E), Revenue (R), and Expenses (X).

The company has now made a sale. Sale transaction records have two parts. One part represents the $125 revenue to be received from the customer, and the other part represents the $100 cost of the goods that have been sold. Although payment has not yet been received from the customer in payment for the goods, the company has delivered the goods (five books) and so revenue is recorded. A corresponding asset, accounts receivable, is recorded to reflect amounts due from the customer. Simultaneously, the company reduces its inventory balance by the cost of the five books sold and also records this amount as an expense termed **cost of goods sold**.

	15 January 2006	
#	**Business Activity**	**Accounting Treatment**
10	■ Sell for cash 10 books at $25 per book at an investment conference.	■ **Cash[A]** is increased by $250, and **revenue[R]** is increased by $250. Additionally, **inventory[A]** is decreased by $200, and **cost of goods sold [X]** is increased by $200.

Accounting elements: Assets (A), Liabilities (L), Equity (E), Revenue (R), and Expenses (X).

Similar to the previous sale transaction, both the $250 sales proceeds and the $200 cost of the goods sold must be recorded. In contrast with the previous sale, however, the sales proceeds are received in cash. Subtotals from Exhibit 6 can once again be used to prepare a preliminary income statement and balance sheet to evaluate the business to date:

**Investment Advisers, Ltd. Income Statement For the Period
1 January through 15 January 2006**

Total revenue		$ 375
Expenses		
Cost of goods sold	300	
Advertising	600	
Total expenses		900

(continued)

Net income (loss)	$ (525)

Investment Advisers, Ltd. Balance Sheet As of 15 January 2006

Assets	
Cash	$ 53,850
Accounts receivable	125
Investments	100,000
Inventory	9,700
Prepaid rent	1,000
Deposits	2,000
Office equipment	6,000
Total assets	$172,675
Liabilities and owners' equity	
Liabilities	
Accounts payable	$ 10,000
Unearned fees	1,200
Bank debt	12,000
Total liabilities	23,200
Equity	
Contributed capital	150,000
Retained earnings	(525)
Total equity	149,475
Total liabilities and owners' equity	$172,675

An income statement covering Transactions 1–10 would reflect revenue to date of $375 for the sale of books minus the $300 cost of those books and minus the $600 advertising expense. The net loss is $525, which is shown in the income statement as $(525) using the accounting convention that indicates a negative number using parentheses. This net loss is also reflected on the balance sheet in retained earnings. The amount in retained earnings at this point equals the net loss of $525 because retained earnings had $0 beginning balance and no dividends have been distributed. The balance sheet reflects total assets of $172,675 and claims on the assets of $23,200 in liabilities and $149,475 owners' equity. Within assets, the inventory balance represents the cost of the 485 remaining books (a total of 15 have been sold) at $20 each.

Transactions 1–10 occurred throughout the month and involved cash, accounts receivable, or accounts payable; accordingly, these transactions clearly required an entry into the accounting system. The other transactions, items 11–13, have also occurred and need to be reflected in the financial statements, but these transactions may not be so obvious. In order to prepare complete financial statements at the end of a reporting period, an entity needs to review its operations to determine whether any accruals or other adjustments are required. A more complete discussion of accruals and adjustments is set forth in the next section, but generally speaking, such entries serve to allocate revenue and expense items into the correct accounting period. In practice, companies may also make adjustments to correct erroneous entries or to update inventory balances to reflect a physical count.

In this illustration, adjustments are needed for a number of transactions in order to allocate amounts across accounting periods. The accounting treatment for these transactions is shown in Exhibit 7. Transactions are numbered sequentially, and an "a" is added to a transaction number to denote an adjustment relating to a previous transaction. Exhibit 8 presents the completed spreadsheet reflecting these additional entries in the accounting system.

Exhibit 7	Investment Advisers, Ltd. Accruals and Other Adjusting Entries on 31 January 2006

#	Business Activity	Accounting Treatment
11	■ Hire a part-time clerk. The clerk is hired through an agency that also handles all payroll taxes. The company is to pay $15 per hour to the agency. The clerk works six hours prior to 31 January, but no cash will be paid until February.	■ The company owes $90 for wages at month end. Under accrual accounting, expenses are recorded when incurred, not when paid. ■ **Accrued wages [L]** is increased by $90, and **payroll expense [X]** is increased by $90. The accrued wage liability will be eliminated when the wages are paid.
12	■ Mail out the first month's newsletter to customer. This subscription had been sold on 3 January.	■ One month (or 1/12) of the $1,200 subscription has been satisfied, so $100 can be recognized as revenue. ■ **Unearned fees [L]** is decreased by $100, and **fee revenue [R]** is increased by $100.
13	■ Review of the investment portfolio shows that $100 of interest income was earned and the market value of the portfolio has increased by $2,000. The balance in the investment account is now $102,100. The securities are classified as "trading" securities.	■ **Interest income [R]** is increased by $100, and the **investments** account **[A]** is increased by $100. ■ The $2,000 increase in the value of the portfolio represents unrealized gains that are part of income for traded securities. The **investments** account **[A]** is increased by $2,000, and **unrealized gains [R]** is increased by $2,000.
3a	■ In item 3, $3,000 was paid to the landlord for office/warehouse, including a $2,000 refundable deposit and $1,000 for the first month's rent. ■ Now, the first month has ended, so this rent has become a cost of doing business.	■ To reflect the full amount of the first month's rent as a cost of doing business, **prepaid rent [A]** is decreased by $1,000, and **rent expense [X]** is increased by $1,000.
4a	■ In item 4, office equipment was purchased for $6,000 in cash. The equipment has an estimated life of two years with no salvage value. ■ Now, one month (or 1/24) of the useful life of the equipment has ended, so a portion of the equipment cost has become a cost of doing business.	■ A portion (1/24) of the total $6,000 cost of the office equipment is allocated to the current period's cost of doing business. ■ **Depreciation expense [X]** is increased by $250, and **accumulated depreciation [A]** (a contra asset account) is increased by $250. ■ Accumulated depreciation is a contra asset account to office equipment.

(continued)

Exhibit 7	(Continued)

#	Business Activity	Accounting Treatment
8a	▪ The company borrowed $12,000 from a bank on 15 January, with interest payable annually at 10 percent and the principal due in two years. ▪ Now, one-half of one month has passed since the borrowing.	▪ One-half of one month of interest expense has become a cost of doing business. $12,000 × 10% = $1,200 of annual interest, equivalent to $100 per month or $50 for one-half month. ▪ **Interest expense [X]** is increased by $50, and **interest payable [L]** is increased by $50.

Accounting elements: Assets (A), Liabilities (L), Equity (E), Revenue (R), and Expenses (X).

Notes: Items 11–13 are repeated from Exhibit 5. Items 3a, 4a, and 8a reflect adjustments relating to items 3, 4, and 8 from Exhibit 5.

A final income statement and balance sheet can now be prepared reflecting all transactions and adjustments.

Investment Advisers, Ltd. Income Statement For the Period 1 January through 31 January 2006

Revenues	
Fee revenue	$ 100
Book sales	375
Investment income	2,100
Total revenues	$ 2,575
Expenses	
Cost of goods sold	$ 300
Advertising	600
Wage	90
Rent	1,000
Depreciation	250
Interest	50
Total expenses	2,290
Net income (loss)	$ 285

Investment Advisers, Ltd. Balance Sheet As of 31 January 2006

Assets	
Cash	$ 53,850
Accounts receivable	125
Investments	102,100
Inventory	9,700
Prepaid rent	0
Office equipment, net	5,750
Deposits	2,000
Total assets	$173,525

Exhibit 8   Accounting System for Investment Advisers, Ltd.

#	Cash	Other Assets	Account	Amount	Account	Contributed Capital	Beginning Retained Earnings	Revenue	Expense (Enter as Negative)	Dividends (Enter as Negative)
Beg. Balance	0	0		0		0	0	0	0	0
1 Capitalize	150,000					150,000				
2 Investments	(100,000)	100,000	Investments							
3 Pay landlord	(3,000)	1,000	Prepaid rent							
		2,000	Rent deposit							
4 Buy equipment	(6,000)	6,000	Office equipment							
5 Sell subscript.	1,200			1,200	Unearned fees					
6 Buy Books		10,000	Inventory	10,000	Accounts payable					
7 Advertise	(600)								(600)	
8 Borrow	12,000			12,000	Bank debt					
9 Sell books on account		(100)	Inventory					125	(100)	
		125	Accounts receivable							
10 Cash sale	250	(200)	Inventory					250	(200)	
11 Accrue wages				90	Accrued wages				(90)	
12 Earn subscription fees				(100)	Unearned fees			100		
13 Investment income		100	Investments					100		
		2,000	Investments					2,000		
3a Rent expense		(1,000)	Prepaid rent						(1,000)	
4a Depreciate equipment		(250)	Accumulated depreciation (equipment)						(250)	
8a Accrue interest				50	Interest payable				(50)	
Subtotal	**53,850**	**119,675**		**23,240**		**150,000**		**2,575**	**(2,290)**	

Investment Advisers, Ltd. Balance Sheet As of 31 January 2006	
Liabilities and owners' equity	
Liabilities	
Accounts payable	$ 10,000
Accrued wages	90
Interest payable	50
Unearned fees	1,100
Bank debt	12,000
Total liabilities	23,240
Equity	
Contributed capital	150,000
Retained earnings	285
Total equity	150,285
Total liabilities and owners' equity	$173,525

From the income statement, we can determine that the business was profitable for the month. The business earned $285 after expenses. The balance sheet presents the financial position. The company has assets of $173,525, and claims against those assets included liabilities of $23,240 and an owners' claim of $150,285. The owners' claim reflects their initial investment plus reinvested earnings. These statements are explored further in the next section.

4.3 Financial Statements

The spreadsheet in Exhibit 8 is an organized presentation of the company's transactions and can help in preparing the income statement and balance sheet presented above. Exhibit 9 presents all financial statements and demonstrates their relationships. Note that the data for the income statement come from the revenue and expense columns of the spreadsheet (which include gains and losses). The net income of $285 (revenue of $2,575 minus expenses of $2,290) was retained in the business rather than distributed to the owners as dividends. The net income, therefore, becomes part of ending retained earnings on the balance sheet. The detail of retained earnings is shown in the statement of owners' equity.

The balance sheet presents the financial position of the company using the assets, liabilities, and equity accounts from the accounting system spreadsheet. The statement of cash flows summarizes the data from the cash column of the accounting system spreadsheet to enable the owners and others to assess the sources and uses of cash. These sources and uses of cash are categorized according to group of business activity: operating, investing, or financing. The format of the statement of cash flows presented here is known as the **direct format**, which refers to the operating cash section appearing simply as operating cash receipts less operating cash disbursements. An alternative format for the operating cash section, which begins with net income and shows adjustments to derive operating cash flow, is known as the **indirect format**. The alternative formats and detailed rules are discussed in the reading on understanding the statement of cash flows.

Exhibit 9	Investment Advisers, Ltd., Financial Statements

Investment Advisers, Ltd.
Balance Sheet
As of

	12/31/2005	1/31/2006
Assets		
Cash	150,000	53,850
Accounts receivable	0	125
Investments	0	102,100
Inventory		9,700
Office equipment, net		5,750
Deposits		2,000
Total assets	150,000	173,525
Liabilities		
Accounts payable	0	10,000
Accrued expenses		140
Unearned fees		1,100
Bank debt		12,000
Total liabilities		23,240
Owners' equity		
Contributed capital	150,000	150,000
Retained earnings	0	285
Total equity	150,000	150,285
Total liabilities and equity	150,000	173,525

Investment Advisers, Ltd.
Income Statement
For the Month Ended 1/31/2006

Fee revenue	100
Book sales revenue	375
Investment income	2,100
Total revenue	2,575
Cost of goods sold	300
Other expense	1,990
Total expense	2,290
Net income (loss)	285

Investment Advisers, Ltd.
Statement of Cash Flows
For the Month Ended 1/31/2006

Cash received from customers	1,450
Cash paid to landlord	(3,000)
Cash paid for advertising	(600)
Investments in trading securities	(100,000)
Operating cash flows	(102,150)
Capital expenditures	(6,000)
Investing cash flows	(6,000)
Borrowing	12,000
Financing cash flows	12,000
Net decrease in cash	(96,150)
Cash at 12/31/05	150,000
Cash at 1/31/06	53,850

Investment Advisers, Ltd.
Statement of Owners' Equity
31 January 2006

	Contributed Capital	Retained Earnings	Total
Balance at 12/31/05	150,000	0	150,000
Issuance of stock			
Net income (loss)		285	285
Distributions			
Balance at 1/31/06	150,000	285	150,285

Financial statements use the financial data reported in the accounting system and present this data in a more meaningful manner. Each statement reports on critical areas. Specifically, a review of the financial statements for the IAL illustration provides the following information:

▪ **Balance Sheet**. This statement provides information about a company's financial position at a point in time. It shows an entity's assets, liabilities, and owners' equity at a particular date. Two years are usually presented so that comparisons can be made. Less significant accounts can be grouped into a single line item. One observation from the IAL illustration is that although total assets have increased significantly (about 16 percent), equity has increased less than 0.2 percent—most of the increase in total assets is due to the increase in liabilities.

▪ **Income Statement**. This statement provides information about a company's profitability over a period of time. It shows the amount of revenue, expense, and resulting net income or loss for a company during a period of time. Again, less significant accounts can be grouped into a single line item—in this illustration, expenses other than cost of goods sold are grouped into a single line item. The statement shows that IAL has three sources of revenue and made a small profit in its first month of operations. Significantly, most of the revenue came from investments rather than subscriptions or book sales.

▪ **Statement of Cash Flows**. This statement provides information about a company's cash flows over a period of time. It shows a company's cash inflows (receipts) and outflows (payments) during the period. These flows are categorized according to the three groups of business activities: operating, financing, and investing. In the illustration, IAL reported a large negative cash flow from operations ($102,150), primarily because its trading activities involved the purchase of a portfolio of securities but no sales were made from the portfolio. (Note that the purchase of investments for IAL appears in its operating section because the company is in the business of trading securities. In contrast, for a nontrading company, investment activity would be shown as investing cash flows rather than operating cash flows.) IAL's negative operating and investing cash flows were funded by $12,000 bank borrowing and a $96,150 reduction in the cash balance.

▪ **Statement of Owners' Equity**. This statement provides information about the composition and changes in owners' equity during a period of time. In this illustration, the only change in equity resulted from the net income of $285. A **Statement of Retained Earnings** (not shown) would report the changes in a company's retained earnings during a period of time.

These statements again illustrate the interrelationships among financial statements. On the balance sheet, we see beginning and ending amounts for assets, liabilities, and owners' equity. Owners' equity increased from $150,000 to $150,285. The statement of owners' equity presents a breakdown of this $285 change. The arrow from the statement of owners' equity to the owners' equity section of the balance sheet explains that section of the balance sheet. In the IAL illustration, the entire $285 change resulted from an increase in retained earnings. In turn, the increase in retained earnings resulted from $285 net income. The income statement presents a breakdown of the revenues and expenses resulting in this $285. The arrow from the income statement to the net income figure in the owners' equity section explains how reported net income came about.

Also on the balance sheet, we see that cash decreased from $150,000 at the beginning of the month to $53,850 at the end of the month. The statement of cash flows provides information on the increases and decreases in cash by group of business activity. The arrow from the statement of cash flows to the ending cash figure shows that the statement of cash flows explains in detail the ending cash amount.

In summary, the balance sheet provides information at a point in time (financial position), whereas the other statements provide useful information regarding the activity during a period of time (profitability, cash flow, and changes in owners' equity).

ACCRUALS AND VALUATION ADJUSTMENTS

5

In a simple business model such as the investment company discussed in the illustration above, many transactions are handled in cash and settled in a relatively short time frame. Furthermore, assets and liabilities have a fixed and determinable value. Translating business transactions into the accounting system is fairly easy. Difficulty usually arises when a cash receipt or disbursement occurs in a different period than the related revenue or expense, or when the reportable values of assets vary. This section will address the accounting treatment for these situations—namely, accruals and valuation adjustments.

5.1 Accruals

Accrual accounting requires that revenue be recorded when earned and that expenses be recorded when incurred, irrespective of when the related cash movements occur. The purpose of accrual entries is to report revenue and expense in the proper accounting period. Because accrual entries occur due to timing differences between cash movements and accounting recognition of revenue or expense, it follows that there are only a few possibilities. First, cash movement and accounting recognition can occur at the same time, in which case there is no need for accruals. Second, cash movement may occur before or after accounting recognition, in which case accruals are required. The possible situations requiring accrual entries are summarized into four types of accrual entries shown in Exhibit 10 and discussed below. Each type of accrual involves an originating entry and at least one adjusting entry at a later date or dates.

| Exhibit 10 | Accruals |

	Cash Movement prior to Accounting Recognition	Cash Movement in the Same Period as Accounting Recognition	Cash Movement after Accounting Recognition
Revenue	**UNEARNED (DEFERRED) REVENUE** ■ **Originating entry**–record cash receipt and establish a liability (such as unearned revenue) ■ **Adjusting entry**–reduce the liability while recording revenue	Settled transaction– no accrual entry needed	**UNBILLED (ACCRUED) REVENUE** ■ **Originating entry**–record revenue and establish an asset (such as unbilled revenue) ■ **Adjusting entry**–When billing occurs, reduce unbilled revenue and increase accounts receivable. When cash is collected, eliminate the receivable.
Expense	**PREPAID EXPENSE** ■ **Originating entry**–record cash payment and establish an asset (such as prepaid expense) ■ **Adjusting entry**–reduce the asset while recording expense		**ACCRUED EXPENSES** ■ **Originating entry**–establish a liability (such as accrued expenses) and record an expense ■ **Adjusting entry**–reduce the liability as cash is paid

Unearned revenue (or **deferred revenue**) arises when a company receives cash prior to earning the revenue. In the IAL illustration, in Transaction 5, the company received $1,200 for a 12-month subscription to a monthly newsletter. At the time the cash was received, the company had an obligation to deliver 12 newsletters and thus had not yet earned the revenue. Each month, as a newsletter is delivered, this obligation will decrease by 1/12th (i.e., $100). And at the same time, $100 of revenue will be earned. The accounting treatment involves an originating entry (the initial recording of the cash received and the corresponding liability to deliver newsletters) and, subsequently, 12 future adjusting entries, the first one of which was illustrated as Transaction 12. Each adjusting entry reduces the liability and records revenue.

In practice, a large amount of unearned revenue may cause some concern about a company's ability to deliver on this future commitment. Conversely, a positive aspect is that increases in unearned revenue are an indicator of future revenues. For example, a large liability on the balance sheet of an airline relates to cash received for future airline travel. Revenue will be recognized as the travel occurs, so an increase in this liability is an indicator of future increases in revenue.

Unbilled revenue (or **accrued revenue**) arises when a company earns revenue prior to receiving cash but has not yet recognized the revenue at the end of an accounting period. In such cases, the accounting treatment involves an originating entry to record the revenue earned through the end of the accounting period and a related receivable reflecting amounts due from customers. When the company receives payment (or if goods are returned), an adjusting entry eliminates the receivable.

Accrued revenue specifically relates to end-of-period accruals; however, the concept is similar to any sale involving deferred receipt of cash. In the IAL illustration, in Transaction 9, the company sold books on account, so the revenue was recognized prior to cash receipt. The accounting treatment involved an entry to record the revenue and the associated receivable. In the future, when the company receives payment, an adjusting entry (not shown) would eliminate the receivable. In practice, it is important to understand the quality of a company's receivables (i.e., the likelihood of collection).

Prepaid expense arises when a company makes a cash payment prior to recognizing an expense. In the illustration, in Transaction 3, the company prepaid one month's rent. The accounting treatment involves an originating entry to record the payment of cash and the prepaid asset reflecting future benefits, and a subsequent adjusting entry to record the expense and eliminate the prepaid asset. (See the boxes showing the accounting treatment of Transaction 3, which refers to the originating entry, and Transaction 3a, which refers to the adjusting entry.) In other words, prepaid expenses are assets that will be subsequently expensed. In practice, particularly in a valuation, one consideration is that prepaid assets typically have future value only as future operations transpire, unless they are refundable.

Accrued expenses arise when a company incurs expenses that have not yet been paid as of the end of an accounting period. Accrued expenses result in liabilities that usually require future cash payments. In the IAL illustration, the company had incurred wage expenses at month end, but the payment would not be made until after the end of the month (Transaction 11). To reflect the company's position at the end of the month, the accounting treatment involved an originating entry to record wage expense and the corresponding liability for wages payable, and a future adjusting entry to eliminate the liability when cash is paid (not shown because wages will be paid only in February). Similarly, the IAL illustration included interest accrual on the company's bank borrowing. (See the boxes showing the accounting treatment of Transaction 8, where Transaction 8 refers to the originating entry, and Transaction 8a, which refers to the adjusting entry.)

As with accrued revenues, accrued expenses specifically relate to end-of-period accruals. Accounts payable are similar to accrued expenses in that they involve a transaction that occurs now but the cash payment is made later. Accounts payable is also a liability but often relates to the receipt of inventory (or perhaps services) as opposed to recording an immediate expense. Accounts payable should be listed separately from other accrued expenses on the balance sheet because of their different nature.

Overall, in practice, complex businesses require additional accruals that are theoretically similar to the four categories of accruals discussed above but which require considerably more judgment. For example, there may be significant lags between a transaction and cash settlement. In such cases, accruals can span many accounting periods (even 10–20 years!), and it is not always clear when revenue has been earned or an expense has been incurred. Considerable judgment is required to determine how to allocate/distribute amounts across periods. An example of such a complex accrual would be the estimated annual revenue for a contractor on a long-term construction project, such as building a nuclear power plant. In general, however, accruals fall under the four general types and follow essentially the same pattern of originating and adjusting entries as the basic accruals described.

5.2 Valuation Adjustments

In contrast to accrual entries that allocate revenue and expenses into the appropriate accounting periods, valuation adjustments are made to a company's assets or liabilities—only where required by accounting standards—so that the accounting records reflect the current market value rather than the historical cost. In this discussion, we focus on valuation adjustments to assets. For example, in the IAL illustration, Transaction 13 adjusted the value of the company's investment portfolio to its current market value. The income statement reflects the $2,100 increase (including interest), and the ending balance sheets report the investment portfolio at its current market value of $102,100. In contrast, the equipment in the IAL illustration was not reported at its current market value and no valuation adjustment was required.

As this illustration demonstrates, accounting regulations do not require all types of assets to be reported at their current market value. Some assets (e.g., trading securities) are shown on the balance sheet at their current market value, and changes in that market value are reported in the income statement. Some assets are shown at their historical cost (e.g., specific classes of investment securities being held to maturity). Other assets (e.g., a particular class of investment securities) are shown on the balance sheet at their current market value, but changes in market value bypass the income statement and are recorded directly into shareholders' equity under a component referred to as "other comprehensive income." This topic will be discussed in more detail in later readings.

In summary, where valuation adjustment entries are required for assets, the basic pattern is the following for increases in assets: An asset is increased with the other side of the equation being a gain on the income statement or an increase to other comprehensive income. Conversely for decreases: An asset is decreased with the other side of the equation being a loss on the income statement or a decrease to other comprehensive income.

6 ACCOUNTING SYSTEMS

The accounting system set forth for the IAL illustration involved a very simple business, a single month of activity, and a small number of transactions. In practice, most businesses are more complicated and have many more transactions. Accordingly, actual accounting systems, although using essentially the same logic as discussed in the illustration, are both more efficient than a spreadsheet and more complex.

6.1 Flow of Information in an Accounting System

Accounting texts typically discuss accounting systems in detail because accountants need to understand each step in the process. While analysts do not need to know the same details, they should be familiar with the flow of information through a financial reporting system. This flow and the key related documents are described in Exhibit 11.

Exhibit 11	**Accounting System Flow and Related Documents**
Journal entries and adjusting entries	A journal is a document or computer file in which business transactions are recorded in the order in which they occur (chronological order). The general journal is the collection of all business transactions in an accounting system sorted by date. All accounting systems have a general journal to record all transactions. Some accounting systems also include special journals. For example, there may be one journal for recording sales transactions and another for recording inventory purchases.
	Journal entries—recorded in journals—are dated, show the accounts affected, and the amounts. If necessary, the entry will include an explanation of the transaction and documented authorization to record the entry. As the initial step in converting business transactions into financial information, the journal entry is useful for obtaining detailed information regarding a particular transaction.
	Adjusting journal entries, a subset of journal entries, are typically made at the end of an accounting period to record items such as accruals that are not yet reflected in the accounting system.

Exhibit 11	(Continued)

↓

General ledger and T- accounts	A ledger is a document or computer file that shows all business transactions by account. Note that the general ledger, the core of every accounting system, contains all of the same entries as that posted to the general journal—the only difference is that the data are sorted by date in a journal and by account in the ledger. The general ledger is useful for reviewing all of the activity related to a single account. T-accounts, explained in Appendix 23, are representations of ledger accounts and are frequently used to describe or analyze accounting transactions.

↓

Trial balance and adjusted trial balance	A trial balance is a document that lists account balances at a particular point in time. Trial balances are typically prepared at the end of an accounting period as a first step in producing financial statements. A key difference between a trial balance and a ledger is that the trial balance shows only total ending balances. An initial trial balance assists in the identification of any adjusting entries that may be required. Once these adjusting entries are made, an adjusted trial balance can be prepared.

↓

Financial statements	The financial statements, a final product of the accounting system, are prepared based on the account totals from an adjusted trial balance.

6.2 Debits and Credits

Reviewing the example of IAL, it is clear that the accounting treatment of every transaction involved at least two accounts and the transaction either increased or decreased the value of any affected account. Traditionally, accounting systems have used the terms **debit** and **credit** to describe changes in an account resulting from the accounting processing of a transaction. The correct usage of "debit" and "credit" in an accounting context differs from how these terms are used in everyday language.[6] The accounting definitions of debit and credit ensure that, in processing a transaction, the sum of the debits equals the sum of the credits, which is consistent with the accounting equation always remaining in balance.

Although mastering the usage of the terms "debit" and "credit" is essential for an accountant, an analyst can still understand financial reporting mechanics without speaking in terms of debits and credits. In general, this text avoids the use of debit/credit presentation; however, for reference, Appendix 23 presents the IAL illustration in a debit and credit system.

The following section broadly describes some considerations for using financial statements in security analysis.

USING FINANCIAL STATEMENTS IN SECURITY ANALYSIS

7

Financial statements serve as a foundation for credit and equity analysis, including security valuation. Analysts may need to make adjustments to reflect items not reported in the statements (certain assets/liabilities and future earnings). Analysts may also need to assess the reasonableness of management judgment (e.g., in accruals

---

6 In accounting, debits record increases of asset and expense accounts or decreases in liability and owners' equity accounts. Credits record increases in liability, owners' equity, and revenue accounts or decreases in asset accounts. Appendix 23 provides more details.

and valuations). Because analysts typically will not have access to the accounting system or individual entries, they will need to infer what transactions were recorded by examining the financial statements.

7.1 The Use of Judgment in Accounts and Entries

Quite apart from deliberate misrepresentations, even efforts to faithfully represent the economic performance and position of a company require judgments and estimates. Financial reporting systems need to accommodate complex business models by recording accruals and changes in valuations of balance sheet accounts. Accruals and valuation entries require considerable judgment and thus create many of the limitations of the accounting model. Judgments could prove wrong or, worse, be used for deliberate earnings manipulation. An important first step in analyzing financial statements is identifying the types of accruals and valuation entries in an entity's financial statements. Most of these items will be noted in the critical accounting policies/estimates section of management's discussion and analysis (MD&A) and in the significant accounting policies footnote, both found in the annual report. Analysts should use this disclosure to identify the key accruals and valuations for a company. The analyst needs to be aware, as Example 4 shows, that the manipulation of earnings and assets can take place within the context of satisfying the mechanical rules governing the recording of transactions.

EXAMPLE 4

The Manipulation of Accounting Earnings

As discussed in this reading, the accounting equation can be expressed as Assets = Liabilities + Contributed capital + Ending retained earnings (Equation 5a). Although the equation must remain in balance with each transaction, management can improperly record a transaction to achieve a desired result. For example, when a company spends cash and records an expense, assets are reduced on the left side of the equation and expenses are recorded, which lowers retained earnings on the right side. The balance is maintained. If, however, a company spent cash but did not want to record an expense in order to achieve higher net income, the company could manipulate the system by reducing cash and increasing another asset. The equation would remain in balance and the right-hand side of the equation would not be affected at all. This was one of the techniques used by managers at WorldCom to manipulate financial reports, as summarized in a U.S. Securities and Exchange Commission complaint against the company (emphasis added):

> In general, WorldCom manipulated its financial results in two ways. First, WorldCom reduced its operating expenses by improperly releasing certain reserves held against operating expenses. Second, **WorldCom improperly reduced its operating expenses by recharacterizing certain expenses as capital assets**. Neither practice was in conformity with generally accepted accounting principles ("GAAP"). Neither practice was disclosed to WorldCom's investors, despite the fact that both practices constituted changes from WorldCom's previous accounting practices. Both practices falsely reduced WorldCom's

> expenses and, accordingly, had the effect of artificially inflating the income WorldCom reported to the public in its financial statements from 1999 through the first quarter of 2002.[7]
>
> In 2005, the former CEO of WorldCom was sentenced to 25 years in prison for his role in the fraud.[8] The analyst should be aware of the possibility of manipulation of earnings and be on the lookout for large increases in existing assets, new unusual assets, and unexplained changes in financial ratios.

7.2 Misrepresentations

It is rare in this age of computers that the mechanics of an accounting system do not work. Most computer accounting systems will not allow a company to make one-sided entries. It is important to note, however, that just because the mechanics work does not necessarily mean that the judgments underlying the financial statements are correct. An unscrupulous accountant could structure entries to achieve a desired result. For example, if a manager wanted to record fictitious revenue, a fictitious asset (a receivable) could be created to keep the accounting equation in balance. If the manager paid for something but did not want to record an expense, the transaction could be recorded in a prepaid asset account. If cash is received but the manager does not want to record revenue, a liability could be created. Understanding that there has to be another side to every entry is key in detecting inappropriate accounting because—usually in the course of "fixing" one account—there will be another account with a balance that does not make sense. In the case of recording fictitious revenue, there is likely to be a growing receivable whose collectibility is in doubt. Ratio analysis, which is discussed further in later readings, can assist in detecting suspect amounts in these accounts. Furthermore, the accounting equation can be used to detect likely accounts where aggressive or even fraudulent accounting may have occurred.

SUMMARY

The accounting process is a key component of financial reporting. The mechanics of this process convert business transactions into records necessary to create periodic reports on a company. An understanding of these mechanics is useful in evaluating financial statements for credit and equity analysis purposes and in forecasting future financial statements. Key concepts are as follows:

- Business activities can be classified into three groups: operating activities, investing activities, and financing activities.
- Companies classify transactions into common accounts that are components of the five financial statement elements: assets, liabilities, equity, revenue, and expense.
- The core of the accounting process is the basic accounting equation: Assets = Liabilities + Owners' equity.
- The expanded accounting equation is Assets = Liabilities + Contributed capital + Beginning retained earnings + Revenue – Expenses – Dividends.

---

7 SEC vs. WorldCom, 5 November 2002: www.sec.gov/litigation/complaints/comp17829.htm.
8 "Ebbers Is Sentenced to 25 Years For $11 Billion WorldCom Fraud," *Wall Street Journal*, 14 July 2005, A1.

- Business transactions are recorded in an accounting system that is based on the basic and expanded accounting equations.

- The accounting system tracks and summarizes data used to create financial statements: the balance sheet, income statement, statement of cash flows, and statement of owners' equity. The statement of retained earnings is a component of the statement of owners' equity.

- Accruals are a necessary part of the accounting process and are designed to allocate activity to the proper period for financial reporting purposes.

- The results of the accounting process are financial reports that are used by managers, investors, creditors, analysts, and others in making business decisions.

- An analyst uses the financial statements to make judgments on the financial health of a company.

- Company management can manipulate financial statements, and a perceptive analyst can use his or her understanding of financial statements to detect misrepresentations.

APPENDIX 23: A DEBIT/CREDIT ACCOUNTING SYSTEM

The main section of this reading presented a basic accounting system represented as a spreadsheet. An alternative system that underlies most manual and electronic accounting systems uses debits and credits. Both a spreadsheet and a debit/credit system are based on the basic accounting equation:

Assets = Liabilities + Owners' equity

Early generations of accountants desired a system for recording transactions that maintained the balance of the accounting equation and avoided the use of negative numbers (which could lead to errors in recording). The system can be illustrated with T-accounts for every account involved in recording transactions. The T-account is so named for its shape:

T-Account

Debit	Credit

The left-hand side of the T-account is called a "debit," and the right-hand side is termed a "credit." The names should not be construed as denoting value. A debit is not better than a credit and vice versa. Debit simply means the left side of the T-account, and credit simply means the right side. Traditionally, debit is abbreviated as "DR," whereas credit is abbreviated "CR." The T-account is also related to the balance sheet and accounting equation as follows:

Balance Sheet

Assets	Liabilities
	Owners' Equity

Assets are referred to as the left side of the balance sheet (and accounting equation) and hence are on the left side of the T-account. Assets are, therefore, recorded with a debit balance. In other words, to record an increase in an asset, an entry is made to the left-hand side of a T-account. A decrease to an asset is recorded on the right side of a T-account. Liabilities and owners' equity are referred to as the right side of the balance sheet (and accounting equation). Increases to liabilities and owners' equity are recorded on the right side of a T-account; decreases to liabilities and owners' equity are recorded on the left side.

At any point in time, the balance in an account is determined by summing all the amounts on the left side of the account, summing all the amounts on the right side of the account, and calculating the difference. If the sum of amounts on the left side of the account is greater than the sum of amounts on the right side of the account, the account has a debit balance equal to the difference. If the sum of amounts on the right side of the account is greater than the sum of amounts on the left side of the account, the account has a credit balance.

A T-account is created for each asset account, liability account, and owners' equity account. The collection of these T-accounts at the beginning of the year for a fictitious company, Investment Advisers, Ltd. (IAL), is presented in Exhibit 1. Each balance sheet T-account is termed a "permanent" or "real" account because the balance in the account carries over from year-to-year.

Exhibit 1 Balance Sheet T-Accounts for Investment Advisers, Ltd.

Cash	Accounts Receivable	Inventory

Investments	Office Equipment	Accumulated Depreciation

Deposits	Prepaid Rent	Accounts Payable

Accrued Wages	Unearned Fees	Bank Debt

Accrued Interest	Contributed Capital	Retained Earnings

T-accounts are also set up for each income statement account. These T-accounts are referred to as "temporary" or "nominal" accounts because they are transferred at the end of each fiscal year by transferring any net income or loss to the balance sheet account, Retained Earnings. Income statement T-accounts for IAL are presented in Exhibit 2.

Exhibit 2 Income Statement T-Accounts for Investment Advisers, Ltd.

Fee Revenue	Book Sales Revenue	Investment Income

Exhibit 2	(Continued)

Cost of Goods Sold **Advertising Expense** **Rent Expense**

Depreciation Expense **Wage Expense** **Interest Expense**

The collection of all business transactions sorted by account, real and temporary, for a company comprise the general ledger. The general ledger is the core of every accounting system, where all transactions are ultimately entered. To illustrate the use of T-accounts, we will use the transactions for IAL summarized in Exhibit 3. We will first enter each transaction into the general ledger T-accounts, then use the information to prepare financial statements.

Exhibit 3	Business Transactions for Investment Advisers, Ltd.

#	Date	Business Activity
1	31 December 2005	■ File documents with regulatory authorities to establish a separate legal entity. Initially capitalize the company through deposit of $150,000 from the three owners.
2	2 January 2006	■ Set up a $100,000 investment account and purchase a portfolio of equities and fixed-income securities.
3	2 January 2006	■ Pay $3,000 to landlord for office/warehouse. $2,000 represents a refundable deposit, and $1,000 represents the first month's rent.
4	3 January 200	■ Purchase office equipment for $6,000. The equipment has an estimated life of two years with no salvage value.
5	3 January 2006	■ Receive $1,200 cash for a one-year subscription to the monthly newsletter.
6	10 January 2006	■ Purchase and receive 500 books at a cost of $20 per book for a total of $10,000. Invoice terms are that payment from IAL is due in 30 days. No cash changes hands. These books are intended for resale.
7	10 January 2006	■ Spend $600 on newspaper and trade magazine advertising for the month.

(continued)

Exhibit 3	(Continued)

#	Date	Business Activity
8	15 January 2006	■ Borrow $12,000 from a bank for working capital. Interest is payable annually at 10 percent. The principal is due in two years.
9	15 January 2006	■ Ship first order to a customer consisting of five books at $25 per book. Invoice terms are that payment is due in 30 days. No cash changes hands.
10	15 January 2006	■ Sell for cash 10 books at $25 per book at an investment conference.
11	30 January 2006	■ Hire a part-time clerk. The clerk is hired through an agency that also handles all payroll taxes. The company is to pay $15 per hour to the agency. The clerk works six hours prior to 31 January, but no cash will be paid until February.
12	31 January 2006	■ Mail out the first month's newsletter to customer. This subscription had been sold on 3 January. See item 5.
13	31 January 2006	■ Review of the investment portfolio shows that $100 of interest income was earned and the market value of the portfolio has increased by $2,000. The balance in the investment account is now $102,100. Securities are classified as "trading" securities.

Because this is a new business, the company's general ledger T-accounts initially have a zero balance.

31 December 2005 (excerpt from Exhibit 3)	

#	Business Activity	Accounting Treatment
1	■ File documents with regulatory authorities to establish a separate legal entity. Initially capitalize the company through deposit of $150,000 from the three owners.	■ **Cash [A]** is increased by $150,000, and **contributed capital [E]** is increased by $150,000.

Accounting elements: Assets (A), Liabilities (L), Equity (E), Revenue (R), and Expenses (X).

This transaction affects two accounts: cash and contributed capital. (Cash is an asset, and contributed capital is part of equity.) The transaction is entered into the T-accounts as shown below. The number in parenthesis references the transaction number.

Cash		Contributed Capital	
150,000 (1)			150,000 (1)

Cash is an asset account, and assets are on the left-hand side of the balance sheet (and basic accounting equation); therefore, cash is increased by recording the $150,000 on the debit (left) side of the T-account. Contributed capital is an equity account, and equity accounts are on the right-hand side of the balance sheet; therefore, contributed capital is increased by recording $150,000 on the credit (right) side of the T-account. Note that the sum of the debits for this transaction equals the sum of the credits:

DR = $150,000

CR = $150,000

DR = CR

Each transaction must always maintain this equality. This ensures that the accounting system (and accounting equation) is kept in balance. At this point in time, the company has assets (resources) of $150,000, and the owners' claim on the resources equals $150,000 (their contributed capital) because there are no liabilities at this point.

Transactions are recorded in a journal, which is then "posted to" (recorded in) the general ledger. When a transaction is recorded in a journal, it takes the form:

Date	Account	DR	CR
13 Dec 2005	Cash	150,000	
	Contributed Capital		150,000

This kind of entry is referred to as a "journal entry," and it is a summary of the information that will be posted in the general ledger T-accounts.

2 January 2006 (excerpt from Exhibit 3)	

#	Business Activity	Accounting Treatment
2	■ Set up a $100,000 investment account and purchase a portfolio of equities and fixed-income securities.	■ **Investments [A]** were increased by $100,000, and **cash [A]** was decreased by $100,000.

Accounting elements: Assets (A), Liabilities (L), Equity (E), Revenue (R), and Expenses (X).

This transaction affects two accounts but only one side of the accounting equation. Cash is reduced when the investments are purchased. Another type of asset, investments, increases. The T-account entries are shown below:

Cash		Investment	
150,000 (1)	100,000 (2)	100,000 (2)	

The cash account started with a $150,000 debit balance from the previous transaction. Assets are reduced by credit entries, so the reduction in cash is recorded by entering the $100,000 on the credit (right) side of the cash T-account. The investment account is also an asset, and the increase in investments is recorded by entering $100,000 on the debit side of the investments T-account. Transaction 2 balances because Transaction 2 debits equal Transaction 2 credits.

Going forward, we will use the traditional accounting terms of debit (debiting, debited) to indicate the action of entering a number in the debit side of an account, and credit (crediting, credited) to indicate the action of entering an amount on the credit side of an account.

2 January 2006 (excerpt from Exhibit 3)

#	Business Activity	Accounting Treatment
3	▪ Pay $3,000 to landlord for office/warehouse. $2,000 represents a refundable deposit, and $1,000 represents the first month's rent.	▪ **Cash [A]** was decreased by $3,000, **deposits [A]** were increased by $2,000, and **prepaid rent [A]** was increased by $1,000.

Accounting elements: Assets (A), Liabilities (L), Equity (E), Revenue (R), and Expenses (X).

Cash is reduced once again by crediting the account by $3,000. On the other side of the transaction, two asset accounts increase. Deposits are increased by debiting the account for $2,000, while prepaid rent is increased by debiting that account for $1,000:

Cash		Deposits		Prepaid Rent	
150,000 (1)	100,000 (2)	2,000 (3)		1,000 (3)	
	3,000 (3)				

The sum of the debits for Transaction 3 equals the sum of the credits (i.e., $3,000).

3 January 2006 (excerpt from Exhibit 3)

#	Business Activity	Accounting Treatment
4	▪ Purchase office equipment for $6,000 in cash. The equipment has an estimated life of two years with no salvage value.	▪ **Cash [A]** was decreased by $6,000, and **office equipment [A]** was increased by $6,000.

Accounting elements: Assets (A), Liabilities (L), Equity (E), Revenue (R), and Expenses (X).

Cash is credited for $6,000, while office equipment is debited for $6,000. Both are asset accounts, so these entries reflect a reduction in cash and an increase in office equipment.

Cash		Office Equipment	
150,000 (1)	100,000 (2)	6,000 (4)	
	3,000 (3)		
	6,000 (4)		

3 January 2006 (excerpt from Exhibit 3)

#	Business Activity	Accounting Treatment
5	■ Receive $1,200 cash for a one-year subscription to the monthly newsletter.	■ **Cash** [A] was increased by $1,200, and **unearned fees** [L] was increased by $1,200.

Accounting elements: Assets (A), Liabilities (L), Equity (E), Revenue (R), and Expenses (X).

In this transaction, the company has received cash related to the sale of subscriptions. However, the company has not yet actually earned the subscription fees because it has an obligation to deliver newsletters in the future. So, this amount is recorded as a liability called "unearned fees" (or "unearned revenue"). In the future, as the company delivers the newsletters and thus fulfills its obligation, this amount will be transferred to revenue. If they fail to deliver the newsletters, the fees will need to be returned to the customer. To record the transaction, cash is debited (increased), while a liability account, unearned fees, is credited. Liabilities are on the right-hand side of the balance sheet and are, therefore, increased by crediting the T-account.

Cash		Unearned Fees	
150,000 (1)	100,000 (2)		1,200 (5)
1,200 (5)	3,000 (3)		
	6,000 (4)		

The sum of Transaction 5 debits and credits each equal $1,200.

10 January 2006 (excerpt from Exhibit 3)

#	Business Activity	Accounting Treatment
6	■ Purchase and receive 500 books at a cost of $20 per book for a total of $10,000. Invoice terms are that payment from IAL is due in 30 days. No cash changes hands. These books are intended for resale.	■ **Inventory** [A] is increased by $10,000, and **accounts payable** [L] is increased by $10,000.

Accounting elements: Assets (A), Liabilities (L), Equity (E), Revenue (R), and Expenses (X).

The company has obtained an asset, inventory, which can be sold to customers at a later date. Rather than paying cash to the supplier currently, the company has an obligation to do so in 30 days. This represents a liability ("accounts payable") to the supplier. Inventory is debited for $10,000, while the liability, accounts payable, is credited for $10,000. Note that there is no impact on the cash account.

Inventory		Accounts Payable	
10,000 (6)			10,000 (6)

10 January 2006 (excerpt from Exhibit 3)

#	Business Activity	Accounting Treatment
7	▪ Spend $600 on newspaper and trade magazine advertising for the month	▪ **Cash [A]** was decreased by $600, and **advertising expense [X]** was increased by $600.

Accounting elements: Assets (A), Liabilities (L), Equity (E), Revenue (R), and Expenses (X).

Unlike the previous expenditures, advertising is not an asset. Its future economic benefits are unclear, unlike equipment, which is expected to be useful over multiple periods. Expenditures such as advertising are recorded as an expense when they are incurred. To record the advertising expense, cash is credited for $600, and advertising expense is debited for $600. Expenses reduce net income, and thus reduce retained earnings. Decreases in retained earnings, as with any equity account, are recorded as debits. The entries with respect to retained earnings will be presented later in this section after the income statement.

Cash		Advertising Expense	
150,000 (1)	100,000 (2)	600 (7)	
1,200 (5)	3,000 (3)		
	6,000 (4)		
	600 (7)		

15 January 2006 (excerpt from Exhibit 3)

#	Business Activity	Accounting Treatment
8	▪ Borrow $12,000 from a bank for working capital. Interest is payable annually at 10 percent. The principal is due in two years.	▪ **Cash [A]** is increased by $12,000, and **Bank debt [L]** is increased by $12,000.

Accounting elements: Assets (A), Liabilities (L), Equity (E), Revenue (R), and Expenses (X).

Cash is debited, and a corresponding liability is credited. Initially, no entry is made for interest that is expected to be paid on the loan. Interest will be recorded in the future as time passes and interest accrues (accumulates) on the loan.

Cash		Bank Debt	
150,000 (1)	100,000 (2)		12,000 (8)
1,200 (5)	3,000 (3)		

Cash		Bank Debt	
12,000 (8)	6,000 (4)		
	600 (7)		

The debits and credits of Transaction 8 each total $12,000.

15 January 2006 (excerpt from Exhibit 3)

#	Business Activity	Accounting Treatment
9	▪ Ship first order to a customer consisting of five books at $25 per book. Invoice terms are that payment is due in 30 days. No cash changes hands.	▪ **Accounts receivable** [A] increased by $125, and **book sales revenue** [R] increased by $125. Additionally, **inventory** [A] decreased by $100, and **cost of goods sold** [X] increased by $100.

Accounting elements: Assets (A), Liabilities (L), Equity (E), Revenue (R), and Expenses (X).

The company has now made a sale. Sale transaction records have two parts. One part records the $125 revenue to be received from the customer, and the other part records the $100 cost of the goods that have been sold. For the first part, accounts receivable is debited (increased) for $125, and a revenue account is credited for $125.

Accounts Receivable		Book Sales Revenue	
125 (9)			125 (9)

For the second part, inventory is credited (reduced) for $100, and an expense, cost of goods sold, is debited (increased) to reflect the cost of inventory sold.

Inventory		Cost of Goods Sold	
10,000 (6)	100 (9)	100 (9)	

Note that the sum of debits and the sum of credits for Transaction 9 both equal $225. The $225 is not meaningful by itself. What is important is that the debits and credits balance.

15 January 2006 (excerpt from Exhibit 3)

#	Business Activity	Accounting Treatment
10	▪ Sell for cash 10 books at $25 per book at an investment conference.	▪ **Cash** [A] is increased by $250, and **book sales revenue** [R] is increased by $250. Additionally, **inventory** [A] is decreased by $200, and **cost of goods sold** [X] is increased by $200.

Accounting elements: Assets (A), Liabilities (L), Equity (E), Revenue (R), and Expenses (X).

Similar to the previous transaction, both the sales proceeds and cost of the goods sold must be recorded. In this case, however, the sales proceeds are received in cash. To record the sale proceeds, the entries include a debit to cash for $250 and a corresponding credit to book sales revenue for $250. To record cost of goods sold, the entries include a debit to cost of goods sold and a credit to inventory.

Cash		Book Sales Revenue	
150,000 (1)	100,000 (2)		125 (9)
1,200 (5)	3,000 (3)		250 (10)
12,000 (8)	6,000 (4)		
250 (10)	600 (7)		

Inventory		Cost of Goods Sold	
10,000 (6)	100 (9)	100 (9)	
	200 (10)	200 (10)	

Transaction 10's debits and credits are equal, maintaining the accounting system's balance.

30 January 2006 (excerpt from Exhibit 3)

#	Business Activity	Accounting Treatment
11	■ Hire a part-time clerk. The clerk is hired through an agency that also handles all payroll taxes. The company is to pay $15 per hour to the agency. The clerk works six hours prior to 31 January, but no cash will be paid until February.	■ The company owes $90 for wages at month-end. Under accrual accounting, expenses are recorded when incurred, not when paid. ■ **Accrued wages** [L] is increased by $90, and **wage expense** [X] is increased by $90. The accrued wage liability will be eliminated when the wages are paid.

Accounting elements: Assets (A), Liabilities (L), Equity (E), Revenue (R), and Expenses (X).

Accrued wages is a liability that is increased by crediting that account, whereas payroll is an expense account that is increased with a debit.

Accrued Wages		Wage Expense	
	90 (11)	90 (11)	

	31 January 2006 (excerpt from Exhibit 3)

#	Business Activity	Accounting Treatment
12	▪ Mail out the first month's newsletter to customer. This subscription had been sold on 3 January.	▪ One month (or 1/12) of the $1,200 subscription has been satisfied, and thus $100 can be recognized as revenue. ▪ **Unearned fees [L]** is decreased by $100, and **fee revenue [R]** is increased by $100.

Accounting elements: Assets (A), Liabilities (L), Equity (E), Revenue (R), and Expenses (X).

To record the recognition of one month of the subscription fee, the account fee revenue is credited (increased) by $100, and the related liability is debited (decreased) by $100.

Fee Revenue		**Unearned Fees**	
	100 (12)	100 (12)	1,200 (5)

	31 January 2006 (excerpt from Exhibit 3)

#	Business Activity	Accounting Treatment
13	▪ Review of the investment portfolio shows that $100 of interest income was earned and the market value of the portfolio has increased by $2,000. The balance in the investment account is now $102,100. The securities are classified as "trading" securities.	▪ **Investment income [R]** is increased by $100, and the **investments** account **[A]** is increased by $100. ▪ The $2,000 increase in the value of the portfolio represents unrealized gains that are part of income for traded securities. The **investments** account **[A]** is increased by $2,000, and **investment income [R]** is increased by $2,000.

Accounting elements: Assets (A), Liabilities (L), Equity (E), Revenue (R), and Expenses (X).

The investments account is an asset account that is debited (increased) for $2,100, and investment income is a revenue account that is credited (increased) by $2,100.

Investments		**Investment Income**	
100,000 (2)			2,100 (13)
2,100 (13)			

These entries complete the recording of the first 13 transactions. In this illustration, there are three adjustments. An adjustment must be made related to Transaction 3 to account for the fact that a month has passed and rent expense has been incurred. We refer to this as Transaction 3a. Adjustments must also be made for an estimate of the depreciation of the office equipment (Transaction 4a) and for interest that has accrued on the loan (Transaction 8a).

31 January 2006 (excerpt from Exhibit 3)	

#	Business Activity	Accounting Treatment
3a	■ In item 3, $3,000 was paid to the landlord for office/warehouse, including a $2,000 refundable deposit and $1,000 for the first month's rent. ■ Now, the first month has ended, so this rent has become a cost of doing business.	■ To reflect the full amount of the first month's rent as a cost of doing business, **prepaid rent [A]** is decreased by $1,000, and **rent expense [X]** is increased by $1,000.

Accounting elements: Assets (A), Liabilities (L), Equity (E), Revenue (R), and Expenses (X).

Prepaid rent (an asset) is credited for $1,000 to reduce the balance, and rent expense is debited for the same amount to record the fact that the expense has now been incurred. After this entry, the balance of the prepaid rent asset account is $0.

Prepaid Rent		Rent Expense	
1,000 (3)	1,000 (3a)	1,000 (3a)	

31 January 2006 (excerpt from Exhibit 3)	

#	Business Activity	Accounting Treatment
4a	■ In item 4, office equipment was purchased for $6,000 in cash. The equipment has an estimated life of two years with no salvage value. ■ Now, one month (or 1/24) of the useful life of the equipment has ended so a portion of the equipment cost has become a cost of doing business.	■ A portion (1/24) of the total $6,000 cost of the office equipment is allocated to the current period's cost of doing business. ■ **Depreciation expense [X]** is increased by $250, and **accumulated depreciation** is increased by $250. ■ Accumulated depreciation is a contra asset account to office equipment

Accounting elements: Assets (A), Liabilities (L), Equity (E), Revenue (R), and Expenses (X).

Because some time has passed, accounting principles require that the estimated depreciation of the equipment be recorded. In this case, one could directly credit office equipment for $250; however, a preferred method is to credit an account called "accumulated depreciation," which is associated with the office equipment account. This accumulated depreciation account "holds" the cumulative amount of the depreciation related to the office equipment. When financial reports are prepared, a user is able to see both the original cost of the equipment as well as the accumulated depreciation. The user, therefore, has insight into the age of the asset, and perhaps how much time remains before it is likely to be replaced. Accumulated depreciation is termed a "contra" asset account and is credited for $250, while depreciation expense is debited (increased) for $250.

Accumulated Depreciation		Depreciation Expense	
	250 (4a)	250 (4a)	

	31 January 2006 (excerpt from Exhibit 3)

#	**Business Activity**	**Accounting Treatment**
8a	▪ The company borrowed $12,000 from a bank on 15 January, with interest payable annually at 10 percent and the principal due in two years. ▪ Now, one-half of one month has passed since the borrowing.	▪ One-half of one month of interest expense has become a cost of doing business. $12,000 times 10% equals $1,200 of annual interest, equivalent to $100 per month and $50 for one-half month. ▪ **Interest expense [X]** is increased by $50, and **accrued interest [L]** is increased by $50.

Accounting elements: Assets (A), Liabilities (L), Equity (E), Revenue (R), and Expenses (X).

Accrued interest is a liability that is credited (increased) for $50, and interest expense is debited (increased) for $50. Accrued interest is also sometimes referred to as "interest payable."

Accrued Interest		**Interest Expense**	
	50 (8a)	50 (8a)	

Exhibit 4 summarizes the general ledger T-accounts for IAL at this point in time. For accounts with multiple entries, a line is drawn and the debit and credit columns are summed and netted to determine the current balance in the account. The balance is entered below the line. These individual account totals are then summarized in a trial balance as depicted in Exhibit 5. A trial balance is a summary of the account balances at a point in time. An accountant can prepare a trial balance at any time to ensure that the system is in balance and to review current amounts in the accounts. Note that the debit and credit columns each total $176,065, confirming that the system is in balance. Any difference in the column totals would indicate an error had been made. The trial balance totals have no particular significance and are not used in preparing financial statements. These totals are simply the sum of debits and credits in the accounting system at that point in time.

Exhibit 4	General Ledger T-Accounts for Investment Advisors, Ltd.

Cash		**Accounts Receivable**		**Inventory**	
150,000 (1)	100,000 (2)	125 (9)		10,000 (6)	100 (9)
1,200 (5)	3,000 (3)				200 (10)
12,000 (8)	6,000 (4)			9,700	
250 (10)	600 (7)				
53,850					

(continued)

Exhibit 4	(Continued)

Investments		Office Equipment		Accumulated Depreciation	
100,000 (2)		6,000 (4)			250 (4a)
2,100 (13)					
102,100					

Deposits		Prepaid Rent		Accounts Payable	
2,000 (3)		1,000 (3)	1,000 (3a)		10,000 (6)
		0			

Accrued Wages		Unearned Fees		Bank Debt	
	90 (11)	100 (12)	1,200 (5)		12,000 (8)
			1,100		

Accrued Interest		Contributed Capital		Retained Earnings	
	50 (8a)		150,000 (1)		

Fee Revenue		Book Sales Revenue		Investment Income	
	100 (12)		125 (9)		2,100 (13)
			250 (10)		
			375		

Cost of Goods Sold		Advertising Expense		Rent Expense	
100 (9)		600 (7)		1,000 (3a)	
200 (10)					
300					

Exhibit 4	(Continued)

Depreciation Expense	Wage Expense	Interest Expense
250 (4a)	90 (11)	50 (8a)

Exhibit 5	Investment Advisers, Ltd., Trial Balance

	DR	CR
Cash	53,850	
Accounts receivable	125	
Inventory	9,700	
Investments	102,100	
Office equipment	6,000	
Accumulated depreciation		250
Deposits	2,000	
Prepaid rent	0	
Accounts payable		10,000
Accrued wages		90
Unearned fees		1,100
Bank debt		12,000
Accrued interest		50
Contributed capital		150,000
Retained earnings		
Fee revenue		100
Book sales revenue		375
Investment income		2,100
Cost of goods sold	300	
Advertising expense	600	
Rent expense	1,000	
Depreciation expense	250	
Wage expense	90	
Interest expense	50	
Total	**176,065**	**176,065**

After ensuring that the balances in the trial balance are correct (if there are errors, they are corrected and an adjusted trial balance is prepared), we prepare the financial statements. The trial balance provides the information necessary to prepare the balance sheet and the income statement. The detail in the general ledger must be reviewed to prepare the statement of cash flows and statement of owners' equity. After the income statement is prepared, the temporary accounts are closed out (i.e., taken to a zero balance) by transferring each of their balances to retained earnings. This typically occurs at year-end and is termed the "closing process." Exhibits 6 and 7 show the post-closing general ledger and trial balance, respectively.

Exhibit 6	Post-Closing General Ledger T-Accounts for Investment Advisors, Ltd.

Cash		Accounts Receivable		Inventory	
150,000 (1)	100,000 (2)	125 (9)		10,000 (6)	100 (9)
1,200 (5)	3,000 (3)				200 (10)
12,000 (8)	6,000 (4)			9,700	
250 (10)	600 (7)				
53,850					

Investments		Office Equipment		Accumulated Depreciation	
100,000 (2)		6,000 (4)			250 (4a)
2,100 (13)					
102,100					

Deposits		Prepaid Rent		Accounts Payable	
2,000 (3)		1,000 (3)	1,000 (3a)		10,000 (6)
		0			

Accrued Wages		Unearned Fees		Bank Debt	
	90 (11)	100 (12)	1,200 (5)		12,000 (8)
			1,100		

Accrued Interest		Contributed Capital		Retained Earnings	
	50 (8a)		150,000 (1)		285

Fee Revenue		Book Sales Revenue		Investment Income	
	0		0		0

Cost of Goods Sold		Advertising Expense		Rent Expense	
0		0		0	

Exhibit 6	(Continued)

Depreciation Expense		Wage Expense		Interest Expense	
0		0		0	

Exhibit 7	Investment Advisers, Ltd., Post-Closing Trial Balance

	DR	CR
Cash	53,850	
Accounts receivable	125	
Inventory	9,700	
Investments	102,100	
Office equipment	6,000	
Accumulated depreciation		250
Deposits	2,000	
Prepaid rent	0	
Accounts payable		10,000
Accrued wages		90
Unearned fees		1,100
Bank debt		12,000
Accrued interest		50
Contributed capital		150,000
Retained earnings		285
Fee revenue		0
Book sales revenue		0
Investment income		0
Cost of goods sold	0	
Advertising expense	0	
Rent expense	0	
Depreciation expense	0	
Wage expense	0	
Interest expense	0	
Total	**173,775**	**173,775**

**END OPTIONAL
SEGMENT**

Financial statements are identical whether using a spreadsheet approach or a debit/credit approach. Accordingly, the financial statements for IAL that would be prepared using the trial balances are identical to those presented in the main body of the reading as Exhibit 9.

PRACTICE PROBLEMS

1 Which of the following items would most likely be classified as an operating activity?

   A   Issuance of debt.

   B   Acquisition of a competitor.

   C   Sale of automobiles by an automobile dealer.

2 Which of the following items would most likely be classified as a financing activity?

   A   Issuance of debt.

   B   Payment of income taxes.

   C   Investments in the stock of a supplier.

3 Which of the following elements represents an economic resource?

   A   Asset.

   B   Liability.

   C   Owners' equity.

4 Which of the following elements represents a residual claim?

   A   Asset.

   B   Liability.

   C   Owners' equity.

5 An analyst has projected that a company will have assets of €2,000 at year-end and liabilities of €1,200. The analyst's projection of total owners' equity should be *closest* to:

   A   €800.

   B   €2,000.

   C   €3,200.

6 An analyst has collected the following information regarding a company in advance of its year-end earnings announcement (in millions):

Estimated net income	$	200
Beginning retained earnings	$	1,400
Estimated distributions to owners	$	100

The analyst's estimate of ending retained earnings (in millions) should be *closest* to:

   A $1,300.

   B $1,500.

   C $1,700.

7 An analyst has compiled the following information regarding Rubsam, Inc.

Liabilities at year-end	€	1,000
Contributed capital at year-end	€	500
Beginning retained earnings	€	600

(continued)

Revenue during the year	€	5,000
Expenses during the year	€	4,300

There have been no distributions to owners. The analyst's *most likely* estimate of total assets at year-end should be *closest* to:

A   €2,100.

B   €2,300.

C   €2,800.

8   A group of individuals formed a new company with an investment of $500,000. The *most likely* effect of this transaction on the company's accounting equation at the time of the formation is an increase in cash and:

A   an increase in revenue.

B   an increase in liabilities.

C   an increase in contributed capital.

9   HVG, LLC paid $12,000 of cash to a real estate company upon signing a lease on 31 December 2005. The payment represents a $4,000 security deposit and $4,000 of rent for each of January 2006 and February 2006. Assuming that the correct accounting is to reflect both January and February rent as prepaid, the *most likely* effect on HVG's accounting equation in December 2005 is:

A   no net change in assets.

B   a decrease in assets of $8,000.

C   a decrease in assets of $12,000.

10   TRR Enterprises sold products to customers on 30 June 2006 for a total price of €10,000. The terms of the sale are that payment is due in 30 days. The cost of the products was €8,000. The *most likely* net change in TRR's total assets on 30 June 2006 related to this transaction is:

A   €0.

B   €2,000.

C   €10,000.

11   On 30 April 2006, Pinto Products received a cash payment of $30,000 as a deposit on production of a custom machine to be delivered in August 2006. This transaction would *most likely* result in which of the following on 30 April 2006?

A   No effect on liabilities.

B   A decrease in assets of $30,000.

C   An increase in liabilities of $30,000.

12   Squires & Johnson, Ltd., recorded €250,000 of depreciation expense in December 2005. The *most likely* effect on the company's accounting equation is:

A   no effect on assets.

B   a decrease in assets of €250,000.

C   an increase in liabilities of €250,000.

13   An analyst who is interested in assessing a company's financial position is *most likely* to focus on which financial statement?

A   Balance sheet.

B   Income statement.

C   Statement of cash flows.

14 The statement of cash flows presents the flows into which three groups of business activities?

A Operating, Nonoperating, and Financing.

B Operating, Investing, and Financing.

C Operating, Nonoperating, and Investing.

15 Which of the following statements about cash received prior to the recognition of revenue in the financial statements is *most* accurate? The cash is recorded as:

A deferred revenue, an asset.

B accrued revenue, a liability.

C deferred revenue, a liability.

16 When, at the end of an accounting period, a revenue has been recognized in the financial statements but no billing has occurred and no cash has been received, the accrual is to:

A unbilled (accrued) revenue, an asset.

B deferred revenue, an asset.

C unbilled (accrued) revenue, a liability.

17 When, at the end of an accounting period, cash has been paid with respect to an expense, the business should then record:

A an accrued expense, an asset.

B a prepaid expense, an asset.

C an accrued expense, a liability.

18 When, at the end of an accounting period, cash has not been paid with respect to an expense that has been incurred, the business should then record:

A an accrued expense, an asset.

B a prepaid expense, an asset.

C an accrued expense, a liability.

19 The collection of all business transactions sorted by account in an accounting system is referred to as:

A a trial balance.

B a general ledger.

C a general journal.

20 If a company reported fictitious revenue, it could try to cover up its fraud by:

A decreasing assets.

B increasing liabilities.

C creating a fictitious asset.

SOLUTIONS

1 C is correct. Sales of products, a primary business activity, are classified as an operating activity. Issuance of debt would be a financing activity. Acquisition of a competitor and the sale of surplus equipment would both be classified as investing activities.

2 A is correct. Issuance of debt would be classified as a financing activity. B is incorrect because payment of income taxes would be classified as an operating activity. C is incorrect because investments in common stock would be generally classified as investing activities.

3 A is correct. An asset is an economic resource of an entity that will either be converted into cash or consumed.

4 C is correct. Owners' equity is a residual claim on the resources of a business.

5 A is correct. Assets must equal liabilities plus owners' equity and, therefore, €2,000 = €1,200 + Owners' equity. Owners' equity must be €800.

6 B is correct.

Beginning retained earnings	$1,400
+ Net income	200
– Distributions to owners	(100)
= Ending retained earnings	$1,500

7 C is correct.

Assets = Liabilities + Contributed capital + Beginning retained earnings – Distributions to owners + Revenues – Expenses

Liabilities	$1,000
+ Contributed capital	500
+ Beginning retained earnings	600
– Distributions to owners	(0)
+ Revenues	5,000
– Expenses	(4,300)
= Assets	$2,800

8 C is correct. This is a contribution of capital by the owners. Assets would increase by $500,000 and contributed capital would increase by $500,000, maintaining the balance of the accounting equation.

9 A is correct. The payment of January rent represents prepaid rent (an asset), which will be adjusted at the end of January to record rent expense. Cash (an asset) decreases by $12,000. Deposits (an asset) increase by $4,000. Prepaid rent (an asset) increases by $8,000. There is no net change in assets.

10 B is correct. The sale of products without receipt of cash results in an increase in accounts receivable (an asset) of €10,000. The balance in inventory (an asset) decreases by €8,000. The net increase in assets is €2,000. This would be balanced by an increase in revenue of €10,000 and an increase in expenses (costs of goods sold) of €8,000.

11 C is correct. The receipt of cash in advance of delivering goods or services results in unearned revenue, which is a liability. The company has an obligation to deliver $30,000 in goods in the future. This balances the increase in cash (an asset) of $30,000.

12 B is correct. Depreciation is an expense and increases accumulated depreciation. Accumulated depreciation is a contra account which reduces property, plant, and equipment (an asset) by €250,000. Assets decrease by €250,000, and expenses increase by €250,000.

13 A is correct. The balance sheet shows the financial position of a company at a particular point in time. The balance sheet is also known as a "statement of financial position."

14 B is correct. The three sections of the statement of cash flows are operating, investing, and financing activities.

15 C is correct. Cash received prior to revenue recognition increases cash and deferred or unearned revenue. This is a liability until the company provides the promised goods or services.

16 A is correct. When cash is to be received after revenue has been recognized but no billing has actually occurred, an unbilled (accrued) revenue is recorded. Such accruals would usually occur when an accounting period ends prior to a company billing its customer. This type of accrual can be contrasted with a simple credit sale, which is reflected as an increase in revenue and an increase in accounts receivable. No accrual is necessary.

17 B is correct. Payment of expenses in advance is called a prepaid expense which is classified as an asset.

18 C is correct. When an expense is incurred and no cash has been paid, expenses are increased and a liability ("accrued expense") is established for the same amount.

19 B is correct. The general ledger is the collection of all business transactions sorted by account in an accounting system. The general journal is the collection of all business activities sorted by date.

20 C is correct. In order to balance the accounting equation, the company would either need to increase assets or decrease liabilities. Creating a fictitious asset would be one way of attempting to cover up the fraud.

READING

24

Financial Reporting Standards

by Elaine Henry, CFA, Jan Hendrik van Greuning, CFA, and Thomas R. Robinson, CFA

LEARNING OUTCOMES

Mastery	The candidate should be able to:
☐	**a.** describe the objective of financial statements and the importance of financial reporting standards in security analysis and valuation;
☐	**b.** describe roles and desirable attributes of financial reporting standard-setting bodies and regulatory authorities in establishing and enforcing reporting standards, and describe the role of the International Organization of Securities Commissions;
☐	**c.** describe the status of global convergence of accounting standards and ongoing barriers to developing one universally accepted set of financial reporting standards;
☐	**d.** describe the International Accounting Standards Board's conceptual framework, including the objective and qualitative characteristics of financial statements, required reporting elements, and constraints and assumptions in preparing financial statements;
☐	**e.** describe general requirements for financial statements under IFRS;
☐	**f.** compare key concepts of financial reporting standards under IFRS and U.S. GAAP reporting systems;
☐	**g.** identify characteristics of a coherent financial reporting framework and the barriers to creating such a framework;
☐	**h.** describe implications for financial analysis of differing financial reporting systems and the importance of monitoring developments in financial reporting standards;
☐	**i.** analyze company disclosures of significant accounting policies.

Note: New rulings and/or pronouncements issued after the publication of the readings in financial reporting and analysis may cause some of the information in these readings to become dated. Candidates are expected to be familiar with the overall analytical framework contained in the study session readings, as well as the implication of alternative accounting methods for financial analysis and valuation, as provided in the assigned readings. Candidates are not responsible for changes that occur after the material was written.

1   INTRODUCTION

Financial reporting standards provide principles for preparing financial reports and determine the types and amounts of information that must be provided to users of financial statements, including investors and creditors, so that they may make informed decisions. This reading focuses on the framework within which these standards are created. An understanding of the underlying framework of financial reporting standards, which is broader than knowledge of specific accounting rules, will allow an analyst to assess the valuation implications of financial statement elements and transactions—including transactions, such as those that represent new developments, which are not specifically addressed by the standards.

Section 2 of this reading discusses the objective of financial statements and the importance of financial reporting standards in security analysis and valuation. Section 3 describes the roles of financial reporting standard-setting bodies and regulatory authorities and several of the financial reporting standard-setting bodies and regulatory authorities. Section 4 describes the trend toward and barriers to convergence of global financial reporting standards. Section 5 describes the International Financial Reporting Standards (IFRS) framework[1] and general requirements for financial statements. Section 6 discusses the characteristics of an effective financial reporting framework along with some of the barriers to a single coherent framework. Section 7 illustrates some of the specific differences between IFRS and U.S. generally accepted accounting practices (U.S. GAAP), and Section 8 discusses the importance of monitoring developments in financial reporting standards. A summary of the key points and practice problems in the CFA Institute multiple choice format conclude the reading.

2   THE OBJECTIVE OF FINANCIAL REPORTING

The financial reports of a company include financial statements and other supplemental disclosures necessary to assess a company's financial position and periodic financial performance. Financial reporting is based on a simple premise. The International Accounting Standards Board (IASB), which sets financial reporting standards that have been adopted in many countries, expressed it as follows in its *Conceptual Framework for Financial Reporting 2010* (*Conceptual Framework 2010*):[2]

> The objective of general purpose financial reporting is to provide financial information about the reporting entity that is useful to existing and potential investors, lenders, and other creditors in making decisions about providing resources to the entity. Those decisions involve buying, selling or holding equity and debt instruments, and providing or settling loans and other forms of credit.[3]

---

1 The body of standards issued by the International Accounting Standards Board (IASB) is referred to as International Financial Reporting Standards.

2 In September 2010, the IASB adopted the *Conceptual Framework for Financial Reporting* in place of the *Framework for the Preparation and Presentation of Financial Statements* (*1989*). The *Conceptual Framework* represents the partial completion of a joint convergence project between the IASB and FASB on an updated framework. The *Conceptual Framework* (*2010*) contains two updated chapters: *The objective of financial reporting* and *Qualitative characteristics of useful financial information*. The remainder of the material in the *Conceptual Framework* is from the *Framework* (*1989*) and will be updated as the project is completed. Also in September 2010, the FASB issued Concepts Statement 8, *Conceptual Framework for Financial Reporting*, to replace Concepts Statements 1 and 2.

3 *Conceptual Framework (2010)* Chapter 1, OB2. Under U.S. GAAP, the identical statement appears in Concept Statement 8, Chapter 1, OB2.

The objective in the *Conceptual Framework (2010)* differs from the objective of the *Framework for the Preparation and Presentation of Financial Statements (1989)*[4] in a number of key ways. The scope of the objective now extends to financial reporting, which is broader than the previously stated scope that covered financial statements only. Another difference is that the objective now specifies the primary users for whom the reports are intended (existing and potential investors, etc.) while the previously stated objective referred solely to a 'wide range of users.' Also, while the *Conceptual Framework (2010)* identifies information that should be reported—including that about financial position (economic resources and claims), changes in economic resources and claims, and financial performance reflected by accrual accounting and past cash flows—it does not list that information within the objective itself, unlike the previously stated objective.

Standards are developed in accordance with a framework so it is useful to have an agreed upon framework to guide the development of standards. The joint conceptual framework project of the IASB and the U.S. Financial Accounting Standards Board (FASB) aims to develop a common foundation for standards. Standards based on this foundation should be principles-based, internally consistent, and converged. Until recently, financial reporting standards were primarily developed independently by each country's standard-setting body. This independent standard setting created a wide range of standards, some of which were quite comprehensive and complex (often considered to be rules-based standards), and others more general (often considered to be principles-based standards). Recent accounting scandals and the economic crisis of 2008–2009 increased awareness of the need for high quality, more uniform global financial reporting standards and provided the impetus for stronger coordination among the major standard-setting bodies. Such coordination is also a natural outgrowth of the increased globalization of capital markets.

Developing financial reporting standards is complicated because the underlying economic reality is complicated. The financial transactions and financial position that companies aim to represent in their financial reports are also complex. Furthermore, uncertainty about various aspects of transactions often results in the need for accruals and estimates, both of which necessitate judgment. Judgment varies from one preparer to the next. Accordingly, standards are needed to achieve some amount of consistency in these judgments. Even with such standards, there usually will be no single correct answer to the question of how to reflect economic reality in financial reports. Nevertheless, financial reporting standards try to limit the range of acceptable answers in order to increase consistency in financial reports.

EXAMPLE 1

Estimates in Financial Reporting

To facilitate comparisons across companies (cross sectional analysis) and over time for a single company (time series analysis), it is important that accounting methods are comparable and consistently applied. However, accounting standards must be flexible enough to recognize that differences exist in the underlying economics between businesses.

Suppose two companies buy the same model of machinery to be used in their respective businesses. The machine is expected to last for several years. Financial reporting standards typically require that both companies account for this equipment by initially recording the cost of the machinery as an asset. Without such a

---

4 The *Framework (1989)* stated that, "The objective of financial statements is to provide information about the financial position, performance, and changes in financial position of an entity; this information should be useful to a wide range of users for the purpose of making economic decisions."

standard, the companies could report the purchase of the equipment differently. For example, one company might record the purchase as an asset and the other might record the purchase as an expense. An accounting standard ensures that both companies should record the transaction in a similar manner.

Accounting standards typically require the cost of the machine to be apportioned over the estimated useful life of an asset as an expense called depreciation. Because the two companies may be operating the machinery differently, financial reporting standards must retain some flexibility. One company might operate the machinery only a few days per week, whereas the other company operates the equipment continuously throughout the week. Given the difference in usage, it would not be appropriate to require the two companies to report an identical amount of depreciation expense each period. Financial reporting standards must allow for some discretion such that management can match their financial reporting choices to the underlying economics of their business while ensuring that similar transactions are recorded in a similar manner between companies.

Financial statements of two companies with identical transactions in the fiscal year, prepared in accordance with the same set of financial reporting standards, are *most likely* to be:

A   identical.

B   consistent.

C   comparable.

Solution:

C is correct. The companies' financial statements should be comparable (possible to compare) because they should reflect the underlying economics of the transactions for each company. The underlying economics may vary between companies, so the financial statements are not likely to be identical. Choices made by each company with respect to accounting methods should be consistent but the choice across companies is not necessarily consistent. Information about accounting choices will enhance a user's ability to compare the companies' financial statements.

The IASB and the FASB have developed similar financial reporting frameworks which specify the overall objective and qualities of information to be provided. Financial reports are intended to provide information to many users, including investors, creditors, employees, customers, and others. As a result of this multipurpose nature, financial reports are *not* designed solely with asset valuation in mind. However, financial reports provide important inputs into the process of valuing a company or the securities a company issues. Understanding the financial reporting framework—including how and when judgments and estimates can affect the numbers reported—enables an analyst to evaluate the information reported and to use the information appropriately when assessing a company's financial performance. Clearly, such an understanding is also important in assessing the financial impact of business decisions by, and in making comparisons across, entities.

STANDARD-SETTING BODIES AND REGULATORY AUTHORITIES

3

A distinction must be made between standard-setting bodies and regulatory authorities. Standard-setting bodies, such as the IASB and FASB, are typically private sector, self-regulated organizations with board members who are experienced accountants, auditors, users of financial statements, and academics. The requirement to prepare financial reports in accordance with specified accounting standards is the responsibility of regulatory authorities. Regulatory authorities, such as the Accounting and Corporate Regulatory Authority in Singapore, the Securities and Exchange Commission (SEC) in the United States, the Securities and Exchange Commission in Brazil, and the Financial Service Authority (FSA) in the United Kingdom (a new regulatory authority will succeed the FSA in the United Kingdom as of 2012), are governmental entities that have the legal authority to enforce financial reporting requirements and exert other controls over entities that participate in the capital markets within their jurisdiction.

In other words, *generally*, standard-setting bodies set the standards and regulatory authorities recognise and enforce the standards. Without the recognition of the standards by the regulatory authorities, the private sector standard-setting bodies would have no authority. Note, however, that regulators often retain the legal authority to establish financial reporting standards in their jurisdiction and can overrule the private sector standard-setting bodies.

EXAMPLE 2

Industry-Specific Regulation

In certain cases, multiple regulatory bodies affect a company's financial reporting requirements. For example, in almost all jurisdictions around the world, banking-specific regulatory bodies establish requirements related to risk-based capital measurement, minimum capital adequacy, provisions for doubtful loans, and minimum monetary reserves. An awareness of such regulations provides an analyst with the context to understand a bank's business, including the objectives and scope of allowed activities. Insurance is another industry where specific regulations typically are in place. An analyst should be aware of such regulations to understand constraints on an insurance company.

The following are examples of country-specific bank regulators. In Canada, the Office of the Superintendent of Financial Institutions regulates and supervises all banks in Canada as well as some other federally incorporated or registered financial institutions or intermediaries. In Germany, the German Federal Financial Supervisory Authority exercises supervision over financial institutions in accordance with the Banking Act. In Japan, the Financial Services Agency has regulatory authority over financial institutions. In the United States, the Office of the Comptroller of the Currency charters and regulates all national banks. In some countries, a single entity serves both as the central bank and as the regulatory body for the country's financial institutions.

In addition, the Basel Accords establish and promote internationally consistent capital requirements and risk management practices for larger international banks. The Basel Committee on Banking Supervision, among other functions, has evolved into a standard setter for bank supervision. The various regulations that affect banks present a challenge for bank analysts.

> Which of the following statements is *most* accurate?
>
> **A** As a general rule, it is sufficient for an analyst covering an industry to be familiar with financial reporting standards and regulations in his/her country of residence.
>
> **B** An analyst should familiarize him/herself with the regulations and reporting standards that affect the company and/or industry that he/she is analyzing.
>
> **C** An analyst should be aware that financial reporting standards vary among countries and may be industry specific, but standards are so similar that the analyst does not have to be concerned about it.
>
> **Solution:**
>
> B is correct. An analyst should familiarize him/herself with the regulations and reporting standards that affect the company and/or industry being analyzed. This can be quite challenging but, given the potential effects, necessary.

This section provides a brief overview of the International Accounting Standards Board and the U.S. Financial Accounting Standards Board. The overview is followed by descriptions of the International Organization of Securities Commissions, the U.S. Securities and Exchange Commission, and capital markets regulation in the European Union. The topics covered in these overviews were chosen to serve as examples of standard-setting boards, securities commissions, and capital market regulation. After reading these descriptions, the reader should be able to describe the functioning and roles of standard-setting bodies and regulatory authorities in more detail than is given in the introduction to this section.

3.1 Accounting Standards Boards

Accounting standards boards exist in virtually every national market. These boards are typically independent, private, not-for-profit organizations. Most users of financial statements know of the International Accounting Standards Board that issues international financial reporting standards and the U.S. Financial Accounting Standards Board that is the source of U.S. generally accepted accounting principles. Most countries have an accounting standard-setting body. There are certain attributes that are typically common to these standard setters. After discussing the IASB and the FASB, some of the common and desirable attributes of accounting standards boards will be identified.

3.1.1 *International Accounting Standards Board*

The IASB is the independent standard-setting body of the IFRS Foundation,[5] an independent, not-for-profit private sector organization. The Trustees of the IFRS Foundation reflect a diversity of geographical and professional backgrounds. The Trustees appoint the members of the IASB and related entities, ensure the financing of the Foundation, establish the budget, and monitor the IASB's strategy and effectiveness. The Trustees of the Foundation are accountable to a monitoring board composed of public authorities that include representatives from the European Commission, IOSCO, the Japan Financial Services Agency, and the U.S. SEC. The chairman of the Basel Committee on Banking Supervision serves as an observer on the Monitoring Board.

---

5 The IFRS Foundation was previously named the International Accounting Standards Committee Foundation (IASC Foundation).

The Trustees of the IFRS Foundation make a commitment to act in the public interest. The principle objectives of the IFRS Foundation are to develop and promote the use and adoption of a single set of high quality financial standards; to ensure the standards result in transparent, comparable, and decision-useful information while taking into account the needs of a range of sizes and types of entities in diverse economic settings; and to promote the convergence of national accounting standards and IFRS. The Trustees are responsible for ensuring that the IASB is and is perceived as independent. Each member of the IASB is expected to exercise independence of judgment in setting standards.

The members of the IASB are appointed by the Trustees on the basis of professional competence and practical experience. As is true for the Trustees, the members reflect a diversity of geographical and professional backgrounds. The members deliberate, develop, and issue international financial reporting standards.[6] Two related entities, with members appointed by the Trustees, are the IFRS Interpretations Committee and the IFRS Advisory Council.[7] The Interpretations Committee's members are responsible for reviewing accounting issues that arise in the application of IFRS and are not specifically addressed by IFRS, and for issuing appropriate, authoritative, IASB-approved interpretations. Note that the authoritative interpretations must be approved by the IASB. The IFRS Advisory Council's members represent a wide range of organizations and individuals that are affected by and interested in international financial reporting. The Council provides advice to the IASB on, among other items, agenda decisions and priorities.

The IASB has a basic process that it goes through when deliberating, developing, and issuing international financial reporting standards. A simplified version of the typical process is as follows. An issue is identified as a priority for consideration and placed on the IASB's agenda in consultation with the Advisory Council. After considering an issue, which may include soliciting advice from others including national standard-setters, the IASB may publish an exposure draft for public comment. In addition to soliciting public comment, the IASB may hold public hearings to discuss proposed standards. After reviewing the input of others, the IASB may issue a new or revised financial reporting standard. These standards are authoritative to the extent that they are recognised and adopted by regulatory authorities.

3.1.2 Financial Accounting Standards Board

The FASB and its predecessor organizations have been issuing financial reporting standards in the United States since the 1930s. The FASB operates within a structure similar to that of the IASB. The Financial Accounting Foundation oversees, administers, and finances the organization. The Foundation ensures the independence of the standard-setting process and appoints members to the FASB and related entities including the Financial Accounting Standards Advisory Council.

The FASB issues new and revised standards to improve standards of financial reporting so that decision-useful information is provided to users of financial reports. This is done through a thorough and independent process that seeks input from stakeholders and is overseen by the Financial Accounting Foundation. The steps in the process are similar to those described for the IASB. The outputs of the standard-setting process

---

6 Although the name of the IASB incorporates "Accounting Standards" and early standards were titled International Accounting Standards (IAS), the term "International Financial Reporting Standards" (IFRS) is being used for new standards. The use of the words "financial reporting" recognizes the importance of disclosures outside of the core financial statements, such as management discussion of the business, risks, and future plans.

7 The IFRS Interpretations Committee and the IFRS Advisory Council were previously named the International Financial Reporting Interpretations Committee and the Standards Advisory Council.

are contained in the FASB *Accounting Standards Codification*™ (Codification).[8] Effective for periods ending after 15 September 2009, the Codification is the source of authoritative U.S. generally accepted accounting principles to be applied to non-governmental entities. The Codification is organized by topic. Among the specific motivations for the Codification, the FASB mentions that it will facilitate researching accounting issues, improve the usability of the literature, provide accurate updated information on an ongoing basis, and help with convergence efforts.

U.S. GAAP, as established by the FASB, is officially recognized as authoritative by the SEC (Financial Reporting Release No. 1, Section 101, and reaffirmed in the April 2003 Policy Statement). However, the SEC retains the authority to establish standards. Although it has rarely overruled the FASB, the SEC does issue authoritative financial reporting guidance including Staff Accounting Bulletins. These bulletins reflect the SEC's views regarding accounting-related disclosure practices and can be found on the SEC website. Certain portions—but not all portions—of the SEC regulations, releases, interpretations, and guidance are included for reference in the FASB Codification.

3.1.3 *Desirable Attributes of Accounting Standards Boards*

The responsibilities of all parties involved in the standards-setting process—including trustees of a foundation or others that oversee, administer, and finance the organization and members of the standard setting board—should be clearly defined. All parties involved in the standards-setting process should observe high professional standards, including standards of ethics and confidentiality. The organization should have adequate authority, resources, and competencies to fulfill its responsibilities. The processes that guide the organization and the formation of standards should be clear and consistent. The accounting standards board should be guided by a well-articulated framework with a clearly stated objective. The accounting standards board should operate independently, seeking and considering input from stakeholders but making decisions that are consistent with the stated objective of the framework. The decision-setting process should not be compromised by pressure from external forces and should not be influenced by self- or special interests. The decisions and resulting standards should be in the public interest, and culminate in a set of high quality standards that will be recognised and adopted by regulatory authorities.

3.2 Regulatory Authorities

The requirement to prepare financial reports in accordance with specified accounting standards is the responsibility of regulatory authorities. Regulatory authorities are governmental entities that have the legal authority to enforce financial reporting requirements and exert other controls over entities that participate in the capital markets within their jurisdiction. Regulatory authorities may require that financial reports be prepared in accordance with one specific set of accounting standards or may specify acceptable accounting standards. For example in Switzerland, as of 2010, companies listed on the main board of the SIX Swiss Stock Exchange had to prepare their financial statements in accordance with either IFRS or U.S. GAAP. Other registrants in Switzerland could use IFRS, U.S. GAAP, or Swiss GAAP FER.

The International Organization of Securities Commissions (IOSCO) is not a regulatory authority but its members regulate a significant portion of the world's financial capital markets. This organization has established objectives and principles to guide

---

8 The Codification combines literature issued by various standard setters, including the FASB, the Emerging Issues Task Force (EITF), the Derivative Implementation Group (DIG), and the American Institute of Certified Public Accountants (AICPA).

securities and capital market regulation. The U.S. SEC is discussed as an example of a regulatory authority. Aspects of capital market regulation in Europe are discussed to illustrate a co-operative approach to regulation.

3.2.1 *International Organization of Securities Commissions*

IOSCO was formed in 1983 as the successor organization to an inter-American regional association (created in 1974). As of 23 September 2010, IOSCO had 114 ordinary members, 11 associate members, and 74 affiliate members. Ordinary members are the securities commission or similar governmental regulatory authority with primary responsibility for securities regulation in the country.[9] The members regulate more than 90 percent of the world's financial capital markets.

The IOSCO's comprehensive set of *Objectives and Principles of Securities Regulation* is updated as required and is recognized as an international benchmark for all markets. The principles of securities regulation are based upon three core objectives:[10]

- protecting investors;
- ensuring that markets are fair, efficient, and transparent; and
- reducing systemic risk.

IOSCO's principles are grouped into nine categories, including principles for regulators, for enforcement, for auditing, and for issuers, among others. Within the category "Principles for Issuers," two principles relate directly to financial reporting:

- There should be full, accurate, and timely disclosure of financial results, risk, and other information which is material to investors' decisions.
- Accounting standards used by issuers to prepare financial statements should be of a high and internationally acceptable quality.

Historically, regulation and related financial reporting standards were developed within individual countries and were often based on the cultural, economic, and political norms of each country. As financial markets have become more global, it has become desirable to establish comparable financial reporting standards internationally. Ultimately, laws and regulations are established by individual jurisdictions, so this also requires cooperation among regulators. Another IOSCO principle deals with the use of self-regulatory organizations (accounting standards bodies are examples of self-regulating organizations in this context). Principle 9 states:

> Where the regulatory system makes use of Self-Regulatory Organizations (SROs) that exercise some direct oversight responsibility for their respective areas of competence, such SROs should be subject to the oversight of the Regulator and should observe standards of fairness and confidentiality when exercising powers and delegated responsibilities.[11]

To ensure consistent application of international financial standards (such as the Basel Committee on Banking Supervision's standards and IFRS), it is important to have uniform regulation and enforcement across national boundaries. IOSCO assists in attaining this goal of uniform regulation as well as cross-border co-operation in combating violations of securities and derivatives laws.

---

9 The names of the primary securities regulator vary from country to country. For example: China Securities Regulatory Commission, Egyptian Financial Supervisory Authority, Securities and Exchange Board of India, Kingdom of Saudi Arabia Capital Market Authority, and Banco Central del Uruguay.
10 *Objectives and Principles of Securities Regulation*, IOSCO, June 2010.
11 *Objectives and Principles of Securities Regulation*, IOSCO, June 2010.

3.2.2 *The Securities and Exchange Commission (U.S.)*

The U.S. SEC has primary responsibility for securities and capital markets regulation in the United States and is an ordinary member of IOSCO. Any company issuing securities within the United States, or otherwise involved in U.S. capital markets, is subject to the rules and regulations of the SEC. The SEC, one of the oldest and most developed regulatory authorities, originated as a result of reform efforts made after the great stock market crash of 1929, sometimes referred to as simply the "Great Crash."

A number of laws affect reporting companies, broker/dealers, and other market participants. From a financial reporting and analysis perspective, the most significant pieces of legislation are the Securities Acts of 1933 and 1934 and the Sarbanes–Oxley Act of 2002.

- **Securities Act of 1933** (The 1933 Act): This act specifies the financial and other significant information that investors must receive when securities are sold, prohibits misrepresentations, and requires initial registration of all public issuances of securities.

- **Securities Exchange Act of 1934** (The 1934 Act): This act created the SEC, gave the SEC authority over all aspects of the securities industry, and empowered the SEC to require periodic reporting by companies with publicly traded securities.

- **Sarbanes–Oxley Act of 2002**: The Sarbanes–Oxley Act of 2002 created the Public Company Accounting Oversight Board (PCAOB) to oversee auditors. The SEC is responsible for carrying out the requirements of the act and overseeing the PCAOB. The act addresses auditor independence; for example, it prohibits auditors from providing certain non-audit services to the companies they audit. The act strengthens corporate responsibility for financial reports; for example, it requires the chief executive officer and the chief financial officer to certify that the company's financial reports fairly present the company's condition. Furthermore, Section 404 of the Sarbanes–Oxley Act requires management to report on the effectiveness of the company's internal control over financial reporting and to obtain a report from its external auditor attesting to management's assertion about the effectiveness of the company's internal control.

Companies comply with these acts principally through the completion and submission (i.e., filing) of standardized forms issued by the SEC. There are more than 50 different types of SEC forms that are used to satisfy reporting requirements; the discussion herein will be limited to those forms most relevant for financial analysts.

In 1993, the SEC began to mandate electronic filings of the required forms through its Electronic Data Gathering, Analysis, and Retrieval (EDGAR) system. As of 2005, most SEC filings are required to be made electronically. EDGAR has made corporate and financial information more readily available to investors and the financial community. Most of the SEC filings that an analyst would be interested in can be retrieved from the internet from one of many websites, including the SEC's own website. Some filings are required on the initial offering of securities, whereas others are required on a periodic basis thereafter. The following are some of the more common information sources used by analysts.

- **Securities Offerings Registration Statement**: The 1933 Act requires companies offering securities to file a registration statement. New issuers as well as previously registered companies that are issuing new securities are required to file these statements. Required information and the precise form vary depending upon the size and nature of the offering. Typically, required information includes: 1) disclosures about the securities being offered for sale, 2) the relationship of these new securities to the issuer's other capital securities, 3) the information typically provided in the annual filings, 4) recent audited financial statements, and 5) risk factors involved in the business.

- **Forms 10-K, 20-F, and 40-F**: These are forms that companies are required to file *annually*. Form 10-K is for U.S. registrants, Form 40-F is for certain Canadian registrants, and Form 20-F is for all other non-U.S. registrants. These forms require a comprehensive overview, including information concerning a company's business, financial disclosures, legal proceedings, and information related to management. The financial disclosures include a historical summary of financial data (usually 10 years), management's discussion and analysis (MD&A) of the company's financial condition and results of operations, and audited financial statements.[12]

- **Annual Report**: In addition to the SEC's annual filings (e.g., Form 10-K), most companies prepare an annual report to shareholders. This is not a requirement of the SEC. The annual report is usually viewed as one of the most significant opportunities for a company to present itself to shareholders and other external parties; accordingly, it is often a highly polished marketing document with photographs, an opening letter from the chief executive officer, financial data, market segment information, research and development activities, and future corporate goals. In contrast, the Form 10-K is a more legal type of document with minimal marketing emphasis. Although the perspectives vary, there is considerable overlap between a company's annual report and its Form 10-K. Some companies elect to prepare just the Form 10-K or a document that integrates both the 10-K and annual report.

- **Proxy Statement/Form DEF-14A**: The SEC requires that shareholders of a company receive a proxy statement prior to a shareholder meeting. A proxy is an authorization from the shareholder giving another party the right to cast its vote. Shareholder meetings are held at least once a year, but any special meetings also require a proxy statement. Proxies, especially annual meeting proxies, contain information that is often useful to financial analysts. Such information typically includes proposals that require a shareholder vote, details of security ownership by management and principal owners, biographical information on directors, and disclosure of executive compensation. Proxy statement information is filed with the SEC as Form DEF-14A.

- **Forms 10-Q and 6-K**: These are forms that companies are required to submit for interim periods (quarterly for U.S. companies on Form 10-Q, semiannually for many non-U.S. companies on Form 6-K). The filing requires certain financial information, including unaudited financial statements and a MD&A for the interim period covered by the report. Additionally, if certain types of non-recurring events—such as the adoption of a significant accounting policy, commencement of significant litigation, or a material limitation on the rights of any holders of any class of registered securities—take place during the period covered by the report, these events must be included in the Form 10-Q report. Companies may provide the 10-Q report to shareholders or may prepare a separate, abbreviated, quarterly report to shareholders.

---

12 Effective in 2008, the SEC permits foreign private issuers to file financial statements prepared in accordance with IFRS (as issued by the IASB) with no reconciliation to U.S. GAAP. Foreign private issuers using accounting standards other than U.S. GAAP or IFRS must still provide a reconciliation to U.S. GAAP.

EXAMPLE 3

Initial Registration Statement

In 2004, Google filed a Form S-1 registration statement with the U.S. SEC to register its initial public offering of securities (Class A Common Stock). In addition to a large amount of financial and business information, the registration statement provided a 20-page discussion of risks related to Google's business and industry. This type of qualitative information is helpful, if not essential, in making an assessment of a company's credit or investment risk.

Which of the following is *least likely* to have been included in Google's registration statement?

A   Audited financial statements.

B   Assessment of risk factors involved in the business.

C   Projected cash flows and earnings for the business.

Solution:

C is correct. Companies provide information useful in developing these projections but do not typically include these in the registration statement. Information provided includes audited financial statements, an assessment of risk factors involved in the business, names of the underwriters, estimated proceeds from the offering, and use of proceeds.

A company or its officers make other SEC filings—either periodically, or, if significant events or transactions have occurred, in between the periodic reports noted above. By their nature, these forms sometimes contain the most interesting and timely information and may have significant valuation implications.

■ **Form 8-K:** In addition to filing annual and interim reports, SEC registrants must report material corporate events on a more current basis. Form 8-K (6-K for non-U.S. registrants) is the "current report" companies must file with the SEC to announce such major events as acquisitions or disposals of corporate assets, changes in securities and trading markets, matters related to accountants and financial statements, corporate governance and management changes, and Regulation FD disclosures.[13]

■ **Form 144:** This form must be filed with the SEC as notice of the proposed sale of restricted securities or securities held by an affiliate of the issuer in reliance on Rule 144. Rule 144 permits limited sales of restricted securities without registration.

■ **Forms 3, 4, and 5:** These forms are required to report beneficial ownership of securities. These filings are required for any director or officer of a registered company as well as beneficial owners of greater than 10 percent of a class of registered equity securities. Form 3 is the initial statement, Form 4 reports

---

13 Regulation FD provides that when an issuer discloses material non-public information to certain individuals or entities—generally, securities market professionals such as stock analysts or holders of the issuer's securities who may trade on the basis of the information—the issuer must make public disclosure of that information. In this way, the rule aims to promote full and fair disclosure.

changes, and Form 5 is the annual report. These forms, along with Form 144, can be used to examine purchases and sales of securities by officers, directors, and other affiliates of the company.

■ **Form 11-K**: This is the annual report of employee stock purchase, savings, and similar plans. It might be of interest to analysts for companies with significant employee benefit plans because it contains more information than that disclosed in the company's financial statements.

In jurisdictions other than the United States, similar legislation exists for the purpose of regulating securities and capital markets. Regulatory authorities are responsible for enforcing regulation, and securities regulation is intended to be consistent with the IOSCO objectives described in the previous section. Within each jurisdiction, regulators will either establish or, more typically, recognize and adopt a specified set or sets of accounting standards. The regulators will also establish reporting and filing requirements. IOSCO members have agreed to cooperate in the development, implementation, and enforcement of internationally recognised and consistent standards of regulation.

3.2.3 *Capital Markets Regulation in Europe*

Each individual member state of the European Union (EU) regulates capital markets in its jurisdiction. There are, however, certain regulations that have been adopted at the EU level. Importantly, in 2002 the EU agreed that from 1 January 2005, consolidated accounts of EU listed companies would use International Financial Reporting Standards. The endorsement process by which newly issued IFRS are adopted by the EU reflects the balance between the individual member state's autonomy and the need for cooperation and convergence. When the IASB issues a new standard, the European Financial Reporting Advisory Group advises the European Commission on the standard, and the Standards Advice Review Group provides the Commission an opinion about that advice. Based on the input from these two entities, the Commission prepares a draft endorsement regulation. The Accounting Regulatory Committee votes on the proposal; and if the vote is favorable, the proposal proceeds to the European Parliament and the Council of the European Union for approval.[14]

Two committees related to securities regulation, established in 2001 by the European Commission, are the European Securities Committee (ESC) and the Committee of European Securities Regulators (CESR). The ESC consists of high-level representatives of member states and advises the European Commission on securities policy issues. The CESR, an independent advisory body composed of representatives of regulatory authorities of the member states, assists the commission, particularly with technical issues. As noted earlier, regulation still rests with the individual member states and, therefore, requirements for registering shares and filing periodic financial reports vary from country to country.

On 1 January 2011, CESR was replaced by the European Securities and Market Authority (ESMA) as part of a reform of the EU financial supervisory framework. The EU Parliament created ESMA as an EU cross-border supervisor because the CESR's powers were deemed insufficient to co-ordinate supervision of the EU market. ESMA is one of three European supervisory authorities; the two others supervise the banking and insurance industries.

---

14 Source: European Commission.
http://ec.europa.eu/internal_market/accounting/legal_framework/ias_regulation_en.htm.

4   CONVERGENCE OF GLOBAL FINANCIAL REPORTING STANDARDS

Recent activities have moved the goal of one set of universally accepted financial reporting standards out of the theoretical sphere and closer to reality. IFRS have been or are in the process of being adopted in many countries. Other countries maintain their own set of standards but are working with the IASB to converge their standards and IFRS.

In some ways, the movement toward one global set of financial reporting standards has made the challenges related to full convergence or adoption of a single set of global standards more apparent. Standard-setting bodies and regulators can have differing views or use a different framework for developing standards. This can be the result of differences in institutional, regulatory, business, and cultural environments. In addition, there may be resistance to change or advocacy for change from certain constituents; accounting boards may be influenced by strong industry lobbying groups and others that will be subject to these reporting standards. For example, the FASB faced strong opposition when it first attempted to adopt standards requiring companies to expense employee stock compensation plans.[15] The IASB has experienced similar political pressures. The issue of political pressure is compounded when international standards are involved, simply because there are many more interested parties and many more divergent views and objectives. In the financial crisis of 2008 and 2009, both the FASB and the IASB faced political pressure to amend the standards related to financial instrument accounting. Political pressure and its influence create tension as the independence of accounting standards boards are questioned and jeopardized.

The integrity of the financial reporting framework depends on the standard setter's ability to invite and balance various points of view and yet to remain independent of external pressures. For analysts, it is important to be aware of the pace of change in accounting standards and factors potentially influencing those changes.

An additional issue related to convergence involves the application and enforcement of accounting standards. Unless the standards are applied consistently and enforcement is uniform, a single set of standards may only appear to exist but desirable attributes such as comparability may be lacking.

In 2002, the IASB and FASB each acknowledged their commitment to the development of high quality, compatible accounting standards that could be used for both domestic and cross-border financial reporting (in an agreement referred to as "the Norwalk Agreement"). Both the IASB and FASB pledged to use their best efforts to 1) make their existing financial reporting standards fully compatible as soon as practicable, and 2) to coordinate their future work programs to ensure that, once achieved, compatibility is maintained. The Norwalk Agreement was certainly an important milestone, and both bodies began working toward convergence. In 2004, the IASB and FASB agreed that, in principle, any significant accounting standard would be developed cooperatively. In 2006, the IASB and the FASB issued another memorandum of understanding (titled "A Roadmap for Convergence between IFRSs and U.S. GAAP") in which the two Boards identified major projects. They agreed to align their conceptual frameworks; in the short term, to remove selected differences; and in the medium term, to issue joint standards where significant improvements were identified as being required. The joint projects include (but are not limited to): the Conceptual Framework, Fair Value Measurement, Consolidations, Financial Instruments, Financial Statement Presentation, Insurance Contracts, Leases, Post

---

15 The second attempt was successful and U.S. GAAP requires the expensing of stock options. FASB ASC Topic 718 [Compensation–Stock Compensation].

Employment Benefits, and Revenue Recognition. In 2009, the IASB and FASB again reaffirmed their commitment to achieving convergence and affirmed June 2011 as the target completion date for the major projects that had been identified. In mid-2010, however, the Boards acknowledged that all the new standard-setting activity required to achieve that targeted completion would not give stakeholders enough time to provide high quality input in the process. Therefore, the Boards pushed back the target date for some projects to later in 2011.

Meanwhile, as convergence between IFRS and U.S. GAAP continued, the SEC began certain steps regarding the possible adoption of IFRS in the United States. Effective in 2008, the SEC adopted rules to eliminate the reconciliation requirement for foreign private issuers' financial statements prepared in accordance with IFRS as issued by the IASB. Previously, any non-U.S. issuer using accounting standards other than U.S. GAAP was required to provide a reconciliation to U.S. GAAP. In November 2008, the SEC issued a proposed rule concerning a "Roadmap" for the use of financial statements prepared in accordance with IFRS by U.S. issuers; however the rule did not become final. In February 2010, the SEC issued a "Statement in Support of Convergence and Global Accounting Standards" in which it reiterated its commitment to global accounting standards and directed its staff to execute a work plan to enable the "Commission in 2011 to make a determination regarding incorporating IFRS into the financial reporting system for U.S. issuers."[16]

Convergence between IFRS and other local GAAP also continues. For example, convergence between IFRS and Japanese GAAP is underway. In 2008, the IASB and the Accounting Standards Board of Japan published a memorandum of understanding (the "Tokyo Agreement") outlining work to achieve convergence by June 2011. In 2009, the Japanese Business Accounting Council, a key advisory body to the Commissioner of the Japanese Financial Services Agency, approved a roadmap for the adoption of IFRS in Japan.[17]

Exhibit 1 provides a summary of the adoption status of IFRS in selected worldwide locations. As can be seen, adoption ranges from total adoption of IFRS to requiring local GAAP. Between these two extremes, countries demonstrate different levels of commitment to IFRS including adoption of a local version of IFRS, requirement for certain entities to use IFRS, permission to use IFRS, and use of local GAAP that is converging with IFRS.

Exhibit 1	International Adoption Status of IFRS in Selected Locations as of June 2010
Europe	■ The EU requires companies listed in EU countries to adopt IFRS beginning with their 2005 financial statements.
	■ Switzerland requires that Swiss multinational companies listed on the main board of the Swiss Exchange must choose either U.S. GAAP or IFRS.
	■ Some countries (for example, Georgia, Macedonia, Moldova, Serbia) use IFRS as adopted locally. Georgia, for example, uses the IFRS 2007 edition.
	■ Some countries (for example, Czech Republic, Finland, Germany, Ireland, Lithuania, Netherlands, Norway, Poland) permit some foreign companies listing on local exchanges to use other specified and/or well-recognised standards.

(continued)

---

16 Source: www.sec.gov/rules/other/2010/33-9109.pdf.
17 Source: www.iasb.org/Use+around+the+world/Global+convergence/IFRS+global+convergence.htm.

Exhibit 1	(Continued)
North America	■ The U.S. SEC accepts IFRS for non-U.S. registrants and no longer requires a reconciliation to U.S. GAAP for filers using IFRS.
	■ The U.S. FASB is engaged in numerous projects with the IASB to achieve convergence of U.S. GAAP and IFRS.
	■ The U.S. SEC announced its intention to decide by 2011 whether to incorporate IFRS into financial reporting by U.S. issuers.
	■ In Canada, listed companies are required to use IFRS beginning 1 January 2011. The year ending 31 December 2010 is the last year of reporting under current Canadian GAAP.
	■ In November 2008, Mexico announced plans to move to IFRS in 2012.
	■ Most of the island nations off the southeast coast of North America require or permit the use of IFRS by listed companies.
Central and South America	■ Central America, Costa Rica, Honduras and Panama require the use of IFRS. El Salvador, Guatemala, and Nicaragua permit the use of IFRS.
	■ Brazil requires that listed companies and financial institutions use IFRS, starting with periods ending in 2010. Brazilian GAAP continues to converge to IFRS. Ecuador requires listed companies, other than financial institutions, to use IFRS beginning in 2010.
	■ Chile requires major listed companies to use IFRS for 2009 financial statements. Other companies are permitted to use IFRS.
	■ Venezuela permits listed companies to use IFRS. The expectation is that listed companies will be required to use IFRS by 2011.
	■ Peru and Uruguay require the use of IFRS as adopted locally.
	■ In Argentina, convergence of ARG GAAP to IFRS is in progress. Listed foreign companies are permitted to use their primary GAAP, including IFRS, but should also include a reconciliation to ARG GAAP.
	■ Bolivia is moving towards convergence with IFRS.
	■ In Colombia and Paraguay, the adoption of IFRS is in early stages of consideration.

Exhibit 1	(Continued)

Asia and Middle East	■ Listed companies in a number of countries—including India, Indonesia, and Thailand—report under local GAAP, and plans exist to either converge with or transition to IFRS.
	■ Companies in China report under Chinese accounting standards (CAS). CAS are largely converged with IFRS and China's November 2009 proposed Roadmap targeted 2011 as the year for completion of convergence of IFRS and CAS. Financial institutions are required to prepare financial statements in accordance with IFRS in addition to their statements prepared using CAS.
	■ In Japan, some companies that meet certain criteria may use IFRS, otherwise companies report using Japanese GAAP. Japan has launched a joint project with the IASB to reduce differences between Japanese GAAP and IFRS.
	■ In Malaysia, domestic listed companies report using local GAAP and foreign companies listed on Malaysian exchanges are permitted to use IFRS. Malaysia plans to have full convergence with IFRS by January 2012.
	■ In Hong Kong, companies incorporated in Hong Kong normally report under Hong Kong FRS. These are largely converged with IFRS.
	■ Korea requires the use of IFRS beginning 2011. Early adoption was permitted from 2009.
	■ Listed companies are required to report under IFRS in a number of other countries, including Kyrgyz Republic, Lebanon, and Turkey.
	■ A number of countries, including Pakistan, Philippines, and Singapore, require use of IFRS as adopted locally. In Singapore, IFRS is permitted for use by companies that list on other exchanges that require IFRS or if permission is given by the Accounting and Corporate Regulatory Authority.
	■ In a number of countries, IFRS is required for some types of entities and permitted for others. For example, Armenia requires IFRS for financial organizations and permits its use for others, Azerbaijan requires IFRS for banks and state owned public interest entities, Israel requires IFRS for domestic listed companies except for banking institutions, Kazakhstan requires IFRS for domestic listed companies, large business entities and public interest entities, Saudi Arabia requires IFRS for all banks regulated by the Saudi Arabian Monetary Agency (central bank), and Uzbekistan requires IFRS for all commercial banks and permits IFRS for others. Vietnam requires IFRS for state owned banks and permits IFRS for commercial banks; all other listed companies report under Vietnamese accounting standards. Some countries, including Afghanistan and Qatar, permit the use of IFRS.
Oceana	■ Australia requires Australian reporting entities to use IFRS as adopted locally. Foreign companies listing on local exchanges are permitted to use IFRS or their primary GAAP. The Australian regulator may require additional information.
	■ New Zealand requires use of IFRS as adopted locally (NZ-IFRS).
Africa	■ Many African countries, including Botswana, Ghana, Kenya, Malawi, Mauritius, Namibia, South Africa, Swaziland, Tanzania, Uganda, Zambia, and Zimbabwe, require IFRS for listed companies.
	■ Morocco requires the use of IFRS for consolidated financial statements of bank and financial institutions and permits its use for others.
	■ Mozambique requires the use of IFRS for financial and lending institutions and for certain large entities. Use of IFRS is permitted by other entities beginning in 2010.
	■ Egypt requires the use of local GAAP which is partially converged with IFRS.
	■ The Nigerian Federal Executive Council approved 1 January 2012 as the effective date for convergence of accounting standards in Nigeria with IFRS.
	■ In some countries, financial statements are required to be prepared in accordance with the Organization for the Harmonization of Business Law in Africa accounting framework. These countries include Cameroon, Cote D'Ivoire, and Equatorial Guinea.

Sources: Based on data from www.iasb.org, www.sec.gov, www.iasplus.com, and www.pwc.com.

5   THE INTERNATIONAL FINANCIAL REPORTING STANDARDS FRAMEWORK

The *Conceptual Framework for Financial Reporting 2010* sets forth "the concepts that underlie the preparation and presentation of financial statements for external users." The *Conceptual Framework (2010)* is designed to assist standard setters in developing and reviewing standards, to assist preparers of financial statements in applying standards and in dealing with issues not specifically covered by standards, to assist auditors in forming an opinion on financial statements, and to assist users in interpreting financial statement information. It is important to note that an understanding of the *Conceptual Framework (2010)* is expected to assist users of financial statements—including financial analysts—in interpreting the information contained therein.

The *Conceptual Framework (2010)* is diagrammed in Exhibit 2. The top part of the diagram shows the objective of general purpose financial reporting at the center, because other aspects of the framework are based upon this core. The qualitative characteristics of useful financial information surround the objective (fundamental characteristics are listed on the left and enhancing characteristics are listed on the right). The reporting elements are shown next with elements of financial statements shown at the bottom. Beneath the diagram of the framework are the basic constraint (cost) and assumption (going concern) that guide the development of standards and the preparation of financial reports.

Exhibit 2	IFRS Framework for the Preparation and Presentation of Financial Reports

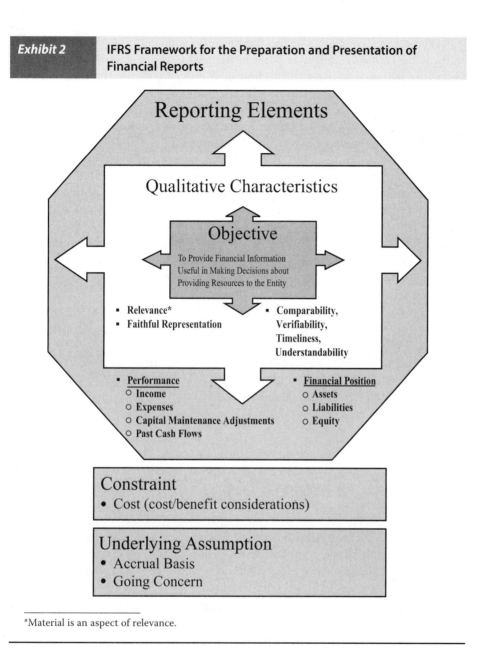

*Material is an aspect of relevance.

In the following, we discuss the *Conceptual Framework (2010)* starting at the core: The objective of financial statements.

5.1 Objective of Financial Reports

At the core of the *Conceptual Framework (2010)* is the objective: The provision of financial information that is useful to current and potential providers of resources in making decisions. All other aspects of the framework flow from that central objective.

The providers of resources are considered to be the primary users of financial reports and include investors, lenders, and other creditors. The purpose of providing the financial information is to be useful in making decisions about providing resources. Other users may find the financial information useful for making economic decisions. The types of economic decisions differ by users, so the specific information needed differs as well. However, although these users may have unique information needs, some information needs are common across all users. Information is needed about the company's financial position: its resources and its financial obligations. Information is needed about a company's financial performance; this information explains how and why the company's financial position changed in the past and can be useful in evaluating potential changes in the future. The third common information need reflected in the *Conceptual Framework* (*2010*) diagram is the need for information about a company's cash. How did the company obtain cash (by selling its products and services, borrowing, other)? How did the company use cash (by paying expenses, investing in new equipment, paying dividends, other)?

The *Conceptual Framework* (*2010*) indicates that to make decisions about providing resources to the company, users need information that is helpful in assessing future net cash inflows to the entity. Such information includes information about the economic resources of (assets) and claims against (liabilities and equity) the entity, and about how well the management and governing board have utilized the resources of the entity. It is specifically noted in the *Conceptual Framework* (*2010*) that users need to consider information from other sources as well in making their decisions. Further, it is noted that the financial reports do not show the value of an entity but are useful in estimating the value of an entity.

5.2 Qualitative Characteristics of Financial Reports

Flowing from the central objective of providing information that is *useful* to providers of resources, the *Conceptual Framework* (*2010*) elaborates on what constitutes usefulness. It identifies two fundamental qualitative characteristics that make financial information useful: relevance and faithful representation.[18] The concept of materiality is discussed within the context of relevance.

1 *Relevance*: Information is relevant if it would potentially affect or make a difference in users' decisions. The information can have predictive value (useful in making forecasts), confirmatory value (useful to evaluate past decisions or forecasts), or both. In other words, relevant information helps users of financial information to evaluate past, present, and future events, or to confirm or correct their past evaluations in a decision-making context. *Materiality:* Information is considered to be material if omission or misstatement of the information could influence users' decisions. Materiality is a function of the nature and/or magnitude of the information.

2 *Faithful representation*: Information that faithfully represents an economic phenomenon that it purports to represent is ideally complete, neutral, and free from error. Complete means that all information necessary to understand the phenomenon is depicted. Neutral means that information is selected and presented without bias. In other words, the information is not presented in such a manner as to bias the users' decisions. Free from error means that there are no errors of commission or omission in the description of the economic phenomenon, and that an appropriate process to arrive at the reported information was selected and was adhered to without error. Faithful representation maximizes the qualities of complete, neutral, and free from error to the extent possible.

Relevance and faithful representation are the fundamental, most critical characteristics of useful financial information. In addition to these two fundamental characteristics, the *Conceptual Framework* (*2010*) identifies four characteristics that

---

18 *Conceptual Framework for Financial Reporting (2010).* paragraphs QC 5–18.

enhance the usefulness of relevant and faithfully represented financial information. These enhancing qualitative characteristics are comparability, verifiability, timeliness, and understandability.[19]

1 *Comparability*: Comparability allows users "to identify and understand similarities and differences of items." Information presented in a consistent manner over time and across entities enables users to make comparisons more easily than information with variations in how similar economic phenomena are represented.

2 *Verifiability*: Verifiability means that different knowledgeable and independent observers would agree that the information presented faithfully represents the economic phenomena it purports to represent.

3 *Timeliness*: Timely information is available to decision makers prior to their making a decision.

4 *Understandability*: Clear and concise presentation of information enhances understandability. The *Conceptual Framework (2010)* specifies that the information is prepared for and should be understandable by users who have a reasonable knowledge of business and economic activities, and who are willing to study the information with diligence. However, some complex economic phenomena cannot be presented in an easily understandable form. Information that is useful should not be excluded simply because it is difficult to understand. It may be necessary for users to seek assistance to understand information about complex economic phenomena.

Financial information exhibiting these qualitative characteristics—fundamental and enhancing—should be useful for making economic decisions.

5.3 Constraints on Financial Reports

Although it would be ideal for financial statements to exhibit all of these qualitative characteristics and thus achieve maximum usefulness, it may be necessary to make tradeoffs across the enhancing characteristics. The application of the enhancing characteristics follows no set order of priority. Depending on the circumstances, each enhancing characteristic may take priority over the others.[20] The aim is an appropriate balance among the enhancing characteristics.

A pervasive constraint on useful financial reporting is the cost of providing and using this information.[21] Optimally, benefits derived from information should exceed the costs of providing and using it. Again, the aim is a balance between costs and benefits.

A limitation of financial reporting not specifically mentioned in the *Conceptual Framework (2010)* involves information not included. Financial statements, by necessity, omit information that is non-quantifiable. For example, the creativity, innovation, and competence of a company's work force are not directly captured in the financial statements. Similarly, customer loyalty, a positive corporate culture, environmental responsibility, and many other aspects about a company may not be directly reflected in the financial statements. Of course, to the extent that these items result in superior financial performance, a company's financial reports will reflect the results.

---

19 Ibid., paragraphs QC19–34.
20 Ibid., paragraph QC34.
21 Ibid., paragraphs QC35–39.

EXAMPLE 4

Balancing Qualitative Characteristics of Useful Information

A tradeoff between enhancing qualitative characteristics often occurs. For example, when a company records sales revenue, it is required to simultaneously estimate and record an expense for potential bad debts (uncollectible accounts). Including this estimated expense is considered to represent the economic event faithfully and to provide relevant information about the net profits for the accounting period. The information is timely and understandable; but because bad debts may not be known with certainty until a later period, inclusion of this estimated expense involves a sacrifice of verifiability. The bad debt expense is simply an estimate. It is apparent that it is not always possible to simultaneously fulfill all qualitative characteristics.

Companies are *most likely* to make tradeoffs between which of the following when preparing financial reports?

A   Relevance and materiality.

B   Timeliness and verifiability.

C   Relevance and faithful representation.

Solution:

B is correct. Providing timely information implies a shorter time frame between the economic event and the information preparation; however, fully verifying information may require a longer time frame. Relevance and faithful representation are fundamental qualitative characteristics that make financial information useful. Both characteristics are required; there is no tradeoff between these. Materiality is an aspect of relevance.

5.4 The Elements of Financial Statements

Financial statements portray the financial effects of transactions and other events by grouping them into broad classes (elements) according to their economic characteristics.[22] Three elements of financial statements are directly related to the measurement of financial position: assets, liabilities, and equity.[23]

- **Assets**: Resources controlled by the enterprise as a result of past events and from which future economic benefits are expected to flow to the enterprise. Assets are what a company owns (e.g., inventory and equipment).

- **Liabilities**: Present obligations of an enterprise arising from past events, the settlement of which is expected to result in an outflow of resources embodying economic benefits. Liabilities are what a company owes (e.g., bank borrowings).

- **Equity** (for public companies, also known as "shareholders' equity" or "stockholders' equity"): Assets less liabilities. Equity is the residual interest in the assets after subtracting the liabilities.

---

22 Chapter 4, the section of *The Conceptual Framework (2010)* which deals with the elements of the financial statements and their recognition and measurement, has not been amended from *The Framework (1989).* This chapter and the proposed Chapter 2, "The Reporting Entity," will be considered further sometime after 2010. The references given will be as they appear in *The Conceptual Framework (2010).*
23 *Conceptual Framework for Financial Reporting (2010)*, paragraphs 4.4–4.23.

The elements of financial statements directly related to the measurement of performance (profit and related measures) are income and expenses.[24]

- **Income**: Increases in economic benefits in the form of inflows or enhancements of assets, or decreases of liabilities that result in an increase in equity (other than increases resulting from contributions by owners). Income includes both revenues and gains. Revenues represent income from the ordinary activities of the enterprise (e.g., the sale of products). Gains may result from ordinary activities or other activities (the sale of surplus equipment).

- **Expenses**: Decreases in economic benefits in the form of outflows or depletions of assets, or increases in liabilities that result in decreases in equity (other than decreases because of distributions to owners). Expenses include losses, as well as those items normally thought of as expenses, such as the cost of goods sold or wages.

5.4.1 *Underlying Assumptions in Financial Statements*

Two important assumptions underlie financial statements: accrual accounting and going concern. These assumptions determine how financial statement elements are recognized and measured.[25]

The use of "accrual accounting" assumes that financial statements should reflect transactions in the period when they actually occur, not necessarily when cash movements occur. For example, accrual accounting specifies that a company reports revenues *when they are earned (when the performance obligations have been satisfied)*, regardless of whether the company received cash before delivering the product, after delivering the product, or at the time of delivery.

"Going concern" refers to the assumption that the company will continue in business for the foreseeable future. To illustrate, consider the value of a company's inventory if it is assumed that the inventory can be sold over a normal period of time versus the value of that same inventory if it is assumed that the inventory must all be sold in a day (or a week). Companies with the intent to liquidate or materially curtail operations would require different information for a fair presentation.

In reporting the financial position of a company that is assumed to be a going concern, it may be appropriate to list assets at some measure of a current value based upon normal market conditions. However, if a company is expected to cease operations and be liquidated, it may be more appropriate to list such assets at an appropriate liquidation value, namely, a value that would be obtained in a forced sale.

5.4.2 *Recognition of Financial Statement Elements*

Recognition means that an item is included in the balance sheet or income statement. Recognition occurs if the item meets the definition of an element and satisfies the criteria for recognition. A financial statement element (assets, liabilities, equity, income, and expenses) should be recognized in the financial statements if:[26]

- it is *probable* that any future economic benefit associated with the item will flow to or from the enterprise; and
- the item has a cost or value that can be *measured with reliability*.

---

24 Ibid., paragraphs 4.24–4.36.
25 Ibid., paragraphs OB17 and 4.1.
26 Ibid., paragraphs 4.37–4.38.

5.4.3 *Measurement of Financial Statement Elements*

Measurement is the process of determining the monetary amounts at which the elements of the financial statements are to be recognized and carried in the balance sheet and income statement. The following alternative bases of measurement are used to different degrees and in varying combinations to measure assets and liabilities:[27]

- **Historical cost**: Historical cost is simply the amount of cash or cash equivalents paid to purchase an asset, including any costs of acquisition and/or preparation. If the asset was not bought for cash, historical cost is the fair value of whatever was given in order to buy the asset. When referring to liabilities, the historical cost basis of measurement means the amount of proceeds received in exchange for the obligation.

- **Amortised cost**: Historical cost adjusted for amortisation, depreciation, or depletion and/or impairment.

- **Current cost**: In reference to assets, current cost is the amount of cash or cash equivalents that would have to be paid to buy the same or an equivalent asset today. In reference to liabilities, the current cost basis of measurement means the undiscounted amount of cash or cash equivalents that would be required to settle the obligation today.

- **Realizable (settlement) value**: In reference to assets, realizable value is the amount of cash or cash equivalents that could currently be obtained by selling the asset in an orderly disposal. For liabilities, the equivalent to realizable value is called "settlement value"—that is, settlement value is the undiscounted amount of cash or cash equivalents expected to be paid to satisfy the liabilities in the normal course of business.

- **Present value (PV)**: For assets, present value is the present discounted value of the future net cash inflows that the asset is expected to generate in the normal course of business. For liabilities, present value is the present discounted value of the future net cash outflows that are expected to be required to settle the liabilities in the normal course of business.

- **Fair value**: is a measure of value mentioned but not specifically defined in the *Conceptual Framework* (*2010*). Fair value is the amount at which an asset could be exchanged, or a liability settled, between knowledgeable, willing parties in an arm's length transaction. This may involve either market measures or present value measures depending on the availability of information.[28]

5.5 General Requirements for Financial Statements

The *Conceptual Framework* (*2010*) provides a basis for establishing standards and the elements of financial statements, but it does not address the contents of the financial statements. Having discussed the *Conceptual Framework* (*2010*), we now address the general requirements for financial statements.

---

27 Ibid., paragraphs 4.54–4.55.
28 IFRS *Glossary of Terms*. Note that the joint IASB/FASB Fair Value project intends to redefine the term "fair value" as an exit price—the price that would be received to sell an asset or paid to transfer a liability in an orderly transaction between market participants at the measurement date. This is the definition in FASB ASC Topic 820 [Fair Value Measurements and Disclosures].

International Accounting Standard (IAS) No. 1, *Presentation of Financial Statements*, specifies the required financial statements, general features of financial statements, and structure and content of financial statements.[29] These general requirements are illustrated in Exhibit 3 and described in the subsections below.

Exhibit 3	IASB General Requirements for Financial Statements

Required Financial Statements
- Statement of financial position (Balance sheet)
- Statement of comprehensive income (Single statement or Income statement + Statement of comprehensive income)
- Statement of changes in equity
- Statement of cash flows
- Notes, summarizing accounting policies and disclosing other items
- In certain cases, Statement of financial position from earliest comparative period

General Features
- Fair presentation
- Going concern
- Accrual basis
- Materiality and aggregation
- No offsetting
- Frequency of reporting
- Comparative information
- Consistency of presentation

Structure and Content
- Classified balance sheet
- Minimum specified information on face
- Minimum specified note disclosures
- Comparative information

In the following sections, we discuss the required financial statements, the general features underlying the preparation of financial statements, and the specified structure and content in greater detail.

5.5.1 *Required Financial Statements*

Under IAS No. 1, a complete set of financial statements includes:[30]

- a statement of financial position (balance sheet);

- a statement of comprehensive income (a single statement of comprehensive income or two statements, an income statement and a statement of comprehensive income that begins with profit or loss from the income statement);

- a statement of changes in equity, separately showing changes in equity resulting from profit or loss, each item of other comprehensive income, and transactions with owners in their capacity as owners;[31]

- a statement of cash flows; and

- notes comprising a summary of significant accounting policies and other explanatory notes that disclose information required by IFRS and not presented elsewhere and that provide information relevant to an understanding of the financial statements.

---

29 For U.S. GAAP, financial statement presentation is covered in Sections 205 through 280 of the Accounting Standards Codification.

30 IAS No. 1, *Presentation of Financial Statements*, paragraph 10.

31 Examples of transactions with owners acting in their capacity as owners include sale of equity securities to investors, distributions of earnings to investors, and repurchases of equity securities from investors.

Entities are encouraged to furnish other related financial and non-financial information in addition to that required. Financial statements need to present fairly the financial position, financial performance, and cash flows of an entity.

5.5.2 *General Features of Financial Statements*

A company that applies IFRS is required to state explicitly in the notes to its financial statements that it is in compliance with the standards. Such a statement is only made when a company is in compliance with *all* requirements of IFRS. In extremely rare circumstances, a company may deviate from a requirement of IFRS if management concludes that complying with IFRS would result in misleading financial statements. In this case, management must disclose details of the departure from IFRS.

IAS No. 1 specifies a number of general features underlying the preparation of financial statements. These features clearly reflect the *Conceptual Framework* (*2010*).

- *Fair Presentation*: The application of IFRS is presumed to result in financial statements that achieve a fair presentation. The IAS describes fair presentation as follows:

    > Fair presentation requires the faithful representation of the effects of transactions, other events and conditions in accordance with the definitions and recognition criteria for assets, liabilities, income and expenses set out in the *Framework*.[32]

- *Going Concern*: Financial statements are prepared on a going concern basis unless management either intends to liquidate the entity or to cease trading, or has no realistic alternative but to do so. If not presented on a going concern basis, the fact and rationale should be disclosed.

- *Accrual Basis*: Financial statements (except for cash flow information) are to be prepared using the accrual basis of accounting.

- *Materiality and Aggregation*: Omissions or misstatements of items are material if they could, individually or collectively, influence the economic decisions that users make on the basis of the financial statements. Each material class of similar items is presented separately. Dissimilar items are presented separately unless they are immaterial.

- *No Offsetting*: Assets and liabilities, and income and expenses, are not offset unless required or permitted by an IFRS.

- *Frequency of Reporting*: Financial statements must be prepared at least annually.

- *Comparative Information*: Financial statements must include comparative information from the previous period. The comparative information of prior periods is disclosed for all amounts reported in the financial statements, unless an IFRS requires or permits otherwise.

- *Consistency*: The presentation and classification of items in the financial statements are usually retained from one period to the next.

---

32 IAS No. 1, *Presentation of Financial Statements*, paragraph 15.

5.5.3 Structure and Content Requirements

IAS No. 1 also specifies structure and content of financial statements. These requirements include the following:

- *Classified Statement of Financial Position (Balance Sheet)*: IAS No. 1 requires the balance sheet to distinguish between current and non-current assets, and between current and non-current liabilities unless a presentation based on liquidity provides more relevant and reliable information (e.g., in the case of a bank or similar financial institution).

- *Minimum Information on the Face of the Financial Statements*: IAS No. 1 specifies the minimum line item disclosures on the face of, or in the notes to, the financial statements. For example, companies are specifically required to disclose the amount of their plant, property, and equipment as a line item on the face of the balance sheet. The specific requirements are listed in Exhibit 4.

- *Minimum Information in the Notes* (or on the face of financial statements): IAS No. 1 specifies disclosures about information to be presented in the financial statements. This information must be provided in a systematic manner and cross-referenced from the face of the financial statements to the notes. The required information is summarized in Exhibit 5.

- *Comparative Information*: For all amounts reported in a financial statement, comparative information should be provided for the previous period unless another standard requires or permits otherwise. Such comparative information allows users to better understand reported amounts.

Exhibit 4	IAS No. 1: Minimum Required Line Items in Financial Statements
On the face of the Statement of Financial Position	■ Plant, property, and equipment ■ Investment property ■ Intangible assets ■ Financial assets (those not included in other specified line items) ■ Investments accounted for using the equity method ■ Biological assets ■ Inventories ■ Trade and other receivables ■ Cash and cash equivalents ■ Total assets in groups held for sale ■ Trade and other payables ■ Provisions ■ Financial liabilities (not listed in other line items) ■ Liabilities and assets for current tax ■ Deferred tax liabilities and deferred tax assets ■ Total liabilities in groups held for sale ■ Non-controlling interest (i.e., minority interest, presented within equity) ■ Issued capital and reserves attributable to owners of the parent

(continued)

Exhibit 4	(Continued)

On the face of the Statement of Comprehensive Income, presented either in a single statement or in two statements (Income statement + Statement of comprehensive income)	▪ Revenue ▪ Specified gains and losses for financial assets ▪ Finance costs ▪ Share of the profit or loss of associates and joint ventures accounted for using the equity method ▪ Pretax gain or loss recognized on the disposal of assets or settlement of liabilities attributable to discontinued operations ▪ Tax expense ▪ Profit or loss ▪ Each component of other comprehensive income ▪ Amount of profit or loss and amount of comprehensive income attributable to non-controlling interest (minority interest) ▪ Amount of profit or loss and amount of comprehensive income attributable to the parent
On the face of the Statement of Changes in Equity	▪ Total comprehensive income for the period, showing separately the total amounts attributable to owners of the parent and to non-controlling interest (minority interest) ▪ For each component of equity, a reconciliation between beginning balances and ending balances, showing separately amounts arising from a) profit or loss, b) each item of other comprehensive income, and c) transactions with owners in their capacity as owners. ▪ For each component of equity, the effects of changes in accounting policies and corrections of errors recognized in accordance with IAS No. 8

Exhibit 5	Summary of IFRS Required Disclosures in the Notes to the Financial Statements

Disclosure of Accounting Policies	▪ Measurement bases used in preparing financial statements ▪ Significant accounting policies used ▪ Judgments made in applying accounting policies that have the most significant effect on the amounts recognized in the financial statements
Sources of Estimation Uncertainty	▪ Key assumptions about the future and other key sources of estimation uncertainty that have a significant risk of causing material adjustment to the carrying amount of assets and liabilities within the next year
Other Disclosures	▪ Information about capital and about certain financial instruments classified as equity ▪ Dividends not recognized as a distribution during the period, including dividends declared before the financial statements were issued and any cumulative preference dividends ▪ Description of the entity, including its domicile, legal form, country of incorporation, and registered office or business address ▪ Nature of operations and principal activities ▪ Name of parent and ultimate parent

5.6 Convergence of Conceptual Framework

One of the joint IASB/FASB projects, begun in 2004, aims to develop an improved, common conceptual framework. The project will be conducted in phases. The Boards' initial, technical work plan included: Objective of and qualitative characteristics of financial reporting; Reporting entity; Elements; and Measurement and recognition of elements. As of the writing of this reading, the objective and qualitative characteristics phase was complete and is incorporated in the reading.

As more countries adopt IFRS, the need to consider other financial reporting systems will be reduced. Additionally, the IASB and FASB are considering frameworks from other jurisdictions in developing their joint framework. Nevertheless, analysts are likely to encounter financial statements that are prepared on a basis other than IFRS. Although the number and relevance of different local GAAP reporting systems are likely to decline, industry-specific financial reports—such as those required for banking or insurance companies—will continue to exist. Differences remain between IFRS and U.S. GAAP that affect the framework and general financial reporting requirements. The readings on individual financial statements and specific topics will review in more detail differences in IFRS and U.S. GAAP as they apply to specific financial statements and topics.

As mentioned earlier, a joint IASB–FASB project was begun in October 2004 to develop a common conceptual framework. The initial focus was to achieve the convergence of the frameworks and improve particular aspects of the framework dealing with objectives, qualitative characteristics, elements and their recognition, and measurement. A December 2004 discussion paper presented the broad differences between the two frameworks. The differences between IFRS and U.S. GAAP that affect the framework and general financial reporting requirements have been reduced by the agreement by the IASB and FASB on the purpose and scope of the *Conceptual Framework* (*2010*), the objective of general purpose financial reporting, and qualitative characteristics of useful financial information. Exhibit 6 summarizes the remaining differences as presented in the December 2004 discussion paper. Some of the differences identified in December 2004 may no longer apply. The readings on individual financial statements and specific topics will discuss relevant and more current differences in greater detail.

Exhibit 6	Summary of Differences between IFRS and U.S. GAAP Frameworks

	U.S. GAAP (FASB) Framework
Financial Statement Elements (definition, recognition, and measurement)	■ *Performance Elements*: The FASB framework includes three elements relating to financial performance in addition to revenue and expenses: gains, losses, and comprehensive income. Comprehensive income is a more encompassing concept than net income, as it includes all changes in equity during a period except those resulting from investments by and distributions to owners.
	■ *Financial Position Elements*: The FASB framework defines an asset as "a future economic benefit" rather than the "resource" from which future economic benefits are expected to flow to the entity as in the IASB framework. It also includes the term "probable" to define the assets and liabilities elements. As discussed below, the term "probable" is part of the IASB framework recognition criteria. Additionally, the frameworks have different meanings of probable.
	■ *Recognition of Elements*: The FASB framework does not discuss the term "probable" in its recognition criteria, whereas the IASB framework requires that it is probable that any future economic benefit flow to/from the entity. The FASB framework also has a separate recognition criterion of relevance.
	■ *Measurement of Elements*: Measurement attributes (historical cost, current cost, settlement value, current market value, and present value) are broadly consistent, and both frameworks lack fully developed measurement concepts. Furthermore, the FASB framework prohibits revaluations except for certain categories of financial instruments, which have to be carried at fair value.

For analysis of financial statements created under different frameworks, reconciliation schedules and disclosures regarding the significant differences between the reporting bases were formerly available to a greater extent. For example, the SEC used to require reconciliation for foreign private issuers that did not prepare financial statements in accordance with U.S. GAAP. The SEC no longer requires reconciliation for foreign private issuers that prepare their financial reports in compliance with IFRS. Such reconciliations can reveal additional information related to the more judgmental components of the financial statements. In the absence of a reconciliation, users of financial statements must be prepared to consider how the use of different reporting standards potentially impact financial reports. This can have important implications for comparing the performance of companies and security valuation.

EFFECTIVE FINANCIAL REPORTING

A discussion of the characteristics of an effective framework and the barriers to the creation of such a framework offer additional perspective on financial reporting.

6.1 Characteristics of an Effective Financial Reporting Framework

Any effective financial reporting system needs to be a coherent one (i.e., a framework in which all the pieces fit together according to an underlying logic). Such frameworks have several characteristics:

- *Transparency*: A framework should enhance the transparency of a company's financial statements. Transparency means that users should be able to see the underlying economics of the business reflected clearly in the company's financial statements. Full disclosure and fair presentation create transparency.

- *Comprehensiveness*: To be comprehensive, a framework should encompass the full spectrum of transactions that have financial consequences. This spectrum includes not only transactions currently occurring, but also new types of transactions as they are developed. So an effective financial reporting framework is based on principles that are universal enough to provide guidance for recording both existing and newly developed transactions.

- *Consistency*: An effective framework should ensure reasonable consistency across companies and time periods. In other words, similar transactions should be measured and presented in a similar manner regardless of industry, company size, geography, or other characteristics. Balanced against this need for consistency, however, is the need for sufficient flexibility to allow companies sufficient discretion to report results in accordance with underlying economic activity.

6.2 Barriers to a Single Coherent Framework

Although effective frameworks all share the characteristics of transparency, comprehensiveness, and consistency, there are some conflicts that create inherent limitations in any financial reporting standards framework. Specifically, it is difficult to completely satisfy all these characteristics concurrently, so any framework represents an attempt to balance the relative importance of these characteristics. Three areas of conflict include valuation, standard-setting approach, and measurement.

- *Valuation*: As discussed, various bases for measuring the value of assets and liabilities exist, such as historical cost, current cost, fair value, realizable value, and present value. Historical cost valuation, under which an asset's value is its initial cost, requires minimal judgment. In contrast, other valuation approaches, such as fair value, require considerable judgment but can provide more relevant information.

- *Standard-Setting Approach*: Financial reporting standards can be established based on 1) principles, 2) rules, or 3) a combination of principles and rules (sometimes referred to as "objectives oriented"). A principles-based approach provides a broad financial reporting framework with little specific guidance on how to report a particular element or transaction. Such principles-based approaches require the preparers of financial reports and auditors to exercise considerable judgment in financial reporting. In contrast, a rules-based approach establishes specific rules for each element or transaction. Rules-based approaches are characterized by a list of yes-or-no rules, specific numerical tests for classifying certain transactions (known as "bright line tests"), exceptions, and alternative treatments. Some suggest that rules are created in response to preparers' needs for specific guidance in implementing principles, so even standards that begin purely as principles evolve into a combination of principles and rules. The third alternative, an objectives-oriented approach, combines the other two approaches by including both a framework of principles and appropriate levels of implementation guidance. The common conceptual framework is likely to be more objectives oriented.

- *Measurement*: The balance sheet presents elements at a point in time, whereas the income statement reflects changes during a period of time. Because these statements are related, standards regarding one of the statements have an effect on the other statement. Financial reporting standards can be established taking an "asset/liability" approach, which gives preference to proper valuation of the balance sheet, or a "revenue/expense" approach that focuses more on the income statement. This conflict can result in one statement being reported in a theoretically sound manner, but the other statement reflecting less relevant information. In recent years, standard setters have predominantly used an asset/liability approach.

EXAMPLE 5

Conflicts between Measurement Approaches

Prime Retailers (PR), a U.S.-based distributor of men's shirts, has a policy of marking its merchandise up by $5 per unit. At the beginning of 2009, PR had 10,000 units of inventory on hand, which cost $15 per unit. During 2009, PR purchased 100,000 units of inventory at a cost of $22 per unit. Also during 2009, PR sold 100,000 units of inventory at $27 per unit. How shall PR reflect the cost of the inventory sold: $15 or $22 or some combination?

In order to match current costs with current revenues, PR (which does not operate in an IFRS jurisdiction; last-in, first-out is not allowed under IFRS) may decide that it is appropriate to use a method of inventory costing that assumes that the most recently purchased inventory is sold first. So, the assumption is that the 100,000 units of sales had a cost of $22. A partial income statement for PR would be:

Sales	$2,700,000
Cost of sales	$2,200,000
Gross profit	$500,000

The gross profit calculated in this manner reflects the current cost of goods matched with the current level of revenues.

But PR still has 10,000 units of inventory on hand. The assumption must be that the 10,000 remaining units had a cost of $15 per unit. Therefore, the value of the inventory reflected on the balance sheet would be $150,000.

Although the income statement reflects current costs, the remaining inventory on the balance sheet does not reflect current information. The inventory is reflected at the older cost of $15 per unit. An analyst would likely find this older cost less relevant than the current cost of that inventory.

COMPARISON OF IFRS WITH ALTERNATIVE REPORTING SYSTEMS

7

The recent adoption of IFRS as the required financial reporting standard by the EU and other countries has advanced the goal of global convergence. Nevertheless, there are still significant differences in financial reporting in the global capital markets. Arguably, the most critical are the differences that exist between IFRS and U.S. GAAP. After the EU adoption of IFRS in 2005, a significant number of the world's listed companies use one of these two reporting standards.

For analyzing financial statements created under different standards, reconciliation schedules and disclosures regarding the significant differences between the reporting bases—historically available in some jurisdictions—were particularly helpful. For example, the SEC historically required reconciliation for foreign private issuers that did not prepare financial statements in accordance with U.S. GAAP. In 2007, however, the SEC eliminated the reconciliation requirement for companies that prepared their financial statements according to IFRS.[33]

Although the disclosures related to any such differences were sometimes dauntingly long, the numerical reconciliations of net income and shareholders' equity appeared in charts that were relatively easy to use. As an example, consider the reconciliation disclosures made by Syngenta AG, a Swiss agribusiness company in 2006, the last year in which reconciliations were required. Syngenta's 2006 U.S. SEC Form 20-F filing discussed these differences in Note 34, "Significant Differences between IFRS and United States Generally Accepted Accounting Principles." This note was roughly 20 pages long! The chart presenting the numerical reconciliation of net income (see Exhibit 7) was, however, relatively easy to use and could be reviewed to identify the significant items; large amounts could be examined in more detail. The Syngenta disclosure indicates that the company's 2006 net income based on U.S. GAAP was $504 million, compared with the $634 million of net income reported under IFRS. The reconciliation indicates that most significant differences relate to accounting for acquisitions (purchase accounting adjustments include a $30 million increase and an $86 million decrease), accounting for pension provisions ($48 million), accounting for put options ($60 million) and accounting for various tax-related items. In some instances, further analysis would be undertaken to determine the implications of each significant difference based on additional disclosures in the notes.

Exhibit 7	Reconciliation of GAAP Income: Syngenta (US$ in Millions)		
	2006	**2005**	**2004**
Net income/(loss) reported under IFRS attributable to Syngenta AG shareholders	634	622	460
U.S. GAAP adjustments:			
Purchase accounting: Zeneca agrochemicals business	30	(7)	62
Purchase accounting: other acquisitions	(86)	(80)	(62)
Restructuring charges	(9)	(9)	47
Pension provisions (including post-retirement benefits)	(48)	15	43
Deferred taxes on share based compensation	—	3	(3)

(continued)

---

33 The SEC issued Rule 33-8879 (available at www.sec.gov/rules/final/2007/33-8879.pdf) on 21 December 2007. The Rule eliminated the reconciliation requirement for companies reporting under IFRS as issued by the IASB and applied to financial years ending after 15 November 2007.

Exhibit 7	(Continued)		
	2006	**2005**	**2004**
Deferred taxes on unrealized profit in inventory	26	(33)	(61)
Impairment losses	2	(7)	(1)
Inventory provisions	(13)	—	—
Revenue recognition	(1)	—	—
Environmental remediation costs	(27)	—	—
Other items	9	28	(17)
Grant of put option to Syngenta AG shareholders	(60)	—	—
Valuation allowance against deferred tax assets	—	26	(34)
Income tax on undistributed earnings of subsidiaries	1	1	(27)
Deferred tax effect of U.S. GAAP adjustments	46	27	(55)
Net income/(loss) reported under U.S. GAAP	504	556	352

Source: 2005 U.S. SEC Form 20-F.

Now that reconciliation disclosures are no longer generally available, an analyst comparing two companies that use different reporting standards must be aware of areas where accounting standards have not converged. For example, data from 2006 SEC reconciliations (the last year available) indicated that pensions and goodwill were the dominant IFRS-to-U.S. GAAP reconciliation items for European companies that listed their stock on an exchange in the United States.[34] In most cases, a user of financial statements prepared under different accounting standards will no longer have enough information to make specific adjustments required to achieve comparability. Instead, an analyst must maintain general caution in interpreting comparative financial measures produced under different accounting standards and monitor significant developments in financial reporting standards.

8

MONITORING DEVELOPMENTS IN FINANCIAL REPORTING STANDARDS

In studying financial reporting and financial statement analysis in general, the analyst must be aware that reporting standards are evolving rapidly. Analysts need to monitor ongoing developments in financial reporting and assess their implications for security analysis and valuation. The need to monitor developments in financial reporting standards does not mean that analysts should be accountants. An accountant monitors these developments from a preparer's perspective; an analyst needs to monitor from a user's perspective. More specifically, analysts need to know how these developments will affect financial reports.

Analysts can remain aware of developments in financial reporting standards by monitoring three areas: new products or transactions, actions of standard setters and other groups representing users of financial statements (such as CFA Institute), and company disclosures regarding critical accounting policies and estimates.

---

34 Henry, Lin, and Yang (2009) "The European-U.S. 'GAAP Gap': IFRS to U.S. GAAP Form 20-F Reconciliations" *Accounting Horizons* 23(2): 121–150.

8.1 New Products or Types of Transactions

New products and new types of transactions can have unusual or unique elements to them such that no explicit guidance in the financial reporting standards exists. New products or transactions typically arise from economic events, such as new businesses (e.g., the internet), or from a newly developed financial instrument or financial structure. Financial instruments, whether exchange traded or not, are typically designed to enhance a company's business or to mitigate inherent risks. However, at times, financial instruments or structured transactions have been developed primarily for purposes of financial report "window dressing."

Although companies might discuss new products and transactions in their financial reports, the analyst can also monitor business journals and the capital markets to identify such items. Additionally, when one company in an industry develops a new product or transaction, other companies in the industry often do the same. Once new products, financial instruments, or structured transactions are identified, it is helpful to gain an understanding of the business purpose. If necessary, an analyst can obtain further information from a company's management, which should be able to describe the economic purpose, the financial statement reporting, significant estimates, judgments applied in determining the reporting, and future cash flow implications for these items. The financial reporting framework described here is useful in evaluating the potential effect on financial statements even though a standard may not have been issued as to how to report a particular transaction.

8.2 Evolving Standards and the Role of CFA Institute

The actions of standard setters and regulators are unlikely to be helpful in identifying new products and transactions, given the lag between new product development and regulatory action. Monitoring the actions of these authorities is nonetheless important for another reason: Changes in regulations can affect companies' financial reports and, thus, valuations. This is particularly true if the financial reporting standards change to require more explicit identification of matters affecting asset/liability valuation or financial performance. For example, one relatively recent regulatory change requires companies to report the value of employee stock options as an expense in the income statement. Prior to the required expensing, an analyst could assess the impact of stock options on a company's performance and the dilutive effect to shareholders by reviewing information disclosed in the notes to the financial statements. As another example, the current standard-setting project on leases will likely result in explicitly recognizing on the balance sheet the assets and liabilities associated with certain types of leases; currently, that lease information is available only in the notes. To the extent that some market participants do not examine financial statement details and thus ignore some items when valuing a company's securities, more explicit identification could affect the value of the company's securities. Additionally, it is plausible to believe that management is more attentive to and rigorous in any calculations/estimates of items that appear in the financial statements, compared to items that are only disclosed in the notes.

The IASB and FASB have numerous major projects underway that will most likely result in new standards. It is important to keep up to date on these evolving standards. The IASB (www.iasb.org) and FASB (www.fasb.org) provide a great deal of information on their websites regarding new standards and proposals for future changes in standards. In addition, the IASB and FASB seek input from the financial analyst community—those who regularly use financial statements in making investment and credit decisions. When a new standard is proposed, an exposure draft is made available and users of financial statements can draft comment letters and position papers for submission to the IASB and FASB in order to evaluate the proposal.

CFA Institute is active in advocating improvements to financial reporting, through its Standards and Financial Market Integrity Division. Volunteer members of CFA Institute serve on several liaison committees that meet regularly to make recommendations to the IASB and FASB on proposed standards and to draft comment letters and position papers. The comment letters and position papers of these groups on financial reporting issues are available at www.cfainstitute.org/ethics/topics/pages/index.aspx.

CFA Institute issued a position paper titled *A Comprehensive Business Reporting Model: Financial Reporting for Investors*, which provides a suggested model for significantly improving financial reporting. The position paper, issued in 2007, states:

> Corporate financial statements and their related disclosures are fundamental to sound investment decision making. The well-being of the world's financial markets, and of the millions of investors who entrust their financial present and future to those markets, depends directly on the information financial statements and disclosures provide. Consequently, the quality of the information drives global financial markets. The quality, in turn, depends directly on the principles and standards managers apply when recognizing and measuring the economic activities and events affecting their companies' operations....
>
> Investors require timeliness, transparency, comparability, and consistency in financial reporting. Investors have a preference for decision relevance over reliability. As CFA Institute stated in 1993 and as reiterated in this paper, "analysts need to know economic reality—what is really going on—to the greatest extent it can be depicted by accounting numbers." Corporate financial statements that fail to reflect this economic reality undermine the investment decision-making process.[35]

Among other principles, the proposed model stresses the importance of information regarding the current fair value of assets and liabilities, of neutrality in financial reporting, and of providing detailed information on cash flows to investors through the choice of the so-called direct format for the cash flow statement.[36]

In summary, analysts can improve their investment decision making by keeping current on financial reporting standards, and various web-based sources provide the means to do so. In addition, analysts can contribute to improving financial reporting by sharing their perspective as users with standard-setting bodies, which typically invite comments concerning proposed changes.

8.3 Company Disclosures

A good source for obtaining information regarding the effect of financial reporting standards on a company's financial statements is typically the company itself. This information is provided in the notes to the financial statements and accompanying discussion.

8.3.1 *Disclosures Relating to Critical and Significant Accounting Policies*

As noted earlier, financial reporting standards need to restrict alternatives but retain flexibility in allowing enterprises to match their accounting methods with underlying economics. As a result, companies choose among alternative accounting policies (e.g., depreciation methods) and use estimates (e.g., depreciable lives of assets). Under both IFRS and U.S. GAAP, companies are required to disclose their accounting policies

---

35 *A Comprehensive Business Reporting Model: Financial Reporting for Investors*, CFA Institute Centre for Financial Market Integrity, July 2007, p. 1, 2.
36 See the reading on cash flow statements for further information on the direct format.

and estimates in the notes to the financial statements. Companies also discuss in the management commentary (or the management's discussion and analysis, MD&A) those policies that management deems most important. Although many of the policies are discussed in both the management commentary and the notes to the financial statement, there is typically a distinction between the two discussions. The management commentary generally relates to aspects of the accounting policies deemed important by management to understand the financial statements, particularly changes. The MD&A disclosure relates to those policies that require significant judgments and estimates, whereas the note discusses all accounting policies, irrespective of whether judgment was required. Each disclosure has value.

In analyzing financial reporting disclosures, the following questions should be addressed:

- What policies have been discussed?
- Do these policies appear to cover all of the significant balances on the financial statements?
- Which policies are identified as requiring significant estimates?
- Have there been any changes in these disclosures from one year to the next?

Exhibit 8 summarizes the accounting policies discussed in the management report section of Volkswagen's annual report.

Exhibit 8	Accounting Policy Discussion in Volkswagen's Management Report

Volkswagen's management report includes the following discussion of accounting policies:

> The application of IFRS 8 led to a reclassification of the segments disclosed in the notes. The following segments are now reported: Passenger Cars and Light Commercial Vehicles, Scania, and Volkswagen Financial Services. The classification of the Group's activities into the Automotive and Financial Services divisions remains unchanged in the management report.
>
> In accordance with the amended IAS 7, as of fiscal year 2009 we are reporting liquidity movements resulting from changes in leasing and rental assets in cash flows from operating activities (previously reported in cash flows from investing activities). Accordingly, changes in financial services receivables are also allocated to cash flows from operating activities. The prior-year presentation has been adjusted accordingly.
>
> The adoption of new or amended accounting standards did not otherwise materially affect the 2009 consolidated financial statements.

Source: Volkswagen's 2009 Annual Report, page 144.

Exhibit 9 lists the items discussed in the note titled "Accounting Policies" in Volkswagen's notes to the financial statements. Note that far more items are described in the notes to the financial statements as compared to the management's commentary, illustrating the broader disclosure of the notes.

| Exhibit 9 | Accounting Policies Described in Volkswagen's Financial Statement Notes |

- Intangible assets
- Property, plant, and equipment
- Leasing and rental assets
- Investment property
- Capitalization of borrowing costs
- Equity-accounted investments
- Financial instruments
- Loans and receivables and financial liabilities
- Available-for-sale financial assets
- Derivatives and hedge accounting
- Receivables from finance leases
- Other receivables and financial assets
- Impairment losses on financial instruments
- Deferred taxes
- Inventories
- Non-current assets held for sale and discontinued operations
- Pension provisions
- Provisions for taxes
- Other provisions
- Liabilities
- Revenue and expense recognition

8.3.2 *Disclosures Regarding Changes in Accounting Policies*

Companies must disclose information about changes in accounting policies. Such changes can occur as a result of initially applying a new accounting standard or as a result of the company voluntarily changing which policy it uses (among those allowable). In addition, IFRS require discussion about pending implementations of new standards and the known or estimable information relevant to assessing the impact of the new standards.[37] These disclosures can alert an analyst to significant changes in reported financial statement amounts that could affect security valuation. Although each discussion will be different, the conclusions that a company can reach about a new standard not yet implemented include:

1 the standard does not apply;
2 the standard will have no material impact;
3 management is still evaluating the impact; or
4 the impact of adoption is discussed.

---

37 IAS No. 8, Accounting Policies, *Changes in Accounting Estimates and Errors.*

Clearly, disclosures indicating the expected impact provide the most meaningful information. In addition, disclosures indicating that the standard does not apply or will not have a material effect are also helpful. However, disclosures indicating that management is still evaluating the impact of a new standard create some uncertainty about whether the change might materially affect the company.

In addition to the disclosures referred to in Exhibits 8 and 9, Volkswagen also provided extensive disclosures about recently issued accounting standards in its 2009 Annual Report. The company confirmed it had adopted all accounting pronouncements required to be applied starting in fiscal year 2009, stated the impact of four new or revised standards, and listed nine other standards that had no material effect on the company's financial reports. In addition, Volkswagen provided a table summarizing standards that had been adopted by the IASB but were not required to be applied for fiscal year 2009. The table listed 17 specific standards changes, of which the company expected 14 to have no impact and the other three to result in non-quantified changes in disclosures or presentations.

In some cases, companies are able to quantify the expected impact of accounting standards that have been changed but are not yet effective at the time of the company's report. As an example of quantified disclosures about accounting changes that would have a future effect on a company's financial statements, consider the disclosures in Exhibit 10.

Exhibit 10	Impact of New and Amended Accounting Standards: General Electric

In its 2009 annual report filed with the SEC in February 2010, General Electric (which reports under U.S. GAAP) included disclosures in its MD&A about an accounting change that would require consolidation of certain entities that previously had not been consolidated. The acronym ASU stands for "Accounting Standards Update" and is the means by which the FASB communicates changes to U.S. GAAP following the Financial Standards Codification in 2009. The acronym ASC stands for "Accounting Standards Codification" and refers to a particular section of the Codification.

> In 2009, the FASB issued ASU 2009–16 and ASU 2009–17, which amended ASC 860, *Transfers and Servicing*, and ASC 810, *Consolidation*, respectively, and are effective for us on January 1, 2010…
>
> Upon adoption of the amendments on January 1, 2010, we will consolidate the assets and liabilities of these entities at the amount they would have been reported in our financial statements had we always consolidated them. We will also deconsolidate certain entities where we do not meet the definition of the primary beneficiary under the revised guidance, the effect of which will be insignificant. The incremental effect of consolidation on total assets and liabilities, net of our investment in these entities, will be an increase of approximately $32 billion and $34 billion, respectively. There also will be a net reduction of equity of approximately $2 billion, principally related to the reversal of previously recognized securitization gains as a cumulative effect adjustment to retained earnings, which will be earned back over the life of the assets.

Source: General Electric 2009 Annual Report.

An analyst could use these disclosures to adjust expectations about the company's assets, liabilities, and equity, and confirm the impact (which in this case appear to be minimal) on the company's leverage ratios. Importantly, because these disclosures relate to expected changes, the analyst could incorporate these disclosures into forecasts of financial statements.

SUMMARY

An awareness of the reporting framework underlying financial reports can assist in security valuation and other financial analysis. The framework describes the objectives of financial reporting, desirable characteristics for financial reports, the elements of financial reports, and the underlying assumptions and constraints of financial reporting. An understanding of the framework, which is broader than knowledge of a particular set of rules, offers an analyst a basis from which to infer the proper financial reporting, and thus security valuation implications, of *any* financial statement element or transaction. The reading discusses the conceptual objectives of financial reporting standards, the parties involved in standard-setting processes, and how financial reporting standards are converging into one global set of standards.

Some key points of the reading are summarized below:

- *The Objective of Financial Reporting*:
  - The objective of general purpose financial reporting is to provide financial information about the reporting entity that is useful to existing and potential investors, lenders, and other creditors in making decisions about providing resources to the entity. Those decisions involve buying, selling, or holding equity and debt instruments, and providing or settling loans and other forms of credit.[38]
  - Financial reporting requires policy choices and estimates. These choices and estimates require judgment, which can vary from one preparer to the next. Accordingly, standards are needed to ensure increased consistency in these judgments.

- *Financial Reporting Standard-Setting Bodies and Regulatory Authorities*: Private sector standard setting bodies and regulatory authorities play significant but different roles in the standard setting process. In general, standard setting bodies make the rules, and regulatory authorities enforce the rules. However, regulators typically retain legal authority to establish financial reporting standards in their jurisdiction.

- *Convergence of Global Financial Reporting Standards*: The IASB and FASB, along with other standard setters, are working to achieve convergence of financial reporting standards. Many countries have adopted or permit the use of IFRS, have indicated that they will adopt IFRS in the future, or have indicated that they are working on convergence with IFRS. Listed companies in many countries are adopting IFRS. Barriers and challenges to full convergence still exist.

---

[38] *Conceptual Framework for Financial Reporting (2010)*, International Accounting Standards Board, 2010, Chapter 1, OB2.

- *The IFRS Framework*: The IFRS *Framework* sets forth the concepts that underlie the preparation and presentation of financial statements for external users, provides further guidance on the elements from which financial statements are constructed, and discusses concepts of capital and capital maintenance.

  - The objective of fair presentation of useful information is the center of the *Conceptual Framework (2010)*. The qualitative characteristics of useful information include fundamental and enhancing characteristics. Information must exhibit the fundamental characteristics of relevance and faithful representation to be useful. The enhancing characteristics identified are comparability, verifiability, timeliness, and understandability.

  - The IFRS *Framework* identifies the following elements of financial statements: assets, liabilities, equity, income, expenses, and capital maintenance adjustments.

  - The *Conceptual Framework (2010)* is constructed based on the underlying assumptions of accrual basis and going concern and acknowledges the inherent constraint of benefit versus cost.

- *IFRS Financial Statements*: IAS No. 1 prescribes that a complete set of financial statements includes a statement of financial position (balance sheet), a statement of comprehensive income (either two statements—one for net income and one for comprehensive income—or a single statement combining both net income and comprehensive income), a statement of changes in equity, a cash flow statement, and notes. The notes include a summary of significant accounting policies and other explanatory information.

  - Financial statements need to reflect certain basic features: fair presentation, going concern, accrual basis, materiality and aggregation, no offsetting, and consistency.

  - Financial statements must be prepared at least annually and must include comparative information from the previous period.

  - Financial statements must follow certain presentation requirements including a classified balance sheet, minimum information on the face of the financial statements and in the notes.

- *Characteristics of a Coherent Financial Reporting Framework*: Effective frameworks share three characteristics: transparency, comprehensiveness, and consistency. Effective standards can, however, differ on appropriate valuation bases, the basis for standard setting (principle or rules based), and resolution of conflicts between balance sheet and income statement focus.

- *Comparison of IFRS with Alternative Reporting Systems*: A significant number of the world's listed companies report under either IFRS or U.S. GAAP.

  - Although these standards are moving toward convergence, there are still significant differences in the framework and individual standards.

  - In most cases, a user of financial statements will lack the information necessary to make specific adjustments required to achieve comparability between companies that use IFRS and companies that use U.S. GAAP. Instead, an analyst must maintain general caution in interpreting comparative financial measures produced under different accounting standards and monitor significant developments in financial reporting standards.

- *Monitoring Developments*: Analysts can remain aware of ongoing developments in financial reporting by monitoring three areas: new products or types of transactions; actions of standard setters, regulators, and other groups; and company disclosures regarding critical accounting policies and estimates.

PRACTICE PROBLEMS

1 Which of the following is *most likely* not an objective of financial statements?

   A To provide information about the performance of an entity.

   B To provide information about the financial position of an entity.

   C To provide information about the users of an entity's financial statements.

2 International financial reporting standards are currently developed by which entity?

   A The IFRS Foundation.

   B The International Accounting Standards Board.

   C The International Organization of Securities Commissions.

3 U.S. generally accepted accounting principles are currently developed by which entity?

   A The Securities and Exchange Commission.

   B The Financial Accounting Standards Board.

   C The Public Company Accounting Oversight Board.

4 Which of the following statements about desirable attributes of accounting standards boards is *most* accurate? Accounting standards boards should:

   A concede to political pressures.

   B be guided by a well articulated framework.

   C be adequately funded by companies to which the standards apply.

5 A core objective of the International Organization of Securities Commissions is to:

   A eliminate systematic risk.

   B protect users of financial statements.

   C ensure that markets are fair, efficient, and transparent.

6 According to the *Conceptual Framework for Financial Reporting (2010)*, which of the following is *not* an enhancing qualitative characteristic of information in financial statements?

   A Accuracy.

   B Timeliness.

   C Comparability.

7 Which of the following is *not* a constraint on the financial statements according to the *Conceptual Framework (2010)*?

   A Understandability.

   B Benefit versus cost.

   C Balancing of qualitative characteristics.

8 The assumption that an entity will continue to operate for the foreseeable future is called:

   A accrual basis.

   B comparability.

   C going concern.

9 The assumption that the effects of transactions and other events are recognized when they occur, not when the cash flows occur, is called:

A relevance.

B accrual basis.

C going concern.

10 Neutrality of information in the financial statements most closely contributes to which qualitative characteristic?

A Relevance.

B Understandability.

C Faithful representation.

11 Valuing assets at the amount of cash or equivalents paid or the fair value of the consideration given to acquire them at the time of acquisition most closely describes which measurement of financial statement elements?

A Current cost.

B Historical cost.

C Realizable value.

12 The valuation technique under which assets are recorded at the amount that would be received in an orderly disposal is:

A current cost.

B present value.

C realizable value.

13 Which of the following is *not* a required financial statement according to IAS No. 1?

A Statement of financial position.

B Statement of changes in income.

C Statement of comprehensive income.

14 Which of the following elements of financial statements is *most* closely related to measurement of performance?

A Assets.

B Expenses.

C Liabilities.

15 Which of the following elements of financial statements is *most* closely related to measurement of financial position?

A Equity.

B Income.

C Expenses.

16 Which of the following is *not* a characteristic of a coherent financial reporting framework?

A Timeliness.

B Consistency.

C Transparency.

17 Which of the following is *not* a recognized approach to standard-setting?

A A rules-based approach.

B An asset/liability approach.

C A principles-based approach.

18 Which of the following disclosures regarding new accounting standards provides the *most* meaningful information to an analyst?

   A The impact of adoption is discussed.

   B The standard will have no material impact.

   C Management is still evaluating the impact.

SOLUTIONS

1 C is correct. Financial statements provide information, including information about the entity's financial position, performance, and changes in financial position, to users. They do not typically provide information about users.

2 B is correct. The IASB is currently charged with developing International Financial Reporting Standards.

3 B is correct. The FASB is responsible for the Accounting Standards Codification™, the single source of nongovernmental authoritative U.S. generally accepted accounting principles.

4 B is correct. Accounting standards boards should be guided by a well articulated framework. They should be independent; and while they consider input from stakeholders, the process should not be compromised by pressure from external forces, including political pressure. Accounting standards boards should have adequate resources.

5 C is correct. A core objective of IOSCO is to ensure that markets are fair, efficient, and transparent. The other core objectives are to reduce, not eliminate, systematic risk and to protect investors, not all users of financial statements.

6 A is correct. Accuracy is not an enhancing qualitative characteristic. Faithful representation, not accuracy, is a fundamental qualitative characteristic.

7 A is correct. Understandability is an enhancing qualitative characteristic of financial information—not a constraint.

8 C is correct. The *Conceptual Framework* (*2010*) identifies two important underlying assumptions of financial statements: accrual basis and going concern. Going concern is the assumption that the entity will continue to operate for the foreseeable future. Enterprises with the intent to liquidate or materially curtail operations would require different information for a fair presentation.

9 B is correct. Accrual basis reflects the effects of transactions and other events being recognized when they occur, not when the cash flows. These effects are recorded and reported in the financial statements of the periods to which they relate.

10 C is correct. The fundamental qualitative characteristic of faithful representation is contributed to by completeness, neutrality, and freedom from error.

11 B is correct. Historical cost is the consideration paid to acquire an asset.

12 C is correct. The amount that would be received in an orderly disposal is realizable value.

13 B is correct. There is no statement of changes in income. Under IAS No. 1, a complete set of financial statements includes a statement of financial position, a statement of comprehensive income, a statement of changes in equity, a statement of cash flows, and notes comprising a summary of significant accounting policies and other explanatory information.

14 B is correct. The elements of financial statements related to the measure of performance are income and expenses.

15 A is correct. The elements of financial statements related to the measurement of financial position are assets, liabilities, and equity.

16 A is correct. Timeliness is not a characteristic of a coherent financial reporting framework. Consistency, transparency, and comprehensiveness are characteristics of a coherent financial reporting framework.

17 B is correct. Rules-based, principles-based, and objectives-oriented approaches are recognized approaches to standard-setting.

18 A is correct. A discussion of the impact would be the most meaningful, although B would also be useful.

Financial Reporting and Analysis

Income Statements, Balance Sheets, and Cash Flow Statements

The first three readings in this study session focus on the three major financial statements: the income statement, the balance sheet, and the cash flow statement. For each financial statement, the reading describes its purpose, construction, pertinent ratios, and common-size analysis. These readings provide a background for evaluating trends in a company's performance over several measurement periods and for comparing the performance of different companies over a given period. The final reading covers in greater depth financial analysis techniques based on the financial reports.

READING ASSIGNMENTS

Reading 25	Understanding Income Statements by Elaine Henry, CFA, and Thomas R. Robinson, CFA
Reading 26	Understanding Balance Sheets by Elaine Henry, CFA, and Thomas R. Robinson, CFA
Reading 27	Understanding Cash Flow Statements by Elaine Henry, CFA, Thomas R. Robinson, CFA, Jan Hendrik van Greuning, CFA, and Michael A. Broihahn, CFA
Reading 28	Financial Analysis Techniques by Elaine Henry, CFA, Thomas R. Robinson, CFA, and Jan Hendrik van Greuning, CFA

Note: New rulings and/or pronouncements issued after the publication of the readings in financial reporting and analysis may cause some of the information in these readings to become dated. Candidates are expected to be familiar with the overall analytical framework contained in the study session readings, as well as the implications of alternative accounting methods for financial analysis and valuation, as provided in the assigned readings. Candidates are not responsible for changes that occur after the material was written.

Understanding Income Statements

by Elaine Henry, CFA, and Thomas R. Robinson, CFA

LEARNING OUTCOMES

Mastery	The candidate should be able to:
☐	**a.** describe the components of the income statement and alternative presentation formats of that statement;
☐	**b.** describe general principles of revenue recognition and accrual accounting, specific revenue recognition applications (including accounting for long-term contracts, installment sales, barter transactions, gross and net reporting of revenue), and implications of revenue recognition principles for financial analysis;
☐	**c.** calculate revenue given information that might influence the choice of revenue recognition method;
☐	**d.** describe general principles of expense recognition, specific expense recognition applications, and implications of expense recognition choices for financial analysis;
☐	**e.** describe the financial reporting treatment and analysis of non-recurring items (including discontinued operations, extraordinary items, unusual or infrequent items) and changes in accounting standards;
☐	**f.** distinguish between the operating and non-operating components of the income statement;
☐	**g.** describe how earnings per share is calculated and calculate and interpret a company's earnings per share (both basic and diluted earnings per share) for both simple and complex capital structures;
☐	**h.** distinguish between dilutive and antidilutive securities, and describe the implications of each for the earnings per share calculation;
☐	**i.** convert income statements to common-size income statements;
☐	**j.** evaluate a company's financial performance using common-size income statements and financial ratios based on the income statement;

(continued)

Note: New rulings and/or pronouncements issues after the publication of the readings in financial reporting and analysis may cause some of the information in these readings to become dated. Candidates are expected to be familiar with the overall analytical framework contained in the study session readings, as well as the implications of alternative accounting methods for financial analysis and valuation, as provided in the assigned readings. Candidates are not responsible for changes that occur after the material was written.

LEARNING OUTCOMES	
Mastery	*The candidate should be able to:*
☐	**k.** describe, calculate, and interpret comprehensive income;
☐	**l.** describe other comprehensive income, and identify major types of items included in it.

1 INTRODUCTION

The income statement presents information on the financial results of a company's business activities over a period of time. The income statement communicates how much revenue the company generated during a period and what costs it incurred in connection with generating that revenue. The basic equation underlying the income statement, ignoring gains and losses, is Revenue minus Expenses equals Net income. The income statement is also sometimes referred to as the "statement of operations," "statement of earnings," or "profit and loss (P&L) statement." Under International Financial Reporting Standards (IFRS), the income statement may be presented as a separate statement followed by a statement of comprehensive income that begins with the profit or loss from the income statement or as a section of a single statement of comprehensive income.[1] Under U.S. generally accepted accounting principles (U.S. GAAP), the income statement may be presented as a separate statement or as a section of a single statement of income and comprehensive income.[2] This reading focuses on the income statement, but also discusses comprehensive income (profit or loss from the income statement plus other comprehensive income).

Investment analysts intensely scrutinize companies' income statements.[3] Equity analysts are interested in them because equity markets often reward relatively high- or low-earnings growth companies with above-average or below-average valuations, respectively, and because inputs into valuation models often include estimates of earnings. Fixed-income analysts examine the components of income statements, past and projected, for information on companies' abilities to make promised payments on their debt over the course of the business cycle. Corporate financial announcements frequently emphasize information reported in income statements, particularly earnings, more than information reported in the other financial statements.

This reading is organized as follows: Section 2 describes the components of the income statement and its format. Section 3 describes basic principles and selected applications related to the recognition of revenue, and Section 4 describes basic principles and selected applications related to the recognition of expenses. Section 5 covers non-recurring items and non-operating items. Section 6 explains the calculation

---

1 The International Accounting Standards Board (IASB) issues International Financial Reporting Standards (IFRS), which have been adopted as the accounting standards in many countries in the world. International Accounting Standard (IAS) 1, *Presentation of Financial Statements*, establishes the presentation and minimum content requirements of financial statements and guidelines for the structure of financial statements.
2 The single authoritative source of U.S. GAAP is the Financial Accounting Standards Board (FASB) Accounting Standards Codification™ (FASB ASC). FASB ASC Section 220-10-45 [Comprehensive Income–Overall–Other Presentation Matters] discusses acceptable formats in which to present income, other comprehensive income, and comprehensive income.
3 In this reading, the term *income statement* will be used to describe either the separate statement that reports profit or loss used for earnings per share calculations or that section of a statement of comprehensive income that reports the same profit or loss.

of earnings per share. Section 7 introduces income statement analysis, and Section 8 explains comprehensive income and its reporting. A summary of the key points and practice problems in the CFA Institute multiple choice format complete the reading.

COMPONENTS AND FORMAT OF THE INCOME STATEMENT

2

On the top line of the income statement, companies typically report revenue. **Revenue** generally refers to amounts charged (and expected to be received) for the delivery of goods or services in the *ordinary activities* of a business. The term **net revenue** means that the revenue number is reported after adjustments (e.g., for cash or volume discounts, or for estimated returns). Revenue may be called sales or turnover.[4] Exhibits 1 and 2 show the income statements for Groupe Danone (Euronext Paris: BN), a French food manufacturer, and Kraft Foods (NYSE:KFT), a U.S. food manufacturer.[5] For the year ended 31 December 2009, Danone reports €14.98 billion of net revenue, whereas Kraft reports $40.39 billion of net revenue.

Exhibit 1	Groupe Danone Consolidated Income Statement (in Millions of Euros)	
	Year Ended 31 December	
	2008	**2009**
Net revenue	15,220	14,982
Cost of goods sold	(7,172)	(6,749)
Selling expenses	(4,197)	(4,212)
General and administrative expenses	(1,297)	(1,356)
Research and development expenses	(198)	(206)
Other revenue (expense)	(86)	(165)
Trading operating income	**2,270**	**2,294**
Other operating income (expense)	(83)	217
Operating income	**2,187**	**2,511**
Interest revenue	58	76
Interest expense	(497)	(340)
Cost of net debt	(439)	(264)
Other financial revenue (expense)	(145)	(225)
Income before tax	**1,603**	**2,022**
Income tax	(443)	(424)
Income from fully consolidated companies	**1,160**	**1,598**
Share of profits of associates	62	(77)

(continued)

---

4 **Sales** is sometimes understood to refer to the sale of goods, whereas *revenue* can include the sale of goods or services; however, the terms are often used interchangeably. In some countries, such as South Africa, turnover may be used in place of revenue. For an example of this, the reader can look at the Sasol (JSE: SOL) Annual Financial Statements 2009.

5 Following net income, the income statement will also present **earnings per share**, the amount of earnings per common share of the company. Earnings per share will be discussed in detail later in this reading, and the per-share display has been omitted from these exhibits to focus on the core income statement.

Exhibit 1 (Continued)

	Year Ended 31 December	
	2008	**2009**
Net income from continuing operations	1,222	1,521
Net income from discontinued operations	269	—
NET INCOME	1,491	1,521
Attributable to the Group	1,313	1,361
Attributable to minority interests	178	160

Exhibit 2 Kraft Foods and Subsidiaries Consolidated Statements of Earnings (in Millions of Dollars, except Per-Share Data)

	Year Ended 31 December		
	2009	**2008**	**2007**
Net revenues	$40,386	$41,932	$35,858
Cost of sales	25,786	28,088	23,656
Gross profit	14,600	13,844	12,202
Marketing, administration, and research costs	9,108	8,862	7,587
Asset impairment and exit costs	(64)	1,024	440
(Gains)/Losses on divestitures, net	6	92	(14)
Amortisation of intangibles	26	23	13
Operating income	5,524	3,843	4,176
Interest and other expense, net	1,237	1,240	604
Earnings from continuing operations before income taxes	4,287	2,603	3,572
Provision for income taxes	1,259	755	1,080
Earnings from continuing operations	3,028	1,848	2,492
Earnings and gain from discontinued operations, net of income taxes (Note 2)	—	1,045	232
Net earnings	3,028	2,893	2,724
Non-controlling interest	7	9	3
Net earnings attributable to Kraft Foods	$3,021	$2,884	$2,721

Note that Danone lists the years in increasing order from left to right with the most recent year in the right-most column, whereas Kraft lists the years in decreasing order with the most recent year listed in the left-most column. Different orderings of chronological information are common. Differences in presentations of items, such as expenses, are also common. **Expenses** reflect outflows, depletions of assets, and incurrences of liabilities in the course of the activities of a business. Expenses may be grouped and reported in different formats, subject to some specific requirements.

For example, Danone reports research and development expenses as a separate line item whereas Kraft combines research costs with marketing and administration costs and reports the total in a single line item.

Another difference is how the companies indicate that an amount on the income statement results in a reduction in net income. Danone shows expenses, such as cost of goods sold and selling expenses, in parentheses to explicitly indicate that these are subtracted from revenue and reduce net income. Kraft, on the other hand, does not place cost of sales in parentheses. Rather, Kraft assumes that the user implicitly understands that this is an expense and is subtracted in arriving at gross profit, subtotals such as operating earnings, and, ultimately, in net income. In general, companies may or may not enclose an amount in parentheses (or use a negative sign) to indicate that it is a reduction in net income. Furthermore, within a list of items that normally reduce net income, an item that increases net income may be shown as a negative. In this case, the item is actually added rather than subtracted in calculating net income. In summary, because there is flexibility in how companies may present the income statement, the analyst should always verify the order of years, how expenses are grouped and reported, and how to treat items presented as negatives.

At the bottom of the income statement, companies report net income (companies may use other terms such as "net earnings" or "profit or loss"). For 2009, Danone reports €1,521 million of net income and Kraft reports $3,028 million of net earnings. Net income is often referred to as the "bottom line." The basis for this expression is that net income is the final—or bottom—line item in an income statement. Because net income is often viewed as the single most relevant number to describe a company's performance over a period of time, the term "bottom line" sometimes is used in business to refer to any final or most relevant result.

Despite this customary terminology, note that the companies both present another item below net income: information about how much of that net income is attributable to the company itself and how much of that income is attributable to minority interests, or non-controlling interests. Danone and Kraft both consolidate subsidiaries over which they have control. Consolidation means that they include all of the revenues and expenses of the subsidiaries even if they own less than 100 percent. Minority interest represents the portion of income that "belongs" to minority shareholders of the consolidated subsidiaries, as opposed to the parent company itself. For Danone, €1,361 million of the net income amount is attributable to shareholders of Groupe Danone and €160 million is attributable to minority interests. For Kraft, $3,021 million of the net earnings amount is attributable to the shareholders of Kraft Foods and $7 million is attributable to the non-controlling interest.

Net income also includes **gains** and **losses,** which are increases and decreases in economic benefits, respectively, which may or may not arise in the ordinary activities of the business. For example, when a manufacturing company sells its products, these transactions are reported as revenue, and the costs incurred to generate these revenues are expenses and are presented separately. However, if a manufacturing company sells surplus land that is not needed, the transaction is reported as a gain or a loss. The amount of the gain or loss is the difference between the carrying value of the land and the price at which the land is sold. For example, in Exhibit 2, Kraft reports a loss (proceeds, net of carrying value) of $6 million on divestitures in fiscal 2009. Kraft discloses in the notes to consolidated financial statements that the assets sold included a nutritional energy bar operation in the United States, a juice operation in Brazil, and a plant in Spain.

The definition of income encompasses both revenue and gains and the definition of expenses encompasses both expenses that arise in the ordinary activities of the business and losses.[6] Thus, **net income** (profit or loss) can be defined as: a) income minus expenses, or equivalently b) revenue plus other income plus gains minus expenses, or equivalently c) revenue plus other income plus gains minus expenses in the ordinary activities of the business minus other expenses, and minus losses. The last definition can be rearranged as follows: net income equals (i) revenue minus expenses in the ordinary activities of the business, plus (ii) other income minus other expenses, plus (iii) gains minus losses.

In addition to presenting the net income, income statements also present items, including subtotals, which are significant to users of financial statements. Some of the items are specified by IFRS but other items are not specified.[7] Certain items, such as revenue, finance costs, and tax expense, are required to be presented separately on the face of the income statement. IFRS additionally require that line items, headings, and subtotals relevant to understanding the entity's financial performance should be presented even if not specified. Expenses may be grouped together either by their nature or function. Grouping together expenses such as depreciation on manufacturing equipment and depreciation on administrative facilities into a single line item called "depreciation" is an example of a **grouping by nature** of the expense. An example of **grouping by function** would be grouping together expenses into a category such as cost of goods sold, which may include labour and material costs, depreciation, some salaries (e.g., salespeople's), and other direct sales related expenses.[8] Both Danone and Kraft present their expenses by function, which is sometimes referred to "cost of sales" method.

One subtotal often shown in an income statement is **gross profit** or **gross margin** (that is revenue less cost of sales). When an income statement shows a gross profit subtotal, it is said to use a **multi-step format** rather than a **single-step format**. The Kraft Foods income statement is an example of the multi-step format, whereas the Groupe Danone income statement is in a single-step format. For manufacturing and merchandising companies, gross profit is a relevant item and is calculated as revenue minus the cost of the goods that were sold. For service companies, gross profit is calculated as revenue minus the cost of services that were provided. In summary, gross profit is the amount of revenue available after subtracting the costs of delivering goods or services. Other expenses related to running the business are subtracted after gross profit.

Another important subtotal which may be shown on the income statement is **operating profit** (or, synonymously, operating income). Operating profit results from deducting operating expenses such as selling, general, administrative, and research and development expenses from gross profit. Operating profit reflects a company's profits on its usual business activities before deducting taxes, and for non-financial companies, before deducting interest expense. For financial companies, interest expense would be included in operating expenses and subtracted in arriving at operating profit because it relates to the operating activities for such companies. For some companies composed of a number of separate business segments, operating profit can be useful in evaluating the performance of the individual business segments, because interest and tax expenses may be more relevant at the level of the overall company rather than an individual segment level. The specific calculations of gross profit and operating profit may vary by company, and a reader of financial statements can consult the notes to the statements to identify significant variations across companies.

---

6 IASB *Framework for the Preparation and Presentation of Financial Statements*, paragraphs 74 to 80.
7 Requirements are presented in IAS 1, *Presentation of Financial Statements*.
8 Later readings will provide additional information about alternative methods to calculate cost of goods sold.

Operating profit is sometimes referred to as EBIT (earnings before interest and taxes). However, operating profit and EBIT are not necessarily the same. Note that in both Exhibits 1 and 2, interest and taxes do not represent the only differences between earnings (net income, net earnings) and operating income. For example, both companies separately report some income from discontinued operations.

Exhibit 3 shows an excerpt from the income statement of CRA International (NASDAQ GS: CRAI), a company providing management consulting services. Accordingly, CRA deducts cost of services (rather than cost of goods) from revenues to derive gross profit. CRA's fiscal year ends on the last Saturday in November, and periodically (for example in 2008) its fiscal year will contain 53 weeks rather than 52 weeks. Although the extra week is likely immaterial in computing year-to-year growth rates, it may have a material impact on a quarter containing the extra week. In general, an analyst should be alert to the effect of an extra week when making historical comparisons and forecasting future performance.

Exhibit 3	CRA International Inc. Consolidated Statements of Income (Excerpt) (in Thousands of Dollars, except Per-Share Data)		
	Year Ended		
	28 Nov 2009 (52 weeks)	**29 Nov 2008 (53 weeks)**	**24 Nov 2007 (52 weeks)**
Revenues	$301,639	$376,751	$394,645
Costs of services	199,861	251,263	248,514
Gross profit	101,778	125,488	146,131
Selling, general, and administrative expenses	76,124	92,797	90,079
Depreciation and amortisation	8,521	12,699	9,782
Income from operations	$17,133	$19,992	$46,270

Note: Remaining items omitted

Exhibits 1, 2, and 3 illustrate basic points about the income statement, including variations across the statements—some of which depend on the industry and/or country, and some of which reflect differences in accounting policies and practices of a particular company. In addition, some differences within an industry are primarily differences in terminology, whereas others are more fundamental accounting differences. Notes to the financial statements are helpful in identifying such differences.

Having introduced the components and format of an income statement, the next objective is to understand the actual reported numbers in it. To accurately interpret reported numbers, the analyst needs to be familiar with the principles of revenue and expense recognition—that is, how revenue and expenses are measured and attributed to a given accounting reporting period.

REVENUE RECOGNITION

3

Revenue is the top line in an income statement, so we begin the discussion of line items in the income statement with revenue recognition. A first task is to explain some relevant accounting terminology.

The terms revenue, sales, gains, losses, and net income (profit, net earnings) have been briefly defined. The IASB *Framework for the Preparation andPresentation of Financial Statements* (referred to hereafter as "the Framework") further defines and discusses these income statement items. The *Framework* explains that profit is a frequently used measure of performance and is composed of income and expenses.[9] It defines **income** as follows:

> Income is increases in economic benefits during the accounting period in the form of inflows or enhancements of assets or decreases of liabilities that result in increases in equity, other than those relating to contributions from equity participants.[10]

In IFRS, the term "income" includes revenue and gains. Gains are similar to revenue, but they typically arise from secondary or peripheral activities rather than from a company's primary business activities. For example, for a restaurant, the sale of surplus restaurant equipment for more than its carrying value is referred to as a gain rather than as revenue. Similarly, a loss typically arises from secondary activities. Gains and losses may be considered part of operating activities (e.g., a loss due to a decline in the value of inventory) or may be considered part of non-operating activities (e.g., the sale of non-trading investments).

In the following simple hypothetical scenario, revenue recognition is straightforward: a company sells goods to a buyer for cash and does not allow returns, so the company recognizes revenue when the exchange of goods for cash takes place and measures revenue at the amount of cash received. In practice, however, determining when revenue should be recognized and at what amount is considerably more complex for reasons discussed in the following sections.

3.1 General Principles

An important aspect concerning revenue recognition is that it can occur independently of cash movements. For example, assume a company sells goods to a buyer on credit, so does not actually receive cash until some later time. A fundamental principle of accrual accounting is that revenue is recognized (reported on the income statement) when it is earned, so the company's financial records reflect revenue from the sale when the risk and reward of ownership is transferred; this is often when the company delivers the goods or services. If the delivery was on credit, a related asset, such as trade or accounts receivable, is created. Later, when cash changes hands, the company's financial records simply reflect that cash has been received to settle an account receivable. Similarly, there are situations when a company receives cash in advance and actually delivers the product or service later, perhaps over a period of time. In this case, the company would record a liability for **unearned revenue** when the cash is initially received, and revenue would be recognized as being earned over time as products and services are delivered. An example would be a subscription payment received for a publication that is to be delivered periodically over time.

---

9 IASB *Framework for the Preparation and Presentation of Financial Statements (1989)*, paragraph 69. The text on the elements of financial statements and their recognition and measurement is the same in the 1989 *Framework* and the IASB *Conceptual Frameworkfor Financial Reporting (2010)*.
10 Ibid., paragraph 70.

When to recognize revenue (when to report revenue on the income statement) is a critical issue in accounting.[11] IFRS specify that revenue from the sale of goods is to be recognized (reported on the income statement) when the following conditions are satisfied:[12]

- the entity has transferred to the buyer the significant risks and rewards of ownership of the goods;
- the entity retains neither continuing managerial involvement to the degree usually associated with ownership nor effective control over the goods sold;
- the amount of revenue can be measured reliably;
- it is probable that the economic benefits associated with the transaction will flow to the entity; and
- the costs incurred or to be incurred in respect of the transaction can be measured reliably.

In simple words, this basically says revenue is recognized when the seller no longer bears risks with respect to the goods (for example, if the goods were destroyed by fire, it would be a loss to the purchaser), the seller cannot tell the purchaser what to do with the goods, the seller knows what it expects to collect and is reasonably certain of collection, and the seller knows how much the goods cost.

IFRS note that the transfer of the risks and rewards of ownership normally occurs when goods are delivered to the buyer or when legal title to goods transfers. However, as noted by the above remaining conditions, physical transfer of goods will not always result in the recognition of revenue. For example, if goods are delivered to a retail store to be sold on consignment and title is not transferred, the revenue would not yet be recognized.[13]

IFRS specify similar criteria for recognizing revenue for the rendering of services.[14] When the outcome of a transaction involving the rendering of services can be estimated reliably, revenue associated with the transaction shall be recognized by reference to the stage of completion of the transaction at the balance sheet date. The outcome of a transaction can be estimated reliably when all the following conditions are satisfied:

- the amount of revenue can be measured reliably;
- it is probable that the economic benefits associated with the transaction will flow to the entity;
- the stage of completion of the transaction at the balance sheet date can be measured reliably; and
- the costs incurred for the transaction and the costs to complete the transaction can be measured reliably.

IFRS criteria for recognizing interest, royalties, and dividends are that it is probable that the economic benefits associated with the transaction will flow to the entity and the amount of the revenue can be reliably measured.

---

11 In June 2010, IASB and FASB issued a joint proposal for a standard on revenue recognition. If adopted, there will be a single revenue recognition standard for IFRS and U.S. GAAP. The standards in this reading are those in effect 30 June 2010 and do not reflect the proposed standard.
12 IAS No. 18, *Revenue*, paragraph 14.
13 IAS 18 IE describes a "consignment sale" as one in which the recipient undertakes to sell the goods on behalf of the shipper (seller). Revenue is recognized by the shipper when the recipient sells the goods to a third party. IAS 18 IE, *Illustrative Examples*, paragraph 2.
14 IAS No. 18, *Revenue*, paragraph 20.

U.S. GAAP[15] specify that revenue should be recognized when it is "realized or realizable and earned." The U.S. Securities and Exchange Commission (SEC),[16] motivated in part because of the frequency with which overstating revenue occurs in connection with fraud and/or misstatements, provides guidance on how to apply the accounting principles. This guidance lists four criteria to determine when revenue is realized or realizable and earned:

1 There is evidence of an arrangement between buyer and seller. For instance, this would disallow the practice of recognizing revenue in a period by delivering the product just before the end of an accounting period and then completing a sales contract *after* the period end.

2 The product has been delivered, or the service has been rendered. For instance, this would preclude revenue recognition when the product has been shipped but the *risks and rewards of ownership have not actually passed* to the buyer.

3 The price is determined, or determinable. For instance, this would preclude a company from recognizing revenue that is based on some *contingency*.

4 The seller is reasonably sure of collecting money. For instance, this would preclude a company from recognizing revenue when the customer is *unlikely to pay*.

Companies must disclose their revenue recognition policies in the notes to their financial statements (sometimes referred to as footnotes). Analysts should review these policies carefully to understand how and when a company recognizes revenue, which may differ depending on the types of product sold and services rendered. Exhibit 4 presents a portion of the summary of significant accounting policies note that discusses revenue recognition for DaimlerChrysler (DB-F: DAI) from its 2009 annual report, prepared under IFRS.

Exhibit 4	Excerpt from DaimlerChrysler Notes

Revenue from sales of vehicles, service parts and other related products is recognized when the risks and rewards of ownership of the goods are transferred to the customer, the amount of revenue can be estimated reliably and collectability is reasonably assured. Revenue is recognized net of discounts, cash sales incentives, customer bonuses and rebates granted.

Daimler uses price discounts in response to a number of market and product factors, including pricing actions and incentives offered by competitors, the amount of excess industry production capacity, the intensity of market competition and consumer demand for the product. The Group may offer a variety of sales incentive programs at any point in time, including cash offers to dealers and consumers, lease subsidies which reduce the consumers' monthly lease payment, or reduced financing rate programs offered to consumers.

---

15 FASB ASC Section 605-10-25 [Revenue Recognition-Overall-Recognition].
16 The content of SEC Staff Accounting Bulletin 101 is contained in FASB ASC Section 605-10-S99 [Revenue Recognition–Overall–SEC Materials].

An analyst comparing Daimler with another company would likely want to ensure that revenue recognition policies are similar. For example, Daimler notes that it recognizes its revenue net of certain items. Does the comparison company deduct the same items from revenue? Exhibit 5 presents excerpts from the 2009 annual report's notes to the financial statements of Ford Motor Company (NYSE:F) prepared under U.S. GAAP. In Ford's Note 2, Summary of Accounting Policies, the section titled *revenue recognition* mentions the criteria and timing of revenue recognition, but not the recognition of revenue net of certain items. In a subsequent section of Note 2, Ford states that its marketing incentives are recognized as revenue reductions. A comparison of the disclosed revenue recognition policies suggests that the companies do have similar revenue recognition policies despite minor differences in presentation.

Exhibit 5	Excerpt from Ford Motor Company Notes

Revenue Recognition — Automotive Sector

Automotive sales consist primarily of revenue generated from the sale of vehicles. Sales are recorded when the risks and rewards of ownership are transferred to our customers (generally dealers and distributors). For the majority of our sales, this occurs when products are shipped from our manufacturing facilities or delivered to our customers. When vehicles are shipped to customers or vehicle modifiers on consignment, revenue is recognized when the vehicle is sold to the ultimate customer.

[*portions omitted*]

Marketing Incentives and Interest Supplements

Marketing incentives generally are recognized by the Automotive sector as revenue reductions in Automotive sales. These include customer and dealer cash payments and costs for special financing and leasing programs paid to the Financial Services sector. The revenue reductions are accrued at the later of the date the related vehicle sales to the dealers are recorded or the date the incentive program is both approved and communicated. We generally estimate these accruals using marketing programs that are approved as of the balance sheet date and are expected to be effective at the beginning of the subsequent period. The Financial Services sector identifies payments for special financing and leasing programs as interest supplements or other support costs and recognizes them consistent with the earnings process of the underlying receivable or operating lease.

The topic of revenue recognition remains important and new challenges have evolved, particularly in areas of e-commerce and services such as software development. Standard setters continue to evaluate current revenue recognition standards and issue new guidance periodically to deal with new types of transactions.[17] Additionally, there are occasional special cases for revenue recognition, as discussed in the next section.

3.2 Revenue Recognition in Special Cases

The general principles discussed above are helpful for dealing with most revenue recognition issues. There are some instances where revenue recognition is more difficult to determine. For example, in limited circumstances, revenue may be recognized before or after goods are delivered or services are rendered, as summarized in Exhibit 6.

Exhibit 6	Revenue Recognition in Special Cases	
Before Goods Are Fully Delivered or Services Completely Rendered	**At the Time** Goods Are Delivered or Services Rendered	**After** Goods Are Delivered or Services Rendered
For example, with long-term contracts where the outcome can be reliably measured, the percentage-of-completion method is used.	Recognize revenues using normal revenue recognition criteria.	For example, with real estate sales where there is doubt about the buyer's ability to complete payments, the installment method and cost recovery method are appropriate.

The following sections discuss revenue recognition in the case of long-term contracts, installment sales, and barter.

3.2.1 Long-Term Contracts

A **long-term contract** is one that spans a number of accounting periods. Such contracts raise issues in determining when the earnings process has been completed and revenue recognition should occur. How should a company apportion the revenue earned under a long-term contract to each accounting period? If, for example, the contract is a service contract or a licensing arrangement, the company may recognize the revenue on a prorated basis over the period of time of the contract rather than at the end of the contract term. Under IFRS, this may be done using the percentage-of-completion method.[18] Under the percentage-of-completion method, revenue is recognized based on the stage of completion of a transaction or contract and is, thus, recognized when the services are rendered. Construction contracts are examples of contracts that may span a number of accounting periods and that may use the percentage-of-completion method.[19] IFRS provide that when the outcome of a construction contract can be measured reliably, revenue and expenses should be recognized in reference to the stage of completion. U.S. GAAP have similar requirements for long-term contracts including construction contracts.

---

17 In June 2010, IASB and FASB issued a joint proposal for a standard on revenue recognition. If adopted, there will be a single revenue recognition standard for IFRS and U.S. GAAP. The standards in this reading are those in effect 30 June 2010 and do not reflect the proposed standard.
18 IAS No. 18, *Revenue*, paragraph 21.
19 IAS No. 11, *Construction Contracts*.

Under the **percentage-of-completion** method, in each accounting period, the company estimates what percentage of the contract is complete and then reports that percentage of the total contract revenue in its income statement. Contract costs for the period are expensed against the revenue. Therefore, net income or profit is reported each year as work is performed.

Under IFRS, if the outcome of the contract cannot be measured reliably, then revenue may be recognized to the extent of contract costs incurred (but only if it is probable the costs will be recovered). Costs are expensed in the period incurred. Under this method, no profit is recognized until all the costs had been recovered. Under U.S. GAAP, but not under IFRS, a revenue recognition method used when the outcome cannot be measured reliably is the completed contract method. Under the **completed contract** method, the company does not report any income until the contract is substantially finished (the remaining costs and potential risks are insignificant in amount), although provision should be made for expected losses. Billings and costs are accumulated on the balance sheet rather than flowing through the income statement. Under U.S. GAAP, the completed contract method is also acceptable when the entity has primarily short-term contracts. Note that if a contract is started and completed in the same period, there is no difference between the percentage-of-completion and completed contract methods.

Examples 1, 2, and 3 provide illustrations of these revenue recognition methods. As shown, the percentage-of-completion method results in revenue recognition sooner than the completed contract method and thus may be considered a less conservative approach. In addition, the percentage-of-completion method relies on management estimates and is thus not as objective as the completed contract method. However, an advantage of the percentage-of-completion method is that it results in better matching of revenue recognition with the accounting period in which it was earned. Because of better matching with the periods in which work is performed, the percentage-of-completion method is the preferred method of revenue recognition for long-term contracts and is required when the outcome can be measured reliably under both IFRS and U.S. GAAP. Under both IFRS and U.S. GAAP, if a loss is expected on the contract, the loss is reported immediately, not upon completion of the contract, regardless of the method used (e.g., percentage-of-completion or completed contract).

EXAMPLE 1

Revenue Recognition for Long-Term Contracts: Recognizing Revenue on a Prorated Basis

New Era Network Associates has a five-year license to provide networking support services to a customer. The total amount of the license fee to be received by New Era is $1 million. New Era recognizes license revenue on a prorated basis regardless of the time at which cash is received. How much revenue will New Era recognize for this license in each year?

Solution:

For this license, New Era Network Associates will recognize $200,000 each year for five years (calculated as $1 million divided by 5).

EXAMPLE 2

Revenue Recognition for Long-Term Contracts: Percentage-of-Completion Method

Stelle Technology has a contract to build a network for a customer for a total sales price of €10 million. The network will take an estimated three years to build, and total building costs are estimated to be €6 million. Stelle recognizes long-term contract revenue using the percentage-of-completion method and estimates percentage complete based on expenditure incurred as a percentage of total estimated expenditures.

1 At the end of Year 1, the company had spent €3 million. Total costs to complete are estimated to be another €3 million. How much revenue will Stelle recognize in Year 1?

2 At the end of Year 2, the company had spent an additional €2.4 million for an accumulated total of €5.4 million. Total costs to complete are estimated to be another €0.6 million. How much revenue will Stelle recognize in Year 2?

3 At the end of Year 3, the contract is complete. The company spent an accumulated total of €6 million. How much revenue will Stelle recognize in Year 3?

Solution to 1:

Stelle has spent 50 percent of the total project costs (€3 million divided by €6 million), so in Year 1, the company will recognize 50 percent of the total contract revenue (i.e., €5 million).

Solution to 2:

Because Stelle has spent 90 percent of the total project costs (€5.4 million divided by €6 million), by the end of Year 2, it will need to have recognized 90 percent of the total contract revenue (i.e., €9 million). Stelle has already recognized €5 million of revenue in Year 1, so in Year 2, the company will recognize €4 million revenue (€9 million minus €5 million).

Solution to 3:

Because Stelle has spent 100 percent of the total project costs, by the end of Year 3, it will need to have recognized 100 percent of the total contract revenue (i.e., €10 million). Stelle had already recognized €9 million of revenue by the end of Year 2, so in Year 3, the company will recognize €1 million revenue (€10 million minus €9 million).

	Year 1	Year 2	Year 3	Total
Revenue	€5 million	€4 million	€1 million	€10 million

EXAMPLE 3

Revenue Recognition for Long-Term Contracts: Outcome Cannot Be Reliably Measured

Kolenda Technology Group has a contract to build a network for a customer for a total sales price of $10 million. This network will take an estimated three years to build, but considerable uncertainty surrounds total building costs because new technologies are involved. In other words, the outcome cannot be reliably measured, but it is probable that the costs up to the agreed upon price will be recovered.

Assuming the following expenditures, how much revenue, expense (cost of construction), and income would the company recognize each year under IFRS and using the completed contract method under U.S. GAAP? The amounts periodically billed to the customer and received from the customer are not necessarily equivalent to the amount of revenue being recognized in the period. For simplicity, assume Kolenda pays cash for all expenditures.

1   At the end of Year 1, Kolenda has spent $3 million.

2   At the end of Year 2, Kolenda has spent a total of $5.4 million.

3   At the end of Year 3, the contract is complete. Kolenda spent a total of $6 million.

Solution:

Under IFRS, revenue may be recognized to the extent of contract costs incurred if the outcome of the contract cannot be measured reliably and it is probable that costs will be recovered. In this example, the outcome is uncertain but it is probable that Kolenda will recover the costs up to $10 million. Under U.S. GAAP, the company would use the completed contract method. No revenue will be recognized until the contract is complete.

Year 1. Under IFRS, Kolenda would recognize $3 million cost of construction, $3 million revenue, and thus $0 income. Under U.S. GAAP, Kolenda would recognize $0 cost of construction, $0 revenue, and thus $0 income. The $3 million expenditure would be reported as an increase in the inventory account "construction in progress" and a decrease in cash.

Year 2. Under IFRS, Kolenda would recognize $2.4 million cost of construction, $2.4 million revenue, and thus $0 income. Under U.S. GAAP, Kolenda would recognize $0 cost of construction, $0 revenue, and thus $0 income. The $2.4 million expenditures would be reported as an increase in the inventory account "construction in progress" and a decrease in cash.

Year 3. Under IFRS, Kolenda would recognize the $0.6 million cost of construction incurred in the period. Because the contract has been completed and the outcome is now measurable, the company would recognize the remaining $4.6 million revenue on the contract, and thus $4 million income. Under U.S. GAAP, because the contract has been completed, Kolenda would recognize the total contract revenue (i.e., $10 million). Kolenda would recognize $6 million cost of construction and thus $4 million income. The inventory account "construction in progress" would be eliminated.

Summary

Revenue recognition to the extent of contract costs incurred: IFRS

	Year 1	Year 2	Year 3	Total
Revenue	$3 million	$2.4 million	$4.6 million	$10 million
Cost of construction	$3 million	$2.4 million	$0.6 million	$6 million
Profit	$0 million	$0 million	$4 million	$4 million

Completed Contract Method: U.S. GAAP

	Year 1	Year 2	Year 3	Total
Revenue	$0 million	$0 million	$10 million	$10 million
Cost of construction	$0 million	$0 million	$6 million	$6 million
Profit	$0 million	$0 million	$4 million	$4 million

3.2.2 Installment Sales

As noted above, revenue is normally reported when goods are delivered or services are rendered, independent of the period in which cash payments for those goods or services are received. This principle applies even to **installment sales**—sales in which proceeds are to be paid in installments over an extended period. For installment sales, IFRS separate the installments into the sale price, which is the discounted present value of the installment payments, and an interest component. Revenue attributable to the sale price is recognized at the date of sale, and revenue attributable to the interest component is recognized over time.[20] International standards note, however, that the guidance for revenue recognition must be considered in light of local laws regarding the sale of goods in a particular country. Under limited circumstances, recognition of revenue or profit may be required to be deferred for some installment sales. An example of such deferral arises for certain sales of real estate on an installment basis. Revenue recognition for sales of real estate varies depending on specific aspects of the sale transaction.[21]

Under U.S. GAAP, when the seller has completed the significant activities in the earnings process and is either assured of collecting the selling price or able to estimate amounts that will not be collected, a sale of real estate is reported at the time of sale using the normal revenue recognition conditions.[22] When those two conditions are not fully met, under U.S. GAAP some of the profit is deferred. Two of the methods may be appropriate in these limited circumstances and relate to the amount of profit to be recognized each year from the transaction: the **installment method** and the **cost recovery method**. Under the installment method, the portion of the total profit of the sale that is recognized in each period is determined by the percentage of the total sales price for which the seller has received cash. Under the cost recovery method, the seller does not report any profit until the cash amounts paid by the buyer—including

---

20 IAS No. 18 IE, *Illustrative Examples*, paragraph 8.
21 IFRIC Interpretation 15, *Agreements for the Construction of Real Estate*, distinguishes three types of agreements for real estate construction (construction contract, rendering services, sale of goods) to determine whether the revenue recognition methods described under long-term contracts apply.
22 FASB ASC Section 360-20-55 [Property, Plant, and Equipment–Real Estate Sales–Implementation Guidance and Illustrations].

principal and interest on any financing from the seller—are greater than all the seller's costs of the property. Note that the cost recovery method is similar to the revenue recognition method under international standards, described above, when the outcome of a contract cannot be measured reliably (although the term cost recovery method is not used in the international standard).

Example 4 illustrates the differences between the installment method and the cost recovery method. Installment sales and cost recovery treatment of revenue recognition are rare for financial reporting purposes, especially for assets other than real estate.

EXAMPLE 4

The Installment and Cost Recovery Methods of Revenue Recognition

Assume the total sales price and cost of a property are $2,000,000 and $1,100,000, respectively, so that the total profit to be recognized is $900,000. The amount of cash received by the seller as a down payment is $300,000, with the remainder of the sales price to be received over a 10-year period. It has been determined that there is significant doubt about the ability and commitment of the buyer to complete all payments. How much profit will be recognized attributable to the down payment if:

1 The installment method is used?

2 The cost recovery method is used?

Solution to 1:

The installment method apportions the cash receipt between cost recovered and profit using the ratio of profit to sales value; here, this ratio equals $900,000/$2,000,000 = 0.45 or 45 percent. Therefore, the seller will recognize the following profit attributable to the down payment: 45 percent of $300,000 = $135,000.

Solution to 2:

Under the cost recovery method of revenue recognition, the company would not recognize any profit attributable to the down payment because the cash amounts paid by the buyer still do not exceed the cost of $1,100,000.

3.2.3 *Barter*

Revenue recognition issues related to barter transactions became particularly important as e-commerce developed. As an example, if Company A exchanges advertising space for computer equipment from Company B but no cash changes hands, can Company A and B both report revenue? Such an exchange is referred to as a "barter transaction."

An even more challenging revenue recognition issue evolved from a specific type of barter transaction, a round-trip transaction. As an example, if Company A sells advertising services (or energy contracts, or commodities) to Company B and almost simultaneously buys an almost identical product from Company B, can Company A report revenue at the fair value of the product sold? Because the company's revenue would be approximately equal to its expense, the net effect of the transaction would have no impact on net income or cash flow. However, the amount of revenue reported would be higher, and the amount of revenue can be important to a company's valuation. In the earlier stages of e-commerce, for example, some equity valuations were based on sales (because many early internet companies reported no net income).

Under IFRS, revenue from barter transactions must be measured based on the fair value of revenue from similar non-barter transactions with unrelated parties (parties other than the barter partner).[23] U.S.GAAP state that revenue can be recognized at fair value only if a company has historically received cash payments for such services and can thus use this historical experience as a basis for determining fair value; otherwise, the revenue from the barter transaction is recorded at the carrying amount of the asset surrendered.[24]

3.2.4 *Gross versus Net Reporting*

Another revenue recognition issue that became particularly important with the emergence of e-commerce is the issue of gross versus net reporting. Merchandising companies typically sell products that they purchased from a supplier. In accounting for their sales, the company records the amount of the sale proceeds as sales revenue and their cost of the products as the cost of goods sold. As internet-based merchandising companies developed, many sold products that they had never held in inventory; they simply arranged for the supplier to ship the products directly to the end customer. In effect, many such companies were agents of the supplier company, and the net difference between their sales proceeds and their costs was equivalent to a sales commission. What amount should these companies record as their revenues—the gross amount of sales proceeds received from their customers, or the net difference between sales proceeds and their cost?

U.S. GAAP indicate that the approach should be based on the specific situation and provides guidance for determining when revenue should be reported gross versus net.[25] To report gross revenues, the following criteria are relevant: the company is the primary obligor under the contract, bears inventory risk and credit risk, can choose its supplier, and has reasonable latitude to establish price. If these criteria are not met, the company should report revenues net. Example 5 provides an illustration.

EXAMPLE 5

Gross versus Net Reporting of Revenues

Flyalot has agreements with several major airlines to obtain airline tickets at reduced rates. The company pays only for tickets it sells to customers. In the most recent period, Flyalot sold airline tickets to customers over the internet for a total of $1.1 million. The cost of these tickets to Flyalot was $1 million. The company's direct selling costs were $2,000. Once the customers receive their ticket, the airline is responsible for providing all services associated with the customers' flights.

1 Demonstrate the reporting of revenues under:

   A gross reporting.

   B net reporting.

2 Determine and justify the appropriate method for reporting revenues.

Solution to 1:

The table below shows how reporting would appear on a gross and a net basis:

---

23 IASB, SIC Interpretation 31, *Revenue—Barter Transactions Involving Advertising Services*, paragraph 5.
24 FASB ASC paragraph 605-20-25-14 [Revenue Recognition–Services–Recognition–Advertising Barter Services].
25 FASB ASC Section 605-45-45 [Revenue Recognition–Principal Agent Considerations–Other Presentation Matters].

	A. Gross Reporting	B. Net Reporting
Revenues	$1,100,000	$100,000
Cost of sales	1,002,000	2,000
Gross margin	$ 98,000	$ 98,000

Solution to 2:

Flyalot should report revenue on a net basis. Flyalot pays only for tickets it sells to customers and thus does not bear inventory risk. In addition, the airline—not Flyalot—is the primary obligor under the contract. Revenues should be reported as $100,000.

3.3 Implications for Financial Analysis

As we have seen, companies use a variety of revenue recognition methods. Furthermore, a single company may use different revenue recognition policies for different businesses. Companies disclose their revenue recognition policies in the notes to their financial statement, often in the first note.

The following aspects of a company's revenue recognition policy are particularly relevant to financial analysis: whether a policy results in recognition of revenue sooner rather than later (sooner is less conservative), and to what extent a policy requires the company to make estimates. In order to analyze a company's financial statements, and particularly to compare one company's financial statements with those of another company, it is helpful to understand any differences in their revenue recognition policies. Although it may not be possible to calculate the monetary effect of differences between particular companies' revenue recognition policies and estimates, it is generally possible to characterize the relative conservatism of a company's policies and to qualitatively assess how differences in policies might affect financial ratios.

EXAMPLE 6

Revenue Recognition Policy for Apple

As disclosed in the excerpt from notes to the consolidated financial statements shown below (emphasis added), Apple Inc. (NasdaqGS: AAPL) uses different revenue recognition policies depending on the type of revenue producing activity, including product sales, service and support contracts, and products obtained from other companies. Note that these are only the first three paragraphs of Apple's disclosure on revenue recognition; the entire revenue recognition portion has nine paragraphs.

Revenue Recognition

Net sales consist primarily of revenue from the sale of hardware, software, digital content and applications, peripherals, and service and support contracts. The Company recognizes revenue when persuasive evidence of an arrangement exists, delivery has occurred, the sales price is fixed or determinable, and collection is probable. Product is considered delivered to the customer once it has been shipped and title and risk of loss have been transferred. For most of the Company's *product sales*, these criteria are met at the time the product is shipped. For online sales to individuals, for some sales to education customers in the U.S., and for certain other sales, the Company defers revenue until the customer receives the product because the Company legally retains a portion of the risk of loss on these sales during transit *[portions omitted]*.

Revenue from *service and support contracts* is deferred and recognized ratably over the service coverage periods. These contracts typically include extended phone support, repair services, web-based support resources, diagnostic tools, and extend the service coverage offered under the Company's standard limited warranty.

The Company sells software and peripheral *products obtained from other companies*. The Company generally establishes its own pricing and retains related inventory risk, is the primary obligor in sales transactions with its customers, and assumes the credit risk for amounts billed to its customers. Accordingly, the Company generally recognizes revenue for the sale of products obtained from other companies based on the gross amount billed.

Source: Apple Inc. 10-K/A for the year ended 26 September 2009, as filed with the SEC on 25 January 2010. Emphasis added.

1   What criteria does Apple apply to determine when to recognize revenue from product sales?

2   What principle underpins the company's deferral of revenue from service and support contracts?

Solution to 1:

Apple recognizes revenue when persuasive evidence of an arrangement exists, delivery has occurred, the sales price is fixed or determinable, and collection is probable. Note that these are just the four U.S. GAAP revenue recognition criteria described in Section 3.1. Note also that Apple recognizes revenue on some product sales at the time of shipment and others at the time of delivery, depending on when its risk of loss ends.

Solution to 2:

The basic principle underpinning the company's deferral of revenue for service and sales contracts is that revenue should be recognized in the period it is earned. Because service under these contracts will be performed in future periods, the company defers the revenue and then recognizes it over the time it is earned.

With familiarity of the basic principles of revenue recognition in hand, the next section begins a discussion of expense recognition.

EXPENSE RECOGNITION

4

Expenses are deducted against revenue to arrive at a company's net profit or loss. Under the IASB *Framework*, **expenses** are "decreases in economic benefits during the accounting period in the form of outflows or depletions of assets or incurrences of liabilities that result in decreases in equity, other than those relating to distributions to equity participants."[26]

The IASB *Framework* also states:

> The definition of expenses encompasses losses as well as those expenses that arise in the course of the ordinary activities of the enterprise. Expenses that arise in the course of the ordinary activities of the enterprise include, for example, cost of sales, wages and depreciation. They usually take the form of an outflow or depletion of assets such as cash and cash equivalents, inventory, property, plant and equipment.
>
> Losses represent other items that meet the definition of expenses and may, or may not, arise in the course of the ordinary activities of the enterprise. Losses represent decreases in economic benefits and as such they are no different in nature from other expenses. Hence, they are not regarded as a separate element in this *Framework*.
>
> Losses include, for example, those resulting from disasters such as fire and flood, as well as those arising on the disposal of non-current assets.[27]

Similar to the issues with revenue recognition, in a simple hypothetical scenario, expense recognition would not be an issue. For instance, assume a company purchased inventory for cash and sold the entire inventory in the same period. When the company paid for the inventory, absent indications to the contrary, it is clear that the inventory cost has been incurred and when that inventory is sold, it should be recognized as an expense (cost of goods sold) in the financial records. Assume also that the company paid all operating and administrative expenses in cash within each accounting period. In such a simple hypothetical scenario, no issues of expense recognition would arise. In practice, however, as with revenue recognition, determining when expenses should be recognized can be somewhat more complex.

4.1 General Principles

In general, a company recognizes expenses in the period that it consumes (i.e., uses up) the economic benefits associated with the expenditure, or loses some previously recognized economic benefit.[28]

A general principle of expense recognition is the **matching principle.** Strictly speaking, IFRS do not refer to a "matching principle" but rather to a "matching concept" or to a process resulting in "matching of costs with revenues."[29] The distinction is relevant in certain standard setting deliberations. Under matching, a company recognizes some expenses (e.g., cost of goods sold) when associated revenues are recognized and thus, expenses and revenues are matched. Associated revenues and expenses are those that result directly and jointly from the same transactions or events. Unlike the simple scenario in which a company purchases inventory and sells all of the inventory within the same accounting period, in practice, it is more likely that some of the current period's sales are made from inventory purchased in a previous

---

26 IASB *Framework for the Preparation and Presentation of Financial Statements*, paragraph 70.
27 Ibid., paragraphs 78–80.
28 Ibid., paragraph 94.
29 Ibid., paragraph 95.

period or previous periods. It is also likely that some of the inventory purchased in the current period will remain unsold at the end of the current period and so will be sold in a following period. Matching requires that a company recognizes cost of goods sold in the same period as revenues from the sale of the goods.

Period costs, expenditures that less directly match revenues, are reflected in the period when a company makes the expenditure or incurs the liability to pay. Administrative expenses are an example of period costs. Other expenditures that also less directly match revenues relate more directly to future expected benefits; in this case, the expenditures are allocated systematically with the passage of time. An example is depreciation expense.

Examples 7 and 8 demonstrate matching applied to inventory and cost of goods sold.

EXAMPLE 7

The Matching of Inventory Costs with Revenues

Kahn Distribution Limited (KDL) purchases inventory items for resale. At the beginning of 2009, Kahn had no inventory on hand. During 2009, Kahn had the following transactions:

Inventory Purchases		
First quarter	2,000	units at $40 per unit
Second quarter	1,500	units at $41 per unit
Third quarter	2,200	units at $43 per unit
Fourth quarter	1,900	units at $45 per unit
Total	7,600	units at a total cost of $321,600

KDL sold 5,600 units of inventory during the year at $50 per unit, and received cash. KDL determines that there were 2,000 remaining units of inventory and specifically identifies that 1,900 were those purchased in the fourth quarter and 100 were purchased in the third quarter. What are the revenue and expense associated with these transactions during 2009 based on specific identification of inventory items as sold or remaining in inventory?

Solution:

The revenue for 2009 would be $280,000 (5,600 units × $50 per unit). Initially, the total cost of the goods purchased would be recorded as inventory (an asset) in the amount of $321,600. During 2009, the cost of the 5,600 units sold would be expensed (matched against the revenue) while the cost of the 2,000 remaining unsold units would remain in inventory as follows:

Cost of Goods Sold		
From the first quarter	2,000 units at $40 per unit =	$ 80,000
From the second quarter	1,500 units at $41 per unit =	$ 61,500
From the third quarter	2,100 units at $43 per unit =	$ 90,300
Total cost of goods sold		$231,800
Cost of Goods Remaining in Inventory		
From the third quarter	100 units at $43 per unit =	$ 4,300
From the fourth quarter	1,900 units at $45 per unit =	$85,500
Total remaining (or ending) inventory cost		$89,800

To confirm that total costs are accounted for: $231,800 + $89,800 = $321,600. The cost of the goods sold would be expensed against the revenue of $280,000 as follows:

Revenue	$280,000
Cost of goods sold	231,800
Gross profit	$ 48,200

An alternative way to think about this is that the company created an asset (inventory) of $321,600 as it made its purchases. At the end of the period, the value of the company's inventory on hand is $89,800. Therefore, the amount of the Cost of goods sold expense recognized for the period should be the difference: $231,800.

The remaining inventory amount of $89,800 will be matched against revenue in a future year when the inventory items are sold.

EXAMPLE 8

Alternative Inventory Costing Methods

In Example 7, KDL was able to specifically identify which inventory items were sold and which remained in inventory to be carried over to later periods. This is called the **specific identification method** and inventory and cost of goods sold are based on their physical flow. It is generally not feasible to specifically identify which items were sold and which remain on hand, so accounting standards permit the assignment of inventory costs to costs of goods sold and to ending inventory using cost formulas (IFRS terminology) or cost flow assumptions (U.S. GAAP). The cost formula or cost flow assumption determines which goods are assumed to be sold and which goods are assumed to remain in inventory. Both IFRS and U.S. GAAP permit the use of the first in, first out (FIFO) method, and the weighted average cost method to assign costs.

Under the **FIFO method**, the oldest goods purchased (or manufactured) are assumed to be sold first and the newest goods purchased (or manufactured) are assumed to remain in inventory. Cost of goods in beginning inventory and costs of the first items purchased (or manufactured) flow into cost of goods sold first, as if the earliest items purchased sold first. Ending inventory would, therefore, include the most recent purchases. It turns out that those items specifically identified as sold in Example 7 were also the first items purchased, so in this example, under FIFO, the cost of goods sold would also be $231,800, calculated as above.

The **weighted average cost method** assigns the average cost of goods available for sale to the units sold and remaining in inventory. The assignment is based on the average cost per unit (total cost of goods available for sale/total units available for sale) and the number of units sold and the number remaining in inventory.

For KDL, the weighted average cost per unit would be

$321,600/7,600 units = $42.3158 per unit

Cost of goods sold using the weighted average cost method would be

5,600 units at $42.3158 = $236,968

Ending inventory using the weighted average cost method would be

> 2,000 units at $42.3158 = $84,632
>
> Another method is permitted under U.S. GAAP but is not permitted under IFRS. This is the last in, first out (LIFO) method. Under the **LIFO method**, the newest goods purchased (or manufactured) are assumed to be sold first and the oldest goods purchased (or manufactured) are assumed to remain in inventory. Costs of the latest items purchased flow into cost of goods sold first, as if the most recent items purchased were sold first. Although this may seem contrary to common sense, it is logical in certain circumstances. For example, lumber in a lumberyard may be stacked up with the oldest lumber on the bottom. As lumber is sold, it is sold from the top of the stack, so the last lumber purchased and put in inventory is the first lumber out. Theoretically, a company should choose a method linked to the physical inventory flows.[30] Under the LIFO method, in the KDL example, it would be assumed that the 2,000 units remaining in ending inventory would have come from the first quarter's purchases:[31]
>
> Ending inventory 2,000 units at $40 per unit = $80,000
>
> The remaining costs would be allocated to cost of goods sold under LIFO:
>
> Total costs of $321,600 less $80,000 remaining in ending inventory = $241,600
>
> Alternatively, the cost of the last 5,600 units purchased is allocated to cost of goods sold under LIFO:
>
> 1,900 units at $45 per unit + 2,200 units at $43 per unit + 1,500 units at $41 per unit = $241,600
>
> An alternative way to think about expense recognition is that the company created an asset (inventory) of $321,600 as it made its purchases. At the end of the period, the value of the company's inventory is $80,000. Therefore, the amount of the Cost of goods sold expense recognized for the period should be the difference: $241,600.

Exhibit 7 summarizes and compares inventory costing methods.

---

30 Practically, the reason some companies choose to use LIFO in the United States is to reduce taxes. When prices and inventory quantities are rising, LIFO will normally result in higher cost of goods sold and lower income and hence lower taxes. U.S. tax regulations require that if LIFO is used on a company's tax return, it must also be used on the company's GAAP financial statements.

31 If data on the precise timing of quarterly sales were available, the answer would differ because the cost of goods sold would be determined during the quarter rather than at the end of the quarter.

Exhibit 7	Summary Table on Inventory Costing Methods		
Method	**Description**	**Cost of Goods Sold When Prices Are Rising, Relative to Other Two Methods**	**Ending Inventory When Prices Are Rising, Relative to Other Two Methods**
FIFO (first in, first out)	Costs of the earliest items purchased flow to cost of goods sold first	Lowest	Highest
LIFO (last in, first out)	Costs of the most recent items purchased flow to cost of goods sold first	Highest*	Lowest*
Weighted average cost	Averages total costs over total units available	Middle	Middle

*Assumes no LIFO layer liquidation. **LIFO layer liquidation** occurs when the volume of sales exceeds the volume of purchases in the period so that some sales are assumed to be made from existing, relatively low-priced inventory rather than from more recent purchases.

4.2 Issues in Expense Recognition

The following sections cover applications of the principles of expense recognition to certain common situations.

4.2.1 Doubtful Accounts

When a company sells its products or services on credit, it is likely that some customers will ultimately default on their obligations (i.e., fail to pay). At the time of the sale, it is not known which customer will default. (If it were known that a particular customer would ultimately default, presumably a company would not sell on credit to that customer.) One possible approach to recognizing credit losses on customer receivables would be for the company to wait until such time as a customer defaulted and only then recognize the loss (**direct write-off method**). Such an approach would usually not be consistent with generally accepted accounting principles.

Under the matching principle, at the time revenue is recognized on a sale, a company is required to record an estimate of how much of the revenue will ultimately be uncollectible. Companies make such estimates based on previous experience with uncollectible accounts. Such estimates may be expressed as a proportion of the overall amount of sales, the overall amount of receivables, or the amount of receivables overdue by a specific amount of time. The company records its estimate of uncollectible amounts as an expense on the income statement, not as a direct reduction of revenues.

4.2.2 Warranties

At times, companies offer warranties on the products they sell. If the product proves deficient in some respect that is covered under the terms of the warranty, the company will incur an expense to repair or replace the product. At the time of sale, the company does not know the amount of future expenses it will incur in connection with its warranties. One possible approach would be for a company to wait until actual expenses are incurred under the warranty and to reflect the expense at that time. However, this would not result in a matching of the expense with the associated revenue.

Under the matching principle, a company is required to estimate the amount of future expenses resulting from its warranties, to recognize an estimated warranty expense in the period of the sale, and to update the expense as indicated by experience over the life of the warranty.

4.2.3 *Depreciation and Amortisation*

Companies commonly incur costs to obtain long-lived assets. **Long-lived assets** are assets expected to provide economic benefits over a future period of time greater than one year. Examples are land (property), plant, equipment, and **intangible assets** (assets lacking physical substance) such as trademarks. The costs of most long-lived assets are allocated over the period of time during which they provide economic benefits. The two main types of long-lived assets whose costs are *not* allocated over time are land and those intangible assets with indefinite useful lives.

Depreciation is the process of systematically allocating costs of long-lived assets over the period during which the assets are expected to provide economic benefits. "Depreciation" is the term commonly applied to this process for physical long-lived assets such as plant and equipment (land is not depreciated), and **amortisation** is the term commonly applied to this process for intangible long-lived assets with a finite useful life.[32] Examples of intangible long-lived assets with a finite useful life include an acquired mailing list, an acquired patent with a set expiration date, and an acquired copyright with a set legal life. The term "amortisation" is also commonly applied to the systematic allocation of a premium or discount relative to the face value of a fixed-income security over the life of the security.

IFRS allow two alternative models for valuing property, plant, and equipment: the cost model and the revaluation model.[33] Under the cost model, the depreciable amount of that asset (cost less residual value) is allocated on a systematic basis over the remaining useful life of the asset. Under the cost model, the asset is reported at its cost less any accumulated depreciation. Under the revaluation model, the asset is reported at its fair value. The revaluation model is not permitted under U.S. GAAP. Here, we will focus only on the cost model. There are two other differences between IFRS and U.S. GAAP to note: IFRS require each component of an asset to be depreciated separately and U.S. GAAP do not require component depreciation; and IFRS require an annual review of residual value and useful life, and U.S. GAAP do not explicitly require such a review.

The method used to compute depreciation should reflect the pattern over which the economic benefits of the asset are expected to be consumed. IFRS do not prescribe a particular method for computing depreciation but note that several methods are commonly used, such as the straight-line method, diminishing balance method (accelerated depreciation), and the units of production method (depreciation varies depending upon production or usage).

The **straight-line method** allocates evenly the cost of long-lived assets less estimated residual value over the estimated useful life of an asset. (The term "straight line" derives from the fact that the annual depreciation expense, if represented as a line graph over time, would be a straight line. In addition, a plot of the cost of the asset minus the cumulative amount of annual depreciation expense, if represented as a line graph over time, would be a straight line with a negative downward slope.) Calculating depreciation and amortisation requires two significant estimates: the estimated useful life of an asset and the estimated residual value (also known as "salvage value") of an asset. Under IFRS, the residual value is the amount that the company expects to receive upon sale of the asset at the end of its useful life. Example 9 assumes that an item of equipment is depreciated using the straight-line method and illustrates how

---

32 Intangible assets with indefinite life are not amortised. Instead, they are reviewed each period as to the reasonableness of continuing to assume an indefinite useful life and are tested at least annually for impairment (i.e., if the recoverable or fair value of an intangible asset is materially lower than its value in the company's books, the value of the asset is considered to be impaired and its value must be decreased). IAS 38, *Intangible Assets* and FASB ASC Topic 350 [Intangibles–Goodwill and Other].
33 IAS No. 16, *Property, Plant, and Equipment.*

the annual depreciation expense varies under different estimates of the useful life and estimated residual value of an asset. As shown, annual depreciation expense is sensitive to both the estimated useful life and to the estimated residual value.

EXAMPLE 9

Sensitivity of Annual Depreciation Expense to Varying Estimates of Useful Life and Residual Value

Using the straight-line method of depreciation, annual depreciation expense is calculated as:

$$\frac{\text{Cost} - \text{Residual value}}{\text{Estimated useful life}}$$

Assume the cost of an asset is $10,000. If, for example, the residual value of the asset is estimated to be $0 and its useful life is estimated to be 5 years, the annual depreciation expense under the straight-line method would be ($10,000 − $0)/5 years = $2,000. In contrast, holding the estimated useful life of the asset constant at 5 years but increasing the estimated residual value of the asset to $4,000 would result in annual depreciation expense of only $1,200 [calculated as ($10,000 − $4,000)/5 years]. Alternatively, holding the estimated residual value at $0 but increasing the estimated useful life of the asset to 10 years would result in annual depreciation expense of only $1,000 [calculated as ($10,000 − $0)/10 years]. Exhibit 8 shows annual depreciation expense for various combinations of estimated useful life and residual value.

Exhibit 8	Annual Depreciation Expense (in Dollars)					
Estimated Useful Life (Years)			**Estimated Residual Value**			
	0	1,000	2,000	3,000	4,000	5,000
2	5,000	4,500	4,000	3,500	3,000	2,500
4	2,500	2,250	2,000	1,750	1,500	1,250
5	2,000	1,800	1,600	1,400	1,200	1,000
8	1,250	1,125	1,000	875	750	625
10	1,000	900	800	700	600	500

Generally, alternatives to the straight-line method of depreciation are called **accelerated methods** of depreciation because they accelerate (i.e., speed up) the timing of depreciation. Accelerated depreciation methods allocate a greater proportion of the cost to the early years of an asset's useful life. These methods are appropriate if the plant or equipment is expected to be used up faster in the early years (e.g., an automobile). A commonly used accelerated method is the **diminishing balance method**, (also known as the declining balance method). The diminishing balance method is demonstrated in Example 10.

EXAMPLE 10

An Illustration of Diminishing Balance Depreciation

Assume the cost of computer equipment was $11,000, the estimated residual value is $1,000, and the estimated useful life is five years. Under the diminishing or declining balance method, the first step is to determine the straight-line rate, the rate at which the asset would be depreciated under the straight-line method. This rate is measured as 100 percent divided by the useful life or 20 percent for a five-year useful life. Under the straight-line method, 1/5 or 20 percent of the depreciable cost of the asset (here, $11,000 – $1,000 = $10,000) would be expensed each year for five years: The depreciation expense would be $2,000 per year.

The next step is to determine an acceleration factor that approximates the pattern of the asset's wear. Common acceleration factors are 150 percent and 200 percent. The latter is known as **double declining balance depreciation** because it depreciates the asset at double the straight-line rate. Using the 200 percent acceleration factor, the diminishing balance rate would be 40 percent (20 percent × 2.0). This rate is then applied to the remaining undepreciated balance of the asset each period (known as the **net book value**).

At the beginning of the first year, the net book value is $11,000. Depreciation expense for the first full year of use of the asset would be 40 percent of $11,000, or $4,400. Under this method, the residual value, if any, is generally not used in the computation of the depreciation each period (the 40 percent is applied to $11,000 rather than to $11,000 minus residual value). However, the company will stop taking depreciation when the salvage value is reached.

At the beginning of Year 2, the net book value is measured as

Asset cost	$11,000
Less: Accumulated depreciation	(4,400)
Net book value	$ 6,600

For the second full year, depreciation expense would be $6,600 × 40 percent, or $2,640. At the end of the second year (i.e., beginning of the third year), a total of $7,040 ($4,400 + $2,640) of depreciation would have been recorded. So, the remaining net book value at the beginning of the third year would be

Asset cost	$11,000
Less: Accumulated depreciation	(7,040)
Net book value	$ 3,960

For the third full year, depreciation would be $3,960 × 40 percent, or $1,584. At the end of the third year, a total of $8,624 ($4,400 + $2,640 + $1,584) of depreciation would have been recorded. So, the remaining net book value at the beginning of the fourth year would be

Asset cost	$11,000
Less: Accumulated depreciation	(8,624)
Net book value	$ 2,376

For the fourth full year, depreciation would be $2,376 × 40 percent, or $950. At the end of the fourth year, a total of $9,574 ($4,400 + $2,640 + $1,584 + $950) of depreciation would have been recorded. So, the remaining net book value at the beginning of the fifth year would be

Asset cost	$11,000
Less: Accumulated depreciation	(9,574)
Net book value	$ 1,426

For the fifth year, if deprecation were determined as in previous years, it would amount to $570 ($1,426 × 40 percent). However, this would result in a remaining net book value of the asset below its estimated residual value of $1,000. So, instead, only $426 would be depreciated, leaving a $1,000 net book value at the end of the fifth year.

Asset cost	$11,000
Less: Accumulated depreciation	(10,000)
Net book value	$ 1,000

Companies often use a zero or small residual value, which creates problems for diminishing balance depreciation because the asset never fully depreciates. In order to fully depreciate the asset over the initially estimated useful life when a zero or small residual value is assumed, companies often adopt a depreciation policy that combines the diminishing balance and straight-line methods. An example would be a deprecation policy of using double-declining balance depreciation and switching to the straight-line method halfway through the useful life.

Under accelerated depreciation methods, there is a higher depreciation expense in early years relative to the straight-line method. This results in higher expenses and lower net income in the early depreciation years. In later years, there is a reversal with accelerated depreciation expense lower than straight-line depreciation. Accelerated depreciation is sometimes referred to as a conservative accounting choice because it results in lower net income in the early years of asset use.

For those intangible assets that must be amortised (those with an identifiable useful life), the process is the same as for depreciation; only the name of the expense is different. IFRS state that if a pattern cannot be determined over the useful life, then the straight-line method should be used.[34] In most cases under IFRS and U.S. GAAP, amortisable intangible assets are amortised using the straight-line method with no residual value. **Goodwill**[35] and intangible assets with indefinite life are not amortised. Instead, they are tested at least annually for impairment (i.e., if the current value of an intangible asset or goodwill is materially lower than its value in the company's books, the value of the asset is considered to be impaired and its value in the company's books must be decreased).

In summary, to calculate depreciation and amortisation, a company must choose a method, estimate the asset's useful life, and estimate residual value. Clearly, different choices have a differing effect on depreciation or amortisation expense and, therefore, on reported net income.

---

34 IAS 38, *Intangible Assets.*
35 Goodwill is recorded in acquisitions and is the amount by which the price to purchase an entity exceeds the amount of net identifiable assets acquired (the total amount of identifiable assets acquired less liabilities assumed).

4.3 Implications for Financial Analysis

A company's estimates for doubtful accounts and/or for warranty expenses can affect its reported net income. Similarly, a company's choice of depreciation or amortisation method, estimates of assets' useful lives, and estimates of assets' residual values can affect reported net income. These are only a few of the choices and estimates that affect a company's reported net income.

As with revenue recognition policies, a company's choice of expense recognition can be characterized by its relative conservatism. A policy that results in recognition of expenses later rather than sooner is considered less conservative. In addition, many items of expense require the company to make estimates that can significantly affect net income. Analysis of a company's financial statements, and particularly comparison of one company's financial statements with those of another, requires an understanding of differences in these estimates and their potential impact.

If, for example, a company shows a significant year-to-year change in its estimates of uncollectible accounts as a percentage of sales, warranty expenses as a percentage of sales, or estimated useful lives of assets, the analyst should seek to understand the underlying reasons. Do the changes reflect a change in business operations (e.g., lower estimated warranty expenses reflecting recent experience of fewer warranty claims because of improved product quality)? Or are the changes seemingly unrelated to changes in business operations and thus possibly a signal that a company is manipulating estimates in order to achieve a particular effect on its reported net income?

As another example, if two companies in the same industry have dramatically different estimates for uncollectible accounts as a percentage of their sales, warranty expenses as a percentage of sales, or estimated useful lives as a percentage of assets, it is important to understand the underlying reasons. Are the differences consistent with differences in the two companies' business operations (e.g., lower uncollectible accounts for one company reflecting a different, more creditworthy customer base or possibly stricter credit policies)? Another difference consistent with differences in business operations would be a difference in estimated useful lives of assets if one of the companies employs newer equipment. Or, alternatively, are the differences seemingly inconsistent with differences in the two companies' business operations, possibly signaling that a company is manipulating estimates?

Information about a company's accounting policies and significant estimates are described in the notes to the financial statements and in the management discussion and analysis section of a company's annual report.

When possible, the monetary effect of differences in expense recognition policies and estimates can facilitate more meaningful comparisons with a single company's historical performance or across a number of companies. An analyst can use the monetary effect to adjust the reported expenses so that they are on a comparable basis.

Even when the monetary effects of differences in policies and estimates cannot be calculated, it is generally possible to characterize the relative conservatism of the policies and estimates and, therefore, to qualitatively assess how such differences might affect reported expenses and thus financial ratios.

5   NON-RECURRING ITEMS AND NON-OPERATING ITEMS

From a company's income statements, we can see its earnings from last year and in the previous year. Looking forward, the question is: What will the company earn next year and in the years after?

To assess a company's future earnings, it is helpful to separate those prior years' items of income and expense that are likely to continue in the future from those items that are less likely to continue.[36] Some items from prior years are clearly not expected to continue in the future periods and are separately disclosed on a company's income statement. This is consistent with "An entity shall present additional line items, headings, and subtotals … when such presentation is relevant to an understanding of the entity's financial performance."[37] IFRS describe considerations that enter into the decision to present information other than that explicitly specified by a standard. U.S. GAAP specify some of the items that should be reported separately. Two such items are 1) discontinued operations, and 2) extraordinary items (the latter category is not permitted under IFRS). These two items, if applicable, must be reported separately from continuing operations under U.S. GAAP.[38] For other items on a company's income statement, such as unusual items, accounting changes, and non-operating income, the likelihood of their continuing in the future is somewhat less clear and requires the analyst to make some judgments.

5.1 Discontinued Operations

When a company disposes of or establishes a plan to dispose of one of its component operations and will have no further involvement in the operation, the income statement reports separately the effect of this disposal as a "discontinued" operation under both IFRS and U.S. GAAP. Financial standards provide various criteria for reporting the effect separately, which are generally that the discontinued component must be separable both physically and operationally.[39]

Because the discontinued operation will no longer provide earnings (or cash flow) to the company, an analyst can eliminate discontinued operations in formulating expectations about a company's future financial performance.

In Exhibit 2, Kraft reported earnings and gains from discontinued operations of $1,045 million in 2008 and $232 million in 2007. In Note 2 of its financial statements, Kraft explains that it split off its Post Cereals business. The earnings and gains from discontinued operations of $1,045 million in 2008 and $232 million in 2007 refer to the amount of earnings of the cereal business in each of those years, up to the date it was split off.

5.2 Extraordinary Items

IFRS prohibit classification of any income or expense items as being "extraordinary."[40] Under U.S. GAAP, an extraordinary item is one that is both unusual in nature and infrequent in occurrence. Extraordinary items are presented separately on the income statement and allow a reader of the statements to see that these items are not part of a company's operating activities and are not expected to occur on an ongoing basis. Extraordinary items are shown net of tax and appear on the income statement below discontinued operations. An example of an extraordinary item is provided in Exhibit 9.

---

36 In business writing, items expected to continue in the future are often described as "persistent" or "permanent," whereas those not expected to continue are described as "transitory."
37 IAS No. 1, *Presentation of Financial Statements*, paragraph 85.
38 These requirements apply to material amounts.
39 IFRS No. 5, *Non-Current Assets Held for Sale and Discontinued Operations*, paragraphs 31–33.
40 IAS No. 1, *Presentation of Financial Statements*, paragraph 87.

Exhibit 9	Extraordinary Gain on Debt Forgiveness

In its annual report, ForgeHouse, Inc. (OTCBB: FOHE) made the following disclosure describing an extraordinary gain on debt forgiveness:

> On September 30, 2009, the Company entered into a Debt Forgiveness Agreement with Insurance Medical Group Limited (f/k/a After All Limited), Bryan Irving, and Ian Morl, pursuant to which $785,000 (plus accrued and unpaid interest and any penalties of $80,141) of the Company's outstanding obligations in favor of Arngrove Group Holdings were forgiven and all $200,000 (plus accrued and unpaid interest and any penalties of $23,418) of the Company's outstanding obligations in favor of After All Group, Limited, was forgiven. Gain on these two debt restructurings was a gross of $1,088,559 for the year ended December 31, 2009.
>
> In December 2009, the Company entered into agreements with two of its vendors to reduce the amounts owed to the vendors in exchange for upfront payments. Gain on the restructure of amounts owed to the two vendors was $244,041.
>
> These amounts are presented in the statement of operations net of income taxes of $453,084 for a net extraordinary gain on debt restructuring of $879,516.

Source: ForgeHouse, Inc. 10-K for fiscal year ended 31 December 2009, filed 14 May 2010: Note 6.

Companies apply judgment to determine whether an item is extraordinary based on guidance from accounting standards.[41] Judgment on whether an item is unusual in nature requires consideration of the company's environment, including its industry and geography. Determining whether an item is infrequent in occurrence is based on expectations of whether it will occur again in the near future. Standard setters offer specific guidance in some cases. For example, following Hurricanes Katrina and Rita in 2005, the American Institute of Certified Public Accountants issued Technical Practice Aid 5400.05, which states (the material in square brackets has been added): "A natural disaster [such as a hurricane, tornado, fire, or earthquake] of a type that is reasonably expected to re-occur would not meet both conditions [for classification as an extraordinary item]."

Given the requirements for classification of an item as extraordinary—unusual and infrequent—an analyst can generally eliminate extraordinary items from expectations about a company's future financial performance unless there is some indication that such an extraordinary item may reoccur.

5.3 Unusual or Infrequent Items

IFRS require that items of income or expense that are material and/or relevant to the understanding of the entity's financial performance should be disclosed separately. Unusual or infrequent items are likely to meet these criteria. Under U.S. GAAP, which allow items to be shown as extraordinary, items that are unusual or infrequent—but not both—cannot be shown as extraordinary. Items that are unusual or infrequent are shown as part of a company's continuing operations. For example, restructuring

---

[41] FASB ASC Section 225–20–45 [Income Statement-Extraordinary and Unusual Items–Other Presentation Matters].

charges, such as costs to close plants and employee termination costs, are considered part of a company's ordinary activities. As another example, gains and losses arising when a company sells an asset or part of a business, for more or less than its carrying value, are also disclosed separately on the income statement. These are not considered extraordinary under U.S. GAAP because such sales are considered ordinary business activities.

Highlighting the unusual or infrequent nature of these items assists an analyst in judging the likelihood that such items will reoccur. This meets the IFRS criteria of disclosing items that are relevant to the understanding of an entity's financial performance. Exhibit 10 shows such disclosure.

Exhibit 10	Highlighting Infrequent Nature of Items Excerpt from Roche Group Consolidated Income Statement (in millions of CHF, Year ended 31 December 2009)

[portions omitted]	
Operating profit before exceptional items	15,012
Major legal cases	(320)
Changes in Group organisation	(2,415)
Operating profit	12,277
[portions omitted]	

In Exhibit 10, Roche Group (SWX: ROG), a Swiss healthcare company, shows operating profit before and after exceptional items. The exceptional items relate to major legal cases and changes in the organization. The company's notes explain both items further. The costs for changes in the organization relate to Roche's acquisition of Genentech and major changes to certain manufacturing and commercial centers. Generally, in forecasting future operations, an analyst would assess whether the items reported are likely to reoccur and also possible implications for future earnings. It is generally not advisable simply to ignore all unusual items.

5.4 Changes in Accounting Policies

At times, standard setters issue new standards that require companies to change accounting policies. Companies may be permitted to adopt the standards prospectively (in the future) or retrospectively (restate financial statements as though the standard existed in the past). In other cases, changes in accounting policies (e.g., from one acceptable inventory costing method to another) are made for other reasons, such as providing a better reflection of the company's performance. Changes in accounting policies are reported through retrospective application[42] unless it is impractical to do so.

Retrospective application means that the financial statements for all fiscal years shown in a company's financial report are presented as if the newly adopted accounting principle had been used throughout the entire period. Notes to the financial statements describe the change and explain the justification for the change. Because changes in accounting principles are retrospectively applied, the financial statements

---

42 IAS No. 8, *Accounting Policies, Changes in Accounting Estimates and Errors,* and FASB ASC Topic 250 [Accounting Changes and Error Corrections].

that appear within a financial report are comparable. So, if a company's annual report for 2009 includes its financial statements for fiscal years 2007, 2008, and 2009, all of these statements will be comparable.

Example 11 presents an excerpt from the 25 January 2010 10-K/A of Apple Inc. (NasdaqGS: AAPL). Apple amended its previously filed 10-K to reflect the company's retrospective adoption of a new FASB accounting standard related to revenue recognition for multi-deliverables. An example of a multi-deliverable is the sale of an iPhone with the right to receive future upgrades. The change described in Example 11 brings U.S. GAAP closer to IFRS although differences remain. For example, IFRS do not provide detailed guidance and instead require that revenue should be allocated to separately identifiable components if doing so reflects the substance of the transaction. In contrast, U.S. GAAP provide details about how the separation of revenue should be done and how the revenue should be allocated to each component.

EXAMPLE 11

Revenue Recognition: A Change in Accounting Principle

Apple's amended 10-K for the year ended 26 September 2009 explains how a change in accounting standards (the company refers to these as accounting principles) affects its financial statements. The following excerpt (emphasis added) is from the explanatory note included in the amendment.

> Under the historical accounting principles, the Company was required to account for sales of both iPhone and Apple TV using subscription accounting because the Company indicated it might from time-to-time provide future unspecified software upgrades and features for those products free of charge. Under **subscription accounting**, revenue and associated product cost of sales for iPhone and Apple TV were deferred at the time of sale and recognized on a straight-line basis over each product's estimated economic life. This resulted in the deferral of significant amounts of revenue and cost of sales related to iPhone and Apple TV. Costs incurred by the Company for engineering, sales, marketing and warranty were expensed as incurred. As of September 26, 2009, based on the historical accounting principles, total accumulated deferred revenue and deferred costs associated with past iPhone and Apple TV sales were $12.1 billion and $5.2 billion, respectively.
>
> The **new accounting principles generally require the Company to account for the sale of both iPhone and Apple TV as two deliverables**. The first deliverable is the hardware and software delivered at the time of sale, and the second deliverable is the right included with the purchase of iPhone and Apple TV to receive on a when-and-if-available basis future unspecified software upgrades and features relating to the product's software. **The new accounting principles result in the recognition of substantially all of the revenue and product costs from sales of iPhone and Apple TV at the time of sale**. Additionally, the Company is required to estimate a standalone selling price for the unspecified software upgrade right included with the sale of iPhone and Apple TV and recognizes that amount ratably over the 24-month estimated life of the related hardware device. For all periods presented, the Company's estimated selling price for the software upgrade right included with each iPhone and Apple TV sold is $25 and $10, respectively. The adoption of the new accounting principles increased the Company's net sales by $6.4 billion,

$5.0 billion and $572 million for 2009, 2008 and 2007, respectively. As of September 26, 2009, the revised total accumulated deferred revenue associated with iPhone and Apple TV sales to date was $483 million; revised accumulated deferred costs for such sales were zero.

Source: Apple Inc. 10-K/A for the year ended 26 September 2009, as filed with the SEC on 25 January 2010. Emphasis added.

1 Under the historical accounting principle, how would the revenue from a sale of an iPhone be reflected in Apple's financial statements?

2 How and why did adoption of the new accounting principles affect Apple's revenues in 2009?

Solution to 1:

Under the historical accounting principle (standard), a sale of an iPhone was treated as a subscription sale and revenue was not recognized at the time of sale. Rather, the sale would result in a liability entitled "deferred revenue." In subsequent periods, the company would recognize as revenue a portion of the revenue from that sale and reduce the amount of deferred revenue by the same amount. Disclosures about deferred revenue can be helpful to an analyst in developing expectations about future revenues.

Solution to 2:

Adoption of the new accounting principles (standards) increased the company's 2009 net sales (revenue) by $6.4 billion. The reason for the increase is that the new standard allowed the company to separate the revenue from the iPhone into two separate components and to report revenue from them separately.

In years prior to 2005, under both IFRS and U.S. GAAP, the cumulative effect of changes in accounting policies was typically shown at the bottom of the income statement in the year of change instead of using retrospective application. It is possible that future accounting standards may occasionally require a company to report the change differently than retrospective application. Note disclosures are required to explain how the transition from the old standard to the new one is handled. During the period when companies make the transition from the old standard to the new, an analyst can examine disclosures to ensure comparability across companies.

In contrast to changes in accounting policies (such as whether to expense the cost of employee stock options), companies sometimes make *changes in accounting estimates* (such as the useful life of a depreciable asset). Changes in accounting estimates are handled prospectively, with the change affecting the financial statements for the period of change and future periods. No adjustments are made to prior statements, and the adjustment is not shown on the face of the income statement. Significant changes should be disclosed in the notes.

Another possible adjustment is a *correction of an error for a prior period* (e.g., in financial statements issued for an earlier year). This cannot be handled by simply adjusting the current period income statement. Correction of an error for a prior period is handled by restating the financial statements (including the balance sheet, statement of owners' equity, and cash flow statement) for the prior periods presented in the current financial statements.[43] Note disclosures are required regarding the error. These disclosures should be examined carefully because they may reveal weaknesses in the company's accounting systems and financial controls.

5.5 Non-Operating Items

Non-operating items are typically reported separately from operating income because they are material and/or relevant to the understanding of the entity's financial performance. Under IFRS, there is no definition of operating activities, and companies that choose to report operating income or the results of operating activities should ensure that these represent activities that are normally regarded as operating. Under U.S. GAAP, operating activities generally involve producing and delivering goods and providing services and include all transactions and other events that are not defined as investing or financing activities.[44] For example, if a non-financial service company invests in equity or debt securities issued by another company, any interest, dividends, or profits from sales of these securities will be shown as non-operating income. In general, for non-financial services companies,[45] non-operating income that is disclosed separately on the income statement (or in the notes) includes amounts earned through investing activities.

Among non-operating items on the income statement (or accompanying notes), non-financial service companies also disclose the interest expense on their debt securities, including amortisation of any discount or premium. The amount of interest expense is related to the amount of a company's borrowings and is generally described in the notes to the financial statements. For financial service companies, interest income and expense are likely components of operating activities. (Note that the characterization of interest and dividends as non-operating items on the income statement is not necessarily consistent with the classification on the statement of cash flows. Specifically, under IFRS, interest and dividends received can be shown either as operating or as investing on the statement of cash flows, while under U.S. GAAP interest and dividends received are shown as operating cash flows. Under IFRS, interest and dividends paid can be shown either as operating or as financing on the statement of cash flows, while under U.S. GAAP, interest paid is shown as operating and dividends paid are shown as financing.)

In practice, investing and financing activities may be disclosed on a net basis, with the components disclosed separately in the notes. In its income statement for 2009 (Exhibit 1), Groupe Danone, for example, disclosed net interest expense (cost of net debt) of €264 million. The net amount is the €340 million of interest expense minus €76 million interest revenue. The financial statement notes (not shown) provide further disclosure about the expense.

For purposes of assessing a company's future performance, the amount of financing expense will depend on the company's financing policy (target capital structure) and borrowing costs. The amount of investing income will depend on the purpose and success of investing activities. For a non-financial company, a significant amount of financial income would typically warrant further exploration. What are the reasons underlying the company's investments in the securities of other companies? Is the company simply investing excess cash in short-term securities to generate income higher than cash deposits, or is the company purchasing securities issued by other companies for strategic reasons, such as access to raw material supply or research?

---

43 Ibid.
44 FASB ASC *Master Glossary.*
45 Examples of financial services companies are insurance companies, banks, brokers, dealers, and investment companies.

# EARNINGS PER SHARE											**6**

One metric of particular importance to an equity investor is earnings per share (EPS). EPS is an input into ratios such as the price/earnings ratio. Additionally, each shareholder in a company owns a different number of shares. IFRS require the presentation of EPS on the face of the income statement for net profit or loss (net income) and profit or loss (income) from continuing operations.[46] Similar presentation is required under U.S. GAAP.[47] This section outlines the calculations for EPS and explains how the calculation differs for a simple versus complex capital structure.

6.1 Simple versus Complex Capital Structure

A company's capital is composed of its equity and debt. Some types of equity have preference over others, and some debt (and other instruments) may be converted into equity. Under IFRS, the type of equity for which EPS is presented is referred to as ordinary. **Ordinary shares** are those equity shares that are subordinate to all other types of equity. The ordinary shareholders are basically the owners of the company—the equity holders who are paid last in a liquidation of the company and who benefit the most when the company does well. Under U.S. GAAP, this ordinary equity is referred to as **common stock** or **common shares**, reflecting U.S. language usage. The terms "ordinary shares," "common stock," and "common shares" are used interchangeably in the following discussion.

When a company has issued any financial instruments that are potentially convertible into common stock, it is said to have a complex capital structure. Examples of financial instruments that are potentially convertible into common stock include convertible bonds, convertible preferred stock, employee stock options, and warrants.[48] If a company's capital structure does not include such potentially convertible financial instruments, it is said to have a simple capital structure.

The distinction between simple versus complex capital structure is relevant to the calculation of EPS because financial instruments that are potentially convertible into common stock could, as a result of conversion or exercise, potentially dilute (i.e., decrease) EPS. Information about such a potential dilution is valuable to a company's current and potential shareholders; therefore, accounting standards require companies to disclose what their EPS would be if all dilutive financial instruments were converted into common stock. The EPS that would result if all dilutive financial instruments were converted is called **diluted EPS**. In contrast, **basic EPS** is calculated using the reported earnings available to common shareholders of the parent company and the weighted average number of shares outstanding.

Companies are required to report both basic and diluted EPS. For example, Danone reported basic EPS ("before dilution") and diluted EPS ("after dilution") of €2.57 for 2009, somewhat lower than 2008. Kraft reported basic EPS of $2.04 and diluted EPS of $2.03 for 2009, much higher than basic and diluted EPS (from continuing operations) of $1.22 and $1.21 for 2008. (The EPS information appears at the bottom of Danone's and Kraft's income statements.) An analyst would try to determine the causes underlying the changes in EPS, a topic we will address following an explanation of the calculations of both basic and diluted EPS.

---

46 IAS No. 33, *Earnings Per Share.*
47 FASB ASC Topic 260 [Earnings Per Share].
48 A warrant is a call option typically attached to securities issued by a company, such as bonds. A warrant gives the holder the right to acquire the company's stock from the company at a specified price within a specified time period. IFRS and U.S. GAAP standards regarding earnings per share apply equally to call options, warrants, and equivalent instruments.

6.2 Basic EPS

Basic EPS is the amount of income available to common shareholders divided by the weighted average number of common shares outstanding over a period. The amount of income available to common shareholders is the amount of net income remaining after preferred dividends (if any) have been paid. Thus, the formula to calculate basic EPS is:

$$\text{Basic EPS} = \frac{\text{Net income} - \text{Preferred dividends}}{\text{Weighted average number of shares outstanding}} \tag{1}$$

The weighted average number of shares outstanding is a time weighting of common shares outstanding. For example, assume a company began the year with 2,000,000 common shares outstanding and repurchased 100,000 common shares on 1 July. The weighted average number of common shares outstanding would be the sum of 2,000,000 shares × 1/2 year + 1,900,000 shares × 1/2 year, or 1,950,000 shares. So the company would use 1,950,000 shares as the weighted average number of shares in calculating its basic EPS.

If the number of shares of common stock increases as a result of a stock dividend or a stock split, the EPS calculation reflects the change retroactively to the beginning of the period.

Examples 12, 13, and 14 illustrate the computation of basic EPS.

EXAMPLE 12

A Basic EPS Calculation (1)

For the year ended 31 December 2009, Shopalot Company had net income of $1,950,000. The company had 1,500,000 shares of common stock outstanding, no preferred stock, and no convertible financial instruments. What is Shopalot's basic EPS?

Solution:

Shopalot's basic EPS is $1.30 ($1,950,000 divided by 1,500,000 shares).

EXAMPLE 13

A Basic EPS Calculation (2)

For the year ended 31 December 2009, Angler Products had net income of $2,500,000. The company declared and paid $200,000 of dividends on preferred stock. The company also had the following common stock share information:

Shares outstanding on 1 January 2009	1,000,000
Shares issued on 1 April 2009	200,000
Shares repurchased (treasury shares) on 1 October 2009	(100,000)
Shares outstanding on 31 December 2009	1,100,000

1   What is the company's weighted average number of shares outstanding?

2   What is the company's basic EPS?

Solution to 1:

The weighted average number of shares outstanding is determined by the length of time each quantity of shares was outstanding:

1,000,000 × (3 months/12 months) =	250,000
1,200,000 × (6 months/12 months) =	600,000
1,100,000 × (3 months/12 months) =	275,000
Weighted average number of shares outstanding	1,125,000

Solution to 2:

Basic EPS = (Net income − Preferred dividends)/Weighted average number of shares = ($2,500,000 − $200,000)/1,125,000 = $2.04

EXAMPLE 14

A Basic EPS Calculation (3)

Assume the same facts as in Example 13 except that on 1 December 2009, a previously declared 2 for 1 stock split took effect. Each shareholder of record receives two shares in exchange for each current share that he or she owns. What is the company's basic EPS?

Solution:

For EPS calculation purposes, a stock split is treated as if it occurred at the beginning of the period. The weighted average number of shares would, therefore, be 2,250,000, and the basic EPS would be $1.02 [= ($2,500,000 − $200,000)/2,250,000].

6.3 Diluted EPS

If a company has a simple capital structure (in other words, one that includes no potentially dilutive financial instruments), then its basic EPS is equal to its diluted EPS. However, if a company has potentially dilutive financial instruments, its diluted EPS may differ from its basic EPS. Diluted EPS, by definition, is always equal to or less than basic EPS. The sections below describe the effects of three types of potentially dilutive financial instruments on diluted EPS: convertible preferred, convertible debt, and employee stock options. The final section explains why not all potentially dilutive financial instruments actually result in a difference between basic and diluted EPS.

6.3.1 *Diluted EPS When a Company Has Convertible Preferred Stock Outstanding*

When a company has convertible preferred stock outstanding, diluted EPS is calculated using the **if-converted method**. The if-converted method is based on what EPS would have been if the convertible preferred securities had been converted at the beginning of the period. In other words, the method calculates what the effect would have been if the convertible preferred shares converted at the beginning of the period. If the convertible shares had been converted, there would be two effects. First, the convertible preferred securities would no longer be outstanding; instead, additional common stock would be outstanding. Thus, under the if-converted method, the weighted average number of shares outstanding would be higher than in the basic

EPS calculation. Second, if such a conversion had taken place, the company would not have paid preferred dividends. Thus, under the if-converted method, the net income available to common shareholders would be higher than in the basic EPS calculation.

Diluted EPS using the if-converted method for convertible preferred stock is equal to net income divided by the weighted average number of shares outstanding from the basic EPS calculation plus the additional shares of common stock that would be issued upon conversion of the preferred. Thus, the formula to calculate diluted EPS using the if-converted method for preferred stock is:

$$\text{Diluted EPS} = \frac{(\text{Net income})}{\begin{pmatrix}\text{Weighted average number of shares} \\ \text{outstanding} + \text{New common shares that} \\ \text{would have been issued at conversion}\end{pmatrix}} \qquad (2)$$

A diluted EPS calculation using the if-converted method for preferred stock is provided in Example 15.

EXAMPLE 15

A Diluted EPS Calculation Using the If-Converted Method for Preferred Stock

For the year ended 31 December 2009, Bright-Warm Utility Company had net income of $1,750,000. The company had an average of 500,000 shares of common stock outstanding, 20,000 shares of convertible preferred, and no other potentially dilutive securities. Each share of preferred pays a dividend of $10 per share, and each is convertible into five shares of the company's common stock. Calculate the company's basic and diluted EPS.

Solution:

If the 20,000 shares of convertible preferred had each converted into 5 shares of the company's common stock, the company would have had an additional 100,000 shares of common stock (5 shares of common for each of the 20,000 shares of preferred). If the conversion had taken place, the company would not have paid preferred dividends of $200,000 ($10 per share for each of the 20,000 shares of preferred). As shown in Exhibit 11, the company's basic EPS was $3.10 and its diluted EPS was $2.92.

Exhibit 11	Calculation of Diluted EPS for Bright-Warm Utility Company Using the If-Converted Method: Case of Preferred Stock

	Basic EPS	Diluted EPS Using If-Converted Method
Net income	$1,750,000	$1,750,000
Preferred dividend	−200,000	0
Numerator	$1,550,000	$1,750,000
Weighted average number of shares outstanding	500,000	500,000
Additional shares issued if preferred converted	0	100,000
Denominator	500,000	600,000

	Basic EPS	Diluted EPS Using If-Converted Method
Exhibit 11 **(Continued)**		
EPS	$3.10	$2.92

6.3.2 Diluted EPS When a Company Has Convertible Debt Outstanding

When a company has convertible debt outstanding, the diluted EPS calculation also uses the if-converted method. Diluted EPS is calculated as if the convertible debt had been converted at the beginning of the period. If the convertible debt had been converted, the debt securities would no longer be outstanding; instead, additional shares of common stock would be outstanding. Also, if such a conversion had taken place, the company would not have paid interest on the convertible debt, so the net income available to common shareholders would increase by the after-tax amount of interest expense on the debt converted.

Thus, the formula to calculate diluted EPS using the if-converted method for convertible debt is:

$$\text{Diluted EPS} = \frac{\left(\begin{array}{c}\text{Net income} + \text{After-tax interest on} \\ \text{convertible debt} - \text{Preferred dividends}\end{array}\right)}{\left(\begin{array}{c}\text{Weighted average number of shares} \\ \text{outstanding} + \text{Additional common} \\ \text{shares that would have been} \\ \text{issued at conversion}\end{array}\right)} \qquad (3)$$

A diluted EPS calculation using the if-converted method for convertible debt is provided in Example 16.

EXAMPLE 16

A Diluted EPS Calculation Using the If-Converted Method for Convertible Debt

Oppnox Company reported net income of $750,000 for the year ended 31 December 2009. The company had a weighted average of 690,000 shares of common stock outstanding. In addition, the company has only one potentially dilutive security: $50,000 of 6 percent convertible bonds, convertible into a total of 10,000 shares. Assuming a tax rate of 30 percent, calculate Oppnox's basic and diluted EPS.

Solution:

If the debt securities had been converted, the debt securities would no longer be outstanding and instead, an additional 10,000 shares of common stock would be outstanding. Also, if the debt securities had been converted, the company would not have paid interest of $3,000 on the convertible debt, so net income available to common shareholders would have increased by $2,100 [= $3,000(1 − 0.30)] on an after-tax basis. Exhibit 12 illustrates the calculation of diluted EPS using the if-converted method for convertible debt.

Exhibit 12	Calculation of Diluted EPS for Oppnox Company Using the If-Converted Method: Case of a Convertible Bond	

	Basic EPS	Diluted EPS Using If-Converted Method
Net income	$750,000	$750,000
After-tax cost of interest		2,100
Numerator	$750,000	$752,100
Weighted average number of shares outstanding	690,000	690,000
If converted	0	10,000
Denominator	690,000	700,000
EPS	**$1.09**	**$1.07**

6.3.3 *Diluted EPS When a Company Has Stock Options, Warrants, or Their Equivalents Outstanding*

When a company has stock options, warrants, or their equivalents[49] outstanding, diluted EPS is calculated as if the financial instruments had been exercised and the company had used the proceeds from exercise to repurchase as many shares of common stock as possible at the average market price of common stock during the period. The weighted average number of shares outstanding for diluted EPS is thus increased by the number of shares that would be issued upon exercise minus the number of shares that would have been purchased with the proceeds. This method is called the **treasury stock method** under U.S. GAAP because companies typically hold repurchased shares as treasury stock. The same method is used under IFRS but is not named.

For the calculation of diluted EPS using this method, the assumed exercise of these financial instruments would have the following effects:

▪ The company is assumed to receive cash upon exercise and, in exchange, to issue shares.

▪ The company is assumed to use the cash proceeds to repurchase shares at the weighted average market price during the period.

As a result of these two effects, the number of shares outstanding would increase by the incremental number of shares issued (the difference between the number of shares issued to the holders and the number of shares assumed to be repurchased by the company). For calculating diluted EPS, the incremental number of shares is weighted based upon the length of time the financial instrument was outstanding in the year. If the financial instrument was issued prior to the beginning of the year, the weighted average number of shares outstanding increases by the incremental number of shares. If the financial instruments were issued during the year, then the incremental shares are weighted by the amount of time the financial instruments were outstanding during the year.

---

49 Hereafter, options, warrants, and their equivalents will be referred to simply as "options" because the accounting treatment for EPS calculations is interchangeable for these instruments under IFRS and U.S. GAAP.

The assumed exercise of these financial instruments would not affect net income. For calculating EPS, therefore, no change is made to the numerator. The formula to calculate diluted EPS using the treasury stock method (same method as used under IFRS but not named) for options is:

$$\text{Diluted EPS} = \frac{(\text{Net income} - \text{Preferred dividends})}{\begin{bmatrix}\text{Weighted average number of shares} \\ \text{outstanding} + (\text{New shares that would} \\ \text{have been issued at option exercise} - \\ \text{Shares that could have been purchased} \\ \text{with cash received upon exercise}) \times \\ (\text{Proportion of year during which the} \\ \text{financial instruments were outstanding})\end{bmatrix}} \quad (4)$$

A diluted EPS calculation using the treasury stock method for options is provided in Example 17.

EXAMPLE 17

A Diluted EPS Calculation Using the Treasury Stock Method for Options

Hihotech Company reported net income of $2.3 million for the year ended 30 June 2009 and had a weighted average of 800,000 common shares outstanding. At the beginning of the fiscal year, the company has outstanding 30,000 options with an exercise price of $35. No other potentially dilutive financial instruments are outstanding. Over the fiscal year, the company's market price has averaged $55 per share. Calculate the company's basic and diluted EPS.

Solution:

Using the treasury stock method, we first calculate that the company would have received $1,050,000 ($35 for each of the 30,000 options exercised) if all the options had been exercised. The options would no longer be outstanding; instead, 30,000 shares of common stock would be outstanding. Under the treasury stock method, we assume that shares would be repurchased with the cash received upon exercise of the options. At an average market price of $55 per share, the $1,050,000 proceeds from option exercise, the company could have repurchased 19,091 shares. Therefore, the incremental number of shares issued is 10,909 (calculated as 30,000 minus 19,091). For the diluted EPS calculation, no change is made to the numerator. As shown in Exhibit 13, the company's basic EPS was $2.88 and the diluted EPS was $2.84.

Exhibit 13	Calculation of Diluted EPS for Hihotech Company Using the Treasury Stock Method: Case of Stock Options	
	Basic EPS	**Diluted EPS Using Treasury Stock Method**
Net income	$2,300,000	$2,300,000
Numerator	$2,300,000	$2,300,000

(continued)

Exhibit 13	(Continued)	

	Basic EPS	Diluted EPS Using Treasury Stock Method
Weighted average number of shares outstanding	800,000	800,000
If converted	0	10,909
Denominator	800,000	810,909
EPS	**$2.88**	**$2.84**

As noted, IFRS require a similar computation but does not refer to it as the "treasury stock method." The company is required to consider that any assumed proceeds are received from the issuance of new shares at the average market price for the period. These new "inferred" shares would be disregarded in the computation of diluted EPS, but the excess of the new shares that would be issued under options contracts minus the new inferred shares would be added to the weighted average number of shares outstanding. The results are the same as the treasury stock method, as shown in Example 18.

EXAMPLE 18

Diluted EPS for Options under IFRS

Assuming the same facts as in Example 17, calculate the weighted average number of shares outstanding for diluted EPS under IFRS.

Solution:

If the options had been exercised, the company would have received $1,050,000. If this amount had been received from the issuance of new shares at the average market price of $55 per share, the company would have issued 19,091 shares. IFRS refer to the 19,091 shares the company would have issued at market prices as the inferred shares. The number of shares issued under options (30,000) minus the number of inferred shares (19,091) equals 10,909. This amount is added to the weighted average number of shares outstanding of 800,000 to get diluted shares of 810,909. Note that this is the same result as that obtained under U.S. GAAP; it is just derived in a different manner.

6.3.4 *Other Issues with Diluted EPS*

It is possible that some potentially convertible securities could be **antidilutive** (i.e., their inclusion in the computation would result in an EPS higher than the company's basic EPS). Under IFRS and U.S. GAAP, antidilutive securities are not included in the calculation of diluted EPS. Diluted EPS should reflect the maximum potential dilution from conversion or exercise of potentially dilutive financial instruments. Diluted EPS will always be less than or equal to basic EPS. Example 19 provides an illustration of an antidilutive security.

EXAMPLE 19

An Antidilutive Security

For the year ended 31 December 2009, Dim-Cool Utility Company had net income of $1,750,000. The company had an average of 500,000 shares of common stock outstanding, 20,000 shares of convertible preferred, and no other potentially dilutive securities. Each share of preferred pays a dividend of $10 per share, and each is convertible into three shares of the company's common stock. What was the company's basic and diluted EPS?

Solution:

If the 20,000 shares of convertible preferred had each converted into 3 shares of the company's common stock, the company would have had an additional 60,000 shares of common stock (3 shares of common for each of the 20,000 shares of preferred). If the conversion had taken place, the company would not have paid preferred dividends of $200,000 ($10 per share for each of the 20,000 shares of preferred). The effect of using the if-converted method would be EPS of $3.13, as shown in Exhibit 14. Because this is greater than the company's basic EPS of $3.10, the securities are said to be antidilutive and the effect of their conversion would not be included in diluted EPS. Diluted EPS would be the same as basic EPS (i.e., $3.10).

Exhibit 14	Calculation for an Antidilutive Security

	Basic EPS	Diluted EPS Using If-Converted Method	
Net income	$1,750,000	$1,750,000	
Preferred dividend	−200,000	0	
Numerator	$1,550,000	$1,750,000	
Weighted average number of shares outstanding	500,000	500,000	
If converted	0	60,000	
Denominator	500,000	560,000	
EPS	**$3.10**	**$3.13**	←Exceeds basic EPS; security is antidilutive and, therefore, **not** included. **Reported diluted EPS= $3.10**.

6.4 Changes in EPS

Having explained the calculations of both basic and diluted EPS, we return to an examination of changes in EPS. As noted above, Kraft's fully diluted EPS from continuing operations increased from $1.21 in 2008 to $2.03 in 2009. One cause of the increase in EPS is found in the notes to the financial statements (not shown). The note describing the calculation of EPS indicates that the number of weighted-average shares decreased, and another note indicates that one reason for the decrease was the company's repurchase of some of its own shares during the year. A more important cause of the increase in EPS—shown on the income statement itself—was the significant increase in earnings from continuing operations, from $1,848 million to $3,028 million. Changes in the numerator and denominator explain the changes in

EPS arithmetically. To understand the business drivers of those changes requires further research. The next section presents analytical tools that an analyst can use to highlight areas for further examination.

7   ANALYSIS OF THE INCOME STATEMENT

In this section, we apply two analytical tools to analyze the income statement: common-size analysis and income statement ratios. The objective of this analysis is to assess a company's performance over a period of time—compared with its own past performance or the performance of another company.

7.1 Common-Size Analysis of the Income Statement

Common-size analysis of the income statement can be performed by stating each line item on the income statement as a percentage of revenue.[50] Common-size statements facilitate comparison across time periods (time series analysis) and across companies (cross-sectional analysis) because the standardization of each line item removes the effect of size.

To illustrate, Panel A of Exhibit 15 presents an income statement for three hypothetical companies in the same industry. Company A and Company B, each with $10 million in sales, are larger (as measured by sales) than Company C, which has only $2 million in sales. In addition, Companies A and B both have higher operating profit: $2 million and $1.5 million, respectively, compared with Company C's operating profit of only $400,000.

How can an analyst meaningfully compare the performance of these companies? By preparing a common-size income statement, as illustrated in Panel B, an analyst can readily see that the percentages of Company C's expenses and profit relative to its sales are exactly the same as for Company A. Furthermore, although Company C's operating profit is lower than Company B's in absolute dollars, it is higher in percentage terms (20 percent for Company C compared with only 15 percent for Company B). For each $100 of sales, Company C generates $5 more operating profit than Company B. In other words, Company C is relatively more profitable than Company B based on this measure.

The common-size income statement also highlights differences in companies' strategies. Comparing the two larger companies, Company A reports significantly higher gross profit as a percentage of sales than does Company B (70 percent compared with 25 percent). Given that both companies operate in the same industry, why can Company A generate so much higher gross profit? One possible explanation is found by comparing the operating expenses of the two companies. Company A spends significantly more on research and development and on advertising than Company B. Expenditures on research and development likely result in products with superior technology. Expenditures on advertising likely result in greater brand awareness. So, based on these differences, it is likely that Company A is selling technologically superior products with a better brand image. Company B may be selling its products more cheaply (with a lower gross profit as a percentage of sales) but saving money by not investing in research and development or advertising. In practice, differences across

---

50 This format can be distinguished as "vertical common-size analysis." As the reading on financial statement analysis discusses, there is another type of common-size analysis, known as "horizontal common-size analysis," that states items in relation to a selected base year value. Unless otherwise indicated, text references to "common-size analysis" refer to vertical analysis.

companies are more subtle, but the concept is similar. An analyst, noting significant differences, would do more research and seek to understand the underlying reasons for the differences and their implications for the future performance of the companies.

Exhibit 15			

Panel A: Income Statements for Companies A, B, and C ($)			
	A	B	C
Sales	$10,000,000	$10,000,000	$2,000,000
Cost of sales	3,000,000	7,500,000	600,000
Gross profit	7,000,000	2,500,000	1,400,000
Selling, general, and administrative expenses	1,000,000	1,000,000	200,000
Research and development	2,000,000	–	400,000
Advertising	2,000,000	–	400,000
Operating profit	2,000,000	1,500,000	400,000

Panel B: Common-Size Income Statements for Companies A, B, and C (%)			
	A	B	C
Sales	100%	100%	100%
Cost of sales	30	75	30
Gross profit	70	25	70
Selling, general, and administrative expenses	10	10	10
Research and development	20	0	20
Advertising	20	0	20
Operating profit	20	15	20

Note: Each line item is expressed as a percentage of the company's sales.

For most expenses, comparison to the amount of sales is appropriate. However, in the case of taxes, it is more meaningful to compare the amount of taxes with the amount of pretax income. Using note disclosure, an analyst can then examine the causes for differences in effective tax rates. To project the companies' future net income, an analyst would project the companies' pretax income and apply an estimated effective tax rate determined in part by the historical tax rates.

Vertical common-size analysis of the income statement is particularly useful in cross-sectional analysis—comparing companies with each other for a particular time period or comparing a company with industry or sector data. The analyst could select individual peer companies for comparison, use industry data from published sources, or compile data from databases based on a selection of peer companies or broader industry data. For example, Exhibit 16 presents median common-size income statement data compiled for the components of the S&P 500 classified into the 10 S&P/MSCI Global Industrial Classification System (GICS) sectors using 2008 data. Note that when compiling aggregate data such as this, some level of aggregation is necessary and less detail may be available than from peer company financial statements. The performance of an individual company can be compared with industry or peer company data to evaluate its relative performance.

Exhibit 16	Median Common-Size Income Statement Statistics for the S&P 500 Classified by S&P/MSCI GICS Sector Data for 2008				
	Energy	**Materials**	**Industrials**	**Consumer Discretionary**	**Consumer Staples**
No. observations	40	29	59	86	40
Operating margin	20.81	10.59	12.47	8.65	13.19
Pretax margin	17.73	7.11	10.92	5.37	9.49
Profit margin	10.76	5.01	7.22	3.35	6.03
Cost of goods sold/sales	63.03	73.93	69.56	62.82	59.18
Selling, general, and administrative expenses/sales	5.21	8.91	14.70	23.78	21.79
Taxes/Pretax income	33.30	30.72	32.30	32.56	33.51

	Health Care	**Financials**	**Information Technology**	**Telecom. Services**	**Utilities**
No. observations	55	87	77	9	33
Operating margin	19.77	16.69	16.91	27.76	17.22
Pretax margin	14.13	4.43	13.19	16.35	12.80
Profit margin	9.42	4.62	9.63	10.37	8.09
Cost of goods sold/sales	40.19	71.53	42.74	36.71	72.72
Selling, general, and administrative expenses/sales	33.13	26.36	35.76	24.04	4.42
Taxes/Pretax income	24.27	25.63	25.81	36.43	32.71

Source: Based on data from Compustat.

7.2 Income Statement Ratios

One aspect of financial performance is profitability. One indicator of profitability is **net profit margin**, also known as **profit margin** and **return on sales**, which is calculated as net income divided by revenue (or sales).[51]

$$\text{Net profit margin} = \frac{\text{Net income}}{\text{Revenue}}$$

Net profit margin measures the amount of income that a company was able to generate for each dollar of revenue. A higher level of net profit margin indicates higher profitability and is thus more desirable. Net profit margin can also be found directly on the common-size income statements.

For Kraft Foods, net profit margin for 2009 was 7.5 percent (calculated as earnings from continuing operations, net of non-controlling interests, of $3,021 million, divided by net revenues of $40,386 million). To judge this ratio, some comparison is needed. Kraft's profitability can be compared with that of another company or with its own previous performance. Compared with previous years, Kraft's profitability is higher than in 2008 and roughly equivalent to 2007. In 2008, net profit margin was 6.9 percent, and in 2007, it was 7.6 percent.

---

51 In the definition of margin ratios of this type, "sales" is often used interchangeably with "revenue." "Return on sales" has also been used to refer to a class of profitability ratios having revenue in the denominator.

Another measure of profitability is the gross profit margin. Gross profit (gross margin) is calculated as revenue minus cost of goods sold, and the **gross profit margin** is calculated as the gross profit divided by revenue.

$$\text{Gross profit margin} = \frac{\text{Gross profit}}{\text{Revenue}}$$

The gross profit margin measures the amount of gross profit that a company generated for each dollar of revenue. A higher level of gross profit margin indicates higher profitability and thus is generally more desirable, although differences in gross profit margins across companies reflect differences in companies' strategies. For example, consider a company pursuing a strategy of selling a differentiated product (e.g., a product differentiated based on brand name, quality, superior technology, or patent protection). The company would likely be able to sell the differentiated product at a higher price than a similar, but undifferentiated, product and, therefore, would likely show a higher gross profit margin than a company selling an undifferentiated product. Although a company selling a differentiated product would likely show a higher gross profit margin, this may take time. In the initial stage of the strategy, the company would likely incur costs to create a differentiated product, such as advertising or research and development, which would not be reflected in the gross margin calculation.

Kraft's gross profit (shown in Exhibit 2) was $14,600 million in 2009, $13,844 million in 2008, and $12,202 million in 2007. Expressing gross profit as a percentage of net revenues, we see that the gross profit margin was 36.2 percent in 2009, 33.0 percent in 2008, and 34.0 percent in 2007. In absolute terms, Kraft's gross profit was higher in 2008 than in 2007. However Kraft's gross profit *margin* was lower in 2008.

Exhibit 17 presents a common-size income statement for Kraft, and highlights certain profitability ratios. The net profit margin and gross profit margin described above are just two of the many subtotals that can be generated from common-size income statements. Other "margins" used by analysts include the **operating profit margin** (operating income divided by revenue) and the **pretax margin** (earnings before taxes divided by revenue).

Exhibit 17	Kraft's Margins Abbreviated Common-Size Income Statement

	Year Ended 31 December					
	2009		**2008**		**2007**	
	$ millions	Percent	$ millions	Percent	$ millions	Percent
Net revenues	40,386	100.0	41,932	100.0	35,858	100.0
Cost of sales	25,786	63.8	28,088	67.0	23,656	66.0
Gross profit	14,600	**36.2** [a]	13,844	**33.0** [a]	12,202	**34.0** [a]
Marketing, administration and research costs	9,108	22.6	8,862	21.1	7,587	21.2
Asset impairment and exit costs	−64	−0.2	1,024	2.4	440	1.2
(Gains) / losses on divestitures, net	6	0.0	92	0.2	−14	0.0
Amortisation of intangibles	26	0.1	23	0.1	13	0.0
Operating income	5,524	**13.7** [b]	3,843	**9.2** [b]	4,176	**11.6** [b]
Interest and other expense, net	1,237	3.1	1,240	3.0	604	1.7
Earnings from continuing operations before income taxes	4,287	**10.6** [c]	2,603	**6.2** [c]	3,572	**10.0** [c]

(continued)

Exhibit 17	(Continued)

	Year Ended 31 December					
	2009		**2008**		**2007**	
	$ millions	**Percent**	**$ millions**	**Percent**	**$ millions**	**Percent**
[Portions omitted]						
Net earnings attributable to Kraft Foods	3,021	7.5 [d]	2,884	6.9 [d]	2,721	7.6 [d]

Notes:
[a] Gross profit margin
[b] Operating profit margin
[c] Pretax margin
[d] Net profit margin

The profitability ratios and the common-size income statement yield quick insights about changes in a company's performance. For example, Kraft's increase in profitability in 2009 was not driven by an increase in revenues. (In fact, net revenues were lower than in 2008.) Instead the company's improved profitability in 2009 was driven primarily by its higher gross profit margins. Given the economic climate in 2008, the company likely had to lower prices and/or incur higher promotional costs in order to stimulate demand for its products (downward pressure on net revenues). Another driver of the company's improved profitability in 2009 was a lower amount of asset impairment and exit costs. The profitability ratios and the common-size income statement thus serve to highlight areas about which an analyst might wish to gain further understanding.

8   COMPREHENSIVE INCOME

The general expression for net income is revenue minus expenses. There are, however, certain items of revenue and expense that, by accounting convention, are excluded from the net income calculation. To understand how reported shareholders' equity of one period links with reported shareholders' equity of the next period, we must understand these excluded items, known as **other comprehensive income**.

Under IFRS, **total comprehensive income** is "the change in equity during a period resulting from transaction and other events, other than those changes resulting from transactions with owners in their capacity as owners."[52] Under U.S. GAAP, **comprehensive income** is defined as "the change in equity [net assets] of a business enterprise during a period from transactions and other events and circumstances from non-owner sources. It includes all changes in equity during a period except those resulting from investments by owners and distributions to owners."[53] While the wording differs, comprehensive income includes the same items under IFRS and U.S. GAAP. So, comprehensive income includes *both* net income and other revenue and expense items that are excluded from the net income calculation (other comprehensive income). Assume, for example, a company's beginning shareholders' equity is €110 million, its net income for the year is €10 million, its cash dividends for the year are €2 million, and there was no issuance or repurchase of common stock. If the

---

[52] IAS 1, *Presentation of Financial Statements*, paragraph 7.
[53] FASB ASC Section 220-10-05 [Comprehensive Income–Overall–Overview and Background].

company's actual ending shareholders' equity is €123 million, then €5 million [€123 – (€110 + €10 – €2)] has bypassed the net income calculation by being classified as other comprehensive income. If the company had no other comprehensive income, its ending shareholders' equity would have been €118 million [€110 + €10 – €2].

Four types of items are treated as other comprehensive income under both IFRS and U.S. GAAP.[54] (The specific treatment of some of these items differs between the two sets of standards, but these types of items are common to both.)

- Foreign currency translation adjustments. In consolidating the financial statements of foreign subsidiaries, the effects of translating the subsidiaries' balance sheet assets and liabilities at current exchange rates are included as other comprehensive income.

- Unrealized gains or losses on derivatives contracts accounted for as hedges. Changes in the fair value of derivatives are recorded each period, but these changes in value for certain derivatives (those considered hedges) are treated as other comprehensive income and thus bypass the income statement.

- Unrealized holding gains and losses on a certain category of investment securities, namely, available-for-sale securities.

- Certain costs of a company's defined benefit post-retirement plans that are not recognized in the current period.

In addition, under IFRS, other comprehensive income includes certain changes in the value of long-lived assets that are measured using the revaluation model rather than the cost model.

The third type of item is perhaps the simplest to illustrate. Holding gains on securities arise when a company owns securities over an accounting period, during which time the securities' value increases. Similarly, holding losses on securities arise when a company owns securities over a period during which time the securities' value decreases. If the company has not sold the securities (i.e., realized the gain or loss), its holding gain or loss is said to be unrealized. The question is: Should the company reflect these unrealized holding gains and losses in its income statement?

According to accounting standards, the answer depends on how the company has categorized the securities. Categorization depends on what the company intends to do with the securities. If the company intends to actively trade the securities, the answer is yes; the company should categorize the securities as **trading securities** and reflect unrealized holding gains and losses in its income statement. However, if the company does not intend to actively trade the securities, the securities may be categorized as **available-for-sale** securities. For available-for-sale securities, the company does not reflect unrealized holding gains and losses in its income statement. Instead, unrealized holding gains and losses on available-for-sale securities bypass the income statement and go directly to shareholders' equity.

Even though unrealized holding gains and losses on available-for-sale securities are excluded from a company's net income, they are *included* in a company's comprehensive income.

---

54 IAS 1, *Presentation of Financial Statements*, paragraph 7, and FASB ASC Section 220-10-55-02 [Comprehensive Income–Overall–Implementation Guidance and Illustrations].

EXAMPLE 20

Other Comprehensive Income

Assume a company's beginning shareholders' equity is €200 million, its net income for the year is €20 million, its cash dividends for the year are €3 million, and there was no issuance or repurchase of common stock. The company's actual ending shareholders' equity is €227 million.

1 What amount has bypassed the net income calculation by being classified as other comprehensive income?

     A   €0.

     B   €7 million.

     C   €10 million.

2 Which of the following statements *best* describes other comprehensive income?

     A   Income earned from diverse geographic and segment activities.

     B   Income that increases stockholders' equity but is not reflected as part of net income.

     C   Income earned from activities that are not part of the company's ordinary business activities.

Solution to 1:

C is correct. If the company's actual ending shareholders' equity is €227 million, then €10 million [€227– (€200 + €20 – €3)] has bypassed the net income calculation by being classified as other comprehensive income.

Solution to 2:

B is correct. Answers A and C are not correct because they do not specify whether such income is reported as part of net income and shown in the income statement.

EXAMPLE 21

Other Comprehensive Income in Analysis

An analyst is looking at two comparable companies. Company A has a lower price/earnings (P/E) ratio than Company B, and the conclusion that has been suggested is that Company A is undervalued. As part of examining this conclusion, the analyst decides to explore the question: What would the company's P/E look like if total comprehensive income per share—rather than net income per share—were used as the relevant metric?

	Company A	Company B
Price	$35	$30
EPS	$1.60	$0.90
P/E ratio	21.9×	33.3×
Other comprehensive income (loss) $ million	($16.272)	$(1.757)
Shares (millions)	22.6	25.1

Solution:

As shown in the following table, part of the explanation for Company A's lower P/E ratio may be that its significant losses—accounted for as other comprehensive income (OCI)—are not included in the P/E ratio.

	Company A	Company B
Price	$35	$30
EPS	$1.60	$0.90
OCI (loss) $ million	($16.272)	$(1.757)
Shares (millions)	22.6	25.1
OCI (loss) per share	$(0.72)	$(0.07)
Comprehensive EPS = EPS + OCI per share	$ 0.88	$0.83
Price/Comprehensive EPS ratio	39.8×	36.1×

Both IFRS and U.S. GAAP currently provide companies with some flexibility in reporting comprehensive income. IFRS currently allow companies two alternative presentations: either two statements—a separate income statement and a second statement additionally including other comprehensive income—or a single statement of other comprehensive income.[55] U.S. GAAP give companies both of those alternatives plus another. Under U.S. GAAP, a company can report comprehensive income at the bottom of the income statement, on a separate statement of comprehensive income, or as a column in the statement of shareholders' equity.[56] Particularly in comparing financial statements of two companies, it is relevant to examine significant differences in comprehensive income.

SUMMARY

This reading has presented the elements of income statement analysis. The income statement presents information on the financial results of a company's business activities over a period of time; it communicates how much revenue the company generated during a period and what costs it incurred in connection with generating that revenue. A company's net income and its components (e.g., gross margin, operating earnings, and pretax earnings) are critical inputs into both the equity and credit analysis processes. Equity analysts are interested in earnings because equity markets often reward relatively high- or low-earnings growth companies with above-average or below-average valuations, respectively. Fixed-income analysts examine the components of income statements, past and projected, for information on companies' abilities to make promised payments on their debt over the course of the business cycle. Corporate financial announcements frequently emphasize income statements more than the other financial statements.

---

55 IAS 1, *Presentation of Financial Statements*, paragraph 81.
56 FASB ASC 220-10-45 [Comprehensive Income–Overall–Other Presentation Matters] and FASB ASC 220-10-55 [Comprehensive Income–Overall–Implementation Guidance and Illustrations].

Key points to this reading include the following:

- The income statement presents revenue, expenses, and net income.

- The components of the income statement include: revenue; cost of sales; sales, general, and administrative expenses; other operating expenses; non-operating income and expenses; gains and losses; non-recurring items; net income; and EPS.

- An income statement that presents a subtotal for gross profit (revenue minus cost of goods sold) is said to be presented in a multi-step format. One that does not present this subtotal is said to be presented in a single-step format.

- Revenue is recognized in the period it is earned, which may or may not be in the same period as the related cash collection. Recognition of revenue when earned is a fundamental principal of accrual accounting.

- In limited circumstances, specific revenue recognition methods may be applicable, including percentage of completion, completed contract, installment sales, and cost recovery.

- An analyst should identify differences in companies' revenue recognition methods and adjust reported revenue where possible to facilitate comparability. Where the available information does not permit adjustment, an analyst can characterize the revenue recognition as more or less conservative and thus qualitatively assess how differences in policies might affect financial ratios and judgments about profitability.

- The general principles of expense recognition include a process to match expenses either to revenue (such as, cost of goods sold) or to the time period in which the expenditure occurs (period costs such as, administrative salaries) or to the time period of expected benefits of the expenditures (such as, depreciation).

- In expense recognition, choice of method (i.e., depreciation method and inventory cost method), as well as estimates (i.e., uncollectible accounts, warranty expenses, assets' useful life, and salvage value) affect a company's reported income. An analyst should identify differences in companies' expense recognition methods and adjust reported financial statements where possible to facilitate comparability. Where the available information does not permit adjustment, an analyst can characterize the policies and estimates as more or less conservative and thus qualitatively assess how differences in policies might affect financial ratios and judgments about companies' performance.

- To assess a company's future earnings, it is helpful to separate those prior years' items of income and expense that are likely to continue in the future from those items that are less likely to continue.

- Under IFRS, a company should present additional line items, headings, and subtotals beyond those specified when such presentation is relevant to an understanding of the entity's financial performance. Some items from prior years clearly are not expected to continue in future periods and are separately disclosed on a company's income statement. Under U.S. GAAP, two such items are specified 1) discontinued operations and 2) extraordinary items (IFRS prohibit reporting any item of income or expense as extraordinary). Both of these items are required to be reported separately from continuing operations, under U.S. GAAP.

- For other items on a company's income statement, such as unusual items and accounting changes, the likelihood of their continuing in the future is somewhat less clear and requires the analyst to make some judgments.

- Non-operating items are reported separately from operating items on the income statement.

- Basic EPS is the amount of income available to common shareholders divided by the weighted average number of common shares outstanding over a period. The amount of income available to common shareholders is the amount of net income remaining after preferred dividends (if any) have been paid.

- If a company has a simple capital structure (i.e., one with no potentially dilutive securities), then its basic EPS is equal to its diluted EPS. If, however, a company has dilutive securities, its diluted EPS is lower than its basic EPS.

- Diluted EPS is calculated using the if-converted method for convertible securities and the treasury stock method for options.

- Common-size analysis of the income statement involves stating each line item on the income statement as a percentage of sales. Common-size statements facilitate comparison across time periods and across companies of different sizes.

- Two income-statement-based indicators of profitability are net profit margin and gross profit margin.

- Comprehensive income includes *both* net income and other revenue and expense items that are excluded from the net income calculation.

PRACTICE PROBLEMS

1   Expenses on the income statement may be grouped by:

    A   nature, but not by function.

    B   function, but not by nature.

    C   either function or nature.

2   An example of an expense classification by function is:

    A   tax expense.

    B   interest expense.

    C   cost of goods sold.

3   Denali Limited, a manufacturing company, had the following income statement information:

Revenue	$4,000,000
Cost of goods sold	$3,000,000
Other operating expenses	$500,000
Interest expense	$100,000
Tax expense	$120,000

    Denali's gross profit is equal to

    A $280,000.

    B $500,000.

    C $1,000,000.

4   Under IFRS, income includes increases in economic benefits from:

    A   increases in liabilities not related to owners' contributions.

    B   enhancements of assets not related to owners' contributions.

    C   increases in owners' equity related to owners' contributions.

5   Fairplay had the following information related to the sale of its products during 2009, which was its first year of business:

Revenue	$1,000,000
Returns of goods sold	$100,000
Cash collected	$800,000
Cost of goods sold	$700,000

    Under the accrual basis of accounting, how much net revenue would be reported on Fairplay's 2009 income statement?

    A $200,000.

    B $900,000.

    C $1,000,000.

6   If the outcome of a long-term contract can be measured reliably, the preferred accounting method under both IFRS and U.S. GAAP is:

    A   the cost recovery method.

    B   the completed contract method.

C the percentage-of-completion method.

7 At the beginning of 2009, Florida Road Construction entered into a contract to build a road for the government. Construction will take four years. The following information as of 31 December 2009 is available for the contract:

Total revenue according to contract	$10,000,000
Total expected cost	$8,000,000
Cost incurred during 2009	$1,200,000

Assume that the company estimates percentage complete based on costs incurred as a percentage of total estimated costs. Under the completed contract method, how much revenue will be reported in 2009?

A None.

B $300,000.

C $1,500,000.

8 During 2009, Argo Company sold 10 acres of prime commercial zoned land to a builder for $5,000,000. The builder gave Argo a $1,000,000 down payment and will pay the remaining balance of $4,000,000 to Argo in 2010. Argo purchased the land in 2002 for $2,000,000. Using the installment method, how much profit will Argo report for 2009?

A $600,000.

B $1,000,000.

C $3,000,000.

9 Using the same information as in Question 8, how much profit will Argo report for 2009 using the cost recovery method?

A None.

B $600,000.

C $1,000,000.

10 Under IFRS, revenue from barter transactions should be measured based on the fair value of revenue from:

A similar barter transactions with unrelated parties.

B similar non-barter transactions with related parties.

C similar non-barter transactions with unrelated parties.

11 Apex Consignment sells items over the internet for individuals on a consignment basis. Apex receives the items from the owner, lists them for sale on the internet, and receives a 25 percent commission for any items sold. Apex collects the full amount from the buyer and pays the net amount after commission to the owner. Unsold items are returned to the owner after 90 days. During 2009, Apex had the following information:

● Total sales price of items sold during 2009 on consignment was €2,000,000.

● Total commissions retained by Apex during 2009 for these items was €500,000.

How much revenue should Apex report on its 2009 income statement?

A €500,000.

B €2,000,000.

C €1,500,000.

12 During 2009, Accent Toys Plc., which began business in October of that year, purchased 10,000 units of a toy at a cost of £10 per unit in October. The toy sold well in October. In anticipation of heavy December sales, Accent purchased 5,000 additional units in November at a cost of £11 per unit. During 2009, Accent sold 12,000 units at a price of £15 per unit. Under the first in, first out (FIFO) method, what is Accent's cost of goods sold for 2009?

   A £120,000.

   B £122,000.

   C £124,000.

13 Using the same information as in Question 12, what would Accent's cost of goods sold be under the weighted average cost method?

   A £120,000.

   B £122,000.

   C £124,000.

14 Which inventory method is least likely to be used under IFRS?

   A First in, first out (FIFO).

   B Last in, first out (LIFO).

   C Weighted average.

15 At the beginning of 2009, Glass Manufacturing purchased a new machine for its assembly line at a cost of $600,000. The machine has an estimated useful life of 10 years and estimated residual value of $50,000. Under the straight-line method, how much depreciation would Glass take in 2010 for financial reporting purposes?

   A $55,000.

   B $60,000.

   C $65,000.

16 Using the same information as in Question 15, how much depreciation would Glass take in 2009 for financial reporting purposes under the double-declining balance method?

   A $60,000.

   B $110,000.

   C $120,000.

17 Which combination of depreciation methods and useful lives is most conservative in the year a depreciable asset is acquired?

   A Straight-line depreciation with a short useful life.

   B Declining balance depreciation with a long useful life.

   C Declining balance depreciation with a short useful life.

18 Under IFRS, a loss from the destruction of property in a fire would most likely be classified as:

   A an extraordinary item.

   B continuing operations.

   C discontinued operations.

19 For 2009, Flamingo Products had net income of $1,000,000. At 1 January 2009, there were 1,000,000 shares outstanding. On 1 July 2009, the company issued 100,000 new shares for $20 per share. The company paid $200,000 in dividends to common shareholders. What is Flamingo's basic earnings per share for 2009?

   A $0.80.

B $0.91.

C $0.95.

20 Cell Services Inc. (CSI) had 1,000,000 average shares outstanding during all of 2009. During 2009, CSI also had 10,000 options outstanding with exercise prices of $10 each. The average stock price of CSI during 2009 was $15. For purposes of computing diluted earnings per share, how many shares would be used in the denominator?

A 1,003,333.

B 1,006,667.

C 1,010,000.

SOLUTIONS

1 C is correct. IAS No. 1 states that expenses may be categorized by either nature or function.

2 C is correct. Cost of goods sold is a classification by function. The other two expenses represent classifications by nature.

3 C is correct. Gross margin is revenue minus cost of goods sold. Answer A represents net income and B represents operating income.

4 B is correct. Under IFRS, income includes increases in economic benefits from increases in assets, enhancement of assets, and decreases in liabilities.

5 B is correct. Net revenue is revenue for goods sold during the period less any returns and allowances, or $1,000,000 minus $100,000 = $900,000.

6 C is correct. The preferred method is the percentage-of-completion method. The completed contract method should be used under U.S. GAAP only when the outcome cannot be measured reliably. A method similar to, but not referred to as, the cost recovery method is used under IFRS when the outcome cannot be measured reliably.

7 A is correct. Under the completed contract method, no revenue would be reported until the project is completed.

8 A is correct. The installment method apportions the cash receipt between cost recovered and profit using the ratio of profit to sales value (i.e., $3,000,000 ÷ $5,000,000 = 60 percent). Argo will, therefore, recognize $600,000 in profit for 2009 ($1,000,000 cash received × 60 percent).

9 A is correct. Under the cost recovery method, the company would not recognize any profit until the cash amounts paid by the buyer exceeded Argo's cost of $2,000,000.

10 C is correct. Revenue for barter transactions should be measured based on the fair value of revenue from similar non-barter transactions with unrelated parties.

11 A is correct. Apex is not the owner of the goods and should only report its net commission as revenue.

12 B is correct. Under the first in, first out (FIFO) method, the first 10,000 units sold came from the October purchases at £10, and the next 2,000 units sold came from the November purchases at £11.

13 C is correct. Under the weighted average cost method:

October purchases	10,000 units	$100,000
November purchases	5,000 units	$55,000
Total	15,000 units	$155,000

$155,000/15,000 units = $10.3333 × 12,000 units = $124,000.

14 B is correct. The last in, first out (LIFO) method is not permitted under IFRS. The other two methods are permitted.

15 A is correct. Straight-line depreciation would be ($600,000 − $50,000)/10, or $55,000.

16 C is correct. Double-declining balance depreciation would be $600,000 ×
20 percent (twice the straight-line rate). The residual value is not subtracted
from the initial book value to calculate depreciation. However, the book value
(carrying amount) of the asset will not be reduced below the estimated residual
value.

17 C is correct. This would result in the highest amount of depreciation in the first
year and hence the lowest amount of net income relative to the other choices.

18 B is correct. A fire may be infrequent, but it would still be part of continuing operations. IFRS do not permit classification of an item as extraordinary.
Discontinued operations relate to a decision to dispose of an operating division.

19 C is correct. The weighted average number of shares outstanding for 2009 is
1,050,000. Basic earnings per share would be $1,000,000 divided by 1,050,000,
or $0.95.

20 A is correct. With stock options, the treasury stock method must be used.
Under that method, the company would receive $100,000 (10,000 × $10) and
would repurchase 6,667 shares ($100,000/$15). The shares for the denominator
would be:

Shares outstanding	1,000,000
Options exercises	100,000
Treasury shares purchased	(6,667)
Denominator	1,003,333

Understanding Balance Sheets

by Elaine Henry, CFA, and Thomas R. Robinson, CFA

LEARNING OUTCOMES

Mastery	The candidate should be able to:
☐	**a.** describe the elements of the balance sheet: assets, liabilities, and equity;
☐	**b.** describe uses and limitations of the balance sheet in financial analysis;
☐	**c.** describe alternative formats of balance sheet presentation;
☐	**d.** distinguish between current and non-current assets, and current and non-current liabilities;
☐	**e.** describe different types of assets and liabilities and the measurement bases of each;
☐	**f.** describe the components of shareholders' equity;
☐	**g.** analyze balance sheets and statements of changes in equity;
☐	**h.** convert balance sheets to common-size balance sheets and interpret common-size balance sheets;
☐	**i.** calculate and interpret liquidity and solvency ratios.

Note: New rulings and/ or pronouncements issued after the publication of the readings in financial reporting and analysis may cause some of the information in these readings to become dated. Candidates are expected to be familiar with the overall analytical framework contained in the study session readings, as well as the implications of alternative accounting methods for financial analysis and valuation, as provided in the assigned readings. Candidates are not responsible for changes that occur after the material was written.

1 INTRODUCTION

The balance sheet provides information on a company's resources (assets) and its sources of capital (equity and liabilities/debt). This information helps an analyst assess a company's ability to pay for its near-term operating needs, meet future debt obligations, and make distributions to owners. The basic equation underlying the balance sheet is Assets = Liabilities + Equity.

Analysts should be aware that different items of assets and liabilities may be measured differently. For example, some items are measured at historical cost or a variation thereof and others at fair value.[1] An understanding of the measurement issues will facilitate analysis. The balance sheet measurement issues are, of course, closely linked to the revenue and expense recognition issues affecting the income statement. Throughout this reading, we describe and illustrate some of the linkages between the measurement issues affecting the balance sheet and the revenue and expense recognition issues affecting the income statement.

This reading is organized as follows: In Section 2, we describe and give examples of the elements and formats of balance sheets. Section 3 discusses current assets and current liabilities. Section 4 focuses on assets, and Section 5 focuses on liabilities. Section 6 describes the components of equity and illustrates the statement of changes in shareholders' equity. Section 7 introduces balance sheet analysis. A summary of the key points and practice problems in the CFA Institute multiple-choice format conclude the reading.

2 COMPONENTS AND FORMAT OF THE BALANCE SHEET

The **balance sheet** (also called the **statement of financial position** or **statement of financial condition**) discloses what an entity owns (or controls), what it owes, and what the owners' claims are at a specific point in time.[2]

The financial position of a company is described in terms of its basic elements (assets, liabilities, and equity):

- **Assets** (A) are what the company owns (or controls). More formally, assets are resources controlled by the company as a result of past events and from which future economic benefits are expected to flow *to* the entity.

- **Liabilities** (L) are what the company owes. More formally, liabilities represent obligations of a company arising from past events, the settlement of which is expected to result in an outflow of economic benefits *from* the entity.

- **Equity** (E) represents the owners' residual interest in the company's assets after deducting its liabilities. Commonly known as **shareholders' equity** or **owners' equity**, equity is determined by subtracting the liabilities from the assets of a company, giving rise to the accounting equation: **A − L = E** or **A = L + E**.

---

[1] IFRS defines the term "fair value" as the amount for which an asset could be exchanged or a liability settled between knowledgeable, willing parties in an arm's length transaction (IAS 39, *Financial Instruments: Recognition and Measurement*, paragraph 9). U.S. GAAP defines "fair value" as an exit price, i.e., the price that would be received to sell an asset or paid to transfer a liability in an orderly transaction between market participants at the measurement date (FASB ASC Glossary).

[2] IFRS uses the term "statement of financial position" (IAS 1 *Presentation of Financial Statements*), although U.S. GAAP uses the two terms interchangeably (ASC 210-10-05 [Balance Sheet–Overall–Overview and Background).

The equation A = L + E is sometimes summarized as follows: The left side of the equation reflects the resources controlled by the company and the right side reflects how those resources were financed. For all financial statement items, an item should only be recognized in the financial statements if it is probable that any future economic benefit associated with the item will flow to or from the entity and if the item has a cost or value that can be measured with reliability.[3]

The balance sheet provides important information about a company's financial condition, but the balance sheet amounts of equity (assets, net of liabilities) should not be viewed as a measure of either the market or intrinsic value of a company's equity for several reasons. First, the balance sheet under current accounting standards is a mixed model with respect to measurement. Some assets and liabilities are measured based on historical cost, sometimes with adjustments, whereas other assets and liabilities are measured based on a current value. The measurement bases may have a significant effect on the amount reported. Second, even the items measured at current value reflect the value that was current at the end of the reporting period. The values of those items obviously can change after the balance sheet is prepared. Third, the value of a company is a function of many factors, including future cash flows expected to be generated by the company and current market conditions. Important aspects of a company's ability to generate future cash flows—for example, its reputation and management skills—are not included in its balance sheet.

2.1 Balance Sheet Components

To illustrate the components and formats of balance sheets, we show the major subtotals from two companies' balance sheets. Exhibit 1 and Exhibit 2 are based on the balance sheets of SAP Group (Frankfurt: SAP) and Apple Inc. (Nasdaq: AAPL). SAP Group is a leading business software company based in Germany and prepares its financial statements in accordance with IFRS. Apple is a technology manufacturer based in the United States and prepares its financial statements in accordance with U.S. GAAP. For purposes of discussion, Exhibits 1 and 2 show only the main subtotals and totals of these companies' balance sheets. Additional exhibits throughout this reading will expand on these subtotals.

Exhibit 1	SAP Group Consolidated Statements of Financial Position (Excerpt) (in millions of €)	
	31 December	
Assets	**2009**	**2008**
Total current assets	5,255	5,571
Total non-current assets	8,119	8,329
Total assets	13,374	13,900
Equity and liabilities		
Total current liabilities	3,416	5,824
Total non-current liabilities	1,467	905
Total liabilities	4,883	6,729

(continued)

---

3 *Framework for the Preparation and Presentation of Financial Statements*, International Accounting Standards Committee, 1989, adopted by IASB 2001, paragraph 83.

Exhibit 1	(Continued)		

		31 December	
Assets		2009	2008
Total equity		8,491	7,171
Equity and liabilities		13,374	13,900

Source: SAP Group 2009 annual report.

Exhibit 2	Apple Inc. Consolidated Balance Sheet (Excerpt)* (in millions of $)

Assets	26 September 2009	27 September 2008
Total current assets	31,555	30,006
[All other assets]	15,946	6,165
Total assets	47,501	36,171
Liabilities and shareholders' equity		
Total current liabilities	11,506	11,361
[Total non-current liabilities]	4,355	2,513
Total liabilities	15,861	13,874
Total shareholders' equity	31,640	22,297
Total liabilities and shareholders' equity	47,501	36,171

Note: The italicized subtotals presented in this excerpt are not explicitly shown on the face of the financial statement as prepared by the company.
Source: Apple Inc. 2009 annual report (Form 10K/A).

SAP Group uses the title Statement of Financial Position, consistent with IFRS, and Apple uses the title Balance Sheet. Despite their different titles, both statements report the three basic elements: assets, liabilities, and equity. Both companies are reporting on a consolidated basis, i.e., including all their controlled subsidiaries. The numbers in SAP Group's balance sheet are in millions of euro, and the numbers in Apple's balance sheet are in millions of dollars.

Balance sheet information is as of a specific point in time. These exhibits are from the companies' annual financial statements, so the balance sheet information is as of the last day of their respective fiscal years. SAP Group's fiscal year is the same as the calendar year and the balance sheet information is as of 31 December. Apple's fiscal year ends on the last Saturday of September so the actual date changes from year to year. About every six years, Apple's fiscal year will include 53 weeks rather than 52 weeks. This feature of Apple's fiscal year should be noted, but in general, the extra week is more relevant to evaluating statements spanning a period of time (the income and cash flow statements) rather than the balance sheet which captures information as of a specific point in time.

A company's ability to pay for its short term operating needs relates to the concept of **liquidity**. With respect to a company overall, liquidity refers to the availability of cash to meet those short-term needs. With respect to a particular asset or liability, liquidity refers to its "nearness to cash." A liquid asset is one that can be easily converted into cash in a short period of time at a price close to fair market value. For example, a small holding of an actively traded stock is much more liquid than an asset such as a commercial real estate property in a weak property market.

The separate presentation of current and non-current assets and liabilities enables an analyst to examine a company's liquidity position (at least as of the end of the fiscal period). Both IFRS and U.S. GAAP require that the balance sheet distinguish between current and non-current assets and between current and non-current liabilities and present these as separate classifications. An exception to this requirement, under IFRS, is that the current and non-current classifications are not required if a liquidity-based presentation provides reliable and more relevant information. Presentations distinguishing between current and non-current elements are shown in Exhibits 1 and 2. Exhibit 3 in Section 2.3 shows a liquidity-based presentation.

2.2 Current and Non-Current Classification

Assets held primarily for the purpose of trading or expected to be sold, used up, or otherwise realized in cash within one year or one operating cycle of the business, whichever is greater, after the reporting period are classified as **current assets**. A company's operating cycle is the average amount of time that elapses between acquiring inventory and collecting the cash from sales to customers. For a manufacturer, this is the average amount of time between acquiring raw materials and converting these into cash from a sale. Examples of companies that might be expected to have operating cycles longer than one year include those operating in the tobacco, distillery, and lumber industries. Even though these types of companies often hold inventories longer than one year, the inventory is classified as a current asset because it is expected to be sold within an operating cycle. Assets not expected to be sold or used up within one year or one operating cycle of the business, whichever is greater, are classified as **non-current assets** (long-term, long-lived assets).

Current assets are generally maintained for operating purposes, and these assets include—in addition to cash—items expected to be converted into cash (e.g., trade receivables), used up (e.g., office supplies, prepaid expenses), or sold (e.g., inventories) in the current period. Current assets provide information about the operating activities and the operating capability of the entity. For example, the item "trade receivables" or "accounts receivable" would indicate that a company provides credit to its customers. Non-current assets represent the infrastructure from which the entity operates and are not consumed or sold in the current period. Investments in such assets are made from a strategic and longer term perspective.

Similarly, liabilities expected to be settled within one year or within one operating cycle of the business, whichever is greater, after the reporting period are classified as **current liabilities**. The specific criteria for classification of a liability as current include the following:

- It is expected to be settled in the entity's normal operating cycle;
- It is held primarily for the purpose of being traded;[4]
- It is due to be settled within one year after the balance sheet date; or
- The entity does not have an unconditional right to defer settlement of the liability for at least one year after the balance sheet date.[5]

---

4 Examples of these are financial liabilities classified as held for trading in accordance with IAS 39.
5 IAS 1, *Presentation of Financial Statements*, paragraph 69.

IFRS specify that some current liabilities, such as trade payables and some accruals for employee and other operating costs, are part of the working capital used in the entity's normal operating cycle. Such operating items are classified as current liabilities even if they will be settled more than one year after the balance sheet date. When the entity's normal operating cycle is not clearly identifiable, its duration is assumed to be one year. All other liabilities are classified as **non-current liabilities**. Non-current liabilities include financial liabilities that provide financing on a long-term basis.

The excess of current assets over current liabilities is called **working capital**. The level of working capital tells analysts something about the ability of an entity to meet liabilities as they fall due. Although adequate working capital is essential, working capital should not be too large because funds may be tied up that could be used more productively elsewhere.

A balance sheet with separately classified current and non-current assets and liabilities is referred to as a **classified balance sheet**. Classification also refers generally to the grouping of accounts into subcategories. Both companies' balance sheets that are summarized in Exhibits 1 and 2 are classified balance sheets. Although both companies' balance sheets present current assets before non-current assets and current liabilities before non-current liabilities, this is not required. IFRS does not specify the order or format in which a company presents items on a current/non-current classified balance sheet.

2.3 Liquidity-Based Presentation

A liquidity-based presentation, rather than a current/non-current presentation, is used when such a presentation provides information that is reliable and more relevant. With a liquidity-based presentation, all assets and liabilities are presented broadly in order of liquidity.

Entities such as banks are candidates to use a liquidity-based presentation. Exhibit 3 presents the assets portion of the balance sheet of China Construction Bank, a commercial bank based in Beijing that reports using IFRS. [The Bank's H-shares are listed on the Hong Kong Stock Exchange (Stock Code: 939), and the Bank's A-shares are listed on the Shanghai Stock Exchange (Stock Code: 601939).] Its balance sheet is ordered using a liquidity-based presentation. As shown, the asset section begins with Cash and deposits with central banks. Less liquid items such as fixed assets and land use rights appear near the bottom of the asset listing.

Exhibit 3	China Construction Bank Corporation Consolidated Statement of Financial Position (Excerpt: Assets Only) as of 31 December (in millions of RMB)		
Assets		**2009**	**2008**
Cash and deposits with central banks		1,458,648	1,247,450
Deposits with banks and non-bank financial institutions		101,163	33,096
Precious metals		9,229	5,160
Placements with banks and non-bank financial institutions		22,217	16,836
Financial assets at fair value through profit or loss		18,871	50,309
Positive fair value of derivatives		9,456	21,299
Financial assets held under resale agreements		589,606	208,548
Interest receivable		40,345	38,317

Exhibit 3	(Continued)	

Assets	2009	2008
Loans and advances to customers	4,692,947	3,683,575
Available-for-sale financial assets	651,480	550,838
Held-to-maturity investments	1,408,873	1,041,783
Debt securities classified as receivables	499,575	551,818
Interests in associates and jointly controlled entities	1,791	1,728
Fixed assets	74,693	63,957
Land use rights	17,122	17,295
Intangible assets	1,270	1,253
Goodwill	1,590	1,527
Deferred tax assets	10,790	7,855
Other assets	13,689	12,808
Total assets	9,623,355	7,555,452

Source: China Construction Bank 2009 Annual Report.

CURRENT ASSETS AND CURRENT LIABILITIES

3

This section examines current assets and current liabilities in greater detail.

3.1 Current Assets

Accounting standards require that certain specific line items, if they are material, must be shown on a balance sheet. Among the current assets' required line items are cash and cash equivalents, trade and other receivables, inventories, and financial assets (with short maturities). Companies present other line items as needed, consistent with the requirements to separately present each material class of similar items. As examples, Exhibit 4 and Exhibit 5 present balance sheet excerpts for SAP Group and Apple Inc. showing the line items for the companies' current assets.

Exhibit 4	SAP Group Consolidated Statements of Financial Position (Excerpt: Current Assets Detail) (in millions of €)	

	as of 31 December	
Assets	2009	2008
Cash and cash equivalents	1,884	1,280
Other financial assets	486	588
Trade and other receivables	2,546	3,178
Other non-financial assets	147	126
Tax assets	192	399
Total current assets	5,255	5,571
Total non-current assets	8,119	8,329
Total assets	13,374	13,900

(continued)

Exhibit 4	(Continued)		

		as of 31 December	
Assets		**2009**	**2008**
Equity and liabilities			
Total current liabilities		3,416	5,824
Total non-current liabilities		1,467	905
Total liabilities		4,883	6,729
Total equity		8,491	7,171
Equity and liabilities		13,374	13,900

Source: SAP Group 2009 annual report.

Exhibit 5	Apple Inc. Consolidated Balance Sheet (Excerpt: Current Assets Detail) * (in millions of $)

Assets	**26 September 2009**	**27 September 2008**
Cash and cash equivalents	5,263	11,875
Short-term marketable securities	18,201	10,236
Accounts receivable, less allowances of $52 and $47, respectively	3,361	2,422
Inventories	455	509
Deferred tax assets	1,135	1,044
Other current assets	3,140	3,920
Total current assets	31,555	30,006
[All other assets]	15,946	6,165
Total assets	47,501	36,171
Liabilities and shareholders' equity		
Total current liabilities	11,506	11,361
[Total non-current liabilities]	4,355	2,513
Total liabilities	15,861	13,874
Total shareholders' equity	31,640	22,297
Total liabilities and shareholders' equity	47,501	36,171

*Note: The italicized subtotals presented in this excerpt are not explicitly shown on the face of the financial statement as prepared by the company.
Source: Apple Inc. 2009 annual report (Form 10K/A).

3.1.1 Cash and Cash Equivalents

Cash equivalents are highly liquid, short-term investments that are so close to maturity,[6] the risk is minimal that their value will change significantly with changes in interest rates. Cash and cash equivalents are financial assets. Financial assets, in general, are

---

6 Generally, three months or less.

measured and reported at either **amortised cost** or **fair value**. Amortised cost is the historical cost (initially recognised cost) of the asset adjusted for amortisation and impairment. Under IFRS, fair value is the amount at which an asset could be exchanged or a liability settled in an arm's length transaction between knowledgeable and willing parties. Under U.S. GAAP, the definition is similar but it is based on an exit price, the price received to sell an asset or paid to transfer a liability, rather than an entry price.[7]

For cash and cash equivalents, amortised cost and fair value are likely to be immaterially different. Examples of cash equivalents are demand deposits with banks and highly liquid investments (such as U.S. Treasury bills, commercial paper, and money market funds) with original maturities of three months or less. Cash and cash equivalents excludes amounts that are restricted in use for at least 12 months. For all companies, the Statement of Cash Flows presents information about the changes in cash over a period. For the fiscal year 2009, SAP Group's cash and cash equivalents increased from €1,280 million to €1,844 million, and Apple's cash and cash equivalents decreased from $11,875 million to $5,263 million.

3.1.2 *Marketable Securities*

Marketable securities are also financial assets and include investments in debt or equity securities that are traded in a public market, and whose value can be determined from price information in a public market. Examples of marketable securities include treasury bills, notes, bonds, and equity securities, such as common stocks and mutual fund shares. Companies disclose further detail in the notes to their financial statements about their holdings. For example, SAP Group discloses that its other financial assets consist mainly of time deposits, investment in insurance policies, and loans to employees. Apple's short-term marketable securities, totaling $18.2 billion and $10.2 billion at the end of fiscal 2009 and 2008, respectively, consist of fixed-income securities with a maturity of less than one year. Financial assets such as investments in debt and equity securities involve a variety of measurement issues and will be addressed in Section 4.5.

3.1.3 *Trade Receivables*

Trade receivables, also referred to as accounts receivable, are another type of financial asset. These are amounts owed to a company by its customers for products and services already delivered. They are typically reported at net realisable value, an approximation of fair value, based on estimates of collectability. Several aspects of accounts receivable are usually relevant to an analyst. First, the overall level of accounts receivable relative to sales (a topic to be addressed further in ratio analysis) is important because a significant increase in accounts receivable relative to sales could signal that the company is having problems collecting cash from its customers.

A second relevant aspect of accounts receivable is the allowance for doubtful accounts. The allowance for doubtful accounts reflects the company's estimate of amounts that will ultimately be uncollectible. Additions to the allowance in a particular period are reflected as bad debt expenses, and the balance of the allowance for doubtful accounts reduces the gross receivables amount to a net amount that is an estimate of fair value. When specific receivables are deemed to be uncollectible, they are written off by reducing accounts receivable and the allowance for doubtful accounts. The allowance for doubtful accounts is called a **contra account** because it is netted against (i.e., reduces) the balance of accounts receivable, which is an asset account. SAP Group's balance sheet, for example, reports current net trade and other receivables of €2,546 million as of 31 December 2009. The amount of the allowance for

---

7 The joint IASB/FASB Fair Value project has expressed the intent to adopt an exit price definition of fair value.

doubtful accounts (€48 million) is disclosed in the notes to the financial statements. Apple discloses the allowance for doubtful accounts on the balance sheet; as of 26 September 2009, the allowance was $52 million. The $3,361 million of accounts receivable on that date is net of the allowance. Apple's disclosures state that the allowance is based on "historical experience, the age of the accounts receivable balances, credit quality of the Company's customers, current economic conditions, and other factors that may affect customers' ability to pay." The age of an accounts receivable balance refers to the length of time the receivable has been outstanding, including how many days past the due date.

Another relevant aspect of accounts receivable is the concentration of credit risk. For example, SAP Group's note on trade and other receivables discloses that concentration of credit risk is limited because they have a large customer base diversified across various industries and countries, and because no single customer accounted for 10 percent or more of either revenue or receivables.

EXAMPLE 1

Analysis of Accounts Receivable

1 Based on the balance sheet excerpt for Apple Inc. in Exhibit 5, what percentage of its total accounts receivable in 2009 and 2008 does Apple estimate will be uncollectible?

2 In general, how does the amount of allowance for doubtful accounts relate to bad debt expense?

3 In general, what are some factors that could cause a company's allowance for doubtful accounts to decrease?

Solution to 1:

($ millions) The percentage of 2009 accounts receivable estimated to be uncollectible is 1.5 percent, calculated as $52/($3,361 + $52). Note that the $3,361 is net of the $52 allowance, so the gross amount of accounts receivable is determined by adding the allowance to the net amount. The percentage of 2008 accounts receivable estimated to be uncollectible is 1.9 percent [$47/($2,422 + $47)].

Solution to 2:

Bad debt expense is an expense of the period, based on a company's estimate of the percentage of credit sales in the period, for which cash will ultimately not be collected. The allowance for bad debts is a contra asset account, which is netted against the asset accounts receivable.

To record the estimated bad debts, a company recognizes a bad debt expense (which affects net income) and increases the balance in the allowance for doubtful accounts by the same amount. To record the write off of a particular account receivable, a company reduces the balance in the allowance for doubtful accounts and reduces the balance in accounts receivable by the same amount.

Solution to 3:

In general, a decrease in a company's allowance for doubtful accounts in absolute terms could be caused by a decrease in the amount of credit sales.

Some factors that could cause a company's allowance for doubtful accounts to decrease as a percentage of accounts receivable include the following:

■ Improvements in the credit quality of the company's existing customers (whether driven by a customer-specific improvement or by an improvement in the overall economy);

- Stricter credit policies (for example, refusing to allow less creditworthy customers to make credit purchases and instead requiring them to pay cash, to provide collateral, or to provide some additional form of financial backing); and/or

- Stricter risk management policies (for example, buying more insurance against potential defaults).

In addition to the business factors noted above, because the allowance is based on management's estimates of collectability, management can potentially bias these estimates to manipulate reported earnings. For example, a management team aiming to increase reported income could intentionally over-estimate collectability and under-estimate the bad debt expense for a period. Conversely, in a period of good earnings, management could under-estimate collectability and over-estimate the bad debt expense with the intent of reversing the bias in a period of poorer earnings.

3.1.4 *Inventories*

Inventories are physical products that will eventually be sold to the company's customers, either in their current form (finished goods) or as inputs into a process to manufacture a final product (raw materials and work-in-process). Like any manufacturer, Apple holds inventories. The 2009 balance sheet of Apple Inc. shows $455 million of inventories. SAP Group's balance sheet does not include a line item for inventory, but its note disclosures indicate that inventory is included as a part of other non-financial assets on its balance sheet. SAP Group is primarily a software and services provider and the amount of its inventory is not material enough to require disclosure as a separate line item on the balance sheet.

Inventories are measured at the lower of cost and net realisable value under IFRS, and the lower of cost or market under U.S. GAAP. The cost of inventories comprises all costs of purchase, costs of conversion, and other costs incurred in bringing the inventories to their present location and condition. The following amounts are excluded from the determination of inventory costs:

- abnormal amounts of wasted materials, labor, and overheads;

- storage costs, unless they are necessary prior to a further production process;

- administrative overheads; and

- selling costs.

The following techniques can be used to measure the cost of inventories if the resulting valuation amount approximates cost:

- **Standard cost**, which should take into account the normal levels of materials, labor, and actual capacity. The standard cost should be reviewed regularly to ensure that it approximates actual costs.

- The **retail method** in which the sales value is reduced by the gross margin to calculate cost. An average gross margin percentage should be used for each homogeneous group of items. In addition, the impact of marked-down prices should be taken into consideration.

Net realisable value (NRV), the measure used by IFRS, is the estimated selling price less the estimated costs of completion and costs necessary to make the sale. Under U.S. GAAP, market value is current replacement cost but with upper and lower limits: It cannot exceed NRV and cannot be lower than NRV less a normal profit margin.

If the net realisable value (under IFRS) or market value (under U.S. GAAP) of a company's inventory falls below its carrying amount, the company must write down the value of the inventory. The loss in value is reflected in the income statement. For example, within its Management's Discussion and Analysis and notes, Apple indicates that the company reviews its inventory each quarter and records write-downs of inventory that has become obsolete, exceeds anticipated demand, or is carried at a value higher than its market value. Under IFRS, if inventory that was written down in a previous period subsequently increases in value, the amount of the original write-down is reversed. Subsequent reversal of an inventory write-down is not permitted under U.S. GAAP.

When inventory is sold, the cost of that inventory is reported as an expense, "cost of goods sold." Accounting standards allow different valuation methods for determining the amounts that are included in cost of goods sold on the income statement and thus the amounts that are reported in inventory on the balance sheet. (Inventory valuation methods are referred to as cost formulas and cost flow assumptions under IFRS and U.S. GAAP, respectively.) IFRS allows only the first-in, first-out (FIFO), weighted average cost, and specific identification methods. Some accounting standards (such as U.S. GAAP) also allow last-in, first-out (LIFO) as an additional inventory valuation method. The LIFO method is not allowed under IFRS.

EXAMPLE 2

Analysis of Inventory

Cisco Systems is a global provider of networking equipment. In its third quarter 2001 Form 10-Q filed with the U.S. Securities and Exchange Commission (U.S. SEC) on 1 June 2001, the company made the following disclosure:

> We recorded a provision for inventory, including purchase commitments, totaling $2.36 billion in the third quarter of fiscal 2001, of which $2.25 billion related to an additional excess inventory charge. Inventory purchases and commitments are based upon future sales forecasts. To mitigate the component supply constraints that have existed in the past, we built inventory levels for certain components with long lead times and entered into certain longer-term commitments for certain components. Due to the sudden and significant decrease in demand for our products, inventory levels exceeded our requirements based on current 12-month sales forecasts. This additional excess inventory charge was calculated based on the inventory levels in excess of 12-month demand for each specific product. We do not currently anticipate that the excess inventory subject to this provision will be used at a later date based on our current 12-month demand forecast.

After the inventory charge, Cisco reported approximately $2 billion of inventory on the balance sheet, suggesting that the write-off amounted to approximately half of its inventory. In addition to the obvious concerns raised as to management's poor performance in anticipating how much inventory was required, many analysts were concerned about how the write-off would affect Cisco's future reported earnings. If this inventory is sold in a future period, a "gain" could be reported based on a lower cost basis for the inventory. In this case, management indicated that the intent was to scrap the inventory. When the company subsequently released its annual earnings, the press release stated:[8]

---

8 Cisco press release dated 7 August 2001 from www.cisco.com.

Net sales for fiscal 2001 were $22.29 billion, compared with $18.93 billion for fiscal 2000, an increase of 18%. Pro forma net income, which excludes the effects of acquisition charges, payroll tax on stock option exercises, restructuring costs and other special charges, excess inventory charge (benefit), and net gains realized on minority investments, was $3.09 billion or $0.41 per share for fiscal 2001, compared with pro forma net income of $3.91 billion or $0.53 per share for fiscal 2000, decreases of 21% and 23%, respectively.

Actual net loss for fiscal 2001 was $1.01 billion or $0.14 per share, compared with actual net income of $2.67 billion or $0.36 per share for fiscal 2000.

1   What concerns would an analyst likely have about the company's $2.3 billion write-off of inventory? What is the significance of the company indicating its intent to scrap the written off inventory?

2   What concerns might an analyst have about the company's earnings press release when the company subsequently released its annual earnings?

Solution to 1:

First, an analyst would likely have concerns about management's abilities to anticipate how much and what type of inventory was required. While errors in forecasting demand are understandable, the amount of inventory written off represented about half of the company's inventory. A second concern would relate to how the write-off would affect the company's future reported earnings. If the inventory that had been written off were sold in a future period, a "gain" could be reported based on a lower cost basis for the inventory. The company's intent to scrap the written off inventory would alleviate but not eliminate concerns about distortions to future reported earnings.

Solution to 2:

An analyst might be concerned that the company's press release focused mainly on "pro forma earnings," which excluded the impact of many items, including the inventory write-off. The company only gave a brief mention of actual (U.S. GAAP) results.

Note: A 2003 SEC regulation now requires companies to give at least equal emphasis to GAAP measures (for example, reported net income) when using a non-GAAP measure (for example, pro forma net income) and to provide a reconciliation of the two measures.[9]

3.1.5 *Other Current Assets*

The amounts shown in "other current assets" reflect items that are individually not material enough to require a separate line item on the balance sheet and so are aggregated into a single amount. Companies usually disclose the components in a note to the financial statements. A typical item included in other current assets is prepaid expenses. **Prepaid expenses** are normal operating expenses that have been paid in advance. Because expenses are recognized in the period in which they are incurred—and not necessarily the period in which the payment is made—the advance payment of a future expense creates an asset. The asset (prepaid expenses) will be recognized as an expense in future periods as it is used up. For example, consider prepaid insurance.

9 U.S. Securities and Exchange Commission. (January 2003). *Final rule: Conditions for use of non-GAAP financial measures* (Releases 33-8176 and 34-47226, File S7-43-02).

Assume a company pays its insurance premium for coverage over the next calendar year on 31 December of the current year. At the time of the payment, the company recognizes an asset (prepaid insurance expense). The expense is not incurred at that date; the expense is incurred as time passes (in this example, one-twelfth, 1/12, in each following month). Therefore, the expense is recognized and the value of the asset is reduced in the financial statements over the course of the year.

Portions of the amounts shown as tax assets on SAP's balance sheet and **deferred tax assets** on Apple's balance sheet represent income taxes incurred prior to the time that the income tax expense will be recognized on the income statement. Deferred tax assets may result when the actual **income tax payable** based on income for tax purposes in a period exceeds the amount of income tax expense based on the reported financial statement income due to temporary timing differences. For example, a company may be required to report certain income for tax purposes in the current period but to defer recognition of that income for financial statement purposes to subsequent periods. In this case, the company will pay income tax as required by tax laws, and the difference between the taxes payable and the tax expense related to the income for which recognition was deferred on the financial statements will be reported as a deferred tax asset. When the income is subsequently recognized on the income statement, the related tax expense is also recognised which will reduce the deferred tax asset.

Also, a company may claim certain expenses for financial statement purposes that it is only allowed to claim in subsequent periods for tax purposes. In this case, as in the previous example, the financial statement income before taxes is less than taxable income. Thus, income taxes payable based on taxable income exceeds income tax expense based on accounting net income before taxes. The difference is expected to reverse in the future when the income reported on the financial statements exceeds the taxable income as a deduction for the expense becomes allowed for tax purposes. Deferred tax assets may also result from carrying forward unused tax losses and credits (these are not temporary timing differences). Deferred tax assets are only to be recognised if there is an expectation that there will be taxable income in the future, against which the temporary difference or carried forward tax losses or credits can be applied to reduce taxes payable.

3.2 Current Liabilities

Current liabilities are those liabilities that are expected to be settled in the entity's normal operating cycle, held primarily for trading, or due to be settled within 12 months after the balance sheet date. Exhibit 6 and Exhibit 7 present balance sheet excerpts for SAP Group and Apple Inc. showing the line items for the companies' current liabilities. Some of the common types of current liabilities, including trade payables, financial liabilities, accrued expenses, and deferred income, are discussed below.

Exhibit 6	SAP Group Consolidated Statements of Financial Position (Excerpt: Current Liabilities Detail) (in millions of €)

	as of 31 December	
Assets	**2009**	**2008**
Total current assets	5,255	5,571
Total non-current assets	8,119	8,329
Total assets	13,374	13,900
Equity and liabilities		

Exhibit 6 (Continued)

Assets	as of 31 December	
	2009	2008
Trade and other payables	638	599
Tax liabilities	125	363
Bank loans and other financial liabilities	146	2,563
Other non-financial liabilities	1,577	1,428
Provisions	332	248
Deferred income	598	623
Total current liabilities	3,416	5,824
Total non-current liabilities	1,467	905
Total liabilities	4,883	6,729
Total equity	8,491	7,171
Equity and liabilities	13,374	13,900

Source: SAP Group 2009 annual report.

Exhibit 7 Apple Inc. Consolidated Balance Sheet (Excerpt: Current Liabilities Detail)* (in millions of $)

Assets	26 September 2009	27 September 2008
Total current assets	31,555	30,006
[All other assets]	15,946	6,165
Total assets	47,501	36,171
Liabilities and shareholders' equity		
Accounts payable	5,601	5,520
Accrued expenses	3,852	4,224
Deferred revenue	2,053	1,617
Total current liabilities	11,506	11,361
[Total non-current liabilities]	4,355	2,513
Total liabilities	15,861	13,874
Total shareholders' equity	31,640	22,297
Total liabilities and shareholders' equity	47,501	36,171

Note: The italicized subtotals presented in this excerpt are not explicitly shown on the face of the financial statement as prepared by the company.
Source: Apple Inc. 2009 annual report (Form 10K/A).

Trade payables, also called **accounts payable**, are amounts that a company owes its vendors for purchases of goods and services. In other words, these represent the unpaid amount as of the balance sheet date of the company's purchases on credit. An issue relevant to analysts is the trend in overall levels of trade payables relative to purchases (a topic to be addressed further in ratio analysis). Significant changes in accounts payable relative to purchases could signal potential changes in the company's credit relationships with its suppliers. The general term "trade credit" refers to credit provided to a company by its vendors. Trade credit is a source of financing that allows the company to make purchases and then pay for those purchases at a later date.

Notes payable are financial liabilities owed by a company to creditors, including trade creditors and banks, through a formal loan agreement. Any notes payable, loans payable, or other financial liabilities that are due within one year (or the operating cycle, whichever is longer) appear in the current liability section of the balance sheet. In addition, any portions of long-term liabilities that are due within one year (i.e., the current portion of long-term liabilities) are also shown in the current liability section of the balance sheet. On SAP Group's balance sheet, current liabilities include bank loans and other financial liabilities. Apple Inc. does not have any current notes payable or loans payable.

Income taxes payable reflect taxes, based on taxable income, that have not yet been paid. SAP Group's balance sheet shows €125 million of tax liabilities in its current liabilities. Apple Inc.'s balance sheet does not show a separate line item for current taxes payable; instead a note discloses that income taxes payable of $430 million are included within the $3,852 million of "Accrued expenses." **Accrued expenses** (also called accrued expenses payable, accrued liabilities, and other non-financial liabilities) are expenses that have been recognized on a company's income statement but which have not yet been paid as of the balance sheet date. In addition to income taxes payable, other common examples of accrued expenses are accrued interest payable, accrued warranty costs, and accrued employee compensation (i.e., wages payable). SAP Group's notes disclose that the €1,577 million line item of other non-financial liabilities, for example, includes €1,343 million of employee-related liabilities.

Deferred income (also called **deferred revenue** and **unearned revenue**) arises when a company receives payment in advance of delivery of the goods and services associated with the payment. The company has an obligation either to provide the goods or services or to return the cash received. Examples include lease payments received at the beginning of a lease, fees for servicing office equipment received at the beginning of the service period, and payments for magazine subscriptions received at the beginning of the subscription period. SAP Group's balance sheet shows deferred income of €598 million at the end of 2009, down slightly from €623 million at the end of 2008. Apple Inc.'s balance sheet shows deferred revenue of $2,053 million at the end of fiscal 2009, up 27 percent from $1,617 million at the end of fiscal 2008. Example 3 presents each company's disclosures about deferred revenue and discusses some of the implications.

EXAMPLE 3

Analysis of Deferred Revenue

In the notes to its 2009 financial statements, SAP Group describes its deferred income as follows:

> Deferred income consists mainly of prepayments made by our customers for support services and professional services, fees for multiple element arrangements allocated to undelivered elements, and amounts … for obligations to perform under acquired support contracts in connection with acquisitions.

Apple's deferred revenue arises from sales involving components, some delivered at the time of sale and others to be delivered in the future. In its 2009 financial statements, Apple Inc. explains that accounting for sale of some of its products is treated as two deliverables:

...The first deliverable is the hardware and software delivered at the time of sale, and the second deliverable is the right included with the purchase of iPhone and Apple TV to receive on a when-and-if-available basis future unspecified software upgrades and features relating to the product's software... the Company is required to estimate a standalone selling price for the unspecified software upgrade right included with the sale of iPhone and Apple TV and recognizes that amount ratably over the 24-month estimated life of the related hardware device...

1 In general, in the period a transaction occurs, how would a company's balance sheet reflect $100 of deferred revenue resulting from a sale? (Assume, for simplicity, that the company receives cash for all sales, the company's income tax payable is 30 percent based on cash receipts, and the company pays cash for all relevant income tax obligations as they arise. Ignore any associated deferred costs.)

2 In general, how does deferred revenue impact a company's financial statements in the periods following its initial recognition?

3 Interpret the amounts shown by SAP Group as deferred income and by Apple Inc. as deferred revenue.

4 Both accounts payable and deferred revenue are classified as current liabilities. Discuss the following statements:

   A When assessing a company's liquidity, the implication of amounts in accounts payable differs from the implication of amounts in deferred revenue.

   B Some investors monitor amounts in deferred revenue as an indicator of future revenue growth.

Solution to 1:

In the period that deferred revenue arises, the company would record a $100 increase in the asset Cash and a $100 increase in the liability Deferred Revenues. In addition, because the company's income tax payable is based on cash receipts and is paid in the current period, the company would record a $30 decrease in the asset Cash and a $30 increase in the asset Deferred Tax Assets. Deferred tax assets increase because the company has paid taxes on revenue it has not yet recognised for accounting purposes. In effect, the company has prepaid taxes from an accounting perspective.

Solution to 2:

In subsequent periods, the company will recognize the deferred revenue as it is earned. When the revenue is recognized, the liability Deferred Revenue will decrease. In addition, the tax expense is recognized on the income statement as the revenue is recognised and thus the associated amounts of Deferred Tax Assets will decrease.

Solution to 3:

The deferred income on SAP Group's balance sheet and deferred revenue on Apple Inc.'s balance sheet at the end of their respective 2009 fiscal years will be recognized as revenue, sales, or a similar item in income statements subsequent to the 2009 fiscal year, as the goods or services are provided or the obligation is reduced. The costs of delivering the goods or services will also be recognised.

Solution to 4A:

The amount of accounts payable represents a future obligation to pay cash to suppliers. In contrast, the amount of deferred revenue represents payments that the company has already received from its customers, and the future obligation is to deliver the related services. With respect to liquidity, settling accounts payable will require cash outflows whereas settling deferred revenue obligations will not.

Solution to 4B:

Some investors monitor amounts in deferred revenue as an indicator of future growth because the amounts in deferred revenue will be recognized as revenue in the future. Thus, growth in the amount of deferred revenue implies future growth of that component of a company's revenue.

4   NON-CURRENT ASSETS

This section provides an overview of assets other than current assets, sometimes collectively referred to as non-current, long-term, or long-lived assets. The categories discussed are property, plant, and equipment; investment property; intangible assets; goodwill; and financial assets. Exhibit 8 and Exhibit 9 present balance sheet excerpts for SAP Group and Apple Inc. showing the line items for the companies' non-current assets.

Exhibit 8   SAP Group Consolidated Statements of Financial Position (Excerpt: Non-Current Assets Detail) (in millions of €)

| | as of 31 December | |
Assets	2009	2008
Total current assets	5,255	5,571
Goodwill	4,994	4,975
Intangible assets	894	1,140
Property, plant, and equipment	1,371	1,405
Other financial assets	284	262
Trade and other receivables	52	41
Other non-financial assets	35	32
Tax assets	91	33
Deferred tax assets	398	441
Total non-current assets	8,119	8,329
Total assets	13,374	13,900
Equity and liabilities		
Total current liabilities	3,416	5,824
Total non-current liabilities	1,467	905
Total liabilities	4,883	6,729
Total equity	8,491	7,171
Equity and liabilities	13,374	13,900

Source: SAP Group 2009 annual report.

Exhibit 9	Apple Inc. Consolidated Balance Sheet (Excerpt: Non-Current Assets Detail)* (in millions of $)	
Assets	**26 September 2009**	**27 September 2008**
Total current assets	31,555	30,006
Long-term marketable securities	10,528	2,379
Property, plant and equipment, net	2,954	2,455
Goodwill	206	207
Acquired intangible assets, net	247	285
Other assets	2,011	839
Total assets	47,501	36,171
Liabilities and shareholders' equity		
Total current liabilities	11,506	11,361
[Total non-current liabilities]	4,355	2,513
Total liabilities	15,861	13,874
Total shareholders' equity	31,640	22,297
Total liabilities and shareholders' equity	47,501	36,171

*Note: The italicized subtotals presented in this excerpt are not explicitly shown on the face of the financial statement as prepared by the company.
Source: Apple Inc. 2009 annual report (Form 10K/A).

4.1 Property, Plant, and Equipment

Property, plant, and equipment (PPE) are tangible assets that are used in company operations and expected to be used (provide economic benefits) over more than one fiscal period. Examples of tangible assets treated as property, plant, and equipment, include land, buildings, equipment, machinery, furniture, and natural resources such as mineral and petroleum resources. IFRS permits companies to report PPE using either a cost model or a revaluation model.[10] While IFRS permits companies to use the cost model for some classes of assets and the revaluation model for others, the company must apply the same model to all assets within a particular class of assets. U.S. GAAP permits only the cost model for reporting PPE.

Under the cost model, PPE is carried at amortised cost (historical cost less any accumulated depreciation or accumulated depletion, and less any impairment losses). Historical cost generally consists of an asset's purchase price, its delivery cost, and any other additional costs incurred to make the asset operable (such as costs to install a machine). Depreciation and depletion is the process of allocating (recognizing as an expense) the cost of a long-lived asset over its useful life. Land is not depreciated. Because PPE is presented on the balance sheet net of depreciation and depreciation expense is recognised in the income statement, the choice of depreciation method and the related estimates of useful life and salvage value impact both a company's balance sheet and income statement.

---

10 IAS 16, *Property, Plant and Equipment*, paragraphs 29-31.

Whereas depreciation is the systematic allocation of cost over an asset's useful life, impairment losses reflect an unanticipated decline in value. Impairment occurs when the asset's recoverable amount is less than its carrying amount, with terms defined as follows under IFRS:[11]

- Recoverable amount: The higher of an asset's fair value less cost to sell, and its value in use.

- Fair value less cost to sell: The amount obtainable in a sale of the asset in an arms-length transaction between knowledgeable willing parties, less the costs of the sale.

- Value in use: The present value of the future cash flows expected to be derived from the asset.

When an asset is considered impaired, the company recognizes the impairment loss in the income statement. Reversals of impairment losses are permitted under IFRS but not under U.S. GAAP.

Under the revaluation model, the reported and carrying value for PPE is the fair value at the date of revaluation less any subsequent accumulated depreciation. Changes in the value of PPE under the revaluation model affect equity directly or profit and loss depending upon the circumstances.

In Exhibits 8 and 9, SAP Group reports €1,371 million of PPE and Apple Inc. reports $2,954 million of PPE at the end of fiscal year 2009. For SAP Group, PPE represents approximately 10 percent of total assets and for Apple, PPE represents approximately 6 percent of total assets. SAP Group discloses in its notes that land is not depreciated, that they use a cost model for PPE, and that PPE are generally depreciated over their expected useful lives using the straight line method. Apple Inc. discloses similar policies but does not specifically disclose that land is not depreciated.

4.2 Investment Property

Some property is not used in the production of goods or services or for administrative purposes. Instead, it is used to earn rental income or capital appreciation (or both). Under IFRS, such property is considered to be **investment property**.[12] U.S. GAAP does not include a specific definition for investment property. IFRS provides companies with the choice to report investment property using either a cost model or a fair value model. In general, a company must apply its chosen model (cost or fair value) to all of its investment property. The cost model for investment property is identical to the cost model for PPE: In other words, investment property is carried at cost less any accumulated depreciation and any accumulated impairment losses. Under the fair value model, investment property is carried at its fair value. When a company uses the fair value model to measure the value of its investment property, any gain or loss arising from a change in the fair value of the investment property is recognized in profit and loss, i.e., on the income statement, in the period in which it arises.[13]

Neither SAP Group nor Apple disclose ownership of investment property. The types of companies that typically hold investment property are real estate investment companies or property management companies. Entities such as life insurance companies and endowment funds may also hold investment properties as part of their investment portfolio.

---

11 IAS 36, *Impairment of Assets*, paragraph 6. U.S. GAAP uses a different approach to impairment.
12 IAS 40, *Investment Property*.
13 IAS 40, *Investment Property*, paragraph 35.

4.3 Intangible Assets

Intangible assets are identifiable non-monetary assets without physical substance.[14] An identifiable asset can be acquired singly (can be separated from the entity) or is the result of specific contractual or legal rights or privileges. Examples include patents, licenses, and trademarks. The most common asset that is not a separately identifiable asset is accounting goodwill, which arises in business combinations and is discussed further in Section 4.4.

IFRS allows companies to report intangible assets using either a cost model or a revaluation model. The revaluation model can only be selected when there is an active market for an intangible asset. These measurement models are essentially the same as described for PPE. U.S. GAAP permits only the cost model.

For each intangible asset, a company assesses whether the useful life of the asset is finite or indefinite. Amortisation and impairment principles apply as follows:

- An intangible asset with a finite useful life is amortised on a systematic basis over the best estimate of its useful life, with the amortisation method and useful life estimate reviewed at least annually.

- Impairment principles for an intangible asset with a finite useful life are the same as for PPE.

- An intangible asset with an indefinite useful life is not amortised. Instead, at least annually, the reasonableness of assuming an indefinite useful life for the asset is reviewed and the asset is tested for impairment.

Financial analysts have traditionally viewed the values assigned to intangible assets, particularly goodwill, with caution. Consequently, in assessing financial statements, analysts often exclude the book value assigned to intangibles, reducing net equity by an equal amount and increasing pretax income by any amortisation expense or impairment associated with the intangibles. An arbitrary assignment of zero value to intangibles is not advisable; instead, an analyst should examine each listed intangible and assess whether an adjustment should be made. Note disclosures about intangible assets may provide useful information to the analyst. These disclosures include information about useful lives, amortisation rates and methods, and impairment losses recognised or reversed.

Further, a company may have developed intangible assets internally that can only be recognised in certain circumstances. Companies may also have assets that are never recorded on a balance sheet because they have no physical substance and are non-identifiable. These assets might include management skill, name recognition, a good reputation, and so forth. Such assets are valuable and are, in theory, reflected in the price at which the company's equity securities trade in the market (and the price at which the entirety of the company's equity would be sold in an acquisition transaction). Such assets may be recognised as goodwill if a company is acquired, but are not recognised until an acquisition occurs.

4.3.1 Identifiable Intangibles

Under IFRS, identifiable intangible assets are recognised on the balance sheet if it is probable that future economic benefits will flow to the company and the cost of the asset can be measured reliably. Examples of identifiable intangible assets include patents, trademarks, copyrights, franchises, licenses, and other rights. Identifiable intangible assets may have been created internally or purchased by a company. Determining the

---

14 IAS 38, *Intangible Assets*, paragraph 8.

cost of internally created intangible assets can be difficult and subjective. For these reasons, under IFRS and U.S. GAAP, the general requirement is that internally created identifiable intangibles are expensed rather than reported on the balance sheet.

IFRS provides that for internally created intangible assets, the company must separately identify the research phase and the development phase.[15] The research phase includes activities that seek new knowledge or products. The development phase occurs after the research phase and includes design or testing of prototypes and models. IFRS require that costs to internally generate intangible assets during the research phase must be expensed on the income statement. Costs incurred in the development stage can be capitalized as intangible assets if certain criteria are met, including technological feasibility, the ability to use or sell the resulting asset, and the ability to complete the project.

U.S. GAAP prohibits the capitalization as an asset of most costs of internally developed intangibles and research and development. All such costs usually must be expensed. Costs related to the following categories are typically expensed under IFRS and U.S. GAAP. They include:

- internally generated brands, mastheads, publishing titles, customer lists, etc.;
- start-up costs;
- training costs;
- administrative and other general overhead costs;
- advertising and promotion;
- relocation and reorganization expenses; and
- redundancy and other termination costs.

Generally, acquired intangible assets are reported as separately identifiable intangibles (as opposed to goodwill) if they arise from contractual rights (such as a licensing agreement), other legal rights (such as patents), or have the ability to be separated and sold (such as a customer list).

EXAMPLE 4

Measuring Intangible Assets

Alpha Inc., a motor vehicle manufacturer, has a research division that worked on the following projects during the year:

Project 1   Research aimed at finding a steering mechanism that does not operate like a conventional steering wheel but reacts to the impulses from a driver's fingers.

Project 2   The design of a prototype welding apparatus that is controlled electronically rather than mechanically. The apparatus has been determined to be technologically feasible, salable, and feasible to produce.

The following is a summary of the expenses of the research division (in thousands of €):

	General	Project 1	Project 2
Material and services	128	935	620
Labor			

---

15 IAS 38, *Intangible Assets*, paragraphs 51–67.

	General	Project 1	Project 2
• Direct labor	—	630	320
• Administrative personnel	720	—	—
Overhead			
• Direct	—	340	410
• Indirect	270	110	60

Five percent of administrative personnel costs can be attributed to each of Projects 1 and 2. Explain the accounting treatment of Alpha's costs for Projects 1 and 2 under IFRS and U.S. GAAP.

Solution:

Under IFRS, the capitalization of development costs for Projects 1 and 2 would be as follows:

		Amount Capitalized as an Asset (€'000)
Project 1:	Classified as in the research stage, so all costs are recognized as expenses	NIL
Project 2:	Classified as in the development stage, so costs may be capitalized. Note that administrative costs are not capitalized.	(620 + 320 + 410 + 60) = 1,410

Under U.S. GAAP, the costs of Projects 1 and 2 are expensed.

As presented in Exhibits 8 and 9, SAP Group's 2009 balance sheet shows €894 million of intangible assets, and Apple's 2009 balance sheet shows acquired intangible assets, net of $247 million.

4.4 Goodwill

When one company acquires another, the purchase price is allocated to all the identifiable assets (tangible and intangible) and liabilities acquired, based on fair value. If the purchase price is greater than the acquirer's interest in the fair value of the identifiable assets and liabilities acquired, the excess is described as **goodwill** and is recognized as an asset. To understand why an acquirer would pay more to purchase a company than the fair value of the target company's identifiable assets and liabilities, consider the following three observations. First, as noted, certain items not recognized in a company's own financial statements (e.g., its reputation, established distribution system, trained employees) have value. Second, a target company's expenditures in research and development may not have resulted in a separately identifiable asset that meets the criteria for recognition but nonetheless may have created some value. Third, part of the value of an acquisition may arise from strategic positioning versus a competitor or from perceived synergies. The purchase price might not pertain solely to the separately identifiable assets and liabilities acquired and thus may exceed the value of those net assets due to the acquisition's role in protecting the value of all of the acquirer's existing assets or to cost savings and benefits from combining the companies.

The subject of recognizing goodwill in financial statements has found both proponents and opponents among professionals. The proponents of goodwill recognition assert that goodwill is the present value of excess returns that a company is able to earn. This group claims that determining the present value of these excess returns is analogous to determining the present value of future cash flows associated with other assets and projects. Opponents of goodwill recognition claim that the prices paid for acquisitions often turn out to be based on unrealistic expectations, thereby leading to future write-offs of goodwill.

Analysts should distinguish between accounting goodwill and economic goodwill. Economic goodwill is based on the economic performance of the entity, whereas accounting goodwill is based on accounting standards and is reported only in the case of acquisitions. Economic goodwill is important to analysts and investors, and it is not necessarily reflected on the balance sheet. Instead, economic goodwill is reflected in the stock price (at least in theory). Some financial statement users believe that goodwill should not be listed on the balance sheet, because it cannot be sold separately from the entity. These financial statement users believe that only assets that can be separately identified and sold should be reflected on the balance sheet. Other financial statement users analyze goodwill and any subsequent impairment charges to assess management's performance on prior acquisitions.

Under both IFRS and U.S. GAAP, accounting goodwill arising from acquisitions is capitalized. Goodwill is not amortised but is tested for impairment annually. If goodwill is deemed to be impaired, an impairment loss is charged against income in the current period. An impairment loss reduces current earnings. An impairment loss also reduces total assets, so some performance measures, such as return on assets (net income divided by average total assets), may actually increase in future periods. An impairment loss is a non-cash item.

Accounting standards' requirements for recognizing goodwill can be summarized by the following steps:

A The total cost to purchase the target company (the acquiree) is determined.

B The acquiree's identifiable assets are measured at fair value. The acquiree's liabilities and contingent liabilities are measured at fair value. The difference between the fair value of identifiable assets and the fair value of the liabilities and contingent liabilities equals the net identifiable assets acquired.

C Goodwill arising from the purchase is the excess of a) the cost to purchase the target company and b) the net identifiable assets acquired. Occasionally, a transaction will involve the purchase of net identifiable assets with a value greater than the cost to purchase. Such a transaction is called a "bargain purchase." Any gain from a bargain purchase is recognized in profit and loss in the period in which it arises.[16]

Companies are also required to disclose information that enables users to evaluate the nature and financial effect of business combinations. The required disclosures include, for example, the acquisition date fair value of the total cost to purchase the target company, the acquisition date amount recognized for each major class of assets and liabilities, and a qualitative description of the factors that make up the goodwill recognized.

---

16 IFRS 3 *Business Combinations* and FASB ASC 805 [Business Combinations].

Despite the guidance incorporated in accounting standards, analysts should be aware that the estimations of fair value involve considerable management judgment. Values for intangible assets, such as computer software, might not be easily validated when analyzing acquisitions. Management judgment about valuation in turn impacts current and future financial statements because identifiable intangible assets with definite lives are amortized over time. In contrast, neither goodwill nor identifiable intangible assets with indefinite lives are amortized; instead both are tested annually for impairment.

The recognition and impairment of goodwill can significantly affect the comparability of financial statements between companies. Therefore, analysts often adjust the companies' financial statements by removing the impact of goodwill. Such adjustments include:

- excluding goodwill from balance sheet data used to compute financial ratios, and
- excluding goodwill impairment losses from income data used to examine operating trends.

In addition, analysts can develop expectations about a company's performance following an acquisition by taking into account the purchase price paid relative to the net assets and earnings prospects of the acquired company.

EXAMPLE 5

Goodwill Impairment

Safeway, Inc., (NYSE:SWY) is a North American food and drug retailer. On 25 February 2010, Safeway issued a press release that included the following information:

> Safeway Inc. today reported a net loss of $1,609.1 million ($4.06 per diluted share) for the 16-week fourth quarter of 2009. Excluding a non-cash goodwill impairment charge of $1,818.2 million, net of tax ($4.59 per diluted share), net income would have been $209.1 million ($0.53 per diluted share). Net income was $338.0 million ($0.79 per diluted share) for the 17-week fourth quarter of 2008.
>
> In the fourth quarter of 2009, Safeway recorded a non-cash goodwill impairment charge of $1,974.2 million ($1,818.2 million, net of tax). The impairment was due primarily to Safeway's reduced market capitalization and a weak economy....The goodwill originated from previous acquisitions.
>
> Safeway's balance sheet as of 2 January 2010 showed goodwill of $426.6 million and total assets of $14,963.6 million. The company's balance sheet as of 3 January 2009 showed goodwill of $2,390.2 million and total assets of $17,484.7 million.

1 How significant is this goodwill impairment charge?
2 With reference to acquisition prices, what might this goodwill impairment indicate?

> **Solution to 1:**
>
> The goodwill impairment was more than 80 percent of the total value of goodwill and 11 percent of total assets, so it was clearly significant. (The charge of $1,974.2 million equals 82.6 percent of the $2,390.2 million of goodwill at the beginning of the year and 11.3 percent of the $17,484.7 million total assets at the beginning of the year.)
>
> **Solution to 2:**
>
> The goodwill had originated from previous acquisitions. The impairment charge implies that the acquired operations are now worth less than the price that was paid for their acquisition.

As presented in Exhibits 8 and 9, SAP Group's 2009 balance sheet shows €4,994 million of goodwill, and Apple's 2009 balance sheet shows goodwill of $206 million. Goodwill represents 37.3 percent of SAP Group's total assets and only 0.4 percent of Apple's total assets. An analyst may be concerned that goodwill represents such a high proportion of SAP Group's total assets.

4.5 Financial Assets

IFRS define a financial instrument as a contract that gives rise to a financial asset of one entity, and a financial liability or equity instrument of another entity.[17] This section will focus on financial assets such as a company's investments in stocks issued by another company or its investments in the notes, bonds, or other fixed-income instruments issued by another company (or issued by a governmental entity). Financial liabilities such as notes payable and bonds payable issued by the company itself will be discussed in the liability portion of this reading. Some financial instruments may be classified as either an asset or a liability depending on the contractual terms and current market conditions. One example of such a financial instrument is a derivative. **Derivatives** are financial instruments for which the value is derived based on some underlying factor (interest rate, exchange rate, commodity price, security price, or credit rating) and for which little or no initial investment is required.

All financial instruments are recognized when the entity becomes a party to the contractual provisions of the instrument. In general, there are two basic alternative ways that financial instruments are measured: fair value or amortised cost.[18] Recall that fair value is the arm's length transaction price at which an asset could be exchanged or a liability settled between knowledgeable and willing parties under IFRS, and the price that would be received to sell an asset or paid to transfer a liability under U.S. GAAP. The amortised cost of a financial asset (or liability) is the amount at which it was initially recognized, minus any principal repayments, plus or minus any amortisation of discount or premium, and minus any reduction for impairment.

Financial assets are measured at amortised cost if the asset's cash flows occur on specified dates and consist solely of principal and interest, and if the business model is to hold the asset to maturity. This category of asset is referred to as **held-to-maturity**. An example is an investment in a long-term bond issued by another company; the value of the bond will fluctuate, for example with interest rate movements, but if the bond is classified as held-to-maturity, it will be measured at amortised cost. Other types of financial assets measured at historical cost are loans (to other companies).

---

17 IAS 32, *Financial Instruments: Presentation*, paragraph 11.
18 Both IFRS and U.S. GAAP are working on projects related to financial instruments; this reading is current as of June 2010.

Financial assets not measured at amortised cost are measured at fair value. For financial instruments measured at fair value, there are two basic alternatives in how net changes in fair value are recognized: as profit or loss on the income statement, or as other comprehensive income (loss) which bypasses the income statement. Note that these alternatives refer to unrealized changes in fair value, i.e., changes in the value of a financial asset that has not been sold and is still owned at the end of the period. Unrealized gains and losses are also referred to as holding period gains and losses. If a financial asset is sold within the period, a gain is realized if the selling price is greater than the carrying value and a loss is realized if the selling price is less than the carrying value. When a financial asset is sold, any realized gain or loss is reported on the income statement. The category **held for trading** (or "trading securities" under U.S. GAAP) refers to a category of financial assets that is acquired primarily for the purpose of selling in the near term. These assets are likely to be held only for a short period of time. These trading assets are measured at fair value, and any unrealized holding gains or losses are recognized as profit or loss on the income statement. **Mark to market** refers to the process whereby the value of a financial instrument is adjusted to reflect current fair value based on market prices.

Some financial assets are not classified as held for trading, even though they are available to be sold. Such **available-for-sale** assets are measured at fair value, with any unrealized holding gains or losses recognized in other comprehensive income. The "available-for-sale" classification no longer appears in IFRS as of 2010, although the relevant standard (IFRS 9 *Financial Instruments)* is not effective until 2013. However, although the available-for-sale category will not exist, IFRS still permit certain equity investments to be measured at fair value with any unrealized holding gains or losses recognized in other comprehensive income. Specifically, at the time a company buys an equity investment that is not held for trading, the company is permitted to make an irrevocable election to measure the asset in this manner. These assets are referred to as "financial assets measured at fair value through other comprehensive income."[19]

Exhibit 10 summarizes how various financial assets are classified and measured.

Exhibit 10	Measurement of Financial Assets
Measured at Fair Value	**Measured at Cost or Amortised Cost**
■ Financial assets held for trading (e.g., stocks and bonds issued by another company)	■ Unquoted equity instruments (in limited circumstances where the fair value is not reliably measurable, cost may serve as a proxy (estimate) for fair value)
■ Available-for-sale financial assets (e.g., stocks and bonds issued by another company)*	
■ Derivatives whether stand-alone or embedded in non-derivative instruments	■ Held-to-maturity investments (investments in bonds issued by another company, intended to be held to maturity)
■ Non-derivative instruments (including financial assets) with fair value exposures hedged by derivatives	■ Loans to and receivables from another company

*As described above, the available-for-sale category will no longer be a choice under IFRS when IFRS 9 becomes effective in 2013.

---

19 IFRS 7 *Financial Instruments: Disclosures*, paragraph 8(h).

To illustrate the different accounting treatments of the gains and losses on financial assets, consider an entity that invests €100,000,000 on 1 January 200X in a fixed-income security investment, with a 5 percent coupon paid semi-annually. After six months, the company receives the first coupon payment of €2,500,000. Additionally, market interest rates have declined such that the value of the fixed-income investment has increased by €2,000,000 as of 30 June 200X. Exhibit 11 illustrates how this situation will be portrayed in the balance sheet assets and equity, as well as the income statement (ignoring taxes) of the entity concerned, under each of the following three accounting policies for financial assets: assets held for trading purposes, assets available for sale, and held-to-maturity assets.

Exhibit 11	Accounting for Gains and Losses on Marketable Securities		
Balance Sheet As of 30 June 200X	Trading Portfolio	Available-for-Sale Portfolio	Held to Maturity
Assets			
Cash and cash equivalents	2,500,000	2,500,000	2,500,000
Cost of securities	100,000,000	100,000,000	100,000,000
Unrealized gains on securities	2,000,000	2,000,000	—
	104,500,000	104,500,000	102,500,000
Liabilities			
Equity			
Paid-in capital	100,000,000	100,000,000	100,000,000
Retained earnings	4,500,000	2,500,000	2,500,000
Accumulated other comprehensive income	—	2,000,000	—
	104,500,000	104,500,000	102,500,000

Income Statement For period 1 January–30 June 200X			
Interest income	2,500,000	2,500,000	2,500,000
Unrealized gains	2,000,000	—	—
Impact on profit and loss	4,500,000	2,500,000	2,500,000

In the case of marketable securities classified as either trading or available-for-sale, the investments are listed under assets and measured at fair market value. To highlight the impact of the change in value, Exhibit 11 shows the unrealized gain on a separate line. Practically, the investments would be listed at their fair value of €102,000,000 on one line within assets. In the case of trading securities, the unrealized gain is included on the income statement and thus reflected in retained earnings within owners' equity. In the case of available-for-sale securities, the unrealized gain is not included on the income statement as profit and loss; rather, it is treated as part of other comprehensive income and thus reflected in accumulated other comprehensive income within owners' equity. Other comprehensive income includes gains and losses that have not been reported on the income statement due to particular accounting standards.

In the case of held-to-maturity securities, the securities are measured at cost rather than fair value; therefore, no unrealized gain is reflected on either the balance sheet or income statement or through comprehensive income.

In Exhibits 4 and 8, SAP Group's 2009 balance sheet shows other financial assets of €486 million (current) and €284 million (non-current). The company's notes disclose that most of these financial assets are loans and receivables, €422 million (current) and €168 million (non-current). Also, €87 million of the non-current other financial assets are classified as available-for-sale equity investments, of which €62 million are venture capital investments without quoted market prices. The notes disclose that fair values could not be estimated by reference to quoted market prices or by discounting estimated future cash flows and that "such investments are accounted for at cost approximating fair value with impairment being assessed …"

In Exhibits 5 and 9, Apple's 2009 balance sheet shows $18,201 million of short-term marketable securities and $10,528 million of long-term marketable securities. In total, marketable securities represent around 60 percent of Apple's $47.5 billion in total assets. Marketable securities plus cash and cash equivalents represent around 72 percent of the company's total assets. Apple's notes disclose that most of the company's marketable securities are fixed-income securities issued by the U.S. government ($3,327 million) or its agencies ($10,835 million), and by other companies including commercial paper ($12,602 million). In accordance with its investment policy, Apple invests in highly rated securities (which the company defines as investment grade, primarily rated single A or better). The company classifies its marketable securities as available for sale and reports them on the balance sheet at fair value. Unrealized gains and losses are reported in other comprehensive income.

NON-CURRENT LIABILITIES

5

All liabilities that are not classified as current are considered to be non-current or long-term. Exhibits 12 and 13 present balance sheet excerpts for SAP Group and Apple Inc. showing the line items for the companies' non-current liabilities.

Both companies' balance sheets show non-current unearned revenue (deferred income for SAP Group and deferred revenue for Apple). These amounts represent the amounts of unearned revenue relating to goods and services expected to be delivered in periods beyond twelve months following the reporting period. The sections that follow focus on two common types of non-current (long-term) liabilities: long-term financial liabilities and deferred tax liabilities.

| Exhibit 12 | SAP Group Consolidated Statements of Financial Position (Excerpt: Non-Current Liabilities Detail) (in millions of €) |

	as of 31 December	
Assets	**2009**	**2008**
Total current assets	5,255	5,571
Total non-current assets	8,119	8,329
Total assets	13,374	13,900
Equity and liabilities		
Total current liabilities	3,416	5,824
Trade and other payables	35	42
Tax liabilities	239	278

(continued)

Exhibit 12	(Continued)		

	as of 31 December	
Assets	**2009**	**2008**
Bank loans	699	2
Other financial liabilities	30	38
Financial liabilities	729	40
Other non-financial liabilities	12	13
Provisions	198	232
Deferred tax liabilities	190	239
Deferred income	64	61
Total non-current liabilities	1,467	905
Total liabilities	4,883	6,729
Total equity	8,491	7,171
Equity and liabilities	13,374	13,900

Source: SAP Group 2009 annual report.

Exhibit 13	Apple Inc. Consolidated Balance Sheet (Excerpt: Non-Current Liabilities Detail)* (in millions of $)

Assets	**26 September 2009**	**27 September 2008**
Total current assets	31,555	30,006
[All other assets]	15,946	6,165
Total assets	47,501	36,171
Liabilities and shareholders' equity		
Total current liabilities	11,506	11,361
Deferred revenue non-current	853	768
Other non-current liabilities	3,502	1,745
Total liabilities	15,861	13,874
Total shareholders' equity	31,640	22,297
Total liabilities and shareholders' equity	47,501	36,171

Note: The italicized subtotals presented in this excerpt are not explicitly shown on the face of the financial statement as prepared by the company.
Source: Apple Inc. 2009 annual report (Form 10K/A).

5.1 Long-term Financial Liabilities

Typical long-term financial liabilities include loans (i.e., borrowings from banks) and notes or bonds payable (i.e., fixed-income securities issued to investors). Liabilities such as loans payable and bonds payable are usually reported at amortised cost on the balance sheet. At maturity, the amortised cost of the bond (carrying amount) will be equal to the face value of the bond. For example, if a company issues $10,000,000 of bonds at par, the bonds are reported as a long-term liability of $10 million. The carrying amount (amortised cost) from issue to maturity remains at $10 million. As another example, if a company issues $10,000,000 of bonds at a price of 97.50 (a discount to par), the bonds are reported as a liability of $9,750,000. Over the bond's life, the discount of $250,000 is amortised so that the bond will be listed as a liability of $10,000,000 at maturity. Similarly, any bond premium would be amortised for bonds issued at a price in excess of face or par value.

In certain cases, liabilities such as bonds issued by a company are reported at fair value. Those cases include financial liabilities held for trading, derivatives that are a liability to the company, and some non-derivative instruments such as those which are hedged by derivatives.

SAP Group's balance sheet in Exhibit 12 shows €699 million of bank loans and €30 million of other financial liabilities. Apple's balance sheet does not show any non-current financial liabilities.

5.2 Deferred Tax Liabilities

Deferred tax liabilities result from temporary timing differences between a company's income as reported for tax purposes (taxable income) and income as reported for financial statement purposes (reported income). Deferred tax liabilities result when taxable income and the actual income tax payable in a period based on it is less than the reported financial statement income before taxes and the income tax expense based on it. Deferred tax liabilities are defined as the amounts of income taxes payable in future periods in respect of taxable temporary differences.[20] In the previous discussion of unearned revenue, inclusion of revenue in taxable income in an earlier period created a deferred tax asset (essentially prepaid tax).

Deferred tax liabilities typically arise when items of expense are included in taxable income in earlier periods than for financial statement net income. This results in taxable income being less than income before taxes in the earlier periods. As a result, taxes payable based on taxable income are less than income tax expense based on accounting income before taxes. The difference between taxes payable and income tax expense results in a deferred tax liability—for example, when companies use accelerated depreciation methods for tax purposes and straight-line depreciation methods for financial statement purposes. Deferred tax liabilities also arise when items of income are included in taxable income in later periods—for example, when a company's subsidiary has profits that have not yet been distributed and thus have not yet been taxed.

SAP Group's balance sheet in Exhibit 12 shows €190 million of deferred tax liabilities. Apple's balance sheet in Exhibit 13 does not show a separate line item for deferred tax liabilities, however, note disclosures indicate that the $3,502 million of non-current liabilities reported on Apple's balance sheet includes deferred tax liabilities of $2,216 million.

---

20 IAS 12, *Income Taxes*, paragraph 5.

6   EQUITY

Equity is the owners' residual claim on a company's assets after subtracting its lia-bilities.[21] It represents the claim of the owner against the company. Equity includes funds directly invested in the company by the owners, as well as earnings that have been reinvested over time. Equity can also include items of gain or loss that are not yet recognized on the company's income statement.

6.1 Components of Equity

Six potential components comprise total owners' equity. The first five components listed below comprise equity attributable to owners of parent. The sixth component is the equity attributable to non-controlling interests.

1   *Capital contributed by owners* (or common stock, or issued capital). The amount contributed to the company by owners. Ownership of a corporation is evidenced through the issuance of common shares. Common shares may have a par value (or stated value) or may be issued as no par shares (depending on reg-ulations governing the incorporation). Where par or stated value requirements exist, it must be disclosed in the equity section of the balance sheet. In addition, the number of shares authorized, issued, and outstanding must be disclosed for each class of share issued by the company. The number of authorized shares is the number of shares that may be sold by the company under its articles of incorporation. The number of issued shares refers to those shares that have been sold to investors. The number of outstanding shares consists of the issued shares less treasury shares.

2   *Preferred shares*. Classified as equity or financial liabilities based upon their characteristics rather than legal form. For example, perpetual, non-redeemable preferred shares are classified as equity. In contrast, preferred shares with man-datory redemption at a fixed amount at a future date are classified as financial liabilities. Preferred shares have rights that take precedence over the rights of common shareholders—rights that generally pertain to receipt of dividends and receipt of assets if the company is liquidated.

3   *Treasury shares* (or treasury stock or own shares repurchased). Shares in the company that have been repurchased by the company and are held as treasury shares, rather than being cancelled. The company is able to sell (reissue) these shares. A company may repurchase its shares when management considers the shares undervalued, needs shares to fulfill employees' stock options, or wants to limit the effects of dilution from various employee stock compensation plans. A purchase of treasury shares reduces shareholders' equity by the amount of the acquisition cost and reduces the number of total shares outstanding. If treasury shares are subsequently reissued, a company does not recognize any gain or loss from the reissuance on the income statement. Treasury shares are non-voting and do not receive any dividends declared by the company.

4   *Retained earnings*. The cumulative amount of earnings recognized in the company's income statements which have not been paid to the owners of the company as dividends.

5   *Accumulated other comprehensive income* (or other reserves). The cumula-tive amount of *other* comprehensive income or loss. Comprehensive income includes both a) net income, which is recognized on the income statement and

---

21   IAS *Framework*, paragraph 49 (c) and FASB ASC 505-10-05-3 [Equity–Overview and Background].

is reflected in retained earnings, and b) other comprehensive income which is not recognized as part of net income and is reflected in accumulated other comprehensive income.[22]

6 *Noncontrolling interest* (or minority interest). The equity interests of minority shareholders in the subsidiary companies that have been consolidated by the parent (controlling) company but that are not wholly owned by the parent company.

Exhibits 14 and 15 present excerpts of the balance sheets of SAP Group and Apple Inc., respectively, with detailed line items for each company's equity section. SAP's balance sheet indicates that the company has 1,226 million shares of no-par common stock outstanding with a corresponding amount shown in issued capital of €1,226 million. Presentation of the amount of treasury shares, −€1,320 million, is explained in the company's notes:

> Treasury shares are recorded at acquisition cost and are presented as a deduction from total equity. Gains and losses on the subsequent reissuance of treasury shares are credited or charged to share premium on an after-tax basis.

Source: SAP Group 2009 annual report

Thus, the line item share premium of €317 million includes amounts from treasury share transactions (and certain other transactions). The amount of retained earnings, €8,571 million, represents the cumulative amount of earnings that the company has recognized in its income statements, net of dividends. SAP Group's −€317 million of "Other components of equity" includes the company's accumulated other comprehensive income. The consolidated statement of changes in equity shows that this is composed of €319 million of losses on exchange differences in translation, €13 million gains on remeasuring available-for-sale financial assets, and €11 million losses on cash flow hedges. The balance sheet presents a subtotal for the amount of equity attributable to the parent company €8,477 million followed by the amount of equity attributable to non-controlling interests. Total equity includes both equity attributable to the parent company and equity attributable to non-controlling interests.

The equity section of Apple's balance sheet consists of only three line items: common stock, retained earnings, and accumulated other comprehensive income/(loss). The company holds no treasury stock and has no minority interests.

Exhibit 14	SAP Group Consolidated Statements of Financial Position (Excerpt: Equity Detail) (in millions of €)	

| | as of 31 December | |
Assets	**2009**	**2008**
Total assets	13,374	13,900
Equity and liabilities		

(continued)

---

22 Comprehensive income is defined as "the change in equity [net assets] of a business enterprise during a period from transactions and other events and circumstances from non-owner sources. It includes all changes in equity during a period except those resulting from investments by owners and distributions to owners." FASB ASC Section 220-10-05 [Comprehensive Income–Overall–Overview and Background]. There is no explicit definition of comprehensive income in IFRS; the implicit definition is similar to that above. IFRS defines income in the glossary as "increases in economic benefits during the accounting period in the form of inflows or enhancements of assets or decreases of liabilities that result in increases in equity, other than those relating to contributions from equity participants."

Exhibit 14	(Continued)		

| | | as of 31 December | |
Assets		2009	2008
Total liabilities		4,883	6,729
Issued capital[1]		1,226	1,226
Treasury shares		−1,320	−1,362
Share premium		317	320
Retained earnings		8,571	7,422
Other components of equity		−317	−437
Equity attributable to owners of parent		8,477	7,169
Non-controlling interests		14	2
Total equity		8,491	7,171
Equity and liabilities		13,374	13,900

[1]Authorized–not issued or outstanding: 480 million no-par shares at 31 December 2009 and 2008. Authorized–issued and outstanding: 1,226 million no-par shares at 31 December 2009 and 2008. *Source:* SAP Group 2009 annual report.

Exhibit 15	Apple Inc. Consolidated Balance Sheet (Excerpt: Equity Detail) (in millions of $)

Assets	26 September 2009	27 September 2008
Total assets	47,501	36,171
Liabilities and shareholders' equity		
Total liabilities	15,861	13,874
Common stock, no par value; 1,800,000,000 shares authorized; 899,805,500 and 888,325,973 shares issued and outstanding, respectively	8,210	7,177
Retained earnings	23,353	15,129
Accumulated other comprehensive income/(loss)	77	(9)
Total shareholders' equity	31,640	22,297
Total liabilities and shareholders' equity	47,501	36,171

Source: Apple Inc. 2009 annual report (10K/A).

6.2 Statement of Changes in Equity

The **statement of changes in equity** (or statement of shareholders' equity) presents information about the increases or decreases in a company's equity over a period. IFRS requires the following information in the statement of changes in equity:

■ total comprehensive income for the period;

- the effects of any accounting changes that have been retrospectively applied to previous periods;
- capital transactions with owners and distributions to owners; and
- reconciliation of the carrying amounts of each component of equity at the beginning and end of the year.[23]

Under U.S. GAAP, the requirement as specified by the SEC is for companies to provide an analysis of changes in each component of stockholders' equity that is shown in the balance sheet.[24]

Exhibit 16 presents an excerpt from Apple's Consolidated Statements of Changes in Shareholders' Equity. The excerpt shows only one of the years presented on the actual statement. It begins with the balance as of 27 September 2008 (i.e., the beginning of fiscal 2009) and presents the analysis of changes to 26 September 2009 in each component of equity that is shown on Apple's balance sheet. As shown, the company issued 11.48 million new shares in connection with its employee stock plans, increasing the number of shares outstanding from 888.326 million to 899.806 million. The dollar balance in common stock also increased in connection with stock-based compensation. Retained earnings increased by $8,235 million net income, net of an $11 million adjustment in connection with stock plans. For companies that pay dividends, the amount of dividends are shown separately as a deduction from retained earnings. Apple did not pay dividends. The statement also provides details on the $86 million change in Apple's Accumulated other comprehensive income. Note that the statement provides a subtotal for total comprehensive income that includes net income and each of the components of other comprehensive income.

Exhibit 16	Excerpt from Apple Inc.'s Consolidated Statements of Changes in Shareholders' Equity (in millions, except share amounts which are reflected in thousands)

| | Common Stock | | Retained Earnings | Accumulated Other Comprehensive Income | Total Shareholders' Equity |
	Shares	Amount			
Balances as of 27 September 2008	888,326	$ 7,177	$ 15,129	$ (9)	$ 22,297
Components of comprehensive income:					
Net income	—	—	8,235	—	8,235
Change in foreign currency translation	—	—	—	(14)	(14)
Change in unrealized loss on available-for-sale securities, net of tax	—	—	—	118	118
Change in unrealized gain on derivative instruments, net of tax	—	—	—	(18)	(18)
Total comprehensive income					8,321

(continued)

---

23 IAS 1, *Presentation of Financial Statements*, paragraph 106.
24 FASB ASC 505-10-S99 [Equity–Overall–SEC materials] indicates that a company can present the analysis of changes in stockholders' equity either in the notes or in a separate statement.

Exhibit 16	(Continued)

	Common Stock		Retained Earnings	Accumulated Other Comprehensive Income	Total Share-holders' Equity
	Shares	Amount			
Stock-based compensation	—	707	—	—	707
Common stock issued under stock plans, net of shares withheld for employee taxes	11,480	404	(11)	—	393
Tax benefit from employee stock plan awards, including transfer pricing adjustments	—	(78)	—	—	(78)
Balances as of 26 September 2009	**899,806**	**$ 8,210**	**$ 23,353**	**$ 77**	**$ 31,640**

7 ANALYSIS OF THE BALANCE SHEET

This section describes two tools for analyzing the balance sheet: common-size analysis and balance sheet ratios. Analysis of a company's balance sheet can provide insight into the company's liquidity and solvency—as of the balance sheet date—as well as the economic resources the company controls. **Liquidity** refers to a company's ability to meet its short-term financial commitments. Assessments of liquidity focus a company's ability to convert assets to cash and to pay for operating needs. **Solvency** refers to a company's ability to meet its financial obligations over the longer term. Assessments of solvency focus on the company's financial structure and its ability to pay long-term financing obligations.

7.1 Common-Size Analysis of the Balance Sheet

The first technique, vertical common-size analysis, involves stating each balance sheet item as a percentage of total assets.[25] Common-size statements are useful in comparing a company's balance sheet composition over time (time-series analysis) and across companies in the same industry. To illustrate, Panel A of Exhibit 17 presents a balance sheet for three hypothetical companies. Company C, with assets of $9.75 million is much larger than Company A and Company B, each with only $3.25 million in assets. The common-size balance sheet presented in Panel B facilitates a comparison of these different sized companies.

---

25 As discussed in the curriculum reading on financial statement analysis, another type of common-size analysis, known as "horizontal common-size analysis," states quantities in terms of a selected base-year value. Unless otherwise indicated, text references to "common-size analysis" refer to vertical analysis.

Exhibit 17

Panel A: Balance Sheets for Companies A, B, and C			
($ Thousands)	A	B	C
ASSETS			
Current assets			
Cash and cash equivalents	1,000	200	3,000
Short-term marketable securities	900	—	300
Accounts receivable	500	1,050	1,500
Inventory	100	950	300
Total current assets	2,500	2,200	5,100
Property, plant, and equipment, net	750	750	4,650
Intangible assets	—	200	—
Goodwill	—	100	—
Total assets	3,250	3,250	9,750
LIABILITIES AND SHAREHOLDERS' EQUITY			
Current liabilities			
Accounts payable	—	2,500	600
Total current liabilities	—	2,500	600
Long term bonds payable	10	10	9,000
Total liabilities	10	2,510	9,600
Total shareholders' equity	3,240	740	150
Total liabilities and shareholders' equity	3,250	3,250	9,750

Panel B: Common-Size Balance Sheets for Companies A, B, and C			
(Percent)	A	B	C
ASSETS			
Current assets			
Cash and cash equivalents	30.8	6.2	30.8
Short-term marketable securities	27.7	0.0	3.1
Accounts receivable	15.4	32.3	15.4
Inventory	3.1	29.2	3.1
Total current assets	76.9	67.7	52.3
Property, plant and equipment, net	23.1	23.1	47.7
Intangible assets	0.0	6.2	0.0
Goodwill	0.0	3.1	0.0
Total assets	100.0	100.0	100.0
LIABILITIES AND SHAREHOLDERS' EQUITY			
Current liabilities			
Accounts payable	0.0	76.9	6.2
Total current liabilities	0.0	76.9	6.2

(continued)

Exhibit 17	(Continued)

Panel B: Common-Size Balance Sheets for Companies A, B, and C			
(Percent)	**A**	**B**	**C**
Long term bonds payable	0.3	0.3	92.3
Total liabilities	0.3	77.2	98.5
Total shareholders' equity	99.7	22.8	1.5
Total liabilities and shareholders' equity	100.0	100.0	100.0

Most of the assets of Company A and B are current assets; however, Company A has nearly 60 percent of its total assets in cash and short-term marketable securities while Company B has only 6 percent of its assets in cash. Company A is more liquid than Company B. Company A shows no current liabilities (its current liabilities round to less than $10 thousand), and it has cash on hand of $1.0 million to meet any near-term financial obligations it might have. In contrast, Company B has $2.5 million of current liabilities which exceed its available cash of only $200 thousand. To pay those near-term obligations, Company B will need to collect some of its accounts receivables, sell more inventory, borrow from a bank, and/or raise more long-term capital (e.g., by issuing more bonds or more equity). Company C also appears more liquid than Company B. It holds over 30 percent of its total assets in cash and short-term marketable securities, and its current liabilities are only 6.2 percent of the amount of total assets.

Company C's $3.3 million in cash and short-term marketable securities is substantially more than its current liabilities of $600 thousand. Turning to the question of solvency, however, note that 98.5 percent of Company C's assets are financed with liabilities. If Company C experiences significant fluctuations in cash flows, it may be unable to pay the interest and principal on its long-term bonds. Company A is far more solvent than Company C, with less than one percent of its assets financed with liabilities.

Note that these examples are hypothetical only. Other than general comparisons, little more can be said without further detail. In practice, a wide range of factors affect a company's liquidity management and capital structure. The study of optimal **capital structure** is a fundamental issue addressed in corporate finance. Capital refers to a company's long-term debt and equity financing; capital structure refers to the proportion of debt versus equity financing.

Common-size balance sheets can also highlight differences in companies' strategies. Comparing the asset composition of the companies, Company C has made a greater proportional investment in property, plant, and equipment—possibly because it manufactures more of its products in-house. The presence of goodwill on Company B's balance sheet signifies that it has made one or more acquisitions in the past. In contrast, the lack of goodwill on the balance sheets of Company A and Company C suggests that these two companies may have pursued a strategy of internal growth rather than growth by acquisition. Company A may be in either a start-up or liquidation stage of operations as evidenced by the composition of its balance sheet. It has relatively little inventory and no accounts payable. It either has not yet established trade credit or it is in the process of paying off its obligations in the process of liquidating.

EXAMPLE 6

Common-Size Analysis

Applying common-size analysis to the excerpts of SAP Group's balance sheets presented in Exhibits 4, 6, 8, and 12, answer the following: In 2009 relative to 2008, which two of the following line items increased as a percentage of assets?

A Cash and cash equivalents.

B Other financial assets.

C Trade and other receivables.

D Tax assets.

E Bank loans classified as current (i.e., due within one year).

F Bank loans classified as non-current (i.e., due after one year).

Solution:

(€ amounts shown are in millions.) A and F are correct. Both cash and longer-term bank loans increased as a percentage of total assets. Cash and cash equivalents increased from 9.2 percent of total assets in 2008 (€1,280 ÷ €13,900) to 14.1 percent in 2009 (€1,884 ÷ €13,374). Bank loans due after one year increased from 0.01 percent in 2008 (€2 ÷ €13,900) to 5.2 percent in 2009 (€699 ÷ €13,374). The company may have borrowed funds for a strategic purpose that it has not yet acted upon.

The other items (other financial assets, trade and other receivables, tax assets, and bank loans classified as current) all decreased both in absolute Euro amounts and as a percentage of total assets when compared with the previous year. Note that some amounts of the company's other financial assets, trade and other receivables, and tax assets are classified as current assets (shown in Exhibit 4) and some amounts are classified as non-current assets (shown in Exhibit 8). The total amounts—current and non-current—of other financial assets, trade and other receivables, and tax assets, therefore, are obtained by summing the amounts in Exhibits 4 and 8.

Overall, the company strengthened its liquidity position in 2009. Total current assets were approximately the same percentage of total assets, whereas cash was a much higher percentage of total assets; total current liabilities were a much smaller percentage of the amount of total assets.

Common-size analysis of the balance sheet is particularly useful in cross-sectional analysis—comparing companies to each other for a particular time period or comparing a company with industry or sector data. The analyst could select individual peer companies for comparison, use industry data from published sources, or compile data from databases. When analyzing a company, many analysts prefer to select the peer companies for comparison or to compile their own industry statistics.

Exhibit 18 presents common-size balance sheet data compiled for the 10 sectors of the S&P 500 using 2008 data. The sector classification follows the S&P/MSCI Global Industrial Classification System (GICS). The exhibit presents mean and median common-size balance sheet data for those companies in the S&P 500 for which 2008 data was available in the Compustat database.[26]

---

26 An entry of zero for an item (e.g., current assets) was excluded from the data, except in the case of preferred stock. Note that most financial institutions did not provide current asset or current liability data, so these are reported as not available in the database.

Some interesting general observations can be made from these data:

- Energy and utility companies have the largest amounts of property, plant, and equipment (PPE). Telecommunication services, followed by utilities, have the highest level of long-term debt. Utilities also use some preferred stock.

- Financial companies have the greatest percentage of total liabilities. Financial companies typically have relatively high financial leverage.

- Telecommunications services and utility companies have the lowest level of receivables.

- Inventory levels are highest for consumer discretionary. Materials and consumer staples have the next highest inventories.

- Information technology companies use the least amount of leverage as evidenced by the lowest percentages for long-term debt and total liabilities and highest percentages for common and total equity.

Example 7 discusses an analyst using cross-sectional common-size balance sheet data.

EXAMPLE 7

Cross-Sectional Common-Size Analysis

Jason Lu is examining three companies in the computer industry to evaluate their relative financial position as reflected on their balance sheets. He has compiled the following vertical common-size data for Apple, Dell, and Hewlett-Packard.

Cross-Sectional Analysis Consolidated Balance Sheets (in Percent of Total Assets)			
	AAPL 30 Sept 2009	DELL 29 Jan 2010	HPQ 31 Oct 2009
ASSETS:			
Current assets:			
Cash and cash equivalents	11.1	31.6	11.6
Short-term marketable securities	38.3	1.1	0.0
Accounts receivable and financing receivables	7.1	25.4	16.7
Inventories	1.0	3.1	5.3
Deferred tax assets	2.4	0.0	0.0
Other current assets	6.6	10.8	12.1
Total current assets	66.4	72.0	45.8
Long-term marketable securities	22.2	2.3	0.0
Long-term financing receivables	0.0	0.0	9.8
Property, plant and equipment, net	6.2	6.5	9.8
Goodwill	0.4	12.1	28.8
Acquired intangible assets, net	0.5	5.0	5.7
Other assets	4.2	2.0	0.0
Total assets	100.0	100.0	100.0
LIABILITIES AND SHAREHOLDERS' EQUITY:			
Current liabilities:			
Accounts payable	11.8	33.8	12.9
Short-term debt	0.0	2.0	1.6
Accrued expenses	8.1	11.5	17.6

Exhibit 18   Common-Size Balance Sheet Statistics for the S&P 500 Grouped by S&P/MSCI GICS Sector (in percent except No. of Observations; data for 2008)

Panel A. Median Data

	10	15	20	25	30	35	40	45	50	55
	Energy	Materials	Industrials	Consumer Discretionary	Consumer Staples	Health Care	Financials	Information Technology	Telecommunication Services	Utilities
Number of observations	40	29	59	86	40	55	87	77	9	33
Cash	4.31	4.50	5.90	5.92	4.09	11.62	7.36	26.12	2.85	1.66
Receivables	8.34	12.22	16.41	9.43	8.82	11.45	18.25	9.44	5.77	5.29
Inventories	3.33	12.06	8.71	15.20	12.81	6.07	0.00	3.17	0.32	2.27
Other current	2.59	2.29	2.79	3.78	2.70	4.30	0.00	4.88	1.26	3.10
Total current assets	19.88	35.07	35.65	41.24	30.05	39.43	31.07	49.53	8.85	13.77
PPE	69.25	32.46	15.85	21.84	22.69	11.04	1.09	9.79	42.77	61.67
Intangibles	3.39	13.53	27.99	18.45	30.58	33.22	2.34	18.46	40.43	3.95
Accounts payable	6.05	6.28	6.43	7.84	7.88	3.61	9.37	3.17	2.06	3.46
Current liabilities	15.81	17.63	24.55	26.38	26.27	17.94	24.00	22.59	10.70	13.52
LT debt	17.86	22.94	19.15	22.50	26.75	18.66	11.86	9.64	52.75	30.86
Total liabilities	50.74	66.89	63.44	64.08	68.46	53.34	88.16	49.00	66.34	74.53
Preferred stock	0.00	0.00	0.00	0.00	0.00	0.00	0.00	0.00	0.00	0.18
Common equity	47.68	30.88	36.55	35.56	31.48	46.43	9.45	49.88	20.61	25.43
Total equity	47.68	31.03	36.55	35.56	31.48	46.43	11.81	49.88	20.61	25.47

Exhibit 18 (Continued)

Panel B. Mean Data

	10	15	20	25	30	35	40	45	50	55
	Energy	Materials	Industrials	Consumer Discretionary	Consumer Staples	Health Care	Financials	Information Technology	Telecommunication Services	Utilities
Number of observations	40	29	59	86	40	55	87	77	9	33
Cash	5.66	6.72	7.82	10.06	6.81	15.00	10.18	27.63	3.08	2.43
Receivables	9.43	11.80	18.76	11.40	9.62	13.24	29.68	12.16	4.63	5.92
Inventories	5.98	13.64	10.49	17.93	13.44	8.04	2.39	4.70	0.43	2.82
Other current	3.17	2.87	3.44	4.09	3.62	4.75	3.18	7.56	1.77	4.64
Total current assets	23.94	34.98	38.35	39.88	33.31	41.07	34.25	51.97	9.91	15.73
PPE	62.93	37.88	24.15	26.83	27.09	13.52	2.75	13.41	48.81	61.62
Intangibles	7.43	16.52	28.04	21.40	32.75	33.80	9.30	23.08	35.95	5.16
Accounts payable	7.02	6.64	7.69	10.51	8.65	8.50	26.87	5.03	2.46	3.90
Current liabilities	16.33	20.33	25.82	27.48	27.65	22.73	32.76	25.89	10.27	16.02
LT debt	20.08	22.83	20.48	24.94	28.01	19.76	21.04	14.84	49.17	30.99
Total liabilities	52.29	64.02	64.23	66.31	69.32	53.36	79.79	51.21	80.00	73.73
Preferred stock	0.12	0.58	0.00	0.15	0.00	0.16	1.47	0.00	0.00	0.44
Common equity	46.77	35.55	35.41	33.00	30.04	46.08	18.02	48.69	17.95	25.44
Total equity	46.89	36.14	35.41	33.15	30.04	46.25	19.49	48.69	17.95	25.88

PPE = Property, plant, and equipment, LT = Long term.
Source: Based on data from Compustat.

Cross-Sectional Analysis Consolidated Balance Sheets (in Percent of Total Assets)			
	AAPL 30 Sept 2009	DELL 29 Jan 2010	HPQ 31 Oct 2009
Deferred revenue	4.3	9.0	5.4
Total current liabilities	24.2	56.3	37.5
Long-term debt	0.0	10.2	12.2
Deferred revenue non-current	1.8	9.0	0.0
Other non-current liabilities	7.4	7.7	15.1
Total liabilities	33.4	83.2	64.7
Commitments and contingencies			
Total shareholders' equity	66.6	16.8	35.3
Total liabilities and shareholders' equity	100.0	100.0	100.0

APPL = Apple Inc.; DELL = Dell Inc.; HPQ = Hewlett-Packard Co.
Source: Based on data from companies' annual reports.

From this data, Lu learns the following:

- Apple and Dell have a high level of cash and short-term marketable securities, consistent with the information technology sector as reported in Exhibit 18. Hewlett-Packard's percentage of cash and marketable securities is lower, perhaps reflecting its broader range of information technology products and services. Apple has a higher balance in cash and investments combined than Dell, Hewlett-Packard, or the industry sector as reported in Exhibit 18. This may reflect the success of the company's business model, which has generated large operating cash flows in recent years.

- Apple has the lowest level of accounts receivable. Further research is necessary to learn the extent to which this is related to Apple's cash sales through its own retail stores. An alternative explanation would be that the company has been selling/factoring receivables to a greater degree than the other companies; however, that explanation is unlikely given Apple's cash position.

- Apple and Dell both have low levels of inventory compared to the industry sector as reported in Exhibit 18. Both utilize a just-in-time inventory system and rely on suppliers to hold inventory until needed. Additional scrutiny of the notes accompanying their annual reports reveals Apple regularly makes purchase commitments that are not currently recorded as inventory and uses contract manufacturers to assemble and test some finished products. All of the companies have some purchase commitments and make some use of contract manufacturers, which implies that inventory may be "understated."

- Apple and Dell have a level of property, plant, and equipment below that of the sector, whereas Hewlett-Packard is very close to the sector median as reported in Exhibit 18.

- Hewlett-Packard has a large amount of goodwill from its steady stream of acquisitions over the last decade.

- Dell has a large amount of accounts payable. Because of Dell's high level of cash and investments, this is likely not a problem for Dell.

- Consistent with the industry, Dell and Hewlett-Packard have very low levels of long-term debt. Apple has no long term debt.

7.2 Balance Sheet Ratios

Ratios facilitate time-series and cross-sectional analysis of a company's financial position. **Balance sheet ratios** are those involving balance sheet items only. Each of the line items on a vertical common-size balance sheet is a ratio in that it expresses a balance sheet amount in relation to total assets. Other balance sheet ratios compare one balance sheet item to another. For example, the current ratio expresses current assets in relation to current liabilities as an indicator of a company's liquidity. Balance sheet ratios include **liquidity ratios** (measuring the company's ability to meet its short-term obligations) and **solvency ratios** (measuring the company's ability to meet long-term and other obligations). These ratios and others are discussed in a later reading. Exhibit 19 summarizes the calculation and interpretation of selected balance sheet ratios.

Exhibit 19	Balance Sheet Ratios	
Liquidity Ratios	**Calculation**	**Indicates**
Current	Current assets ÷ Current liabilities	Ability to meet current liabilities
Quick (acid test)	(Cash + Marketable securities + Receivables) ÷ Current liabilities	Ability to meet current liabilities
Cash	(Cash + Marketable securities) ÷ Current liabilities	Ability to meet current liabilities
Solvency Ratios		
Long-term debt-to-equity	Total long-term debt ÷ Total equity	Financial risk and financial leverage
Debt-to-equity	Total debt ÷ Total equity	Financial risk and financial leverage
Total debt	Total debt ÷ Total assets	Financial risk and financial leverage
Financial leverage	Total assets ÷ Total equity	Financial risk and financial leverage

EXAMPLE 8

Ratio Analysis

For the following ratio questions, refer to the balance sheet information for the SAP Group presented in Exhibits 1, 4, 6, 8, and 12.

1   The current ratio for SAP Group at 31 December 2009 is *closest* to

   A   1.54.

   B   1.86.

   C   2.33.

2   Which two of the following ratios decreased in 2009 relative to 2008?

   A   Cash.

   B   Quick.

   C   Current.

   D   Debt-to-equity.

   E   Financial leverage.

F Long-term debt-to-equity.

3 For the ratios listed in Question 2, how are the changes interpreted?

Solution to 1:

A is correct. SAP Group's current ratio (Current assets ÷ Current liabilities) at 31 December 2009 is 1.54 (€5,255 million ÷ €3,416 million).

Solution to 2:

D and E are correct. The ratios are shown in the table below. The debt-to-equity and financial leverage ratios are lower in 2009 than in 2008. Bank loans (short-term debt) were reduced and equity increased. All other ratios are higher.

Liquidity Ratios	Calculation	2009 € in millions	2008 € in millions
Current	Current assets ÷ Current liabilities	€5,255 ÷ €3,416 = **1.54**	€5, 571 ÷ €5,824 = **0.96**
Quick (acid test)	(Cash + Marketable securities + Receivables) ÷ Current liabilities	(€1,884 + €486 + €2,546) ÷ €3,416 = **1.44**	(€1,280 + €588 + €3,178) ÷ €5,824 = **0.87**
Cash	(Cash + Marketable securities) ÷ Current liabilities	(€1,884 + €486) ÷ €3,416 = **0.69**	(€1,280 + €588) ÷ €5,824 = **0.32**
Solvency Ratios			
Long-term debt-to-equity	Total long-term debt ÷ Total equity	€729 ÷ €8,491 = **8.6%**	€40 ÷ €7,171 = **0.6%**
Debt-to-equity	Total debt ÷ Total equity	(€146 + €729) ÷ €8,491 = **10.3%**	(€ 2,563 + €40) ÷ €7,171 = **36.3%**
Financial Leverage	Total assets ÷ Total equity	€13,374 ÷ €8,491 = **1.58**	€13,900 ÷ €7,171 = **1.94**

Solution to 3:

- The increase in each of the liquidity ratios (current, quick, and cash) in 2009 indicates that the company's liquidity position strengthened. Compared with the end of 2008, the company reported a greater amount of current assets relative to current liabilities.

- The long-term debt-to-equity ratio indicates the amount of long-term debt capital relative to the amount of equity capital. In general, an increase in the long-term debt-to-equity ratio implies that a company's solvency has weakened. In this case, however, several points should be noted. First, despite the increase, this company's ratio remains very low, indicating its solvency position is strong. Second, securing long-term financing in 2009—when credit market disruptions had caused difficulty for some companies seeking to borrow—could be considered a very prudent action. Third, the company's overall financial leverage decreased, i.e., improved.

- The debt-to-equity ratio indicates the amount of total debt capital relative to the amount of equity capital. Financial leverage indicates the amount of total asset relative to equity. A decrease in the debt-to-equity and financial leverage ratios implies that a company's total leverage decreased and thus its solvency has improved. In this case, the company's total leverage decreased largely because the company repaid most of its short-term bank loans and increased its equity in 2009.

Cross-sectional financial ratio analysis can be limited by differences in accounting methods. In addition, lack of homogeneity of a company's operating activities can limit comparability. For diversified companies operating in different industries, using industry-specific ratios for different lines of business can provide better comparisons. Companies disclose information on operating segments. The financial position and performance of the operating segments can be compared to the relevant industry.

Ratio analysis requires a significant amount of judgment. One key area requiring judgment is understanding the limitations of any ratio. The current ratio, for example, is only a rough measure of liquidity at a specific point in time. The ratio captures only the amount of current assets, but the components of current assets differ significantly in their nearness to cash (e.g., marketable securities versus inventory). Another limitation of the current ratio is its sensitivity to end-of-period financing and operating decisions that can potentially impact current asset and current liability amounts. Another overall area requiring judgment is determining whether a ratio for a company is within a reasonable range for an industry. Yet another area requiring judgment is evaluating whether a ratio signifies a persistent condition or reflects only a temporary condition. Overall, evaluating specific ratios requires an examination of the entire operations of a company, its competitors, and the external economic and industry setting in which it is operating.

SUMMARY

The balance sheet (also referred to as the statement of financial position) discloses what an entity owns (assets) and what it owes (liabilities) at a specific point in time. Equity is the owners' residual interest in the assets of a company, net of its liabilities. The amount of equity is increased by income earned during the year, or by the issuance of new equity. The amount of equity is decreased by losses, by dividend payments, or by share repurchases.

An understanding of the balance sheet enables an analyst to evaluate the liquidity, solvency, and overall financial position of a company.

- The balance sheet distinguishes between current and non-current assets and between current and non-current liabilities unless a presentation based on liquidity provides more relevant and reliable information.

- The concept of liquidity relates to a company's ability to pay for its near-term operating needs. With respect to a company overall, liquidity refers to the availability of cash to pay those near-term needs. With respect to a particular asset or liability, liquidity refers to its "nearness to cash."

- Some assets and liabilities are measured on the basis of fair value and some are measured at historical cost. Notes to financial statements provide information that is helpful in assessing the comparability of measurement bases across companies.

- Assets expected to be liquidated or used up within one year or one operating cycle of the business, whichever is greater, are classified as current assets. Assets not expected to be liquidated or used up within one year or one operating cycle of the business, whichever is greater, are classified as non-current assets.

- Liabilities expected to be settled or paid within one year or one operating cycle of the business, whichever is greater, are classified as current liabilities. Liabilities not expected to be settled or paid within one year or one operating cycle of the business, whichever is greater, are classified as non-current liabilities.

- Trade receivables, also referred to as accounts receivable, are amounts owed to a company by its customers for products and services already delivered. Receivables are reported net of the allowance for doubtful accounts.

- Inventories are physical products that will eventually be sold to the company's customers, either in their current form (finished goods) or as inputs into a process to manufacture a final product (raw materials and work-in-process). Inventories are reported at the lower of cost or net realizable value. If the net realizable value of a company's inventory falls below its carrying amount, the company must write down the value of the inventory and record an expense.

- Inventory cost is based on specific identification or estimated using the first-in, first-out or weighted average cost methods. Some accounting standards (including U.S. GAAP but not IFRS) also allow last-in, first-out as an additional inventory valuation method.

- Accounts payable, also called trade payables, are amounts that a business owes its vendors for purchases of goods and services.

- Deferred revenue (also known as unearned revenue) arises when a company receives payment in advance of delivery of the goods and services associated with the payment received.

- Property, plant, and equipment (PPE) are tangible assets that are used in company operations and expected to be used over more than one fiscal period. Examples of tangible assets include land, buildings, equipment, machinery, furniture, and natural resources such as mineral and petroleum resources.

- IFRS provide companies with the choice to report PPE using either a historical cost model or a revaluation model. U.S. GAAP permit only the historical cost model for reporting PPE.

- Depreciation is the process of recognizing the cost of a long-lived asset over its useful life. (Land is not depreciated.)

- Under IFRS, property used to earn rental income or capital appreciation is considered to be investment property. IFRS provide companies with the choice to report investment property using either a historical cost model or a fair value model.

- Intangible assets refer to identifiable non-monetary assets without physical substance. Examples include patents, licenses, and trademarks. For each intangible asset, a company assesses whether the useful life is finite or indefinite.

- An intangible asset with a finite useful life is amortized on a systematic basis over the best estimate of its useful life, with the amortisation method and useful-life estimate reviewed at least annually. Impairment principles for an intangible asset with a finite useful life are the same as for PPE.

- An intangible asset with an indefinite useful life is not amortised. Instead, it is tested for impairment at least annually.

- For internally generated intangible assets, IFRS require that costs incurred during the research phase must be expensed. Costs incurred in the development stage can be capitalized as intangible assets if certain criteria are met, including technological feasibility, the ability to use or sell the resulting asset, and the ability to complete the project.

- The most common asset that is not a separately identifiable asset is goodwill, which arises in business combinations. Goodwill is not amortized; instead it is tested for impairment at least annually.

- Financial instruments are contracts that give rise to both a financial asset of one entity and a financial liability or equity instrument of another entity. In general, there are two basic alternative ways that financial instruments are measured: fair value or amortised cost. For financial instruments measured at fair value, there are two basic alternatives in how net changes in fair value are recognized: as profit or loss on the income statement, or as other comprehensive income (loss) which bypasses the income statement.

- Typical long-term financial liabilities include loans (i.e., borrowings from banks) and notes or bonds payable (i.e., fixed-income securities issued to investors). Liabilities such as bonds issued by a company are usually reported at amortised cost on the balance sheet.

- Deferred tax liabilities arise from temporary timing differences between a company's income as reported for tax purposes and income as reported for financial statement purposes.

- Six potential components that comprise the owners' equity section of the balance sheet include: contributed capital, preferred shares, treasury shares, retained earnings, accumulated other comprehensive income, and non-controlling interest.

- The statement of changes in equity reflects information about the increases or decreases in each component of a company's equity over a period.

- Vertical common-size analysis of the balance sheet involves stating each balance sheet item as a percentage of total assets.

- Balance sheet ratios include liquidity ratios (measuring the company's ability to meet its short-term obligations) and solvency ratios (measuring the company's ability to meet long-term and other obligations).

PRACTICE PROBLEMS

1 Resources controlled by a company as a result of past events are:

   A equity.

   B assets.

   C liabilities.

2 Equity equals:

   A Assets – Liabilities.

   B Liabilities – Assets.

   C Assets + Liabilities.

3 Distinguishing between current and non-current items on the balance sheet and presenting a subtotal for current assets and liabilities is referred to as:

   A a classified balance sheet.

   B an unclassified balance sheet.

   C a liquidity-based balance sheet.

4 All of the following are current assets *except*:

   A cash.

   B goodwill.

   C inventories.

5 Debt due within one year is considered:

   A current.

   B preferred.

   C convertible.

6 Money received from customers for products to be delivered in the future is recorded as:

   A revenue and an asset.

   B an asset and a liability.

   C revenue and a liability.

7 The carrying value of inventories reflects:

   A their historical cost.

   B their current value.

   C the lower of historical cost or net realizable value.

8 When a company pays its rent in advance, its balance sheet will reflect a reduction in:

   A assets and liabilities.

   B assets and shareholders' equity.

   C one category of assets and an increase in another.

9 Accrued expenses (accrued liabilities) are:

   A expenses that have been paid.

   B created when another liability is reduced.

   C expenses that have been reported on the income statement but not yet paid.

10 The initial measurement of goodwill is *most likely* affected by:

    A   an acquisition's purchase price.

    B   the acquired company's book value.

    C   the fair value of the acquirer's assets and liabilities.

11 Defining total asset turnover as revenue divided by average total assets, all else equal, impairment write-downs of long-lived assets owned by a company will *most likely* result in an increase for that company in:

    A   the debt-to-equity ratio but not the total asset turnover.

    B   the total asset turnover but not the debt-to-equity ratio.

    C   both the debt-to-equity ratio and the total asset turnover.

12 For financial assets classified as trading securities, how are unrealized gains and losses reflected in shareholders' equity?

    A   They are not recognized.

    B   They flow through income into retained earnings.

    C   They are a component of accumulated other comprehensive income.

13 For financial assets classified as available for sale, how are unrealized gains and losses reflected in shareholders' equity?

    A   They are not recognized.

    B   They flow through retained earnings.

    C   They are a component of accumulated other comprehensive income.

14 For financial assets classified as held to maturity, how are unrealized gains and losses reflected in shareholders' equity?

    A   They are not recognized.

    B   They flow through retained earnings.

    C   They are a component of accumulated other comprehensive income.

15 The non-controlling (minority) interest in consolidated subsidiaries is presented on the balance sheet:

    A   as a long-term liability.

    B   separately, but as a part of shareholders' equity.

    C   as a mezzanine item between liabilities and shareholders' equity.

16 The item "retained earnings" is a component of:

    A   assets.

    B   liabilities.

    C   shareholders' equity.

17 When a company buys shares of its own stock to be held in treasury, it records a reduction in:

    A   both assets and liabilities.

    B   both assets and shareholders' equity.

    C   assets and an increase in shareholders' equity.

18 Which of the following would an analyst *most likely* be able to determine from a common-size analysis of a company's balance sheet over several periods?

    A   An increase or decrease in sales.

    B   An increase or decrease in financial leverage.

    C   A more efficient or less efficient use of assets.

19 An investor concerned whether a company can meet its near-term obligations is *most likely* to calculate the:

> **A** current ratio.
>
> **B** return on total capital.
>
> **C** financial leverage ratio.

20 The most stringent test of a company's liquidity is its:

    A cash ratio.

    B quick ratio.

    C current ratio.

21 An investor worried about a company's long-term solvency would *most likely* examine its:

    A current ratio.

    B return on equity.

    C debt-to-equity ratio.

22 Using the information presented in Exhibit 4, the quick ratio for SAP Group at 31 December 2009 is *closest* to:

    A 1.01.

    B 1.44.

    C 1.54.

23 Using the information presented in Exhibit 12, the financial leverage ratio for SAP Group at 31 December 2009 is *closest* to:

    A 0.08.

    B 0.58.

    C 1.58.

SOLUTIONS

1 B is correct. Assets are resources controlled by a company as a result of past events.

2 A is correct. Assets = Liabilities + Equity and, therefore, Assets − Liabilities = Equity.

3 A is correct. A classified balance sheet is one that classifies assets and liabilities as current or non-current and provides a subtotal for current assets and current liabilities. A liquidity-based balance sheet broadly presents assets and liabilities in order of liquidity.

4 B is correct. Goodwill is a long-term asset, and the others are all current assets.

5 A is correct. Current liabilities are those liabilities, including debt, due within one year. Preferred refers to a class of stock. Convertible refers to a feature of bonds (or preferred stock) allowing the holder to convert the instrument into common stock.

6 B is correct. The cash received from customers represents an asset. The obligation to provide a product in the future is a liability called "unearned income" or "unearned revenue." As the product is delivered, revenue will be recognized and the liability will be reduced.

7 C is correct. Under IFRS, inventories are carried at historical cost, unless net realizable value of the inventory is less. Under U.S. GAAP, inventories are carried at the lower of cost or market.

8 C is correct. Paying rent in advance will reduce cash and increase prepaid expenses, both of which are assets.

9 C is correct. Accrued liabilities are expenses that have been reported on a company's income statement but have not yet been paid.

10 A is correct. Initially, goodwill is measured as the difference between the purchase price paid for an acquisition and the fair value of the acquired, not acquiring, company's net assets (identifiable assets less liabilities).

11 C is correct. Impairment write-downs reduce equity in the denominator of the debt-to-equity ratio but do not affect debt, so the debt-to-equity ratio is expected to increase. Impairment write-downs reduce total assets but do not affect revenue. Thus, total asset turnover is expected to increase.

12 B is correct. For financial assets classified as trading securities, unrealized gains and losses are reported on the income statement and flow to shareholders' equity as part of retained earnings.

13 C is correct. For financial assets classified as available for sale, unrealized gains and losses are not recorded on the income statement and instead are part of *other* comprehensive income. Accumulated other comprehensive income is a component of Shareholders' equity

14 A is correct. Financial assets classified as held to maturity are measured at amortised cost. Gains and losses are recognized only when realized.

15 B is correct. The non-controlling interest in consolidated subsidiaries is shown separately as part of shareholders' equity.

16 C is correct. The item "retained earnings" is a component of shareholders' equity.

17 B is correct. Share repurchases reduce the company's cash (an asset). Shareholders' equity is reduced because there are fewer shares outstanding and treasury stock is an offset to owners' equity.

18 B is correct. Common-size analysis (as presented in the reading) provides information about composition of the balance sheet and changes over time. As a result, it can provide information about an increase or decrease in a company's financial leverage.

19 A is correct. The current ratio provides a comparison of assets that can be turned into cash relatively quickly and liabilities that must be paid within one year. The other ratios are more suited to longer-term concerns.

20 A is correct. The cash ratio determines how much of a company's near-term obligations can be settled with existing amounts of cash and marketable securities.

21 C is correct. The debt-to-equity ratio, a solvency ratio, is an indicator of financial risk.

22 B is correct. The quick ratio ([Cash + Marketable securities + Receivables] ÷ Current liabilities) is 1.44 ([= 1,884 + 486 + 2,546] ÷ 3,416). Given the placement of other financial assets between cash and receivables, it is reasonable to assume these are highly liquid and are probably marketable securities.

23 C is correct. The financial leverage ratio (Total assets ÷ Total equity) is 1.58 (= 13,374 ÷ 8,491).

Understanding Cash Flow Statements

by Elaine Henry, CFA, Thomas R. Robinson, CFA,
Jan Hendrik van Greuning, CFA, and Michael A. Broihahn, CFA

LEARNING OUTCOMES

Mastery	The candidate should be able to:
☐	a. compare cash flows from operating, investing, and financing activities and classify cash flow items as relating to one of those three categories given a description of the items;
☐	b. describe how non-cash investing and financing activities are reported;
☐	c. contrast cash flow statements prepared under International Financial Reporting Standards (IFRS) and U.S. generally accepted accounting principles (U.S. GAAP);
☐	d. distinguish between the direct and indirect methods of presenting cash from operating activities and describe arguments in favor of each method;
☐	e. describe how the cash flow statement is linked to the income statement and the balance sheet;
☐	f. describe the steps in the preparation of direct and indirect cash flow statements, including how cash flows can be computed using income statement and balance sheet data;
☐	g. convert cash flows from the indirect to direct method;
☐	h. analyze and interpret both reported and common-size cash flow statements;
☐	i. calculate and interpret free cash flow to the firm, free cash flow to equity, and performance and coverage cash flow ratios.

Note: New rulings and/or pronouncements issued after the publication of the readings in financial reporting and analysis may cause some of the information in these readings to become dated. Candidates are expected to be familiar with the overall analytical framework contained in the study session readings, as well as the implications of alternative accounting methods for financial analysis and valuation, as provided in the assigned readings. Candidates are not responsible for changes that occur after the material was written.

1   INTRODUCTION

The cash flow statement provides information about a company's *cash receipts* and *cash payments* during an accounting period. The cash-based information provided by the cash flow statement contrasts with the accrual-based information from the income statement. For example, the income statement reflects revenues when earned rather than when cash is collected; in contrast, the cash flow statement reflects cash receipts when collected as opposed to when the revenue was earned. A reconciliation between reported income and cash flows from operating activities provides useful information about when, whether, and how a company is able to generate cash from its operating activities. Although income is an important measure of the results of a company's activities, cash flow is also essential. As an extreme illustration, a hypothetical company that makes all sales on account, without regard to whether it will ever collect its accounts receivable, would report healthy sales on its income statement and might well report significant income; however, with zero cash inflow, the company would not survive. The cash flow statement also provides a reconciliation of the beginning and ending cash on the balance sheet.

In addition to information about cash generated (or, alternatively, cash used) in operating activities, the cash flow statement provides information about cash provided (or used) in a company's investing and financing activities. This information allows the analyst to answer such questions as:

- Does the company generate enough cash from its operations to pay for its new investments, or is the company relying on new debt issuance to finance them?

- Does the company pay its dividends to common stockholders using cash generated from operations, from selling assets, or from issuing debt?

Answers to these questions are important because, in theory, generating cash from operations can continue indefinitely, but generating cash from selling assets, for example, is possible only as long as there are assets to sell. Similarly, generating cash from debt financing is possible only as long as lenders are willing to lend, and the lending decision depends on expectations that the company will ultimately have adequate cash to repay its obligations. In summary, information about the sources and uses of cash helps creditors, investors, and other statement users evaluate the company's liquidity, solvency, and financial flexibility.

This reading explains how cash flow activities are reflected in a company's cash flow statement. The reading is organized as follows. Section 2 describes the components and format of the cash flow statement, including the classification of cash flows under International Financial Reporting Standards (IFRS) and U.S. generally accepted accounting principles (GAAP) and the direct and indirect formats for presenting the cash flow statement. Section 3 discusses the linkages of the cash flow statement with the income statement and balance sheet and the steps in the preparation of the cash flow statement. Section 4 demonstrates the analysis of cash flow statements, including the conversion of an indirect cash flow statement to the direct method and how to use common-size cash flow analysis, free cash flow measures, and cash flow ratios used in security analysis. A summary of the key points and practice problems in the CFA Institute multiple-choice format conclude the reading.

COMPONENTS AND FORMAT OF THE CASH FLOW STATEMENT

2

The analyst needs to be able to extract and interpret information on cash flows from financial statements. The basic components and allowable formats of the cash flow statement are well established.

- The cash flow statement has subsections relating specific items to the operating, investing, and financing activities of the company.
- Two presentation formats for the operating section are allowable: direct and indirect.

The following discussion presents these topics in greater detail.

2.1 Classification of Cash Flows and Non-Cash Activities

All companies engage in operating, investing, and financing activities. These activities are the classifications used in the cash flow statement under both IFRS and U.S. GAAP and are described as follows:[1]

- **Operating activities** include the company's day-to-day activities that create revenues, such as selling inventory and providing services, and other activities not classified as investing or financing. Cash inflows result from cash sales and from collection of accounts receivable. Examples include cash receipts from the provision of services and royalties, commissions, and other revenue. To generate revenue, companies undertake such activities as manufacturing inventory, purchasing inventory from suppliers, and paying employees. Cash outflows result from cash payments for inventory, salaries, taxes, and other operating-related expenses and from paying accounts payable. Additionally, operating activities include cash receipts and payments related to **dealing securities** or **trading securities** (as opposed to buying or selling securities as investments, as discussed below).

- **Investing activities** include purchasing and selling long-term assets and other investments. These long-term assets and other investments include property, plant, and equipment; intangible assets; other long-term assets; and both long-term and short-term investments in the equity and debt (bonds and loans) issued by other companies. For this purpose, investments in equity and debt securities exclude a) any securities considered cash equivalents (very short-term, highly liquid securities) and b) securities held for dealing or trading purposes, the purchase and sale of which are considered operating activities even for companies where this is not a primary business activity. Cash inflows in the investing category include cash receipts from the sale of non-trading securities; property, plant, and equipment; intangibles; and other long-term assets. Cash outflows include cash payments for the purchase of these assets.

- **Financing activities** include obtaining or repaying capital, such as equity and long-term debt. The two primary sources of capital are shareholders and creditors. Cash inflows in this category include cash receipts from issuing stock (common or preferred) or bonds and cash receipts from borrowing. Cash outflows include cash payments to repurchase stock (e.g., treasury stock) and to

---

1 IAS 7 *Statement of Cash Flows.*

repay bonds and other borrowings. Note that indirect borrowing using accounts payable is not considered a financing activity—such borrowing is classified as an operating activity.

EXAMPLE 1

Net Cash Flow from Investing Activities

A company recorded the following in Year 1:

Proceeds from issuance of long-term debt	€300,000
Purchase of equipment	€200,000
Loss on sale of equipment	€70,000
Proceeds from sale of equipment	€120,000
Equity in earnings of affiliate	€10,000

On the Year 1 statement of cash flows, the company would report net cash flow from investing activities *closest* to:

A   (€150,000).

B   (€80,000).

C   €200,000.

Solution

B is correct. The only two items that would affect the investing section are the purchase of equipment and the proceeds from sale of equipment: (€200,000) + €120,000 = (€80,000). The loss on sale of equipment and the equity in earnings of affiliate affect net income but are not cash flows. The issuance of debt is a financing cash flow.

IFRS provide companies with choices in reporting some items of cash flow, particularly interest and dividends. IFRS explain that although for a financial institution interest paid and received would normally be classified as operating activities, for other entities, alternative classifications may be appropriate. For this reason, under IFRS, interest received may be classified either as an operating activity or as an investing activity. Under IFRS, interest paid may be classified as either an operating activity or a financing activity. Furthermore, under IFRS, dividends received may be classified as either an operating activity or an investing activity and dividends paid may be classified as either an operating activity or a financing activity. Companies must use a consistent classification from year to year and disclose separately the amounts of interest and dividends received and paid and where the amounts are reported.

Under U.S. GAAP, discretion is not permitted in classifying interest and dividends. Interest received and interest paid are reported as operating activities for all companies.[2] Under U.S. GAAP, dividends received are always reported as operating activities and dividends paid are always reported as financing activities.

---

2 FASB ASC Topic 230 [Statement of Cash Flows].

EXAMPLE 2

Operating versus Financing Cash Flows

On 31 December 2009, a company issued a £30,000 180-day note at 8 percent and used the cash received to pay for inventory and issued £110,000 long-term debt at 11 percent annually and used the cash received to pay for new equipment. Which of the following *most* accurately reflects the combined effect of both transactions on the company's cash flows for the year ended 31 December 2009 under IFRS? Cash flows from:

A operations are unchanged.

B financing increase £110,000.

C operations decrease £30,000.

Solution:

C is correct. The payment for inventory would decrease cash flows from operations. The issuance of debt (both short-term and long-term debt) is part of financing activities and would increase cash flows from financing activities by £140,000. The purchase of equipment is an investing activity. Note that the treatment under U.S. GAAP would be the same for these transactions.

Companies may also engage in non-cash investing and financing transactions. A non-cash transaction is any transaction that does not involve an inflow or outflow of cash. For example, if a company exchanges one non-monetary asset for another non-monetary asset, no cash is involved. Similarly, no cash is involved when a company issues common stock either for dividends or in connection with conversion of a convertible bond or convertible preferred stock. Because no cash is involved in non-cash transactions (by definition), these transactions are not incorporated in the cash flow statement. However, because such transactions may affect a company's capital or asset structures, any significant non-cash transaction is required to be disclosed, either in a separate note or a supplementary schedule to the cash flow statement.

2.2 A Summary of Differences between IFRS and U.S. GAAP

As highlighted in the previous section, there are some differences in cash flow statements prepared under IFRS and U.S. GAAP that the analyst should be aware of when comparing the cash flow statements of companies prepared in accordance with different sets of standards. The key differences are summarized in Exhibit 1. Most significantly, IFRS allow more flexibility in the reporting of such items as interest paid or received and dividends paid or received and in how income tax expense is classified.

U.S. GAAP classify interest and dividends received from investments as operating activities, whereas IFRS allow companies to classify those items as either operating or investing cash flows. Likewise, U.S. GAAP classify interest expense as an operating activity, even though the principal amount of the debt issued is classified as a financing activity. IFRS allow companies to classify interest expense as either an operating activity or a financing activity. U.S. GAAP classify dividends paid to stockholders as a financing activity, whereas IFRS allow companies to classify dividends paid as either an operating activity or a financing activity.

U.S. GAAP classify all income tax expenses as an operating activity. IFRS also classify income tax expense as an operating activity, unless the tax expense can be specifically identified with an investing or financing activity (e.g., the tax effect of the sale of a discontinued operation could be classified under investing activities).

Exhibit 1	Cash Flow Statements: Differences between IFRS and U.S. GAAP	
Topic	**IFRS**	**U.S. GAAP**
Classification of cash flows:		
■ Interest received	Operating or investing	Operating
■ Interest paid	Operating or financing	Operating
■ Dividends received	Operating or investing	Operating
■ Dividends paid	Operating or financing	Financing
■ Bank overdrafts	Considered part of cash equivalents	Not considered part of cash and cash equivalents and classified as financing
■ Taxes paid	Generally operating, but a portion can be allocated to investing or financing if it can be specifically identified with these categories	Operating
Format of statement	Direct or indirect; direct is encouraged	Direct or indirect; direct is encouraged. A reconciliation of net income to cash flow from operating activities must be provided regardless of method used

Sources: IAS 7; FASB ASC Topic 230; and "IFRS and U.S. GAAP: Similarities and Differences," PricewaterhouseCoopers (September 2009), available at www.pwc.com.

Under either set of standards, companies currently have a choice of formats for presenting cash flow statements, as discussed in the next section.

2.3 Direct and Indirect Methods for Reporting Cash Flow from Operating Activities

There are two acceptable formats for reporting **cash flow from operating activities** (also known as **cash flow from operations** or **operating cash flow**), defined as the net amount of cash provided from operating activities: the direct and the indirect methods. The *amount* of operating cash flow is identical under both methods; only the *presentation format* of the operating cash flow section differs. The presentation format of the cash flows from investing and financing is exactly the same, regardless of which method is used to present operating cash flows.

The **direct method** shows the specific cash inflows and outflows that result in reported cash flow from operating activities. It shows each cash inflow and outflow related to a company's cash receipts and disbursements. In other words, the direct method eliminates any impact of accruals and shows only cash receipts and cash payments. The primary argument in favor of the direct method is that it provides information on the specific sources of operating cash receipts and payments. This is in contrast to the indirect method, which shows only the net result of these receipts and payments. Just as information on the specific sources of revenues and expenses is more useful than knowing only the net result—net income—the analyst gets additional information from a direct-format cash flow statement. The additional information is useful in understanding historical performance and in predicting future operating cash flows.

The **indirect method** shows how cash flow from operations can be obtained from reported net income as the result of a series of adjustments. The **indirect format** begins with net income. To reconcile net income with operating cash flow, adjustments are made for non-cash items, for non-operating items, and for the net changes in operating accruals. The main argument for the indirect approach is that it shows the reasons for differences between net income and operating cash flows. (However, the differences between net income and operating cash flows are equally visible on an indirect-format cash flow statement and in the supplementary reconciliation required under U.S. GAAP if the company uses the direct method.) Another argument for the indirect method is that it mirrors a forecasting approach that begins by forecasting future income and then derives cash flows by adjusting for changes in balance sheet accounts that occur because of the timing differences between accrual and cash accounting.

IFRS and U.S. GAAP both encourage the use of the direct method but permit either method. U.S. GAAP encourage the use of the direct method but also require companies to present a reconciliation between net income and cash flow (which is equivalent to the indirect method).[3] If the indirect method is chosen, no direct-format disclosures are required. The majority of companies, reporting under IFRS or U.S. GAAP, present using the indirect method for operating cash flows.

Many users of financial statements prefer the **direct format**, particularly analysts and commercial lenders, because of the importance of information about operating receipts and payments in assessing a company's financing needs and capacity to repay existing obligations. Preparers argue that adjusting net income to operating cash flow, as in the indirect format, is easier and less costly than reporting gross operating cash receipts and payments, as in the direct format. With advances in accounting systems and technology, it is not clear that gathering the information required to use the direct method is difficult or costly. CFA Institute has advocated that standard setters require the use of the direct format for the main presentation of the cash flow statement, with indirect cash flows as supplementary disclosure.[4]

2.3.1 *An Indirect-Format Cash Flow Statement Prepared under IFRS*

Exhibit 2 presents the consolidated cash flow statement prepared under IFRS from Unilever Group's 2009 annual report.[5] The statement, covering the fiscal years ended 31 December 2009, 2008, and 2007, shows the use of the indirect method. Unilever is an Anglo-Dutch consumer products company with headquarters in the United Kingdom and the Netherlands.[6]

---

3 FASB ASC Section 230-10-45 [Statement of Cash Flows–Overall–Other Presentation Matters].

4 *A Comprehensive Business Reporting Model: Financial Reporting for Investors*, CFA Institute Centre for Financial Market Integrity (July 2007), p. 13.

5 The cash flow statement presented here includes a reconciliation of net income to cash generated from operations, which Unilever Group reports in Note 28 to the financial statement rather than on the statement itself.

6 Unilever NV (Amsterdam: UNA; NYSE: UN) and Unilever PLC (London: ULVR; NYSE: UL) have independent legal structures, but a series of agreements enable the companies to operate as a single economic entity.

Exhibit 2	Unilever Group Consolidated Cash Flow Statement (€ millions)		
	For the year ended 31 December		
	2009	**2008**	**2007**
Cash flow from operating activities			
Net profit	3,659	5,285	4,136
Taxation	1,257	1,844	1,137
Share of net profit of joint ventures/associates and other income from non-current investments	(489)	(219)	(191)
Net finance costs:	593	257	252
Finance income	(75)	(106)	(147)
Finance cost	504	506	550
Preference shares provision	—	—	7
Pensions and similar obligations	164	(143)	(158)
Operating profit (continuing and discontinued operations)	5,020	7,167	5,334
Depreciation, amortisation and impairment	1,032	1,003	943
Changes in working capital:	1,701	(161)	27
Inventories	473	(345)	(333)
Trade and other current receivables	640	(248)	(43)
Trade payables and other current liabilities	588	432	403
Pensions and similar provisions less payments	(1,028)	(502)	(910)
Provisions less payments	(258)	(62)	145
Elimination of (profits)/losses on disposals	13	(2,259)	(459)
Non-cash charge for share-based compensation	195	125	118
Other adjustments	58	15	(10)
Cash flow from operating activities	**6,733**	**5,326**	**5,188**
Income tax paid	(959)	(1,455)	(1,312)
Net cash flow from operating activities	**5,774**	**3,871**	**3,876**
Interest received	73	105	146
Purchase of intangible assets	(121)	(147)	(136)
Purchase of property, plant and equipment	(1,248)	(1,142)	(1,046)
Disposal of property, plant and equipment	111	190	163
Sale and leaseback transactions resulting in operating leases	—	—	36
Acquisition of group companies, joint ventures and associates	(409)	(211)	(214)
Disposal of group companies, joint ventures and associates	270	2,476	164
Acquisition of other non-current investments	(95)	(126)	(50)
Disposal of other non-current investments	224	47	33
Dividends from joint ventures, associates and other non-current investments	201	132	188
(Purchase)/sale of financial assets	(269)	91	93
Net cash flow (used in)/from investing activities	**(1,263)**	**1,415**	**(623)**
Dividends paid on ordinary share capital	(2,106)	(2,086)	(2,182)
Interest and preference dividends paid	(517)	(487)	(552)
Additional financial liabilities	2,913	4,544	4,283

Exhibit 2	(Continued)			
		For the year ended 31 December		
		2009	**2008**	**2007**
Repayment of financial liabilities		(4,456)	(3,427)	(2,896)
Sale and leaseback transactions resulting in finance leases		—	(1)	25
Capital element of finance lease rental payments		(24)	(66)	(74)
Share buy-back programme		—	(1,503)	(1,500)
Other movements on treasury stock		103	103	442
Other financing activities		(214)	(207)	(555)
Net cash flow (used in)/from financing activities		**(4,301)**	**(3,130)**	**(3,009)**
Net increase/(decrease) in cash and cash equivalents		**210**	**2,156**	**244**
Cash and cash equivalents at the beginning of the year		**2,360**	**901**	**710**
Effect of foreign exchange rate changes		(173)	(697)	(53)
Cash and cash equivalents at the end of the year		**2,397**	**2,360**	**901**

Beginning first at the bottom of the statement, we note that cash increased from €710 million at the beginning of 2007 to €2,397 million at the end of 2009, with the largest increase occurring in 2008. To understand the changes, we next examine the sections of the statement. In each year, the primary cash inflow derived from operating activities, as would be expected for a mature company in a relatively stable industry. In each year, the operating cash flow was more than the reported net profit, again, as would be expected from a mature company, with the largest differences primarily arising from the add-back of depreciation. Also, in each year, the operating cash flow was more than enough to cover the company's capital expenditures. For example, in 2009, the company generated €5,774 million in net cash from operating activities and—as shown in the investing section—spent €1,137 million on property, plant, and equipment (€1,248 million, net of €111 million proceeds from disposals). Also, as shown in the investing section, the main reason for the large increase in cash in 2008 was the €2,476 million inflow from the disposal of group companies, joint ventures, and associates.

The financing section of the statement shows that each year the company returned about €2.1 billion to its common shareholders and around €500 million to its debt holders and preferred shareholders via interest and dividends. The company also repurchased about €1.5 billion in common stock in both 2007 and 2008. In 2009, the company repaid debt (repayments of €4,456 million exceeded additional financing liabilities of €2,913 million).

Having examined each section of the statement, we return to the operating activities section of Unilever's cash flow statement, which presents a reconciliation of net profit to net cash flow from operating activities (i.e., uses the indirect method). The following discussion of certain adjustments to reconcile net profit to operating cash flows explains some of the main reconciliation adjustments and refers to the amounts in 2009. The first adjustment adds back the €1,257 million income tax expense (labeled "Taxation") that had been recognized as an expense in the computation of net profit. A €959 million deduction for the (cash) income taxes paid is then shown separately, as the last item in the operating activities section, consistent with the IFRS requirement that cash flows arising from income taxes be separately disclosed. The classification of taxes on income paid should be indicated. The classification is in operating activities unless the taxes can be specifically identified with financing or investing activities.

The next adjustment "removes" from the operating cash flow section the €489 million representing Unilever's share of joint ventures' income that had been included in the computation of net profit. A €201 million inflow of (cash) dividends received from those joint ventures is then shown in the investing activities section. Similarly, a €593 million adjustment removes the net finance costs from the operating activities section. Unilever then reports its €73 million (cash) interest received in the investing activities section and its €517 million (cash) interest paid (and preference dividends paid) in the financing activities section. The next adjustment in the operating section of this indirect-method statement adds back €1,032 million depreciation, amortisation, and impairment, all of which are expenses that had been deducted in the computation of net income but which did not involve any outflow of cash in the period. The €1,701 million adjustment for changes in working capital is necessary because these changes result from applying accrual accounting and thus do not necessarily correspond to the actual cash movement. These adjustments are described in greater detail in a later section.

In summary, some observations from an analysis of Unilever's cash flow statement include:

■ Total cash increased from €710 million at the beginning of 2007 to €2,397 million at the end of 2009, with the largest increase occurring in 2008.

■ In each year, the operating cash flow was more than the reported net profit, as would generally be expected from a mature company.

■ In each year, the operating cash flow was more than enough to cover the company's capital expenditures.

■ The company returned cash to its equity investors through dividends in each year and through share buybacks in 2007 and 2008.

2.3.2 A Direct-Format Cash Flow Statement Prepared under IFRS

In the direct format of the cash flow statement, the cash received from customers, as well as other operating items, is clearly shown.

Exhibit 3 presents a direct-method format cash flow statement prepared under IFRS for Telefónica Group (SM: TEF), a diversified telecommunications company based in Madrid.[7]

Exhibit 3	**Telefónica Group Consolidated Statement of Cash Flows (€ millions)**		
for the years ended 31 December	**2009**	**2008**	**2007**
Cash flows from operating activities			
Cash received from customers	67,358	69,060	67,129
Cash paid to suppliers and employees	(46,198)	(48,500)	(47,024)
Dividends received	100	113	124
Net interest and other financial expenses paid	(2,170)	(2,894)	(3,221)
Taxes paid	(2,942)	(1,413)	(1,457)
Net cash from operating activities	**16,148**	**16,366**	**15,551**
Cash flows from investing activities			

---

7 This statement excludes the supplemental cash flow reconciliation provided at the bottom of the original cash flow statement by the company.

Exhibit 3	(Continued)		
Proceeds on disposals of property, plant and equipment and intangible assets	242	276	198
Payments on investments in property, plant and equipment and intangible assets	(7,593)	(7,889)	(7,274)
Proceeds on disposals of companies, net of cash and cash equivalents disposed	34	686	5,346
Payments on investments in companies, net of cash and cash equivalents acquired	(48)	(2,178)	(2,798)
Proceeds on financial investments not included under cash equivalents	6	31	14
Payments made on financial investments not included under cash equivalents	(1,411)	(114)	(179)
Interest (paid) received on cash surpluses not included under cash equivalents	(548)	76	74
Government grants received	18	11	27
Net cash used in investing activities	**(9,300)**	**(9,101)**	**(4,592)**
Cash flows from financing activities			
Dividends paid	(4,838)	(4,440)	(3,345)
Transactions with equity holders	(947)	(2,241)	(2,152)
Proceeds on issue of debentures and bonds	8,617	1,317	4,209
Proceeds on loans, borrowings and promissory notes	2,330	3,693	6,658
Cancellation of debentures and bonds	(1,949)	(1,167)	(1,756)
Repayments of loans, borrowings and promissory notes	(5,494)	(4,927)	(13,039)
Net cash flow used in financing activities	**(2,281)**	**(7,765)**	**(9,425)**
Effect of foreign exchange rate changes on collections and payments	269	(302)	(261)
Effect of changes in consolidation methods and other non-monetary effects	—	14	—
Net increase (decrease) in cash and cash equivalents during the period	**4,836**	**(788)**	**1,273**
Cash and cash equivalents at 1 January	4,277	5,065	3,792
Cash and cash equivalents at 31 December	9,113	4,277	5,065

As shown at the bottom of the statement, cash and cash equivalents increased from €3,792 million at the beginning of 2007 to €9,113 million at the end of 2009. The largest increase in cash occurred in 2009, with 2008 showing a decrease. Cash from operations was the primary source of cash, consistent with the profile of a mature company in a relatively stable industry. Each year, the company generated significantly more cash from operations than it required for its capital expenditures. For example, in 2009, the company generated €16.1 billion cash from operations and spent—as shown in the investing section—only €7.4 billion on property, plant, and equipment (€7,593 million, net of €242 million from disposals). Another notable item from the investing section is the company's limited acquisition activity in 2009 compared with 2008 and 2007. In both 2007 and 2008, the company made over €2 billion of acquisitions, and in 2007, the company also received €5.5 billion from disposals. Instead of using cash for acquisition activity in 2009 when net acquisitions used only €14 million

(€48 million acquisitions, net of €34 million from disposals), the company invested €1,411 million in financial investments excluded from cash and cash equivalents (i.e., long-term financial investments).

As shown in the financing section, in 2009, the net cash inflow from debt issuance was €3,504 million (€8,617 million proceeds from debentures and bonds plus €2,330 million proceeds from loans, borrowings, and promissory notes, net of repayments and cancellations totaling €7,443 million).

In summary, some observations from an analysis of Telefónica's cash flow statement include

■ Total cash and cash equivalents increased over the three-year period, with 2009 showing the biggest increase.

■ Cash from operating activities was large enough in each year to cover the company's capital expenditures.

■ The amount paid for property, plant, and equipment and intangible assets was the largest investing expenditure each year and did not significantly vary from year to year.

■ The company had a significant amount of acquisition and divestiture activity in 2007 and 2008 but not in 2009.

■ The company paid an increasing amount of dividends over the three-year period.

An analyst can also make some comparisons between the income statement (not shown here) and the statement of cash flows. For example, contrast the change in revenues from the income statement to the change in cash received from customers. An increase in revenues coupled with a decrease in cash received from customers, for example, could signal collection problems. As shown in Exhibit 3, cash received from customers in 2009 decreased 2.46 percent compared with 2008, from €69,060 million to €67,358 million. The company reported revenues on the income statement of €56,731 million and €57,946 million for 2009 and 2008, respectively. Thus, the decrease in cash received from customers was slightly greater than the 2.10 percent decrease in total revenue and would not in itself indicate any collection issue.

2.3.3 Illustrations of Cash Flow Statements Prepared under U.S. GAAP

Previously, we presented cash flow statements prepared under IFRS. In this section, we illustrate cash flow statements prepared under U.S. GAAP. This section presents the cash flow statements of two companies, Tech Data Corporation (NASDAQ: TECD) and Walmart (NYSE: WMT). Tech Data reports its operating activities using the direct method, whereas Walmart reports its operating activities using the more common indirect method.

Tech Data Corporation is a leading distributor of information technology products. Exhibit 4 presents comparative cash flow statements from the company's annual report for the fiscal years ended 31 January 2008 through 2010.

Exhibit 4	Tech Data Corporation and Subsidiaries Consolidated Cash Flow Statements (in Thousands)		
Years Ended 31 January	**2010**	**2009**	**2008**
Cash flows from operating activities:			
Cash received from customers	$21,927,372	$23,989,567	$23,473,295
Cash paid to vendors and employees	(21,320,637)	(23,636,388)	(23,053,048)
Interest paid, net	(14,015)	(20,382)	(14,273)

Exhibit 4	(Continued)		

Years Ended 31 January	2010	2009	2008
Income taxes paid	(48,790)	(52,987)	(48,552)
Net cash provided by operating activities	**543,930**	**279,810**	**357,422**
Cash flows from investing activities:			
Acquisition of business, net of cash acquired	(8,153)	(78,266)	(21,503)
Proceeds from sale of business	0	0	7,161
Proceeds from sale of property and equipment	5,491	0	0
Expenditures for property and equipment	(14,486)	(17,272)	(21,474)
Software and software development costs	(14,379)	(15,275)	(16,885)
Net cash used in investing activities	**(31,527)**	**(110,813)**	**(52,701)**
Cash flows from financing activities:			
Proceeds from the issuance of common stock and reissuance of treasury stock	37,959	1,530	12,542
Cash paid for purchase of treasury stock	0	(100,000)	(100,019)
Capital contributions and net borrowings from joint venture partner	23,208	10,810	9,000
Net (repayments) borrowings on revolving credit loans	(19,116)	42,834	(56,297)
Principal payments on long-term debt	(5,654)	(1,786)	(2,371)
Excess tax benefit from stock-based compensation	963	0	212
Net cash provided by (used in) financing activities	**37,360**	**(46,612)**	**(136,933)**
Effect of exchange rate changes on cash and cash equivalents	38,793	(41,702)	14,546
Net increase in cash and cash equivalents	588,556	80,683	182,334
Cash and cash equivalents at beginning of year	528,023	447,340	265,006
Cash and cash equivalents at end of year	**$1,116,579**	**$528,023**	**$447,340**

Reconciliation of net income to net cash provided by operating activities:

Net income attributable to shareholders of Tech Data Corporation	$180,155	$117,278	$102,129
Net income (loss) attributable to non-controlling interest	1,045	(1,822)	(3,559)
Consolidated net income	**181,200**	**115,456**	**98,570**
Adjustments to reconcile net income to net cash provided by (used in) operating activities:			
Loss on disposal of subsidiaries	0	0	14,471
Depreciation and amortization	45,954	51,234	53,881
Provision for losses on accounts receivable	10,953	15,000	11,200
Stock-based compensation expense	11,225	11,990	10,287
Accretion of debt discount on convertible senior debentures	10,278	10,278	10,278

(continued)

Exhibit 4	(Continued)		
Years Ended 31 January	**2010**	**2009**	**2008**
Deferred income taxes	(2,541)	18,221	2,629
Excess tax benefit from stock-based compensation	(963)	0	(212)
Changes in operating assets and liabilities:			
Accounts receivable	(168,152)	(86,423)	57,419
Inventories	116,543	(261,974)	57,904
Prepaid expenses and other assets	21,290	(18,761)	(40,951)
Accounts payable	336,587	374,696	83,845
Accrued expenses and other liabilities	(18,444)	50,093	(1,899)
Total adjustments	362,730	164,354	258,852
Net cash provided by operating activities	$543,930	$279,810	$357,422

Tech Data Corporation prepares its cash flow statements under the direct method. The company's cash increased from $265 million at the beginning of 2008 to $1.1 billion at the end of January 2010, with the biggest increase occurring in the most recent year. The 2010 increase was driven by changes across all three sections of the statement. In the cash flows from operating activities section of Tech Data's cash flow statements, the company identifies the amount of cash it received from customers, $21.9 billion for 2010, and the amount of cash that it paid to suppliers and employees, $21.3 billion for 2010. Cash receipts decreased from $24.0 billion in the prior year, but cash paid decreased by even more such that cash provided by operating activities increased in 2010 compared with 2009. Net cash provided by operating activities of $543.9 million was adequate to cover the company's investing activities, primarily purchases of property and equipment ($14.5 million) and software development ($14.4 million). Overall, investing activities in 2010 used far less cash than in 2009, primarily because of reduced amounts of cash used for acquisition of businesses. In 2010, the company issued $38 million of common stock and received $23.2 million in contributions and borrowings from its joint venture partner, providing net cash from financing activities of $37.4 million after its debt repayments.

Whenever the direct method is used, U.S. GAAP require a disclosure note and a schedule that reconciles net income with the net cash flow from operating activities. Tech Data shows this reconciliation at the bottom of its consolidated statements of cash flows. The disclosure note and reconciliation schedule are exactly the information that would have been presented in the body of the cash flow statement if the company had elected to use the indirect method rather than the direct method. For 2009, the reconciliation highlights an increase in the company's accounts receivable, a decrease in inventory, and a significant increase in payables.

In summary, some observations from an analysis of Tech Data's cash flow statement include:

- The company's cash increased by $852 (= 1,117 − 265 or = 589 + 81 + 182) million over the three years ending in January 2010, with the biggest increase occurring in the most recent year.

- The company's operating cash was adequate to cover the company's investments in all three years.
- In 2009, the company issued stock and received financing from its joint venture partner, which provided the company with a stronger cash cushion.

Walmart is a global retailer that conducts business under the names of Walmart and Sam's Club. Exhibit 5 presents the comparative cash flow statements from the company's annual report for the fiscal years ended 31 January 2010, 2009, and 2008.

Exhibit 5	Walmart Cash Flow Statements Fiscal Years Ended 31 January ($ millions)		
Fiscal Year Ended 31 January	**2010**	**2009**	**2008**
Cash flows from operating activities:			
Consolidated net income	14,848	13,899	13,137
Loss (income) from discontinued operations, net of tax	79	(146)	132
Income from continuing operations	14,927	13,753	13,269
Adjustments to reconcile income from continuing operations to net cash provided by operating activities:			
Depreciation and amortization	7,157	6,739	6,317
Deferred income taxes	(504)	581	(8)
Other operating activities	301	769	504
Changes in certain assets and liabilities, net of effects of acquisitions:			
Increase in accounts receivable	(297)	(101)	(564)
Decrease (increase) in inventories	2,265	(220)	(775)
Increase (decrease) in accounts payable	1,052	(410)	865
Increase in accrued liabilities	1,348	2,036	1,034
Net cash provided by operating activities	26,249	23,147	20,642
Cash flows from investing activities:			
Payments for property and equipment	(12,184)	(11,499)	(14,937)
Proceeds from disposal of property and equipment	1,002	714	957
Proceeds from (payments for) disposal of certain international operations, net	—	838	(257)
Investment in international operations, net of cash acquired	—	(1,576)	(1,338)
Other investing activities	(438)	781	(95)
Net cash used in investing activities	(11,620)	(10,742)	(15,670)
Cash flows from financing activities:			
Increase (decrease) in short-term borrowings, net	(1,033)	(3,745)	2,376
Proceeds from issuance of long-term debt	5,546	6,566	11,167
Payment of long-term debt	(6,033)	(5,387)	(8,723)
Dividends paid	(4,217)	(3,746)	(3,586)
Purchase of Company stock	(7,276)	(3,521)	(7,691)
Purchase of redeemable non-controlling interest	(436)	—	—
Payment of capital lease obligations	(346)	(352)	(343)
Other financing activities	(396)	267	(622)
Net cash used in financing activities	(14,191)	(9,918)	(7,422)

(continued)

Exhibit 5	(Continued)			
Fiscal Year Ended 31 January		**2010**	**2009**	**2008**
Effect of exchange rates on cash and cash equivalents		194	(781)	252
Net increase (decrease) in cash and cash equivalents		632	1,706	(2,198)
Cash and cash equivalents at beginning of year[1]		7,275	5,569	7,767
Cash and cash equivalents at end of year[2]		**7,907**	**7,275**	**5,569**
Supplemental disclosure of cash flow information				
Income tax paid		7,389	6,596	6,299
Interest paid		2,141	1,787	1,622
Capital lease obligations incurred		61	284	447

[1] Includes cash and cash equivalents of discontinued operations of $51 million at 1 February 2007.
[2] Includes cash and cash equivalents of discontinued operations of $77 million at 31 January 2008.

Walmart's cash flow statement indicates the following:

■ Cash and cash equivalents changed only slightly over the three years, from $7.8 billion at the beginning of fiscal 2008 to $7.9 billion at the end of fiscal 2010, but year-to-year cash flows varied significantly.

■ Operating cash flow increased steadily from $20.6 billion in fiscal 2008 to $26.2 billion in 2010 and was significantly greater than the company's expenditures on property and equipment in every year.

■ In 2009 and 2010, the company used cash to repay borrowing, to pay dividends, and to repurchase its common stock.

Walmart prepares its cash flow statements under the indirect method. In the cash flows from operating activities section of Walmart's cash flow statement, the company reconciles its net income of $14.8 billion to net cash provided by operating activities of $26.2 billion. Whenever the indirect method is used, U.S. GAAP mandate disclosure of how much cash was paid for interest and income taxes. Note that these are line items in cash flow statements using the direct method, so disclosure does not have to be mandated. Walmart discloses the amount of cash paid for income tax ($7.4 billion), interest ($2.1 billion), and capital lease obligations ($61 million) at the bottom of its cash flow statements.

3   THE CASH FLOW STATEMENT: LINKAGES AND PREPARATION

The indirect format of the cash flow statement demonstrates that changes in balance sheet accounts are an important factor in determining cash flows. The next section addresses the linkages between the cash flow statement and other financial statements.

3.1 Linkages of the Cash Flow Statement with the Income Statement and Balance Sheet

Recall the accounting equation that summarizes the balance sheet:

Assets = Liabilities + Equity

Cash is an asset. The statement of cash flows ultimately shows the change in cash during an accounting period. The beginning and ending balances of cash are shown on the company's balance sheets for the previous and current years, and the bottom of the cash flow statement reconciles beginning cash with ending cash. The relationship, stated in general terms, is as shown below.

Beginning Balance Sheet at 31 December 20X8	Statement of Cash Flows for Year Ended 31 December 20X9		Ending Balance Sheet at 31 December 20X9
Beginning cash	Plus: Cash receipts (from operating, investing, and financing activities)	Less: Cash payments (for operating, investing, and financing activities)	Ending cash

In the case of cash held in foreign currencies, there would also be an impact from changes in exchange rates. For example, Walmart's cash flow statement for 2010, presented in Exhibit 5, shows cash flows from operating, investing, and financing activities that total $438 million during the year ($26,249 – $11,620 – $14,191). Combined with the $194 million net effect of exchange rates on cash and cash equivalents, the net increase in cash and cash equivalents was $632 million, the amount by which end-of-year cash and cash equivalents ($7,907) exceeds beginning-of-year cash and cash equivalents ($7,275).

The body of Walmart's cash flow statement shows why the change in cash occurred; in other words, it shows the company's operating, investing, and financing activities (as well as the impact of foreign currency translation). The beginning and ending balance sheet values of cash and cash equivalents are linked through the cash flow statement.

The current assets and current liabilities sections of the balance sheet typically reflect a company's operating decisions and activities. Because a company's operating activities are reported on an accrual basis in the income statement, any differences between the accrual basis and the cash basis of accounting for an operating transaction result in an increase or decrease in some (usually) short-term asset or liability on the balance sheet. For example, if revenue reported using accrual accounting is higher than the cash actually collected, the result will typically be an increase in accounts receivable. If expenses reported using accrual accounting are lower than cash actually paid, the result will typically be a decrease in accounts payable or another accrued liability account[8]. As an example of how items on the balance sheet are related to the income statement and/or cash flow statement through the change in the beginning and ending balances, consider accounts receivable:

Beginning Balance Sheet at 31 December 20X8	Income Statement for Year Ended 31 December 20X9	Statement of Cash Flows for Year Ended 31 December 20X9	Ending Balance Sheet at 31 December 20X9
Beginning accounts receivable	Plus: Revenues	Minus: Cash collected from customers	Equals: Ending accounts receivable

Knowing any three of these four items makes it easy to compute the fourth. For example, if you know beginning accounts receivable, revenues, and cash collected from customers, you can easily compute ending accounts receivable. Understanding

---

8 There are other less typical explanations of the differences. For example, if revenue reported using accrual accounting is higher than the cash actually collected, it is possible that it is the result of a decrease in an unearned revenue liability account. If expenses reported using accrual accounting are lower than cash actually paid, it is possible that it is the result of an increase in prepaid expenses, inventory, or another asset account.

the interrelationships between the balance sheet, income statement, and cash flow statement is useful in not only understanding the company's financial health but also in detecting accounting irregularities. Recall the extreme illustration of a hypothetical company that makes sales on account without regard to future collections and thus reports healthy sales and significant income on its income statement yet lacks cash inflow. Such a pattern would occur if a company improperly recognized revenue.

A company's investing activities typically relate to the long-term asset section of the balance sheet, and its financing activities typically relate to the equity and long-term debt sections of the balance sheet. The next section demonstrates the preparation of cash flow information based on income statement and balance sheet information.

3.2 Steps in Preparing the Cash Flow Statement

The preparation of the cash flow statement uses data from both the income statement and the comparative balance sheets.

As noted earlier, companies often only disclose indirect operating cash flow information, whereas analysts prefer direct-format information. Understanding how cash flow information is put together will enable you to take an indirect statement apart and reconfigure it in a more useful manner. The result is an approximation of a direct cash flow statement, which—while not perfectly accurate—can be helpful to an analyst. The following demonstration of how an approximation of a direct cash flow statement is prepared uses the income statement and the comparative balance sheets for Acme Corporation (a fictitious retail company) shown in Exhibits 6 and 7.

Exhibit 6	Acme Corporation Income Statement Year Ended 31 December 2009		
Revenue			$23,598
Cost of goods sold			11,456
Gross profit			12,142
Salary and wage expense	$4,123		
Depreciation expense	1,052		
Other operating expenses	3,577		
Total operating expenses			8,752
Operating profit			3,390
Other revenues (expenses):			
Gain on sale of equipment	205		
Interest expense	(246)		(41)
Income before tax			3,349
Income tax expense			1,139
Net income			$2,210

Exhibit 7	Acme Corporation Comparative Balance Sheets 31 December 2009 and 2008

	2009	2008	Net Change
Cash	$ 1,011	$ 1,163	$(152)
Accounts receivable	1,012	957	55
Inventory	3,984	3,277	707
Prepaid expenses	155	178	(23)
Total current assets	6,162	5,575	587
Land	510	510	—
Buildings	3,680	3,680	—
Equipment*	8,798	8,555	243
Less: accumulated depreciation	(3,443)	(2,891)	(552)
Total long-term assets	9,545	9,854	(309)
Total assets	$15,707	$15,429	$278
Accounts payable	$3,588	$3,325	$ 263
Salary and wage payable	85	75	10
Interest payable	62	74	(12)
Income tax payable	55	50	5
Other accrued liabilities	1,126	1,104	22
Total current liabilities	4,916	4,628	288
Long-term debt	3,075	3,575	(500)
Common stock	3,750	4,350	(600)
Retained earnings	3,966	2,876	1,090
Total liabilities and equity	$15,707	$15,429	$278

*During 2009, Acme purchased new equipment for a total cost of $1,300. No items impacted retained earnings other than net income and dividends.

The first step in preparing the cash flow statement is to determine the total cash flows from operating activities. The direct method of presenting cash from operating activities is illustrated in sections 3.2.1 through 3.2.4. Section 3.2.5 illustrates the indirect method of presenting cash flows from operating activities. Cash flows from investing activities and from financing activities are identical under either method.

3.2.1 Operating Activities: Direct Method

We first determine how much cash Acme received from its customers, followed by how much cash was paid to suppliers and to employees as well as how much cash was paid for other operating expenses, interest, and income taxes.

3.2.1.1 Cash Received from Customers   The income statement for Acme reported revenue of $23,598 for the year ended 31 December 2009. To determine the approximate cash receipts from its customers, it is necessary to adjust this revenue amount by the net change in accounts receivable for the year. If accounts receivable increase during the year, revenue on an accrual basis is higher than cash receipts from customers, and vice versa. For Acme Corporation, accounts receivable increased by $55, so cash received from customers was $23,543, as follows:

Revenue	$23,598
Less: Increase in accounts receivable	(55)
Cash received from customers	**$23,543**

Cash received from customers affects the accounts receivable account as follows:

Beginning accounts receivable	$ 957
Plus revenue	23,598
Minus cash collected from customers	**(23,543)**
Ending accounts receivable	$1,012

The accounts receivable account information can also be presented as follows:

Beginning accounts receivable	$ 957
Plus revenue	23,598
Minus ending accounts receivable	(1,012)
Cash collected from customers	**$23,543**

EXAMPLE 3

Computing Cash Received from Customers.

Blue Bayou, a fictitious advertising company, reported revenues of $50 million, total expenses of $35 million, and net income of $15 million in the most recent year. If accounts receivable decreased by $12 million, how much cash did the company receive from customers?

A $38 million.

B $50 million.

C $62 million.

Solution:

C is correct. Revenues of $50 million plus the decrease in accounts receivable of $12 million equals $62 million cash received from customers. The decrease in accounts receivable means that the company received more in cash than the amount of revenue it reported.

"Cash received from customers" is sometimes referred to as "cash collections from customers" or "cash collections."

3.2.1.2 Cash Paid to Suppliers For Acme, the cash paid to suppliers was $11,900, determined as follows:

Cost of goods sold	$11,456
Plus: Increase in inventory	707
Equals purchases from suppliers	$12,163
Less: Increase in accounts payable	(263)
Cash paid to suppliers	**$11,900**

There are two pieces to this calculation: the amount of inventory purchased and the amount paid for it. To determine purchases from suppliers, cost of goods sold is adjusted for the change in inventory. If inventory increased during the year, then purchases during the year exceeded cost of goods sold, and vice versa. Acme reported cost of goods sold of $11,456 for the year ended 31 December 2009. For Acme Corporation, inventory increased by $707, so purchases from suppliers was $12,163. Purchases from suppliers affect the inventory account, as shown below:

Beginning inventory	$ 3,277
Plus purchases	12,163
Minus cost of goods sold	(11,456)
Ending inventory	$3,984

Acme purchased $12,163 of inventory from suppliers in 2009, but is this the amount of cash that Acme paid to its suppliers during the year? Not necessarily. Acme may not have yet paid for all of these purchases and may yet owe for some of the purchases made this year. In other words, Acme may have paid less cash to its suppliers than the amount of this year's purchases, in which case Acme's liability (accounts payable) will have increased by the difference. Alternatively, Acme may have paid even more to its suppliers than the amount of this year's purchases, in which case Acme's accounts payable will have decreased.

Therefore, once purchases have been determined, cash paid to suppliers can be calculated by adjusting purchases for the change in accounts payable. If the company made all purchases with cash, then accounts payable would not change and cash outflows would equal purchases. If accounts payable increased during the year, then purchases on an accrual basis would be higher than they would be on a cash basis, and vice versa. In this example, Acme made more purchases than it paid in cash, so the balance in accounts payable increased. For Acme, the cash paid to suppliers was $11,900, determined as follows:

Purchases from suppliers	$12,163
Less: Increase in accounts payable	(263)
Cash paid to suppliers	**$11,900**

The amount of cash paid to suppliers is reflected in the accounts payable account, as shown below:

Beginning accounts payable	$ 3,325
Plus purchases	12,163
Minus cash paid to suppliers	**(11,900)**
Ending accounts payable	$3,588

EXAMPLE 4

Computing Cash Paid to Suppliers.

Orange Beverages Plc., a fictitious manufacturer of tropical drinks, reported cost of goods sold for the year of $100 million. Total assets increased by $55 million, but inventory declined by $6 million. Total liabilities increased by $45 million, but accounts payable decreased by $2 million. How much cash did the company pay to its suppliers during the year?

A $96 million.

B $104 million.

C $108 million.

Solution:

A is correct. Cost of goods sold of $100 million less the decrease in inventory of $6 million equals purchases from suppliers of $94 million. The decrease in accounts payable of $2 million means that the company paid $96 million in cash ($94 million plus $2 million).

3.2.1.3 Cash Paid to Employees   To determine the cash paid to employees, it is necessary to adjust salary and wages expense by the net change in salary and wages payable for the year. If salary and wages payable increased during the year, then salary and wages expense on an accrual basis would be higher than the amount of cash paid for this expense, and vice versa. For Acme, salary and wages payable increased by $10, so cash paid for salary and wages was $4,113, as follows:

Salary and wages expense	$4,123
Less: Increase in salary and wages payable	(10)
Cash paid to employees	**$4,113**

The amount of cash paid to employees is reflected in the salary and wages payable account, as shown below:

Beginning salary and wages payable	$ 75
Plus salary and wages expense	4,123
Minus cash paid to employees	**(4,113)**
Ending salary and wages payable	$85

3.2.1.4 Cash Paid for Other Operating Expenses   To determine the cash paid for other operating expenses, it is necessary to adjust the other operating expenses amount on the income statement by the net changes in prepaid expenses and accrued expense liabilities for the year. If prepaid expenses increased during the year, other operating expenses on a cash basis would be higher than on an accrual basis, and vice versa. Likewise, if accrued expense liabilities increased during the year, other operating expenses on a cash basis would be lower than on an accrual basis, and vice versa. For Acme Corporation, the amount of cash paid for operating expenses in 2009 was $3,532, as follows:

Other operating expenses	$3,577
Less: Decrease in prepaid expenses	(23)
Less: Increase in other accrued liabilities	(22)
Cash paid for other operating expenses	**$3,532**

EXAMPLE 5

Computing Cash Paid for Other Operating Expenses

Black Ice, a fictitious sportswear manufacturer, reported other operating expenses of $30 million. Prepaid insurance expense increased by $4 million, and accrued utilities payable decreased by $7 million. Insurance and utilities are the only two components of other operating expenses. How much cash did the company pay in other operating expenses?

A $19 million.

B $33 million.

C $41 million.

Solution:

C is correct. Other operating expenses of $30 million plus the increase in prepaid insurance expense of $4 million plus the decrease in accrued utilities payable of $7 million equals $41 million.

3.2.1.5 Cash Paid for Interest   The cash paid for interest is included in operating cash flows under U.S. GAAP and may be included in operating or financing cash flows under IFRS. To determine the cash paid for interest, it is necessary to adjust interest expense by the net change in interest payable for the year. If interest payable increases during the year, then interest expense on an accrual basis will be higher than the amount of cash paid for interest, and vice versa. For Acme Corporation, interest payable decreased by $12, and cash paid for interest was $258, as follows:

Interest expense	$246
Plus: Decrease in interest payable	12
Cash paid for interest	**$258**

Alternatively, cash paid for interest may also be determined by an analysis of the interest payable account, as shown below:

Beginning interest payable	$ 74
Plus interest expense	246
Minus cash paid for interest	**(258)**
Ending interest payable	$62

3.2.1.6 Cash Paid for Income Taxes   To determine the cash paid for income taxes, it is necessary to adjust the income tax expense amount on the income statement by the net changes in taxes receivable, taxes payable, and deferred income taxes for the year. If taxes receivable or deferred tax assets increase during the year, income taxes on a cash basis will be higher than on an accrual basis, and vice versa. Likewise, if taxes payable or deferred tax liabilities increase during the year, income tax expense on a cash basis will be lower than on an accrual basis, and vice versa. For Acme Corporation, the amount of cash paid for income taxes in 2009 was $1,134, as follows:

Income tax expense	$1,139
Less: Increase in income tax payable	(5)
Cash paid for income taxes	**$1,134**

3.2.2 *Investing Activities*

The second and third steps in preparing the cash flow statement are to determine the total cash flows from investing activities and from financing activities. The presentation of this information is identical, regardless of whether the direct or indirect method is used for operating cash flows.

Purchases and sales of equipment were the only investing activities undertaken by Acme in 2009, as evidenced by the fact that the amounts reported for land and buildings were unchanged during the year. An informational note in Exhibit 7 tells us that Acme *purchased* new equipment in 2009 for a total cost of $1,300. However, the amount of equipment shown on Acme's balance sheet increased by only $243 (ending balance of $8,798 minus beginning balance of $8,555); therefore, Acme must have also *sold or otherwise disposed of* some equipment during the year. To determine the cash inflow from the sale of equipment, we analyze the equipment and accumulated depreciation accounts as well as the gain on the sale of equipment from Exhibits 6 and 7. Assuming that the entire accumulated depreciation is related to equipment, the cash received from sale of equipment is determined as follows.

The historical cost of the equipment sold was $1,057. This amount is determined as follows:

Beginning balance equipment (from balance sheet)	$ 8,555
Plus equipment purchased (from informational note)	1,300
Minus ending balance equipment (from balance sheet)	(8,798)
Equals historical cost of equipment sold	$1,057

The accumulated depreciation on the equipment sold was $500, determined as follows:

Beginning balance accumulated depreciation (from balance sheet)	$ 2,891
Plus depreciation expense (from income statement)	1,052
Minus ending balance accumulated depreciation (from balance sheet)	(3,443)
Equals accumulated depreciation on equipment sold	$500

The historical cost information, accumulated depreciation information, and information from the income statement about the gain on the sale of equipment can be used to determine the cash received from the sale.

Historical cost of equipment sold (calculated above)	$1,057
Less accumulated depreciation on equipment sold (calculated above)	(500)
Equals book value of equipment sold	$557
Plus gain on sale of equipment (from the income statement)	205
Equals cash received from sale of equipment	**$762**

EXAMPLE 6

Computing Cash Received from the Sale of Equipment

Copper, Inc., a fictitious brewery and restaurant chain, reported a gain on the sale of equipment of $12 million. In addition, the company's income statement shows depreciation expense of $8 million and the cash flow statement shows capital expenditure of $15 million, all of which was for the purchase of new equipment.

Balance sheet item	12/31/2009	12/31/2010	Change
Equipment	$100 million	$109 million	$9 million
Accumulated depreciation—equipment	$30 million	$36 million	$6 million

Using the above information from the comparative balance sheets, how much cash did the company receive from the equipment sale?

A $12 million.

B $16 million.

C $18 million.

Solution:

B is correct. Selling price (cash inflow) minus book value equals gain or loss on sale; therefore, gain or loss on sale plus book value equals selling price (cash inflow). The amount of gain is given, $12 million. To calculate the book value of the equipment sold, find the historical cost of the equipment and the accumulated depreciation on the equipment.

- Beginning balance of equipment of $100 million plus equipment purchased of $15 million minus ending balance of equipment of $109 million equals historical cost of equipment sold, or $6 million.

- Beginning accumulated depreciation on equipment of $30 million plus depreciation expense for the year of $8 million minus ending balance of accumulated depreciation of $36 million equals accumulated depreciation on the equipment sold, or $2 million.

- Therefore, the book value of the equipment sold was $6 million minus $2 million, or $4 million.

- Because the gain on the sale of equipment was $12 million, the amount of cash received must have been $16 million.

3.2.3 Financing Activities

As with investing activities, the presentation of financing activities is identical, regardless of whether the direct or indirect method is used for operating cash flows.

3.2.3.1 Long-Term Debt and Common Stock   The change in long-term debt, based on the beginning 2009 (ending 2008) and ending 2009 balances in Exhibit 7, was a decrease of $500. Absent other information, this indicates that Acme retired $500 of long-term debt. Retiring long-term debt is a cash outflow relating to financing activities.

Similarly, the change in common stock during 2009 was a decrease of $600. Absent other information, this indicates that Acme repurchased $600 of its common stock. Repurchase of common stock is also a cash outflow related to financing activity.

3.2.3.2 Dividends   Recall the following relationship:

Beginning retained earnings + Net income – Dividends = Ending retained earnings

Based on this relationship, the amount of cash dividends paid in 2009 can be determined from an analysis of retained earnings, as follows:

Beginning balance of retained earnings (from the balance sheet)	$ 2,876
Plus net income (from the income statement)	2,210
Minus ending balance of retained earnings (from the balance sheet)	(3,966)
Equals dividends paid	**$1,120**

Note that dividends paid are presented in the statement of changes in equity.

3.2.4 Overall Statement of Cash Flows: Direct Method

Exhibit 8 summarizes the information about Acme's operating, investing, and financing cash flows in the statement of cash flows. At the bottom of the statement, the total net change in cash is shown to be a decrease of $152 (from $1,163 to $1,011). This decrease can also be seen on the comparative balance sheet in Exhibit 7. The cash provided by operating activities of $2,606 was adequate to cover the net cash used in investing activities of $538; however, the company's debt repayments, cash payments for dividends, and repurchase of common stock (i.e., its financing activities) of $2,220 resulted in an overall decrease in cash of $152.

Exhibit 8	Acme Corporation Cash Flow Statement (Direct Method) for Year Ended 31 December 2009

Cash flow from operating activities:	
Cash received from customers	$ 23,543
Cash paid to suppliers	(11,900)
Cash paid to employees	(4,113)
Cash paid for other operating expenses	(3,532)
Cash paid for interest	(258)
Cash paid for income tax	(1,134)
Net cash provided by operating activities	2,606
Cash flow from investing activities:	
Cash received from sale of equipment	762
Cash paid for purchase of equipment	(1,300)
Net cash used for investing activities	(538)
Cash flow from financing activities:	
Cash paid to retire long-term debt	(500)
Cash paid to retire common stock	(600)
Cash paid for dividends	(1,120)
Net cash used for financing activities	(2,220)

Exhibit 8	(Continued)

Net increase (decrease) in cash	(152)
Cash balance, 31 December 2008	1,163
Cash balance, 31 December 2009	$1,011

3.2.5 Overall Statement of Cash Flows: Indirect Method

Using the alternative approach to reporting cash from operating activities, the indirect method, we will present the same amount of cash provided by operating activities. Under this approach, we reconcile Acme's net income of $2,210 to its operating cash flow of $2,606.

To perform this reconciliation, net income is adjusted for the following: a) any non-operating activities, b) any non-cash expenses, and c) changes in operating working capital items.

The only non-operating activity in Acme's income statement, the sale of equipment, resulted in a gain of $205. This amount is removed from the operating cash flow section; the cash effects of the sale are shown in the investing section.

Acme's only non-cash expense was depreciation expense of $1,052. Under the indirect method, depreciation expense must be added back to net income because it was a non-cash deduction in the calculation of net income.

Changes in working capital accounts include increases and decreases in the current operating asset and liability accounts. The changes in these accounts arise from applying accrual accounting; that is, recognizing revenues when they are earned and expenses when they are incurred instead of when the cash is received or paid. To make the working capital adjustments under the indirect method, any increase in a current operating asset account is subtracted from net income and a net decrease is added to net income. As described above, the increase in accounts receivable, for example, resulted from Acme recording income statement revenue higher than the amount of cash received from customers; therefore, to reconcile back to operating cash flow, that increase in accounts receivable must be deducted from net income. For current operating liabilities, a net increase is added to net income and a net decrease is subtracted from net income. As described above, the increase in wages payable, for example, resulted from Acme recording income statement expenses higher than the amount of cash paid to employees.

Exhibit 9 presents a tabulation of the most common types of adjustments that are made to net income when using the indirect method to determine net cash flow from operating activities.

Exhibit 9	Adjustments to Net Income Using the Indirect Method

Additions	■ Non-cash items
	● Depreciation expense of tangible assets
	● Amortisation expense of intangible assets
	● Depletion expense of natural resources
	● Amortisation of bond discount

(continued)

Exhibit 9	(Continued)

                ■ Non-operating losses

                    ● Loss on sale or write-down of assets

                    ● Loss on retirement of debt

                    ● Loss on investments accounted for under the equity method

                ■ Increase in deferred income tax liability

                ■ Changes in working capital resulting from accruing higher amounts for expenses than the amounts of cash payments or lower amounts for revenues than the amounts of cash receipts

                    ● Decrease in current operating assets (e.g., accounts receivable, inventory, and prepaid expenses)

                    ● Increase in current operating liabilities (e.g., accounts payable and accrued expense liabilities)

Subtractions   ■ Non-cash items (e.g., amortisation of bond premium)

                ■ Non-operating items

                    ● Gain on sale of assets

                    ● Gain on retirement of debt

                    ● Income on investments accounted for under the equity method

                ■ Decrease in deferred income tax liability

                ■ Changes in working capital resulting from accruing lower amounts for expenses than for cash payments or higher amounts for revenues than for cash receipts

                    ● Increase in current operating assets (e.g., accounts receivable, inventory, and prepaid expenses)

                    ● Decrease in current operating liabilities (e.g., accounts payable and accrued expense liabilities)

Accordingly, for Acme Corporation, the $55 increase in accounts receivable and the $707 increase in inventory are subtracted from net income and the $23 decrease in prepaid expenses is added to net income. For Acme's current liabilities, the increases in accounts payable, salary and wage payable, income tax payable, and other accrued liabilities ($263, $10, $5, and $22, respectively) are added to net income and the $12 decrease in interest payable is subtracted from net income. Exhibit 10 presents the cash flow statement for Acme Corporation under the indirect method by using the information that we have determined from our analysis of the income statement and the comparative balance sheets. Note that the investing and financing sections are identical to the statement of cash flows prepared using the direct method.

Exhibit 10	Acme Corporation Cash Flow Statement (Indirect Method) Year Ended 31 December 2009

Cash flow from operating activities:	
Net income	$ 2,210
Depreciation expense	1,052
Gain on sale of equipment	(205)
Increase in accounts receivable	(55)

Exhibit 10	(Continued)	

Increase in inventory	(707)
Decrease in prepaid expenses	23
Increase in accounts payable	263
Increase in salary and wage payable	10
Decrease in interest payable	(12)
Increase in income tax payable	5
Increase in other accrued liabilities	22
Net cash provided by operating activities	2,606
Cash flow from investing activities:	
Cash received from sale of equipment	762
Cash paid for purchase of equipment	(1,300)
Net cash used for investing activities	(538)
Cash flow from financing activities:	
Cash paid to retire long-term debt	(500)
Cash paid to retire common stock	(600)
Cash paid for dividends	(1,120)
Net cash used for financing activities	(2,220)
Net decrease in cash	(152)
Cash balance, 31 December 2008	1,163
Cash balance, 31 December 2009	$1,011

EXAMPLE 7

Adjusting Net Income to Compute Operating Cash Flow

Based on the following information for Pinkerly Inc., a fictitious company, what are the total adjustments that the company would make to net income in order to derive operating cash flow?

	Year Ended	
Income statement item	12/31/2009	
Net income	$30 million	
Depreciation	$7 million	

Balance sheet item	12/31/2008	12/31/2009	Change
Accounts receivable	$15 million	$30 million	$15 million
Inventory	$16 million	$13 million	($3 million)
Accounts payable	$10 million	$20 million	$10 million

A Add $5 million.

B   Add $21 million.

C   Subtract $9 million.

Solution:

A is correct. To derive operating cash flow, the company would make the following adjustments to net income: add depreciation (a non-cash expense) of $7 million; add the decrease in inventory of $3 million; add the increase in accounts payable of $10 million; and subtract the increase in accounts receivable of $15 million. Total additions of $20 million and total subtractions of $15 million result in net total additions of $5 million.

3.3 Conversion of Cash Flows from the Indirect to the Direct Method

An analyst may desire to review direct-format operating cash flow to review trends in cash receipts and payments (such as cash received from customers or cash paid to suppliers). If a direct-format statement is not available, cash flows from operating activities reported under the indirect method can be converted to the direct method. Accuracy of conversion depends on adjustments using data available in published financial reports. The method described here is sufficiently accurate for most analytical purposes.

The three-step conversion process is demonstrated for Acme Corporation in Exhibit 11. Referring again to Exhibits 6 and 7 for Acme Corporation's income statement and balance sheet information, begin by disaggregating net income of $2,210 into total revenues and total expenses (Step 1). Next, remove any non-operating and non-cash items (Step 2). For Acme, we therefore remove the non-operating gain on the sale of equipment of $205 and the non-cash depreciation expense of $1,052. Then, convert accrual amounts of revenues and expenses to cash flow amounts of receipts and payments by adjusting for changes in working capital accounts (Step 3). The results of these adjustments are the items of information for the direct format of operating cash flows. These line items are shown as the results of Step 3.

Exhibit 11	Conversion from the Indirect to the Direct Method		
Step 1	Total revenues		$23,803
Aggregate all revenue and all expenses	Total expenses		21,593
	Net income		$2,210
Step 2	Total revenue less noncash item revenues:		
Remove all noncash items from aggregated revenues and expenses and break out remaining items into relevant cash flow items		($23,803 − $205) =	$23,598
		Revenue	$23,598
	Total expenses less noncash item expenses:		
		($21,593 − $1,052) =	$20,541
	Cost of goods sold		$11,456
	Salary and wage expenses		4,123
	Other operating expenses		3,577
	Interest expense		246
	Income tax expense		1,139

Exhibit 11	(Continued)	

	Total	$20,541
Step 3	Cash received from customers[a]	$23,543
Convert accrual amounts to cash flow amounts by adjusting for working capital changes	Cash paid to suppliers[b]	(11,900)
	Cash paid to employees[c]	(4,113)
	Cash paid for other operating expenses[d]	(3,532)
	Cash paid for interest[e]	(258)
	Cash paid for income tax[f]	(1,134)
	Net cash provided by operating activities	$2,606

Calculations for Step 3:
[a] Revenue of $23,598 less increase in accounts receivable of $55.
[b] Cost of goods sold of $11,456 plus increase in inventory of $707 less increase in accounts payable of $263.
[c] Salary and wage expense of $4,123 less increase in salary and wage payable of $10.
[d] Other operating expenses of $3,577 less decrease in prepaid expenses of $23 less increase in other accrued liabilities of $22.
[e] Interest expense of $246 plus decrease in interest payable of $12.
[f] Income tax expense of $1,139 less increase in income tax payable of $5.

CASH FLOW STATEMENT ANALYSIS

4

The analysis of a company's cash flows can provide useful information for understanding a company's business and earnings and for predicting its future cash flows. This section describes tools and techniques for analyzing the statement of cash flows, including the analysis of sources and uses of cash and cash flow, common-size analysis, and calculation of free cash flow measures and cash flow ratios.

4.1 Evaluation of the Sources and Uses of Cash

Evaluation of the cash flow statement should involve an overall assessment of the sources and uses of cash between the three main categories as well as an assessment of the main drivers of cash flow within each category, as follows:

1 Evaluate where the major sources and uses of cash flow are between operating, investing, and financing activities.

2 Evaluate the primary determinants of operating cash flow.

3 Evaluate the primary determinants of investing cash flow.

4 Evaluate the primary determinants of financing cash flow.

Step 1 The major sources of cash for a company can vary with its stage of growth. For a mature company, it is expected and desirable that operating activities are the primary source of cash flows. Over the long term, a company must generate cash from its operating activities. If operating cash flow were consistently negative, a company would need to borrow money or issue stock (financing activities) to fund the shortfall. Eventually, these providers of capital need to be repaid from operations or they will no longer be willing to provide capital. Cash generated from operating activities can be used in either investing or financing activities. If the company has good opportunities to grow the business or other investment opportunities, it is desirable to use the cash in investing activities. If the company does not have profitable investment opportunities, the cash should be returned to capital providers, a financing activity. For a new or growth stage company, operating cash flow may be negative for some period of time as it invests in such assets as inventory and receivables (extending credit to new customers) in order to grow the business. This situation is not sustainable over the long term, so eventually the cash must start to come primarily from operating activities so that capital can be returned to the providers of capital. Lastly, it is desirable that operating cash flows are sufficient to cover capital expenditures (in other words, the company has free cash flow as discussed further in Section 4.3). In summary, major points to consider at this step are:

- What are the major sources and uses of cash flow?
- Is operating cash flow positive and sufficient to cover capital expenditures?

Step 2 Turning to the operating section, the analysts should examine the most significant determinants of operating cash flow. Companies need cash for use in operations (for example, to hold receivables and inventory and to pay employees and suppliers) and receive cash from operating activities (for example, payments from customers). Under the indirect method, the increases and decreases in receivables, inventory, payables, and so on can be examined to determine whether the company is using or generating cash in operations and why. It is also useful to compare operating cash flow with net income. For a mature company, because net income includes non-cash expenses (depreciation and amortisation), it is expected and desirable that operating cash flow exceeds net income. The relationship between net income and operating cash flow is also an indicator of earnings quality. If a company has large net income but poor operating cash flow, it may be a sign of poor earnings quality. The company may be making aggressive accounting choices to increase net income but not be generating cash for its business. You should also examine the variability of both earnings and cash flow and consider the impact of this variability on the company's risk as well as the ability to forecast future cash flows for valuation purposes. In summary:

- What are the major determinants of operating cash flow?
- Is operating cash flow higher or lower than net income? Why?
- How consistent are operating cash flows?

Step 3 Within the investing section, you should evaluate each line item. Each line item represents either a source or use of cash. This enables you to understand where the cash is being spent (or received). This section will tell you how much cash is being invested for the future in property, plant, and equipment; how much is used to acquire entire companies; and how much is put aside in liquid investments, such as stocks and bonds. It will also tell you how much cash is being raised by selling these types of assets. If the company is making major capital investments, you should consider where the cash is coming from to cover these investments (e.g., is the cash coming from excess operating cash flow or from the financing activities described in Step 4). If assets are being sold, it is important to determine why and to assess the effects on the company.

Step 4 Within the financing section, you should examine each line item to understand whether the company is raising capital or repaying capital and what the nature of its capital sources are. If the company is borrowing each year, you should consider when repayment may be required. This section will also present dividend payments and repurchases of stock that are alternative means of returning capital to owners. It is important to assess why capital is being raised or repaid.

We now provide an example of a cash flow statement evaluation.

EXAMPLE 8

Analysis of the Cash Flow Statement

Derek Yee, CFA, is preparing to forecast cash flow for Groupe Danone (FP: BN) as an input into his valuation model. He has asked you to evaluate the historical cash flow statement of Groupe Danone, which is presented in Exhibit 12. Groupe Danone prepares its financial statements in conformity with IFRS. Note that Groupe Danone presents the most recent period on the right.

Exhibit 12	Groupe Danone Consolidated Financial Statements Consolidated Statements of Cash Flows (in € Millions)		
Years Ended 31 December		**2008**	**2009**
Net income attributable to the Group		1,313	1,361
Net income attributable to minority interests		178	160
Net income from discontinued operations		(269)	—
Share of profits of associates		(62)	77
Depreciation and amortization		525	549
Dividends received from associates		29	174
Other flows with impact on cash		(113)	(157)
Other flows with no impact on cash		93	(93)
Cash flows provided by operating activities, excluding changes in net working capital		**1,699**	**2,092**
(Increase) decrease in inventories		3	37
(Increase) decrease in trade accounts receivable		(74)	(112)
Increase (decrease) in trade accounts payable		36	(127)
Changes in other accounts receivable and payable		90	110
Change in other working capital requirements		55	(92)
Cash flows provided by (used in) operating activities		**1,754**	**2,000**
Capital expenditure		(706)	(699)
Purchase of businesses and other investments, net of cash and cash equivalents acquired		(259)	(147)
Proceeds from the sale of businesses and other investments, including indebtedness of companies sold		329	1,024
(Increase) decrease in long-term loans and other long-term assets		67	36
Cash flows provided by (used in) investing activities		**(569)**	**214**
Increase in capital and additional paid-in capital		48	2,977
Purchases of treasury stock (net of disposals)		46	100
Dividends paid to Danone shareholders and to minority interests		(705)	(451)
Settlement of debt hedge financial instruments (mainly equalization payments)			(154)
Increase (decrease) in non-current financial liabilities		1,338	(4,154)
Increase (decrease) in current financial liabilities		(1,901)	(427)
Increase (decrease) in marketable securities		63	(60)
Cash flows provided by (used in) financing activities		**(1,111)**	**(2,169)**
Effect of exchange rate changes		(31)	8
Increase (decrease) in cash and cash equivalents		**43**	**53**
Cash and cash equivalents at beginning of period		548	591

(continued)

| Exhibit 12 | (Continued) |

Years Ended 31 December	2008	2009
Cash and cash equivalents at end of period	591	644
Supplemental disclosures		
Payments during the year of:		
• net interest	433	272
• income tax	430	413

Yee would like answers to the following questions:

- What are the major sources of cash for Groupe Danone?
- What are the major uses of cash for Groupe Danone?
- What is the relationship between net income and cash flow from operating activities?
- Is cash flow from operating activities sufficient to cover capital expenditures?
- Other than capital expenditures, is cash being used or generated in investing activities?
- What types of financing cash flows does Groupe Danone have?

Solution:

The major categories of cash flows can be summarized as follows (in € millions):

	2008	2009
Cash flows provided by operating activities	1,754	2,000
Cash flows provided by (used in) investing activities	(569)	214
Cash flows provided by (used in) financing activities	(1,111)	(2,169)
Exchange rate effects on cash	(31)	8
Increase in cash	43	53

The primary source of cash for Groupe Danone is operating activities. In 2009, investing activities provided cash as the result of the sale of businesses and other investments. Cash flow is being used in financing activities, primarily to repay financial liabilities and to pay dividends. The fact that the primary source of cash is from operations is positive and desirable for a mature company. Additionally, the fact that operating cash flow exceeds net income in both years is a positive sign. Finally, operating cash flows exceed capital expenditures, indicating that the company can fund capital expenditures from operations.

4.2 Common-Size Analysis of the Statement of Cash Flows

In common-size analysis of a company's income statement, each income and expense line item is expressed as a percentage of net revenues (net sales). For the common-size balance sheet, each asset, liability, and equity line item is expressed as a percentage of total assets. For the common-size cash flow statement, there are two alternative approaches. The first approach is to express each line item of cash inflow (outflow) as a percentage of total inflows (outflows) of cash, and the second approach is to express each line item as a percentage of net revenue.

Exhibit 13 demonstrates the total cash inflows/total cash outflows method for Acme Corporation. Under this approach, each of the cash inflows is expressed as a percentage of the total cash inflows, whereas each of the cash outflows is expressed as a percentage of the total cash outflows. In Panel A, Acme's common-size statement is based on a cash flow statement using the direct method of presenting operating cash flows. Operating cash inflows and outflows are separately presented on the cash flow statement, and therefore, the common-size cash flow statement shows each of these operating inflows (outflows) as a percentage of total inflows (outflows). In Panel B, Acme's common-size statement is based on a cash flow statement using the indirect method of presenting operating cash flows. When a cash flow statement has been presented using the indirect method, operating cash inflows and outflows are not separately presented; therefore, the common-size cash flow statement shows only the net operating cash flow (net cash provided by or used in operating activities) as a percentage of total inflows or outflows, depending on whether the net amount was a cash inflow or outflow. Because Acme's net operating cash flow is positive, it is shown as a percentage of total inflows.

Exhibit 13	Acme Corporation Common-Size Cash Flow Statement Year Ended 31 December 2009

Panel A. Direct Format for Cash Flow

Inflows		Percentage of Total Inflows
Receipts from customers	$23,543	96.86%
Sale of equipment	762	3.14
Total	$24,305	100.00%

Outflows		Percentage of Total Outflows
Payments to suppliers	$11,900	48.66%
Payments to employees	4,113	16.82
Payments for other operating expenses	3,532	14.44
Payments for interest	258	1.05
Payments for income tax	1,134	4.64
Purchase of equipment	1,300	5.32
Retirement of long-term debt	500	2.04
Retirement of common stock	600	2.45
Dividend payments	1,120	4.58
Total	$24,457	100.00%
Net increase (decrease) in cash	($152)	

(continued)

Exhibit 13	(Continued)

Panel B. Indirect Format for Cash Flow

Inflows		Percentage of Total Inflows
Net cash provided by operating activities	$2,606	77.38%
Sale of equipment	762	22.62
Total	$3,368	100.00%

Outflows		Percentage of Total Outflows
Purchase of equipment	$1,300	36.93%
Retirement of long-term debt	500	14.20
Retirement of common stock	600	17.05
Dividend payments	1,120	31.82
Total	$3,520	100.00%
Net increase (decrease) in cash	($152)	

Exhibit 14 demonstrates the net revenue common-size cash flow statement for Acme Corporation. Under the net revenue approach, each line item in the cash flow statement is shown as a percentage of net revenue. The common-size statement in this exhibit has been developed based on Acme's cash flow statement using the indirect method for operating cash flows and using net revenue of $23,598 as shown in Exhibit 6. Each line item of the reconciliation between net income and net operating cash flows is expressed as a percentage of net revenue. The common-size format makes it easier to see trends in cash flow rather than just looking at the total amount. This method is also useful to the analyst in forecasting future cash flows because individual items in the common-size statement (e.g., depreciation, fixed capital expenditures, debt borrowing, and repayment) are expressed as a percentage of net revenue. Thus, once the analyst has forecast revenue, the common-size statement provides a basis for forecasting cash flows for those items with an expected relation to net revenue.

Exhibit 14	Acme Corporation Common-Size Cash Flow Statement: Indirect Format Year Ended 31 December 2009

		Percentage of Net Revenue
Cash flow from operating activities:		
Net income	$2,210	9.37%
Depreciation expense	1,052	4.46
Gain on sale of equipment	(205)	(0.87)
Increase in accounts receivable	(55)	(0.23)
Increase in inventory	(707)	(3.00)
Decrease in prepaid expenses	23	0.10
Increase in accounts payable	263	1.11

Exhibit 14	(Continued)	

		Percentage of Net Revenue
Increase in salary and wage payable	10	0.04
Decrease in interest payable	(12)	(0.05)
Increase in income tax payable	5	0.02
Increase in other accrued liabilities	22	0.09
Net cash provided by operating activities	$2,606	11.04%
Cash flow from investing activities:		
Cash received from sale of equipment	$ 762	3.23%
Cash paid for purchase of equipment	(1,300)	(5.51)
Net cash used for investing activities	$(538)	(2.28)%
Cash flow from financing activities:		
Cash paid to retire long-term debt	$ (500)	(2.12)%
Cash paid to retire common stock	(600)	(2.54)
Cash paid for dividends	(1,120)	(4.75)
Net cash used for financing activities	$(2,220)	(9.41)%
Net decrease in cash	$(152)	(0.64)%

EXAMPLE 9

Analysis of a Common-Size Cash Flow Statement

Andrew Potter is examining an abbreviated common-size cash flow statement for Dell Inc. (NASDAQ: DELL), a provider of technological products and services. The common-size cash flow statement was prepared by dividing each line item by total net revenue for the same year. The terminology is that used by Dell. "Change in cash from" is used instead of "cash provided by (used in)."

	29 Jan 10	30 Jan 09	1 Feb 08
Cash flows from operating activities:			
Net income	**2.71%**	**4.06%**	**4.82%**
Adjustments to reconcile net income to net cash provided by operating activities:			
Depreciation and amortization	1.61	1.26	0.99
Stock-based compensation	0.59	0.68	0.54
In-process research and development charges	0.00	0.00	0.14
Effects of exchange rate changes on monetary assets and liabilities denominated in foreign currencies	0.11	(0.19)	0.05
Deferred income taxes	(0.10)	0.14	(0.50)
Provision for doubtful accounts—including financing receivables	0.81	0.51	0.31
Other	0.19	0.05	0.05

(continued)

	29 Jan 10	30 Jan 09	1 Feb 08
Changes in operating assets and liabilities, net of effects from acquisitions:			
Accounts receivable	(1.25)	0.79	(1.78)
Financing receivables	(2.05)	(0.49)	(0.64)
Inventories	(0.35)	0.51	(0.81)
Other assets	(0.43)	(0.17)	(0.20)
Accounts payable	5.36	(5.10)	1.37
Deferred services revenue	0.26	1.09	1.69
Accrued and other liabilities	(0.08)	(0.02)	0.45
Change in cash from operating activities	**7.38**	**3.10**	**6.46**
Cash flows from investing activities:			
Investments: Purchases	(2.61)	(2.59)	(3.92)
Investments: Maturities and sales	2.91	3.82	6.02
Capital expenditures	(0.69)	(0.72)	(1.36)
Proceeds from sale of facility and land	0.03	0.07	0.00
Acquisition of business, net of cash received	(6.83)	(0.29)	(3.63)
Change in cash from investing activities	**(7.20)**	**0.29**	**(2.88)**
Cash flows from financing activities:			
Repurchase of common stock	0.00	(4.69)	(6.55)
Issuance of common stock under employee plans	0.00	0.13	0.22
Issuance of commercial paper (maturity 90 days or less), net	0.14	0.16	(0.16)
Proceeds from debt	3.89	2.49	0.11
Repayments of debt	(0.23)	(0.39)	(0.27)
Other	0.00	0.00	(0.09)
Change in cash from financing activities	**3.80**	**(2.30)**	**(6.74)**
Effect of exchange rate changes on cash and cash equivalents	0.33	−0.13	0.25
Change in cash and cash equivalents	**4.32%**	**0.96%**	**−2.91%**

Based on the information in the above exhibit:

1   Discuss the significance of

   A   depreciation and amortization.

   B   capital expenditures.

2   Compare Dell's operating cash flow as a percentage of revenue with Dell's net profit margin.

3   Discuss Dell's use of its positive operating cash flow.

Solution to 1:

A Dell's depreciation and amortization expense is less than 2 percent of total net revenue in the year ended 29 January 2010. However, as a percentage of total revenue, it has been increasing each year. In the year ended 29 January 2010, adding this expense back to determine operating cash flow has a significant impact on cash flow from operations as a percentage of total revenue because its size was approximately 60 percent of net profit margin (net income/total net revenue).

B Dell's level of capital expenditures is relatively small, less than 1 percent of revenues in the most recent years. Cash flow from operations as a percentage of total revenue indicates that operating cash flows are more than sufficient to cover these expenditures.

Solution to 2:

Dell's operating cash flow as a percentage of revenue is usually much higher than net profit margin, with the exception of the year ended 30 January 2009. In that year, the net profit margin was 4.06 percent and operating cash flow as a percentage of total revenue was 3.10 percent. The primary difference between that year and the other years appears to have been a significant reduction in accounts payable; in each of the other years, accounts payable increased. For the year ended 29 January 2010, operating cash flow as a percentage of total revenue was 7.38 percent and net profit margin was 2.71 percent.

Solution to 3:

In the year ended 29 January 2010, the largest cash outflow was for an acquisition of business (investing activities). In prior years, much of Dell's operating cash flow was used to repurchase its own stock (financing activities). In each of the three years, Dell's purchases of investments (investing activities) were less than the amounts of maturities and sales; thus, on a net basis, investments provided a net source of cash.

4.3 Free Cash Flow to the Firm and Free Cash Flow to Equity

It was mentioned earlier that it is desirable that operating cash flows are sufficient to cover capital expenditures. The excess of operating cash flow over capital expenditures is known generically as **free cash flow**. For purposes of valuing a company or its equity securities, an analyst may want to determine and use other cash flow measures, such as free cash flow to the firm (FCFF) or free cash flow to equity (FCFE).

FCFF is the cash flow available to the company's suppliers of debt and equity capital after all operating expenses (including income taxes) have been paid and necessary investments in working capital and fixed capital have been made. FCFF can be computed starting with net income as[9]

$$FCFF = NI + NCC + Int(1 - \text{Tax rate}) - FCInv - WCInv$$

where

NI = Net income

NCC = Non-cash charges (such as depreciation and amortisation)

Int = Interest expense

---

[9] See Pinto et al., *Equity Asset Valuation* (2010) for a detailed discussion of free cash flow computations.

FCInv = Capital expenditures (fixed capital, such as equipment)

WCInv = Working capital expenditures

The reason for adding back interest is that FCFF is the cash flow available to the suppliers of debt capital as well as equity capital. Conveniently, FCFF can also be computed from cash flow from operating activities as

FCFF = CFO + Int(1 − Tax rate) − FCInv

CFO represents cash flow from operating activities under U.S. GAAP or under IFRS where the company has included interest paid in operating activities. If interest paid was included in financing activities, then CFO does not have to be adjusted for Int(1 − Tax rate). Under IFRS, if the company has placed interest and dividends received in investing activities, these should be added back to CFO to determine FCFF. Additionally, if dividends paid were subtracted in the operating section, these should be added back in to compute FCFF.

The computation of FCFF for Acme Corporation (based on the data from Exhibits 6, 7, and 8) is as follows:

CFO	$2,606
Plus: Interest paid times (1 − income tax rate)	
{$258 [1 − 0.34[a]]}	170
Less: Net investments in fixed capital	
($1,300 − $762)	(538)
FCFF	$2,238

[a] Income tax rate of 0.34 = (Tax expense ÷ Pretax income) = ($1,139 ÷ $3,349).

FCFE is the cash flow available to the company's common stockholders after all operating expenses and borrowing costs (principal and interest) have been paid and necessary investments in working capital and fixed capital have been made. FCFE can be computed as

FCFE = CFO − FCInv + Net borrowing

When net borrowing is negative, debt repayments exceed receipts of borrowed funds. In this case, FCFE can be expressed as

FCFE = CFO − FCInv − Net debt repayment

The computation of FCFE for Acme Corporation (based on the data from Exhibits 6, 7, and 8) is as follows:

CFO	$2,606
Less: Net investments in fixed capital ($1,300 − $762)	(538)
Less: Debt repayment	(500)
FCFE	$1,568

Positive FCFE means that the company has an excess of operating cash flow over amounts needed for capital expenditures and repayment of debt. This cash would be available for distribution to owners.

4.4 Cash Flow Ratios

The statement of cash flows provides information that can be analyzed over time to obtain a better understanding of the past performance of a company and its future prospects. This information can also be effectively used to compare the performance and prospects of different companies in an industry and of different industries. There are several ratios based on cash flow from operating activities that are useful in this analysis. These ratios generally fall into cash flow performance (profitability) ratios and cash flow coverage (solvency) ratios. Exhibit 15 summarizes the calculation and interpretation of some of these ratios.

Exhibit 15	**Cash Flow Ratios**	
Performance Ratios	**Calculation**	**What It Measures**
Cash flow to revenue	CFO ÷ Net revenue	Operating cash generated per dollar of revenue
Cash return on assets	CFO ÷ Average total assets	Operating cash generated per dollar of asset investment
Cash return on equity	CFO ÷ Average shareholders' equity	Operating cash generated per dollar of owner investment
Cash to income	CFO ÷ Operating income	Cash generating ability of operations
Cash flow per share[a]	(CFO – Preferred dividends) ÷ Number of common shares outstanding	Operating cash flow on a per-share basis
Coverage Ratios	**Calculation**	**What It Measures**
Debt coverage	CFO ÷ Total debt	Financial risk and financial leverage
Interest coverage[b]	(CFO + Interest paid + Taxes paid) ÷ Interest paid	Ability to meet interest obligations
Reinvestment	CFO ÷ Cash paid for long-term assets	Ability to acquire assets with operating cash flows
Debt payment	CFO ÷ Cash paid for long-term debt repayment	Ability to pay debts with operating cash flows
Dividend payment	CFO ÷ Dividends paid	Ability to pay dividends with operating cash flows
Investing and financing	CFO ÷ Cash outflows for investing and financing activities	Ability to acquire assets, pay debts, and make distributions to owners

Notes:

[a] If the company reports under IFRS and includes total dividends paid as a use of cash in the operating section, total dividends should be added back to CFO as reported and then preferred dividends should be subtracted. Recall that CFO reported under U.S. GAAP and IFRS may differ depending on the treatment of interest and dividends, received and paid.

[b] If the company reports under IFRS and included interest paid as a use of cash in the financing section, then interest paid should not be added back to the numerator.

EXAMPLE 10

A Cash Flow Analysis of Comparables

Andrew Potter is comparing the cash-flow-generating ability of Dell Inc. with that of other computer manufacturers: Hewlett Packard (NYSE: HPQ) and Apple Inc. (NASDAQ: AAPL). He collects information from the companies' annual reports and prepares the following table.

Cash Flow from Operating Activities As a Percentage of Total Net Revenue			
	2009 (%)	2008 (%)	2007 (%)
DELL	7.38	3.10	6.46
HPQ	11.68	12.33	9.22
AAPL	23.68	29.55	22.79

As a Percentage of Ending Total Assets			
	2009 (%)	2008 (%)	2007 (%)
DELL	11.61	7.15	14.33
HPQ	11.65	12.87	10.84
AAPL	21.39	24.25	21.58

AAPL = Apple; HPQ = Hewlett Packard.

What is Potter likely to conclude about the relative cash-flow-generating ability of these companies?

Solution:

On both measures—operating cash flow divided by revenue and operating cash flow divided by assets—Apple's performance was much stronger than the two comparable companies. Dell's operating cash flow divided by revenue is lower than HP's for all three years. Dell's operating cash flow relative to assets is similar to HP's in 2009, lower than HP's in 2008, and higher than HP's in 2007. Apple's measures are significantly higher than the others, indicating that it has the best cash generating ability. Note that Apple's cash generating ability presumably reflects the company's successful introduction and sales of new products (including the iPhone), tightly managed inventory, and ability to generate revenues (and operating cash flow) from businesses not requiring significant investment in such assets as service contracts and sales of third-party compatible products. Overall, Potter should undertake additional research to understand the underlying business reasons for the differences in the companies' cash flow profiles.

SUMMARY

The cash flow statement provides important information about a company's cash receipts and cash payments during an accounting period as well as information about a company's operating, investing, and financing activities. Although the income statement provides a measure of a company's success, cash and cash flow are also vital to a company's long-term success. Information on the sources and uses of cash helps creditors, investors, and other statement users evaluate the company's liquidity, solvency, and financial flexibility. Key concepts are as follows:

- Cash flow activities are classified into three categories: operating activities, investing activities, and financing activities. Significant non-cash transaction activities (if present) are reported by using a supplemental disclosure note to the cash flow statement.

- Cash flow statements under IFRS and U.S. GAAP are similar; however, IFRS provide companies with more choices in classifying some cash flow items as operating, investing, or financing activities.

- Companies can use either the direct or the indirect method for reporting their operating cash flow:

    - The direct method discloses operating cash inflows by source (e.g., cash received from customers, cash received from investment income) and operating cash outflows by use (e.g., cash paid to suppliers, cash paid for interest) in the operating activities section of the cash flow statement.

    - The indirect method reconciles net income to operating cash flow by adjusting net income for all non-cash items and the net changes in the operating working capital accounts.

- The cash flow statement is linked to a company's income statement and comparative balance sheets and to data on those statements.

- Although the indirect method is most commonly used by companies, an analyst can generally convert it to an approximation of the direct format by following a simple three-step process.

- An evaluation of a cash flow statement should involve an assessment of the sources and uses of cash and the main drivers of cash flow within each category of activities.

- The analyst can use common-size statement analysis for the cash flow statement. Two approaches to developing the common-size statements are the total cash inflows/total cash outflows method and the percentage of net revenues method.

- The cash flow statement can be used to determine free cash flow to the firm (FCFF) and free cash flow to equity (FCFE).

- The cash flow statement may also be used in financial ratios that measure a company's profitability, performance, and financial strength.

REFERENCES

Pinto, Jerald E., Elaine Henry, Thomas R. Robinson, and John D. Stowe. 2010. *Equity Asset Valuation*, 2nd edition. Hoboken, NJ: John Wiley & Sons.

PRACTICE PROBLEMS

1   The three major classifications of activities in a cash flow statement are:

   A   inflows, outflows, and net flows.

   B   operating, investing, and financing.

   C   revenues, expenses, and net income.

2   The sale of a building for cash would be classified as what type of activity on the cash flow statement?

   A   Operating.

   B   Investing.

   C   Financing.

3   Which of the following is an example of a financing activity on the cash flow statement under U.S. GAAP?

   A   Payment of interest.

   B   Receipt of dividends.

   C   Payment of dividends.

4   A conversion of a face value $1 million convertible bond for $1 million of common stock would most likely be:

   A   reported as a $1 million investing cash inflow and outflow.

   B   reported as a $1 million financing cash outflow and inflow.

   C   reported as supplementary information to the cash flow statement.

5   Interest paid is classified as an operating cash flow under:

   A   U.S. GAAP but may be classified as either operating or investing cash flows under IFRS.

   B   IFRS but may be classified as either operating or investing cash flows under U.S. GAAP.

   C   U.S. GAAP but may be classified as either operating or financing cash flows under IFRS.

6   Cash flows from taxes on income must be separately disclosed under:

   A   IFRS only.

   B   U.S. GAAP only.

   C   both IFRS and U.S GAAP.

7   Which of the following components of the cash flow statement may be prepared under the indirect method under both IFRS and U.S. GAAP?

   A   Operating.

   B   Investing.

   C   Financing.

8   Which of the following is *most likely* to appear in the operating section of a cash flow statement under the indirect method?

   A   Net income.

   B   Cash paid to suppliers.

   C   Cash received from customers.

9 Red Road Company, a consulting company, reported total revenues of $100 million, total expenses of $80 million, and net income of $20 million in the most recent year. If accounts receivable increased by $10 million, how much cash did the company receive from customers?

A $90 million.

B $100 million.

C $110 million.

10 Green Glory Corp., a garden supply wholesaler, reported cost of goods sold for the year of $80 million. Total assets increased by $55 million, including an increase of $5 million in inventory. Total liabilities increased by $45 million, including an increase of $2 million in accounts payable. The cash paid by the company to its suppliers is most likely *closest* to:

A $73 million.

B $77 million.

C $83 million.

11 Purple Fleur S.A., a retailer of floral products, reported cost of goods sold for the year of $75 million. Total assets increased by $55 million, but inventory declined by $6 million. Total liabilities increased by $45 million, and accounts payable increased by $2 million. The cash paid by the company to its suppliers is most likely *closest* to:

A $67 million.

B $79 million.

C $83 million.

12 White Flag, a women's clothing manufacturer, reported salaries expense of $20 million. The beginning balance of salaries payable was $3 million, and the ending balance of salaries payable was $1 million. How much cash did the company pay in salaries?

A $18 million.

B $21 million.

C $22 million.

13 An analyst gathered the following information from a company's 2010 financial statements (in $ millions):

Year ended 31 December	2009	2010
Net sales	245.8	254.6
Cost of goods sold	168.3	175.9
Accounts receivable	73.2	68.3
Inventory	39.0	47.8
Accounts payable	20.3	22.9

Based only on the information above, the company's 2010 statement of cash flows in the direct format would include amounts (in $ millions) for cash received from customers and cash paid to suppliers, respectively, that are *closest* to:

	cash received from customers	cash paid to suppliers
A	249.7	169.7
B	259.5	174.5
C	259.5	182.1

14 Golden Cumulus Corp., a commodities trading company, reported interest expense of $19 million and taxes of $6 million. Interest payable increased by $3 million, and taxes payable decreased by $4 million over the period. How much cash did the company pay for interest and taxes?

   A $22 million for interest and $10 million for taxes.

   B $16 million for interest and $2 million for taxes.

   C $16 million for interest and $10 million for taxes.

15 An analyst gathered the following information from a company's 2010 financial statements (in $ millions):

Balances as of Year Ended 31 December	2009	2010
Retained earnings	120	145
Accounts receivable	38	43
Inventory	45	48
Accounts payable	36	29

   In 2010, the company declared and paid cash dividends of $10 million and recorded depreciation expense in the amount of $25 million. The company considers dividends paid a financing activity. The company's 2010 cash flow from operations (in $ millions) was *closest* to

   A 25.

   B 45.

   C 75.

16 Silverago Incorporated, an international metals company, reported a loss on the sale of equipment of $2 million in 2010. In addition, the company's income statement shows depreciation expense of $8 million and the cash flow statement shows capital expenditure of $10 million, all of which was for the purchase of new equipment. Using the following information from the comparative balance sheets, how much cash did the company receive from the equipment sale?

Balance Sheet Item	12/31/2009	12/31/2010	Change
Equipment	$100 million	$105 million	$5 million
Accumulated depreciation—equipment	$40 million	$46 million	$6 million

   A $1 million.

   B $2 million.

   C $3 million.

17 Jaderong Plinkett Stores reported net income of $25 million. The company has no outstanding debt. Using the following information from the comparative balance sheets (in millions), what should the company report in the financing section of the statement of cash flows in 2010?

Balance Sheet Item	12/31/2009	12/31/2010	Change
Common stock	$100	$102	$2
Additional paid-in capital common stock	$100	$140	$40
Retained earnings	$100	$115	$15
Total stockholders' equity	$300	$357	$57

    A Issuance of common stock of $42 million; dividends paid of $10 million.

    B Issuance of common stock of $38 million; dividends paid of $10 million.

    C Issuance of common stock of $42 million; dividends paid of $40 million.

18 Based on the following information for Star Inc., what are the total net adjustments that the company would make to net income in order to derive operating cash flow?

Income Statement Item	Year Ended 12/31/2010
Net income	$20 million
Depreciation	$2 million

Balance Sheet Item	12/31/2009	12/31/2010	Change
Accounts receivable	$25 million	$22 million	($3 million)
Inventory	$10 million	$14 million	$4 million
Accounts payable	$8 million	$13 million	$5 million

    A Add $2 million.

    B Add $6 million.

    C Subtract $6 million.

19 The first step in cash flow statement analysis should be to:

    A evaluate consistency of cash flows.

    B determine operating cash flow drivers.

    C identify the major sources and uses of cash.

20 Which of the following would be valid conclusions from an analysis of the cash flow statement for Telefónica Group presented in Exhibit 3?

    A The primary use of cash is financing activities.

    B The primary source of cash is operating activities.

    C Telefónica classifies interest received as an operating activity.

21 Which is an appropriate method of preparing a common-size cash flow statement?

    A Show each item of revenue and expense as a percentage of net revenue.

    B Show each line item on the cash flow statement as a percentage of net revenue.

    C Show each line item on the cash flow statement as a percentage of total cash outflows.

22 Which of the following is an appropriate method of computing free cash flow to the firm?

    A Add operating cash flows to capital expenditures and deduct after-tax interest payments.

    B Add operating cash flows to after-tax interest payments and deduct capital expenditures.

    C Deduct both after-tax interest payments and capital expenditures from operating cash flows.

23 An analyst has calculated a ratio using as the numerator the sum of operating cash flow, interest, and taxes and as the denominator the amount of interest. What is this ratio, what does it measure, and what does it indicate?

    A This ratio is an interest coverage ratio, measuring a company's ability to meet its interest obligations and indicating a company's solvency.

    B This ratio is an effective tax ratio, measuring the amount of a company's operating cash flow used for taxes and indicating a company's efficiency in tax management.

    C This ratio is an operating profitability ratio, measuring the operating cash flow generated accounting for taxes and interest and indicating a company's liquidity.

SOLUTIONS

1 B is correct. Operating, investing, and financing are the three major classifications of activities in a cash flow statement. Revenues, expenses, and net income are elements of the income statement. Inflows, outflows, and net flows are items of information in the statement of cash flows.

2 B is correct. Purchases and sales of long-term assets are considered investing activities. Note that if the transaction had involved the exchange of a building for other than cash (for example, for another building, common stock of another company, or a long-term note receivable), it would have been considered a significant non-cash activity.

3 C is correct. Payment of dividends is a financing activity under U.S. GAAP. Payment of interest and receipt of dividends are included in operating cash flows under U.S. GAAP. Note that IFRS allow companies to include receipt of interest and dividends as either operating or investing cash flows and to include payment of interest and dividends as either operating or financing cash flows.

4 C is correct. Non-cash transactions, if significant, are reported as supplementary information, not in the investing or financing sections of the cash flow statement.

5 C is correct. Interest expense is always classified as an operating cash flow under U.S. GAAP but may be classified as either an operating or financing cash flow under IFRS.

6 C is correct. Taxes on income are required to be separately disclosed under IFRS and U.S. GAAP. The disclosure may be in the cash flow statement or elsewhere.

7 A is correct. The operating section may be prepared under the indirect method. The other sections are always prepared under the direct method.

8 A is correct. Under the indirect method, the operating section would begin with net income and adjust it to arrive at operating cash flow. The other two items would appear in the operating section under the direct method.

9 A is correct. Revenues of $100 million minus the increase in accounts receivable of $10 million equal $90 million cash received from customers. The increase in accounts receivable means that the company received less in cash than it reported as revenue.

10 C is correct. Cost of goods sold of $80 million plus the increase in inventory of $5 million equals purchases from suppliers of $85 million. The increase in accounts payable of $2 million means that the company paid $83 million in cash ($85 million minus $2 million) to its suppliers.

11 A is correct. Cost of goods sold of $75 million less the decrease in inventory of $6 million equals purchases from suppliers of $69 million. The increase in accounts payable of $2 million means that the company paid $67 million in cash ($69 million minus $2 million).

12 C is correct. Beginning salaries payable of $3 million plus salaries expense of $20 million minus ending salaries payable of $1 million equals $22 million. Alternatively, the expense of $20 million plus the $2 million decrease in salaries payable equals $22 million.

13 C is correct. Cash received from customers = Sales + Decrease in accounts receivable = 254.6 + 4.9 = 259.5. Cash paid to suppliers = Cost of goods sold + Increase in inventory − Increase in accounts payable = 175.9 + 8.8 − 2.6 = 182.1.

14 C is correct. Interest expense of $19 million less the increase in interest payable of $3 million equals interest paid of $16 million. Tax expense of $6 million plus the decrease in taxes payable of $4 million equals taxes paid of $10 million.

15 B is correct. All dollar amounts are in millions. Net income (NI) for 2010 is $35. This amount is the increase in retained earnings, $25, plus the dividends paid, $10. Depreciation of $25 is added back to net income, and the increases in accounts receivable, $5, and in inventory, $3, are subtracted from net income because they are uses of cash. The decrease in accounts payable is also a use of cash and, therefore, a subtraction from net income. Thus, cash flow from operations is $25 + $10 + $25 − $5 − $3 − $7 = $45.

16 A is correct. Selling price (cash inflow) minus book value equals gain or loss on sale; therefore, gain or loss on sale plus book value equals selling price (cash inflow). The amount of loss is given—$2 million. To calculate the book value of the equipment sold, find the historical cost of the equipment and the accumulated depreciation on the equipment.

- Beginning balance of equipment of $100 million plus equipment purchased of $10 million minus ending balance of equipment of $105 million equals the historical cost of equipment sold, or $5 million.

- Beginning accumulated depreciation of $40 million plus depreciation expense for the year of $8 million minus ending balance of accumulated depreciation of $46 million equals accumulated depreciation on the equipment sold, or $2 million.

- Therefore, the book value of the equipment sold was $5 million minus $2 million, or $3 million.

- Because the loss on the sale of equipment was $2 million, the amount of cash received must have been $1 million.

17 A is correct. The increase of $42 million in common stock and additional paid-in capital indicates that the company issued stock during the year. The increase in retained earnings of $15 million indicates that the company paid $10 million in cash dividends during the year, determined as beginning retained earnings of $100 million plus net income of $25 million minus ending retained earnings of $115 million, which equals $10 million in cash dividends.

18 B is correct. To derive operating cash flow, the company would make the following adjustments to net income: Add depreciation (a non-cash expense) of $2 million; add the decrease in accounts receivable of $3 million; add the increase in accounts payable of $5 million; and subtract the increase in inventory of $4 million. Total additions would be $10 million, and total subtractions would be $4 million, which gives net additions of $6 million.

19 C is correct. An overall assessment of the major sources and uses of cash should be the first step in evaluating a cash flow statement.

20 B is correct. The primary source of cash is operating activities. The primary use of cash is investing activities. Interest received for Telefónica is classified as an investing activity.

21 B is correct. An appropriate method to prepare a common-size cash flow statement is to show each line item on the cash flow statement as a percentage of net revenue. An alternative way to prepare a statement of cash flows is to show each item of cash inflow as a percentage of total inflows and each item of cash outflows as a percentage of total outflows.

22 B is correct. Free cash flow to the firm can be computed as operating cash flows plus after-tax interest expense less capital expenditures.

23 A is correct. This ratio is an interest coverage ratio, measuring a company's ability to meet its interest obligations and indicating a company's solvency. This coverage ratio is based on cash flow information; another common coverage ratio uses a measure based on the income statement (earnings before interest, taxes, depreciation, and amortisation).

28

Financial Analysis Techniques

by Elaine Henry, CFA, Thomas R. Robinson, CFA, and Jan Hendrik van Greuning, CFA

LEARNING OUTCOMES

Mastery	The candidate should be able to:
☐	a. describe tools and techniques used in financial analysis, including their uses and limitations;
☐	b. classify, calculate, and interpret activity, liquidity, solvency, profitability, and valuation ratios;
☐	c. describe relationships among ratios and evaluate a company using ratio analysis;
☐	d. demonstrate the application of DuPont analysis of return on equity, and calculate and interpret effects of changes in its components;
☐	e. calculate and interpret ratios used in equity analysis and credit analysis;
☐	f. explain the requirements for segment reporting, and calculate and interpret segment ratios;
☐	g. describe how ratio analysis and other techniques can be used to model and forecast earnings.

INTRODUCTION

1

Financial analysis tools can be useful in assessing a company's performance and trends in that performance. In essence, an analyst converts data into financial metrics that assist in decision making. Analysts seek to answer such questions as: How successfully has the company performed, relative to its own past performance and relative to its competitors? How is the company likely to perform in the future? Based on expectations about future performance, what is the value of this company or the securities it issues?

A primary source of data is a company's annual report, including the financial statements and notes, and management commentary (operating and financial review or management's discussion and analysis). This reading focuses on data presented in financial reports prepared under International Financial Reporting Standards (IFRS) and United States generally accepted accounting principles (U.S. GAAP). However, financial reports do not contain all the information needed to perform effective financial analysis. Although financial statements do contain data about the *past* performance of a company (its income and cash flows) as well as its *current* financial condition (assets, liabilities, and owners' equity), such statements do not necessarily provide all the information useful for analysis nor do they forecast *future* results. The financial analyst must be capable of using financial statements in conjunction with other information to make projections and reach valid conclusions. Accordingly, an analyst typically needs to supplement the information found in a company's financial reports with other information, including information on the economy, industry, comparable companies, and the company itself.

This reading describes various techniques used to analyze a company's financial statements. Financial analysis of a company may be performed for a variety of reasons, such as valuing equity securities, assessing credit risk, conducting due diligence related to an acquisition, or assessing a subsidiary's performance. This reading will describe techniques common to any financial analysis and then discuss more specific aspects for the two most common categories: equity analysis and credit analysis.

Equity analysis incorporates an owner's perspective, either for valuation or performance evaluation. Credit analysis incorporates a creditor's (such as a banker or bondholder) perspective. In either case, there is a need to gather and analyze information to make a decision (ownership or credit); the focus of analysis varies because of the differing interest of owners and creditors. Both equity and credit analyses assess the entity's ability to generate and grow earnings, and cash flow, as well as any associated risks. Equity analysis usually places a greater emphasis on growth, whereas credit analysis usually places a greater emphasis on risks. The difference in emphasis reflects the different fundamentals of these types of investments: The value of a company's equity generally increases as the company's earnings and cash flow increase, whereas the value of a company's debt has an upper limit.[1]

The balance of this reading is organized as follows: Section 2 recaps the framework for financial statements and the place of financial analysis techniques within the framework. Section 3 provides a description of analytical tools and techniques. Section 4 explains how to compute, analyze, and interpret common financial ratios. Sections 5 through 8 explain the use of ratios and other analytical data in equity analysis, credit analysis, segment analysis, and forecasting, respectively. A summary of the key points and practice problems in the CFA Institute multiple-choice format conclude the reading.

2   THE FINANCIAL ANALYSIS PROCESS

In financial analysis, it is essential to clearly identify and understand the final objective and the steps required to reach that objective. In addition, the analyst needs to know where to find relevant data, how to process and analyze the data (in other words, know the typical questions to address when interpreting data), and how to communicate the analysis and conclusions.

---

[1] The upper limit is equal to the undiscounted sum of the principal and remaining interest payments (i.e., the present value of these contractual payments at a zero percent discount rate).

2.1 The Objectives of the Financial Analysis Process

Because of the variety of reasons for performing financial analysis, the numerous available techniques, and the often substantial amount of data, it is important that the analytical approach be tailored to the specific situation. Prior to beginning any financial analysis, the analyst should clarify the purpose and context, and clearly understand the following:

- What is the purpose of the analysis? What questions will this analysis answer?
- What level of detail will be needed to accomplish this purpose?
- What data are available for the analysis?
- What are the factors or relationships that will influence the analysis?
- What are the analytical limitations, and will these limitations potentially impair the analysis?

Having clarified the purpose and context of the analysis, the analyst can select the set of techniques (e.g., ratios) that will best assist in making a decision. Although there is no single approach to structuring the analysis process, a general framework is set forth in Exhibit 1.[2] The steps in this process were discussed in more detail in an earlier reading; the primary focus of this reading is on Phases 3 and 4, processing and analyzing data.

Exhibit 1	A Financial Statement Analysis Framework	
Phase	**Sources of Information**	**Output**
1 Articulate the purpose and context of the analysis.	■ The nature of the analyst's function, such as evaluating an equity or debt investment or issuing a credit rating. ■ Communication with client or supervisor on needs and concerns. ■ Institutional guidelines related to developing specific work product.	■ Statement of the purpose or objective of analysis. ■ A list (written or unwritten) of specific questions to be answered by the analysis. ■ Nature and content of report to be provided. ■ Timetable and budgeted resources for completion.
2 Collect input data.	■ Financial statements, other financial data, questionnaires, and industry/economic data. ■ Discussions with management, suppliers, customers, and competitors. ■ Company site visits (e.g., to production facilities or retail stores).	■ Organized financial statements. ■ Financial data tables. ■ Completed questionnaires, if applicable.
3 Process data.	■ Data from the previous phase.	■ Adjusted financial statements. ■ Common-size statements. ■ Ratios and graphs. ■ Forecasts.

(continued)

---

2 Components of this framework have been adapted from van Greuning and Bratanovic (2003, p. 300) and Benninga and Sarig (1997, pp. 134–156).

Exhibit 1	(Continued)

Phase	Sources of Information	Output
4 Analyze/interpret the processed data.	■ Input data as well as processed data.	■ Analytical results.
5 Develop and communicate conclusions and recommendations (e.g., with an analysis report).	■ Analytical results and previous reports. ■ Institutional guidelines for published reports.	■ Analytical report answering questions posed in Phase 1. ■ Recommendation regarding the purpose of the analysis, such as whether to make an investment or grant credit.
6 Follow-up.	■ Information gathered by periodically repeating above steps as necessary to determine whether changes to holdings or recommendations are necessary.	■ Updated reports and recommendations.

2.2 Distinguishing between Computations and Analysis

An effective analysis encompasses both computations and interpretations. A well-reasoned analysis differs from a mere compilation of various pieces of information, computations, tables, and graphs by integrating the data collected into a cohesive whole. Analysis of past performance, for example, should address not only what happened but also why it happened and whether it advanced the company's strategy. Some of the key questions to address include:

- What aspects of performance are critical for this company to successfully compete in this industry?
- How well did the company's performance meet these critical aspects? (Established through computation and comparison with appropriate benchmarks, such as the company's own historical performance or competitors' performance.)
- What were the key causes of this performance, and how does this performance reflect the company's strategy? (Established through analysis.)

If the analysis is forward looking, additional questions include:

- What is the likely impact of an event or trend? (Established through interpretation of analysis.)
- What is the likely response of management to this trend? (Established through evaluation of quality of management and corporate governance.)
- What is the likely impact of trends in the company, industry, and economy on future cash flows? (Established through assessment of corporate strategy and through forecasts.)
- What are the recommendations of the analyst? (Established through interpretation and forecasting of results of analysis.)
- What risks should be highlighted? (Established by an evaluation of major uncertainties in the forecast and in the environment within which the company operates.)

Example 1 demonstrates how a company's financial data can be analyzed in the context of its business strategy and changes in that strategy. An analyst must be able to understand the "why" behind the numbers and ratios, not just what the numbers and ratios are.

EXAMPLE 1

Strategy Reflected in Financial Performance

Apple Inc. (NasdaqGS: AAPL) and Dell Inc. (NasdaqGS: DELL) engage in the design, manufacture, and sale of computer hardware and related products and services. Selected financial data for 2007 through 2009 for these two competitors are given below. Apple's fiscal year (FY) ends on the final Saturday in September (for example, FY2009 ended on 26 September 2009). Dell's fiscal year ends on the Friday nearest 31 January (for example, FY2009 ended on 29 January 2010 and FY2007 ended on 1 February 2008).

Selected Financial Data for Apple (Dollars in Millions)

Fiscal year	2009	2008	2007
Net sales	42,905	37,491	24,578
Gross margin	17,222	13,197	8,152
Operating income	11,740	8,327	4,407

Selected Financial Data for Dell (Dollars in Millions)

Fiscal year	2009	2008	2007
Net sales	52,902	61,101	61,133
Gross margin	9,261	10,957	11,671
Operating income	2,172	3,190	3,440

Source: Apple's Forms 10-K and 10-K/A and Dell's Form 10-K.

Apple reported a 53 percent increase in net sales from FY2007 to FY2008 and a further increase in FY2009 of approximately 14 percent. Gross margin increased 62 percent from FY2007 to FY2008 and increased 30 percent from FY2008 to FY2009. From FY2007 to FY2009, the gross margin more than doubled. Also, the company's operating income almost tripled over the three year period. From FY2007 to 2009, Dell reported a decrease in sales, gross margin, and operating income

What caused Apple's dramatic growth in sales and operating income and Dell's comparatively sluggish performance? One of the most important factors was the introduction of innovative and stylish products, the linkages with iTunes, and expansion of the distinctive Apple stores. Among the company's most important and most successful new products was the iPhone. Apple's 2009 10-K indicates that iPhone unit sales grew 78 percent from 11.6 million units in 2008 to 20.7 million units in 2009. By 2009, the company's revenues from iPhones and related services had grown to $13.0 billion and were nearly as large as the company's $13.8 billion revenues from sales of Mac computers. The new products and linkages among the products not only increased demand but also increased the potential for higher pricing. As a result, gross profit margins and operating profit margins increased over the period because costs did not increase at the same pace as sales. Moreover, the company's products revolutionized the delivery channel for music and video. The financial results reflect a successful execution of the company's strategy to deliver integrated, innovative products by controlling the design and development of both hardware and software.

Dell continued to concentrate in the personal computer market, which arguably is in the market maturity stage of the product life cycle. Dell's results are consistent with a market maturity stage where industry sales level off and competition increases so that industry profits decline. With increased competition, some companies cannot compete and drop out of the market.

Analysts often need to communicate the findings of their analysis in a written report. Their reports should communicate how conclusions were reached and why recommendations were made. For example, a report might present the following:[3]

- the purpose of the report, unless it is readily apparent;
- relevant aspects of the business context:
  - economic environment (country, macro economy, sector);
  - financial and other infrastructure (accounting, auditing, rating agencies);
  - legal and regulatory environment (and any other material limitations on the company being analyzed);
- evaluation of corporate governance and assessment of management strategy, including the company's competitive advantage(s);
- assessment of financial and operational data, including key assumptions in the analysis; and
- conclusions and recommendations, including limitations of the analysis and risks.

An effective narrative and well supported conclusions and recommendations are normally enhanced by using 3–10 years of data, as well as analytic techniques appropriate to the purpose of the report.

3 ANALYTICAL TOOLS AND TECHNIQUES

The tools and techniques presented in this section facilitate evaluations of company data. Evaluations require comparisons. It is difficult to say that a company's financial performance was "good" without clarifying the basis for comparison. In assessing a company's ability to generate and grow earnings and cash flow, and the risks related to those earnings and cash flows, the analyst draws comparisons to other companies (cross-sectional analysis) and over time (trend or time-series analysis).

For example, an analyst may wish to compare the profitability of companies competing in a global industry. If the companies differ significantly in size and/or report their financial data in different currencies, comparing net income as reported is not useful. Ratios (which express one number in relation to another) and common-size financial statements can remove size as a factor and enable a more relevant comparison. To achieve comparability across companies reporting in different currencies, one

---

3 The nature and content of reports will vary depending upon the purpose of the analysis and the ultimate recipient of the report. For an example of the contents of an equity research report, see Pinto et al. (2010).

approach is to translate all reported numbers into a common currency using exchange rates at the end of a period. Others may prefer to translate reported numbers using the average exchange rates during the period. Alternatively, if the focus is primarily on ratios, comparability can be achieved without translating the currencies.

The analyst may also want to examine comparable performance over time. Again, the nominal currency amounts of sales or net income may not highlight significant changes. However, using ratios (see Example 2), horizontal financial statements where quantities are stated in terms of a selected base year value, and graphs can make such changes more apparent. Another obstacle to comparison is differences in fiscal year end. To achieve comparability, one approach is to develop trailing twelve months data, which will be described in a section below. Finally, it should be noted that differences in accounting standards can limit comparability.

EXAMPLE 2

Ratio Analysis

An analyst is examining the profitability of three Asian companies with large shares of the global personal computer market: Acer Inc. (Taiwan SE: ACER), Lenovo Group Limited (HKSE: 0992), and Toshiba Corporation (Tokyo SE: 6502). Taiwan-based Acer has pursued a strategy of selling its products at affordable prices. In contrast, China-based Lenovo aims to achieve higher selling prices by stressing the high engineering quality of its personal computers for business use. Japan-based Toshiba is a conglomerate with varied product lines in addition to computers. For its personal computer business, one aspect of Toshiba's strategy has been to focus on laptops only, in contrast with other manufacturers that also make desktops. Acer reports in New Taiwan dollars (TW$), Lenovo reports in U.S. dollars (US$), and Toshiba reports in Japanese yen (JP¥). For Acer, fiscal year end is 31 December. For both Lenovo and Toshiba, fiscal year end is 31 March; thus, for these companies, FY2009 ended 31 March 2010.

The analyst collects the data shown in Exhibit 2 below. Use this information to answer the following questions:

1 Which of the three companies is largest based on the amount of revenue, in US$, reported in fiscal year 2009? For FY2009, assume the relevant, average exchange rates were 32.2 TW$/US$ and 92.5 JP¥/US$.

2 Which company had the highest revenue growth from FY2005 to FY2009?

3 How do the companies compare, based on profitability?

Exhibit 2

ACER

TW$ Millions	**FY2005**	**FY2006**	**FY2007**	**FY2008**	**FY2009**
Revenue	318,088	350,816	462,066	546,274	573,983
Gross profit	34,121	38,171	47,418	57,286	58,328
Net income	8,478	10,218	12,959	11,742	11,353

LENOVO

US$ Millions	**FY2005**	**FY2006**	**FY2007**	**FY2008**	**FY2009**
Revenue	13,276	14,590	16,352	14,901	16,605
Gross profit	1,858	2,037	2,450	1,834	1,790
Net income (Loss)	22	161	484	(226)	129

(continued)

| Exhibit 2 | (Continued) |

TOSHIBA

JP¥ Millions	FY2005	FY2006	FY2007	FY2008	FY2009
Revenue	6,343,506	7,116,350	7,665,332	6,654,518	6,381,599
Gross profit	1,683,711	1,804,171	1,908,729	1,288,431	1,459,362
Net income (Loss)	78,186	137,429	127,413	(343,559)	(19,743)

Solution to 1:

Toshiba is far larger than the other two companies based on FY2009 revenues in US$. Toshiba's FY2009 revenues of US$69.0 billion are far higher than either Acer's US$17.8 billion or Lenovo's US$16.6 billion.

Acer: At the assumed average exchange rate of 32.2 TW$/US$, Acer's FY2009 revenues are equivalent to US$17.8 billion (= TW$573.983 billion ÷ 32.2 TW$/US$).

Lenovo: Lenovo's FY2009 revenues totaled US$16.6 billion.

Toshiba: At the assumed average exchange rate of 92.5 JP¥/US$, Toshiba's revenues for FY2009 are equivalent to US$69.0 billion (= JP¥ 6,381.599 billion ÷ 92.5 JP¥/US$).

Note: Comparing the size of companies reporting in different currencies requires translating reported numbers into a common currency using exchange rates at some point in time. This solution converts the revenues of Acer and Toshiba to billions of U.S. dollars using the average exchange rate of the fiscal period. It would be equally informative (and would yield the same conclusion) to convert the revenues of Acer and Lenovo to Japanese yen, or to convert the revenues of Toshiba and Lenovo to New Taiwan dollars.

Solution to 2:

The growth in Acer's revenue was much higher than either of the other two companies.

	Change in Revenue FY2009 versus FY2005 (%)	Compound Annual Growth Rate from FY2005 to FY2009 (%)
Acer	80.4	15.9
Lenovo	25.1	5.8
Toshiba	0.6	0.1

The table shows two growth metrics. Calculations are illustrated using the revenue data for Acer:

The change in Acer's revenue for FY2009 versus FY2005 is 80.4 percent calculated as $(573,983 - 318,088) \div 318,088$ or equivalently $(573,983 \div 318,088) - 1$.

The compound annual growth rate in Acer's revenue from FY2005 to FY2009 is 15.9 percent, calculated using a financial calculator with the following inputs: Present Value = − 318,088; Future value = 573,983; N = 4; Payment = 0; and then Interest = ? to solve for growth.

Calculation of the compound annual growth rate can also be expressed as follows: $[(\text{Ending value} \div \text{Beginning value})^{(1/\text{number of periods})}] - 1 = [(573,983 \div 318,088)^{(1/4)} - 1 = 0.159$ or 15.9 percent.

Solution to 3:

Profitability can be assessed by comparing the amount of gross profit to revenue and the amount of net income to revenue. The following table presents these two profitability ratios—**gross profit margin** (gross profit divided by revenue) and **net profit margin** (net income divided by revenue)—for each year.

ACER	**FY2005 (%)**	**FY2006 (%)**	**FY2007 (%)**	**FY2008 (%)**	**FY2009 (%)**
Gross profit margin	10.7	10.9	10.3	10.5	10.2
Net profit margin	2.7	2.9	2.8	2.1	2.0

LENOVO	**FY2005 (%)**	**FY2006 (%)**	**FY2007 (%)**	**FY2008 (%)**	**FY2009 (%)**
Gross profit margin	14.0	14.0	15.0	12.3	10.8
Net profit margin	0.2	1.1	3.0	−1.5	0.8

TOSHIBA	**FY2005 (%)**	**FY2006 (%)**	**FY2007 (%)**	**FY2008 (%)**	**FY2009 (%)**
Gross profit margin	26.5	25.4	24.9	19.4	22.9
Net profit margin	1.2	1.9	1.7	−5.2	−0.3

The net profit margins indicate that Acer has been the most profitable of the three companies. The company's net profit margin was somewhat lower in the most recent two years (only 2.1 percent and 2.0 percent in FY2008 and FY2009, respectively, compared to 2.7 percent, 2.9 percent and 2.8 percent in FYs 2005, 2006, and 2007, respectively), but has nonetheless remained positive and has remained higher than the competing companies.

Acer's gross profit margin has remained consistently above 10 percent in all 5 fiscal years. In contrast, Lenovo's gross profit margin has declined markedly over the 5-year period, but remains higher than Acer's, which is consistent with the company's strategic objective to achieve higher selling prices by stressing the high engineering quality of its personal computers. However, Lenovo's net profit margin has typically been lower than Acer's. Further analysis is needed to determine the cause of Lenovo's gross profitability decline over the period FY2005 to 2009 (lower selling prices and/or higher costs), to assess whether this decline is likely to persist in future years, and to determine the reason Lenovo's net profit margins are generally lower than Acer's despite Lenovo's higher gross profit margins.

Because Toshiba is a conglomerate, profit ratios based on data for the entire company give limited information about the company's personal computer business. Ratios based on segment data would likely be more useful than profit ratios for the entire company. Based on the aggregate information, Toshiba's gross profit margins are higher than either Acer's or Lenovo's gross profit margins, whereas Toshiba's net profit margins are generally lower than the net profit margins of either of the other two companies.

Section 3.1 describes the tools and techniques of ratio analysis in more detail. Sections 3.2 to 3.4 describe other tools and techniques.

3.1 Ratios

There are many relationships between financial accounts and between expected relationships from one point in time to another. Ratios are a useful way of expressing these relationships. Ratios express one quantity in relation to another (usually as a quotient).

Extensive academic research has examined the importance of ratios in predicting stock returns (Ou and Penman, 1989; Abarbanell and Bushee, 1998) or credit failure (Altman, 1968; Ohlson, 1980; Hopwood et al., 1994). This research has found that financial statement ratios are effective in selecting investments and in predicting financial distress. Practitioners routinely use ratios to derive and communicate the value of companies and securities.

Several aspects of ratio analysis are important to understand. First, the computed ratio is not "the answer." The ratio is an *indicator* of some aspect of a company's performance, telling what happened but not why it happened. For example, an analyst might want to answer the question: Which of two companies was more profitable?

As demonstrated in the previous example, the net profit margin, which expresses profit relative to revenue, can provide insight into this question. Net profit margin is calculated by dividing net income by revenue:[4]

$$\frac{\text{Net income}}{\text{Revenue}}$$

Assume Company A has €100,000 of net income and Company B has €200,000 of net income. Company B generated twice as much income as Company A, but was it more profitable? Assume further that Company A has €2,000,000 of revenue, and thus a net profit margin of 5 percent, and Company B has €6,000,000 of revenue, and thus a net profit margin of 3.33 percent. Expressing net income as a percentage of revenue clarifies the relationship: For each €100 of revenue, Company A earns €5 in net income, whereas Company B earns only €3.33 for each €100 of revenue. So, we can now answer the question of which company was more profitable in percentage terms: Company A was more profitable, as indicated by its higher net profit margin of 5 percent. Note that Company A was more *profitable* despite the fact that Company B reported higher absolute amounts of net income and revenue. However, this ratio by itself does not tell us *why* Company A has a higher profit margin. Further analysis is required to determine the reason (perhaps higher relative sales prices or better cost control or lower effective tax rates).

Company size sometimes confers economies of scale, so the absolute amounts of net income and revenue are useful in financial analysis. However, ratios reduce the effect of size, which enhances comparisons between companies and over time.

A second important aspect of ratio analysis is that differences in accounting policies (across companies and across time) can distort ratios, and a meaningful comparison may, therefore, involve adjustments to the financial data. Third, not all ratios are necessarily relevant to a particular analysis. The ability to select a relevant ratio or ratios to answer the research question is an analytical skill. Finally, as with financial analysis in general, ratio analysis does not stop with computation; interpretation of the result is essential. In practice, differences in ratios across time and across companies can be subtle, and interpretation is situation specific.

3.1.1 *The Universe of Ratios*

There are no authoritative bodies specifying exact formulas for computing ratios or providing a standard, comprehensive list of ratios. Formulas and even names of ratios often differ from analyst to analyst or from database to database. The number of different ratios that can be created is practically limitless. There are, however, widely accepted ratios that have been found to be useful. Section 4 of this reading will focus primarily on these broad classes and commonly accepted definitions of key ratios. However, the analyst should be aware that different ratios may be used in practice and that certain industries have unique ratios tailored to the characteristics of that industry. When faced with an unfamiliar ratio, the analyst can examine the underlying formula to gain insight into what the ratio is measuring. For example, consider the following ratio formula:

$$\frac{\text{Operating income}}{\text{Average total assets}}$$

---

4 The term "sales" is often used interchangeably with the term "revenues." Other times it is used to refer to revenues derived from **sales** of products versus services. The income statement usually reflects "revenues" or "sales" after returns and allowances (e.g., returns of products or discounts offered after a sale to induce the customer to not return a product). Additionally, in some countries, including the United Kingdom and South Africa, the term "turnover" is used in the sense of "revenue."

Never having seen this ratio, an analyst might question whether a result of 12 percent is better than 8 percent. The answer can be found in the ratio itself. The numerator is operating income and the denominator is average total assets, so the ratio can be interpreted as the amount of operating income generated per unit of assets. For every €100 of average total assets, generating €12 of operating income is better than generating €8 of operating income. Furthermore, it is apparent that this particular ratio is an indicator of profitability (and, to a lesser extent, efficiency in use of assets in generating operating profits). When facing a ratio for the first time, the analyst should evaluate the numerator and denominator to assess what the ratio is attempting to measure and how it should be interpreted. This is demonstrated in Example 3.

EXAMPLE 3

Interpreting a Financial Ratio

A U.S. insurance company reports that its "combined ratio" is determined by dividing losses and expenses incurred by net premiums earned. It reports the following combined ratios:

Fiscal Year	5	4	3	2	1
Combined ratio	90.1%	104.0%	98.5%	104.1%	101.1%

Explain what this ratio is measuring and compare the results reported for each of the years shown in the chart. What other information might an analyst want to review before making any conclusions on this information?

Solution:

The combined ratio is a profitability measure. The ratio is explaining how much costs (losses and expenses) were incurred for every dollar of revenue (net premiums earned). The underlying formula indicates that a lower ratio is better. The Year 5 ratio of 90.1 percent means that for every dollar of net premiums earned, the costs were $0.901, yielding a gross profit of $0.099. Ratios greater than 100 percent indicate an overall loss. A review of the data indicates that there does not seem to be a consistent trend in this ratio. Profits were achieved in Years 5 and 3. The results for Years 4 and 2 show the most significant costs at approximately 104 percent.

The analyst would want to discuss this data further with management and understand the characteristics of the underlying business. He or she would want to understand why the results are so volatile. The analyst would also want to determine what should be used as a benchmark for this ratio.

The Operating income/Average total assets ratio shown above is one of many versions of the **return on assets (ROA)** ratio. Note that there are other ways of specifying this formula based on how assets are defined. Some financial ratio databases compute ROA using the ending value of assets rather than average assets. In limited cases, one may also see beginning assets in the denominator. Which one is right? It depends on what you are trying to measure and the underlying company trends. If the company has a stable level of assets, the answer will not differ greatly under the three measures of assets (beginning, average, and ending). However, if the assets are growing (or shrinking), the results will differ among the three measures. When assets are growing, operating income divided by ending assets may not make sense because some of the income would have been generated before some assets were purchased, and this would understate the company's performance. Similarly, if beginning assets are used, some of the operating income later in the year may have been generated only because of the addition of assets; therefore, the ratio would overstate the company's performance. Because operating income occurs throughout the period, it generally makes sense to use some average measure of assets. A good general rule is that when an income statement or cash flow statement number is in the numerator of a ratio and a balance sheet number is in the denominator, then an average should be used for the denominator. It is generally not necessary to use averages when only balance sheet numbers are used in both the numerator and denominator because both are determined as of the same date. However, in some instances, even ratios that only use balance sheet data may use averages. For example, **return on equity (ROE)**, which is defined as net income divided by average shareholders' equity, can be decomposed into other ratios, some of which only use balance sheet data. In decomposing ROE into component ratios, if an average is used in one of the component ratios then it should be used in the other component ratios. The decomposition of ROE is discussed further in Section 4.6.2.

If an average is used, judgment is also required about what average should be used. For simplicity, most ratio databases use a simple average of the beginning and end-of-year balance sheet amounts. If the company's business is seasonal so that levels of assets vary by interim period (semiannual or quarterly), then it may be beneficial to take an average over all interim periods, if available. (If the analyst is working within a company and has access to monthly data, this can also be used.)

3.1.2 Value, Purposes, and Limitations of Ratio Analysis

The value of ratio analysis is that it enables a financial analyst to evaluate past performance, assess the current financial position of the company, and gain insights useful for projecting future results. As noted previously, the ratio itself is not "the answer" but is an indicator of some aspect of a company's performance. Financial ratios provide insights into:

- microeconomic relationships within a company that help analysts project earnings and free cash flow;

- a company's financial flexibility, or ability to obtain the cash required to grow and meet its obligations, even if unexpected circumstances develop;

- management's ability;

- changes in the company and/or industry over time; and

- comparability with peer companies or the relevant industry(ies).

There are also limitations to ratio analysis. Factors to consider include:

- *The heterogeneity or homogeneity of a company's operating activities.* Companies may have divisions operating in many different industries. This can make it difficult to find comparable industry ratios to use for comparison purposes.

- *The need to determine whether the results of the ratio analysis are consistent.* One set of ratios may indicate a problem, whereas another set may indicate that the potential problem is only short term in nature.

- *The need to use judgment.* A key issue is whether a ratio for a company is within a reasonable range. Although financial ratios are used to help assess the growth potential and risk of a company, they cannot be used alone to directly value a company or its securities, or to determine its creditworthiness. The entire operation of the company must be examined, and the external economic and industry setting in which it is operating must be considered when interpreting financial ratios.

- *The use of alternative accounting methods.* Companies frequently have latitude when choosing certain accounting methods. Ratios taken from financial statements that employ different accounting choices may not be comparable unless adjustments are made. Some important accounting considerations include the following:

  - FIFO (first in, first out), LIFO (last in, first out), or average cost inventory valuation methods (IFRS does not allow LIFO);
  - Cost or equity methods of accounting for unconsolidated affiliates;
  - Straight line or accelerated methods of depreciation; and
  - Capital or operating lease treatment.

The expanding use of IFRS and the ongoing convergence between IFRS and U.S. GAAP seeks to make the financial statements of different companies comparable and may overcome some of these difficulties. Nonetheless, there will remain accounting choices that the analyst must consider.

3.1.3 Sources of Ratios

Ratios may be computed using data obtained directly from companies' financial statements or from a database such as Bloomberg, Compustat, FactSet, or Thomson Reuters. The information provided by the database may include information as reported in companies' financial statements and ratios calculated based on the information. These databases are popular because they provide easy access to many years of historical data so that trends over time can be examined. They also allow for ratio calculations based on periods other than the company's fiscal year, such as for the trailing 12 months (TTM) or most recent quarter (MRQ).

EXAMPLE 4

Trailing Twelve Months

On 15 July, an analyst is examining a company with a fiscal year ending on 31 December. Use the following data to calculate the company's trailing 12 month earnings (for the period ended 30 June 2010):

- Earnings for the year ended 31 December, 2009: $1,200;
- Earnings for the six months ended 30 June 2009: $550; and
- Earnings for the six months ended 30 June 2010: $750.

Solution:

The company's trailing 12 months earnings is $1,400, calculated as $1,200 − $550 + $750.

Analysts should be aware that the underlying formulas for ratios may differ by vendor. The formula used should be obtained from the vendor, and the analyst should determine whether any adjustments are necessary. Furthermore, database providers often exercise judgment when classifying items. For example, operating income may not appear directly on a company's income statement, and the vendor may use judgment to classify income statement items as "operating" or "non-operating." Variation in such judgments would affect any computation involving operating income. It is therefore a good practice to use the same source for data when comparing different companies or when evaluating the historical record of a single company. Analysts should verify the consistency of formulas and data classifications by the data source.

Analysts should also be mindful of the judgments made by a vendor in data classifications and refer back to the source financial statements until they are comfortable that the classifications are appropriate.

Systems are under development that collect financial data from regulatory filings and can automatically compute ratios. The eXtensible Business Reporting Language (XBRL) is a mechanism that attaches "smart tags" to financial information (e.g., total assets), so that software can automatically collect the data and perform desired computations. The organization developing XBRL (www.xbrl.org) is an international nonprofit consortium of over 600 members from companies, associations, and agencies, including the International Accounting Standards Board. Many stock exchanges and regulatory agencies around the world now use XBRL for receiving and distributing public financial reports from listed companies.

Analysts can compare a subject company to similar (peer) companies in these databases or use aggregate industry data. For non-public companies, aggregate industry data can be obtained from such sources as Annual Statement Studies by the Risk Management Association or Dun & Bradstreet. These publications typically provide industry data with companies sorted into quartiles. By definition, twenty-five percent of companies' ratios fall within the lowest quartile, 25 percent have ratios between the lower quartile and median value, and so on. Analysts can then determine a company's relative standing in the industry.

3.2 Common-Size Analysis

Common-size analysis involves expressing financial data, including entire financial statements, in relation to a single financial statement item, or base. Items used most frequently as the bases are total assets or revenue. In essence, common-size analysis creates a ratio between every financial statement item and the base item.

Common-size analysis was demonstrated in readings for the income statement, balance sheet, and cash flow statement. In this section, we present common-size analysis of financial statements in greater detail and include further discussion of their interpretation.

3.2.1 *Common-Size Analysis of the Balance Sheet*

A vertical[5] common-size balance sheet, prepared by dividing each item on the balance sheet by the same period's total assets and expressing the results as percentages, highlights the composition of the balance sheet. What is the mix of assets being used? How is the company financing itself? How does one company's balance sheet composition compare with that of peer companies, and what are the reasons for any differences?

A horizontal common-size balance sheet, prepared by computing the increase or decrease in percentage terms of each balance sheet item from the prior year or prepared by dividing the quantity of each item by a base year quantity of the item, highlights changes in items. These changes can be compared to expectations. The section on trend analysis below will illustrate a horizontal common-size balance sheet.

Exhibit 3 presents a vertical common-size (partial) balance sheet for a hypothetical company in two time periods. In this example, receivables have increased from 35 percent to 57 percent of total assets and the ratio has increased by 63 percent from Period 1 to Period 2. What are possible reasons for such an increase? The increase might indicate that the company is making more of its sales on a credit basis rather than a cash basis, perhaps in response to some action taken by a competitor. Alternatively,

---

5 The term **vertical analysis** is used to denote a common-size analysis using only one reporting period or one base financial statement, whereas **horizontal analysis** refers to an analysis comparing a specific financial statement with prior or future time periods or to a cross-sectional analysis of one company with another.

the increase in receivables as a percentage of assets may have occurred because of a change in another current asset category, for example, a decrease in the level of inventory; the analyst would then need to investigate why that asset category has changed. Another possible reason for the increase in receivables as a percentage of assets is that the company has lowered its credit standards, relaxed its collection procedures, or adopted more aggressive revenue recognition policies. The analyst can turn to other comparisons and ratios (e.g., comparing the rate of growth in accounts receivable with the rate of growth in sales) to help determine which explanation is most likely.

Exhibit 3	Vertical Common-Size (Partial) Balance Sheet for a Hypothetical Company	
	Period 1 **Percent of Total Assets**	**Period 2** **Percent of Total Assets**
Cash	25	15
Receivables	35	57
Inventory	35	20
Fixed assets, net of depreciation	5	8
Total assets	100	100

3.2.2 Common-Size Analysis of the Income Statement

A vertical common-size income statement divides each income statement item by revenue, or sometimes by total assets (especially in the case of financial institutions). If there are multiple revenue sources, a decomposition of revenue in percentage terms is useful. Exhibit 4 presents a hypothetical company's vertical common-size income statement in two time periods. Revenue is separated into the company's four services, each shown as a percentage of total revenue.

In this example, revenues from Service A have become a far greater percentage of the company's total revenue (30 percent in Period 1 and 45 percent in Period 2). What are possible reasons for and implications of this change in business mix? Did the company make a strategic decision to sell more of Service A, perhaps because it is more profitable? Apparently not, because the company's earnings before interest, taxes, depreciation, and amortisation (EBITDA) declined from 53 percent of sales to 45 percent, so other possible explanations should be examined. In addition, we note from the composition of operating expenses that the main reason for this decline in profitability is that salaries and employee benefits have increased from 15 percent to 25 percent of total revenue. Are more highly compensated employees required for Service A? Were higher training costs incurred in order to increase revenues from Service A? If the analyst wants to predict future performance, the causes of these changes must be understood.

In addition, Exhibit 4 shows that the company's income tax as a percentage of sales has declined dramatically (from 15 percent to 8 percent). Furthermore, taxes as a percentage of earnings before tax (EBT) (the effective tax rate, which is usually the more relevant comparison), have decreased from 36 percent (= 15/42) to 24 percent (= 8/34). Is Service A, which in Period 2 is a greater percentage of total revenue, provided in a jurisdiction with lower tax rates? If not, what is the explanation for the change in effective tax rate?

The observations based on Exhibit 4 summarize the issues that can be raised through analysis of the vertical common-size income statement.

| Exhibit 4 | Vertical Common-Size Income Statement for Hypothetical Company |

	Period 1 Percent of Total Revenue	Period 2 Percent of Total Revenue
Revenue source: Service A	30	45
Revenue source: Service B	23	20
Revenue source: Service C	30	30
Revenue source: Service D	17	5
Total revenue	**100**	**100**
Operating expenses (excluding depreciation)		
Salaries and employee benefits	15	25
Administrative expenses	22	20
Rent expense	10	10
EBITDA	**53**	**45**
Depreciation and amortisation	4	4
EBIT	**49**	**41**
Interest paid	7	7
EBT	**42**	**34**
Income tax provision	15	8
Net income	**27**	**26**

EBIT = earnings before interest and tax.

3.2.3 Cross-Sectional Analysis

As noted previously, ratios and common-size statements derive part of their meaning through comparison to some benchmark. **Cross-sectional analysis** (sometimes called "relative analysis") compares a specific metric for one company with the same metric for another company or group of companies, allowing comparisons even though the companies might be of significantly different sizes and/or operate in different currencies. This is illustrated in Exhibit 5.

| Exhibit 5 | Vertical Common-Size (Partial) Balance Sheet for Two Hypothetical Companies |

Assets	Company 1 Percent of Total Assets	Company 2 Percent of Total Assets
Cash	38	12
Receivables	33	55
Inventory	27	24
Fixed assets net of depreciation	1	2
Investments	1	7
Total Assets	**100**	**100**

Exhibit 5 presents a vertical common-size (partial) balance sheet for two hypothetical companies at the same point in time. Company 1 is clearly more liquid (liquidity is a function of how quickly assets can be converted into cash) than Company 2, which has only 12 percent of assets available as cash, compared with the highly liquid Company 1, which has 38 percent of assets available as cash. Given that cash is generally a relatively low-yielding asset and thus not a particularly efficient use of excess funds, why does Company 1 hold such a large percentage of total assets in cash? Perhaps the company is preparing for an acquisition, or maintains a large cash position as insulation from a particularly volatile operating environment. Another issue highlighted by the comparison in this example is the relatively high percentage of receivables in Company 2's assets, which may indicate a greater proportion of credit sales, overall changes in asset composition, lower credit or collection standards, or aggressive accounting policies.

3.2.4 *Trend Analysis*[6]

When looking at financial statements and ratios, trends in the data, whether they are improving or deteriorating, are as important as the current absolute or relative levels. Trend analysis provides important information regarding historical performance and growth and, given a sufficiently long history of accurate seasonal information, can be of great assistance as a planning and forecasting tool for management and analysts.

Exhibit 6A presents a partial balance sheet for a hypothetical company over five periods. The last two columns of the table show the changes for Period 5 compared with Period 4, expressed both in absolute currency (in this case, dollars) and in percentages. A small percentage change could hide a significant currency change and vice versa, prompting the analyst to investigate the reasons despite one of the changes being relatively small. In this example, the largest percentage change was in investments, which decreased by 33.3 percent.[7] However, an examination of the absolute currency amount of changes shows that investments changed by only $2 million, and the more significant change was the $12 million increase in receivables.

Another way to present data covering a period of time is to show each item in relation to the same item in a base year (i.e., a horizontal common-size balance sheet). Exhibits 6B and 6C illustrate alternative presentations of horizontal common-size balance sheets. Exhibit 6B presents the information from the same partial balance sheet as in Exhibit 6A, but indexes each item relative to the same item in Period 1. For example, in Period 2, the company had $29 million cash, which is 74 percent or 0.74 of the amount of cash it had in Period 1. Expressed as an index relative to Period 1, where each item in Period 1 is given a value of 1.00, the value in Period 2 would be 0.74 ($29/$39 = 0.74). In Period 3, the company had $27 million cash, which is 69 percent of the amount of cash it had in Period 1 ($27/$39 = 0.69).

Exhibit 6C presents the percentage change in each item, relative to the previous year. For example, the change in cash from Period 1 to Period 2 was −25.6 percent ($29/$39 − 1 = −0.256), and the change in cash from Period 2 to Period 3 was −6.9 percent ($27/$29 − 1 = −0.069). An analyst will select the horizontal common-size balance that addresses the particular period of interest. Exhibit 6B clearly highlights that in Period 5 compared to Period 1, the company has less than half the amount of cash, four times the amount of investments, and eight times the amount of property, plant, and equipment. Exhibit 6C highlights year-to-year changes: For example, cash

---

6 In financial statement analysis, the term "trend analysis" usually refers to comparisons across time periods of 3–10 years not involving statistical tools. This differs from the use of the term in the quantitative methods portion of the CFA curriculum, where "trend analysis" refers to statistical methods of measuring patterns in time-series data.
7 Percentage change is calculated as (Ending value − Beginning value)/Beginning value, or equivalently, (Ending value/Beginning value) − 1.

has declined in each period. Presenting data this way highlights significant changes. Again, note that a mathematically big change is not necessarily an important change. For example, fixed assets increased 100 percent, i.e., doubled between Period 1 and 2; however, as a proportion of total assets, fixed assets increased from 1 percent of total assets to 2 percent of total assets. The company's working capital assets (receivables and inventory) are a far higher proportion of total assets and would likely warrant more attention from an analyst.

An analysis of horizontal common-size balance sheets highlights structural changes that have occurred in a business. Past trends are obviously not necessarily an accurate predictor of the future, especially when the economic or competitive environment changes. An examination of past trends is more valuable when the macroeconomic and competitive environments are relatively stable and when the analyst is reviewing a stable or mature business. However, even in less stable contexts, historical analysis can serve as a basis for developing expectations. Understanding of past trends is helpful in assessing whether these trends are likely to continue or if the trend is likely to change direction.

Exhibit 6A	**Partial Balance Sheet for a Hypothetical Company over Five Periods**						
	Period					**Change 4 to 5**	**Change 4 to 5**
Assets ($ Millions)	**1**	**2**	**3**	**4**	**5**	**($ Million)**	**(Percent)**
Cash	39	29	27	19	16	−3	−15.8
Investments	1	7	7	6	4	−2	−33.3
Receivables	44	41	37	67	79	12	17.9
Inventory	15	25	36	25	27	2	8.0
Fixed assets net of depreciation	1	2	6	9	8	−1	−11.1
Total assets	100	104	113	126	134	8	6.3

Exhibit 6B	**Horizontal Common-Size (Partial) Balance Sheet for a Hypothetical Company over Five Periods, with Each Item Expressed Relative to the Same Item in Period One**				
	Period				
Assets	**1**	**2**	**3**	**4**	**5**
Cash	1.00	0.74	0.69	0.49	0.41
Investments	1.00	7.00	7.00	6.00	4.00
Receivables	1.00	0.93	0.84	1.52	1.80
Inventory	1.00	1.67	2.40	1.67	1.80
Fixed assets net of depreciation	1.00	2.00	6.00	9.00	8.00
Total assets	1.00	1.04	1.13	1.26	1.34

Exhibit 6C	Horizontal Common-Size (Partial) Balance Sheet for a Hypothetical Company over Five Periods, with Percent Change in Each Item Relative to the Prior Period

	Period			
Assets	**2 (%)**	**3 (%)**	**4 (%)**	**5 (%)**
Cash	−25.6	−6.9	−29.6	−15.8
Investments	600.0	0.0	−14.3	−33.3
Receivables	−6.8	−9.8	81.1	17.9
Inventory	66.7	44.0	−30.6	8.0
Fixed assets net of depreciation	100.0	200.0	50.0	−11.1
Total assets	4.0	8.7	11.5	6.3

One measure of success is for a company to grow at a rate greater than the rate of the overall market in which it operates. Companies that grow slowly may find themselves unable to attract equity capital. Conversely, companies that grow too quickly may find that their administrative and management information systems cannot keep up with the rate of expansion.

3.2.5 Relationships among Financial Statements

Trend data generated by a horizontal common-size analysis can be compared across financial statements. For example, the growth rate of assets for the hypothetical company in Exhibit 6 can be compared with the company's growth in revenue over the same period of time. If revenue is growing more quickly than assets, the company may be increasing its efficiency (i.e., generating more revenue for every dollar invested in assets).

As another example, consider the following year-over-year percentage changes for a hypothetical company:

Revenue	+20%
Net income	+25%
Operating cash flow	−10%
Total assets	+30%

Net income is growing faster than revenue, which indicates increasing profitability. However, the analyst would need to determine whether the faster growth in net income resulted from continuing operations or from non-operating, non-recurring items. In addition, the 10 percent decline in operating cash flow despite increasing revenue and net income clearly warrants further investigation because it could indicate a problem with earnings quality (perhaps aggressive reporting of revenue). Lastly, the fact that assets have grown faster than revenue indicates the company's efficiency may be declining. The analyst should examine the composition of the increase in assets and the reasons for the changes. Example 5 illustrates a company where comparisons of trend data from different financial statements were actually indicative of aggressive accounting policies.

EXAMPLE 5

Use of Comparative Growth Information[8]

In July 1996, Sunbeam, a U.S. company, brought in new management to turn the company around. In the following year, 1997, using 1996 as the base, the following was observed based on reported numbers:

Revenue	+19%
Inventory	+58%
Receivables	+38%

It is generally more desirable to observe inventory and receivables growing at a slower (or similar) rate compared to revenue growth. Receivables growing faster than revenue can indicate operational issues, such as lower credit standards or aggressive accounting policies for revenue recognition. Similarly, inventory growing faster than revenue can indicate an operational problem with obsolescence or aggressive accounting policies, such as an improper overstatement of inventory to increase profits.

In this case, the explanation lay in aggressive accounting policies. Sunbeam was later charged by the U.S. Securities and Exchange Commission with improperly accelerating the recognition of revenue and engaging in other practices, such as billing customers for inventory prior to shipment.

3.3 The Use of Graphs as an Analytical Tool

Graphs facilitate comparison of performance and financial structure over time, highlighting changes in significant aspects of business operations. In addition, graphs provide the analyst (and management) with a visual overview of risk trends in a business. Graphs may also be used effectively to communicate the analyst's conclusions regarding financial condition and risk management aspects.

Exhibit 7 presents the information from Exhibit 6A in a stacked column format. The graph makes the significant decline in cash and growth in receivables (both in absolute terms and as a percentage of assets) readily apparent. In Exhibit 7, the vertical axis shows US$ millions and the horizontal axis denotes the period.

Choosing the appropriate graph to communicate the most significant conclusions of a financial analysis is a skill. In general, pie graphs are most useful to communicate the composition of a total value (e.g., assets over a limited amount of time, say one or two periods). Line graphs are useful when the focus is on the change in amount for a limited number of items over a relatively longer time period. When the composition and amounts, as well as their change over time, are all important, a stacked column graph can be useful.

---

8 Adapted from Robinson and Munter (2004, pp. 2–15).

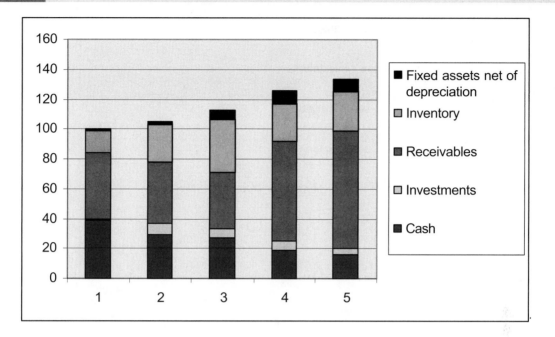

| Exhibit 7 | Stacked Column Graph of Asset Composition of Hypothetical Company over Five Periods |

When comparing Period 5 with Period 4, the growth in receivables appears to be within normal bounds; but when comparing Period 5 with earlier periods, the dramatic growth becomes apparent. In the same manner, a simple line graph will also illustrate the growth trends in key financial variables. Exhibit 8 presents the information from Exhibit 6A as a line graph, illustrating the growth of assets of a hypothetical company over five periods. The steady decline in cash, volatile movements of inventory, and dramatic growth of receivables is clearly illustrated. Again, the vertical axis is shown in US$ millions and the horizontal axis denotes periods.

| Exhibit 8 | Line Graph of Growth of Assets of Hypothetical Company over Five Periods |

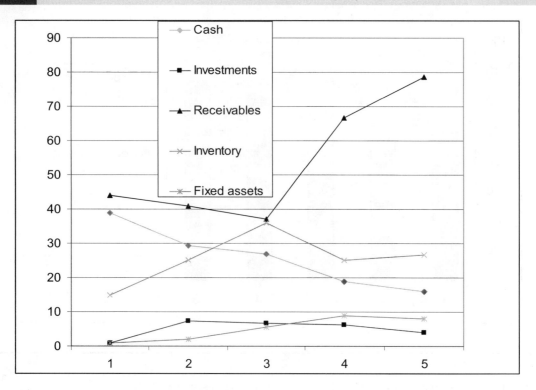

3.4 Regression Analysis

When analyzing the trend in a specific line item or ratio, frequently it is possible simply to visually evaluate the changes. For more complex situations, regression analysis can help identify relationships (or correlation) between variables. For example, a regression analysis could relate a company's sales to GDP over time, providing insight into whether the company is cyclical. In addition, the statistical relationship between sales and GDP could be used as a basis for forecasting sales.

Other examples include the relationship between a company's sales and inventory over time, or the relationship between hotel occupancy and a company's hotel revenues. In addition to providing a basis for forecasting, regression analysis facilitates identification of items or ratios that are not behaving as expected, given historical statistical relationships.

4   COMMON RATIOS USED IN FINANCIAL ANALYSIS

In the previous section, we focused on ratios resulting from common-size analysis. In this section, we expand the discussion to include other commonly used financial ratios and the broad classes into which they are categorized. There is some overlap with common-size financial statement ratios. For example, a common indicator of profitability is the net profit margin, which is calculated as net income divided by sales. This ratio appears on a vertical common-size income statement. Other ratios involve information from multiple financial statements or even data from outside the financial statements.

Because of the large number of ratios, it is helpful to think about ratios in terms of broad categories based on what aspects of performance a ratio is intended to detect. Financial analysts and data vendors use a variety of categories to classify ratios. The category names and the ratios included in each category can differ. Common ratio categories include activity, liquidity, solvency, profitability, and valuation. These categories are summarized in Exhibit 9. Each category measures a different aspect of the company's business, but all are useful in evaluating a company's overall ability to generate cash flows from operating its business and the associated risks.

Exhibit 9	Categories of Financial Ratios
Category	**Description**
Activity	**Activity ratios** measure how efficiently a company performs day-to-day tasks, such as the collection of receivables and management of inventory.
Liquidity	**Liquidity ratios** measure the company's ability to meet its short-term obligations.
Solvency	**Solvency ratios** measure a company's ability to meet long-term obligations. Subsets of these ratios are also known as "leverage" and "long-term debt" ratios.
Profitability	**Profitability ratios** measure the company's ability to generate profits from its resources (assets).
Valuation	**Valuation ratios** measure the quantity of an asset or flow (e.g., earnings) associated with ownership of a specified claim (e.g., a share or ownership of the enterprise).

These categories are not mutually exclusive; some ratios are useful in measuring multiple aspects of the business. For example, an activity ratio measuring how quickly a company collects accounts receivable is also useful in assessing the company's liquidity because collection of revenues increases cash. Some profitability ratios also reflect the operating efficiency of the business. In summary, analysts appropriately use certain ratios to evaluate multiple aspects of the business. Analysts also need to be aware of variations in industry practice in the calculation of financial ratios. In the text that follows, alternative views on ratio calculations are often provided.

4.1 Interpretation and Context

Financial ratios can only be interpreted in the context of other information, including benchmarks. In general, the financial ratios of a company are compared with those of its major competitors (cross-sectional and trend analysis) and to the company's prior periods (trend analysis). The goal is to understand the underlying causes of divergence between a company's ratios and those of the industry. Even ratios that remain consistent require understanding because consistency can sometimes indicate accounting policies selected to smooth earnings. An analyst should evaluate financial ratios based on the following:

1 *Company goals and strategy*. Actual ratios can be compared with company objectives to determine whether objectives are being attained and whether the results are consistent with the company's strategy.

2 *Industry norms* (*cross-sectional analysis*). A company can be compared with others in its industry by relating its financial ratios to industry norms or to a subset of the companies in an industry. When industry norms are used to make judgments, care must be taken because:

- Many ratios are industry specific, and not all ratios are important to all industries.
- Companies may have several different lines of business. This will cause aggregate financial ratios to be distorted. It is better to examine industry-specific ratios by lines of business.
- Differences in accounting methods used by companies can distort financial ratios.
- Differences in corporate strategies can affect certain financial ratios.

3 *Economic conditions*. For cyclical companies, financial ratios tend to improve when the economy is strong and weaken during recessions. Therefore, financial ratios should be examined in light of the current phase of the business cycle.

The following sections discuss activity, liquidity, solvency, and profitability ratios in turn. Selected valuation ratios are presented later in the section on equity analysis.

4.2 Activity Ratios

Activity ratios are also known as **asset utilization ratios** or **operating efficiency ratios**. This category is intended to measure how well a company manages various activities, particularly how efficiently it manages its various assets. Activity ratios are analyzed as indicators of ongoing operational performance—how effectively assets are used by a company. These ratios reflect the efficient management of both working capital and longer term assets. As noted, efficiency has a direct impact on liquidity (the ability of a company to meet its short-term obligations), so some activity ratios are also useful in assessing liquidity.

4.2.1 *Calculation of Activity Ratios*

Exhibit 10 presents the most commonly used activity ratios. The exhibit shows the numerator and denominator of each ratio.

Exhibit 10	Definitions of Commonly Used Activity Ratios	
Activity Ratios	**Numerator**	**Denominator**
Inventory turnover	Cost of sales or cost of goods sold	Average inventory
Days of inventory on hand (DOH)	Number of days in period	Inventory turnover
Receivables turnover	Revenue	Average receivables
Days of sales outstanding (DSO)	Number of days in period	Receivables turnover

Exhibit 10	(Continued)	

Activity Ratios	Numerator	Denominator
Payables turnover	Purchases	Average trade payables
Number of days of payables	Number of days in period	Payables turnover
Working capital turnover	Revenue	Average working capital
Fixed asset turnover	Revenue	Average net fixed assets
Total asset turnover	Revenue	Average total assets

Activity ratios measure how efficiently the company utilizes assets. They generally combine information from the income statement in the numerator with balance sheet items in the denominator. Because the income statement measures what happened *during* a period whereas the balance sheet shows the condition only at the end of the period, average balance sheet data are normally used for consistency. For example, to measure inventory management efficiency, cost of sales or cost of goods sold (from the income statement) is divided by average inventory (from the balance sheet). Most databases, such as Bloomberg and Baseline, use this averaging convention when income statement and balance sheet data are combined. These databases typically average only two points: the beginning of the year and the end of the year. The examples that follow based on annual financial statements illustrate that practice. However, some analysts prefer to average more observations if they are available, especially if the business is seasonal. If a semiannual report is prepared, an average can be taken over three data points (beginning, middle, and end of year). If quarterly data are available, a five-point average can be computed (beginning of year and end of each quarterly period) or a four-point average using the end of each quarterly period. Note that if the company's year ends at a low or high point for inventory for the year, there can still be bias in using three or five data points, because the beginning and end of year occur at the same time of the year and are effectively double counted.

Because cost of goods sold measures the cost of inventory that has been sold, this ratio measures how many times per year the entire inventory was theoretically turned over, or sold. (We say that the entire inventory was "theoretically" sold because in practice companies do not generally sell out their entire inventory.) If, for example, a company's cost of goods sold for a recent year was €120,000 and its average inventory was €10,000, the inventory turnover ratio would be 12. The company theoretically turns over (i.e., sells) its entire inventory 12 times per year (i.e., once a month). (Again, we say "theoretically" because in practice the company likely carries some inventory from one month into another.) Turnover can then be converted to days of inventory on hand (DOH) by dividing inventory turnover into the number of days in the accounting period. In this example, the result is a DOH of 30.42 (365/12), meaning that, on average, the company's inventory was on hand for about 30 days, or, equivalently, the company kept on hand about 30 days' worth of inventory, on average, during the period.

Activity ratios can be computed for any annual or interim period, but care must be taken in the interpretation and comparison across periods. For example, if the same company had cost of goods sold for the first quarter (90 days) of the following year of €35,000 and average inventory of €11,000, the inventory turnover would be 3.18 times. However, this turnover rate is 3.18 times per quarter, which is not directly comparable to the 12 times per year in the preceding year. In this case, we can annualize the quarterly inventory turnover rate by multiplying the quarterly turnover by 4 (12 months/3 months; or by 4.06, using 365 days/90 days) for comparison to the annual turnover rate. So, the quarterly inventory turnover is equivalent to a 12.72 annual inventory turnover (or 12.91 if we annualize the ratio using a 90-day quarter and a 365-day year). To compute the DOH using quarterly data, we can use the quarterly turnover rate and the number of days in the quarter for the numerator—or, we can use the annualized turnover rate and 365 days; either results in DOH of around 28.3, with slight differences due to rounding (90/3.18 = 28.30 and 365/12.91 = 28.27). Another time-related computational detail is that for companies using a 52/53-week annual period and for leap years, the actual days in the year should be used rather than 365.

In some cases, an analyst may want to know how many days of inventory are on hand at the end of the year rather than the average for the year. In this case, it would be appropriate to use the year-end inventory balance in the computation rather than the average. If the company is growing rapidly or if costs are increasing rapidly, analysts should consider using cost of goods sold just for the fourth quarter in this computation because the cost of goods sold of earlier quarters may not be relevant. Example 6 further demonstrates computation of activity ratios using Hong Kong Exchange-listed Lenovo Group Limited.

EXAMPLE 6

Computation of Activity Ratios

An analyst would like to evaluate Lenovo Group's efficiency in collecting its trade accounts receivable during the fiscal year ended 31 March 2010 (FY2009). The analyst gathers the following information from Lenovo's annual and interim reports:

	US$ in Thousands
Trade receivables as of 31 March 2009	482,086
Trade receivables as of 31 March 2010	1,021,062
Revenue for year ended 31 March 2010	16,604,815

Calculate Lenovo's receivables turnover and number of days of sales outstanding (DSO) for the fiscal year ended 31 March 2010.

Solution:

$$
\begin{aligned}
\text{Receivables turnover} \ &= \ \text{Revenue/Average receivables} \\
&= \ 16,604,815/\ [(1,021,062 + 482,086)/2] \\
&= \ 16,604,815/751,574 \\
&= \ 22.0934 \text{ times, or } 22.1 \text{ rounded} \\
\text{DSO} \ &= \ \text{Number of days in period/Receivables} \\
& \quad\ \ \text{turnover} \\
&= \ 365/22.1 \\
&= \ 16.5 \text{ days}
\end{aligned}
$$

On average, it took Lenovo 16.5 days to collect receivables during the fiscal year ended 31 March 2010.

4.2.2 *Interpretation of Activity Ratios*

In the following section, we further discuss the activity ratios that were defined in Exhibit 10.

Inventory Turnover and DOH   Inventory turnover lies at the heart of operations for many entities. It indicates the resources tied up in inventory (i.e., the carrying costs) and can, therefore, be used to indicate inventory management effectiveness. A higher inventory turnover ratio implies a shorter period that inventory is held, and thus a lower DOH. In general, inventory turnover and DOH should be benchmarked against industry norms.

A high inventory turnover ratio relative to industry norms might indicate highly effective inventory management. Alternatively, a high inventory turnover ratio (and commensurately low DOH) could possibly indicate the company does not carry adequate inventory, so shortages could potentially hurt revenue. To assess which explanation is more likely, the analyst can compare the company's revenue growth with that of the industry. Slower growth combined with higher inventory turnover could indicate inadequate inventory levels. Revenue growth at or above the industry's growth supports the interpretation that the higher turnover reflects greater inventory management efficiency.

A low inventory turnover ratio (and commensurately high DOH) relative to the rest of the industry could be an indicator of slow-moving inventory, perhaps due to technological obsolescence or a change in fashion. Again, comparing the company's sales growth with the industry can offer insight.

Receivables Turnover and DSO.   The number of DSO represents the elapsed time between a sale and cash collection, reflecting how fast the company collects cash from customers to whom it offers credit. Although limiting the numerator to sales made on credit in the receivables turnover would be more appropriate, credit sales information is not always available to analysts; therefore, revenue as reported in the income statement is generally used as an approximation.

A relatively high receivables turnover ratio (and commensurately low DSO) might indicate highly efficient credit and collection. Alternatively, a high receivables turnover ratio could indicate that the company's credit or collection policies are too stringent, suggesting the possibility of sales being lost to competitors offering more lenient terms. A relatively low receivables turnover ratio would typically raise questions about the efficiency of the company's credit and collections procedures. As with inventory management, comparison of the company's sales growth relative to the industry can help the analyst assess whether sales are being lost due to stringent credit policies. In addition, comparing the company's estimates of uncollectible accounts receivable and actual credit losses with past experience and with peer companies can help assess whether low turnover reflects credit management issues. Companies often provide details of receivables aging (how much receivables have been outstanding by age). This can be used along with DSO to understand trends in collection, as demonstrated in Example 7.

EXAMPLE 7

Evaluation of an Activity Ratio

An analyst has computed the average DSO for Lenovo for fiscal years ended 31 March 2010 and 2009:

	2010	2009
Days of sales outstanding	16.5	15.2

Revenue increased from US$14.901 billion for fiscal year ended 31 March 2009 (FY2008) to US$16.605 billion for fiscal year ended 31 March 2010 (FY2009). The analyst would like to better understand the change in the company's DSO from FY2008 to FY2009 and whether the increase is indicative of any issues with the customers' credit quality. The analyst collects accounts receivable aging information from Lenovo's annual reports and computes the percentage of accounts receivable by days outstanding. This information is presented in Exhibit 11:

Exhibit 11

	FY2009		FY2008		FY2007	
	US$000	Percent	US$000	Percent	US$000	Percent
Accounts receivable						
0–30 days	907,412	87.39	391,098	76.41	691,428	89.32
31–60 days	65,335	6.29	9,014	1.76	0	0.00
61–90 days	32,730	3.15	21,515	4.20	32,528	4.20
Over 90 days	32,904	3.17	90,214	17.63	50,168	6.48
Total	1,038,381	100.00	511,841	100.00	774,124	100.00
Less: Provision for impairment	−17,319	−1.67	−29,755	−5.81	−13,885	−1.79
Trade receivables, net	1,021,062	98.33	482,086	94.19	760,239	98.21
Total sales	*16,604,815*		*14,900,931*		*16,351,503*	

Note: Lenovo's footnotes disclose that general trade customers are provided with 30-day credit terms.

These data indicate that total accounts receivable more than doubled in FY2009 versus FY2008, while total sales increased by only 11.4 percent. This suggests that, overall, the company has been increasing customer financing to drive its sales growth. The significant increase in accounts receivable in total was the primary reason for the increase in DSO. The percentage of receivables older than 61 days has declined significantly which is generally positive. However, the large increase in 0–30 day receivables may be indicative of aggressive accounting policies or sales practices. Perhaps Lenovo offered incentives to generate a large amount of year-end sales. While the data may suggest that the quality of receivables improved in FY2009 versus FY2008, with a much lower percentage of receivables (and a much lower absolute amount) that are more than 90 days outstanding and, similarly, a lower percentage of estimated uncollectible receivables, this should be investigated further by the analyst.

Payables Turnover and the Number of Days of Payables　The number of days of payables reflects the average number of days the company takes to pay its suppliers, and the payables turnover ratio measures how many times per year the company theoretically pays off all its creditors. For purposes of calculating these ratios, an implicit assumption is that the company makes all its purchases using credit. If the amount of purchases is not directly available, it can be computed as cost of goods sold plus ending inventory less beginning inventory. Alternatively, cost of goods sold is sometimes used as an approximation of purchases.

A payables turnover ratio that is high (low days payable) relative to the industry could indicate that the company is not making full use of available credit facilities; alternatively, it could result from a company taking advantage of early payment discounts. An excessively low turnover ratio (high days payable) could indicate trouble making payments on time, or alternatively, exploitation of lenient supplier terms. This is another example where it is useful to look simultaneously at other ratios. If liquidity ratios indicate that the company has sufficient cash and other short-term assets to pay obligations and yet the days payable ratio is relatively high, the analyst would favor the lenient supplier credit and collection policies as an explanation.

Working Capital Turnover **Working capital** is defined as current assets minus current liabilities. Working capital turnover indicates how efficiently the company generates revenue with its working capital. For example, a working capital turnover ratio of 4.0 indicates that the company generates €4 of revenue for every €1 of working capital. A high working capital turnover ratio indicates greater efficiency (i.e., the company is generating a high level of revenues relative to working capital). For some companies, working capital can be near zero or negative, rendering this ratio incapable of being interpreted. The following two ratios are more useful in those circumstances.

Fixed Asset Turnover This ratio measures how efficiently the company generates revenues from its investments in fixed assets. Generally, a higher fixed asset turnover ratio indicates more efficient use of fixed assets in generating revenue. A low ratio can indicate inefficiency, a capital-intensive business environment, or a new business not yet operating at full capacity—in which case the analyst will not be able to link the ratio directly to efficiency. In addition, asset turnover can be affected by factors other than a company's efficiency. The fixed asset turnover ratio would be lower for a company whose assets are newer (and, therefore, less depreciated and so reflected in the financial statements at a higher carrying value) than the ratio for a company with older assets (that are thus more depreciated and so reflected at a lower carrying value). The fixed asset ratio can be erratic because, although revenue may have a steady growth rate, increases in fixed assets may not follow a smooth pattern; so, every year-to-year change in the ratio does not necessarily indicate important changes in the company's efficiency.

Total Asset Turnover The total asset turnover ratio measures the company's overall ability to generate revenues with a given level of assets. A ratio of 1.20 would indicate that the company is generating €1.20 of revenues for every €1 of average assets. A higher ratio indicates greater efficiency. Because this ratio includes both fixed and current assets, inefficient working capital management can distort overall interpretations. It is therefore helpful to analyze working capital and fixed asset turnover ratios separately.

A low asset turnover ratio can be an indicator of inefficiency or of relative capital intensity of the business. The ratio also reflects strategic decisions by management—for example, the decision whether to use a more labor-intensive (and less capital-intensive) approach to its business or a more capital-intensive (and less labor-intensive) approach.

When interpreting activity ratios, the analysts should examine not only the individual ratios but also the collection of relevant ratios to determine the overall efficiency of a company. Example 8 demonstrates the evaluation of activity ratios, both narrow (e.g., days of inventory on hand) and broad (e.g., total asset turnover) for a hypothetical manufacturer.

EXAMPLE 8

Evaluation of Activity Ratios

ZZZ Company is a hypothetical manufacturing company. As part of an analysis of management's operating efficiency, an analyst collects the following activity ratios from a data provider:

Ratio	2009	2008	2007	2006
DOH	35.68	40.70	40.47	48.51
DSO	45.07	58.28	51.27	76.98
Total asset turnover	0.36	0.28	0.23	0.22

These ratios indicate that the company has improved on all three measures of activity over the four-year period. The company appears to be managing its inventory more efficiently, is collecting receivables faster, and is generating a higher level of revenues relative to total assets. The overall trend appears good, but thus far, the analyst has only determined *what* happened. A more important question is *why* the ratios improved, because understanding good changes as well as bad ones facilitates judgments about the company's future performance. To answer this question, the analyst examines company financial reports as well as external information about the industry and economy. In examining the annual report, the analyst notes that in the fourth quarter of 2009, the company experienced an "inventory correction" and that the company recorded an allowance for the decline in market value and obsolescence of inventory of about 15 percent of year-end inventory value (compared with about a 6 percent allowance in the prior year). This reduction in the value of inventory accounts for a large portion of the decline in DOH from 40.70 in 2008 to 35.68 in 2009. Management claims that this inventory obsolescence is a short-term issue; analysts can watch DOH in future interim periods to confirm this assertion. In any event, all else being equal, the analyst would likely expect DOH to return to a level closer to 40 days going forward.

More positive interpretations can be drawn from the total asset turnover. The analyst finds that the company's revenues increased more than 35 percent while total assets only increased by about 6 percent. Based on external information about the industry and economy, the analyst attributes the increased revenues both to overall growth in the industry and to the company's increased market share. Management was able to achieve growth in revenues with a comparatively modest increase in assets, leading to an improvement in total asset turnover. Note further that part of the reason for the increase in asset turnover is lower DOH and DSO.

4.3 Liquidity Ratios

Liquidity analysis, which focuses on cash flows, measures a company's ability to meet its short-term obligations. Liquidity measures how quickly assets are converted into cash. Liquidity ratios also measure the ability to pay off short-term obligations. In day-to-day operations, liquidity management is typically achieved through efficient use of assets. In the medium term, liquidity in the non-financial sector is also addressed by managing the structure of liabilities. (See the discussion on financial sector below.)

The level of liquidity needed differs from one industry to another. A particular company's liquidity position may vary according to the anticipated need for funds at any given time. Judging whether a company has adequate liquidity requires analysis of its historical funding requirements, current liquidity position, anticipated future funding needs, and options for reducing funding needs or attracting additional funds (including actual and potential sources of such funding).

Larger companies are usually better able to control the level and composition of their liabilities than smaller companies. Therefore, they may have more potential funding sources, including public capital and money markets. Greater discretionary access to capital markets also reduces the size of the liquidity buffer needed relative to companies without such access.

Contingent liabilities, such as letters of credit or financial guarantees, can also be relevant when assessing liquidity. The importance of contingent liabilities varies for the non-banking and banking sector. In the non-banking sector, contingent liabilities (usually disclosed in the footnotes to the company's financial statements) represent potential cash outflows, and when appropriate, should be included in an assessment of a company's liquidity. In the banking sector, contingent liabilities represent potentially significant cash outflows that are not dependent on the bank's financial condition. Although outflows in normal market circumstances typically may be low, a general macroeconomic or market crisis can trigger a substantial increase in cash outflows related to contingent liabilities because of the increase in defaults and business bankruptcies that often accompany such events. In addition, such crises are usually characterized by diminished levels of overall liquidity, which can further exacerbate funding shortfalls. Therefore, for the banking sector, the effect of contingent liabilities on liquidity warrants particular attention.

4.3.1 Calculation of Liquidity Ratios

Common liquidity ratios are presented in Exhibit 12. These liquidity ratios reflect a company's position at a point in time and, therefore, typically use data from the ending balance sheet rather than averages. The current, quick, and cash ratios reflect three measures of a company's ability to pay current liabilities. Each uses a progressively stricter definition of liquid assets.

The **defensive interval ratio** measures how long a company can pay its daily cash expenditures using only its existing liquid assets, without additional cash flow coming in. This ratio is similar to the "burn rate" often computed for start-up internet companies in the late 1990s or for biotechnology companies. The numerator of this ratio includes the same liquid assets used in the quick ratio, and the denominator is an estimate of daily cash expenditures. To obtain daily cash expenditures, the total of cash expenditures for the period is divided by the number of days in the period. Total cash expenditures for a period can be approximated by summing all expenses on the income statement—such as cost of goods sold; selling, general, and administrative expenses; and research and development expenses—and then subtracting any non-cash expenses, such as depreciation and amortisation. (Typically, taxes are not included.)

The **cash conversion cycle**, a financial metric not in ratio form, measures the length of time required for a company to go from cash paid (used in its operations) to cash received (as a result of its operations). The cash conversion cycle is sometimes expressed as the length of time funds are tied up in working capital. During this period of time, the company needs to finance its investment in operations through other sources (i.e., through debt or equity).

Exhibit 12	Definitions of Commonly Used Liquidity Ratios	
Liquidity Ratios	**Numerator**	**Denominator**
Current ratio	Current assets	Current liabilities
Quick ratio	Cash + Short-term marketable investments + Receivables	Current liabilities

(continued)

Exhibit 12	(Continued)	
Liquidity Ratios	**Numerator**	**Denominator**
Cash ratio	Cash + Short-term marketable investments	Current liabilities
Defensive interval ratio	Cash + Short-term marketable investments + Receivables	Daily cash expenditures
Additional Liquidity Measure		
Cash conversion cycle (net operating cycle)	DOH + DSO − Number of days of payables	

4.3.2 Interpretation of Liquidity Ratios

In the following, we discuss the interpretation of the five basic liquidity measures presented in Exhibit 12.

Current Ratio   This ratio expresses current assets in relation to current liabilities. A higher ratio indicates a higher level of liquidity (i.e., a greater ability to meet short-term obligations). A current ratio of 1.0 would indicate that the book value of its current assets exactly equals the book value of its current liabilities.

A lower ratio indicates less liquidity, implying a greater reliance on operating cash flow and outside financing to meet short-term obligations. Liquidity affects the company's capacity to take on debt. The current ratio implicitly assumes that inventories and accounts receivable are indeed liquid (which is presumably not the case when related turnover ratios are low).

Quick Ratio   The quick ratio is more conservative than the current ratio because it includes only the more liquid current assets (sometimes referred to as "quick assets") in relation to current liabilities. Like the current ratio, a higher quick ratio indicates greater liquidity.

The quick ratio reflects the fact that certain current assets—such as prepaid expenses, some taxes, and employee-related prepayments—represent costs of the current period that have been paid in advance and cannot usually be converted back into cash. This ratio also reflects the fact that inventory might not be easily and quickly converted into cash, and furthermore, that a company would probably not be able to sell all of its inventory for an amount equal to its carrying value, especially if it were required to sell the inventory quickly. In situations where inventories are illiquid (as indicated, for example, by low inventory turnover ratios), the quick ratio may be a better indicator of liquidity than is the current ratio.

Cash Ratio   The cash ratio normally represents a reliable measure of an entity's liquidity in a crisis situation. Only highly marketable short-term investments and cash are included. In a general market crisis, the fair value of marketable securities could decrease significantly as a result of market factors, in which case even this ratio might not provide reliable information.

Defensive Interval Ratio   This ratio measures how long the company can continue to pay its expenses from its existing liquid assets without receiving any additional cash inflow. A defensive interval ratio of 50 would indicate that the company can continue to pay its operating expenses for 50 days before running out of quick assets, assuming no additional cash inflows. A higher defensive interval ratio indicates greater liquidity.

If a company's defensive interval ratio is very low relative to peer companies or to the company's own history, the analyst would want to ascertain whether there is sufficient cash inflow expected to mitigate the low defensive interval ratio.

Cash Conversion Cycle (Net Operating Cycle) This metric indicates the amount of time that elapses from the point when a company invests in working capital until the point at which the company collects cash. In the typical course of events, a merchandising company acquires inventory on credit, incurring accounts payable. The company then sells that inventory on credit, increasing accounts receivable. Afterwards, it pays out cash to settle its accounts payable, and it collects cash in settlement of its accounts receivable. The time between the outlay of cash and the collection of cash is called the "cash conversion cycle." A shorter cash conversion cycle indicates greater liquidity. A short cash conversion cycle implies that the company only needs to finance its inventory and accounts receivable for a short period of time. A longer cash conversion cycle indicates lower liquidity; it implies that the company must finance its inventory and accounts receivable for a longer period of time, possibly indicating a need for a higher level of capital to fund current assets. Example 9 demonstrates the advantages of a short cash conversion cycle as well as how a company's business strategies are reflected in financial ratios.

EXAMPLE 9

Evaluation of Liquidity Measures

An analyst is evaluating the liquidity of Dell and finds that Dell's 10-K provides a computation of the number of days of receivables, inventory, and accounts payable, as well as the overall cash conversion cycle, as follows:

Fiscal Year Ended	29 Jan 2010	30 Jan 2009	1 Feb 2008
DSO	38	35	36
DOH	8	7	8
Less: Number of days of payables	82	67	80
Equals: Cash conversion cycle	(36)	(25)	(36)

The minimal DOH indicates that Dell maintains lean inventories, which is attributable to key aspects of the company's business model. The company does not build a computer until it is ordered and maintains a just-in-time approach to inventory management. In isolation, the increase in number of days payable (from 67 days in 2009 to 82 days in 2010) might suggest an inability to pay suppliers; however, in Dell's case, the balance sheet indicates that the company has more than $10 billion of cash and short-term investments, which would be more than enough to pay suppliers sooner if Dell chose to do so. Instead, Dell takes advantage of the favorable credit terms granted by its suppliers. The overall effect is a negative cash cycle, a somewhat unusual result. Instead of requiring additional capital to fund working capital as is the case for most companies, Dell has excess cash to invest for about 37 days (reflected on the balance sheet as short-term investments) on which it is earning, rather than paying, interest.

For comparison, the analyst finds the cash conversion cycle reported in the annual reports of two of Dell's competitors, Lenovo and Hewlett-Packard (NYSE: HPQ):

Fiscal Year	2009	2008	2007
Lenovo	(30)	(23)	(28)
Hewlett-Packard	14	20	24

The analyst notes that of the three, only Hewlett-Packard has to raise capital for working capital purposes. While both Dell and Lenovo have consistently negative cash conversion cycles, Lenovo has been slightly less liquid than Dell, evidenced by its slightly less negative cash conversion cycle.

EXAMPLE 10

Bounds and Context of Financial Measures

The previous example focused on the cash conversion cycle, which many companies identify as a key performance metric. The less positive the number of days in the cash conversion cycle, typically, the better it is considered to be. However, is this always true?

This example considers the following question: If a larger negative number of days in a cash conversion cycle is considered to be a desirable performance metric, does identifying a company with a large negative cash conversion cycle necessarily imply good performance?

Using the Compustat database, the company identified as the U.S. computer technology company with the most negative number of days in its cash conversion cycle during the 2005 to 2009 period is National Datacomputer Inc. (OTC: NDCP), which had a negative cash conversion cycle of 275.5 days in 2008.

Exhibit 13	National Datacomputer Inc. ($ millions)					
Fiscal year	**2004**	**2005**	**2006**	**2007**	**2008**	**2009**
Sales	3.248	2.672	2.045	1.761	1.820	1.723
Cost of goods sold	1.919	1.491	0.898	1.201	1.316	1.228
Receivables, Total	0.281	0.139	0.099	0.076	0.115	0.045
Inventories, Total	0.194	0.176	0.010	0.002	0.000	0.000
Accounts payable	0.223	0.317	0.366	1.423	0.704	0.674
DSO		28.69	21.24	18.14	19.15	16.95
DOH		45.29	37.80	1.82	0.28	0.00
*Less: Number of days of payables**		66.10	138.81	271.85	294.97	204.79
Equals: Cash conversion cycle		7.88	−79.77	−251.89	−275.54	−187.84

*Notes: Calculated using Cost of goods sold as an approximation of purchases. Ending inventories 2008 and 2009 are reported as $0 million; therefore, inventory turnover for 2009 cannot be measured. However, given inventory and average sales per day, DOH in 2009 is 0.00.
Source: Raw data from Compustat. Ratios calculated.

The reason for the negative cash conversion cycle is that the company's accounts payable increased substantially over the period. An increase from approximately 66 days in 2005 to 295 days in 2008 to pay trade creditors is clearly a negative signal. In addition, the company's inventories disappeared, most likely because the company did not have enough cash to purchase new inventory and was unable to get additional credit from its suppliers.

Of course, an analyst would have immediately noted the negative trends in these data, as well as additional data throughout the company's financial statements. In its MD&A, the company clearly reports the risks as follows:

> Because we have historically had losses and only a limited amount of cash has been generated from operations, we have funded our operating activities to date primarily from the sale of securities and from the sale of a product line in 2009. In order to continue to fund our operations, we may need to raise additional capital, through the sale of securities. We cannot be certain that any such financing will be available on acceptable terms, or at all. Moreover, additional equity financing, if available, would likely be dilutive to the holders of our common stock, and debt financing, if available, would likely involve restrictive covenants and a security interest in all or substantially all of our assets. If we fail to obtain acceptable financing when needed, we may not have sufficient resources to fund our normal operations which would have a material adverse effect on our business.
>
> IF WE ARE UNABLE TO GENERATE ADEQUATE WORKING CAPITAL FROM OPERATIONS OR RAISE ADDITIONAL CAPITAL THERE IS SUBSTANTIAL DOUBT ABOUT THE COMPANY'S ABILITY TO CONTINUE AS A GOING CONCERN. (emphasis added by company)
>
> *Source*: National Datacomputer Inc., 2009 Form 10-K, page 7.

In summary, it is always necessary to consider ratios within bounds of reasonability and to understand the reasons underlying changes in ratios. Ratios must not only be calculated but must also be interpreted by an analyst.

4.4 Solvency Ratios

Solvency refers to a company's ability to fulfill its long-term debt obligations. Assessment of a company's ability to pay its long-term obligations (i.e., to make interest and principal payments) generally includes an in-depth analysis of the components of its financial structure. Solvency ratios provide information regarding the relative amount of debt in the company's capital structure and the adequacy of earnings and cash flow to cover interest expenses and other fixed charges (such as lease or rental payments) as they come due.

Analysts seek to understand a company's use of debt for several main reasons. One reason is that the amount of debt in a company's capital structure is important for assessing the company's risk and return characteristics, specifically its financial leverage. Leverage is a magnifying effect that results from the use of **fixed costs**—costs that stay the same within some range of activity—and can take two forms: operating leverage and financial leverage.

Operating leverage results from the use of fixed costs in conducting the company's business. Operating leverage magnifies the effect of changes in sales on operating income. Profitable companies may use operating leverage because when revenues increase, with operating leverage, their operating income increases at a faster rate. The explanation is that, although **variable costs** will rise proportionally with revenue, fixed costs will not.

When financing a company (i.e., raising capital for it), the use of debt constitutes **financial leverage** because interest payments are essentially fixed financing costs. As a result of interest payments, a given percent change in EBIT results in a larger percent change in earnings before taxes (EBT). Thus, financial leverage tends to magnify the effect of changes in EBIT on returns flowing to equity holders. Assuming that a company can earn more on funds than it pays in interest, the inclusion of some level of debt in a company's capital structure may lower a company's overall cost of capital and increase returns to equity holders. However, a higher level of debt in a company's capital structure increases the risk of default and results in higher borrowing costs for the company to compensate lenders for assuming greater credit risk. Starting with Modigliani and Miller (1958, 1963), a substantial amount of research has focused on determining a company's optimal capital structure and the subject remains an important one in corporate finance.

In analyzing financial statements, an analyst aims to understand levels and trends in a company's use of financial leverage in relation to past practices and the practices of peer companies. Analysts also need to be aware of the relationship between operating leverage (results from the use of non-current assets with fixed costs) and financial leverage (results from the use of long-term debt with fixed costs). The greater a company's operating leverage, the greater the risk of the operating income stream available to cover debt payments; operating leverage can thus limit a company's capacity to use financial leverage.

A company's relative solvency is fundamental to valuation of its debt securities and its creditworthiness. Finally, understanding a company's use of debt can provide analysts with insight into the company's future business prospects because management's decisions about financing may signal their beliefs about a company's future. For example, the issuance of long-term debt to repurchase common shares may indicate that management believes the market is underestimating the company's prospects and that the shares are undervalued.

4.4.1 *Calculation of Solvency Ratios*

Solvency ratios are primarily of two types. Debt ratios, the first type, focus on the balance sheet and measure the amount of debt capital relative to equity capital. Coverage ratios, the second type, focus on the income statement and measure the ability of a company to cover its debt payments. These ratios are useful in assessing a company's solvency and, therefore, in evaluating the quality of a company's bonds and other debt obligations.

Exhibit 14 describes commonly used solvency ratios. The first three of the debt ratios presented use total debt in the numerator. The definition of total debt used in these ratios varies among informed analysts and financial data vendors, with some using the total of interest-bearing short-term and long-term debt, excluding liabilities such as accrued expenses and accounts payable. (For calculations in this reading, we use this definition.) Other analysts use definitions that are more inclusive (e.g., all liabilities) or restrictive (e.g., long-term debt only, in which case the ratio is sometimes qualified as "long-term," as in "long-term debt-to-equity ratio"). If using different definitions of total debt materially changes conclusions about a company's solvency, the reasons for the discrepancies warrant further investigation.

Exhibit 14	Definitions of Commonly Used Solvency Ratios	

Solvency Ratios	Numerator	Denominator
Debt Ratios		
Debt-to-assets ratio[a]	Total debt[b]	Total assets
Debt-to-capital ratio	Total debt[b]	Total debt[b] + Total shareholders' equity
Debt-to-equity ratio	Total debt[b]	Total shareholders' equity
Financial leverage ratio	Average total assets	Average total equity
Coverage Ratios		
Interest coverage	EBIT	Interest payments
Fixed charge coverage	EBIT + Lease payments	Interest payments + Lease payments

[a] "Total debt ratio" is another name sometimes used for this ratio.

[b] In this reading, we take total debt in this context to be the sum of interest-bearing short-term and long-term debt.

4.4.2 *Interpretation of Solvency Ratios*

In the following, we discuss the interpretation of the basic solvency ratios presented in Exhibit 14.

Debt-to-Assets Ratio This ratio measures the percentage of total assets financed with debt. For example, a **debt-to-assets ratio** of 0.40 or 40 percent indicates that 40 percent of the company's assets are financed with debt. Generally, higher debt means higher financial risk and thus weaker solvency.

Debt-to-Capital Ratio The **debt-to-capital ratio** measures the percentage of a company's capital (debt plus equity) represented by debt. As with the previous ratio, a higher ratio generally means higher financial risk and thus indicates weaker solvency.

Debt-to-Equity Ratio The **debt-to-equity ratio** measures the amount of debt capital relative to equity capital. Interpretation is similar to the preceding two ratios (i.e., a higher ratio indicates weaker solvency). A ratio of 1.0 would indicate equal amounts of debt and equity, which is equivalent to a debt-to-capital ratio of 50 percent. Alternative definitions of this ratio use the market value of stockholders' equity rather than its book value (or use the market values of both stockholders' equity and debt).

Financial Leverage Ratio This ratio (often called simply the "leverage ratio") measures the amount of total assets supported for each one money unit of equity. For example, a value of 3 for this ratio means that each €1 of equity supports €3 of total assets. The higher the **financial leverage ratio**, the more leveraged the company is in the sense of using debt and other liabilities to finance assets. This ratio is often defined in terms of average total assets and average total equity and plays an important role in the DuPont decomposition of return on equity that will be presented in Section 4.6.2.

Interest Coverage This ratio measures the number of times a company's EBIT could cover its interest payments. Thus, it is sometimes referred to as "times interest earned." A higher **interest coverage** ratio indicates stronger solvency, offering greater assurance that the company can service its debt (i.e., bank debt, bonds, notes) from operating earnings.

Fixed Charge Coverage   This ratio relates fixed charges, or obligations, to the cash flow generated by the company. It measures the number of times a company's earnings (before interest, taxes, and lease payments) can cover the company's interest and lease payments.[9] Similar to the interest coverage ratio, a higher **fixed charge coverage** ratio implies stronger solvency, offering greater assurance that the company can service its debt (i.e., bank debt, bonds, notes, and leases) from normal earnings. The ratio is sometimes used as an indication of the quality of the preferred dividend, with a higher ratio indicating a more secure preferred dividend.

Example 11 demonstrates the use of solvency ratios in evaluating the creditworthiness of a company.

EXAMPLE 11

Evaluation of Solvency Ratios

A credit analyst is evaluating the solvency of Alcatel-Lucent (Euronext Paris: ALU) as of the beginning of 2010. The following data are gathered from the company's 2009 annual report (in € millions):

	2009	2008
Total equity	4,309	5,224
Accrued pension	5,043	4,807
Long-term debt	4,179	3,998
Other long term liabilities*	1,267	1,595
Current liabilities*	9,050	11,687
Total equity + Liabilities (equals Total assets)	23,848	27,311

*For purposes of this example, assume that these items are non-interest bearing, and that long-term debt equals total debt. In practice, an analyst could refer to Alcatel's footnotes to confirm details, rather than making an assumption.

---

1 A Calculate the company's financial leverage ratio for 2009.

　　B Interpret the financial leverage ratio calculated in Part A.

2 A What are the company's debt-to-assets, debt-to-capital, and debt-to-equity ratios for the two years?

　　B Is there any discernable trend over the two years?

Solutions to 1:

(Amounts are millions of euro.)

A Average total assets was (27,311 + 23,848)/2 = 25,580 and average total equity was (5,224 + 4,309)/2 = 4,767. Thus, financial leverage was 25,580/4,767 = 5.37.

B For 2009, every €1 in total equity supported €5.37 in total assets, on average.

---

9 For computing this ratio, an assumption sometimes made is that one-third of the lease payment amount represents interest on the lease obligation and that the rest is a repayment of principal on the obligation. For this variant of the fixed charge coverage ratio, the numerator is EBIT plus one-third of lease payments and the denominator is interest payments plus one-third of lease payments.

> **Solutions to 2:**
>
> (Amounts are millions of euro.)
>
> **A** Debt-to-assets for 2008 = 3,998/27,311 = 14.64%
>
>   Debt-to-assets for 2009 = 4,179/23,848 = 17.52%
>
>   Debt-to-capital for 2008 = 3,998/(3,998 + 5,224) = 43.35%
>
>   Debt-to-capital for 2009 = 4,179/(4,179 + 4,309) = 49.23%
>
>   Debt-to-equity for 2008 = 3,998/5,224 = 0.77
>
>   Debt-to-equity for 2009 = 4,179/4,309 = 0.97
>
> **B** On all three metrics, the company's leverage has increased. The increase in debt as part of the company's capital structure indicates that the company's solvency has weakened. From a creditor's perspective, lower solvency (higher debt) indicates higher risk of default on obligations.

As with all ratio analysis, it is important to consider leverage ratios in a broader context. In general, companies with lower business risk and operations that generate steady cash flows are better positioned to take on more leverage without a commensurate increase in the risk of insolvency. In other words, a higher proportion of debt financing poses less risk of non-payment of interest and debt principal to a company with steady cash flows than to a company with volatile cash flows.

4.5 Profitability Ratios

The ability to generate profit on capital invested is a key determinant of a company's overall value and the value of the securities it issues. Consequently, many equity analysts would consider profitability to be a key focus of their analytical efforts.

Profitability reflects a company's competitive position in the market, and by extension, the quality of its management. The income statement reveals the sources of earnings and the components of revenue and expenses. Earnings can be distributed to shareholders or reinvested in the company. Reinvested earnings enhance solvency and provide a cushion against short-term problems.

4.5.1 Calculation of Profitability Ratios

Profitability ratios measure the return earned by the company during a period. Exhibit 15 provides the definitions of a selection of commonly used profitability ratios. Return-on-sales profitability ratios express various subtotals on the income statement (e.g., gross profit, operating profit, net profit) as a percentage of revenue. Essentially, these ratios constitute part of a common-size income statement discussed earlier. Return on investment profitability ratios measure income relative to assets, equity, or total capital employed by the company. For operating ROA, returns are measured as operating income, i.e., prior to deducting interest on debt capital. For ROA and ROE, returns are measured as net income, i.e., after deducting interest paid on debt capital. For return on common equity, returns are measured as net income minus preferred dividends (because preferred dividends are a return to preferred equity).

Exhibit 15	Definitions of Commonly Used Profitability Ratios	
Profitability Ratios	**Numerator**	**Denominator**
Return on Sales[a]		
Gross profit margin	Gross profit	Revenue
Operating profit margin	Operating income[b]	Revenue
Pretax margin	EBT (earnings before tax but after interest)	Revenue
Net profit margin	Net income	Revenue
Return on Investment		
Operating ROA	Operating income	Average total assets
ROA	Net income	Average total assets
Return on total capital	EBIT	Short- and long-term debt and equity
ROE	Net income	Average total equity
Return on common equity	Net income – Preferred dividends	Average common equity

[a] "Sales" is being used as a synonym for "revenue."

[b] Some analysts use EBIT as a shortcut representation of operating income. Note that EBIT, strictly speaking, includes non-operating items such as dividends received and gains and losses on investment securities. Of utmost importance is that the analyst compute ratios consistently whether comparing different companies or analyzing one company over time.

4.5.2 Interpretation of Profitability Ratios

In the following, we discuss the interpretation of the profitability ratios presented in Exhibit 15. For each of the profitability ratios, a higher ratio indicates greater profitability.

Gross Profit Margin   **Gross profit margin** indicates the percentage of revenue available to cover operating and other expenses and to generate profit. Higher gross profit margin indicates some combination of higher product pricing and lower product costs. The ability to charge a higher price is constrained by competition, so gross profits are affected by (and usually inversely related to) competition. If a product has a competitive advantage (e.g., superior branding, better quality, or exclusive technology), the company is better able to charge more for it. On the cost side, higher gross profit margin can also indicate that a company has a competitive advantage in product costs.

Operating Profit Margin   Operating profit is calculated as gross profit minus operating costs. So, an **operating profit margin** increasing faster than the gross profit margin can indicate improvements in controlling operating costs, such as administrative overheads. In contrast, a declining operating profit margin could be an indicator of deteriorating control over operating costs.

Pretax Margin   Pretax income (also called "earnings before tax" or "EBT") is calculated as operating profit minus interest, and the **pretax margin** is the ratio of pretax income to revenue. The pretax margin reflects the effects on profitability of leverage and other (non-operating) income and expenses. If a company's pretax margin is increasing primarily as a result of increasing amounts of non-operating income, the analyst should evaluate whether this increase reflects a deliberate change in a company's business focus and, therefore, the likelihood that the increase will continue.

Net Profit Margin Net profit, or net income, is calculated as revenue minus all expenses. Net income includes both recurring and non-recurring components. Generally, the net income used in calculating the net profit margin is adjusted for non-recurring items to offer a better view of a company's potential future profitability.

ROA ROA measures the return earned by a company on its assets. The higher the ratio, the more income is generated by a given level of assets. Most databases compute this ratio as:

$$\frac{\text{Net income}}{\text{Average total assets}}$$

An issue with this computation is that net income is the return to equity holders, whereas assets are financed by both equity holders and creditors. Interest expense (the return to creditors) has already been subtracted in the numerator. Some analysts, therefore, prefer to add back interest expense in the numerator. In such cases, interest must be adjusted for income taxes because net income is determined after taxes. With this adjustment, the ratio would be computed as:

$$\frac{\text{Net income} + \text{Interest expense} (1 - \text{Tax rate})}{\text{Average total assets}}$$

Alternatively, some analysts elect to compute ROA on a pre-interest and pre-tax basis (operating ROA in Exhibit 15) as:

$$\frac{\text{Operating income or EBIT}}{\text{Average total assets}}$$

In this ROA calculation, returns are measured prior to deducting interest on debt capital (i.e., as operating income or EBIT). This measure reflects the return on all assets invested in the company, whether financed with liabilities, debt, or equity. Whichever form of ROA is chosen, the analyst must use it consistently in comparisons to other companies or time periods.

Return on Total Capital **Return on total capital** measures the profits a company earns on all of the capital that it employs (short-term debt, long-term debt, and equity). As with operating ROA, returns are measured prior to deducting interest on debt capital (i.e., as operating income or EBIT).

ROE ROE measures the return earned by a company on its equity capital, including minority equity, preferred equity, and common equity. As noted, return is measured as net income (i.e., interest on debt capital is not included in the return on equity capital). A variation of ROE is return on common equity, which measures the return earned by a company only on its common equity.

Both ROA and ROE are important measures of profitability and will be explored in more detail in section 4.6.2. As with other ratios, profitability ratios should be evaluated individually and as a group to gain an understanding of what is driving profitability (operating versus non-operating activities). Example 12 demonstrates the evaluation of profitability ratios and the use of the management report (sometimes called management's discussion and analysis or management commentary) that accompanies financial statements to explain the trend in ratios.

EXAMPLE 12

Evaluation of Profitability Ratios

An analyst is evaluating the profitability of Daimler AG (Xetra: DAI) over a recent five-year period. He gathers the following revenue data and calculates the following profitability ratios from information in Daimler's annual reports:

	2009	2008	2007	2006	2005
Revenues (€ millions)	78,924	98,469	101,569	99,222	95,209
Gross profit margin	16.92%	21.89%	23.62%	20.60%	19.48%
Operating profit (EBIT) margin[a]	−1.92%	2.77%	8.58%	5.03%	3.02%
Pretax margin	−2.91%	2.84%	9.04%	4.94%	2.55%
Net profit margin	−3.35%	1.73%	4.78%	3.19%	2.37%

[a]EBIT (Earnings before interest and taxes) is the operating profit metric used by Daimler.

Daimler's revenue declined from 2007 to 2008 and from 2008 to 2009. Further, Daimler's 2009 revenues were the lowest of the five years. Management's discussion of the decline in revenue and EBIT in the 2009 Annual Report notes the following:

> The main reason for the decline [in EBIT] was a significant drop in revenue due to markedly lower unit sales in all vehicle segments as a result of the global economic downturn. Cost savings achieved through permanent and temporary cost reductions and efficiency improvements realized through ongoing optimization programs could only partially compensate for the drop in revenue.

1 Compare gross profit margins and operating profit margins over the 2005 to 2009 period.

2 Explain the decline in operating profit margin in 2009.

3 Explain why the pretax margin might have decreased to a greater extent than the operating profit margin in 2009.

4 Compare net profit margins and pretax margins over 2007 to 2009

Solution to 1:

Gross profit margin improved from 2005 to 2007 as a result of some combination of price increases and/or cost control. However, gross profit margin declined from 2007 to 2009. Operating profit margin showed a similar trend. In 2009, the operating profit margin was negative.

Solution to 2:

The decline in operating profit from 2.77 percent in 2008 to −1.92 percent in 2009 appears to be the result of Daimler's operating leverage. Management indicated that revenue declined in 2009 and reductions in expenses were not enough to offset the revenue decline. Management tried to increase efficiency and reduce costs, including personnel expenses, but this did not sufficiently counteract the decrease in revenues. Expenses thus increased as a proportion of revenue, lowering the gross and operating profit margins. This is an example of the effects of operating leverage (fixed costs that could not be reduced) on profitability. In general, as revenue increases, to the extent that costs remain fixed, operating profit margins should increase. As revenue declines, the opposite occurs.

Solution to 3:

Pretax margin was down substantially in 2009, indicating that the company may have had some non-operating losses or high interest expense in that year. A review of the company's annual report confirms that the cause was higher net interest expense. Specifically, the company increased financing liabilities, faced higher financing costs because of higher risk premiums on borrowing, and had lower interest income on investments. This is an example of the effects of financial leverage on profitability.

Solution to 4:

Net profit margin followed the same pattern as pretax margin, increasing from 2005 to 2007 and then decreasing from 2007 to 2009. In the absence of major variation in the applicable tax rates, this would be expected as net profit margin is based on net income while pretax margin is based on EBT, and net income is EBT(1 − Tax rate).

4.6 Integrated Financial Ratio Analysis

In prior sections, the text presented separately activity, liquidity, solvency, and profitability ratios. Prior to discussing valuation ratios, the following sections demonstrate the importance of examining a variety of financial ratios—not a single ratio or category of ratios in isolation—to ascertain the overall position and performance of a company. Experience shows that the information from one ratio category can be helpful in answering questions raised by another category and that the most accurate overall picture comes from integrating information from all sources. Section 4.6.1 provides some introductory examples of such analysis and Section 4.6.2 shows how return on equity can be analyzed into components related to profit margin, asset utilization (activity), and financial leverage.

4.6.1 *The Overall Ratio Picture: Examples*

This section presents two simple illustrations to introduce the use of a variety of ratios to address an analytical task. Example 13 shows how the analysis of a pair of activity ratios resolves an issue concerning a company's liquidity. Example 14 shows that examining the overall ratios of multiple companies can assist an analyst in drawing conclusions about their relative performances.

EXAMPLE 13

A Variety of Ratios

An analyst is evaluating the liquidity of a Canadian manufacturing company and obtains the following liquidity ratios:

Fiscal Year	10	9	8
Current ratio	2.1	1.9	1.6
Quick ratio	0.8	0.9	1.0

The ratios present a contradictory picture of the company's liquidity. Based on the increase in its current ratio from 1.6 to 2.1, the company appears to have strong and improving liquidity; however, based on the decline of the quick ratio from 1.0 to 0.8, its liquidity appears to be deteriorating. Because both ratios have exactly the same denominator, current liabilities, the difference must be the result of changes in some asset that is included in the current ratio but not in the quick ratio (e.g., inventories). The analyst collects the following activity ratios:

DOH	55	45	30
DSO	24	28	30

The company's DOH has deteriorated from 30 days to 55 days, meaning that the company is holding increasingly larger amounts of inventory relative to sales. The decrease in DSO implies that the company is collecting receivables faster. If the proceeds from these collections were held as cash, there would be no effect on either the current ratio or the quick ratio. However, if the proceeds from the collections were used to purchase inventory, there would be no effect on the current ratio and a decline in the quick ratio (i.e., the pattern shown in this example). Collectively, the ratios suggest that liquidity is declining and that the company may have an inventory problem that needs to be addressed.

EXAMPLE 14

A Comparison of Two Companies (1)

An analyst collects the information[10] shown in Exhibit 16 for two companies:

Exhibit 16

Anson Industries	Fiscal Year	5	4	3	2
Inventory turnover		76.69	89.09	147.82	187.64
DOH		4.76	4.10	2.47	1.95
Receivables turnover		10.75	9.33	11.14	7.56
DSO		33.95	39.13	32.77	48.29
Accounts payable turnover		4.62	4.36	4.84	4.22
Days payable		78.97	83.77	75.49	86.56
Cash from operations/Total liabilities		31.41%	11.15%	4.04%	8.81%
ROE		5.92%	1.66%	1.62%	−0.62%
ROA		3.70%	1.05%	1.05%	−0.39%
Net profit margin (Net income/Revenue)		3.33%	1.11%	1.13%	−0.47%

---

10 Note that ratios are expressed in terms of two decimal places and are rounded. Therefore, expected relationships may not hold perfectly.

Exhibit 16 (Continued)

Anson Industries	Fiscal Year	5	4	3	2
Total asset turnover (Revenue/Average assets)		1.11	0.95	0.93	0.84
Leverage (Average assets/Average equity)		1.60	1.58	1.54	1.60

Clarence Corporation	Fiscal Year	5	4	3	2
Inventory turnover		9.19	9.08	7.52	14.84
DOH		39.73	40.20	48.51	24.59
Receivables turnover		8.35	7.01	6.09	5.16
DSO		43.73	52.03	59.92	70.79
Accounts payable turnover		6.47	6.61	7.66	6.52
Days payable		56.44	55.22	47.64	56.00
Cash from operations/Total liabilities		13.19%	16.39%	15.80%	11.79%
ROE		9.28%	6.82%	−3.63%	−6.75%
ROA		4.64%	3.48%	−1.76%	−3.23%
Net profit margin (Net income/ Revenue)		4.38%	3.48%	−1.60%	−2.34%
Total asset turnover (Revenue/Average assets)		1.06	1.00	1.10	1.38
Leverage (Average assets/Average equity)		2.00	1.96	2.06	2.09

Which of the following choices best describes reasonable conclusions an analyst might make about the companies' efficiency?

A   Over the past four years, Anson has shown greater improvement in efficiency than Clarence, as indicated by its total asset turnover ratio increasing from 0.84 to 1.11.

B   In FY5, Anson's DOH of only 4.76 indicated that it was less efficient at inventory management than Clarence, which had DOH of 39.73.

C   In FY5, Clarence's receivables turnover of 8.35 times indicated that it was more efficient at receivables management than Anson, which had receivables turnover of 10.75.

Solution:

A is correct. Over the past four years, Anson has shown greater improvement in efficiency than Clarence, as indicated by its total asset turnover ratio increasing from 0.84 to 1.11. Over the same period of time, Clarence's total asset turnover ratio has declined from 1.38 to 1.06. Choices B and C are incorrect because DOH and receivables turnover are misinterpreted.

4.6.2 *DuPont Analysis: The Decomposition of ROE*

As noted earlier, ROE measures the return a company generates on its equity capital. To understand what drives a company's ROE, a useful technique is to decompose ROE into its component parts. (Decomposition of ROE is sometimes referred to as **DuPont analysis** because it was developed originally at that company.) Decomposing ROE involves expressing the basic ratio (i.e., net income divided by average shareholders' equity) as the product of component ratios. Because each of these component ratios is an indicator of a distinct aspect of a company's performance that affects ROE, the decomposition allows us to evaluate how these different aspects of performance affected the company's profitability as measured by ROE.[11]

Decomposing ROE is useful in determining the reasons for changes in ROE over time for a given company and for differences in ROE for different companies in a given time period. The information gained can also be used by management to determine which areas they should focus on to improve ROE. This decomposition will also show why a company's overall profitability, measured by ROE, is a function of its efficiency, operating profitability, taxes, and use of financial leverage. DuPont analysis shows the relationship between the various categories of ratios discussed in this reading and how they all influence the return to the investment of the owners.

Analysts have developed several different methods of decomposing ROE. The decomposition presented here is one of the most commonly used and the one found in popular research databases, such as Bloomberg. Return on equity is calculated as:

ROE = Net income/Average shareholders' equity

The decomposition of ROE makes use of simple algebra and illustrates the relationship between ROE and ROA. Expressing ROE as a product of only two of its components, we can write:

$$
\text{ROE} = \frac{\text{Net income}}{\text{Average shareholders' equity}}
$$

$$
= \frac{\text{Net income}}{\text{Average total assets}} \times \frac{\text{Average total assets}}{\text{Average shareholders' equity}}
$$

(1a)

which can be interpreted as:

ROE = ROA × Leverage

In other words, ROE is a function of a company's ROA and its use of financial leverage ("leverage" for short, in this discussion). A company can improve its ROE by improving ROA or making more effective use of leverage. Consistent with the definition given earlier, leverage is measured as average total assets divided by average shareholders' equity. If a company had no leverage (no liabilities), its leverage ratio would equal 1.0 and ROE would exactly equal ROA. As a company takes on liabilities, its leverage increases. As long as a company is able to borrow at a rate lower than the marginal rate it can earn investing the borrowed money in its business, the company is making an effective use of leverage and ROE would increase as leverage increases. If a company's borrowing cost exceeds the marginal rate it can earn on investing in the business, ROE would decline as leverage increased because the effect of borrowing would be to depress ROA.

Using the data from Example 14 for Anson Industries, an analyst can examine the trend in ROE and determine whether the increase from an ROE of −0.625 percent in FY2 to 5.925 percent in FY5 is a function of ROA or the use of leverage:

---

11 For purposes of analyzing ROE, this method usually uses average balance sheet factors; however, the math will work out if beginning or ending balances are used throughout. For certain purposes, these alternative methods may be appropriate. See Stowe et al. (2002, pp. 85–88).

	ROE	=	ROA	×	Leverage
FY5	5.92%		3.70%		1.60
FY4	1.66%		1.05%		1.58
FY3	1.62%		1.05%		1.54
FY2	−0.62%		−0.39%		1.60

Over the four-year period, the company's leverage factor was relatively stable. The primary reason for the increase in ROE is the increase in profitability measured by ROA.

Just as ROE can be decomposed, the individual components such as ROA can be decomposed. Further decomposing ROA, we can express ROE as a product of three component ratios:

$$\frac{\text{Net income}}{\text{Average shareholders' equity}} = \frac{\text{Net income}}{\text{Revenue}} \times \frac{\text{Revenue}}{\text{Average total assets}} \times \frac{\text{Average total assets}}{\text{Average shareholders' equity}} \quad \text{(1b)}$$

which can be interpreted as:

ROE = Net profit margin × Total asset turnover × Leverage

The first term on the right-hand side of this equation is the net profit margin, an indicator of profitability: how much income a company derives per one monetary unit (e.g., euro or dollar) of sales. The second term on the right is the asset turnover ratio, an indicator of efficiency: how much revenue a company generates per one money unit of assets. Note that ROA is decomposed into these two components: net profit margin and total asset turnover. A company's ROA is a function of profitability (net profit margin) and efficiency (total asset turnover). The third term on the right-hand side of Equation 1b is a measure of financial leverage, an indicator of solvency: the total amount of a company's assets relative to its equity capital. This decomposition illustrates that a company's ROE is a function of its net profit margin, its efficiency, and its leverage. Again, using the data from Example 14 for Anson Industries, the analyst can evaluate in more detail the reasons behind the trend in ROE:[12]

	ROE	=	Net profit margin	×	Total asset turnover	×	Leverage
FY5	5.92%		3.33%		1.11		1.60
FY4	1.66%		1.11%		0.95		1.58
FY3	1.62%		1.13%		0.93		1.54
FY2	−0.62%		−0.47%		0.84		1.60

This further decomposition confirms that increases in profitability (measured here as net profit margin) are indeed an important contributor to the increase in ROE over the four-year period. However, Anson's asset turnover has also increased steadily. The increase in ROE is, therefore, a function of improving profitability and improving efficiency. As noted above, ROE decomposition can also be used to compare the ROEs of peer companies, as demonstrated in Example 15.

---

12 Ratios are expressed in terms of two decimal places and are rounded. Therefore, ROE may not be the exact product of the three ratios.

EXAMPLE 15

A Comparison of Two Companies (2)

Referring to the data for Anson Industries and Clarence Corporation in Example 14, which of the following choices best describes reasonable conclusions an analyst might make about the companies' ROE?

A   Anson's inventory turnover of 76.69 indicates it is more profitable than Clarence.

B   The main driver of Clarence's superior ROE in FY5 is its more efficient use of assets.

C   The main drivers of Clarence's superior ROE in FY5 are its greater use of debt financing and higher net profit margin.

Solution:

C is correct. The main driver of Clarence's superior ROE (9.28 percent compared with only 5.92 percent for Anson) in FY5 is its greater use of debt financing (leverage of 2.00 compared with Anson's leverage of 1.60) and higher net profit margin (4.38 percent compared with only 3.33 percent for Anson). A is incorrect because inventory turnover is not a direct indicator of profitability. An increase in inventory turnover may indicate more efficient use of inventory which in turn could affect profitability; however, an increase in inventory turnover would also be observed if a company was selling more goods even if it was not selling those goods at a profit. B is incorrect because Clarence has less efficient use of assets than Anson, indicated by turnover of 1.06 for Clarence compared with Anson's turnover of 1.11.

To separate the effects of taxes and interest, we can further decompose the net profit margin and write:

$$
\begin{aligned}
\frac{\text{Net income}}{\text{Average shareholders' equity}} &= \frac{\text{Net income}}{\text{EBT}} \times \frac{\text{EBT}}{\text{EBIT}} \times \frac{\text{EBIT}}{\text{Revenue}} \\
&\times \frac{\text{Revenue}}{\text{Average total assets}} \times \frac{\text{Average total assets}}{\text{Average shareholders' equity}}
\end{aligned}
$$

(1c)

which can be interpreted as:

$$
\begin{aligned}
\text{ROE} = \text{Tax burden} &\times \text{Interest burden} \times \text{EBIT margin} \\
&\times \text{Total asset turnover} \times \text{Leverage}
\end{aligned}
$$

This five-way decomposition is the one found in financial databases such as Bloomberg. The first term on the right-hand side of this equation measures the effect of taxes on ROE. Essentially, it reflects one minus the average tax rate, or how much of a company's pretax profits it gets to keep. This can be expressed in decimal or percentage form. So, a 30 percent tax rate would yield a factor of 0.70 or 70 percent. A higher value for the tax burden implies that the company can keep a higher percentage of its pretax profits, indicating a lower tax rate. A decrease in the tax burden ratio implies the opposite (i.e., a higher tax rate leaving the company with less of its pretax profits).

The second term on the right-hand side captures the effect of interest on ROE. Higher borrowing costs reduce ROE. Some analysts prefer to use operating income instead of EBIT for this term and the following term. Either operating income or EBIT is acceptable as long as it is applied consistently. In such a case, the second term would measure both the effect of interest expense and non-operating income on ROE.

The third term on the right-hand side captures the effect of operating margin (if operating income is used in the numerator) or EBIT margin (if EBIT is used) on ROE. In either case, this term primarily measures the effect of operating profitability on ROE.

The fourth term on the right-hand side is again the total asset turnover ratio, an indicator of the overall efficiency of the company (i.e., how much revenue it generates per unit of total assets). The fifth term on the right-hand side is the financial leverage ratio described above—the total amount of a company's assets relative to its equity capital.

This decomposition expresses a company's ROE as a function of its tax rate, interest burden, operating profitability, efficiency, and leverage. An analyst can use this framework to determine what factors are driving a company's ROE. The decomposition of ROE can also be useful in forecasting ROE based upon expected efficiency, profitability, financing activities, and tax rates. The relationship of the individual factors, such as ROA to the overall ROE, can also be expressed in the form of an ROE tree to study the contribution of each of the five factors, as shown in Exhibit 17 for Anson Industries.[13]

Exhibit 17 shows that Anson's ROE of 5.92 percent in FY5 can be decomposed into ROA of 3.70 percent and leverage of 1.60. ROA can further be decomposed into a net profit margin of 3.33 percent and total asset turnover of 1.11. Net profit margin can be decomposed into a tax burden of 0.70 (an average tax rate of 30 percent), an interest burden of 0.90, and an EBIT margin of 5.29 percent. Overall ROE is decomposed into five components.

Exhibit 17	DuPont Analysis of Anson Industries' ROE: Fiscal Year 5

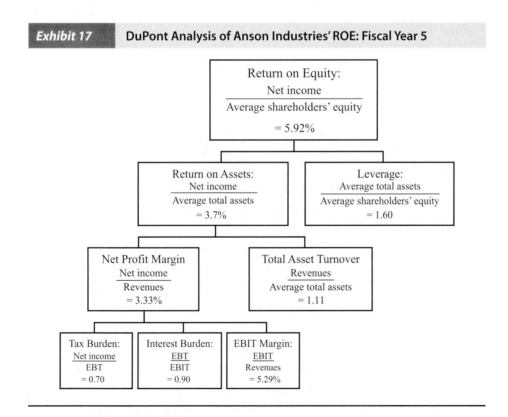

Example 16 demonstrates how the five-component decomposition can be used to determine reasons behind the trend in a company's ROE.

---

13 Note that a breakdown of net profit margin was not provided in Example 14, but is added here.

EXAMPLE 16

Five-Way Decomposition of ROE

An analyst examining Royal Dutch Shell PLC (Amsterdam and London SEs: RDSA) wishes to understand the factors driving the trend in ROE over a recent four-year period. The analyst obtains and calculates the following data from Shell's annual reports:

	2009	2008	2007	2006
ROE	9.53%	20.78%	26.50%	24.72%
Tax burden	60.50%	52.10%	63.12%	58.96%
Interest burden	97.49%	97.73%	97.86%	97.49%
EBIT margin[a]	7.56%	11.04%	13.98%	13.98%
Asset turnover	0.99	1.71	1.47	1.44
Leverage	2.15	2.17	2.10	2.14

[a] Shell's income statement does not present a separate subtotal for operating income. EBIT was calculated as Earnings before taxes plus interest.

What might the analyst conclude?

Solution:

The tax burden measure has varied, with no obvious trend. In the most recent year, 2009, taxes declined as a percentage of pretax profit. (Because the tax burden reflects the relation of after-tax profits to pretax profits, the increase from 52.10 percent in 2008 to 60.50 percent in 2009 indicates that taxes declined as a percentage of pretax profits.) This decline in average tax rates could be a result of lower tax rates from new legislation or revenue in a lower tax jurisdiction. The interest burden has remained fairly constant over the four-year period indicating that the company maintains a fairly constant capital structure. Operating margin (EBIT margin) declined over the period, indicating the company's operations were less profitable. This decline is generally consistent with declines in oil prices in 2009 and declines in refining industry gross margins in 2008 and 2009. The company's efficiency (asset turnover) decreased in 2009. The company's leverage remained constant, consistent with the constant interest burden. Overall, the trend in ROE (declining substantially over the recent years) resulted from decreases in operating profits and a lower asset turnover. Additional research on the causes of these changes is required in order to develop expectations about the company's future performance.

The most detailed decomposition of ROE that we have presented is a five-way decomposition. Nevertheless, an analyst could further decompose individual components of a five-way analysis. For example, EBIT margin (EBIT/Revenue) could be further decomposed into a non-operating component (EBIT/Operating income) and an operating component (Operating income/Revenue). The analyst can also examine which other factors contributed to these five components. For example, an improvement in efficiency (total asset turnover) may have resulted from better management of inventory (DOH) or better collection of receivables (DSO).

EQUITY ANALYSIS

One application of financial analysis is to select securities as part of the equity portfolio management process. Analysts are interested in valuing a security to assess its merits for inclusion or retention in a portfolio. The valuation process has several steps, including:[14]

1 understanding the business and the existing financial profile

2 forecasting company performance

3 selecting the appropriate valuation model

4 converting forecasts to a valuation

5 making the investment decision

Financial analysis assists in providing the core information to complete the first two steps of this valuation process: understanding the business and forecasting performance.

Fundamental equity analysis involves evaluating a company's performance and valuing its equity in order to assess its relative attractiveness as an investment. Analysts use a variety of methods to value a company's equity, including valuation ratios (e.g., the price-to-earnings or P/E ratio), discounted cash flow approaches, and residual income approaches (ROE compared with the cost of capital), among others. The following section addresses the first of these approaches—the use of valuation ratios.

5.1 Valuation Ratios

Valuation ratios have long been used in investment decision making. A well known example is the **price to earnings ratio** (P/E ratio)—probably the most widely cited indicator in discussing the value of equity securities—which relates share price to the earnings per share (EPS). Additionally, some analysts use other market multiples, such as price to book value (P/B) and price to cash flow (P/CF). The following sections explore valuation ratios and other quantities related to valuing equities.

5.1.1 *Calculation of Valuation Ratios and Related Quantities*

Exhibit 18 describes the calculation of some common valuation ratios and related quantities.

Exhibit 18	**Definitions of Selected Valuation Ratios and Related Quantities**	
	Numerator	**Denominator**
Valuation Ratios		
P/E	Price per share	Earnings per share
P/CF	Price per share	Cash flow per share
P/S	Price per share	Sales per share
P/BV	Price per share	Book value per share

(continued)

---

14 Stowe et al. (2002, p. 6).

Exhibit 18	(Continued)

Per-Share Quantities

Basic EPS	Net income minus pre-ferred dividends	Weighted average number of ordinary shares outstanding
Diluted EPS	Adjusted income available for ordinary shares, reflecting conversion of dilutive securities	Weighted average number of ordinary and potential ordinary shares outstanding
Cash flow per share	Cash flow from operations	Weighted average number of shares outstanding
EBITDA per share	EBITDA	Weighted average number of shares outstanding
Dividends per share	Common dividends declared	Weighted average number of ordinary shares outstanding

Dividend-Related Quantities

Dividend payout ratio	Common share dividends	Net income attributable to common shares
Retention rate (b)	Net income attributable to common shares – Common share dividends	Net income attributable to common shares
Sustainable growth rate	$b \times$ ROE	

The P/E ratio expresses the relationship between the price per share and the amount of earnings attributable to a single share. In other words, the P/E ratio tells us how much an investor in common stock pays per dollar of earnings.

Because P/E ratios are calculated using net income, the ratios can be sensitive to non-recurring earnings or one-time earnings events. In addition, because net income is generally considered to be more susceptible to manipulation than are cash flows, analysts may use **price to cash flow** as an alternative measure—particularly in situations where earnings quality may be an issue. EBITDA per share, because it is calculated using income before interest, taxes, and depreciation, can be used to eliminate the effect of different levels of fixed asset investment across companies. It facilitates comparison between companies in the same sector but at different stages of infrastructure maturity. **Price to sales** is calculated in a similar manner and is sometimes used as a comparative price metric when a company does not have positive net income.

Another price-based ratio that facilitates useful comparisons of companies' stock prices is **price to book value**, or P/B, which is the ratio of price to book value per share. This ratio is often interpreted as an indicator of market judgment about the relationship between a company's required rate of return and its actual rate of return. Assuming that book values reflect the fair values of the assets, a price to book ratio of one can be interpreted as an indicator that the company's future returns are expected to be exactly equal to the returns required by the market. A ratio greater than one would indicate that the future profitability of the company is expected to exceed the required rate of return, and values of this ratio less than one indicate that the company is not expected to earn excess returns.[15]

5.1.2 *Interpretation of Earnings per Share*

Exhibit 18 presented a number of per-share quantities that can be used in valuation ratios. In this section, we discuss the interpretation of one such critical quantity, earnings per share or EPS.[16]

EPS is simply the amount of earnings attributable to each share of common stock. In isolation, EPS does not provide adequate information for comparison of one company with another. For example, assume that two companies have only common stock outstanding and no dilutive securities outstanding. In addition, assume the two companies have identical net income of $10 million, identical book equity of $100 million and, therefore, identical profitability (10 percent, using ending equity in this case for simplicity). Furthermore, assume that Company A has 100 million weighted average common shares outstanding, whereas Company B has 10 million weighted average common shares outstanding. So, Company A will report EPS of $0.10 per share, and Company B will report EPS of $1 per share. The difference in EPS does not reflect a difference in profitability—the companies have identical profits and profitability. The difference reflects only a different number of common shares outstanding. Analysts should understand in detail the types of EPS information that companies report:

Basic EPS provides information regarding the earnings attributable to each share of common stock.[17] To calculate basic EPS, the weighted average number of shares outstanding during the period is first calculated. The weighted average number of shares consists of the number of ordinary shares outstanding at the beginning of the period, adjusted by those bought back or issued during the period, multiplied by a time-weighting factor.

Accounting standards generally require the disclosure of basic as well as **diluted EPS** (diluted EPS includes the effect of all the company's securities whose conversion or exercise would result in a reduction of basic EPS; dilutive securities include convertible debt, convertible preferred, warrants, and options). Basic EPS and diluted EPS must be shown with equal prominence on the face of the income statement for each class of ordinary share. Disclosure includes the amounts used as the numerators in calculating basic and diluted EPS, and a reconciliation of those amounts to the company's profit or loss for the period. Because both basic and diluted EPS are presented in a company's financial statements, an analyst does not need to calculate these measures for reported financial statements. Understanding the calculations is, however, helpful for situations requiring an analyst to calculate expected future EPS.

To calculate diluted EPS, earnings are adjusted for the after-tax effects assuming conversion, and the following adjustments are made to the weighted number of shares:

- The weighted average number of shares for basic EPS, *plus* those that would be issued on conversion of all dilutive potential ordinary shares. Potential ordinary shares are treated as dilutive when their conversion would decrease net profit per share from continuing ordinary operations.

---

15 For more detail on valuation ratios as used in equity analysis, see the curriculum reading "Equity Valuation: Concepts and Basic Tools."

16 For more detail on EPS calculation, see the reading "Understanding Income Statements."

17 IAS 33, *Earnings per Share* and FASB ASC Topic 260 [Earnings per Share].

- These shares are deemed to have been converted into ordinary shares at the beginning of the period or, if later, at the date of the issue of the shares.

- Options, warrants (and their equivalents), convertible instruments, contingently issuable shares, contracts that can be settled in ordinary shares or cash, purchased options, and written put options should be considered.

5.1.3 *Dividend-Related Quantities*

In this section, we discuss the interpretation of the dividend-related quantities presented in Exhibit 18. These quantities play a role in some present value models for valuing equities.

Dividend Payout Ratio   The **dividend payout ratio** measures the percentage of earnings that the company pays out as dividends to shareholders. The amount of dividends per share tends to be relatively fixed because any reduction in dividends has been shown to result in a disproportionately large reduction in share price. Because dividend amounts are relatively fixed, the dividend payout ratio tends to fluctuate with earnings. Therefore, conclusions about a company's dividend payout policies should be based on examination of payout over a number of periods. Optimal dividend policy, similar to optimal capital structure, has been examined in academic research and continues to be a topic of significant interest in corporate finance.

Retention Rate   The retention rate, or earnings retention rate, is the complement of the payout ratio or dividend payout ratio (i.e., 1 – payout ratio). Whereas the payout ratio measures the percentage of earnings that a company pays out as dividends, the retention rate is the percentage of earnings that a company retains. (Note that both the payout ratio and retention rate are both percentages of earnings. The difference in terminology—"ratio" versus "rate" versus "percentage"—reflects common usage rather than any substantive differences.)

Sustainable Growth Rate   A company's **sustainable growth rate** is viewed as a function of its profitability (measured as ROE) and its ability to finance itself from internally generated funds (measured as the retention rate). The sustainable growth rate is ROE times the retention rate. A higher ROE and a higher retention rate result in a higher sustainable growth rate. This calculation can be used to estimate a company's growth rate, a factor commonly used in equity valuation.

5.2 Industry-Specific Ratios

As stated earlier in this reading, a universally accepted definition and classification of ratios does not exist. The purpose of ratios is to serve as indicators of important aspects of a company's performance and value. Aspects of performance that are considered important in one industry may be irrelevant in another, and industry-specific ratios reflect these differences. For example, companies in the retail industry may report same-store sales changes because, in the retail industry, it is important to distinguish between growth that results from opening new stores and growth that results from generating more sales at existing stores. Industry-specific metrics can be especially important to the value of equity in early stage industries, where companies are not yet profitable.

In addition, regulated industries—especially in the financial sector—often are required to comply with specific regulatory ratios. For example, the banking sector's liquidity and cash reserve ratios provide an indication of banking liquidity and reflect monetary and regulatory requirements. Banking capital adequacy requirements attempt to relate banks' solvency requirements directly to their specific levels of risk exposure.

Exhibit 19 presents, for illustrative purposes only, some industry-specific and task-specific ratios.[18]

Exhibit 19	Definitions of Some Common Industry- and Task-Specific Ratios	
Ratio	**Numerator**	**Denominator**
Business Risk		
Coefficient of variation of operating income	Standard deviation of operating income	Average operating income
Coefficient of variation of net income	Standard deviation of net income	Average net income
Coefficient of variation of revenues	Standard deviation of revenue	Average revenue
Financial Sector Ratios		
Capital adequacy—banks	Various components of capital	Various measures such as risk-weighted assets, market risk exposure, or level of operational risk assumed
Monetary reserve requirement (Cash reserve ratio)	Reserves held at central bank	Specified deposit liabilities
Liquid asset requirement	Approved "readily marketable" securities	Specified deposit liabilities
Net interest margin	Net interest income	Total interest-earning assets
Retail Ratios		
Same (or comparable) store sales	Average revenue growth year over year for stores open in both periods	Not applicable
Sales per square meter (or square foot)	Revenue	Total retail space in square meters (or square feet)
Service Companies		
Revenue per employee	Revenue	Total number of employees
Net income per employee	Net income	Total number of employees

(continued)

---

18 There are many other industry- and task-specific ratios that are outside the scope of this reading. Resources such as Standard and Poor's Industry Surveys present useful ratios for each industry. Industry organizations may present useful ratios for the industry or a task specific to the industry.

Exhibit 19	(Continued)	
Hotel		
Average daily rate	Room revenue	Number of rooms sold
Occupancy rate	Number of rooms sold	Number of rooms available

5.3 Research on Ratios in Equity Analysis

Some ratios may be particularly useful in equity analysis. The end product of equity analysis is often a valuation and investment recommendation. Theoretical valuation models are useful in selecting ratios that would be useful in this process. For example, a company's P/B is theoretically linked to ROE, growth, and the required return. ROE is also a primary determinant of residual income in a residual income valuation model. In both cases, higher ROE relative to the required return denotes a higher valuation. Similarly, profit margin is related to justified price-to-sales (P/S) ratios. Another common valuation method involves forecasts of future cash flows that are discounted back to the present. Trends in ratios can be useful in forecasting future earnings and cash flows (e.g., trends in operating profit margin and collection of customer receivables). Future growth expectations are a key component of all of these valuation models. Trends may be useful in assessing growth prospects (when used in conjunction with overall economic and industry trends). The variability in ratios and common-size data can be useful in assessing risk, an important component of the required rate of return in valuation models. A great deal of academic research has focused on the use of these fundamental ratios in evaluating equity investments.

A classic study, Ou and Penman (1989a and 1989b), found that ratios and common-size metrics generated from accounting data were useful in forecasting earnings and stock returns. Ou and Penman examined 68 such metrics and found that these could be reduced to a more parsimonious list of relevant variables, including percentage changes in a variety of measures such as current ratio, inventory, and sales; gross and pretax margins; and returns on assets and equity. These variables were found to be useful in forecasting earnings and stock returns.

Subsequent studies have also demonstrated the usefulness of ratios in evaluation of equity investments and valuation. Lev and Thiagarajan (1993) examined fundamental financial variables used by analysts to assess whether they are useful in security valuation. They found that fundamental variables add about 70 percent to the explanatory power of earnings alone in predicting excess returns (stock returns in excess of those expected). The fundamental variables they found useful included percentage changes in inventory and receivables relative to sales, gross margin, sales per employee, and the change in bad debts relative to the change in accounts receivable, among others. Abarbanell and Bushee (1997) found some of the same variables useful in predicting future accounting earnings. Abarbanell and Bushee (1998) devised an investment strategy using these same variables and found that they can generate excess returns under this strategy.

Piotroski (2000) used financial ratios to supplement a value investing strategy and found that he can generate significant excess returns. Variables used by Piotroski include ROA, cash flow ROA, change in ROA, change in leverage, change in liquidity, change in gross margin, and change in inventory turnover.

This research shows that in addition to being useful in evaluating the past performance of a company, ratios can be useful in predicting future earnings and equity returns.

CREDIT ANALYSIS

6

Credit risk is the risk of loss caused by a counterparty's or debtor's failure to make a promised payment. For example, credit risk with respect to a bond is the risk that the obligor (the issuer of the bond) is not able to pay interest and principal according to the terms of the bond indenture (contract). **Credit analysis** is the evaluation of credit risk.

Approaches to credit analysis vary and, as with all financial analysis, depend on the purpose of the analysis and the context in which it is done. Credit analysis for specific types of debt (e.g., acquisition financing and other highly leveraged financing) often involves projections of period-by-period cash flows similar to projections made by equity analysts. Whereas the equity analyst may discount projected cash flows to determine the value of the company's equity, a credit analyst would use the projected cash flows to assess the likelihood of a company complying with its financial covenants in each period and paying interest and principal as due.[19] The analysis would also include expectations about asset sales and refinancing options open to the company.

Credit analysis may relate to the borrower's credit risk in a particular transaction or to its overall creditworthiness. In assessing overall creditworthiness, one general approach is credit scoring, a statistical analysis of the determinants of credit default.

Another general approach to credit analysis is the credit rating process that is used, for example, by credit rating agencies to assess and communicate the probability of default by an issuer on its debt obligations (e.g., commercial paper, notes, and bonds). A credit rating can be either long term or short term and is an indication of the rating agency's opinion of the creditworthiness of a debt issuer with respect to a specific debt security or other obligation. Where a company has no debt outstanding, a rating agency can also provide an issuer credit rating that expresses an opinion of the issuer's overall capacity and willingness to meet its financial obligations. The following sections review research on the use of ratios in credit analysis and the ratios commonly used in credit analysis.

6.1 The Credit Rating Process

The rating process involves both the analysis of a company's financial reports as well as a broad assessment of a company's operations. The credit evaluation process by any analyst includes many of the following procedures performed by analysts at credit rating agencies:[20]

- Meeting with management, typically including the chief financial officer, to discuss, for example, industry outlook, overview of major business segments, financial policies and goals, distinctive accounting practices, capital spending plans, and financial contingency plans.
- Tours of major facilities, time permitting.
- Meeting of a ratings committee where the analyst's recommendations are voted on, after considering factors that include:
  - Business risk, including the evaluation of:

---

19 Financial covenants are clauses in bond indentures relating to the financial condition of the bond issuer.
20 Based on Standard & Poor's *Corporate Ratings Criteria* (2008).

- operating environment;
- industry characteristics (e.g., cyclicality and capital intensity);
- success factors and areas of vulnerability; and
- company's competitive position, including size and diversification.
- Financial risk, including:
  - the evaluation of capital structure, interest coverage, and profitability using ratio analysis, and
  - the examination of debt covenants.
- Evaluation of management.
- Monitoring of publicly distributed ratings—including reconsideration of ratings due to changing conditions.

In assigning credit ratings, rating agencies emphasize the importance of the relationship between a company's business risk profile and its financial risk. "The company's business risk profile determines the level of financial risk appropriate for any rating category."[21]

When analyzing financial ratios, rating agencies normally investigate deviations of ratios from the median ratios of the universe of companies for which such ratios have been calculated and also use the median ratings as an indicator for the ratings grade given to a specific debt issuer. This so-called universe of rated companies changes constantly, and any calculations are obviously affected by economic factors as well as by mergers and acquisitions. International ratings include the influence of country and economic risk factors. Exhibit 20 presents key financial ratios used by Standard & Poor's in evaluating industrial companies. Note that before calculating ratios, rating agencies make certain adjustments to reported financials such as adjusting debt to include off-balance sheet debt in a company's total debt.

Exhibit 20	Selected Credit Ratios Used by Standard & Poor's	
Credit Ratio	**Numerator[b]**	**Denominator[c]**
EBIT interest coverage	EBIT	Gross interest (prior to deductions for capitalized interest or interest income)
EBITDA interest coverage	EBITDA	Gross interest (prior to deductions for capitalized interest or interest income)
FFO[a] (Funds from operations) interest coverage	FFO plus interest paid, minus operating lease adjustments	Gross interest (prior to deductions for capitalized interest or interest income)
Return on capital	EBIT	Average capital, where capital = equity, plus non-current deferred taxes, plus debt
FFO (Funds from operations) to debt	FFO	Total debt
Free operating cash flow to debt	CFO (adjusted) minus capital expenditures	Total debt

---

21 Standard & Poor's *Corporate Ratings Criteria* (2008), p. 23.

Exhibit 20   (Continued)

Credit Ratio	Numerator[b]	Denominator[c]
Discretionary cash flow to debt	CFO minus capital expenditures minus dividends paid	Total debt
Net cash flow to capital expenditures	FFO minus dividends	Capital expenditures
Debt to EBITDA	Total debt	EBITDA
Total debt to total debt plus equity	Total debt	Total debt plus equity

[a] FFO = funds from operations, defined as net income adjusted for non-cash items; CFO = cash flow from operations.
[b] Emphasis is on earnings from *continuing* operations.
[c] Note that both the numerator and denominator definitions are adjusted from ratio to ratio and may not correspond to the definitions used elsewhere in this reading.
Source: Based on data from *Standard & Poor's Corporate Ratings Criteria* (2008), p. 52.

6.2 Research on Ratios in Credit Analysis

A great deal of academic and practitioner research has focused on determining which ratios are useful in assessing the credit risk of a company, including the risk of bankruptcy.

One of the earliest studies examined individual ratios to assess their ability to predict failure of a company up to five years in advance. Beaver (1967) found that six ratios could correctly predict company failure one year in advance 90 percent of the time and five years in advance at least 65 percent of the time. The ratios found effective by Beaver were cash flow to total debt, ROA, total debt to total assets, working capital to total assets, the current ratio, and the no-credit interval ratio (the length of time a company could go without borrowing). Altman (1968) and Altman, Haldeman, and Narayanan (1977) found that financial ratios could be combined in an effective model for predicting bankruptcy. Altman's initial work involved creation of a Z-score that was able to correctly predict financial distress. The Z-score was computed as

$$
\begin{aligned}
Z ={}& 1.2 \times (\text{Current assets} - \text{Current liabilities})/\text{Total assets} \\
& + 1.4 \times (\text{Retained earnings/Total assets}) \\
& + 3.3 \times (\text{EBIT/Total assets}) \\
& + 0.6 \times (\text{Market value of stock/Book value of liabilities}) \\
& + 1.0 \times (\text{Sales/Total assets})
\end{aligned}
$$

In his initial study, a Z-score of lower than 1.81 predicted failure and the model was able to accurately classify 95 percent of companies studied into a failure group and a non-failure group. The original model was designed for manufacturing companies. Subsequent refinements to the models allow for other company types and time periods. Generally, the variables found to be useful in prediction include profitability ratios, coverage ratios, liquidity ratios, capitalization ratios, and earnings variability (Altman 2000).

Similar research has been performed on the ability of ratios to predict bond ratings and bond yields. For example, Ederington, Yawtiz, and Roberts (1987) found that a small number of variables (total assets, interest coverage, leverage, variability of coverage, and subordination status) were effective in explaining bond yields. Similarly,

Ederington (1986) found that nine variables in combination could correctly classify more than 70 percent of bond ratings. These variables included ROA, long-term debt to assets, interest coverage, cash flow to debt, variability of coverage and cash flow, total assets, and subordination status. These studies have shown that ratios are effective in evaluating credit risk, bond yields, and bond ratings.

7 BUSINESS AND GEOGRAPHIC SEGMENTS

Analysts often need to evaluate the performance underlying business segments (subsidiary companies, operating units, or simply operations in different geographic areas) to understand in detail the company as a whole. Although companies are not required to provide full financial statements for segments, they are required to provide segment information under both IFRS and U.S. GAAP.[22]

7.1 Segment Reporting Requirements

An operating segment is defined as a component of a company: a) that engages in activities that may generate revenue and create expenses, including a start-up segment that has yet to earn revenues, b) whose results are regularly reviewed by the company's senior management, and c) for which discrete financial information is available.[23] A company must disclose separate information about any operating segment which meets certain quantitative criteria—namely, the segment constitutes 10 percent or more of the combined operating segments' revenue, assets, or profit. (For purposes of determining whether a segment constitutes 10 percent or more of combined profits or losses, the criteria is expressed in terms of the absolute value of the segment's profit or loss as a percentage of the greater of (i) the combined profits of all profitable segments and (ii) the absolute amount of the combined losses of all loss-making segments.) If, after applying these quantitative criteria, the combined revenue from external customers for all reportable segments combined is less than 75 percent of the total company revenue, the company must identify additional reportable segments until the 75 percent level is reached. Small segments might be combined as one if they share a substantial number of factors that define a business or geographical segment, or they might be combined with a similar significant reportable segment. Information about operating segments and businesses that are not reportable is combined in an "all other segments" category.

Companies may internally report business results in a variety of ways (e.g., product segments and geographical segments). Companies identify the segments for external reporting purposes considering the definition of an operating segment and using factors such as what information is reported to the board of directors and whether a manager is responsible for each segment. Companies must disclose the factors used to identify reportable segments and the types and products and services sold by each reportable segment.

For each reportable segment, the following should also be disclosed:

■ a measure of profit or loss;

---

22 IFRS 8, *Operating Segments* and FASB ASC Topic 280 [Segment Reporting].
23 IFRS 8, *Operating Segments*, paragraph 5.

- a measure of total assets and liabilities[24] (if these amounts are regularly reviewed by the company's chief decision-making officer);
- segment revenue, distinguishing between revenue to external customers and revenue from other segments;
- interest revenue and interest expense;
- cost of property, plant, and equipment, and intangible assets acquired;
- depreciation and amortisation expense;
- other non-cash expenses;
- income tax expense or income; and
- share of the net profit or loss of an investment accounted for under the equity method.

Companies also must provide a reconciliation between the information of reportable segments and the consolidated financial statements in terms of segment revenue, profit or loss, assets, and liabilities.

Another disclosure required is the company's reliance on any single customer. If any single customer represents 10 percent or more of the company's total revenues, the company must disclose that fact. From an analysts' perspective, information about a concentrated customer base can be useful in assessing the risks faced by the company.

7.2 Segment Ratios

Based on the segment information that companies are required to present, a variety of useful ratios can be computed, as shown in Exhibit 21.

Exhibit 21	Definitions of Segment Ratios	
Segment Ratios	**Numerator**	**Denominator**
Segment margin	Segment profit (loss)	Segment revenue
Segment turnover	Segment revenue	Segment assets
Segment ROA	Segment profit (loss)	Segment assets
Segment debt ratio	Segment liabilities	Segment assets

The segment margin measures the operating profitability of the segment relative to revenues, whereas the segment ROA measures the operating profitability relative to assets. Segment turnover measures the overall efficiency of the segment: how much revenue is generated per unit of assets. The segment debt ratio examines the level of liabilities (hence solvency) of the segment. Example 17 demonstrates the evaluation of segment ratios.

---

24 IFRS 8 and FASB ASC Topic 280 are largely converged. One notable difference is that U.S. GAAP does not require disclosure of segment liabilities, while IFRS requires disclosure of segment liabilities if that information is regularly provided to the company's "chief operating decision maker."

EXAMPLE 17

The Evaluation of Segment Ratios

The information contained in Exhibit 22 relates to the business segments of Groupe Danone (EuronextParis:BN) for 2008 and 2009 in millions of euro. According to the company's 2009 annual report:

> Over the course of the past 10 years, the Group has refocused its activities on the health food industry. On October 31, 2007, the acquisition of Royal Numico N.V. and its subsidiaries ("Numico"), a group specialized in baby nutrition and medical nutrition, marked a new phase in the Group's development by adding these lines of business to Danone's portfolio. The Group has since operated in four markets corresponding to its four business lines: (i) Fresh Dairy Products, (ii) Waters, (iii) Baby Nutrition, and (iv) Medical Nutrition.

Evaluate the performance of the segments using the segment margin, segment ROA, and segment turnover.

Exhibit 22

	2009			2008		
(In € millions)	Revenue (3rd party)	Operating income	Assets	Revenue (3rd party)	Operating income	Assets
Fresh Dairy Products	8,555	1,240	7,843	8,697	1,187	7,145
Waters	2,578	646	2,773	2,874	323	3,426
Baby Nutrition	2,924	547	10,203	2,795	462	9,999
Medical Nutrition	925	190	4,781	854	217	4,450
Business Line Total	14,982	2,623	25,600	15,220	2,189	25,020

Segment Ratios							
	2009				2008		
	Segment Revenue as percent of total	Segment Margin	Segment ROA[a]	Segment Turnover	Segment Revenue as percent of total	Segment Margin	Segment ROA[a]	Segment Turnover

	Segment Revenue as percent of total	Segment Margin	Segment ROA[a]	Segment Turnover	Segment Revenue as percent of total	Segment Margin	Segment ROA[a]	Segment Turnover
Fresh Dairy Products	57.1%	14.5%	15.8%	1.1	57.1%	13.6%	16.6%	1.2
Waters	17.2%	25.1%	23.3%	0.9	18.9%	11.2%	9.4%	0.8
Baby Nutrition	19.5%	18.7%	5.4%	0.3	18.4%	16.5%	4.6%	0.3
Medical Nutrition	6.2%	20.5%	4.0%	0.2	5.6%	25.4%	4.9%	0.2

[a]As used in this table, ROA refers to operating income divided by ending assets.

Solution:

The waters segment (Evian and Volvic) was the most profitable in 2009 as measured by margin and ROA; however, in 2009 the segment did not grow as fast as the company's other segments. In 2008, the segment represented 18.9 percent of total segment revenues, but in 2009 the percentage was only 17.2 percent.

The company's largest segment by revenue, fresh dairy products had the lowest margin in 2009 but a much higher segment ROA than the baby and medical nutrition segments. Medical nutrition is the second highest segment in terms of segment margin but lowest in turnover (an indicator of efficiency, i.e., the ability to generate revenue from assets). As a result, medical nutrition had the lowest segment ROA (Segment ROA = Segment operating income/Segment assets = (Segment operating income/Segment revenue) × (Segment revenue × Segment Assets) = Segment margin × Segment turnover. Reported percentages may differ due to rounding). Part of the explanation for segment differences in ROA may be that the medical and baby nutrition businesses were acquired in 2007. In an acquisition, the acquiring company reports the acquired assets at fair value at the time of the acquisition. Most of a company's other assets are reported at historical costs, and over time, most long-term assets are depreciated. Thus, compared to assets in other segments, it is likely that the assets of the nutrition segments are reported at amounts more reflective of current prices.

MODEL BUILDING AND FORECASTING

8

Analysts often need to forecast future financial performance. For example, EPS forecasts of analysts are widely followed by Wall Street. Analysts use data about the economy, industry, and company in arriving at a company's forecast. The results of an analyst's financial analysis, including common-size and ratio analyses, are integral to this process, along with the judgment of the analysts.

Based upon forecasts of growth and expected relationships among the financial statement data, the analyst can build a model (sometimes referred to as an "earnings model") to forecast future performance. In addition to budgets, pro forma financial statements are widely used in financial forecasting within companies, especially for use by senior executives and boards of directors. Last but not least, these budgets and forecasts are also used in presentations to credit analysts and others in obtaining external financing.

For example, based on a revenue forecast, an analyst may budget expenses based on expected common-size data. Forecasts of balance sheet and cash flow statements can be derived from expected ratio data, such as DSO. Forecasts are not limited to a single point estimate but should involve a range of possibilities. This can involve several techniques:

- **Sensitivity analysis**: Also known as "what if" analysis, sensitivity analysis shows the range of possible outcomes as specific assumptions are changed; this could, in turn, influence financing needs or investment in fixed assets.

- **Scenario analysis**: This type of analysis shows the changes in key financial quantities that result from given (economic) events, such as the loss of customers, the loss of a supply source, or a catastrophic event. If the list of events is mutually exclusive and exhaustive and the events can be assigned probabilities, the analyst can evaluate not only the range of outcomes but also standard statistical measures such as the mean and median value for various quantities of interest.

- **Simulation**: This is computer-generated sensitivity or scenario analysis based on probability models for the factors that drive outcomes. Each event or possible outcome is assigned a probability. Multiple scenarios are then run using the probability factors assigned to the possible values of a variable.

SUMMARY

Financial analysis techniques, including common-size and ratio analysis, are useful in summarizing financial reporting data and evaluating the performance and financial position of a company. The results of financial analysis techniques provide important inputs into security valuation. Key facets of financial analysis include the following:

▪ Common-size financial statements and financial ratios remove the effect of size, allowing comparisons of a company with peer companies (cross-sectional analysis) and comparison of a company's results over time (trend or time-series analysis).

▪ Activity ratios measure the efficiency of a company's operations, such as collection of receivables or management of inventory. Major activity ratios include inventory turnover, days of inventory on hand, receivables turnover, days of sales outstanding, payables turnover, number of days of payables, working capital turnover, fixed asset turnover, and total asset turnover.

▪ Liquidity ratios measure the ability of a company to meet short-term obligations. Major liquidity ratios include the current ratio, quick ratio, cash ratio, and defensive interval ratio.

▪ Solvency ratios measure the ability of a company to meet long-term obligations. Major solvency ratios include debt ratios (including the debt-to-assets ratio, debt-to-capital ratio, debt-to-equity ratio, and financial leverage ratio) and coverage ratios (including interest coverage and fixed charge coverage).

▪ Profitability ratios measure the ability of a company to generate profits from revenue and assets. Major profitability ratios include return on sales ratios (including gross profit margin, operating profit margin, pretax margin, and net profit margin) and return on investment ratios (including operating ROA, ROA, return on total capital, ROE, and return on common equity).

▪ Ratios can also be combined and evaluated as a group to better understand how they fit together and how efficiency and leverage are tied to profitability.

▪ ROE can be analyzed as the product of the net profit margin, asset turnover, and financial leverage. This decomposition is sometimes referred to as DuPont analysis.

▪ Valuation ratios express the relation between the market value of a company or its equity (for example, price per share) and some fundamental financial metric (for example, earnings per share).

▪ Ratio analysis is useful in the selection and valuation of debt and equity securities and is a part of the credit rating process.

▪ Ratios can also be computed for business segments to evaluate how units within a business are performing.

▪ The results of financial analysis provide valuable inputs into forecasts of future earnings and cash flow.

REFERENCES

Abarbanell, J.S., and B. J. Bushee. 1997. "Fundamental Analysis, Future Earnings, and Stock Prices." *Journal of Accounting Research*, vol. 35, no. 1:1–24.

Abarbanell, J.S., and B.J. Bushee. 1998. "Abnormal Returns to a Fundamental Analysis Strategy." *Accounting Review*, vol. 73, no. 1:19–46.

Altman, E. 1968. "Financial Ratios, Discriminant Analysis and the Prediction of Corporate Bankruptcy." *Journal of Finance*, vol. 23, no. 4:589–609.

Altman, E. 2000, "Predicting Financial Distress of Companies: Revisiting the Z-Score and Zeta Models." Working paper at www.stern.nyu.edu/~ealtman/Zscores.pdf

Altman, E., R. Haldeman, and P. Narayanan. 1977. "Zeta Analysis: A New Model to Identify Bankruptcy Risk of Corporations." *Journal of Banking & Finance*, vol. 1, no. 1.

Beaver, W. 1967. "Financial Ratios as Predictors of Failures." *Empirical Research in Accounting*, selected studies supplement to *Journal of Accounting Research*, 4 (1).

Benninga, Simon Z., and Oded H. Sarig. 1997. *Corporate Finance: A Valuation Approach*. New York: McGraw-Hill Publishing.

Ederington, L.H. 1986. "Why Split Ratings Occur." *Financial Management*, vol. 15, no. 1:37–47.

Ederington, L.H., J.B. Yawitz, and B.E. Robert. 1987. "The Information Content of Bond Ratings." *Journal of Financial Research*, vol. 10, no. 3:211–226.

Lev, B., and S.R. Thiagarajan. 1993. "Fundamental Information Analysis." *Journal of Accounting Research*, vol. 31, no. 2:190–215.

Modigliani, F., and M. Miller. 1958. "The Cost of Capital, Corporation Finance and the Theory of Investment." *American Economic Review*, vol. 48:261–298.

Modigliani, F., and M. Miller. 1963. "Corporate Income Taxes and the Cost of Capital: A Correction." *American Economic Review*, vol. 53:433–444.

Ou, J.A., and S.H. Penman. 1989a. "Financial Statement Analysis and the Prediction of Stock Returns." *Journal of Accounting and Economics*, vol. 11, no. 4:295–329.

Ou, J.A., and S.H. Penman. 1989b. "Accounting Measurement, Price-Earnings Ratio, and the Information Content of Security Prices." *Journal of Accounting Research*, vol. 27, no. Supplement:111–144.

Pinto, Jerald E., Elaine Henry, Thomas R. Robinson, and John D. Stowe. 2010. *Equity Asset Valuation*, 2nd edition. Hoboken, NJ: John Wiley & Sons.

Piotroski, J.D. 2000. "Value Investing: The Use of Historical Financial Statement Information to Separate Winners from Losers." *Journal of Accounting Research*, vol. 38, no. Supplement:1–41.

Robinson, T., and P. Munter. 2004. "Financial Reporting Quality: Red Flags and Accounting Warning Signs." *Commercial Lending Review*, vol. 19, no. 1:2–15.

Stowe, J.D., T.R. Robinson, J.E. Pinto, and D.W. McLeavey. 2002. *Analysis of Equity Investments: Valuation*. Charlottesville, VA: CFA Institute.

van Greuning, H., and S. Brajovic Bratanovic. 2003. *Analyzing and Managing Banking Risk: A Framework for Assessing Corporate Governance and Financial Risk*. Washington, DC: World Bank.

PRACTICE PROBLEMS

1 Comparison of a company's financial results to other peer companies for the same time period is called:

    A technical analysis.

    B time-series analysis.

    C cross-sectional analysis.

2 In order to assess a company's ability to fulfill its long-term obligations, an analyst would *most likely* examine:

    A activity ratios.

    B liquidity ratios.

    C solvency ratios.

3 Which ratio would a company *most likely* use to measure its ability to meet short-term obligations?

    A Current ratio.

    B Payables turnover.

    C Gross profit margin.

4 Which of the following ratios would be *most* useful in determining a company's ability to cover its lease and interest payments?

    A ROA.

    B Total asset turnover.

    C Fixed charge coverage.

5 An analyst is interested in assessing both the efficiency and liquidity of Spherion PLC. The analyst has collected the following data for Spherion:

	FY3	FY2	FY1
Days of inventory on hand	32	34	40
Days sales outstanding	28	25	23
Number of days of payables	40	35	35

Based on this data, what is the analyst *least likely* to conclude?

    A Inventory management has contributed to improved liquidity.

    B Management of payables has contributed to improved liquidity.

    C Management of receivables has contributed to improved liquidity.

6 An analyst is evaluating the solvency and liquidity of Apex Manufacturing and has collected the following data (in millions of euro):

	FY5 (€)	FY4 (€)	FY3 (€)
Total debt	2,000	1,900	1,750
Total equity	4,000	4,500	5,000

Which of the following would be the analyst's *most likely* conclusion?

A The company is becoming increasingly less solvent, as evidenced by the increase in its debt-to-equity ratio from 0.35 to 0.50 from FY3 to FY5.

B The company is becoming less liquid, as evidenced by the increase in its debt-to-equity ratio from 0.35 to 0.50 from FY3 to FY5.

C The company is becoming increasingly more liquid, as evidenced by the increase in its debt-to-equity ratio from 0.35 to 0.50 from FY3 to FY5.

7 With regard to the data in Problem 6, what would be the *most* reasonable explanation of the financial data?

A The decline in the company's equity results from a decline in the market value of this company's common shares.

B The €250 increase in the company's debt from FY3 to FY5 indicates that lenders are viewing the company as increasingly creditworthy.

C The decline in the company's equity indicates that the company may be incurring losses, paying dividends greater than income, and/or repurchasing shares.

8 An analyst observes a decrease in a company's inventory turnover. Which of the following would *most likely* explain this trend?

A The company installed a new inventory management system, allowing more efficient inventory management.

B Due to problems with obsolescent inventory last year, the company wrote off a large amount of its inventory at the beginning of the period.

C The company installed a new inventory management system but experienced some operational difficulties resulting in duplicate orders being placed with suppliers.

9 Which of the following would *best* explain an increase in receivables turnover?

A The company adopted new credit policies last year and began offering credit to customers with weak credit histories.

B Due to problems with an error in its old credit scoring system, the company had accumulated a substantial amount of uncollectible accounts and wrote off a large amount of its receivables.

C To match the terms offered by its closest competitor, the company adopted new payment terms now requiring net payment within 30 days rather than 15 days, which had been its previous requirement.

10 Brown Corporation had average days of sales outstanding of 19 days in the most recent fiscal year. Brown wants to improve its credit policies and collection practices and decrease its collection period in the next fiscal year to match the industry average of 15 days. Credit sales in the most recent fiscal year were $300 million, and Brown expects credit sales to increase to $390 million in the next fiscal year. To achieve Brown's goal of decreasing the collection period, the change in the average accounts receivable balance that must occur is *closest* to:

A +$0.41 million.

B −$0.41 million.

C −$1.22 million.

11 An analyst observes the following data for two companies:

	Company A ($)	Company B ($)
Revenue	4,500	6,000
Net income	50	1,000
Current assets	40,000	60,000
Total assets	100,000	700,000
Current liabilities	10,000	50,000
Total debt	60,000	150,000
Shareholders' equity	30,000	500,000

Which of the following choices *best* describes reasonable conclusions that the analyst might make about the two companies' ability to pay their current and long-term obligations?

A   Company A's current ratio of 4.0 indicates it is more liquid than Company B, whose current ratio is only 1.2, but Company B is more solvent, as indicated by its lower debt-to-equity ratio.

B   Company A's current ratio of 0.25 indicates it is less liquid than Company B, whose current ratio is 0.83, and Company A is also less solvent, as indicated by a debt-to-equity ratio of 200 percent compared with Company B's debt-to-equity ratio of only 30 percent.

C   Company A's current ratio of 4.0 indicates it is more liquid than Company B, whose current ratio is only 1.2, and Company A is also more solvent, as indicated by a debt-to-equity ratio of 200 percent compared with Company B's debt-to-equity ratio of only 30 percent.

The following information relates to Questions 12–15

The data in Exhibit 1 appear in the five-year summary of a major international company. A business combination with another major manufacturer took place in FY13.

Exhibit 1					

	FY10	FY11	FY12	FY13	FY14
Financial statements	GBP m	GBP m	GBP m	GBP m	GBP m
Income statements					
Revenue	4,390	3,624	3,717	8,167	11,366
Profit before interest and taxation (EBIT)	844	700	704	933	1,579
Net interest payable	−80	−54	−98	−163	−188
Taxation	−186	−195	−208	−349	−579
Minorities	−94	−99	−105	−125	−167
Profit for the year	484	352	293	296	645
Balance sheets					

	FY10	FY11	FY12	FY13	FY14
Fixed assets	3,510	3,667	4,758	10,431	11,483
Current asset investments, cash at bank and in hand	316	218	290	561	682
Other current assets	558	514	643	1,258	1,634
Total assets	4,384	4,399	5,691	12,250	13,799
Interest bearing debt (long term)	−602	−1,053	−1,535	−3,523	−3,707
Other creditors and provisions (current)	−1,223	−1,054	−1,102	−2,377	−3,108
Total liabilities	−1,825	−2,107	−2,637	−5,900	−6,815
Net assets	2,559	2,292	3,054	6,350	6,984
Shareholders' funds	2,161	2,006	2,309	5,572	6,165
Equity minority interests	398	286	745	778	819
Capital employed	2,559	2,292	3,054	6,350	6,984
Cash flow					
Working capital movements	−53	5	71	85	107
Net cash inflow from operating activities	864	859	975	1,568	2,292

Exhibit 1 (Continued)

12 The company's total assets at year-end FY9 were GBP 3,500 million. Which of the following choices *best* describes reasonable conclusions an analyst might make about the company's efficiency?

  A Comparing FY14 with FY10, the company's efficiency improved, as indicated by a total asset turnover ratio of 0.86 compared with 0.64.

  B Comparing FY14 with FY10, the company's efficiency deteriorated, as indicated by its current ratio.

  C Comparing FY14 with FY10, the company's efficiency deteriorated due to asset growth faster than turnover revenue growth.

13 Which of the following choices *best* describes reasonable conclusions an analyst might make about the company's solvency?

  A Comparing FY14 with FY10, the company's solvency improved, as indicated by an increase in its debt-to-assets ratio from 0.14 to 0.27.

  B Comparing FY14 with FY10, the company's solvency deteriorated, as indicated by a decrease in interest coverage from 10.6 to 8.4.

  C Comparing FY14 with FY10, the company's solvency improved, as indicated by the growth in its profits to GBP 645 million.

14 Which of the following choices *best* describes reasonable conclusions an analyst might make about the company's liquidity?

  A Comparing FY14 with FY10, the company's liquidity improved, as indicated by an increase in its debt-to-assets ratio from 0.14 to 0.27.

  B Comparing FY14 with FY10, the company's liquidity deteriorated, as indicated by a decrease in interest coverage from 10.6 to 8.4.

  C Comparing FY14 with FY10, the company's liquidity improved, as indicated by an increase in its current ratio from 0.71 to 0.75.

15 Which of the following choices *best* describes reasonable conclusions an analyst might make about the company's profitability?

A Comparing FY14 with FY10, the company's profitability improved, as indicated by an increase in its debt-to-assets ratio from 0.14 to 0.27.

B Comparing FY14 with FY10, the company's profitability deteriorated, as indicated by a decrease in its net profit margin from 11.0 percent to 5.7 percent.

C Comparing FY14 with FY10, the company's profitability improved, as indicated by the growth in its shareholders' equity to GBP 6,165 million.

16 Assuming no changes in other variables, which of the following would decrease ROA?

A A decrease in the effective tax rate.

B A decrease in interest expense.

C An increase in average assets.

17 An analyst compiles the following data for a company:

	FY13	FY14	FY15
ROE	19.8%	20.0%	22.0%
Return on total assets	8.1%	8.0%	7.9%
Total asset turnover	2.0	2.0	2.1

Based only on the information above, the *most* appropriate conclusion is that, over the period FY13 to FY15, the company's:

A net profit margin and financial leverage have decreased.

B net profit margin and financial leverage have increased.

C net profit margin has decreased but its financial leverage has increased.

18 A decomposition of ROE for Integra SA is as follows:

	FY12	FY11
ROE	18.90%	18.90%
Tax burden	0.70	0.75
Interest burden	0.90	0.90
EBIT margin	10.00%	10.00%
Asset turnover	1.50	1.40
Leverage	2.00	2.00

Which of the following choices *best* describes reasonable conclusions an analyst might make based on this ROE decomposition?

A Profitability and the liquidity position both improved in FY12.

B The higher average tax rate in FY12 offset the improvement in profitability, leaving ROE unchanged.

C The higher average tax rate in FY12 offset the improvement in efficiency, leaving ROE unchanged.

19 A decomposition of ROE for Company A and Company B is as follows:

	Company A		Company B	
	FY15	**FY14**	**FY15**	**FY14**
ROE	26.46%	18.90%	26.33%	18.90%
Tax burden	0.7	0.75	0.75	0.75
Interest burden	0.9	0.9	0.9	0.9
EBIT margin	7.00%	10.00%	13.00%	10.00%
Asset turnover	1.5	1.4	1.5	1.4
Leverage	4	2	2	2

An analyst is *most likely* to conclude that:

A Company A's ROE is higher than Company B's in FY15, and one explanation consistent with the data is that Company A may have purchased new, more efficient equipment.

B Company A's ROE is higher than Company B's in FY15, and one explanation consistent with the data is that Company A has made a strategic shift to a product mix with higher profit margins.

C The difference between the two companies' ROE in FY15 is very small and Company A's ROE remains similar to Company B's ROE mainly due to Company A increasing its financial leverage.

20 What does the P/E ratio measure?

A The "multiple" that the stock market places on a company's EPS.

B The relationship between dividends and market prices.

C The earnings for one common share of stock.

21 A creditor *most likely* would consider a decrease in which of the following ratios to be positive news?

A Interest coverage (times interest earned).

B Debt-to-total assets.

C Return on assets.

22 When developing forecasts, analysts should *most likely*:

A develop possibilities relying exclusively on the results of financial analysis.

B use the results of financial analysis, analysis of other information, and judgment.

C aim to develop extremely precise forecasts using the results of financial analysis.

SOLUTIONS

1 C is correct. Cross-sectional analysis involves the comparison of companies with each other for the same time period. Technical analysis uses price and volume data as the basis for investment decisions. Time-series or trend analysis is the comparison of financial data across different time periods.

2 C is correct. Solvency ratios are used to evaluate the ability of a company to meet its long-term obligations. An analyst is more likely to use activity ratios to evaluate how efficiently a company uses its assets. An analyst is more likely to use liquidity ratios to evaluate the ability of a company to meet its short-term obligations.

3 A is correct. The current ratio is a liquidity ratio. It compares the net amount of current assets expected to be converted into cash within the year with liabilities falling due in the same period. A current ratio of 1.0 would indicate that the company would have just enough current assets to pay current liabilities.

4 C is correct. The fixed charge coverage ratio is a coverage ratio that relates known fixed charges or obligations to a measure of operating profit or cash flow generated by the company. Coverage ratios, a category of solvency ratios, measure the ability of a company to cover its payments related to debt and leases.

5 C is correct. The analyst is *unlikely* to reach the conclusion given in Statement C because days of sales outstanding increased from 23 days in FY1 to 25 days in FY2 to 28 days in FY3, indicating that the time required to collect receivables has increased over the period. This is a negative factor for Spherion's liquidity. By contrast, days of inventory on hand dropped over the period FY1 to FY3, a positive for liquidity. The company's increase in days payable, from 35 days to 40 days, shortened its cash conversion cycle, thus also contributing to improved liquidity.

6 A is correct. The company is becoming increasingly less solvent, as evidenced by its debt-to-equity ratio increasing from 0.35 to 0.50 from FY3 to FY5. The amount of a company's debt and equity do not provide direct information about the company's liquidity position.

   Debt to equity:

   FY5: 2,000/4,000 = 0.5000

   FY4: 1,900/4,500 = 0.4222

   FY3: 1,750/5,000 = 0.3500

7 C is correct. The decline in the company's equity indicates that the company may be incurring losses, paying dividends greater than income, or repurchasing shares. Recall that Beginning equity + New shares issuance − Shares repurchased + Comprehensive income − Dividends = Ending equity. The book value of a company's equity is not affected by changes in the market value of its common stock. An increased amount of lending does not necessarily indicate that lenders view a company as increasingly creditworthy. Creditworthiness is not evaluated based on how much a company has increased its debt but rather on its willingness and ability to pay its obligations. (Its financial strength is indicated by its solvency, liquidity, profitability, efficiency, and other aspects of credit analysis.)

8 C is correct. The company's problems with its inventory management system causing duplicate orders would likely result in a higher amount of inventory and would, therefore, result in a decrease in inventory turnover. A more efficient inventory management system and a write off of inventory at the beginning of

the period would both likely decrease the average inventory for the period (the denominator of the inventory turnover ratio), thus increasing the ratio rather than decreasing it.

9 B is correct. A write off of receivables would decrease the average amount of accounts receivable (the denominator of the receivables turnover ratio), thus increasing this ratio. Customers with weaker credit are more likely to make payments more slowly or to pose collection difficulties, which would likely increase the average amount of accounts receivable and thus decrease receivables turnover. Longer payment terms would likely increase the average amount of accounts receivable and thus decrease receivables turnover.

10 A is correct. The average accounts receivable balances (actual and desired) must be calculated to determine the desired change. The average accounts receivable balance can be calculated as an average day's credit sales times the DSO. For the most recent fiscal year, the average accounts receivable balance is $15.62 million [= ($300,000,000/365) × 19]. The desired average accounts receivable balance for the next fiscal year is $16.03 million (= ($390,000,000/365) × 15). This is an increase of $0.41 million (= 16.03 million − 15.62 million). An alternative approach is to calculate the turnover and divide sales by turnover to determine the average accounts receivable balance. Turnover equals 365 divided by DSO. Turnover is 19.21 (= 365/19) for the most recent fiscal year and is targeted to be 24.33 (= 365/15) for the next fiscal year. The average accounts receivable balances are $15.62 million (= $300,000,000/19.21), and $16.03 million (= $390,000,000/24.33). The change is an increase in receivables of $0.41 million

11 A is correct. Company A's current ratio of 4.0 (= $40,000/$10,000) indicates it is more liquid than Company B, whose current ratio is only 1.2 (= $60,000/$50,000). Company B is more solvent, as indicated by its lower debt-to-equity ratio of 30 percent (= $150,000/$500,000) compared with Company A's debt-to-equity ratio of 200 percent (= $60,000/$30,000).

12 C is correct. The company's efficiency deteriorated, as indicated by the decline in its total asset turnover ratio from 1.11 {= 4,390/[(4,384 + 3,500)/2]} for FY10 to 0.87 {= 11,366/[(12,250 + 13,799)/2]} for FY14. The decline in the total asset turnover ratio resulted from an increase in average total assets from GBP3,942 [= (4,384 + 3,500)/2] for FY10 to GBP13,024.5 for FY14, an increase of 230 percent, compared with an increase in revenue from GBP4,390 in FY10 to GBP11,366 in FY14, an increase of only 159 percent. The current ratio is not an indicator of efficiency.

13 B is correct. Comparing FY14 with FY10, the company's solvency deteriorated, as indicated by a decrease in interest coverage from 10.6 (= 844/80) in FY10 to 8.4 (= 1,579/188) in FY14. The debt-to-asset ratio increased from 0.14 (= 602/4,384) in FY10 to 0.27 (= 3,707/13,799) in FY14. This is also indicative of deteriorating solvency. In isolation, the amount of profits does not provide enough information to assess solvency.

14 C is correct. Comparing FY14 with FY10, the company's liquidity improved, as indicated by an increase in its current ratio from 0.71 [= (316 + 558)/1,223] in FY10 to 0.75 [= (682 + 1,634)/3,108] in FY14. Note, however, comparing only current investments with the level of current liabilities shows a decline in liquidity from 0.26 (= 316/1,223) in FY10 to 0.22 (= 682/3,108) in FY14. Debt-to-assets ratio and interest coverage are measures of solvency not liquidity.

15 B is correct. Comparing FY14 with FY10, the company's profitability deteriorated, as indicated by a decrease in its net profit margin from 11.0 percent (=
484/4,390) to 5.7 percent (= 645/11,366). Debt-to-assets ratio is a measure of
solvency not an indicator of profitability. Growth in shareholders' equity, in
isolation, does not provide enough information to assess profitability.

16 C is correct. Assuming no changes in other variables, an increase in average
assets (an increase in the denominator) would decrease ROA. A decrease in
either the effective tax rate or interest expense, assuming no changes in other
variables, would increase ROA.

17 C is correct. The company's net profit margin has decreased and its financial
leverage has increased. ROA = Net profit margin × Total asset turnover. ROA
decreased over the period despite the increase in total asset turnover; therefore,
the net profit margin must have decreased.

ROE = Return on assets × Financial leverage. ROE increased over the period
despite the drop in ROA; therefore, financial leverage must have increased.

18 C is correct. The increase in the average tax rate in FY12, as indicated by the
decrease in the value of the tax burden (the tax burden equals one minus the
average tax rate), offset the improvement in efficiency indicated by higher asset
turnover) leaving ROE unchanged. The EBIT margin, measuring profitability,
was unchanged in FY12 and no information is given on liquidity.

19 C is correct. The difference between the two companies' ROE in 2010 is very
small and is mainly the result of Company A's increase in its financial leverage,
indicated by the increase in its Assets/Equity ratio from 2 to 4. The impact of
efficiency on ROE is identical for the two companies, as indicated by both companies' asset turnover ratios of 1.5. Furthermore, if Company A had purchased
newer equipment to replace older, depreciated equipment, then the company's
asset turnover ratio (computed as sales/assets) would have declined, assuming
constant sales. Company A has experienced a significant decline in its operating
margin, from 10 percent to 7 percent which, all else equal, would not suggest
that it is selling more products with higher profit margins.

20 A is correct. The P/E ratio measures the "multiple" that the stock market places
on a company's EPS.

21 B is correct. In general, a creditor would consider a decrease in debt to total
assets as positive news. A higher level of debt in a company's capital structure
increases the risk of default and will, in general, result in higher borrowing
costs for the company to compensate lenders for assuming greater credit risk. A
decrease in either interest coverage or return on assets is likely to be considered
negative news.

22 B is correct. The results of an analyst's financial analysis are integral to the process of developing forecasts, along with the analysis of other information and
judgment of the analysts. Forecasts are not limited to a single point estimate but
should involve a range of possibilities.

Financial Reporting and Analysis

Inventories, Long-lived Assets, Income Taxes, and Non-current Liabilities

The readings in this study session examine the financial reporting for specific categories of assets and liabilities. Analysts must understand the effects of alternative financial reporting policies on financial statements and ratios and be able to execute appropriate adjustments to enhance comparability between companies. In addition, analysts must be alert to differences between a company's reported financial statements and economic reality.

The description and measurement of inventories require careful attention because investment in inventories is frequently the largest current asset for merchandising and manufacturing companies. For these companies, the measurement of inventory cost (i.e., cost of sales) is a critical factor in determining gross profit and other measures of profitability. Long-lived operating assets are often the largest category of assets on a company's balance sheet. The analyst needs to scrutinize management's choices with respect to recognizing expenses associated with these operating assets because of the potentially large effect such choices can have on reported earnings and the opportunities for financial statement manipulation.

A company's accounting policies (such as depreciation choices) can cause differences in taxes reported in financial statements and taxes reported on tax returns. The reading "Income Taxes" describes several issues relating to deferred taxes.

Non-current liabilities affect a company's liquidity and solvency and have consequences for its long-term growth and viability. The notes to the financial statements must be carefully reviewed to ensure that all potential liabilities (e.g., leasing arrangements and other contractual commitments) are appropriately evaluated for their conformity to economic reality. Adjustments to the financial statements may be required to achieve comparability when evaluating several companies.

Note: New rulings and/or pronouncements issued after the publication of the readings on financial reporting and analysis may cause some of the information in these readings to become dated. Candidates are expected to be familiar with the overall analytical framework contained in the study session readings, as well as the implications of alternative accounting methods for financial analysis and valuation, as provided in the assigned readings. Candidates are not responsible for changes that occur after the material was written.

READING ASSIGNMENTS

Inventories

by Michael A. Broihahn, CFA

LEARNING OUTCOMES

Mastery	*The candidate should be able to:*
☐	**a.** distinguish between costs included in inventories and costs recognized as expenses in the period in which they are incurred;
☐	**b.** describe different inventory valuation methods (cost formulas);
☐	**c.** calculate cost of sales and ending inventory using different inventory valuation methods and explain the effect of the inventory valuation method choice on gross profit;
☐	**d.** calculate and compare cost of sales, gross profit, and ending inventory using perpetual and periodic inventory systems;
☐	**e.** compare cost of sales, ending inventory, and gross profit using different inventory valuation methods;
☐	**f.** describe the measurement of inventory at the lower of cost and net realisable value;
☐	**g.** describe the financial statement presentation of and disclosures relating to inventories;
☐	**h.** calculate and interpret ratios used to evaluate inventory management.

Note: New rulings and/ or pronouncements issues after the publication of the readings in financial reporting and analysis may cause some of the information in these readings to become dated. Candidates are expected to be familiar with the overall analytical framework contained in the study session readings, as well as the implications of alternative accounting methods for financial analysis and valuation, as provided in the assigned readings. Candidates are not responsible for changes that occur after the material was written.

1   INTRODUCTION

Merchandising and manufacturing companies generate revenues and profits through the sale of inventory. Further, inventory may represent a significant asset on these companies' balance sheets. Merchandisers (wholesalers and retailers) purchase inventory, ready for sale, from manufacturers and thus account for only one type of inventory—finished goods inventory. Manufacturers, however, purchase raw materials from suppliers and then add value by transforming the raw materials into finished goods. They typically classify inventory into three different categories:[1] raw materials, work in progress,[2] and finished goods. Work-in-progress inventories have started the conversion process from raw materials but are not yet finished goods ready for sale. Manufacturers may report either the separate carrying amounts of their raw materials, work-in-progress, and finished goods inventories on the balance sheet or simply the total inventory amount. If the latter approach is used, the company must then disclose the carrying amounts of its raw materials, work-in-progress, and finished goods inventories in a footnote to the financial statements.

An important consideration in calculating profits for merchandising and manufacturing companies is measuring the cost of sales (cost of goods sold).[3] The measurement process would be simple if inventory costs remained constant over time; however, that is not economic reality. Financial analysis would also be much easier if all companies used the same inventory valuation method. International Financial Reporting Standards (IFRS) and U.S. generally accepted accounting principles (U.S. GAAP), however, allow more than one inventory valuation method. Inventory valuation methods are referred to as cost formulas and cost flow assumptions under IFRS and U.S. GAAP, respectively. Differences in the choice of inventory valuation method can result in significantly different amounts being assigned to the cost of sales and inventory.

IFRS allow companies to choose from three cost formulas: specific identification; weighted average cost; and first-in, first-out (FIFO). U.S. GAAP allow the same three cost flow assumptions but also allow a fourth method: last-in, first-out (LIFO). Analysts must clearly understand the various inventory valuation methods and the related impact on financial statements and financial ratios in order to evaluate a company's performance over time and relative to industry peers. The company's financial statements and related notes provide important information that the analyst can use in assessing the impact of the choice of inventory valuation method on financial statements and financial ratios.

This reading is organized as follows: Section 2 discusses the costs that are included in inventory and the costs that are recognised as expenses in the period in which they are incurred. Section 3 discusses inventory valuation methods and the measurement of ending inventory and cost of sales under each method. Section 4 discusses the measurement and reporting of inventory when its value changes. Section 5 describes the presentation of inventories on the financial statements and their related disclosures. Section 6 focuses on the calculation and interpretation of inventory management ratios. A summary and practice problems conclude the reading.

---

1 Other classifications are possible. Inventory classifications should be appropriate to the entity.
2 This category is commonly referred to as *work in process* under U.S. GAAP.
3 Typically, *cost of sales* is IFRS terminology and *cost of goods sold* is U.S. GAAP terminology.

COST OF INVENTORIES

2

Under IFRS, the costs to include in inventories are "all costs of purchase, costs of conversion, and other costs incurred in bringing the inventories to their present location and condition."[4] The costs of purchase include the purchase price, import and tax-related duties, transport, insurance during transport, handling, and other costs directly attributable to the acquisition of finished goods, materials, and services. Trade discounts, rebates, and similar items reduce the price paid and the costs of purchase. The costs of conversion include costs directly related to the units produced, such as direct labour, and fixed and variable overhead costs.[5] Including these product-related costs in inventory (i.e., as an asset) means that they will not be recognised as an expense (i.e., as cost of sales) on the income statement until the inventory is sold. U.S. GAAP provide a similar description of the costs to be included in inventory.[6]

Both IFRS and U.S. GAAP exclude the following costs from inventory: abnormal costs incurred as a result of waste of materials, labour or other production conversion inputs, any storage costs (unless required as part of the production process), and all administrative overhead and selling costs. These excluded costs are treated as expenses and recognised on the income statement in the period in which they are incurred. Including costs in inventory defers their recognition as an expense on the income statement until the inventory is sold. Therefore, including costs in inventory that should be expensed will overstate profitability on the income statement (because of the inappropriate deferral of cost recognition) and create an overstated inventory value on the balance sheet.

EXAMPLE 1

Treatment of Inventory-Related Costs

Acme Enterprises, a hypothetical company that prepares its financial statements in accordance with IFRS, manufactures tables. In 2009, the factory produced 900,000 finished tables and scrapped 1,000 tables. For the finished tables, raw material costs were €9 million, direct labour conversion costs were €18 million, and production overhead costs were €1.8 million. The 1,000 scrapped tables (attributable to abnormal waste) had a total production cost of €30,000 (€10,000 raw material costs and €20,000 conversion costs; these costs are not included in the €9 million raw material and €19.8 million total conversion costs of the finished tables). During the year, Acme spent €1 million for freight delivery charges on raw materials and €500,000 for storing finished goods inventory. Acme does not have any work-in-progress inventory at the end of the year.

1 What costs should be included in inventory in 2009?

2 What costs should be expensed in 2009?

Solution to 1:

Total inventory costs for 2009 are as follows:

---

4 International Accounting Standard (IAS) 2 [Inventories].
5 Fixed production overhead costs (depreciation, factory maintenance, and factory management and administration) represent indirect costs of production that remain relatively constant regardless of the volume of production. Variable production overhead costs are indirect production costs (indirect labour and materials) that vary with the volume of production.
6 FASB Accounting Standards Codification™ (ASC) Topic 330 [Inventory].

Raw materials	€9,000,000
Direct labour	18,000,000
Production overhead	1,800,000
Transportation for raw materials	1,000,000
Total inventory costs	€29,800,000

Solution to 2:

Total costs that should be expensed (not included in inventory) are as follows:

Abnormal waste	€30,000
Storage of finished goods inventory	500,000
Total	€530,000

3   INVENTORY VALUATION METHODS

Generally, inventory purchase costs and manufacturing conversion costs change over time. As a result, the allocation of total inventory costs (i.e., cost of goods available for sale) between cost of sales on the income statement and inventory on the balance sheet will vary depending on the inventory valuation method used by the company. As mentioned in the introduction, inventory valuation methods are referred to as cost formulas and cost flow assumptions under IFRS and U.S. GAAP, respectively. If the choice of method results in more cost being allocated to cost of sales and less cost being allocated to inventory than would be the case with other methods, the chosen method will cause, in the current year, reported gross profit, net income, and inventory carrying amount to be lower than if alternative methods had been used. Accounting for inventory, and consequently the allocation of costs, thus has a direct impact on financial statements and their comparability.

Both IFRS and U.S. GAAP allow companies to use the following inventory valuation methods: specific identification; first-in, first-out (FIFO); and weighted average cost. U.S. GAAP allow companies to use an additional method: last-in, first-out (LIFO). A company must use the same inventory valuation method for all items that have a similar nature and use. For items with a different nature or use, a different inventory valuation method can be used.[7] When items are sold, the carrying amount of the inventory is recognised as an expense (cost of sales) according to the cost formula (cost flow assumption) in use.

Specific identification is used for inventory items that are not ordinarily inter-changeable, whereas FIFO, weighted average cost, and LIFO are typically used when there are large numbers of interchangeable items in inventory. Specific identification matches the actual historical costs of the specific inventory items to their physical flow; the costs remain in inventory until the actual identifiable inventory is sold. FIFO, weighted average cost, and LIFO are based on cost flow assumptions. Under these methods, companies must make certain assumptions about which goods are sold

---

7 For example, if a clothing manufacturer produces both a retail line and one-of-a-kind designer garments, the retail line might be valued using FIFO and the designer garments using specific identification.

and which goods remain in ending inventory. As a result, the allocation of costs to the units sold and to the units in ending inventory can be different from the physical movement of the items.

The choice of inventory valuation method would be largely irrelevant if inventory costs remained constant or relatively constant over time. Given relatively constant prices, the allocation of costs between cost of goods sold and ending inventory would be very similar under each of the four methods. Given changing price levels, however, the choice of inventory valuation method can have a significant impact on the amount of reported cost of sales and inventory. And the reported cost of sales and inventory balances affect other items, such as gross profit, net income, current assets, and total assets.

3.1 Specific Identification

The specific identification method is used for inventory items that are not ordinarily interchangeable and for goods that have been produced and segregated for specific projects. This method is also commonly used for expensive goods that are uniquely identifiable, such as precious gemstones. Under this method, the cost of sales and the cost of ending inventory reflect the actual costs incurred to purchase (or manufacture) the items specifically identified as sold and the items specifically identified as remaining in inventory. Therefore, this method matches the physical flow of the specific items sold and remaining in inventory to their actual cost.

3.2 First-In, First-Out (FIFO)

FIFO assumes that the oldest goods purchased (or manufactured) are sold first and the newest goods purchased (or manufactured) remain in ending inventory. In other words, the first units included in inventory are assumed to be the first units sold from inventory. Therefore, cost of sales reflects the cost of goods in beginning inventory plus the cost of items purchased (or manufactured) earliest in the accounting period, and the value of ending inventory reflects the costs of goods purchased (or manufactured) more recently. In periods of rising prices, the costs assigned to the units in ending inventory are higher than the costs assigned to the units sold. Conversely, in periods of declining prices, the costs assigned to the units in ending inventory are lower than the costs assigned to the units sold.

3.3 Weighted Average Cost

Weighted average cost assigns the average cost of the goods available for sale (beginning inventory plus purchase, conversion, and other costs) during the accounting period to the units that are sold as well as to the units in ending inventory. In an accounting period, the weighted average cost per unit is calculated as the total cost of the units available for sale divided by the total number of units available for sale in the period (Total cost of goods available for sale/Total units available for sale).

3.4 Last-In, First-Out (LIFO)

LIFO is permitted only under U.S. GAAP. This method assumes that the newest goods purchased (or manufactured) are sold first and the oldest goods purchased (or manufactured), including beginning inventory, remain in ending inventory. In other words, the last units included in inventory are assumed to be the first units sold from inventory. Therefore, cost of sales reflects the cost of goods purchased (or manufactured) more recently, and the value of ending inventory reflects the cost of older goods. In periods of rising prices, the costs assigned to the units in ending inventory are lower than the costs assigned to the units sold. Conversely, in periods of declining prices, the costs assigned to the units in ending inventory are higher than the costs assigned to the units sold.

3.5 Calculation of Cost of Sales, Gross Profit, and Ending Inventory

In periods of changing prices, the allocation of total inventory costs (i.e., cost of goods available for sale) between cost of sales on the income statement and inventory on the balance sheet will vary depending on the inventory valuation method used by the company. The following example illustrates how cost of sales, gross profit, and ending inventory differ based on the choice of inventory valuation method.

EXAMPLE 2

Inventory Cost Flow Illustration for the Specific Identification, Weighted Average Cost, FIFO, and LIFO Methods

Global Sales, Inc. (GSI) is a hypothetical distributor of consumer products, including bars of violet essence soap. The soap is sold by the kilogram. GSI began operations in 2009, during which it purchased and received initially 100,000 kg of soap at 110 yuan/kg, then 200,000 kg of soap at 100 yuan/kg, and finally 300,000 kg of soap at 90 yuan/kg. GSI sold 520,000 kg of soap at 240 yuan/kg. GSI stores its soap in its warehouse so that soap from each shipment received is readily identifiable. During 2009, the entire 100,000 kg from the first shipment received, 180,000 kg of the second shipment received, and 240,000 kg of the final shipment received was sent to customers. Answers to the following questions should be rounded to the nearest 1,000 yuan.

1 What are the reported cost of sales, gross profit, and ending inventory balances for 2009 under the specific identification method?

2 What are the reported cost of sales, gross profit, and ending inventory balances for 2009 under the weighted average cost method?

3 What are the reported cost of sales, gross profit, and ending inventory balances for 2009 under the FIFO method?

4 What are the reported cost of sales, gross profit, and ending inventory balances for 2009 under the LIFO method?

Solution to 1:

Under the specific identification method, the physical flow of the specific inventory items sold is matched to their actual cost.

Sales = 520,000 × 240 = 124,800,000 yuan

Cost of sales = (100,000 × 110) + (180,000 × 100) + (240,000 × 90) = 50,600,000 yuan

Gross profit = 124,800,000 − 50,600,000 = 74,200,000 yuan

Ending inventory = (20,000 × 100) + (60,000 × 90) = 7,400,000 yuan

Note that in spite of the segregation of inventory within the warehouse, it would be inappropriate to use specific identification for this inventory of interchangeable items. The use of specific identification could potentially result in earnings manipulation through the shipment decision.

Solution to 2:

Under the weighted average cost method, costs are allocated to cost of sales and ending inventory by using a weighted average mix of the actual costs incurred for all inventory items. The weighted average cost per unit is determined by dividing the total cost of goods available for sale by the number of units available for sale.

Weighted average cost = $[(100,000 \times 110) + (200,000 \times 100) + (300,000 \times 90)]/600,000$ = 96.667 yuan/kg

Sales = $520,000 \times 240$ = 124,800,000 yuan

Cost of sales = $520,000 \times 96.667$ = 50,267,000 yuan

Gross profit = $124,800,000 - 50,267,000$ = 74,533,000 yuan

Ending inventory = $80,000 \times 96.667$ = 7,733,000 yuan

Solution to 3:

Under the FIFO method, the oldest inventory units acquired are assumed to be the first units sold. Ending inventory, therefore, is assumed to consist of those inventory units most recently acquired.

Sales = $520,000 \times 240$ = 124,800,000 yuan

Cost of sales = $(100,000 \times 110) + (200,000 \times 100) + (220,000 \times 90)$ = 50,800,000 yuan

Gross profit = $124,800,000 - 50,800,000$ = 74,000,000 yuan

Ending inventory = $80,000 \times 90$ = 7,200,000 yuan

Solution to 4:

Under the LIFO method, the newest inventory units acquired are assumed to be the first units sold. Ending inventory, therefore, is assumed to consist of the oldest inventory units.

Sales = $520,000 \times 240$ = 124,800,000 yuan

Cost of sales = $(20,000 \times 110) + (200,000 \times 100) + (300,000 \times 90)$ = 49,200,000 yuan

Gross profit = $124,800,000 - 49,200,000$ = 75,600,000 yuan

Ending inventory = $80,000 \times 110$ = 8,800,000 yuan

The following table (in thousands of yuan) summarizes the cost of sales, the ending inventory, and the cost of goods available for sale that were calculated for each of the four inventory valuation methods. Note that in the first year of operation, the total cost of goods available for sale is the same under all four methods. Subsequently, the cost of goods available for sale will typically differ because beginning inventories will differ. Also shown is the gross profit figure for each of the four methods. Because the cost of a kg of soap declined over the period, LIFO had the highest ending inventory amount, the lowest cost of sales, and the highest gross profit. FIFO had the lowest ending inventory amount, the highest cost of sales, and the lowest gross profit.

Inventory Valuation Method	Specific ID	Weighted Average Cost	FIFO	LIFO
Cost of sales	50,600	50,267	50,800	49,200
Ending inventory	7,400	7,733	7,200	8,800
Total cost of goods available for sale	58,000	58,000	58,000	58,000
Gross profit	74,200	74,533	74,000	75,600

3.6 Periodic versus Perpetual Inventory Systems

Companies typically record changes to inventory in one of two ways. Under a periodic inventory system, a company determines the quantity of inventory on hand periodically. Purchases are recorded in a purchases account. The total of purchases and beginning inventory is the amount of goods available for sale during the period. The ending inventory amount is subtracted from the goods available for sale to arrive at the cost of sales. The quantity of goods in ending inventory is usually obtained or verified through a physical count of the units in inventory. Under a perpetual inventory system, changes in the inventory account are continuously updated. Purchases and sales of goods are recorded directly in inventory as they occur.

The use of periodic versus perpetual inventory systems will arrive at the same values for cost of sales and ending inventory using the specific identification and FIFO methods of inventory valuation. The choice of system, however, will potentially affect the ending inventory and cost of sales when either the LIFO or weighted average cost method is used. Example 3 illustrates the impact of the choice of system under LIFO.

EXAMPLE 3

Perpetual versus Periodic Inventory Systems

If GSI (the company in Example 2) had used a perpetual inventory system, the timing of purchases and sales would affect the amounts of cost of sales and inventory. Below is a record of the purchases, sales, and quantity of inventory on hand after the transaction in 2009.

Date	Purchased	Sold	Inventory on Hand
5 January	100,000 kg at 110 yuan/kg		100,000 kg
1 February		80,000 kg at 240 yuan/kg	20,000 kg
8 March	200,000 kg at 100 yuan/kg		220,000 kg
6 April		100,000 kg at 240 yuan/kg	120,000 kg
23 May		60,000 kg at 240 yuan/kg	60,000 kg
7 July		40,000 kg at 240 yuan/kg	20,000 kg
2 August	300,000 kg at 90 yuan/kg		320,000 kg
5 September		70,000 kg at 240 yuan/kg	250,000 kg
17 November		90,000 kg at 240 yuan/kg	160,000 kg

Date	Purchased	Sold	Inventory on Hand
8 December		80,000 kg at 240 yuan/kg	80,000 kg
	Total goods available for sale = 58,000,000 yuan	Total sales = 124,800,000 yuan	

The amounts for total goods available for sale and sales are the same under either the perpetual or periodic system in this first year of operation. The carrying amount of the ending inventory, however, may differ because the perpetual system will apply LIFO continuously throughout the year. Under the periodic system, it was assumed that the ending inventory was composed of 80,000 units of the oldest inventory, which cost 110 yuan/kg.

What are the ending inventory, cost of sales, and gross profit amounts using the perpetual system and the LIFO method? How do these compare with the amounts using the periodic system and the LIFO method, as in Example 2?

Solution:

The carrying amounts of the inventory at the different time points using the perpetual inventory system are as follows:

Date	Quantity on Hand	Quantities and Cost	Carrying Amount
5 January	100,000 kg	100,000 kg at 110 yuan/kg	11,000,000 yuan
1 February	20,000 kg	20,000 kg at 110 yuan/kg	2,200,000 yuan
8 March	220,000 kg	20,000 kg at 110 yuan/kg + 200,000 kg at 100 yuan/kg	22,200,000 yuan
6 April	120,000 kg	20,000 kg at 110 yuan/kg + 100,000 kg at 100 yuan/kg	12,200,000 yuan
23 May	60,000 kg	20,000 kg at 110 yuan/kg + 40,000 kg at 100 yuan/kg	6,200,000 yuan
7 July	20,000 kg	20,000 kg at 110 yuan/kg	2,200,000 yuan
2 August	320,000 kg	20,000 kg at 110 yuan/kg + 300,000 kg at 90 yuan/kg	29,200,000 yuan
5 September	250,000 kg	20,000 kg at 110 yuan/kg + 230,000 kg at 90 yuan/kg	22,900,000 yuan
17 November	160,000 kg	20,000 kg at 110 yuan/kg + 140,000 kg at 90 yuan/kg	14,800,000 yuan
8 December	80,000 kg	20,000 kg at 110 yuan/kg + 60,000 kg at 90 yuan/kg	7,600,000 yuan

Perpetual system

Sales = 520,000 × 240 = 124,800,000 yuan

Cost of sales = 58,000,000 − 7,600,000 = 50,400,000 yuan

Gross profit = 124,800,000 − 50,400,000 = 74,400,000 yuan

Ending inventory = 7,600,000 yuan

Periodic system from Example 2

Sales = 520,000 × 240 = 124,800,000 yuan

Cost of sales = (20,000 × 110) + (200,000 × 100) + (300,000 × 90) = 49,200,000 yuan

Gross profit = 124,800,000 − 49,200,000 = 75,600,000 yuan

Ending inventory = 80,000 × 110 = 8,800,000 yuan

In this example, the ending inventory amount is lower under the perpetual system because only 20,000 kg of the oldest inventory with the highest cost is assumed to remain in inventory. The cost of sales is higher and the gross profit is lower under the perpetual system compared to the periodic system.

3.7 Comparison of Inventory Valuation Methods

As shown in Example 2, the allocation of the total cost of goods available for sale to cost of sales on the income statement and to ending inventory on the balance sheet varies under the different inventory valuation methods. In an environment of declining inventory unit costs and constant or increasing inventory quantities, FIFO (in comparison with weighted average cost or LIFO) will allocate a higher amount of the total cost of goods available for sale to cost of sales on the income statement and a lower amount to ending inventory on the balance sheet. Accordingly, because cost of sales will be higher under FIFO, a company's gross profit, operating profit, and income before taxes will be lower.

Conversely, in an environment of rising inventory unit costs and constant or increasing inventory quantities, FIFO (in comparison with weighted average cost or LIFO) will allocate a lower amount of the total cost of goods available for sale to cost of sales on the income statement and a higher amount to ending inventory on the balance sheet. Accordingly, because cost of sales will be lower under FIFO, a company's gross profit, operating profit, and income before taxes will be higher.

The carrying amount of inventories under FIFO will more closely reflect current replacement values because inventories are assumed to consist of the most recently purchased items. The cost of sales under LIFO will more closely reflect current replacement value. LIFO ending inventory amounts are typically not reflective of current replacement value because the ending inventory is assumed to be the oldest inventory and costs are allocated accordingly.

4 MEASUREMENT OF INVENTORY VALUE

Significant financial risk can result from the holding of inventory. The cost of inventory may not be recoverable because of spoilage, obsolescence, or declines in selling prices. Under IFRS, "inventories shall be measured at the lower of cost and net realisable value."[8] **Net realisable value** is the estimated selling price in the ordinary course of business less the estimated costs necessary to get the inventory in condition for sale and to make the sale. The assessment of net realisable value is typically done by item or by groups of similar or related items. In the event that the value of inventory declines below the carrying amount on the balance sheet, the inventory carrying amount must be written down to its net realisable value and the loss (reduction in value) recognised as an expense on the income statement. Rather than write down the inventory through the inventory account, a company may use an inventory valuation allowance (reserve) account. The inventory amount net of the valuation allowance equals the carrying amount of the inventory after write-downs.

In each subsequent period, a new assessment of net realisable value is made. Reversal (limited to the amount of the original write-down) is required for a subsequent increase in value of inventory previously written down. The amount of any

---

8 IAS 2, paragraph 9.

reversal of any write-down of inventory arising from an increase in net realisable value is recognised as a reduction in cost of sales (a reduction in the amount of inventories recognised as an expense).

Under U.S. GAAP, inventory is measured at the lower of cost or market.[9] Market value is defined as current replacement cost subject to upper and lower limits. Market value cannot exceed net realisable value (selling price less reasonably estimated costs of completion and disposal). The lower limit of market value is net realisable value less a normal profit margin. Any write-down reduces the value of the inventory, and the loss in value (expense) is generally reflected in the income statement in cost of goods sold. U.S. GAAP prohibit the reversal of a write-down; this rule is different from the treatment under IFRS.

IAS 2 does not apply to the inventories of producers of agricultural and forest products, producers of minerals and mineral products, and commodity broker–traders whose inventories are measured at net realisable value (fair value less costs to sell and, if necessary, complete) according to well-established industry practices. If an active market exists for these products, the quoted market price in that market is the appropriate basis for determining the fair value of that asset. If an active market does not exist, a company may use market-determined prices or values (such as the most recent market transaction price) when available. Changes in the value of inventory (increases or decreases) are recognised in profit or loss in the period of the change. U.S. GAAP are similar to IFRS in the treatment of inventories of agricultural and forest products and mineral ores. Mark-to-market inventory accounting is allowed for refined bullion of precious metals.

EXAMPLE 4

Accounting for Declines and Recoveries of Inventory Value

Acme Enterprises, a hypothetical company, manufactures computers and prepares its financial statements in accordance with IFRS. In 2008, the cost of ending inventory was €5.2 million but its net realisable value was €4.9 million. The current replacement cost of the inventory is €4.7 million. This figure exceeds the net realisable value less a normal profit margin. In 2009, the net realisable value of Acme's inventory was €0.5 million greater than the carrying amount.

1 What was the effect of the write-down on Acme's 2008 financial statements? What was the effect of the recovery on Acme's 2009 financial statements?

2 Under U.S. GAAP, what would be the effects of the write-down on Acme's 2008 financial statements and of the recovery on Acme's 2009 financial statements?

3 What would be the effect of the recovery on Acme's 2009 financial statements if Acme's inventory were agricultural products instead of computers?

---

9 ASC Section 330-10-35 [Inventory–Overall–Subsequent Measurement].

Solution to 1:

For 2008, Acme would write its inventory down to €4.9 million and record the change in value of €0.3 million as an expense on the income statement. For 2009, Acme would increase the carrying amount of its inventory and reduce the cost of sales by €0.3 million (the recovery is limited to the amount of the original write-down).

Solution to 2:

Under U.S. GAAP, for 2008, Acme would write its inventory down to €4.7 million and typically include the change in value of €0.5 million in cost of goods sold on the income statement. For 2009, Acme would not reverse the write-down.

Solution to 3:

If Acme's inventory were agricultural products instead of computers, inventory would be measured at net realisable value and Acme would, therefore, increase inventory by and record a gain of €0.5 million for 2009.

5   PRESENTATION AND DISCLOSURE

IFRS require the following financial statement disclosures concerning inventory:

a   the accounting policies adopted in measuring inventories, including the cost formula (inventory valuation method) used;

b   the total carrying amount of inventories and the carrying amount in classifications (for example, merchandise, raw materials, production supplies, work in progress, and finished goods) appropriate to the entity;

c   the carrying amount of inventories carried at fair value less costs to sell;

d   the amount of inventories recognised as an expense during the period (cost of sales);

e   the amount of any write-down of inventories recognised as an expense in the period;

f   the amount of any reversal of any write-down that is recognised as a reduction in cost of sales in the period;

g   the circumstances or events that led to the reversal of a write-down of inventories; and

h   the carrying amount of inventories pledged as security for liabilities.

Inventory-related disclosures under U.S. GAAP are very similar to the disclosures above, except that requirements f) and g) are not relevant because U.S. GAAP do not permit the reversal of prior-year inventory write-downs. U.S. GAAP also require disclosure of significant estimates applicable to inventories and of any material amount of income resulting from the liquidation of LIFO inventory.[10]

---

10   LIFO liquidation is a CFA Level II curriculum topic.

5.1 Changes in Inventory Valuation Method

In rare situations, a company may decide that it is appropriate to change its inventory valuation method (cost formula). Under IFRS,[11] a change in accounting policy (including a change in cost formula) is acceptable only if the change results in the financial statements providing reliable and more relevant information about the effects of transactions, other events, or conditions on the business entity's financial position, financial performance, or cash flows. Changes in accounting policy are accounted for retrospectively. If the change is justifiable, historical information is restated for all accounting periods (typically the previous one or two years) that are presented for comparability purposes with the current year in annual financial reports. Adjustments of financial statement information relating to accounting periods prior to those presented are reflected in the beginning balance of retained earnings for the earliest year presented for comparison purposes. This retrospective restatement requirement enhances the comparability of financial statements over time. An exemption to the retrospective restatement requirement applies when it is impracticable to determine either the period-specific effects or the cumulative effect of the change.

Under U.S. GAAP, a company making a change in inventory valuation method is required to explain why the newly adopted inventory valuation method is superior and preferable to the old method. In addition, U.S. tax regulations may also restrict changes in inventory valuation methods and require permission from the Internal Revenue Service (IRS) prior to implementation. If a company decides to change from LIFO to another inventory method, U.S. GAAP require a retrospective restatement of inventory and retained earnings. Historical financial statements are also restated for the effects of the change. If a company decides to change to the LIFO method, it must do so on a prospective basis. Retrospective adjustments are not made to the financial statements. Instead, the carrying value of inventory under the old method will become the initial LIFO layer in the year of LIFO adoption.

EVALUATION OF INVENTORY MANAGEMENT   6

The choice of inventory valuation method impacts the financial statements, as illustrated in Example 2. The financial statement items impacted include cost of sales, gross profit, net income, inventories, current assets, and total assets. Therefore, the choice of inventory valuation method also affects financial ratios that contain these items. Ratios such as current ratio, return on assets, gross profit margin, and inventory turnover are impacted. As a consequence, analysts must carefully consider inventory valuation method differences when evaluating a company's performance over time or when comparing its performance with the performance of the industry or industry competitors. Additionally, the financial statement items and ratios may be impacted by adjustments of inventory carrying amounts to net realisable value or current replacement cost.

6.1 Inventory Ratios

Three ratios often used to evaluate the efficiency and effectiveness of inventory management are **inventory turnover**, **days of inventory on hand (DOH)**, and **gross profit margin**.[12] These ratios are directly impacted by a company's choice of inventory

---

11 IAS 8 [Accounting Policies, Changes in Accounting Estimates and Errors].
12 *Days of inventory on hand* is also referred to as *days in inventory* and *average inventory days outstanding*.

valuation method. Analysts should be aware, however, that many other ratios are also affected by the choice of inventory valuation method, although less directly. These include the current ratio, because inventory is a component of current assets; the return-on-assets ratio, because cost of sales is a key component in deriving net income and inventory is a component of total assets; and even the debt-to-equity ratio, because the cumulative measured net income from the inception of a business is an aggregate component of retained earnings.

The inventory turnover ratio measures the number of times during the year a company sells (i.e., turns over) its inventory. The higher the turnover ratio, the more times that inventory is sold during the year and the lower the relative investment of resources in inventory. Days of inventory on hand can be calculated as days in the period divided by inventory turnover. Thus, inventory turnover and days of inventory on hand are inversely related. It may be that inventory turnover, however, is calculated using average inventory in the year whereas days of inventory on hand is based on the ending inventory amount. In general, inventory turnover and the number of days of inventory on hand should be benchmarked against industry norms and compared across years.

A high inventory turnover ratio and a low number of days of inventory on hand might indicate highly effective inventory management. Alternatively, a high inventory ratio and a low number of days of inventory on hand could indicate that the company does not carry an adequate amount of inventory or that the company has written down inventory values. Inventory shortages could potentially result in lost sales or production problems in the case of the raw materials inventory of a manufacturer. To assess which explanation is more likely, analysts can compare the company's inventory turnover and sales growth rate with those of the industry and review financial statement disclosures. Slower growth combined with higher inventory turnover could indicate inadequate inventory levels. Write-downs of inventory could reflect poor inventory management. Minimal write-downs and sales growth rates at or above the industry's growth rates would support the interpretation that the higher turnover reflects greater efficiency in managing inventory.

A low inventory turnover ratio and a high number of days of inventory on hand relative to industry norms could be an indicator of slow-moving or obsolete inventory. Again, comparing the company's sales growth across years and with the industry and reviewing financial statement disclosures can provide additional insight.

The gross profit margin, the ratio of gross profit to sales, indicates the percentage of sales being contributed to net income as opposed to covering the cost of sales. Firms in highly competitive industries generally have lower gross profit margins than firms in industries with fewer competitors. A company's gross profit margin may be a function of its type of product. A company selling luxury products will generally have higher gross profit margins than a company selling staple products. The inventory turnover of the company selling luxury products, however, is likely to be much lower than the inventory turnover of the company selling staple products.

6.2 Financial Analysis Illustration

Selected excerpts from the consolidated financial statements and notes to consolidated financial statements for Alcatel-Lucent (NYSE: ALU) are presented in Exhibits 1, 2, and 3. Exhibit 1 contains excerpts from the consolidated income statements, and Exhibit 2 contains excerpts from the consolidated balance sheets. Exhibit 3 contains excerpts from three of the notes to consolidated financial statements.

Evaluation of Inventory Management

Exhibit 1	Alcatel-Lucent Consolidated Income Statements (€ Millions)		
For Years Ended 31 December	**2008**	**2007**	**2006**
Revenues	16,984	17,792	12,282
Cost of sales	(11,190)	(12,083)	(8,214)
Gross profit	5,794	5,709	4,068
Administrative and selling expenses	(3,093)	(3,462)	(1,911)
Research and development costs	(2,757)	(2,954)	(1,470)
Income from operating activities before restructuring costs, impairment of assets, gain/(loss) on disposal of consolidated entities, and post-retirement benefit plan amendments	(56)	(707)	687
Restructuring costs	(562)	(856)	(707)
Impairment of assets	(4,725)	(2,944)	(141)
Gain/(loss) on disposal of consolidated entities	(7)	—	15
Post-retirement benefit plan amendments	47	258	—
Income (loss) from operating activities	(5,303)	(4,249)	(146)
⋮	⋮	⋮	⋮
Income (loss) from continuing operations	(5,206)	(4,087)	(219)
Income (loss) from discontinued operations	33	610	158
Net income (loss)	(5,173)	(3,477)	(61)

Exhibit 2	Alcatel-Lucent Consolidated Balance Sheets (€ Millions)		
31 December	**2008**	**2007**	**2006**
Total non-current assets	12,742	20,135	25,665
Inventories and work in progress, net	2,196	2,235	2,259
Amounts due from customers on construction contracts	495	704	615
Trade receivables and related accounts, net	4,330	4,163	3,877
Advances and progress payments	99	110	87
⋮	⋮	⋮	⋮
Total current assets	14,569	13,695	16,225
Total assets	27,311	33,830	41,890
⋮	⋮	⋮	⋮
Retained earnings, fair value, and other reserves	(8,820)	(3,821)	(3,441)
⋮	⋮	⋮	⋮
Total shareholders' equity	5,224	11,702	16,323
Pensions, retirement indemnities, and other post-retirement benefits	4,807	4,447	5,449
Bonds and notes issued, long-term	3,931	4,517	4,901
Other long-term debt	67	48	147
Deferred tax liabilities	1,152	1,897	2,583

(continued)

| Exhibit 2 | (Continued) | | |

31 December	2008	2007	2006
Other non-current liabilities	443	366	276
Total non-current liabilities	10,400	11,275	13,356
Provisions	2,424	2,566	2,366
Current portion of long-term debt	1,097	483	1,161
Customers' deposits and advances	929	847	778
Amounts due to customers on construction contracts	188	407	273
Trade payables and related accounts	4,571	4,514	4,027
Liabilities related to disposal groups held for sale	—	—	1,606
Current income tax liabilities	185	70	66
Other current liabilities	2,293	1,966	1,934
Total current liabilities	11,687	10,853	12,211
Total liabilities and shareholders' equity	27,311	33,830	41,890

| Exhibit 3 | Alcatel-Lucent Selected Notes to Consolidated Financial Statements |

Note 1. Summary of Significant Accounting Policies
(i) Inventories and work in progress

Inventories and work in progress are valued at the lower of cost (including indirect production costs where applicable) or net realizable value.[13] Net realizable value is the estimated sales revenue for a normal period of activity less expected completion and selling costs.

Note 2. Principal uncertainties regarding the use of estimates
(a) Valuation allowance for inventories and work in progress

Inventories and work in progress are measured at the lower of cost or net realizable value. Valuation allowances for inventories and work in progress are calculated based on an analysis of foreseeable changes in demand, technology, or the market, in order to determine obsolete or excess inventories and work in progress.

The valuation allowances are accounted for in cost of sales or in restructuring costs, depending on the nature of the amounts concerned.

	31 December		
(€ millions)	**2008**	**2007**	**2006**
Valuation allowance for inventories and work in progress on construction contracts	(654)	(514)	(378)
Impact of inventory and work in progress write-downs on income (loss) before income tax related reduction of goodwill and discontinued operations	(285)	(186)	(77)

---

13 *Cost* approximates cost on a first-in, first-out basis.

Exhibit 3	(Continued)

Note 19. Inventories and work in progress

(a) Analysis of net value

(€ millions)	2008	2007	2006
Raw materials and goods	649	564	542
Work in progress excluding construction contracts	972	958	752
Finished goods	1,204	1,185	1,320
Gross value (excluding construction contracts)	2,825	2,707	2,614
Valuation allowance	(629)	(472)	(355)
Net value (excluding construction contracts)	2,196	2,235	2,259
Work in progress on construction contracts, gross*	219	272	347
Valuation allowance	(25)	(42)	(23)
Work in progress on construction contracts, net	194	230	324
Total, net	2,390	2,465	2,583

*Included in the amounts due from/to construction contracts

(b) Change in valuation allowance

(€ millions)	2008	2007	2006
At 1 January	(514)	(378)	(423)
(Additions)/reversals	(285)	(186)	(77)
Utilization	69	38	54
Changes in consolidation group	—	—	54
Net effect of exchange rate changes and other changes	75	12	14
At 31 December	(654)	(514)	(378)

Note: Rounding differences may result in totals that are different from the sum.

Note 1 (i) discloses that ALU's finished goods inventories and work in progress are valued at the lower of cost or net realisable value. Note 2 (a) discloses that the impact of inventory and work in progress write-downs on ALU's income before tax was a net reduction of €285 million in 2008, a net reduction of €186 million in 2007, and a net reduction of €77 million in 2006.[14] The inventory impairment loss amounts steadily increased from 2006 to 2008 and are included as a component, (additions)/reversals, of ALU's change in valuation allowance as disclosed in Note 19 (b) from Exhibit 3. Observe also that ALU discloses its valuation allowance at 31 December 2008, 2007, and 2006 in Note 19 (b) and details on the allocation of the allowance are included in Note 19 (a). The €654 million valuation allowance is the total of a €629 million

---

[14] This reduction is often referred to as a *charge*. An accounting charge is the recognition of a loss or expense. In this case, the charge is attributable to the impairment of assets.

allowance for inventories and a €25 million allowance for work in progress on construction contracts. Finally, observe that the €2,196 million net value for inventories (excluding construction contracts) at 31 December 2008 in Note 19 (a) reconciles with the balance sheet amount for inventories and work in progress, net, on 31 December 2008, as presented in Exhibit 2.

The inventory valuation allowance represents the total amount of inventory write-downs taken for the inventory reported on the balance sheet (which is measured at the lower of cost or net realisable value). Therefore, an analyst can determine the historical cost of the company's inventory by adding the inventory valuation allowance to the reported inventory carrying amount on the balance sheet. The valuation allowance increased in magnitude and as a percentage of gross inventory values from 2006 to 2008.

EXAMPLE 5

Financial Analysis Illustration

The consolidated income statements and consolidated balance sheets for Alcatel-Lucent are provided in Exhibits 1 and 2, respectively. Exhibit 3 includes selected financial note disclosures concerning ALU's inventory accounting policies.

1   Calculate ALU's inventory turnover, number of days of inventory on hand, gross profit margin, current ratio, debt-to-equity ratio, and return on total assets for 2008 and 2007 based on the numbers reported. Use an average for inventory and total asset amounts and year-end numbers for other ratio items. For debt, include only bonds and notes issued, long-term; other long-term debt; and current portion of long-term debt.

2   Based on the answer to Question 1, comment on the changes from 2007 to 2008.

3   If ALU had used the weighted average cost method instead of the FIFO method during 2008, 2007, and 2006, what would be the effect on ALU's reported cost of sales and inventory carrying amounts? What would be the directional impact on the financial ratios that were calculated for ALU in Question 1, above?

Solution to 1:

The financial ratios are as follows:

	2008	2007
Inventory turnover ratio	5.05	5.38
Number of days of inventory	72.3 days	67.8 days
Gross profit margin	34.1%	32.1%
Current ratio	1.25	1.26
Debt-to-equity ratio	0.98	0.43
Return on total assets	−16.9%	−9.2%

Inventory turnover ratio = Cost of sales ÷ Average inventory
2008 inventory turnover ratio = 5.05 = 11,190 ÷ [(2,196 + 2,235) ÷ 2]
2007 inventory turnover ratio = 5.38 = 12,083 ÷ [(2,235 + 2,259) ÷ 2]

Number of days of inventory = 365 days ÷ Inventory turnover ratio
2008 number of days of inventory = 72.3 days = 365 days ÷ 5.05

2007 number of days of inventory = 67.8 days = 365 days ÷ 5.38

Gross profit margin = Gross profit ÷ Total revenue
2008 gross profit margin = 34.1% = 5,794 ÷ 16,984
2007 gross profit margin = 32.1% = 5,709 ÷ 17,792

Current ratio = Current assets ÷ Current liabilities
2008 current ratio = 1.25 = 14,569 ÷ 11,687
2007 current ratio = 1.26 = 13,695 ÷ 10,853

Debt-to-equity ratio = Total debt ÷ Total shareholders' equity
2008 debt-to-equity ratio = 0.98 = (3,931 + 67 + 1,097) ÷ 5,224
2007 debt-to-equity ratio = 0.43 = (4,517 + 48 + 483) ÷ 11,702

Return on assets = Net income ÷ Average total assets
2008 return on assets = −16.9% = −5,173 ÷ [(27,311 + 33,830) ÷ 2]
2007 return on assets = −9.2% = −3,477 ÷ [(33,830 + 41,890) ÷ 2]

Solution to 2:

From 2007 to 2008, the inventory turnover ratio declined and the number of days of inventory increased by 4.5 days. ALU appears to be managing inventory less efficiently. The gross profit margin improved by 2.0 percent, from 32.1 percent in 2007 to 34.1 percent in 2008. The current ratio is relatively unchanged from 2007 to 2008. The debt-to-equity ratio has risen significantly in 2008 compared to 2007. Although ALU's total debt has been relatively stable during this time period, the company's equity has been declining rapidly because of the cumulative effect of its net losses on retained earnings.

The return on assets is negative and got worse in 2008 compared to 2007. A larger net loss and lower total assets in 2008 resulted in a higher negative return on assets. The analyst should investigate the underlying reasons for the sharp decline in ALU's return on assets. From Exhibit 1, it is apparent that ALU's gross profit margins were insufficient to cover the administrative and selling expenses and research and development costs in 2007 and 2008. Large restructuring costs and asset impairment losses contributed to the loss from operating activities in both 2007 and 2008.

Solution to 3:

If inventory replacement costs were increasing during 2006, 2007, and 2008 (and inventory quantity levels were stable or increasing), ALU's cost of sales would have been higher and its gross profit margin would have been lower under the weighted average cost inventory method than what was reported under the FIFO method (assuming no inventory write-downs that would otherwise neutralize the differences between the inventory valuation methods). FIFO allocates the oldest inventory costs to cost of sales; the reported cost of sales would be lower under FIFO given increasing inventory costs. Inventory carrying amounts would be higher under the FIFO method than under the weighted average cost method because the more recently purchased inventory items would be included in inventory at their higher costs (again assuming no inventory write-downs that would otherwise neutralize the differences between the inventory valuation methods). Consequently, ALU's reported gross profit, net income, and retained earnings would also be higher for those years under the FIFO method.

The effects on ratios are as follows:

- The inventory turnover ratios would all be higher under the weighted average cost method because the numerator (cost of sales) would be higher and the denominator (inventory) would be lower than what was reported by ALU under the FIFO method.

- The number of days of inventory would be lower under the weighted average cost method because the inventory turnover ratios would be higher.

- The gross profit margin ratios would all be lower under the weighted average cost method because cost of sales would be higher under the weighted average cost method than under the FIFO method.

- The current ratios would all be lower under the weighted average cost method because inventory carrying values would be lower than under the FIFO method (current liabilities would be the same under both methods).

- The return-on-assets ratios would all be lower under the weighted average cost method because the incremental profit added to the numerator (net income) has a greater impact than the incremental increase to the denominator (total assets). By way of example, assume that a company has €3 million in net income and €100 million in total assets using the weighted average cost method. If the company reports another €1 million in net income by using FIFO instead of weighted average cost, it would then also report an additional €1 million in total assets (after tax). Based on this example, the return on assets is 3.00 percent (€3/€100) under the weighted average cost method and 3.96 percent (€4/€101) under the FIFO method.

- The debt-to-equity ratios would all be higher under the weighted average cost method because retained earnings would be lower than under the FIFO method (again assuming no inventory write-downs that would otherwise neutralize the differences between the inventory valuation methods).

Conversely, if inventory replacement costs were decreasing during 2006, 2007, and 2008 (and inventory quantity levels were stable or increasing), ALU's cost of sales would have been lower and its gross profit and inventory would have been higher under the weighted average cost method than were reported under the FIFO method (assuming no inventory write-downs that would otherwise neutralize the differences between the inventory valuation methods). As a result, the ratio assessment that was performed above would result in directly opposite conclusions.

SUMMARY

The choice of inventory valuation method (cost formula or cost flow assumption) can have a potentially significant impact on inventory carrying amounts and cost of sales. These in turn impact other financial statement items, such as current assets, total assets, gross profit, and net income. The financial statements and accompanying notes provide important information about a company's inventory accounting policies that the analyst needs to correctly assess financial performance and compare it with that of other companies.

Key concepts in this reading are as follows:

- Inventories are a major factor in the analysis of merchandising and manufacturing companies. Such companies generate their sales and profits through inventory transactions on a regular basis. An important consideration in determining profits for these companies is measuring the cost of sales when inventories are sold.

- The total cost of inventories comprises all costs of purchase, costs of conversion, and other costs incurred in bringing the inventories to their present location and condition. Storage costs of finished inventory and abnormal costs due to waste are typically treated as expenses in the period in which they occurred.

- IFRS allow three inventory valuation methods (cost formulas): first-in, first-out (FIFO); weighted average cost; and specific identification. The specific identification method is used for inventories of items that are not ordinarily interchangeable and for goods or services produced and segregated for specific projects. U.S. GAAP allow the three methods above plus the last-in, first-out (LIFO) method.

- A company must use the same cost formula for all inventories having a similar nature and use to the entity.

- The inventory accounting system (perpetual or periodic) may result in different values for cost of sales and ending inventory when the weighted average cost or LIFO inventory valuation method is used.

- Under IFRS, inventories are measured at the lower of cost and net realisable value. Net realisable value is the estimated selling price in the ordinary course of business less the estimated costs necessary to make the sale. Under U.S. GAAP, inventories are measured at the lower of cost or market value. Market value is defined as current replacement cost subject to an upper limit of net realisable value and a lower limit of net realisable value less a normal profit margin. Reversals of previous write-downs are permissible under IFRS but not under U.S. GAAP.

- Consistency of inventory accounting policies is required under both U.S. GAAP and IFRS. If a company changes an inventory accounting policy, the change must be justifiable and all financial statements are accounted for retrospectively. The one exception is for a change to the LIFO method under U.S. GAAP; the change is accounted for prospectively, and there is no retrospective adjustment to the financial statements.

- The choice of inventory valuation method affects a number of items on the financial statements and any financial ratios that include inventory or cost of sales, whether directly or indirectly. As a consequence, the analyst must carefully consider differences in inventory valuation methods when evaluating a company's performance in comparison to industry performance or industry competitors' performance.

- The inventory turnover ratio, number of days of inventory ratio, and gross profit margin ratio are useful in evaluating the management of a company's inventory.

- Financial statement disclosures provide information regarding the accounting policies adopted in measuring inventories, the principal uncertainties regarding the use of estimates related to inventories, and details of the inventory carrying amounts and costs. This information can greatly assist analysts in their evaluation of a company's inventory management.

PRACTICE PROBLEMS

1 Inventory cost is *least likely* to include:

A production-related storage costs.

B costs incurred as a result of normal waste of materials.

C transportation costs of shipping inventory to customers.

2 Mustard Seed PLC adheres to IFRS. It recently purchased inventory for €100 million and spent €5 million for storage prior to selling the goods. The amount it charged to inventory expense (€ millions) was *closest* to:

A €95.

B €100.

C €105.

3 Carrying inventory at a value above its historical cost would *most likely* be permitted if:

A the inventory was held by a producer of agricultural products.

B financial statements were prepared using U.S. GAAP.

C the change resulted from a reversal of a previous write-down.

4 Eric's Used Book Store prepares its financial statements in accordance with IFRS. Inventory was purchased for £1 million and later marked down to £550,000. One of the books, however, was later discovered to be a rare collectible item, and the inventory is now worth an estimated £3 million. The inventory is *most likely* reported on the balance sheet at:

A £550,000.

B £1,000,000.

C £3,000,000.

5 Fernando's Pasta purchased inventory and later wrote it down. The current net realisable value is higher than the value when written down. Fernando's inventory balance will *most likely* be:

A higher if it complies with IFRS.

B higher if it complies with U.S. GAAP.

C the same under U.S. GAAP and IFRS.

For questions 6–17, assume the companies use a periodic inventory system.

6 Cinnamon Corp. started business in 2007 and uses the weighted average cost method. During 2007, it purchased 45,000 units of inventory at €10 each and sold 40,000 units for €20 each. In 2008, it purchased another 50,000 units at €11 each and sold 45,000 units for €22 each. Its 2008 cost of sales (€ thousands) was *closest* to:

A €490.

B €491.

C €495.

7 Zimt AG started business in 2007 and uses the FIFO method. During 2007, it purchased 45,000 units of inventory at €10 each and sold 40,000 units for €20 each. In 2008, it purchased another 50,000 units at €11 each and sold 45,000 units for €22 each. Its 2008 ending inventory balance (€ thousands) was *closest* to:

A €105.

B €109.

C €110.

8 Zimt AG uses the FIFO method, and Nutmeg Inc. uses the LIFO method. Compared to the cost of replacing the inventory, during periods of rising prices, the cost of sales reported by:

A Zimt is too low.

B Nutmeg is too low.

C Nutmeg is too high.

9 Zimt AG uses the FIFO method, and Nutmeg Inc. uses the LIFO method. Compared to the cost of replacing the inventory, during periods of rising prices the ending inventory balance reported by:

A Zimt is too high.

B Nutmeg is too low.

C Nutmeg is too high.

10 Like many technology companies, TechnoTools operates in an environment of declining prices. Its reported profits will tend to be *highest* if it accounts for inventory using the:

A FIFO method.

B LIFO method.

C weighted average cost method.

11 Compared to using the weighted average cost method to account for inventory, during a period in which prices are generally rising, the current ratio of a company using the FIFO method would *most likely* be:

A lower.

B higher.

C dependent upon the interaction with accounts payable.

12 Zimt AG wrote down the value of its inventory in 2007 and reversed the write-down in 2008. Compared to the ratios that would have been calculated if the write-down had never occurred, Zimt's reported 2007:

A current ratio was too high.

B gross margin was too high.

C inventory turnover was too high.

13 Zimt AG wrote down the value of its inventory in 2007 and reversed the write-down in 2008. Compared to the results the company would have reported if the write-down had never occurred, Zimt's reported 2008:

A profit was overstated.

B cash flow from operations was overstated.

C year-end inventory balance was overstated.

14 Compared to a company that uses the FIFO method, during periods of rising prices a company that uses the LIFO method will *most likely* appear more:

   A   liquid.

   B   efficient.

   C   profitable.

15 Nutmeg, Inc. uses the LIFO method to account for inventory. During years
   in which inventory unit costs are generally rising and in which the company
   purchases more inventory than it sells to customers, its reported gross profit
   margin will *most likely* be:

   A   lower than it would be if the company used the FIFO method.

   B   higher than it would be if the company used the FIFO method.

   C   about the same as it would be if the company used the FIFO method.

16 Compared to using the FIFO method to account for inventory, during periods of rising prices, a company using the LIFO method is *most likely* to report
   higher:

   A   net income.

   B   cost of sales.

   C   income taxes.

17 Carey Company adheres to U.S. GAAP, whereas Jonathan Company adheres to
   IFRS. It is *least likely* that:

   A   Carey has reversed an inventory write-down.

   B   Jonathan has reversed an inventory write-down.

   C   Jonathan and Carey both use the FIFO inventory accounting method.

The following information relates to Questions 18–25[1]

Hans Annan, CFA, a food and beverage analyst, is reviewing Century Chocolate's
inventory policies as part of his evaluation of the company. Century Chocolate, based
in Switzerland, manufactures chocolate products and purchases and resells other
confectionery products to complement its chocolate line. Annan visited Century
Chocolate's manufacturing facility last year. He learned that cacao beans, imported
from Brazil, represent the most significant raw material and that the work-in-progress
inventory consists primarily of three items: roasted cacao beans, a thick paste produced from the beans (called chocolate liquor), and a sweetened mixture that needs
to be "conched" to produce chocolate. On the tour, Annan learned that the conch-
ing process ranges from a few hours for lower-quality products to six days for the
highest-quality chocolates. While there, Annan saw the facility's climate-controlled
area where manufactured finished products (cocoa and chocolate) and purchased
finished goods are stored prior to shipment to customers. After touring the facility,
Annan had a discussion with Century Chocolate's CFO regarding the types of costs
that were included in each inventory category.

   Annan has asked his assistant, Joanna Kern, to gather some preliminary information
regarding Century Chocolate's financial statements and inventories. He also asked
Kern to calculate the inventory turnover ratios for Century Chocolate and another

---

1 Developed by Karen Rubsam, CFA (Fountain Hills, Arizona, USA).

chocolate manufacturer for the most recent five years. Annan does not know Century Chocolate's most direct competitor, so he asks Kern to do some research and select the most appropriate company for the ratio comparison.

Kern reports back that Century Chocolate prepares its financial statements in accordance with IFRS. She tells Annan that the policy footnote states that raw materials and purchased finished goods are valued at purchase cost whereas work in progress and manufactured finished goods are valued at production cost. Raw material inventories and purchased finished goods are accounted for using the FIFO (first-in, first-out) method, and the weighted average cost method is used for other inventories. An allowance is established when the net realisable value of any inventory item is lower than the value calculated above.

Kern provides Annan with the selected financial statements and inventory data for Century Chocolate shown in Exhibits 1 through 5. The ratio exhibit Kern prepared compares Century Chocolate's inventory turnover ratios to those of Gordon's Goodies, a U.S.-based company. Annan returns the exhibit and tells Kern to select a different competitor that reports using IFRS rather than U.S. GAAP. During this initial review, Annan asks Kern why she has not indicated whether Century Chocolate uses a perpetual or a periodic inventory system. Kern replies that she learned that Century Chocolate uses a perpetual system but did not include this information in her report because inventory values would be the same under either a perpetual or periodic inventory system. Annan tells Kern she is wrong and directs her to research the matter.

While Kern is revising her analysis, Annan reviews the most recent month's Cocoa Market Review from the International Cocoa Organization. He is drawn to the statement that "the ICCO daily price, averaging prices in both futures markets, reached a 29-year high in US\$ terms and a 23-year high in SDRs terms (the SDR unit comprises a basket of major currencies used in international trade: US\$, euro, pound sterling and yen)." Annan makes a note that he will need to factor the potential continuation of this trend into his analysis.

Exhibit 1	Century Chocolate Income Statements (CHF Millions)		
For Years Ended 31 December		**2009**	**2008**
Sales		95,290	93,248
Cost of sales		−41,043	−39,047
Marketing, administration, and other expenses		−35,318	−42,481
Profit before taxes		**18,929**	**11,720**
Taxes		−3,283	−2,962
Profit for the period		**15,646**	**8,758**

Exhibit 2	Century Chocolate Balance Sheets (CHF Millions)		
31 December		**2009**	**2008**
Cash, cash equivalents, and short-term investments		6,190	8,252
Trade receivables and related accounts, net		11,654	12,910
Inventories, net		8,100	7,039
Other current assets		2,709	2,812

(continued)

Exhibit 2	(Continued)		

31 December	2009	2008
Total current assets	**28,653**	**31,013**
Property, plant, and equipment, net	18,291	19,130
Other non-current assets	45,144	49,875
Total assets	**92,088**	**100,018**
Trade and other payables	10,931	12,299
Other current liabilities	17,873	25,265
Total current liabilities	**28,804**	**37,564**
Non-current liabilities	15,672	14,963
Total liabilities	**44,476**	**52,527**
Equity		
Share capital	332	341
Retained earnings and other reserves	47,280	47,150
Total equity	**47,612**	**47,491**
Total liabilities and shareholders' equity	**92,088**	**100,018**

Exhibit 3	Century Chocolate Supplementary Footnote Disclosures: Inventories (CHF Millions)		

31 December	2009	2008
Raw Materials	2,154	1,585
Work in Progress	1,061	1,027
Finished Goods	5,116	4,665
Total inventories before allowance	8,331	7,277
Allowance for write-downs to net realisable value	−231	−238
Total inventories net of allowance	8,100	7,039

Exhibit 4	Century Chocolate Inventory Record for Purchased Lemon Drops		

Date		Cartons	Per Unit Amount (CHF)
	Beginning inventory	100	22
4 Feb 09	Purchase	40	25
3 Apr 09	Sale	50	32
23 Jul 09	Purchase	70	30

Exhibit 4	(Continued)		

Date		Cartons	Per Unit Amount (CHF)
16 Aug 09	Sale	100	32
9 Sep 09	Sale	35	32
15 Nov 09	Purchase	100	28

Exhibit 5	Century Chocolate Net Realisable Value Information for Black Licorice Jelly Beans		

	2009	2008
FIFO cost of inventory at 31 December (CHF)	314,890	374,870
Ending inventory at 31 December (Kilograms)	77,750	92,560
Cost per unit (CHF)	4.05	4.05
Net Realisable Value (CHF per Kilograms)	4.20	3.95

18 The costs *least likely* to be included by the CFO as inventory are:

A storage costs for the chocolate liquor.

B excise taxes paid to the government of Brazil for the cacao beans.

C storage costs for chocolate and purchased finished goods awaiting shipment to customers.

19 What is the *most likely* justification for Century Chocolate's choice of inventory valuation method for its finished goods?

A It is the preferred method under IFRS.

B It allocates the same per unit cost to both cost of sales and inventory.

C Ending inventory reflects the cost of goods purchased most recently.

20 In Kern's comparative ratio analysis, the 2009 inventory turnover ratio for Century Chocolate is *closest* to:

A 5.07.

B 5.42.

C 5.55.

21 The *most accurate* statement regarding Annan's reasoning for requiring Kern to select a competitor that reports under IFRS for comparative purposes is that under U.S. GAAP:

A fair values are used to value inventory.

B the LIFO method is permitted to value inventory.

C the specific identification method is permitted to value inventory.

22 Annan's statement regarding the perpetual and periodic inventory systems is most significant when which of the following costing systems is used?

A LIFO.

    B FIFO.

    C Specific identification.

23 Using the inventory record for purchased lemon drops shown in Exhibit 4, the cost of sales for 2009 will be *closest* to:

    A CHF 3,550.

    B CHF 4,550.

    C CHF 4,850.

24 Ignoring any tax effect, the 2009 net realisable value reassessment for the black licorice jelly beans will *most likely* result in:

    A an increase in gross profit of CHF 7,775.

    B an increase in gross profit of CHF 11,670.

    C no impact on cost of sales because under IFRS, write-downs cannot be reversed.

25 If the trend noted in the ICCO report continues and Century Chocolate plans to maintain constant or increasing inventory quantities, the *most likely* impact on Century Chocolate's financial statements related to its raw materials inventory will be:

    A a cost of sales that more closely reflects current replacement values.

    B a higher allocation of the total cost of goods available for sale to cost of sales.

    C a higher allocation of the total cost of goods available for sale to ending inventory.

SOLUTIONS

1 C is correct. Transportation costs incurred to ship inventory to customers are an expense and may not be capitalized in inventory. (Transportation costs incurred to bring inventory to the business location can be capitalized in inventory.) Storage costs required as part of production, as well as costs incurred as a result of normal waste of materials, can be capitalized in inventory. (Costs incurred as a result of abnormal waste must be expensed.)

2 B is correct. Inventory expense includes costs of purchase, costs of conversion, and other costs incurred in bringing the inventories to their present location and condition. It does not include storage costs not required as part of production.

3 A is correct. IFRS allow the inventories of producers and dealers of agricultural and forest products, agricultural produce after harvest, and minerals and mineral products to be carried at net realisable value even if above historical cost. (U.S. GAAP treatment is similar.)

4 B is correct. Under IFRS, the reversal of write-downs is required if net realisable value increases. The inventory will be reported on the balance sheet at £1,000,000. The inventory is reported at the lower of cost or net realisable value. Under U.S. GAAP, inventory is carried at the lower of cost or market value. After a write-down, a new cost basis is determined and additional revisions may only reduce the value further. The reversal of write-downs is not permitted.

5 A is correct. IFRS require the reversal of inventory write-downs if net realisable values increase; U.S. GAAP do not permit the reversal of write-downs.

6 B is correct. Cinnamon uses the weighted average cost method, so in 2008, 5,000 units of inventory were 2007 units at €10 each and 50,000 were 2008 purchases at €11. The weighted average cost of inventory during 2008 was thus (5,000 × 10) + (50,000 × 11) = 50,000 + 550,000 = €600,000, and the weighted average cost was approximately €10.91 = €600,000/55,000. Cost of sales was €10.91 × 45,000, which is approximately €490,950.

7 C is correct. Zimt uses the FIFO method, and thus the first 5,000 units sold in 2008 depleted the 2007 inventory. Of the inventory purchased in 2008, 40,000 units were sold and 10,000 remain, valued at €11 each, for a total of €110,000.

8 A is correct. Zimt uses the FIFO method, so its cost of sales represents units purchased at a (no longer available) lower price. Nutmeg uses the LIFO method, so its cost of sales is approximately equal to the current replacement cost of inventory.

9 B is correct. Nutmeg uses the LIFO method, and thus some of the inventory on the balance sheet was purchased at a (no longer available) lower price. Zimt uses the FIFO method, so the carrying value on the balance sheet represents the most recently purchased units and thus approximates the current replacement cost.

10 B is correct. In a declining price environment, the newest inventory is the lowest-cost inventory. In such circumstances, using the LIFO method (selling the newer, cheaper inventory first) will result in lower cost of sales and higher profit.

11 B is correct. In a rising price environment, inventory balances will be higher for the company using the FIFO method. Accounts payable are based on amounts due to suppliers, not the amounts accrued based on inventory accounting.

12 C is correct. The write-down reduced the value of inventory and increased cost of sales in 2007. The higher numerator and lower denominator mean that the inventory turnover ratio as reported was too high. Gross margin and the current ratio were both too low.

13 A is correct. The reversal of the write-down shifted cost of sales from 2008 to 2007. The 2007 cost of sales was higher because of the write-down, and the 2008 cost of sales was lower because of the reversal of the write-down. As a result, the reported 2008 profits were overstated. Inventory balance in 2008 is the same because the write-down and reversal cancel each other out. Cash flow from operations is not affected by the non-cash write-down, but the higher profits in 2008 likely resulted in higher taxes and thus lower cash flow from operations.

14 B is correct. LIFO will result in lower inventory and higher cost of sales. Gross margin (a profitability ratio) will be lower, the current ratio (a liquidity ratio) will be lower, and inventory turnover (an efficiency ratio) will be higher.

15 A is correct. LIFO will result in lower inventory and higher cost of sales in periods of rising costs compared to FIFO. Consequently, LIFO results in a lower gross profit margin than FIFO.

16 B is correct. The LIFO method increases cost of sales, thus reducing profits and the taxes thereon.

17 A is correct. U.S. GAAP do not permit inventory write-downs to be reversed.

18 C is correct. The storage costs for inventory awaiting shipment to customers are not costs of purchase, costs of conversion, or other costs incurred in bringing the inventories to their present location and condition and are not included in inventory. The storage costs for the chocolate liquor occur during the production process and are thus part of the conversion costs. Excise taxes are part of the purchase cost.

19 C is correct. The carrying amount of inventories under FIFO will more closely reflect current replacement values because inventories are assumed to consist of the most recently purchased items. FIFO is an acceptable, but not preferred, method under IFRS. Weighted average cost, not FIFO, is the cost formula that allocates the same per unit cost to both cost of sales and inventory.

20 B is correct. Inventory turnover = Cost of sales/Average inventory = 41,043/7,569.5 = 5.42. Average inventory is (8,100 + 7,039)/2 = 7,569.5.

21 B is correct. For comparative purposes, the choice of a competitor that reports under IFRS is requested because LIFO is permitted under U.S. GAAP.

22 A is correct. The carrying amount of the ending inventory may differ because the perpetual system will apply LIFO continuously throughout the year, liquidating layers as sales are made. Under the periodic system, the sales will start from the last layer in the year. Under FIFO, the sales will occur from the same layers regardless of whether a perpetual or periodic system is used. Specific identification identifies the actual products sold and remaining in inventory, and there will be no difference under a perpetual or periodic system.

23 B is correct. The cost of sales is closest to CHF 4,550. Under FIFO, the inventory acquired first is sold first. Using Exhibit 4, a total of 310 cartons were available for sale (100 + 40 + 70 + 100) and 185 cartons were sold (50 + 100 + 35), leaving 125 in ending inventory. The FIFO cost would be as follows:

100 (beginning inventory) × 22 = 2,200

40 (4 February 2009) × 25 = 1,000

45 (23 July 2009) × 30 = 1,350

Cost of sales = 2,200 + 1,000 + 1,350 = CHF 4,550

24 A is correct. Gross profit will most likely increase by CHF 7,775. The net realisable value has increased and now exceeds the cost. The write-down from 2008 can be reversed. The write-down in 2008 was 9,256 [92,560 × (4.05 – 3.95)]. IFRS require the reversal of any write-downs for a subsequent increase in value of inventory previously written down. The reversal is limited to the lower of the subsequent increase or the original write-down. Only 77,750 kilograms remain in inventory; the reversal is 77,750 × (4.05 – 3.95) = 7,775. The amount of any reversal of a write-down is recognised as a reduction in cost of sales. This reduction results in an increase in gross profit.

25 C is correct. Using the FIFO method to value inventories when prices are rising will allocate more of the cost of goods available for sale to ending inventories (the most recent purchases, which are at higher costs, are assumed to remain in inventory) and less to cost of sales (the oldest purchases, which are at lower costs, are assumed to be sold first).

Long-Lived Assets

by Elaine Henry, CFA, and Elizabeth A. Gordon

LEARNING OUTCOMES

Mastery	The candidate should be able to:
☐	**a.** distinguish between costs that are capitalized and costs that are expensed in the period in which they are incurred;
☐	**b.** compare the financial reporting of the following types of intangible assets: purchased, internally developed, acquired in a business combination;
☐	**c.** describe the different depreciation methods for property, plant, and equipment, the effect of the choice of depreciation method on the financial statements, and the effects of assumptions concerning useful life and residual value on depreciation expense;
☐	**d.** calculate depreciation expense;
☐	**e.** describe the different amortization methods for intangible assets with finite lives, the effect of the choice of amortization method on the financial statements, and the effects of assumptions concerning useful life and residual value on amortization expense;
☐	**f.** calculate amortization expense;
☐	**g.** describe the revaluation model;
☐	**h.** explain the imparment of property, plant, and equipment and intangible assets;
☐	**i.** explain the derecognition of property, plant, and equipment and intangible assets;
☐	**j.** describe the financial statement presentation of and disclosures relating to property, plant, and equipment and intangible assets;
☐	**k.** compare the financial reporting of investment property with that of property, plant, and equipment.

Note: New rulings and/or pronouncements issues after the publication of the readings in financial reporting and analysis may cause some of the information in these readings to become dated. Candidates are expected to be familiar with the overall analytical framework contained in the study session readings, as well as the implications of alternative accounting methods for financial analysis and valuation, as provided in the assigned readings. Candidates are not responsible for changes that occur after the material was written.

1 INTRODUCTION

Long-lived assets, also referred to as non-current assets or long-term assets, are assets that are expected to provide economic benefits over a future period of time, typically greater than one year.[1] Long-lived assets may be tangible, intangible, or financial assets. Examples of long-lived tangible assets, typically referred to as **property, plant, and equipment** and sometimes as fixed assets, include land, buildings, furniture and fixtures, machinery and equipment, and vehicles; examples of long-lived **intangible assets** (assets lacking physical substance) include patents and trademarks; and examples of long-lived financial assets include investments in equity or debt securities issued by other companies. The scope of this reading is limited to long-lived tangible and intangible assets (hereafter, referred to for simplicity as long-lived assets).

The first issue in accounting for a long-lived asset is determining its cost at acquisition. The second issue is how to allocate the cost to expense over time. The costs of most long-lived assets are capitalized and then allocated as expenses in the profit or loss (income) statement over the period of time during which they are expected to provide economic benefits. The two main types of long-lived assets with costs that are typically *not* allocated over time are land, which is not depreciated, and those intangible assets with indefinite useful lives. Additional issues that arise are the treatment of subsequent costs incurred related to the asset, the use of the cost model versus the revaluation model, unexpected declines in the value of the asset, classification of the asset with respect to intent (for example, held for use or held for sale), and the derecognition of the asset.

This reading is organised as follows. Section 2 describes and illustrates accounting for the acquisition of long-lived assets. Section 3 describes the allocation of the costs of long-lived assets over their useful lives. Section 4 discusses the revaluation model that is based on changes in the fair value of an asset. Section 5 covers the concepts of impairment (unexpected decline in the value of an asset). Section 6 describes accounting for the derecognition of long-lived assets. Section 7 describes the financial statement presentation of and disclosures about long-lived assets. Section 8 discusses differences in financial reporting of investment property compared with property, plant, and equipment. A summary is followed by practice problems in the CFA Institute multiple-choice format.

2 ACQUISITION OF LONG-LIVED ASSETS

Upon acquisition, property, plant, and equipment (tangible assets with an economic life of longer than one year and intended to be held for the company's own use) are recorded on the balance sheet at cost, which is typically the same as their fair value.[2] Accounting for an intangible asset depends on how the asset is acquired. If several

---

1 In some instances, industry practice is to include as current assets (inventory) some assets that will be held longer than one year (e.g., leaf tobacco, which is cured and aged over a period longer than one year, and whiskey, which is barrel aged for a period longer than one year).

2 Fair value is defined in International Financial Reporting Standards (IFRS) as "the amount for which an asset could be exchanged, or a liability settled, between knowledgeable, willing parties in an arm's length transaction" and under U.S. generally accepted accounting principles (U.S. GAAP) in the Financial Accounting Standards Board (FASB) Accounting Standards Codification (ASC) as "the price that would be received to sell an asset or paid to transfer a liability in an orderly transaction between market participants at the measurement date."

assets are acquired as part of a group, the purchase price is allocated to each asset on the basis of its fair value. An asset's cost potentially includes expenditures additional to the purchase price.

A key concept in accounting for expenditures related to long-lived assets is whether and when such expenditures are capitalized (i.e., included in the asset shown on the balance sheet) versus expensed (i.e., treated as an expense of the period on the income statement). Before turning to specific treatment of expenditures, we consider the general financial statement impact of capitalizing versus expensing and two analytical issues related to the decision—namely, the effects on an individual company's trend analysis and on comparability across companies.

In the period of the expenditure, an expenditure that is capitalized increases the amount of assets on the balance sheet and appears as an investing cash outflow on the statement of cash flows. In subsequent periods, a company usually allocates the capitalized amount over the asset's useful life as depreciation or amortization expense. This depreciation or amortization expense reduces profit on the income statement and reduces the carrying amount of the asset on the balance sheet. Depreciation and amortization are non-cash expenses and, therefore, apart from a potential effect on taxes payable (a reduction in taxes payable), have no impact on cash flows. When the indirect method is used to report cash flows from operating activities, depreciation and amortization expenses appear on the statement of cash flows: In reconciling net income to operating cash flow as required by the indirect method, the company must adjust profit or loss by adding back depreciation and amortization expenses.

When an expenditure does not meet asset recognition criteria, the expenditure is treated as an expense in the period it is made and reduces net income and operating cash flows by the entire after-tax amount of the expenditure. No asset is recorded on the balance sheet, and thus, no depreciation or amortization expense is recognized in future periods. The lower amount of net income in the initial period is reflected in lower retained earnings on the ending balance sheet of the period. There is no additional effect on the financial statements of subsequent periods. Compared with a company that capitalizes an expenditure, a company that expenses an expenditure will have lower net income in the period of expensing and higher net income thereafter.

In general, all else equal, accounting decisions that result in recognising expenses sooner will give the appearance of greater subsequent growth (i.e., a more positive earnings trend in periods following the recognition of the expense). In contrast, capitalizing rather than expensing an expenditure results in a greater amount reported as cash from operations because the capitalized expenditure is shown as an investment cash outflow whereas the expense is an operating cash outflow. Cash from operations is an important consideration in valuation, so companies may aim to maximize reported cash from operations. WorldCom is an infamous example of a company violating accounting standards; in 2001, the company wrongly capitalized more than $3 billion in line costs (charges paid for access to telecommunication lines) that should have been expensed. This action resulted in higher reported cash from operations and net income. Of course, distinguishing between WorldCom's fraudulent financial reporting and allowable accounting discretion is important. Nonetheless, in general, a capitalized expenditure increases investment cash outflows whereas an expenditure treated as an expense would reduce operating cash flows. In cross-company analysis, variations in companies' decisions about expensing or capitalizing expenditures can impede comparability.

Assets can be acquired by methods other than purchase.[3] When an asset is exchanged for another asset, the asset acquired is recorded at fair value if reliable measures of fair value exist. Fair value is the fair value of the asset given up unless the fair value of the asset acquired is more clearly evident. If there is no reliable measure of fair value, the acquired asset is measured at the carrying amount of the asset given up. In this case, the carrying amount of the assets is unchanged, and no gain or loss is reported.

Typically, accounting for the exchange involves removing the carrying amount of the asset given up, adding a fair value for the asset acquired, and reporting any difference between the carrying amount and the fair value as a gain or loss. A gain would be reported when the fair value used for the newly acquired asset exceeds the carrying amount of the asset given up. A loss would be reported when the fair value used for the newly acquired asset is less than the carrying amount of the asset given up.

2.1 Property, Plant, and Equipment

This section discusses the accounting treatment for the acquisition of long-lived tangible assets (property, plant, and equipment) through purchase, with an emphasis on the capitalization versus expensing of expenditures. At acquisition, the buyer records property, plant, and equipment at cost. In addition to the purchase price, the buyer also includes, as part of the cost of an asset, all the expenditures necessary to get the asset ready for its intended use. For example, freight costs borne by the purchaser to get the asset to the purchaser's place of business and special installation and testing costs required to make the asset usable are included in the total cost of the asset.

Subsequent expenditures related to long-lived assets are included as part of the recorded value of the assets on the balance sheet (i.e., capitalized) if they are expected to provide benefits beyond one year in the future and are expensed if they are not expected to provide benefits in future periods. Expenditures that extend the original life of the asset are typically capitalized. Example 1 illustrates the difference between costs that are capitalized and costs that are expensed in a period.

EXAMPLE 1

Capitalizing versus Expensing

Assume a (hypothetical) company, Trofferini S.A., incurred the following expenditures to purchase a towel and tissue roll machine: €10,900 purchase price including taxes, €200 for delivery of the machine, €300 for installation and testing of the machine, and €100 to train staff on maintaining the machine. In addition, the company paid a construction team €350 to reinforce the factory floor and ceiling joists to accommodate the machine's weight. The company also paid €1,500 to repair the factory roof (a repair expected to extend the useful life of the factory by five years) and €1,000 to have the exterior of the factory and adjoining offices repainted for maintenance reasons. The repainting neither extends the life of factory and offices nor improves their usability.

1 Which of these expenditures will be capitalized and which will be expensed?

2 How will the treatment of these expenditures affect the company's financial statements?

---

3 IAS 16 *Property, Plant and Equipment*, paragraphs 24–26 [Measurement of Cost]; IAS 38 *Intangible Assets*, paragraphs 45–47 [Exchange of Assets]; and FASB ASC Section 845-10-30 [Nonmonetary Transactions–Overall–Initial Measurement].

Solution to 1:

The company will capitalize as part of the cost of the machine all costs that are necessary to get the new machine ready for its intended use: €10,900 purchase price, €200 for delivery, €300 for installation and testing, and €350 to reinforce the factory floor and ceiling joists to accommodate the machine's weight (which was necessary to use the machine and does not increase the value of the factory). The €100 to train staff is not necessary to get the asset ready for its intended use and will be expensed.

The company will capitalize the expenditure of €1,500 to repair the factory roof because the repair is expected to extend the useful life of the factory. The company will expense the €1,000 to have the exterior of the factory and adjoining offices repainted because the painting does not extend the life or alter the productive capacity of the buildings.

Solution to 2:

The costs related to the machine that are capitalized—10,900 purchase price, €200 for delivery, €300 for installation and testing, and €350 to prepare the factory—will increase the carrying amount of the machine asset as shown on the balance sheet and will be included as investing cash outflows. The item related to the factory that is capitalized—the €1,500 roof repair—will increase the carrying amount of the factory asset as shown on the balance sheet and is an investing cash outflow. The expenditures of €100 to train staff and 1,000 to paint are expensed in the period and will reduce the amount of income reported on the company's income statement (and thus reduce retained earnings on the balance sheet) and the operating cash flow.

Example 1 describes capitalizing versus expensing in the context of purchasing property, plant, and equipment. When a company constructs an asset (or acquires an asset that requires a long period of time to get ready for its intended use), borrowing costs incurred directly related to the construction are generally capitalized. Constructing a building, whether for sale (in which case, the building is classified as inventory) or for the company's own use (in which case, the building is classified as a long-lived asset), typically requires a substantial amount of time. To finance construction, any borrowing costs incurred prior to the asset being ready for its intended use are capitalized as part of the cost of the asset. The company determines the interest rate to use on the basis of its existing borrowings or, if applicable, on a borrowing specifically incurred for constructing the asset. If a company takes out a loan specifically to construct a building, the interest cost on that loan during the time of construction would be capitalized as part of the building's cost. Under IFRS, but not under U.S. GAAP, income earned on temporarily investing the borrowed monies decreases the amount of borrowing costs eligible for capitalization.

Thus, a company's interest costs for a period are included either on the balance sheet (to the extent they are capitalized as part of an asset) or on the income statement (to the extent they are expensed). If the interest expenditure is incurred in connection with constructing an asset for the company's own use, the capitalized interest appears on the balance sheet as a part of the relevant long-lived asset (i.e., property, plant, and equipment). The capitalized interest is expensed over time as the property is depreciated and is thus part of subsequent years' depreciation expense rather than interest expense of the current period. If the interest expenditure is incurred in connection with constructing an asset to sell (for example, by a home builder), the capitalized interest appears on the company's balance sheet as part of inventory. The capitalized interest is expensed as part of the cost of goods sold when the asset is sold. Interest payments made prior to completion of construction that are capitalized are classified as an investing cash outflow. Expensed interest may be classified as an operating or financing cash outflow under IFRS and is classified as an operating cash outflow under U.S. GAAP.

EXAMPLE 2

Effect of Capitalized Borrowing Costs

BILDA S.A., a hypothetical company, borrows €1,000,000 at an interest rate of 10 percent per year on 1 January 2010 to finance the construction of a factory that will have a useful life of 40 years. Construction is completed after two years, during which time the company earns €20,000 by temporarily investing the loan proceeds.

1   What is the amount of interest that will be capitalized under IFRS, and how would that amount differ from the amount that would be capitalized under U.S. GAAP?

2   Where will the capitalized borrowing cost appear on the company's financial statements?

Solution to 1:

The total amount of interest paid on the loan during construction is €200,000 (= €1,000,000 × 10% × 2 years). Under IFRS, the amount of borrowing cost eligible for capitalization is reduced by the €20,000 interest income from temporarily investing the loan proceeds, so the amount to be capitalized is €180,000. Under U.S. GAAP, the amount to be capitalized is €200,000.

Solution to 2:

The capitalized borrowing costs will appear on the company's balance sheet as a component of property, plant, and equipment. In the years prior to completion of construction, the interest paid will appear on the statement of cash flows as an investment activity. Over time, as the property is depreciated, the capitalized interest component is part of subsequent years' depreciation expense on the company's income statement.

The treatment of capitalized interest raises issues for consideration by an analyst. First, capitalized interest appears as part of investing cash outflows, whereas expensed interest reduces operating or financing cash flow under IFRS and operating cash flow under U.S. GAAP. An analyst may want to examine the impact on reported cash flows of interest expenditures when comparing companies. Second, interest coverage ratios are solvency indicators measuring the extent to which a company's earnings (or cash flow) in a period covered its interest costs. To provide a true picture of a company's interest coverage, the entire amount of interest, both the capitalized portion and the expensed portion, should be used in calculating interest coverage ratios. Generally, including capitalized interest in the calculation of interest coverage ratios provides a better assessment of a company's solvency. In assigning credit ratings, rating agencies include capitalized interest in coverage ratios. For example, Standard & Poor's calculates the earnings before interest and taxes (EBIT) interest coverage ratio as EBIT divided by gross interest (defined as interest prior to deductions for capitalized interest or interest income).

2.2 Intangible Assets

Intangible assets are assets lacking physical substance. Intangible assets include items that involve exclusive rights, such as patents, copyrights, trademarks, and franchises. Under IFRS, identifiable intangible assets must meet three definitional criteria. They must be 1) identifiable (either capable of being separated from the entity or arising from contractual or legal rights), 2) under the control of the company, and 3) expected to generate future economic benefits. In addition, two recognition criteria must be met: 1) It is probable that the expected future economic benefits of the asset will flow to the company, and 2) the cost of the asset can be reliably measured. Goodwill, which is not considered an identifiable intangible asset,[4] arises when one company purchases another and the acquisition price exceeds the fair value of the identifiable assets (both the tangible assets and the identifiable intangible assets) acquired.

Accounting for an intangible asset depends on how it is acquired. The following sections describe accounting for intangible assets obtained in three ways: purchased in situations other than business combinations, developed internally, and acquired in business combinations.

2.2.1 *Intangible Assets Purchased in Situations Other Than Business Combinations*

Intangible assets purchased in situations other than business combinations, such as buying a patent, are treated at acquisition the same as long-lived tangible assets; they are recorded at their fair value when acquired, which is assumed to be equivalent to the purchase price. If several intangible assets are acquired as part of a group, the purchase price is allocated to each asset on the basis of its fair value.

In deciding how to treat individual intangible assets for analytical purposes, analysts are particularly aware that companies must use a substantial amount of judgment and numerous assumptions to determine the fair value of individual intangible assets. For analysis, therefore, understanding the types of intangible assets acquired can often be more useful than focusing on the values assigned to the individual assets. In other words, an analyst would typically be more interested in understanding what assets a company acquired (for example, franchise rights and a mailing list) than in the precise portion of the purchase price a company allocated to each asset. Understanding the types of assets a company acquires can offer insights into the company's strategic direction and future operating potential.

2.2.2 *Intangible Assets Developed Internally*

In contrast with the treatment of construction costs of tangible assets, the costs to internally develop intangible assets are generally expensed when incurred. There are some situations, however, in which the costs incurred to internally develop an intangible asset are capitalized. The general analytical issues related to the capitalizing-versus-expensing decision apply here—namely, comparability across companies and the effect on an individual company's trend analysis.

The general requirement that costs to internally develop intangible assets be expensed should be compared with capitalizing the cost of acquiring intangible assets in situations other than business combinations. Because costs associated with internally developing intangible assets are usually expensed, a company that has internally developed such intangible assets as patents, copyrights, or brands through expenditures on R&D or advertising will recognise a lower amount of assets than a company that has obtained intangible assets through external purchase. In addition, on the statement of

---

4 The IFRS definition of an intangible asset as an "identifiable non-monetary asset without physical substance" applies to intangible assets not specifically dealt with in standards other than IAS 38. The definition of intangible assets under U.S. GAAP—"assets (other than financial assets) that lack physical substance"—includes goodwill in the definition of an intangible asset.

cash flows, costs of internally developing intangible assets are classified as operating cash outflows whereas costs of acquiring intangible assets are classified as investing cash outflows. Differences in strategy (developing versus acquiring intangible assets) can thus impact financial ratios.

IFRS require that expenditures on research (or during the research phase of an internal project) be expensed rather than capitalized as an intangible asset.[5] Research is defined as "original and planned investigation undertaken with the prospect of gaining new scientific or technical knowledge and understanding."[6] The "research phase of an internal project" refers to the period during which a company cannot demonstrate that an intangible asset is being created—for example, the search for alternative materials or systems to use in a production process. IFRS allow companies to recognise an intangible asset arising from development (or the development phase of an internal project) if certain criteria are met, including a demonstration of the technical feasibility of completing the intangible asset and the intent to use or sell the asset. Development is defined as "the application of research findings or other knowledge to a plan or design for the production of new or substantially improved materials, devices, products, processes, systems or services before the start of commercial production or use."[7]

Generally, U.S. GAAP require that both research and development costs be expensed as incurred but require capitalization of certain costs related to software development.[8] Costs incurred to develop a software product for sale are expensed until the product's technological feasibility is established and are capitalized thereafter. Similarly, companies expense costs related to the development of software for internal use until it is probable that the project will be completed and that the software will be used as intended. Thereafter, development costs are capitalized. The probability that the project will be completed is easier to demonstrate than is technological feasibility. The capitalized costs, related directly to developing software for sale or internal use, include the costs of employees who help build and test the software. The treatment of software development costs under U.S. GAAP is similar to the treatment of all costs of internally developed intangible assets under IFRS.

EXAMPLE 3

Software Development Costs

Assume JHH AG, a hypothetical company, incurs expenditures of €1,000 per month during the fiscal year ended 31 December 2009 to develop software for internal use. Under IFRS, the company must treat the expenditures as an expense until the software meets the criteria for recognition as an intangible asset, after which time the expenditures can be capitalized as an intangible asset.

1 What is the accounting impact of the company being able to demonstrate that the software met the criteria for recognition as an intangible asset on 1 February versus 1 December?

2 How would the treatment of expenditures differ if the company reported under U.S. GAAP and it had established in 2008 that the project was likely to be completed?

---

5 IAS 38 *Intangible Assets*.
6 IAS 38 *Intangible Assets*, paragraph 8 [Definitions].
7 IAS 38 *Intangible Assets*, paragraph 8 [Definitions].
8 FASB ASC Section 350-40-25 [Intangibles–Goodwill and Other–Internal-Use Software–Recognition] and FASB ASC Section 985-20-25 [Software–Costs of Software to be Sold, Leased, or Marketed–Recognition] specify U.S. GAAP accounting for software development costs for software for internal use and for software to be sold, respectively.

Solution to 1:

If the company is able to demonstrate that the software met the criteria for recognition as an intangible asset on 1 February, the company would recognise €1,000 of expense (on the income statement) during the fiscal year ended 31 December 2009. The other €11,000 of expenditures would be recognised as an intangible asset (on the balance sheet). Alternatively, if the company is not able to demonstrate that the software met the criteria for recognition as an intangible asset until 1 December, the company would recognise €11,000 of expense during the fiscal year ended 31 December 2009, with the other €1,000 of expenditures recognised as an intangible asset.

Solution to 2:

Under U.S. GAAP, the company would capitalize the entire €12,000 spent to develop software for internal use.

Even though standards require companies to capitalize software development costs after a product's feasibility is established, judgment in determining feasibility means that companies' capitalization practices differ. For example, as illustrated in Exhibit 1, Microsoft judges product feasibility to be established very shortly before manufacturing begins and, therefore, effectively expenses—rather than capitalizes—research and development costs.

Exhibit 1	Disclosure on Software Development Costs

[Excerpt from Management's Discussion and Analysis (MD&A) of Microsoft Corporation (NasdaqGS: MSFT), Application of Critical Accounting Policies, Research and Development Costs]

> SFAS No. 86 specifies that costs incurred internally in researching and developing a computer software product should be charged to expense until technological feasibility has been established for the product. Once technological feasibility is established, all software costs should be capitalized until the product is available for general release to customers. Judgment is required in determining when technological feasibility of a product is established. We have determined that technological feasibility for our software products is reached after all high-risk development issues have been resolved through coding and testing. Generally, this occurs shortly before the products are released to manufacturing. The amortization of these costs is included in cost of revenue over the estimated life of the products.

Source: Microsoft Corporation Annual Report 2009, p. 36.

Expensing rather than capitalizing development costs results in lower net income in the current period. Expensing rather than capitalizing will continue to result in lower net income so long as the amount of the current-period development expenses is higher than the amortization expense that would have resulted from amortizing prior periods' capitalized development costs—the typical situation when a company's development costs are increasing. On the statement of cash flows, expensing rather than capitalizing development costs results in lower net operating cash flows and higher net investing cash flows. This is because the development costs are reflected as operating cash outflows rather than investing cash outflows.

2.2.3 *Intangible Assets Acquired in a Business Combination*

When one company acquires another company, the transaction is accounted for using the **acquisition method** of accounting.[9] Under the acquisition method, the company identified as the acquirer allocates the purchase price to each asset acquired (and each liability assumed) on the basis of its fair value. If the purchase price exceeds the sum of the amounts that can be allocated to individual identifiable assets and liabilities, the excess is recorded as goodwill. Goodwill cannot be identified separately from the business as a whole.

Under IFRS, the acquired individual assets include identifiable intangible assets that meet the definitional and recognition criteria.[10] Otherwise, if the item is acquired in a business combination and cannot be recognised as a tangible or identifiable intangible asset, it is recognised as goodwill. Under U.S. GAAP, there are two criteria to judge whether an intangible asset acquired in a business combination should be recognised separately from goodwill: The asset must be either an item arising from contractual or legal rights or an item that can be separated from the acquired company. Examples of intangible assets treated separately from goodwill include the intangible assets previously mentioned that involve exclusive rights (patents, copyrights, franchises, licenses), as well as such items as internet domain names and video and audiovisual materials.

Exhibit 2 describes how InBev allocated the €40.3 billion purchase price for its acquisition of Anheuser-Busch. The majority of the identifiable intangible asset valuation (€16.473 billion) relates to brands with indefinite life. Another €256 million or €0.256 billion was for the identifiable intangible assets with definite useful lives—distribution agreements and favorable contracts. These assets are being amortized over the life of the associated contracts. In addition, €24.7 billion of goodwill was recognised.

Exhibit 2	Acquisition of Intangible Assets through a Business Combination

[Excerpt from the 2008 annual report of AB InBev (BRU: ABI)]

> On 18 November, InBev has completed the acquisition of Anheuser-Busch, following approval from shareholders of both companies. . . . Effective the date of the closing, InBev has changed its name to AB InBev to reflect the heritage and traditions of Anheuser-Busch. Under the terms of the merger agreement, all shares of Anheuser-Busch were acquired for 70 US dollar per share in cash for an aggregate amount of approximately 52.5b US dollar or 40.3b euro.
>
> The transaction resulted in 24.7b euro goodwill provisionally allocated primarily to the US business on the basis of expected synergies. . . . The valuation of the property, plant and equipment, intangible assets, investment in associates, interest bearing loans and borrowings and employee benefits is based on the valuation performed by independent valuation specialist. The other assets and liabilities are based on the current best estimates of AB InBev's management.

---

9 Both IFRS and U.S. GAAP require the use of the acquisition method in accounting for business combinations (IFRS 3 and FASB ASC Section 805).

10 As previously described, the definitional criteria are identifiability, control by the company, and expected future benefits. The recognition criteria are probable flows of the expected economic benefits to the company and measurability.

| Exhibit 2 | (Continued) |

The majority of the intangible asset valuation relates to brands with indefinite life. The valuation of the brands with indefinite life is based on a series of factors, including the brand history, the operating plan and the countries in which the brands are sold. The brands with indefinite life include the Budweiser family (including Bud and Bud Light), the Michelob brand family, the Busch brand family and the Natural brand family and have been fair valued for a total amount of 16,473m euro. Distribution agreements and favorable contracts have been fair valued for a total amount of 256m euro. These are being amortized over the term of the associated contracts ranging from 3 to 18 years.

Source: AB InBev 2008 Annual Report, pp. 74–75.

Having described the accounting for acquisition of long-lived assets, we now turn to the topic of measuring long-lived assets in subsequent periods.

DEPRECIATION AND AMORTIZATION OF LONG-LIVED ASSETS

3

Under the cost model of reporting long-lived assets, which is permitted under IFRS and required under U.S. GAAP, the capitalized costs of long-lived tangible assets (other than land, which is not depreciated) and intangible assets with finite useful lives are allocated to subsequent periods as depreciation and amortization expenses. Depreciation and amortization are effectively the same concept, with the term depreciation referring to the process of allocating tangible assets' costs and the term amortization referring to the process of allocating intangible assets' costs.[11] The alternative model of reporting long-lived assets is the **revaluation model**, which is permitted under IFRS but not under U.S. GAAP. Under the revaluation model, a company reports the long-lived asset at fair value rather than at acquisition cost (historical cost) less accumulated depreciation or amortization, as in the cost model.

An asset's carrying amount is the amount at which the asset is reported on the balance sheet. Under the cost model, at any point in time, the carrying amount (also called carrying value or net book value) of a long-lived asset is equal to its historical cost minus the amount of depreciation or amortization that has been accumulated since the asset's purchase (assuming that the asset has not been impaired, a topic which will be addressed in Section 5). Companies may present on the balance sheet the total net amount of property, plant, and equipment and the total net amount of intangible assets. However, more detail is disclosed in the notes to financial statements. The details disclosed typically include the acquisition costs, the depreciation and amortization expenses, the accumulated depreciation and amortization amounts, the depreciation and amortization methods used, and information on the assumptions used to depreciate and amortize long-lived assets.

---

11 Depletion is the term applied to a similar concept for natural resources; costs associated with those resources are allocated to a period on the basis of the usage or extraction of those resources.

3.1 Depreciation Methods and Calculation of Depreciation Expense

Depreciation methods include the **straight-line method**, in which the cost of an asset is allocated to expense evenly over its useful life; **accelerated methods**, in which the allocation of cost is greater in earlier years; and the **units-of-production method**, in which the allocation of cost corresponds to the actual use of an asset in a particular period. The choice of depreciation method affects the amounts reported on the financial statements, including the amounts for reported assets and operating and net income. This, in turn, affects a variety of financial ratios, including fixed asset turnover, total asset turnover, operating profit margin, operating return on assets, and return on assets.

Using the straight-line method, depreciation expense is calculated as depreciable cost divided by estimated useful life and is the same for each period. Depreciable cost is the historical cost of the tangible asset minus the estimated residual (salvage) value.[12] A commonly used accelerated method is the declining balance method, in which the amount of depreciation expense for a period is calculated as some percentage of the carrying amount (i.e., cost net of accumulated depreciation at the beginning of the period). When an accelerated method is used, depreciable cost is not used to calculate the depreciation expense but the carrying amount should not be reduced below the estimated residual value. In the units-of-production method, the amount of depreciation expense for a period is based on the proportion of the asset's production during the period compared with the total estimated productive capacity of the asset over its useful life. The depreciation expense is calculated as depreciable cost times production in the period divided by estimated productive capacity over the life of the asset. Equivalently, the company may estimate a depreciation cost per unit (depreciable cost divided by estimated productive capacity) and calculate depreciation expense as depreciation cost per unit times production in the period. Regardless of the depreciation method used, the carrying amount of the asset is not reduced below the estimated residual value. Example 4 provides an example of these depreciation methods.

EXAMPLE 4

Alternative Depreciation Methods

You are analyzing three hypothetical companies: EVEN-LI Co., SOONER Inc., and AZUSED Co. At the beginning of Year 1, each company buys an identical piece of box manufacturing equipment for $2,300 and has the same assumptions about useful life, estimated residual value, and productive capacity. The annual production of each company is the same, but each company uses a different method of depreciation. As disclosed in each company's notes to the financial statements, each company's depreciation method, assumptions, and production are as follows:

Depreciation method

■ EVEN-LI Co.: straight-line method

---

12 The residual value is the estimated amount that an entity will obtain from disposal of the asset at the end of its useful life.

- SOONER Inc.: double-declining balance method (the rate applied to the carrying amount is double the depreciation rate for the straight-line method)
- AZUSED Co.: units-of-production method

Assumptions and production

- Estimated residual value: $100
- Estimated useful life: 4 years
- Total estimated productive capacity: 800 boxes
- Production in each of the four years: 200 boxes in the first year, 300 in the second year, 200 in the third year, and 100 in the fourth year

1 Using the following template for each company, record its beginning and ending net book value (carrying amount), end-of-year accumulated depreciation, and annual depreciation expense for the box manufacturing equipment.

Template:

	Beginning Net Book Value	Depreciation Expense	Accumulated Depreciation	Ending Net Book Value
Year 1				
Year 2				
Year 3				
Year 4				

2 Explain the significant differences in the timing of the recognition of the depreciation expense.

3 For each company, assume that sales, earnings before interest, taxes, and depreciation, and assets other than the box manufacturing equipment are as shown in the following table. Calculate the total asset turnover ratio, the operating profit margin, and the operating return on assets for each company for each of the four years. Discuss the ratios, comparing results within and across companies.

	Sales	Earnings Before Interest, Taxes, and Depreciation	Carrying Amount of Total Assets, Excluding the Box Manufacturing Equipment, at Year End*
Year 1	$300,000	$36,000	$30,000
Year 2	320,000	38,400	32,000
Year 3	340,000	40,800	34,000
Year 4	360,000	43,200	36,000

*Assume that total assets at the beginning of Year 1, *including* the box manufacturing equipment, had a value of $30,300. Assume that depreciation expense on assets other than the box manufacturing equipment totaled $1,000 per year.

Solution to 1:

For *each* company, the following information applies: Beginning net book value in Year 1 equals the purchase price of $2,300; accumulated year-end depreciation equals the balance from the previous year plus the current year's depreciation expense; ending net book value (carrying amount) equals original cost minus accumulated year-end depreciation (which is the same as beginning net book value minus depreciation expense); and beginning net book value in Years 2, 3, and 4 equals the ending net book value of the prior year. The following text and filled-in templates describe how depreciation *expense* is calculated for each company.

EVEN-LI Co. uses the straight-line method, so depreciation expense in each year equals $550, which is calculated as ($2,300 original cost − $100 residual value)/4 years. The net book value at the end of Year 4 is the estimated residual value of $100.

EVEN-LI Co.	Beginning Net Book Value	Depreciation Expense	Accumulated Year-End Depreciation	Ending Net Book Value
Year 1	$2,300	$550	$550	$1,750
Year 2	1,750	550	1,100	1,200
Year 3	1,200	550	1,650	650
Year 4	650	550	2,200	100

SOONER Inc. uses the double-declining balance method. The depreciation rate for the double-declining balance method is double the depreciation rate for the straight-line method. The depreciation rate under the straight-line method is 25 percent (100 percent divided by 4 years). Thus, the depreciation rate for the double-declining balance method is 50 percent (2 times 25 percent). The depreciation expense for the first year is $1,150 (50 percent of $2,300). Note that under this method, the depreciation rate of 50 percent is applied to the carrying amount (net book value) of the asset, without adjustment for expected residual value. Because the carrying amount of the asset is not depreciated below its estimated residual value, however, the depreciation expense in the final year of depreciation decreases the ending net book value (carrying amount) to the estimated residual value.

SOONER Inc.	Beginning Net Book Value	Depreciation Expense	Accumulated Year-End Depreciation	Ending Net Book Value
Year 1	$2,300	$1,150	$1,150	$1,150
Year 2	1,150	575	1,725	575
Year 3	575	288	2,013	287
Year 4	287	187	2,200	100

Another common approach (not required in this question) is to use an accelerated method, such as the double-declining method, for some period (a year or more) and then to change to the straight-line method for the remaining life of the asset. If SOONER had used the double-declining method for the first year and then switched to the straight-line method for Years 2, 3, and 4, the depreciation expense would be $350 [($1,150 − $100 estimated residual value)/3 years] a year for Years 2, 3, and 4. The results for SOONER under this alternative approach are shown below.

SOONER Inc.	Beginning Net Book Value	Depreciation Expense	Accumulated Year-End Depreciation	Ending Net Book Value
Year 1	$2,300	$1,150	$1,150	$1,150
Year 2	1,150	350	1,500	800
Year 3	800	350	1,850	450
Year 4	450	350	2,200	100

AZUSED Co. uses the units-of-production method. Dividing the equipment's total depreciable cost by its total productive capacity gives a cost per unit of $2.75, calculated as ($2,300 original cost − $100 residual value)/800. The depreciation expense recognised each year is the number of units produced times $2.75. For Year 1, the amount of depreciation expense is $550 (200 units times $2.75). For Year 2, the amount is $825 (300 units times $2.75). For Year 3, the amount is $550. For Year 4, the amount is $275.

AZUSED Co.	Beginning Net Book Value	Depreciation Expense	Accumulated Year-End Depreciation	Ending Net Book Value
Year 1	$2,300	$550	$550	$1,750
Year 2	1,750	825	1,375	925
Year 3	925	550	1,925	375
Year 4	375	275	2,200	100

Solution to 2:

All three methods result in the same total amount of accumulated depreciation over the life of the equipment. The significant differences are simply in the timing of the recognition of the depreciation expense. The straight-line method recognises the expense evenly, the accelerated method recognises most of the expense in the first year, and the units-of-production method recognises the expense on the basis of production (or use of the asset). Under all three methods, the ending net book value is $100.

Solution to 3:

Total asset turnover ratio = Total revenue ÷ Average total assets

Operating profit margin = Earnings before interest and taxes ÷ Total revenue

Operating return on assets = Earnings before interest and taxes ÷ Average total assets

Ratios are shown in the table below, and details of the calculations for Years 1 and 2 are described after discussion of the ratios.

Ratio*	EVEN-LI Co.			SOONER Inc.			AZUSED Co.		
	AT	PM (%)	ROA (%)	AT	PM (%)	ROA (%)	AT	PM (%)	ROA (%)
Year 1	9.67	11.48	111.04	9.76	11.28	110.17	9.67	11.48	111.04
Year 2	9.85	11.52	113.47	10.04	11.51	115.57	9.90	11.43	113.10
Year 3	10.02	11.54	115.70	10.17	11.62	118.21	10.10	11.54	116.64
Year 4	10.18	11.57	117.74	10.23	11.67	119.42	10.22	11.65	118.98

*AT = Total asset turnover ratio. PM = Operating profit margin. ROA = Operating return on assets.

For all companies, the asset turnover ratio increased over time because sales grew at a faster rate than that of the assets. SOONER had consistently higher asset turnover ratios than the other two companies, however, because higher depreciation expense in the earlier periods decreased its average total assets. In addition, the higher depreciation in earlier periods resulted in SOONER having lower operating profit margin and operating ROA in the first year and higher operating profit margin and operating ROA in the later periods. SOONER appears to be more efficiently run, on the basis of its higher asset turnover and greater increases in profit margin and ROA over time; however, these comparisons reflect differences in the companies' choice of depreciation method. In addition, an analyst might question the sustainability of the extremely high ROAs for all three companies because such high profitability levels would probably attract new competitors, which would likely put downward pressure on the ratios.

EVEN-LI Co.

Year 1:

Total asset turnover ratio = 300,000/[(30,300 + 30,000 + 1,750)/2]
= 300,000/31,025 = 9.67
Operating profit margin = (36,000 − 1,000 − 550)/300,000
= 34,450/300,000 = 11.48%
Operating ROA = 34,450/31,025 = 111.04%

Year 2:

Total asset turnover ratio = 320,000/[(30,000 + 1,750 + 32,000 + 1,200)/2]
= 320,000/32,475 = 9.85
Operating profit margin = (38,400 − 1,000 − 550)/320,000
= 36,850/320,000 = 11.52%
Operating ROA = 36,850/32,475 = 113.47%

SOONER Inc.

Year 1:

Total asset turnover ratio = 300,000/[(30,300 + 30,000 + 1,150)/2]
= 300,000/30,725 = 9.76
Operating profit margin = (36,000 − 1,000 − 1,150)/300,000
= 33,850/300,000 = 11.28%
Operating ROA = 33,850/30,725 = 110.17%

Year 2:

Total asset turnover ratio = 320,000/[(30,000 + 1,150 + 32,000 + 575)/2]

$$= 320,000/31,862.50 = 10.04$$
$$\text{Operating profit margin} = (38,400 - 1,000 - 575)/320,000$$
$$= 36,825/320,000 = 11.51\%$$
$$\text{Operating ROA} = 36,825/31,862.50 = 115.57\%$$

AZUSED Co.

Year 1:

$$\text{Total asset turnover ratio} = 300,000/[(30,300 + 30,000 + 1,750)/2]$$
$$= 300,000/31,025 = 9.67$$
$$\text{Operating profit margin} = (36,000 - 1,000 - 550)/300,000 =$$
$$34,450/300,000 = 11.48\%$$
$$\text{Operating ROA} = 34,450/31,025 = 111.04\%$$

Year 2:

$$\text{Total asset turnover ratio} = 320,000/[(30,000 + 1,750 + 32,000 + 925)/2]$$
$$= 320,000/32,337.50 = 9.90$$
$$\text{Operating profit margin} = (38,400 - 1,000 - 825)/320,000$$
$$= 36,575/320,000 = 11.43\%$$
$$\text{Operating ROA} = 36,575/32,337.50 = 113.10\%$$

In many countries, a company must use the same depreciation methods for both financial and tax reporting. In other countries, including the United States, a company need not use the same depreciation method for financial reporting and taxes. As a result of using different depreciation methods for financial and tax reporting, pre-tax income on the income statement and taxable income on the tax return may differ. Thus, the amount of tax expense computed on the basis of pre-tax income and the amount of taxes actually owed on the basis of taxable income may differ. Although these differences eventually reverse because the total depreciation is the same regardless of the timing of its recognition in financial statements versus on tax returns, during the period of the difference, the balance sheet will show what is known as deferred taxes. For instance, if a company uses straight-line depreciation for financial reporting and an accelerated depreciation method for tax purposes, the company's financial statements will report lower depreciation expense and higher pre-tax income in the first year, compared with the amount of depreciation expense and taxable income in its tax reporting. (Compare the depreciation expense in Year 1 for EVEN-LI Co. and SOONER Inc. in the previous example.) Tax expense calculated on the basis of the financial statements' pre-tax income will be higher than taxes payable on the basis of taxable income; the difference between the two amounts represents a deferred tax liability. The deferred tax liability will be reduced as the difference reverses (i.e., when depreciation for financial reporting is higher than the depreciation for tax purposes) and the income tax is paid.

Significant estimates required for calculating depreciation include the useful life of the asset (or its total lifetime productive capacity) and its expected residual value at the end of that useful life. A longer useful life and higher expected residual value decrease the amount of annual depreciation expense relative to a shorter useful life and lower expected residual value. Companies should review their estimates periodically to ensure they remain reasonable. IFRS require companies to review estimates annually.

Although no significant differences exist between IFRS and U.S. GAAP with respect to the definition of depreciation and the acceptable depreciation methods, IFRS require companies to use a component method of depreciation.[13] Companies are required to separately depreciate the significant components of an asset (parts of an item with a cost that is significant in relation to the total cost and/or with different useful lives) and thus require additional estimates for the various components. For instance, it may be appropriate to depreciate separately the engine, frame, and interior furnishings of an aircraft. Under U.S. GAAP, the component method of depreciation is allowed but is seldom used in practice.[14] Example 5 illustrates depreciating components of an asset.

EXAMPLE 5

Illustration of Depreciating Components of an Asset

CUTITUP Co., a hypothetical company, purchases a milling machine, a type of machine used for shaping metal, at a total cost of $10,000. $2,000 was estimated to represent the cost of the rotating cutter, a significant component of the machine. The company expects the machine to have a useful life of eight years and a residual value of $3,000 and that the rotating cutter will need to be replaced every two years. Assume the entire residual value is attributable to the milling machine itself, and assume the company uses straight-line depreciation for all assets.

1   How much depreciation expense would the company report in Year 1 if it uses the component method of depreciation, and how much depreciation expense would the company report in Year 1 if it does not use the component method?

2   Assuming a new cutter with an estimated two-year useful life is purchased at the end of Year 2 for $2,000, what depreciation expenses would the company report in Year 3 if it uses the component method and if it does not use the component method?

3   Assuming replacement of the cutter every two years at a price of $2,000, what is the total depreciation expense over the eight years if the company uses the component method compared with the total depreciation expense if the company does not use the component method?

4   How many different items must the company estimate in the first year to compute depreciation expense for the milling machine if it uses the component method, and how does this compare with what would be required if it does not use the component method?

Solution to 1:

Depreciation expense in Year 1 under the component method would be $1,625. For the portion of the machine excluding the cutter, the depreciable base is total cost minus the cost attributable to the cutter minus the estimated residual value = $10,000 − $2,000 − $3,000 = $5,000. Depreciation expense for the machine excluding the cutter in the first year equals $625 (depreciable cost divided by the useful life of the machine = $5,000/8 years). For the cutter, the depreciation expense equals $1,000 (depreciable cost divided by the useful life of the cutter = $2,000/2 years). Thus, the total depreciation expense for Year 1 under the

---

13 IAS 16 *Property, Plant and Equipment*, paragraphs 43–47 [Depreciation].
14 According to the Ernst & Young Academic Resource Center.

component method is $1,625 (the sum of the depreciation expenses of the two components = $625 + $1,000). Depreciation expense in Year 2 would also be $1,625.

If the company does not use the component method, depreciation expense in Year 1 is $875 (the depreciable cost of the total milling machine divided by its useful life = [$10,000 − $3,000]/8 years). Depreciation expense in Year 2 would also be $875.

Solution to 2:

Assuming that at the end of Year 2, the company purchases a new cutter for $2,000 with an estimated two-year life, under the component method, the depreciation expense in Year 3 will remain at $1,625. If the company does not use the component method and purchases a new cutter with an estimated two-year life for $2,000 at the end of Year 2, the depreciation expense in Year 3 will be $1,875 [$875 + ($2,000/2) = $875 + $1,000].

Solution to 3:

Over the eight years, assuming replacement of the cutters every two years at a price of $2,000, the total depreciation expense will be $13,000 [$1,625 × 8 years] when the component method is used. When the component method is not used, the total depreciation expense will also be $13,000 [$875 × 2 years + $1,875 × 6 years]. This amount equals the total expenditures of $16,000 [$10,000 + 3 cutters × $2,000] less the residual value of $3,000.

Solution to 4:

The following table summarizes the estimates required in the first year to compute depreciation expense if the company does or does not use the component method:

Estimate	Required Using Component Method?	Required if Not Using Component Method?
Useful life of milling machine	Yes	Yes
Residual value of milling machine	Yes	Yes
Portion of machine cost attributable to cutter	Yes	No
Portion of residual value attributable to cutter	Yes	No
Useful life of cutter	Yes	No

Total depreciation expense may be allocated between the cost of sales and other expenses. Within the income statement, depreciation expense of assets used in production is usually allocated to the cost of sales, and the depreciation expense of assets not used in production may be allocated to some other expense category. For instance, depreciation expense may be allocated to selling, general, and administrative expenses if depreciable assets are used in those functional areas. Notes to the financial statements sometimes disclose information regarding which income statement line items include depreciation expense, although the exact amount of detail disclosed by individual companies varies.

3.2 Amortization Methods and Calculation of Amortization Expense

Amortization is similar in concept to depreciation. The term amortization applies to intangible assets, and the term depreciation applies to tangible assets. Both terms refer to the process of allocating the cost of an asset over the asset's useful life. Only those intangible assets assumed to have finite useful lives are amortized over their useful lives, following the pattern in which the benefits are used up. Acceptable amortization methods are the same as the methods acceptable for depreciation. Assets assumed to have an indefinite useful life (in other words, without a finite useful life) are not amortized. An intangible asset is considered to have an indefinite useful life when there is "no foreseeable limit to the period over which the asset is expected to generate net cash inflows" for the company.[15]

Intangible assets with finite useful lives include an acquired customer list expected to provide benefits to a direct-mail marketing company for two to three years, an acquired patent or copyright with a specific expiration date, an acquired license with a specific expiration date and no right to renew the license, and an acquired trademark for a product that a company plans to phase out over a specific number of years. Examples of intangible assets with indefinite useful lives include an acquired license that, although it has a specific expiration date, can be renewed at little or no cost and an acquired trademark that, although it has a specific expiration, can be renewed at a minimal cost and relates to a product that a company plans to continue selling for the foreseeable future.

As with depreciation for a tangible asset, the calculation of amortization for an intangible asset requires the original amount at which the intangible asset is recognised and estimates of the length of its useful life and its residual value at the end of its useful life. Useful lives are estimated on the basis of the expected use of the asset, considering any factors that may limit the life of the asset, such as legal, regulatory, contractual, competitive, or economic factors.

EXAMPLE 6

Amortization Expense

IAS 38 *Intangible Assets* provides illustrative examples regarding the accounting for intangible assets, including the following:

> A direct-mail marketing company acquires a customer list and expects that it will be able to derive benefit from the information on the list for at least one year, but no more than three years. The customer list would be amortized over management's best estimate of its useful life, say 18 months. Although the direct-mail marketing company may intend to add customer names and other information to the list in the future, the expected benefits of the acquired customer list relate only to the customers on that list at the date it was acquired.

In this example, in what ways would management's decisions and estimates affect the company's financial statements?

Solution:

Because the acquired customer list is expected to generate future economic benefits for a period greater than one year, the cost of the list should be capitalized and not expensed. The acquired customer list is determined to not have an

---

15 IAS 38 *Intangible Assets*, paragraph 88.

indefinite life and must be amortized. Management must estimate the useful life of the customer list and must select an amortization method. In this example, the list appears to have no residual value. Both the amortization method and the estimated useful life affect the amount of the amortization expense in each period. A shorter estimated useful life, compared with a longer estimated useful life, results in a higher amortization expense each year over a shorter period, but the *total* accumulated amortization expense over the life of the intangible asset is unaffected by the estimate of the useful life. Similarly, the total accumulated amortization expense over the life of the intangible asset is unaffected by the choice of amortization method. The amortization expense per period depends on the amortization method. If the straight-line method is used, the amortization expense is the same for each year of useful life. If an accelerated method is used, the amortization expense will be higher in earlier years.

THE REVALUATION MODEL

4

The revaluation model is an alternative to the cost model for the periodic valuation and reporting of long-lived assets. IFRS permit the use of either the revaluation model or the cost model, but the revaluation model is not allowed under U.S. GAAP. Revaluation changes the carrying amounts of classes of long-lived assets to fair value (the fair value must be measured reliably). Under the cost model, carrying amounts are historical costs less accumulated depreciation or amortization. Under the revaluation model, carrying amounts are the fair values at the date of revaluation less any subsequent accumulated depreciation or amortization.

IFRS allow companies to value long-lived assets either under a cost model at historical cost minus accumulated depreciation or amortization or under a revaluation model at fair value. In contrast, U.S. accounting standards require the cost model be used. A key difference between the two models is that the cost model allows only decreases in the values of long-lived assets compared with historical costs but the revaluation model may result in increases in the values of long-lived assets to amounts greater than historical costs.

IFRS allow a company to use the cost model for some classes of assets and the revaluation model for others, but the company must apply the same model to all assets within a particular class of assets and must revalue all items within a class to avoid selective revaluation. Examples of different classes of assets include land, land and buildings, machinery, motor vehicles, furniture and fixtures, and office equipment. The revaluation model may be used for classes of intangible assets but only if an active market for the assets exists, because the revaluation model may only be used if the fair values of the assets can be measured reliably. For practical purposes, the revaluation model is rarely used for either tangible or intangible assets, but its use is especially rare for intangible assets.

Under the revaluation model, whether an asset revaluation affects earnings depends on whether the revaluation initially increases or decreases an asset class' carrying amount. If a revaluation initially decreases the carrying amount of the asset class, the decrease is recognised in profit or loss. Later, if the carrying amount of the asset class increases, the increase is recognised in profit or loss to the extent that it reverses a revaluation decrease of the same asset class previously recognised in profit or loss. Any increase in excess of the reversal amount will not be recognised in the income statement but will be recorded directly to equity in a revaluation surplus account. An upward revaluation is treated the same as the amount in excess of the reversal amount. In other words, if a revaluation initially increases the carrying amount of the asset class, the increase in the carrying amount of the asset class bypasses the income statement and goes directly to equity under the heading of revaluation surplus. Any subsequent decrease in the asset's value first decreases the revaluation surplus and then goes to income.

The next two examples illustrate revaluation of long-lived assets under IFRS.

EXAMPLE 7

Revaluation Resulting in an Increase in Carrying Amount Followed by Subsequent Revaluation Resulting in a Decrease in Carrying Amount

UPFIRST, a hypothetical manufacturing company, has elected to use the revaluation model for its machinery. Assume for simplicity that the company owns a single machine, which it purchased for €10,000 on the first day of its fiscal period, and that the measurement date occurs simultaneously with the company's fiscal period end.

1   At the end of the first fiscal period after acquisition, assume the fair value of the machine is determined to be €11,000. How will the company's financial statements reflect the asset?

2   At the end of the second fiscal period after acquisition, assume the fair value of the machine is determined to be €7,500. How will the company's financial statements reflect the asset?

Solution to 1:

At the end of the first fiscal period, the company's balance sheet will show the asset at a value of €11,000. The €1,000 increase in the value of the asset will appear in other comprehensive income and be accumulated in equity under the heading of revaluation surplus.

Solution to 2:

At the end of the second fiscal period, the company's balance sheet will show the asset at a value of €7,500. The total decrease in the carrying amount of the asset is €3,500 (€11,000 – €7,500). Of the €3,500 decrease, the first €1,000 will reduce the amount previously accumulated in equity under the heading of revaluation surplus. The other €2,500 will be shown as a loss on the income statement.

EXAMPLE 8

Revaluation Resulting in a Decrease in Asset's Carrying Amount Followed by Subsequent Revaluation Resulting in an Increase in Asset's Carrying Amount

DOWNFIRST, a hypothetical manufacturing company, has elected to use the revaluation model for its machinery. Assume for simplicity that the company owns a single machine, which it purchased for €10,000 on the first day of its fiscal period, and that the measurement date occurs simultaneously with the company's fiscal period end.

1   At the end of the first fiscal period after acquisition, assume the fair value of the machine is determined to be €7,500. How will the company's financial statements reflect the asset?

2   At the end of the second fiscal period after acquisition, assume the fair value of the machine is determined to be €11,000. How will the company's financial statements reflect the asset?

Solution to 1:

At the end of the first fiscal period, the company's balance sheet will show the asset at a value of €7,500. The €2,500 decrease in the value of the asset will appear as a loss on the company's income statement.

Solution to 2:

At the end of the second fiscal period, the company's balance sheet will show the asset at a value of €11,000. The total increase in the carrying amount of the asset is an increase of €3,500 (€11,000 − €7,500). Of the €3,500 increase, the first €2,500 reverses a previously reported loss and will be reported as a gain on the income statement. The other €1,000 will bypass profit or loss and be reported as other comprehensive income and be accumulated in equity under the heading of revaluation surplus.

Exhibit 3 provides an example of a company's disclosures concerning revaluation. The exhibit shows an excerpt from the 2006 annual report of KPN, a Dutch telecommunications and multimedia company. The excerpt is from the section of the annual report in which the company explains differences between its reporting under IFRS and its reporting under U.S. GAAP.[16] One of these differences, as previously noted, is that U.S. GAAP do not allow revaluation of fixed assets held for use. KPN elected to report a class of fixed assets (cables) at fair value and explained that under U.S. GAAP, using the cost model, the value of the class at the end of 2006 would have been €350 million lower.

---

16 On 15 November 2007, the SEC approved rule amendments under which financial statements from foreign private issuers in the United States will be accepted without reconciliation to U.S. GAAP if the financial statements are prepared in accordance with IFRS as issued by the International Accounting Standards Board. The new rule is effective for the 2007 fiscal year. As a result, companies such as KPN no longer need to provide reconciliations to U.S. GAAP.

Exhibit 3	Impact of Revaluation

[Excerpt from the annual report of Koninklijke KPN N.V. (NYSE: KPN) explaining certain differences between IFRS and U.S. GAAP regarding "Deemed cost fixed assets"]

KPN elected the exemption to revalue certain of its fixed assets upon the transition to IFRS to fair value and to use this fair value as their deemed cost. KPN applied the depreciated replacement cost method to determine this fair value. The revalued assets pertain to certain cables, which form part of property, plant & equipment. Under U.S. GAAP, this revaluation is not allowed and therefore results in a reconciling item. As a result, the value of these assets as of December 31, 2006 under U.S. GAAP is EUR 350 million lower (2005: EUR 415 million; 2004: EUR 487 million) than under IFRS.

Source: KPN's Form 20-F, p. 168, filed 1 March 2007.

Clearly, the use of the revaluation model as opposed to the cost model can have a significant impact on the financial statements of companies. This has potential consequences for comparing financial performance using financial ratios of companies that use different models.

5

IMPAIRMENT OF ASSETS

In contrast with depreciation and amortization charges, which serve to allocate the depreciable cost of a long-lived asset over its useful life, impairment charges reflect an unanticipated decline in the value of an asset. Both IFRS and U.S. GAAP require companies to write down the carrying amount of impaired assets. Impairment reversals are permitted under IFRS but not under U.S. GAAP.

An asset is considered to be impaired when its carrying amount exceeds its recoverable amount ("the higher of fair value less cost to sell or value in use" according to IAS 36 *Impairment of Assets*) or under U.S. GAAP when its carrying amount exceeds its fair value. Under U.S. GAAP, however, impairment losses are only recognisable when the carrying amount of the impaired asset is determined to be not recoverable. Therefore, in general, impairment losses are recognised when the asset's carrying amount is not recoverable. However, IFRS and U.S. GAAP define recoverability differently. The following paragraphs describe accounting for impairment for different categories of assets.

5.1 Impairment of Property, Plant, and Equipment

Accounting standards do not require that property, plant, and equipment be tested annually for impairment. Rather, at the end of each reporting period (generally, a fiscal year), a company assesses whether there are indications of asset impairment. If there is no indication of impairment, the asset is not tested for impairment. If there is an indication of impairment, such as evidence of obsolescence, decline in demand for products, or technological advancements, the recoverable amount of the asset should be measured in order to test for impairment. For property, plant, and equipment, impairment losses are recognised when the asset's carrying amount is not recoverable; the carrying amount is more than the recoverable amount. The amount of the impairment loss will reduce the carrying amount of the asset on the balance sheet and will reduce net income on the income statement. The impairment loss is a non-cash item and will not affect cash from operations.

IFRS and U.S. GAAP differ somewhat both in the guidelines for determining that impairment has occurred and in the measurement of an impairment loss. Under IAS 36, an impairment loss is measured as the excess of carrying amount over the recoverable amount of the asset. The recoverable amount of an asset is defined as "the higher of its fair value less costs to sell and its value in use." Value in use is a discounted measure of expected future cash flows. Under U.S. GAAP, assessing recoverability is separate from measuring the impairment loss. An asset's carrying amount is considered not recoverable when it exceeds the undiscounted expected future cash flows. If the asset's carrying amount is considered not recoverable, the impairment loss is measured as the difference between the asset's fair value and carrying amount.

EXAMPLE 9

Impairment of Property, Plant, and Equipment

Sussex, a hypothetical manufacturing company in the United Kingdom, has a machine it uses to produce a single product. The demand for the product has declined substantially since the introduction of a competing product. The company has assembled the following information with respect to the machine:

Carrying amount	£18,000
Undiscounted expected future cash flows	£19,000
Present value of expected future cash flows	£16,000
Fair value if sold	£17,000
Costs to sell	£2,000

1 Under IFRS, what would the company report for the machine?
2 Under U.S. GAAP, what would the company report for the machine?

Solution to 1:

Under IFRS, the company would compare the carrying amount (£18,000) with the higher of its fair value less costs to sell (£15,000) and its value in use (£16,000). The carrying amount exceeds the value in use, the higher of the two amounts, by £2,000. The machine would be written down to the recoverable amount of £16,000, and a loss of £2,000 would be reported in the income statement. The carrying amount of the machine is now £16,000. A new depreciation schedule based on the carrying amount of £16,000 would be developed.

Solution to 2:

Under U.S. GAAP, the carrying amount (£18,000) is compared with the undiscounted expected future cash flows (£19,000). The carrying amount is less than the undiscounted expected future cash flows, so the carrying amount is considered recoverable. The machine would continue to be carried at £18,000, and no loss would be reported.

5.2 Impairment of Intangible Assets with a Finite Life

Intangible assets with a finite life are amortized (carrying amount decreases over time) and may become impaired. As is the case with property, plant, and equipment, the assets are not tested annually for impairment. Instead, they are tested only when significant events suggest the need to test. The company assesses at the end of each reporting period whether a significant event suggesting the need to test for impairment has occurred. Examples of such events include a significant decrease in the market price or a significant adverse change in legal or economic factors. Impairment accounting for intangible assets with a finite life is essentially the same as for tangible assets; the amount of the impairment loss will reduce the carrying amount of the asset on the balance sheet and will reduce net income on the income statement.

5.3 Impairment of Intangibles with Indefinite Lives

Intangible assets with indefinite lives are not amortized. Instead, they are carried on the balance sheet at historical cost but are tested at least annually for impairment. Impairment exists when the carrying amount exceeds its fair value.

5.4 Impairment of Long-Lived Assets Held for Sale

A long-lived (non-current) asset is reclassified as held for sale rather than held for use when it ceases to be used and management's intent is to sell it. For instance, if a building ceases to be used and management's intent is to sell it, the building is reclassified from property, plant, and equipment to non-current assets held for sale. At the time of reclassification, assets previously held for use are tested for impairment. If the carrying amount at the time of reclassification exceeds the fair value less costs to sell, an impairment loss is recognised and the asset is written down to fair value less costs to sell. Long-lived assets held for sale cease to be depreciated or amortized.

5.5 Reversals of Impairments of Long-Lived Assets

After an asset has been deemed impaired and an impairment loss has been reported, the asset's recoverable amount could potentially increase. For instance, a lawsuit appeal may successfully challenge a patent infringement by another company, with the result that a patent previously written down has a higher recoverable amount. IFRS permit impairment losses to be reversed if the recoverable amount of an asset increases regardless of whether the asset is classified as held for use or held for sale. Note that IFRS permit the reversal of impairment losses only. IFRS do not permit the revaluation to the recoverable amount if the recoverable amount exceeds the previous carrying amount. Under U.S. GAAP, the accounting for reversals of impairments depends on whether the asset is classified as held for use or held for sale.[17] Under U.S. GAAP, once an impairment loss has been recognised for assets held for use, it cannot be reversed. In other words, once the value of an asset held for use has been decreased by an impairment charge, it cannot be increased. For assets held for sale, if the fair value increases after an impairment loss, the loss can be reversed.

---

17 FASB ASC Section 360-10-35 [Property, Plant, and Equipment–Overall–Subsequent Measurement].

DERECOGNITION

A company derecognises an asset (i.e., removes it from the financial statements) when the asset is disposed of or is expected to provide no future benefits from either use or disposal. A company may dispose of a long-lived operating asset by selling it, exchanging it, or abandoning it. As previously described, non-current assets that are no longer in use and are to be sold are reclassified as non-current assets held for sale.

6.1 Sale of Long-Lived Assets

The gain or loss on the sale of long-lived assets is computed as the sales proceeds minus the carrying amount of the asset at the time of sale. An asset's carrying amount is typically the net book value (i.e., the historical cost minus accumulated depreciation), unless the asset's carrying amount has been changed to reflect impairment and/or revaluation, as previously discussed.

EXAMPLE 10

Calculation of Gain or Loss on the Sale of Long-Lived Assets

Moussilauke Diners Inc., a hypothetical company, as a result of revamping its menus to focus on healthier food items, sells 450 used pizza ovens and reports a gain on the sale of $1.2 million. The ovens had a carrying amount of $1.9 million (original cost of $5.1 million less $3.2 million of accumulated depreciation). At what price did Moussilauke sell the ovens?

A $0.7 million

B $3.1 million

C $6.3 million

Solution:

B is correct. The ovens had a carrying amount of $1.9 million, and Moussilauke recognised a gain of $1.2 million. Therefore, Moussilauke sold the ovens at a price of $3.1 million. The gain on the sale of $1.2 million is the selling price of $3.1 million minus the carrying amount of $1.9 million. Ignoring taxes, the cash flow from the sale is $3.1 million, which would appear as a cash inflow from investing.

A gain or loss on the sale of an asset is disclosed on the income statement, either as a component of other gains and losses or in a separate line item when the amount is material. A company typically discloses further detail about the sale in the management discussion and analysis and/or financial statement footnotes. In addition, a statement of cash flows prepared using the indirect method adjusts net income to remove any gain or loss on the sale from operating cash flow and to include the amount of proceeds from the sale in cash from investing activities. Recall that the indirect method of the statement of cash flows begins with net income and makes all adjustments to arrive at cash from operations, including removal of gains or losses from non-operating activities.

6.2 Long-Lived Assets Disposed of Other than by a Sale

Long-lived assets to be disposed of other than by a sale (e.g., abandoned, exchanged for another asset, or distributed to owners in a spin-off) are classified as held for use until disposal.[18] Thus, the long-lived assets continue to be depreciated and tested for impairment, unless their carrying amount is zero, as required for other long-lived assets owned by the company.

When an asset is retired or abandoned, the accounting is similar to a sale, except that the company does not record cash proceeds. Assets are reduced by the carrying amount of the asset at the time of retirement or abandonment, and a loss equal to the asset's carrying amount is recorded.

When an asset is exchanged, accounting for the exchange typically involves removing the carrying amount of the asset given up, adding a fair value for the asset acquired, and reporting any difference between the carrying amount and the fair value as a gain or loss. The fair value used is the fair value of the asset given up unless the fair value of the asset acquired is more clearly evident. If no reliable measure of fair value exists, the acquired asset is measured at the carrying amount of the asset given up. A gain is reported when the fair value used for the newly acquired asset exceeds the carrying amount of the asset given up. A loss is reported when the fair value used for the newly acquired asset is less than the carrying amount of the asset given up. If the acquired asset is valued at the carrying amount of the asset given up because no reliable measure of fair value exists, no gain or loss is reported.

When a spin-off occurs, typically, an entire cash generating unit of a company with all its assets is spun off. As an illustration of a spin-off, Altria Group, Inc. effected a spin-off of Kraft Foods on 30 March 2007 by distributing about 89 percent of Kraft's shares to Altria's shareholders. The company prepared unaudited pro forma income statements and balance sheets (for illustrative purposes only) as if the spin-off had occurred at the beginning of the year. Exhibit 4 summarizes information from the asset portion of the company's pro forma balance sheets. The items in the column labeled "Spin-off of Kraft" reflect Kraft's assets being removed from Altria's balance sheet at the time of the spin-off. For example, Kraft's property, plant, and equipment (net of depreciation) totaled $9.7 billion.

| Exhibit 4 | Altria Group, Inc. and Subsidiaries Pro Forma Condensed Consolidated Balance Sheet [Partial] As of 31 December 2006 (Unaudited) |

Assets ($ Millions)	Historical Altria[a]	Spin-off of Kraft[b]	Adjustments[c]	Pro forma Altria
Cash and cash equivalents	$5,020	($239)	$369	$5,150
Receivables, net	6,070	(3,869)		2,201
Inventories	12,186	(3,506)		8,680
Other current assets	2,876	(640)		2,236
Total current assets	$26,152	($8,254)	$369	$18,267
Property, plant, and equipment, net	17,274	(9,693)		7,581
Goodwill	33,235	(25,553)	(1,485)	6,197
Other intangible assets, net	12,085	(10,177)		1,908
Other assets	8,734	(1,897)	305	7,142

---

18 In a spin-off, shareholders of the parent company receive a proportional number of shares in a new, separate entity.

Exhibit 4	(Continued)

Assets ($ Millions)	Historical Altria[a]	Spin-off of Kraft[b]	Adjustments[c]	Pro forma Altria
Total consumer products assets	$97,480	($55,574)	($811)	$41,095
Financial services assets	6,790	0		6,790
Total assets	$104,270	($55,574)	($811)	$47,885

[a]Historical consolidated balance sheet of Altria.

[b] Reflects the removal of Kraft's consolidated balance sheet from the Altria historical consolidated balance sheet.

[c] Represents adjustments, such as for pro forma cash payments by Kraft to Altria, arising from modifications to existing stock awards and tax contingencies, adjustments to goodwill, etc.

Source: Altria's Form 8-K filed with the SEC on 5 April 2007.

PRESENTATION AND DISCLOSURES

7

Under IFRS, for each class of property, plant, and equipment, a company must disclose the measurement bases, the depreciation method, the useful lives (or, equivalently, the depreciation rate) used, the gross carrying amount and the accumulated depreciation at the beginning and end of the period, and a reconciliation of the carrying amount at the beginning and end of the period.[19] In addition, disclosures of restrictions on title and pledges as security of property, plant, and equipment and contractual agreements to acquire property, plant, and equipment are required. If the revaluation model is used, the date of revaluation, details of how the fair value was obtained, the carrying amount under the cost model, and the revaluation surplus must be disclosed.

The disclosure requirements under U.S. GAAP are less exhaustive.[20] A company must disclose the depreciation expense for the period, the balances of major classes of depreciable assets, accumulated depreciation by major classes or in total, and a general description of the depreciation method(s) used in computing depreciation expense with respect to the major classes of depreciable assets.

Under IFRS, for each class of intangible assets, a company must disclose whether the useful lives are indefinite or finite. If finite, for each class of intangible asset, a company must disclose the useful lives (or, equivalently, the amortization rate) used, the amortization methods used, the gross carrying amount and the accumulated amortization at the beginning and end of the period, where amortization is included on the income statement, and a reconciliation of the carrying amount at the beginning and end of the period.[21] If an asset has an indefinite life, the company must disclose the carrying amount of the asset and why it is considered to have an indefinite life. Similar to property, plant, and equipment, disclosures of restrictions on title and pledges as security of intangible assets and contractual agreements to acquire intangible assets are required. If the revaluation model is used, the date of revaluation, details of how the fair value was obtained, the carrying amount under the cost model, and the revaluation surplus must be disclosed.

---

19 IAS 16 *Property, Plant and Equipment*, paragraphs 73–78 [Disclosure].

20 FASB ASC Section 360-10-50 [Property, Plant, and Equipment–Overall–Disclosure].

21 IAS 38 *Intangible Assets*, paragraphs 118–128 [Disclosure].

Under U.S. GAAP, companies are required to disclose the gross carrying amounts and accumulated amortization in total and by major class of intangible assets, the aggregate amortization expense for the period, and the estimated amortization expense for the next five fiscal years.[22]

The disclosures related to impairment losses also differ under IFRS and U.S. GAAP. Under IFRS, a company must disclose for each class of assets the amounts of impairment losses and reversals of impairment losses recognised in the period and where those are recognised on the financial statements.[23] The company must also disclose in aggregate the main classes of assets affected by impairment losses and reversals of impairment losses and the main events and circumstances leading to recognition of these impairment losses and reversals of impairment losses. Under U.S. GAAP, there is no reversal of impairment losses. The company must disclose a description of the impaired asset, what led to the impairment, the method of determining fair value, the amount of the impairment loss, and where the loss is recognised on the financial statements.[24]

To illustrate financial statement presentation and disclosures, Example 11 provides excerpts relating to intangible assets and property, plant, and equipment from the annual report of Vodafone Group Plc for the year ended 31 March 2009.

EXAMPLE 11

Financial Statement Presentation and Disclosures for Long-Lived Assets

The following exhibits include excerpts from the annual report for the year ended 31 March 2009 of Vodafone Group Plc (London: VOD), a global mobile telecommunications company headquartered in the United Kingdom.

Exhibit 5	Vodafone Group Plc Excerpts from the Consolidated Financial Statements

Excerpt from the Consolidated Income Statement For the Years Ended 31 March (Currency in £ Millions)			
	Note	2009	2008
Revenue	3	41,017	35,478
⋮	⋮	⋮	⋮
Impairment losses	10*	(5,900)	—
⋮	⋮	⋮	⋮
Operating profit/(loss)	4	5,857	10,047
⋮	⋮	⋮	⋮
Profit/(loss) before taxation		4,189	9,001
Income tax expense	6	(1,109)	(2,245)
Profit/(loss) for the financial year from continuing operations		3,080	6,756
Loss for the year from discontinued operations	30	—	—

---

22 FASB ASC Section 350-30-50 [Intangibles–General–Disclosure].
23 IAS 36 *Impairment of Assets*, paragraphs 126–131 [Disclosure].
24 FASB ASC Section 360-10-50 [Property, Plant, and Equipment–Overall–Disclosure] and FASB ASC Section 350-30-50 [Intangibles–General–Disclosure].

Exhibit 5	(Continued)

Excerpt from the Consolidated Income Statement For the Years Ended 31 March (Currency in £ Millions)

	Note	2009	2008
Profit/(loss) for the financial year		**3,080**	**6,756**
Attributable to:			
– Equity shareholders	23	3,078	6,660
– Minority interests		2	96
		3,080	**6,756**

*Notes relating to property, plant, and equipment and intangible assets are underlined.

Excerpt from the Consolidated Statement of Recognised Income and Expense For the Years Ended 31 March (Currency in £ Millions)

	Note	2009	2008
(Losses)/gains on revaluation of available-for-sale investments, net of tax	22	(2,383)	1,949
⋮	⋮	⋮	⋮
Revaluation gain	22	68	—
⋮	⋮	⋮	⋮
Net gain/(loss) recognised directly in equity		**9,854**	**6,909**
Profit/(loss) for the financial year		3,080	6,756
Total recognised income and expense relating to the year		**12,934**	**13,665**
Attributable to:			
– Equity shareholders		13,037	13,912
– Minority interests		(103)	(247)
		12,934	**13,665**

Excerpt from the Consolidated Balance Sheet at 31 March (Currency in £ Millions)

	Note	2009	2008
Non-current assets			
Goodwill	9	53,958	51,336
Other intangible assets	9	20,980	18,995
Property, plant and equipment	11	19,250	16,735
⋮	⋮	⋮	⋮
		139,670	118,546
Current assets		13,029	8,724
Total assets		**152,699**	**127,270**

Equity

(continued)

Excerpt from the Consolidated Balance Sheet at 31 March (Currency in £ Millions)			
	Note	**2009**	**2008**
⋮	⋮	⋮	⋮
Accumulated other recognised income and expense	22	20,517	10,588
⋮	⋮	⋮	⋮
Total equity		84,777	76,471
Non-current liabilities		39,975	28,826
Current liabilities		27,947	21,973
Total equity and liabilities		**152,699**	**127,270**

Exhibit 6   **Vodafone Group Plc**
Excerpts from the Notes to the Consolidated Financial Statements

Excerpt from Note 9, Intangible Assets (Currency in £ Millions)					
Intangible assets	**Goodwill**	**Licences and Spectrum**	**Computer Software**	**Other**	**Total**
Cost:					
31 March 2008	91,762	22,040	5,800	1,188	120,790
Exchange movements	14,298	2,778	749	153	17,978
Arising on acquisition	613	199	69	130	1,011
Additions	—	1,138	1,144	—	2,282
Disposals	—	(1)	(403)	—	(404)
Transfer to investments in associated undertakings	(9)	(16)	—	—	(25)
31 March 2009	106,664	26,138	7,359	1,471	141,632
Accumulated impairment losses and amortization:					
31 March 2008	40,426	5,132	4,160	741	50,459
Exchange movements	6,630	659	569	126	7,984
Amortization charge for the year	—	1,522	885	346	2,753
Impairment losses	5,650	250	—	—	5,900
Disposals	—	—	(391)	—	(391)
Transfers to investments in associated undertakings	—	(11)	—	—	(11)
31 March 2009	52,706	7,552	5,223	1,213	66,694
Net book value:					
31 March 2008	51,336	16,908	1,640	447	70,331
31 March 2009	53,958	18,586	2,136	258	74,938

For licences and spectrum and other intangible assets, amortization is included within the cost of sales line within the consolidated income statement. Licences and spectrum with a net book value of £2,765m (2008: £nil) have been pledged as security against borrowings.

Excerpt from Note 10, Impairment Impairment losses

Impairment losses recognised in the consolidated income statement as a separate line item within operating profit, in respect of goodwill and licences and spectrum fees are as follows (£m):

Cash generating unit	Reportable segment	2009	2008	2007
⋮	⋮	⋮	—	—
Turkey	Other Africa and Central Europe	2,250	—	—
⋮	⋮	⋮	—	—
Total		5,900	—	11,600

The impairment losses were based on value in use calculations....

Turkey

At 30 September 2008, the goodwill was impaired by £1,700 million.... During the second half of the 2009 financial year, impairment losses of £300 million in relation to goodwill and £250 million in relation to licences and spectrum resulted from adverse changes in both the discount rate and a fall in the long term GDP growth rate. The cash flow projections ... were substantially unchanged from those used at 30 September 2008....

Sensitivity to changes in assumptions

The estimated recoverable amount of the Group's operations in Spain, Turkey and Ghana equaled their respective carrying value and, consequently, any adverse change in key assumption would, in isolation, cause a further impairment loss to be recognised....

The changes in the following table to assumptions used in the impairment review would, in isolation, lead to an (increase)/decrease to the aggregate impairment loss recognised in the year ended 31 March 2009:

	Spain	Turkey		Ghana	All other
		Increase by 2% £bn	Decrease by 2% £bn		
Pre-tax adjusted discount rate	⋮ ⋮	(0.4)	0.6	⋮ ⋮	⋮ ⋮
Long term growth rate	⋮ ⋮	0.3	(0.2)	⋮ ⋮	⋮ ⋮
Budgeted EBITDA	⋮ ⋮	0.1	(0.1)	⋮ ⋮	⋮ ⋮
Budgeted capital expenditure	⋮ ⋮	(0.1)	0.1	⋮ ⋮	⋮ ⋮

Excerpt from Note 11, Property, Plant, and Equipment

The net book value of land and buildings and equipment, fixtures and fittings includes £106 million and £82 million, respectively (2008: £110 million and £51 million) in relation to assets held under finance leases. Included in the net book value of land and buildings and equipment, fixtures and fittings are assets in the course of construction, which are not depreciated, with a cost of £44 million and £1,186 million, respectively (2008: £28 million and £1,013 million). Property, plant and equipment with a net book value of £148 million (2008: £1,503 million) has been pledged as security against borrowings.

Excerpt from Note 22, Movements in Accumulated Other Recognised Income and Expense, (Currency in £ Millions)

	Translation Reserve	Pensions Reserve	Available-for-Sale Investments Reserve	Asset Revaluation Surplus	Other	Total
⋮	⋮	⋮	⋮	⋮	⋮	⋮
31 March 2008	5,974	(96)	4.531	112	37	10,558
Gains/(losses) arising in the year	⋮	⋮	⋮	68	⋮	10,023
Transfer to the income statement on disposal	⋮	⋮	⋮	—	⋮	(3)
Tax effect	⋮	⋮	⋮	—	⋮	(61)
31 March 2009	18,451	(259)	2,148	180	(3)	20,517

---

1   As of 31 March 2009, what percentage of other intangible assets and property, plant, and equipment is pledged as security against borrowings?

2   What caused the £250 million impairment losses in relation to licences and spectrum during the year ended 31 March 2009?

3   By what amount would impairment losses related to Turkey change if the pre-tax adjusted discount rate decreased by 2 percent?

4   Where are impairment losses reported on the financial statements? Where is amortization included within the consolidated income statement?

5   What percentage of property, plant, and equipment, based on net book value, is held under finance leases rather than owned as of 31 March 2009?

6   The gains and losses arising in the year on asset revaluation *most likely* are:

    A   reflected on the consolidated income statement.

    B   reported in the notes to the financial statements only.

    C   recognised directly in equity and shown on the consolidated statement of recognised income and expense.

Solution to 1:

Assets that have been pledged as security against borrowings are licences and spectrum, with a net book value of £2,765 million (Note 9), and property, plant, and equipment, with a net book value of £148 million (Note 11). These assets represent 7.24 percent [(2,765 + 148)/(20,980 + 19,250)] of the other intangible assets and property, plant, and equipment.

Solution to 2:

The £250 million impairment losses in relation to licences and spectrum resulted from an increase in the pre-tax adjusted discount rate and a decrease in the long-term growth rate in Turkey (Note 10).

Solution to 3:

A 2 percent decrease in the pre-tax adjusted discount rate related to Turkey would reduce impairment losses by £0.6 billion or £600 million (Note 10).

Solution to 4:

Impairment losses are reported on the consolidated income statement (Exhibit 5). Impairment losses reduce the value of the assets impaired (Note 9) and are thus recognised within the consolidated balance sheet. Amortization is included within the cost of sales line within the consolidated income statement (Note 9).

Solution to 5:

The net book value of land and buildings and equipment, fixtures, and fittings includes £106 million and £82 million, respectively, in relation to assets held under finance leases (Note 22). The sum of these values represents 0.98 percent of the property, plant, and equipment [(106 + 82)/19,250].

Solution to 6:

C is correct. The gains and losses arising in the year on asset revaluation are recognised directly in equity and shown on the consolidated statement of recognised income and expense. They are also reported in the notes to the financial statements (Note 22).

Note that the exhibits in the previous example contain relatively brief excerpts from the company's disclosures. The complete text of the disclosures concerning the company's non-current assets spans seven different footnotes, most of which are several pages long. In addition to information about the discount rate and other assumptions used to calculate impairment charges, the disclosures provide information about the sensitivity of impairment charges to changes in the assumptions.

Overall, an analyst can use the disclosures to understand a company's investments in tangible and intangible assets, how those investments changed during a reporting period, how those changes affected current performance, and what those changes might indicate about future performance.

8   INVESTMENT PROPERTY

Investment property is defined under IFRS as property that is owned (or, in some cases, leased under a finance lease) for the purpose of earning rentals or capital appreciation or both.[25] An example of investment property is a building owned by a company and leased out to tenants. In contrast, other long-lived tangible assets (i.e., property considered to be property, plant, and equipment) are owner-occupied properties used for producing the company's goods and services or for housing the company's administrative activities. Investment properties do not include long-lived tangible assets held for sale in the ordinary course of business. For example, the houses and property owned by a housing construction company are considered to be its inventory.

Under IFRS, companies are allowed to value investment properties using either a cost model or a fair value model. The cost model is identical to the cost model used for property, plant, and equipment. The fair value model, however, differs from the revaluation model used for property, plant, and equipment. Under the revaluation model, whether an asset revaluation affects net income depends on whether the revaluation initially increases or decreases the carrying amount of the asset. In contrast, under the fair value model, all changes in the fair value of the asset affect net income. To use the fair value model, a company must be able to reliably determine the property's fair value on a continuing basis.[26] Under U.S. GAAP, there is no specific definition of investment property. Most operating companies and real estate companies in the United States that hold investment-type property use the historical cost model.

Example 12 presents an excerpt from the annual report of a property company reporting under IFRS.

EXAMPLE 12

Financial Statement Presentation and Disclosures for Long-Lived Assets

The following exhibit presents an excerpt from the annual report for the year ended 31 March 2009 of Daejan Holdings PLC (London: DJAN), a property company headquartered in the United Kingdom.

Exhibit 7	Excerpt from the Consolidated Income Statements at 31 March (Currency in £ thousands)	
	2009	**2008**
Gross rental income	83,918	73,590
Service charge income	12,055	13,362
Total Rental and Related Income from Investment Properties	95,973	86,952
Property operating expenses	(53,470)	(46,464)
Net Rental and Related Income from Investment Properties	42,503	40,488
Profit on Disposal of Investment Properties	6,758	6,578

---

25 IAS 40 *Investment Property* prescribes the accounting treatment for investment property.
26 Fair value of investment property is defined as the price at which the property could be exchanged between knowledgeable, willing parties in an arm's length transaction (IAS 40 *Investment Property*, paragraph 36).

	2009	2008
Valuation gains on investment properties	6,646	46,646
Valuation losses on investment properties	(268,249)	(25,982)
Net Valuation (Losses)/Gains on Investment Properties	(261,603)	20,664
Administrative expenses	(12,039)	(8,629)
Net Operating (Loss)/Profit before Net Financing Costs	(224,381)	59,101

Exhibit 7 (Continued)

1 What was the primary cause of the company's £224,381 thousand net operating loss before net financing costs for the year ended 31 March 2009?

2 What was the primary cause of the company's £59,101 thousand net operating profit before financing costs for the year ended 31 March 2008?

3 What was the primary cause of the change from a £59,101 thousand net operating profit in 2008 to a £224,381 thousand net operating loss in 2009?

4 Do the valuation gains and losses on investment properties indicate that the properties have been sold?

Solution to 1:

The primary cause of the company's net operating loss for the year ended 31 March 2009 was the net valuation loss on investment properties. The net valuation loss of £262 million (valuation gain of £6,646 thousand minus the valuation loss of £268,249 thousand) exceeded the company's net rental income plus its profit on disposal of investment properties.

Solution to 2:

The primary cause of the company's net operating profit for the year ended 31 March 2008 was the £40 million net rental income. Additionally, the company reported net valuation gains on investment properties of £21 million (valuation gain of £46,646 thousand minus the valuation loss of £25,982 thousand) and profit on disposal of investment properties of £7 million.

Solution to 3:

The change from a net operating profit to a net operating loss was primarily due to valuation gains exceeding valuation losses (net valuation gains) in 2008 and valuation losses significantly exceeding valuation gains (net valuation losses) in 2009.

Solution to 4:

No. The valuation gains and losses on investment properties arise from changes in the fair value of properties that are owned by the company. The gains and losses on properties that have been sold are reported as Profit (Loss) on Disposal of Investment Properties. In neither 2008 nor 2009 did the company experience a loss on disposal of investment properties so the line item was reported as Profit on Disposal of Investment Properties.

In general, a company must apply its chosen model (cost or fair value) to all of its investment property. If a company chooses the fair value model for its investment property, it must continue to use the fair value model until it disposes of the property or changes its use such that it is no longer considered investment property (e.g., it becomes owner-occupied property or part of inventory). The company must continue to use the fair value model for that property even if transactions on comparable properties, used to estimate fair value, become less frequent.

Certain valuation issues arise when a company changes the use of property such that it moves from being an investment property to owner-occupied property or part of inventory. If a company's chosen model for investment property is the cost model, such transfers do not change the carrying amount of the property transferred. If a company's chosen model is the fair value model, transfers from investment property to owner-occupied property or to inventory are made at fair value. In other words, the property's fair value at the time of transfer is considered to be its cost for ongoing accounting for the property. If a company's chosen model for investment property is the fair value model and it transfers a property from owner-occupied to investment property, the change in measurement of the property from depreciated cost to fair value is treated like a revaluation. If a company's chosen model is the fair value model and it transfers a property from inventory to investment property, any difference between the inventory carrying amount and the property's fair value at the time of transfer is recognised as profit or loss.

Investment property appears as a separate line item on the balance sheet. Companies are required to disclose whether they use the fair value model or the cost model for their investment property. If the company uses the fair value model, it must make additional disclosures about how it determines fair value and must provide reconciliation between the beginning and ending carrying amounts of investment property. If the company uses the cost model, it must make additional disclosures similar to those for property, plant, and equipment—for example, the depreciation method and useful lives must be disclosed. In addition, if the company uses the cost model, it must also disclose the fair value of investment property.

SUMMARY

Understanding the reporting of long-lived assets at inception requires distinguishing between expenditures that are capitalized (i.e., reported as long-lived assets) and those that are expensed. Once a long-lived asset is recognised, it is reported under the cost model at its historical cost less accumulated depreciation (amortization) and less any impairment and under the revaluation model at its fair value. IFRS permit the use of either the cost model or the revaluation model, whereas U.S. GAAP require the use of the cost model. Most companies reporting under IFRS use the cost model. The choice of different methods to depreciate (amortize) long-lived assets can create challenges for analysts comparing companies.

Key points include the following:

- Expenditures related to long-lived assets are capitalized as part of the cost of assets if they are expected to provide future benefits, typically beyond one year. Otherwise, expenditures related to long-lived assets are expensed as incurred.

- Although capitalizing expenditures, rather than expensing them, results in higher reported profitability in the initial year, it results in lower profitability in subsequent years; however, if a company continues to purchase similar or increasing amounts of assets each year, the profitability-enhancing effect of capitalization continues.

- Capitalizing an expenditure rather than expensing it results in a greater amount reported as cash from operations because capitalized expenditures are classified as an investing cash outflow rather than an operating cash outflow.

- Companies must capitalize interest costs associated with acquiring or constructing an asset that requires a long period of time to prepare for its intended use.

- Including capitalized interest in the calculation of interest coverage ratios provides a better assessment of a company's solvency.

- IFRS require research costs be expensed but allow all development costs (not only software development costs) to be capitalized under certain conditions. Generally, U.S. accounting standards require that research and development costs be expensed; however, certain costs related to software development are required to be capitalized.

- When one company acquires another company, the transaction is accounted for using the acquisition method of accounting in which the company identified as the acquirer allocates the purchase price to each asset acquired (and each liability assumed) on the basis of its fair value. Under acquisition accounting, if the purchase price of an acquisition exceeds the sum of the amounts that can be allocated to individual identifiable assets and liabilities, the excess is recorded as goodwill.

- The capitalized costs of long-lived tangible assets and of intangible assets with finite useful lives are allocated to expense in subsequent periods over their useful lives. For tangible assets, this process is referred to as depreciation, and for intangible assets, it is referred to as amortization.

- Long-lived tangible assets and intangible assets with finite useful lives are reviewed for impairment whenever changes in events or circumstances indicate that the carrying amount of an asset may not be recoverable.

- Intangible assets with an indefinite useful life are not amortized but are reviewed for impairment annually.

- Methods of calculating depreciation or amortization expense include the straight-line method, in which the cost of an asset is allocated to expense in equal amounts each year over its useful life; accelerated methods, in which the allocation of cost is greater in earlier years; and the units-of-production method, in which the allocation of cost corresponds to the actual use of an asset in a particular period.

- Estimates required for depreciation and amortization calculations include the useful life of the equipment (or its total lifetime productive capacity) and its expected residual value at the end of that useful life. A longer useful life and higher expected residual value result in a smaller amount of annual depreciation relative to a shorter useful life and lower expected residual value.

- IFRS permit the use of either the cost model or the revaluation model for the valuation and reporting of long-lived assets, but the revaluation model is not allowed under U.S. GAAP.

- Under the revaluation model, carrying amounts are the fair values at the date of revaluation less any subsequent accumulated depreciation or amortization.

- In contrast with depreciation and amortization charges, which serve to allocate the cost of a long-lived asset over its useful life, impairment charges reflect an unexpected decline in the fair value of an asset to an amount lower than its carrying amount.

- IFRS permit impairment losses to be reversed, with the reversal reported in profit. U.S. GAAP do not permit the reversal of impairment losses.

- The gain or loss on the sale of long-lived assets is computed as the sales proceeds minus the carrying amount of the asset at the time of sale.

- Long-lived assets reclassified as held for sale cease to be depreciated or amortized. Long-lived assets to be disposed of other than by a sale (e.g., by abandonment, exchange for another asset, or distribution to owners in a spin-off) are classified as held for use until disposal. Thus, they continue to be depreciated and tested for impairment.

- Investment property is defined as property that is owned (or, in some cases, leased under a finance lease) for the purpose of earning rentals, capital appreciation, or both.

- Under IFRS, companies are allowed to value investment properties using either a cost model or a fair value model. The cost model is identical to the cost model used for property, plant, and equipment, but the fair value model differs from the revaluation model used for property, plant, and equipment. Under the fair value model, all changes in the fair value of investment property affect net income.

- Under U.S. GAAP, investment properties are generally measured using the cost model.

PRACTICE PROBLEMS

1 JOOVI Inc. has recently purchased and installed a new machine for its manufacturing plant. The company incurred the following costs:

Purchase price	$12,980
Freight and insurance	$1,200
Installation	$700
Testing	$100
Maintenance staff training costs	$500

The total cost of the machine to be shown on JOOVI's balance sheet is *closest*
to:

A $14,180.

B $14,980.

C $15,480.

2 BAURU, S.A., a Brazilian corporation, borrows capital from a local bank to
finance the construction of its manufacturing plant. The loan has the following
conditions:

Borrowing date	1 January 2009
Amount borrowed	500 million Brazilian real (BRL)
Annual interest rate	14 percent
Term of the loan	3 years
Payment method	Annual payment of interest only. Principal amortization is due at the end of the loan term.

The construction of the plant takes two years, during which time BAURU
earned BRL 10 million by temporarily investing the loan proceeds. Which of
the following is the amount of interest related to the plant construction (in BRL
million) that can be capitalized in BAURU's balance sheet?

A 130.

B 140.

C 210.

3 After reading the financial statements and footnotes of a company that follows
IFRS, an analyst identified the following intangible assets:

- product patent expiring in 40 years;
- copyright with no expiration date; and
- goodwill acquired 2 years ago in a business combination.

Which of these assets is an intangible asset with a finite useful life?

	Product Patent	Copyright	Goodwill
A	Yes	Yes	No
B	Yes	No	No
C	No	Yes	Yes

4 Intangible assets with finite useful lives *mostly* differ from intangible assets with infinite useful lives with respect to accounting treatment of:

   A revaluation.

   B impairment.

   C amortization.

5 A financial analyst is studying the income statement effect of two alternative depreciation methods for a recently acquired piece of equipment. She gathers the following information about the equipment's expected production life and use:

	Year 1	Year 2	Year 3	Year 4	Year 5	Total
Units of production	2,000	2,000	2,000	2,000	2,500	10,500

Compared with the units-of-production method of depreciation, if the company uses the straight-line method to depreciate the equipment, its net income in Year 1 will *most likely* be:

   A lower.

   B higher.

   C the same.

6 Juan Martinez, CFO of VIRMIN, S.A., is selecting the depreciation method to use for a new machine. The machine has an expected useful life of six years. Production is expected to be relatively low initially but to increase over time. The method chosen for tax reporting must be the same as the method used for financial reporting. If Martinez wants to minimize tax payments in the first year of the machine's life, which of the following depreciation methods is Martinez *most likely* to use?

   A Straight-line method.

   B Units-of-production method.

   C Double-declining balance method.

The following information relates to Questions 7–8

Miguel Rodriguez of MARIO S.A., an Uruguayan corporation, is computing the depreciation expense of a piece of manufacturing equipment for the fiscal year ended 31 December 2009. The equipment was acquired on 1 January 2009. Rodriguez gathers the following information (currency in Uruguayan pesos, UYP):

Cost of the equipment	UYP 1,200,000
Estimated residual value	UYP 200,000

Expected useful life	8 years
Total productive capacity	800,000 units
Production in FY 2009	135,000 units
Expected production for the next 7 years	95,000 units each year

7 If MARIO uses the straight-line method, the amount of depreciation expense on MARIO's income statement related to the manufacturing equipment is *closest* to:

A 125,000.

B 150,000.

C 168,750.

8 If MARIO uses the units-of-production method, the amount of depreciation expense (in UYP) on MARIO's income statement related to the manufacturing equipment is *closest* to:

A 118,750.

B 168,750.

C 202,500.

9 Which of the following amortization methods is *most likely* to evenly distribute the cost of an intangible asset over its useful life?

A Straight-line method.

B Units-of-production method.

C Double-declining balance method.

10 Which of the following will cause a company to show a lower amount of amortization of intangible assets in the first year after acquisition?

A A higher residual value.

B A higher amortization rate.

C A shorter useful life.

11 An analyst in the finance department of BOOLDO S.A., a French corporation, is computing the amortization of a customer list, an intangible asset, for the fiscal year ended 31 December 2009. She gathers the following information about the asset:

Acquisition cost	€2,300,000
Acquisition date	1 January 2008
Expected residual value at time of acquisition	€500,000

The customer list is expected to result in extra sales for three years after acquisition. The present value of these expected extra sales exceeds the cost of the list.

If the analyst uses the straight-line method, the amount of accumulated amortization related to the customer list as of 31 December 2009 is *closest* to:

A €600,000.

B €1,200,000.

C €1,533,333.

12 A financial analyst is analyzing the amortization of a product patent acquired by MAKETTI S.p.A., an Italian corporation. He gathers the following information about the patent:

Acquisition cost	€5,800,000
Acquisition date	1 January 2009
Patent expiration date	31 December 2015
Total plant capacity of patented product	40,000 units per year
Production of patented product in fiscal year ended 31 December 2009	20,000 units
Expected production of patented product during life of the patent	175,000 units

If the analyst uses the units-of-production method, the amortization expense on the patent for fiscal year 2009 is *closest* to:

A €414,286.

B €662,857.

C €828,571.

13 MARU S.A. de C.V., a Mexican corporation that follows IFRS, has elected to use the revaluation model for its property, plant, and equipment. One of MARU's machines was purchased for 2,500,000 Mexican pesos (MXN) at the beginning of the fiscal year ended 31 March 2010. As of 31 March 2010, the machine has a fair value of MXN 3,000,000. Should MARU show a profit for the revaluation of the machine?

A Yes.

B No, because this revaluation is recorded directly in equity.

C No, because value increases resulting from revaluation can never be recognised as a profit.

14 An analyst is studying the impairment of the manufacturing equipment of WLP Corp., a U.K.-based corporation that follows IFRS. He gathers the following information about the equipment:

Fair value	£16,800,000
Costs to sell	£800,000
Value in use	£14,500,000
Net carrying amount	£19,100,000

The amount of the impairment loss on WLP Corp.'s income statement related to its manufacturing equipment is *closest* to:

A £2,300,000.

B £3,100,000.

C £4,600,000.

15 A financial analyst at BETTO S.A. is analyzing the result of the sale of a vehicle for 85,000 Argentine pesos (ARP) on 31 December 2009. The analyst compiles the following information about the vehicle:

Acquisition cost of the vehicle	ARP 100,000
Acquisition date	1 January 2007
Estimated residual value at acquisition date	ARP 10,000
Expected useful life	9 years
Depreciation method	Straight-line

The result of the sale of the vehicle is *most likely*:

A   a loss of ARP 15,000.

B   a gain of ARP 15,000.

C   a gain of ARP 18,333.

16 CROCO S.p.A sells an intangible asset with a historical acquisition cost of €12 million and an accumulated depreciation of €2 million and reports a loss on the sale of €3.2 million. Which of the following amounts is *most likely* the sale price of the asset?

A   €6.8 million

B   €8.8 million

C   €13.2 million

17 According to IFRS, all of the following pieces of information about property, plant, and equipment must be disclosed in a company's financial statements and footnotes *except for*:

A   useful lives.

B   acquisition dates.

C   amount of disposals.

18 According to IFRS, all of the following pieces of information about intangible assets must be disclosed in a company's financial statements and footnotes *except for*:

A   fair value.

B   impairment loss.

C   amortization rate.

19 Which of the following characteristics is *most likely* to differentiate investment property from property, plant, and equipment?

A   It is tangible.

B   It earns rent.

C   It is long-lived.

20 If a company uses the fair value model to value investment property, changes in the fair value of the asset are *least likely* to affect:

A   net income.

B   net operating income.

C   other comprehensive income.

21 Investment property is *most likely* to:

A   earn rent.

B   be held for resale.

C   be used in the production of goods and services.

22 A company is *most likely* to:

A use a fair value model for some investment property and a cost model for other investment property.

B change from the fair value model when transactions on comparable properties become less frequent.

C change from the fair value model when the company transfers investment property to property, plant, and equipment.

SOLUTIONS

1 B is correct. Only costs necessary for the machine to be ready to use can be capitalized. Therefore, Total capitalized costs = 12,980 + 1,200 + 700 + 100 = $14,980.

2 A is correct. Borrowing costs can be capitalized under IFRS until the tangible asset is ready for use. Also, under IFRS, income earned on temporarily investing the borrowed monies decreases the amount of borrowing costs eligible for capitalization. Therefore, Total capitalized interest = (500 million × 14% × 2 years) − 10 million = 130 million.

3 B is correct. A product patent with a defined expiration date is an intangible asset with a finite useful life. A copyright with no expiration date is an intangible asset with an indefinite useful life. Goodwill is no longer considered an intangible asset under IFRS and is considered to have an indefinite useful life.

4 C is correct. An intangible asset with a finite useful life is amortized, whereas an intangible asset with an indefinite useful life is not.

5 A is correct. If the company uses the straight-line method, the depreciation expense will be one-fifth (20 percent) of the depreciable cost in Year 1. If it uses the units-of-production method, the depreciation expense will be 19 percent (2,000/10,500) of the depreciable cost in Year 1. Therefore, if the company uses the straight-line method, its depreciation expense will be higher and its net income will be lower.

6 C is correct. If Martinez wants to minimize tax payments in the first year of the machine's life, he should use an accelerated method, such as the double-declining balance method.

7 A is correct. Using the straight-line method, depreciation expense amounts to

Depreciation expense = (1,200,000 − 200,000)/8 years = 125,000.

8 B is correct. Using the units-of-production method, depreciation expense amounts to

Depreciation expense = (1,200,000 − 200,000) × (135,000/800,000) = 168,750.

9 A is correct. The straight-line method is the method that evenly distributes the cost of an asset over its useful life because amortization is the same amount every year.

10 A is correct. A higher residual value results in a lower total depreciable cost and, therefore, a lower amount of amortization in the first year after acquisition (and every year after that).

11 B is correct. Using the straight-line method, accumulated amortization amounts to

Accumulated amortization = [(2,300,000 − 500,000)/3 years] × 2 years = 1,200,000.

12 B is correct. Using the units-of-production method, depreciation expense amounts to

Depreciation expense = 5,800,000 × (20,000/175,000) = 662,857.

13 B is correct. In this case, the value increase brought about by the revaluation should be recorded directly in equity. The reason is that under IFRS, an increase in value brought about by a revaluation can only be recognised as a profit to the extent that it reverses a revaluation decrease of the same asset previously recognised in the income statement.

14 B is correct. The impairment loss equals £3,100,000.

Impairment = max(Recoverable amount; Value in use) − Net carrying amount

= max(16,800,000 − 800,000; 14,500,000) − 19,100,000

= −3,100,000.

15 B is correct. The result on the sale of the vehicle equals

Gain or loss on the sale = Sale proceeds − Carrying amount

= Sale proceeds − (Acquisition cost − Accumulated depreciation)

= 85,000 − {100,000 − [((100,000 − 10,000)/9 years) × 3 years]}

= 15,000.

16 A is correct. Gain or loss on the sale = Sale proceeds − Carrying amount. Rearranging this equation, Sale proceeds = Carrying amount + Gain or loss on sale. Thus, Sale price = (12 million − 2 million) + (−3.2 million) = 6.8 million.

17 B is correct. IFRS do not require acquisition dates to be disclosed.

18 A is correct. IFRS do not require fair value of intangible assets to be disclosed.

19 B is correct. Investment property earns rent. Investment property and property, plant, and equipment are tangible and long-lived.

20 C is correct. When a company uses the fair value model to value investment property, changes in the fair value of the property are reported in the income statement—not in other comprehensive income.

21 A is correct. Investment property earns rent. Inventory is held for resale, and property, plant, and equipment are used in the production of goods and services.

22 C is correct. A company will change from the fair value model to either the cost model or revaluation model when the company transfers investment property to property, plant, and equipment.

Income Taxes

by Elbie Antonites, CFA, and Michael A. Broihahn, CFA

LEARNING OUTCOMES

Mastery	The candidate should be able to:
☐	a. describe the differences between accounting profit and taxable income, and define key terms, including deferred tax assets, deferred tax liabilities, valuation allowance, taxes payable, and income tax expense;
☐	b. explain how deferred tax liabilities and assets are created and the factors that determine how a company's deferred tax liabilities and assets should be treated for the purposes of financial analysis;
☐	c. calculate the tax base of a company's assets and liabilities;
☐	d. calculate income tax expense, income taxes payable, deferred tax assets, and deferred tax liabilities, and calculate and interpret the adjustment to the financial statements related to a change in the income tax rate;
☐	e. evaluate the impact of tax rate changes on a company's financial statements and ratios;
☐	f. distinguish between temporary and permanent differences in pre-tax accounting income and taxable income;
☐	g. describe the valuation allowance for deferred tax assets—when it is required and what impact it has on financial statements;
☐	h. compare a company's deferred tax items;
☐	i. analyze disclosures relating to deferred tax items and the effective tax rate reconciliation, and explain how information included in these disclosures affects a company's financial statements and financial ratios;
☐	j. identify the key provisions of and differences between income tax accounting under IFRS and U.S. GAAP.

Note: New rulings and/or pronouncements issued after the publication of the readings on financial reporting and analysis may cause some of the information in these readings to become dated. Candidates are expected to be familiar with the overall analytical framework contained in the study session readings, as well as the implications of alternative accounting methods for financial analysis and valuation, as provided in the assigned readings. Candidates are not responsible for changes that occur after the material was written.

International Financial Statement Analysis, by Thomas R. Robinson, CFA, Jan Hendrik van Greuning, CFA, Elaine Henry, CFA, and Michael A. Broihahn, CFA. Copyright © 2008 by CFA Institute.

1 INTRODUCTION

For those companies reporting under International Financial Reporting Standards (IFRS), IAS 12 covers accounting for a company's income taxes and the reporting of deferred taxes. For those companies reporting under United States generally accepted accounting principles (U.S. GAAP), SFAS No. 109[1] is the primary source for information on accounting for income taxes. Although IFRS and U.S. GAAP follow similar conventions on many income tax issues, there are some key differences that will be discussed in the reading.

Differences between how and when transactions are recognized for financial reporting purposes relative to tax reporting can give rise to differences in tax expense and related tax assets and liabilities. To reconcile these differences, companies that report under either IFRS or U.S. GAAP create a provision on the balance sheet called deferred tax assets or deferred tax liabilities, depending on the nature of the situation.

Deferred tax assets or liabilities usually arise when accounting standards and tax authorities recognize the timing of revenues and expenses at different times. Because timing differences such as these will eventually reverse over time, they are called "temporary differences." Deferred tax assets represent taxes that have been recognized for tax reporting purposes (or often the carrying forward of losses from previous periods) but have not yet been recognized on the income statement prepared for financial reporting purposes. Deferred tax liabilities represent tax expense that has appeared on the income statement for financial reporting purposes, but has not yet become payable under tax regulations.

This reading provides a primer on the basics of income tax accounting and reporting. The reading is organized as follows. Section 2 describes the differences between taxable income and accounting profit. Section 3 explains the determination of tax base, which relates to the valuation of assets and liabilities for tax purposes. Section 4 discusses several types of timing differences between the recognition of taxable and accounting profit. Section 5 examines unused tax losses and tax credits. Section 6 describes the recognition and measurement of current and deferred tax. Section 7 discusses the disclosure and presentation of income tax information on companies' financial statements and illustrates its practical implications for financial analysis. Section 8 provides an overview of the similarities and differences for income-tax reporting between IFRS and U.S. GAAP. A summary of the key points and practice problems in the CFA Institute multiple-choice format conclude the reading.

2 DIFFERENCES BETWEEN ACCOUNTING PROFIT AND TAXABLE INCOME

A company's **accounting profit** is reported on its income statement in accordance with prevailing accounting standards. Accounting profit (also referred to as income before taxes or pretax income) does not include a provision for income tax expense.[2] A company's **taxable income** is the portion of its income that is subject to income taxes under the tax laws of its jurisdiction. Because of different guidelines for how income is reported on a company's financial statements and how it is measured for income tax purposes, accounting profit and taxable income may differ.

---

1 FASB ASC Topic 740 [Income Taxes].
2 As defined under IAS 12, paragraph 5.

A company's taxable income is the basis for its **income tax payable** (a liability) or recoverable (an asset), which is calculated on the basis of the company's tax rate and appears on its balance sheet. A company's **tax expense**, or tax benefit in the case of a recovery, appears on its income statement and is an aggregate of its income tax payable (or recoverable in the case of a tax benefit) and any changes in deferred tax assets and liabilities.

When a company's taxable income is greater than its accounting profit, then its income taxes payable will be higher than what would have otherwise been the case had the income taxes been determined based on accounting profit. **Deferred tax assets**, which appear on the balance sheet, arise when an excess amount is paid for income taxes (taxable income higher than accounting profit) and the company expects to recover the difference during the course of future operations. Actual income taxes payable will thus exceed the financial accounting income tax expense (which is reported on the income statement and is determined based on accounting profit). Related to deferred tax assets is a **valuation allowance**, which is a reserve created against deferred tax assets. The valuation allowance is based on the likelihood of realizing the deferred tax assets in future accounting periods. **Deferred tax liabilities**, which also appear on the balance sheet, arise when a deficit amount is paid for income taxes and the company expects to eliminate the deficit over the course of future operations. In this case, financial accounting income tax expense exceeds income taxes payable.

Income tax paid in a period is the actual amount paid for income taxes (not a provision, but the actual cash outflow). The income tax paid may be less than the income tax expense because of payments in prior periods or refunds received in the current period. Income tax paid reduces the income tax payable, which is carried on the balance sheet as a liability.

The **tax base** of an asset or liability is the amount at which the asset or liability is valued for tax purposes, whereas the **carrying amount** is the amount at which the asset or liability is valued according to accounting principles.[3] Differences between the tax base and the carrying amount also result in differences between accounting profit and taxable income. These differences can carry through to future periods. For example, a **tax loss carry forward** occurs when a company experiences a loss in the current period that may be used to reduce future taxable income. The company's tax expense on its income statement must not only reflect the taxes payable based on taxable income, but also the effect of these differences.

2.1 Current Tax Assets and Liabilities

A company's current tax liability is the amount payable in taxes and is based on current taxable income. If the company expects to receive a refund for some portion previously paid in taxes, the amount recoverable is referred to as a current tax asset. The current tax liability or asset may, however, differ from what the liability would have been if it was based on accounting profit rather than taxable income for the period. Differences in accounting profit and taxable income are the result of the application of different rules. Such differences between accounting profit and taxable income can occur in several ways, including:

- Revenues and expenses may be recognized in one period for accounting purposes and a different period for tax purposes;

---

3 The terms "tax base" and "tax basis" are interchangeable. "Tax basis" is more commonly used in the United States. Similarly, "carrying amount" and "book value" refer to the same concept.

- Specific revenues and expenses may be either recognized for accounting purposes and not for tax purposes; or not recognized for accounting purposes but recognized for tax purposes;

- The carrying amount and tax base of assets and/or liabilities may differ;

- The deductibility of gains and losses of assets and liabilities may vary for accounting and income tax purposes;

- Subject to tax rules, tax losses of prior years might be used to reduce taxable income in later years, resulting in differences in accounting and taxable income (tax loss carryforward); and

- Adjustments of reported financial data from prior years might not be recognized equally for accounting and tax purposes or might be recognized in different periods.

2.2 Deferred Tax Assets and Liabilities

Deferred tax assets represent taxes that have been paid (or often the carrying forward of losses from previous periods) but have not yet been recognized on the income statement. Deferred tax liabilities occur when financial accounting income tax expense is greater than regulatory income tax expense. Deferred tax assets and liabilities usually arise when accounting standards and tax authorities recognize the timing of taxes due at different times; for example, when a company uses accelerated depreciation when reporting to the tax authority (to increase expense and lower tax payments in the early years) but uses the straight-line method on the financial statements. Although not similar in treatment on a year-to-year basis (e.g., depreciation of 5 percent on a straight-line basis may be permitted for accounting purposes whereas 10 percent is allowed for tax purposes) over the life of the asset, both approaches allow for the total cost of the asset to be depreciated (or amortized). Because these timing differences will eventually reverse or self-correct over the course of the asset's depreciable life, they are called "temporary differences."

Under IFRS, deferred tax assets and liabilities are always classified as noncurrent. Under U.S. GAAP, however, deferred tax assets and liabilities are classified on the balance sheet as current and noncurrent based on the classification of the underlying asset or liability.

Any deferred tax asset or liability is based on temporary differences that result in an excess or a deficit amount paid for taxes, which the company expects to recover from future operations. Because taxes will be recoverable or payable at a future date, it is only a temporary difference and a deferred tax asset or liability is created. Changes in the deferred tax asset or liability on the balance sheet reflect the difference between the amounts recognized in the previous period and the current period. The changes in deferred tax assets and liabilities are added to income tax payable to determine the company's income tax expense (or credit) as it is reported on the income statement.

At the end of each fiscal year, deferred tax assets and liabilities are recalculated by comparing the tax bases and carrying amounts of the balance sheet items. Identified temporary differences should be assessed on whether the difference will result in future economic benefits. For example, Pinto Construction (a hypothetical company) depreciates equipment on a straight-line basis of 10 percent per year. The tax authorities allow depreciation of 15 percent per year. At the end of the fiscal year, the carrying amount of the equipment for accounting purposes would be greater than the tax base of the equipment thus resulting in a temporary difference. A deferred tax item may only be created if it is not doubtful that the company will realize economic benefits in the future. In our example, the equipment is used in the core business of

Pinto Construction. If the company is a going concern and stable, there should be no doubt that future economic benefits will result from the equipment and it would be appropriate to create the deferred tax item.

Should it be doubtful that future economic benefits will be realized from a temporary difference (such as Pinto Construction being under liquidation), the temporary difference will not lead to the creation of a deferred tax asset or liability. If a deferred tax asset or liability resulted in the past, but the criteria of economic benefits is not met on the current balance sheet date, then, under IFRS, an existing deferred tax asset or liability related to the item will be reversed. Under U.S. GAAP, a valuation allowance is established. In assessing future economic benefits, much is left to the discretion of the auditor in assessing the temporary differences and the issue of future economic benefits.

EXAMPLE 1

The following information pertains to a fictitious company, Reston Partners:

Reston Partners Consolidated Income Statement			
Period Ending 31 March (£ Millions)	2006	2005	2004
Revenue	£40,000	£30,000	£25,000
Other net gains	2,000	0	0
Changes in inventories of finished goods and work in progress	400	180	200
Raw materials and consumables used	(5,700)	(4,000)	(8,000)
Depreciation expense	(2,000)	(2,000)	(2,000)
Other expenses	(6,000)	(5,900)	(4,500)
Interest expense	(2,000)	(3,000)	(6,000)
Profit before tax	**£26,700**	**£15,280**	**£4,700**

The financial performance and accounting profit of Reston Partners on this income statement is based on accounting principles appropriate for the jurisdiction in which Reston Partners operates. The principles used to calculate accounting profit (profit before tax in the example above) may differ from the principles applied for tax purposes (the calculation of taxable income). For illustrative purposes, however, assume that all income and expenses on the income statement are treated identically for tax and accounting purposes *except* depreciation.

The depreciation is related to equipment owned by Reston Partners. For simplicity, assume that the equipment was purchased at the beginning of the 2004 fiscal year. Depreciation should thus be calculated and expensed for the full year. Assume that accounting standards permit equipment to be depreciated on a straight-line basis over a 10-year period, whereas the tax standards in the jurisdiction specify that equipment should be depreciated on a straight-line basis over a 7-year period. For simplicity, assume a salvage value of £0 at the end of the equipment's useful life. Both methods will result in the full depreciation of the asset over the respective tax or accounting life.

The equipment was originally purchased for £20,000. In accordance with accounting standards, over the next 10 years the company will recognize annual depreciation of £2,000 (£20,000 ÷ 10) as an expense on its income statement and for the determination of accounting profit. For tax purposes, however, the company will recognize £2,857 (£20,000 ÷ 7) in depreciation each year. Each fiscal year the depreciation expense related to the use of the equipment will, therefore, differ for tax and accounting purposes (tax base vs. carrying amount), resulting in a difference between accounting profit and taxable income.

The previous income statement reflects accounting profit (depreciation at £2,000 per year). The following table shows the taxable income for each fiscal year.

Taxable Income (£ Millions)	2006	2005	2004
Revenue	£40,000	£30,000	£25,000
Other net gains	2,000	0	0
Changes in inventories of finished goods and work in progress	400	180	200
Raw materials and consumables used	(5,700)	(4,000)	(8,000)
Depreciation expense	(2,857)	(2,857)	(2,857)
Other expenses	(6,000)	(5,900)	(4,500)
Interest expense	(2,000)	(3,000)	(6,000)
Taxable income	**£25,843**	**£14,423**	**£3,843**

The carrying amount and tax base for the equipment is as follows:

(£ Millions)	2006	2005	2004
Equipment value for accounting purposes (*carrying amount*) (depreciation of £2,000/year)	£14,000	£16,000	£18,000
Equipment value for tax purposes (*tax base*) (depreciation of £2,857/year)	£11,429	£14,286	£17,143
Difference	£2,571	£1,714	£857

At each balance sheet date, the tax base and carrying amount of all assets and liabilities must be determined. The income tax payable by Reston Partners will be based on the taxable income of each fiscal year. If a tax rate of 30 percent is assumed, then the income taxes payable for 2004, 2005, and 2006 are £1,153 (30% × 3,843), £4,327 (30% × 14,423), and £7,753 (30% × 25,843).

Remember, though, that if the tax obligation is calculated based on accounting profits, it will differ because of the differences between the tax base and the carrying amount of equipment. The difference in each fiscal year is reflected in the table above. In each fiscal year the carrying amount of the equipment exceeds its tax base. For tax purposes, therefore, the asset tax base is less than its carrying value under financial accounting principles. The difference results in a deferred tax liability.

(£ Millions)	2006	2005	2004
Deferred tax liability	£771	£514	£257
(Difference between tax base and carrying amount)			
2004: £(18,000 − 17,143) × 30% = 257			
2005: £(16,000 − 14,286) × 30% = 514			
2006: £(14,000 − 11,429) × 30% = 771			

The comparison of the tax base and carrying amount of equipment shows what the deferred tax liability should be on a particular balance sheet date. In each fiscal year, only the change in the deferred tax liability should be included in the calculation of the income tax expense reported on the income statement prepared for accounting purposes.

On the income statement, the company's income tax expense will be the sum of the deferred tax liability and income tax payable.

(£ Millions)	2006	2005	2004
Income tax payable (based on tax accounting)	£7,753	£4,327	£1,153
Deferred tax liability	257	257	257
Income tax (based on financial accounting)	£8,010	£4,584	£1,410

(Difference between tax base and carrying amount)

2004: £(18,000 − 17,143) × 30% = 257

2005: £(16,000 − 14,286) × 30% − 257 = 257

2006: £(14,000 − 11,429) × 30% − 514 = 257

Note that because the different treatment of depreciation is a temporary difference, the income tax on the income statement is 30 percent of the accounting profit, although only a part is income tax payable and the rest is a deferred tax liability.

The consolidated income statement of Reston Partners including income tax is presented as follows:

Reston Partners Consolidated Income Statement			
Period Ending 31 March (£ Millions)	2006	2005	2004
Revenue	£40,000	£30,000	£25,000
Other net gains	2,000	0	0
Changes in inventories of finished goods and work in progress	400	180	200
Raw materials and consumables used	(5,700)	(4,000)	(8,000)
Depreciation expense	(2,000)	(2,000)	(2,000)
Other expenses	(6,000)	(5,900)	(4,500)
Interest expense	(2,000)	(3,000)	(6,000)
Profit before tax	£26,700	£15,280	£4,700
Income tax	(8,010)	(4,584)	(1,410)
Profit after tax	£18,690	£10,696	£3,290

Any amount paid to the tax authorities will reduce the liability for income tax payable and be reflected on the statement of cash flows of the company.

3   DETERMINING THE TAX BASE OF ASSETS AND LIABILITIES

As mentioned in Section 2, temporary differences arise from a difference in the tax base and carrying amount of assets and liabilities. The tax base of an asset or liability is the amount attributed to the asset or liability for tax purposes, whereas the carrying amount is based on accounting principles. Such a difference is considered temporary if it is expected that the taxes will be recovered or payable at a future date.

3.1   Determining the Tax Base of an Asset

The tax base of an asset is the amount that will be deductible for tax purposes in future periods as the economic benefits become realized and the company recovers the carrying amount of the asset.

For example, our previously mentioned Reston Partners (from Example 1) depreciates equipment on a straight-line basis at a rate of 10 percent per year. The tax authorities allow depreciation of approximately 15 percent per year. At the end of the fiscal year, the carrying amount of equipment for accounting purposes is greater than the asset tax base thus resulting in a temporary difference.

EXAMPLE 2

Determining the Tax Base of an Asset

The following information pertains to Entiguan Sports, a hypothetical developer of products used to treat sports-related injuries. (The treatment of items for accounting and tax purposes is based on fictitious accounting and tax standards and is not specific to a particular jurisdiction.) Calculate the tax base and carrying amount for each item.

1   *Dividends receivable*: On its balance sheet, Entiguan Sports reports dividends of €1 million receivable from a subsidiary. Assume that dividends are not taxable.

2   *Development costs*: Entiguan Sports capitalized development costs of €3 million during the year. Entiguan amortized €500,000 of this amount during the year. For tax purposes amortization of 25 percent per year is allowed.

3   *Research costs*: Entiguan incurred €500,000 in research costs, which were all expensed in the current fiscal year for financial reporting purposes. Assume that applicable tax legislation requires research costs to be expensed over a four-year period rather than all in one year.

4   *Accounts receivable*: Included on the income statement of Entiguan Sports is a provision for doubtful debt of €125,000. The accounts receivable amount reflected on the balance sheet, after taking the provision into account, amounts to €1,500,000. The tax authorities allow a deduction of 25 percent of the gross amount for doubtful debt.

Solutions:

	Carrying Amount (€)	Tax Base (€)	Temporary Difference (€)
1. Dividends receivable	1,000,000	1,000,000	0
2. Development costs	2,500,000	2,250,000	250,000
3. Research costs	0	375,000	(375,000)
4. Accounts receivable	1,500,000	1,218,750	281,250

Comments:

1 *Dividends receivable*: Although the dividends received are economic benefits from the subsidiary, we are assuming that dividends are not taxable. Therefore, the carrying amount equals the tax base for dividends receivable.

2 *Development costs*: First, we assume that development costs will generate economic benefits for Entiguan Sports. Therefore, it may be included as an asset on the balance sheet for the purposes of this example. Second, the amortization allowed by the tax authorities exceeds the amortization accounted for based on accounting rules. Therefore, the carrying amount of the asset exceeds its tax base. The carrying amount is (€3,000,000 – €500,000) = €2,500,000 whereas the tax base is [€3,000,000 – (25% × €3,000,000)] = €2,250,000.

3 *Research costs*: We assume that research costs will result in future economic benefits for the company. If this were not the case, creation of a deferred tax asset or liability would not be allowed. The tax base of research costs exceeds their carrying amount. The carrying amount is €0 because the full amount has been expensed for financial reporting purposes in the year in which it was incurred. Therefore, there would not have been a balance sheet item "Research costs" for tax purposes, and only a proportion may be deducted in the current fiscal year. The tax base of the asset is (€500,000 – €500,000/4) = €375,000.

4 *Accounts receivable*: The economic benefits that should have been received from accounts receivable have already been included in revenues included in the calculation of the taxable income when the sales occurred. Because the receipt of a portion of the accounts receivable is doubtful, the provision is allowed. The provision, based on tax legislation, results in a greater amount allowed in the current fiscal year than would be the case under accounting principles. This results in the tax base of accounts receivable being lower than its carrying amount. Note that the example specifically states that the balance sheet amount for accounts receivable after the provision for accounting purposes amounts to €1,500,000. Therefore, accounts receivable before any provision was €1,500,000 + €125,000 = €1,625,000. The tax base is calculated as (€1,500,000 + €125,000) – [25% × (€1,500,000 + €125,000)] = €1,218,750.

3.2 Determining the Tax Base of a Liability

The tax base of a liability is the carrying amount of the liability less any amounts that will be deductible for tax purposes in the future. With respect to payments from customers received in advance of providing the goods and services, the tax base of such a liability is the carrying amount less any amount of the revenue that will not be taxable in future. Keep in mind the following fundamental principle: In general, a company will recognize a deferred tax asset or liability when recovery/settlement of the carrying amount will affect future tax payments by either increasing or reducing the taxable profit. Remember, an analyst is not only evaluating the difference between the carrying amount and the tax base, but the relevance of that difference on future profits and losses and thus by implication future taxes.

IFRS offers specific guidelines with regard to revenue received in advance: IAS 12 states that the tax base is the carrying amount less any amount of the revenue that will not be taxed at a future date. Under U.S. GAAP, an analysis of the tax base would result in a similar outcome. The tax legislation within the jurisdiction will determine the amount recognized on the income statement and whether the liability (revenue received in advance) will have a tax base greater than zero. This will depend on how tax legislation recognizes revenue received in advance.

EXAMPLE 3

Determining the Tax Base of a Liability

The following information pertains to Entiguan Sports for the 2006 year-end. The treatment of items for accounting and tax purposes is based on fictitious accounting and tax standards and is not specific to a particular jurisdiction. Calculate the tax base and carrying amount for each item.

1 *Donations*: Entiguan Sports made donations of €100,000 in the current fiscal year. The donations were expensed for financial reporting purposes, but are not tax deductible based on applicable tax legislation.

2 *Interest received in advance*: Entiguan Sports received in advance interest of €300,000. The interest is taxed because tax authorities recognize the interest to accrue to the company (part of taxable income) on the date of receipt.

3 *Rent received in advance*: Entiguan recognized €10 million for rent received in advance from a lessee for an unused warehouse building. Rent received in advance is deferred for accounting purposes but taxed on a cash basis.

4 *Loan*: Entiguan Sports secured a long-term loan for €550,000 in the current fiscal year. Interest is charged at 13.5 percent per annum and is payable at the end of each fiscal year.

Solutions:

	Carrying Amount (€)	Tax Base (€)	Temporary Difference (€)
1. Donations	0	0	0
2. Interest received in advance	300,000	0	(300,000)
3. Rent received in advance	10,000,000	0	(10,000,000)

	Carrying Amount (€)	Tax Base (€)	Temporary Difference (€)
4. Loan (capital)	550,000	550,000	0
Interest paid	0	0	0

Comments:

1 *Donations*: The amount of €100,000 was immediately expensed on Entiguan's income statement; therefore, the carrying amount is €0. Tax legislation does not allow donations to be deducted for tax purposes, so the tax base of the donations equals the carrying amount. Note that while the carrying amount and tax base are the same, the difference in the treatment of donations for accounting and tax purposes (expensed for accounting purposes, but not deductible for tax purposes) represents a permanent difference (a difference that will not be reversed in future). Permanent and temporary differences are elaborated on in Section 4 and it will refer to this particular case with an expanded explanation.

2 *Interest received in advance*: Based on the information provided, for tax purposes, interest is deemed to accrue to the company on the date of receipt. For tax purposes, it is thus irrelevant whether it is for the current or a future accounting period; it must be included in taxable income in the financial year received. Interest received in advance is, for accounting purposes though, included in the financial period in which it is deemed to have been earned. For this reason, the interest income received in advance is a balance sheet liability. It was not included on the income statement because the income relates to a future financial year. Because the full €300,000 is included in taxable income in the current fiscal year, the tax base is €300,000 – 300,000 = €0. Note that although interest received in advance and rent received in advance are both taxed, the timing depends on how the particular item is treated in tax legislation.

3 *Rent received in advance*: The result is similar to interest received in advance. The carrying amount of rent received in advance would be €10,000,000 while the tax base is €0.

4 *Loan*: Repayment of the loan has no tax implications. The repayment of the capital amount does not constitute an income or expense. The interest paid is included as an expense in the calculation of taxable income as well as accounting income. Therefore, the tax base and carrying amount is €0. For clarity, the interest paid that would be included on the income statement for the year amounts to 13.5% × €550,000 = €74,250 if the loan was acquired at the beginning of the current fiscal year.

3.3 Changes in Income Tax Rates

The measurement of deferred tax assets and liabilities is based on current tax law. But if there are subsequent changes in tax laws or new income tax rates, existing deferred tax assets and liabilities must be adjusted for the effects of these changes. The resulting effects of the changes are also included in determining accounting profit in the period of change.

When income tax rates change, the deferred tax assets and liabilities are adjusted to the new tax rate. If income tax rates increase, deferred taxes (that is, the deferred tax assets and liabilities) will also increase. Likewise, if income tax rates decrease, deferred taxes will decrease. A decrease in tax rates decreases deferred tax liabilities, which reduces future tax payments to the taxing authorities. A decrease in tax rates will also decrease deferred tax assets, which reduces their value toward the offset of future tax payments to the taxing authorities.

To illustrate the effect of a change in tax rate, consider Example 1 again. In that illustration, the timing difference that led to the recognition of a deferred tax liability for Reston Partners was attributable to differences in the method of depreciation and the related effects on the accounting carrying value and the asset tax base. The relevant information is restated below.

The carrying amount and tax base for the equipment is:

(£ Millions)	2006	2005	2004
Equipment value for accounting purposes (*carrying amount*) (depreciation of £2,000/year)	£14,000	£16,000	£18,000
Equipment value for tax purposes (*tax base*) (depreciation of £2,857/year)	£11,429	£14,286	£17,143
Difference	£2,571	£1,714	£857

At a 30 percent income tax rate, the deferred tax liability was then determined as follows:

(£ Millions)	2006	2005	2004
Deferred tax liability	£771	£514	£257
(Difference between tax base and carrying amount)			
2004: £(18,000 − 17,143) × 30% = £257			
2005: £(16,000 − 14,286) × 30% = £514			
2006: £(14,000 − 11,429) × 30% = £771			

For this illustration, assume that the taxing authority has changed the income tax rate to 25 percent for 2006. Although the difference between the carrying amount and the tax base of the depreciable asset are the same, the deferred tax liability for 2006 will be £643 (instead of £771 or a reduction of £128 in the liability). 2006: £(14,000 − 11,429) × 25% = £643.

Reston Partners' provision for income tax expense is also affected by the change in tax rates. Taxable income for 2006 will now be taxed at a rate of 25 percent. The benefit of the 2006 accelerated depreciation tax shield is now only £214 (£857 × 25%) instead of the previous £257 (a reduction of £43). In addition, the reduction in the beginning carrying value of the deferred tax liability for 2006 (the year of change) further reduces the income tax expense for 2006. The reduction in income tax expense attributable to the change in tax rate is £85. 2006: (30% − 25%) × £1,714 = £85. Note that these two components together account for the reduction in the deferred tax liability (£43 + £85 = £128).

As may be seen from this discussion, changes in the income tax rate have an effect on a company's deferred tax asset and liability carrying values as well as an effect on the measurement of income tax expense in the year of change. The analyst must thus note that proposed changes in tax law can have a quantifiable effect on these accounts (and any related financial ratios that are derived from them) if the proposed changes are subsequently enacted into law.

TEMPORARY AND PERMANENT DIFFERENCES BETWEEN TAXABLE AND ACCOUNTING PROFIT

4

Temporary differences arise from a difference between the tax base and the carrying amount of assets and liabilities. The creation of a deferred tax asset or liability from a temporary difference is only possible if the difference reverses itself at some future date and to such an extent that the balance sheet item is expected to create future economic benefits for the company. IFRS and U.S. GAAP both prescribe the balance sheet liability method for recognition of deferred tax. This balance sheet method focuses on the recognition of a deferred tax asset or liability should there be a temporary difference between the carrying amount and tax base of balance sheet items.[4]

Permanent differences are differences between tax and financial reporting of revenue (expenses) that *will not* be reversed at some future date. Because they will not be reversed at a future date, these differences do not give rise to deferred tax. These items typically include

- Income or expense items not allowed by tax legislation, and
- Tax credits for some expenditures that directly reduce taxes.

Because no deferred tax item is created for permanent differences, all permanent differences result in a difference between the company's effective tax rate and statutory tax rate. The effective tax rate is also influenced by different statutory taxes should an entity conduct business in more than one tax jurisdiction. The formula for the reported effective tax rate is thus equal to:

$$\text{Reported effective tax rate} = \text{Income tax expense}$$
$$\div \text{Pretax income (accounting profit)}$$

The net change in deferred tax during a reporting period is the difference between the balance of the deferred tax asset or liability for the current period and the balance of the previous period.

4.1 Taxable Temporary Differences

Temporary differences are further divided into two categories, namely taxable temporary differences and deductible temporary differences. **Taxable temporary differences** are temporary differences that result in a taxable amount in a future period when determining the taxable profit as the balance sheet item is recovered or settled. Taxable temporary differences result in a deferred tax liability when the carrying amount of an asset exceeds its tax base and, in the case of a liability, when the tax base of the liability exceeds its carrying amount.

---

4 Previously, IAS 12 required recognition of deferred tax based on the deferred method (also known as the income statement method), which focused on timing differences. Timing differences are differences in the recognition of income and expenses for accounting and tax purposes that originate in one period and will reverse in a future period. Given the definition of timing differences, all timing differences are temporary differences, such as the different treatment of depreciation for tax and accounting purposes (although the timing is different with regard to the allowed depreciation for tax and accounting purposes, the asset will eventually be fully depreciated).

Under U.S. GAAP, a deferred tax asset or liability is not recognized for unamortizable goodwill. Under IFRS, a deferred tax account is not recognized for goodwill arising in a business combination. Since goodwill is a residual, the recognition of a deferred tax liability would increase the carrying amount of goodwill. Discounting deferred tax assets or liabilities is generally not allowed for temporary differences related to business combinations as it is for other temporary differences.

IFRS provides an exemption (that is, deferred tax is not provided on the temporary difference) for the initial recognition of an asset or liability in a transaction that: a) is not a business combination (e.g., joint ventures, branches and unconsolidated investments); and b) affects neither accounting profit nor taxable profit at the time of the transaction. U.S. GAAP does not provide an exemption for these circumstances.

As a simple example of a temporary difference with no recognition of deferred tax liability, assume that a fictitious company, Corporate International, a holding company of various leisure related businesses and holiday resorts, buys an interest in a hotel in the current financial year. The goodwill related to the transaction will be recognized on the financial statements, but the related tax liability will not, as it relates to the initial recognition of goodwill.

4.2 Deductible Temporary Differences

Deductible temporary differences are temporary differences that result in a reduction or deduction of taxable income in a future period when the balance sheet item is recovered or settled. Deductible temporary differences result in a deferred tax asset when the tax base of an asset exceeds its carrying amount and, in the case of a liability, when the carrying amount of the liability exceeds its tax base. The recognition of a deferred tax asset is only allowed to the extent there is a reasonable expectation of future profits against which the asset or liability (that gave rise to the deferred tax asset) can be recovered or settled.

To determine the probability of sufficient future profits for utilization, one must consider the following: 1) Sufficient taxable temporary differences must exist that are related to the same tax authority and the same taxable entity; and 2) The taxable temporary differences that are expected to reverse in the same periods as expected for the reversal of the deductible temporary differences.

As with deferred tax liabilities, IFRS states that deferred tax assets should not be recognized in cases that would arise from the initial recognition of an asset or liability in transactions that are not a business combination and when, at the time of the transaction, there is no impact on either accounting or taxable profit. Subsequent to initial recognition under IFRS and U.S. GAAP, any deferred tax assets that arise from investments in subsidiaries, branches, associates, and interests in joint ventures are recognized as a deferred tax asset.

IFRS and U.S. GAAP allow the creation of a deferred tax asset in the case of tax losses and tax credits. These two unique situations will be further elaborated on in Section 6. IAS 12 *does not* allow the creation of a deferred tax asset arising from negative goodwill. Negative goodwill arises when the amount that an entity pays for an interest in a business is less than the net fair market value of the portion of assets and liabilities of the acquired company, based on the interest of the entity.

4.3 Examples of Taxable and Deductible Temporary Differences

Exhibit 1 summarizes how differences between the tax bases and carrying amounts of assets and liabilities give rise to deferred tax assets or deferred tax liabilities.

Exhibit 1	Treatment of Temporary Differences

Balance Sheet Item	Carrying Amount vs. Tax Base	Results in Deferred Tax Asset/Liability
Asset	Carrying amount > tax base	Deferred tax liability
Asset	Carrying amount < tax base	Deferred tax asset
Liability	Carrying amount > tax base	Deferred tax asset
Liability	Carrying amount < tax base	Deferred tax liability

EXAMPLE 4

Taxable and Deductible Temporary Differences

Examples 2 and 3 illustrated how to calculate the tax base of assets and liabilities, respectively. Based on the information provided in Examples 2 and 3, indicate whether the difference in the tax base and carrying amount of the assets and liabilities are temporary or permanent differences and whether a deferred tax asset or liability will be recognized based on the difference identified.

Solution to Example 2:

	Carrying Amount (€)	Tax Base (€)	Temporary Difference (€)	*Will Result in Deferred Tax Asset/Liability*
1. Dividends receivable	1,000,000	1,000,000	0	*N/A*
2. Development costs	2,500,000	2,250,000	250,000	*Deferred tax liability*
3. Research costs	0	375,000	(375,000)	*Deferred tax asset*
4. Accounts receivable	1,500,000	1,218,750	281,250	*Deferred tax liability*

Example 2 included comments on the calculation of the carrying amount and tax base of the assets.

1 *Dividends receivable*: As a result of non-taxability, the carrying amount equals the tax base of dividends receivable. This constitutes a permanent difference and will not result in the recognition of any deferred tax asset or liability. A temporary difference constitutes a difference that will, at some future date, be reversed. Although the timing of recognition is different for tax and accounting purposes, in the end the full carrying amount will be expensed/recognized as income. A permanent difference will never be reversed. Based on tax legislation, dividends from a subsidiary are not recognized as income. Therefore, no amount will be reflected as dividend income when calculating the taxable income, and the tax base of dividends receivable must be the total amount received, namely €1,000,000. The taxable income and accounting profit will permanently differ with the amount of dividends receivable, even on future financial statements as an effect on the retained earnings reflected on the balance sheet.

2 *Development costs*: The difference between the carrying amount and tax base is a temporary difference that, in the future, will reverse. In this fiscal year, it will result in a deferred tax liability.

3 *Research costs*: The difference between the carrying amount and tax base is a temporary difference that results in a deferred tax asset. Remember the explanation in Section 2 for deferred tax assets—a deferred tax asset arises because of an excess amount paid for taxes (when taxable income is greater than

accounting profit), which is expected to be recovered from future operations. Based on accounting principles, the full amount was deducted resulting in a lower accounting profit, while the taxable income by implication, should be greater because of the lower amount expensed.

4 *Accounts receivable*: The difference between the carrying amount and tax base of the asset is a temporary difference that will result in a deferred tax liability.

Solution to Example 3:

	Carrying Amount (€)	Tax Base (€)	Temporary Difference (€)	*Will Result in Deferred Tax Asset/Liability*
1. Donations	0	0	0	*N/A*
2. Interest received in advance	300,000	0	(300,000)	*Deferred tax asset*
3. Rent received in advance	10,000,000	0	(10,000,000)	*Deferred tax asset*
4. Loan (capital)	550,000	550,000	0	*N/A*
Interest paid	0	0	0	*N/A*

Example 3 included extensive comments on the calculation of the carrying amount and tax base of the liabilities.

1 *Donations*: It was assumed that tax legislation does not allow donations to be deducted for tax purposes. No temporary difference results from donations, and thus a deferred tax asset or liability will not be recognized. This constitutes a permanent difference.

2 *Interest received in advance*: Interest received in advance results in a temporary difference that gives rise to a deferred tax asset. A deferred tax asset arises because of an excess amount paid for taxes (when taxable income is greater than accounting profit), which is expected to be recovered from future operations.

3 *Rent received in advance*: The difference between the carrying amount and tax base is a temporary difference that leads to the recognition of a deferred tax asset.

4 *Loan*: There are no temporary differences as a result of the loan or interest paid, and thus no deferred tax item is recognized.

4.4 Temporary Differences at Initial Recognition of Assets and Liabilities

In some situations the carrying amount and tax base of a balance sheet item may vary at initial recognition. For example, a company may deduct a government grant from the initial carrying amount of an asset or liability that appears on the balance sheet. For tax purposes, such grants may not be deducted when determining the tax base of the balance sheet item. In such circumstances, the carrying amount of the asset or liability will be lower than its tax base. Differences in the tax base of an asset or liability as a result of the circumstances described above may not be recognized as deferred tax assets or liabilities.

For example, a government may offer grants to Small, Medium, and Micro Enterprises (SMME) in an attempt to assist these entrepreneurs in their endeavors that contribute to the country's GDP and job creation. Assume that a particular grant is offered for infrastructure needs (office furniture, property, plant, and equipment, etc). In these circumstances, although the carrying amount will be lower than the tax base of the asset, the related deferred tax may not be recognized. As mentioned earlier, deferred tax assets and liabilities should not be recognized in cases that would arise from the initial recognition of an asset or liability in transactions that are not a business combination and when, at the time of the transaction, there is no impact on either accounting or taxable profit.

A deferred tax liability will also not be recognized at the initial recognition of goodwill. Although goodwill may be treated differently across tax jurisdictions, which may lead to differences in the carrying amount and tax base of goodwill, IAS 12 does not allow the recognition of such a deferred tax liability. Any impairment that an entity should, for accounting purposes, impose on goodwill will again result in a temporary difference between its carrying amount and tax base. Any impairment that an entity should, for accounting purposes, impose on goodwill and if part of the goodwill is related to the initial recognition, that part of the difference in tax base and carrying amount should not result in any deferred taxation because the initial deferred tax liability was not recognized. Any future differences between the carrying amount and tax base as a result of amortization and the deductibility of a portion of goodwill constitute a temporary difference for which provision should be made.

4.5 Business Combinations and Deferred Taxes

The fair value of assets and liabilities acquired in a business combination is determined on the acquisition date and may differ from the previous carrying amount. It is highly probable that the values of acquired intangible assets, including goodwill, would differ from their carrying amounts. This temporary difference will affect deferred taxes as well as the amount of goodwill recognized as a result of the acquisition.

4.6 Investments in Subsidiaries, Branches, Associates and Interests in Joint Ventures

Investments in subsidiaries, branches, associates and interests in joint ventures may lead to temporary differences on the consolidated versus the parent's financial statements. The related deferred tax liabilities as a result of temporary differences will be recognized unless both of the following criterion are satisfied:

- The parent is in a position to control the timing of the future reversal of the temporary difference, and
- It is probable that the temporary difference will not reverse in the future.

With respect to deferred tax assets related to subsidiaries, branches, and associates and interests, deferred tax assets will only be recognized if the following criteria are satisfied:

- The temporary difference will reverse in the future, and
- Sufficient taxable profits exist against which the temporary difference can be used.

UNUSED TAX LOSSES AND TAX CREDITS

5

IAS 12 allows the recognition of unused tax losses and tax credits only to the extent that it is probable that in the future there will be taxable income against which the unused tax losses and credits can be applied. Under U.S. GAAP, a deferred tax asset is recognized in full but is then reduced by a valuation allowance if it is more likely than not that some or all of the deferred tax asset will not be realized. The same requirements for creation of a deferred tax asset as a result of deductible temporary differences also apply to unused tax losses and tax credits. The existence of tax losses may indicate that the entity cannot reasonably be expected to generate sufficient future taxable income. All other things held constant, the greater the history of tax losses, the greater the concern regarding the company's ability to generate future taxable profits.

Should there be concerns about the company's future profitability, then the deferred tax asset may not be recognized until it is realized. When assessing the probability that sufficient taxable profit will be generated in the future, the following criteria can serve as a guide:

- If there is uncertainty as to the probability of future taxable profits, a deferred tax asset as a result of unused tax losses or tax credits is only recognized to the extent of the available taxable temporary differences;

- Assess the probability that the entity will in fact generate future taxable profits before the unused tax losses and/or credits expire pursuant to tax rules regarding the carry forward of the unused tax losses;

- Verify that the above is with the same tax authority and based on the same taxable entity;

- Determine whether the past tax losses were a result of specific circumstances that are unlikely to be repeated; and

- Discover if tax planning opportunities are available to the entity that will result in future profits. These may include changes in tax legislation that is phased in over more than one financial period to the benefit of the entity.

It is imperative that the timing of taxable and deductible temporary differences also be considered before creating a deferred tax asset based on unused tax credits.

6 RECOGNITION AND MEASUREMENT OF CURRENT AND DEFERRED TAX

Current taxes payable or recoverable from tax authorities are based on the applicable tax rates at the balance sheet date. Deferred taxes should be measured at the tax rate that is expected to apply when the asset is realized or the liability settled. With respect to the income tax for a current or prior period not yet paid, it is recognized as a tax liability until paid. Any amount paid in excess of any tax obligation is recognized as an asset. The income tax paid in excess or owed to tax authorities is separate from deferred taxes on the company's balance sheet.

When measuring deferred taxes in a jurisdiction, there are different forms of taxation such as income tax, capital gains tax (any capital gains made), or secondary tax on companies (tax payable on the dividends that a company declares) and possibly different tax bases for a balance sheet item (as in the case of government grants influencing the tax base of an asset such as property). In assessing which tax laws should apply, it is dependent on how the related asset or liability will be settled. It would be prudent to use the tax rate and tax base that is consistent with how it is expected the tax base will be recovered or settled.

Although deferred tax assets and liabilities are related to temporary differences expected to be recovered or settled at some future date, neither are discounted to present value in determining the amounts to be booked. Both must be adjusted for changes in tax rates.

Deferred taxes as well as income taxes should always be recognized on the income statement of an entity unless it pertains to:

- Taxes or deferred taxes charged directly to equity, or
- A possible provision for deferred taxes relates to a business combination.

The carrying amount of the deferred tax assets and liabilities should also be assessed. The carrying amounts may change even though there may have been no change in temporary differences during the period evaluated. This can result from:

- Changes in tax rates;
- Reassessments of the recoverability of deferred tax assets; or
- Changes in the expectations for how an asset will be recovered and what influences the deferred tax asset or liability.

All unrecognized deferred tax assets and liabilities must be reassessed at the balance sheet date and measured against the criteria of probable future economic benefits. If such a deferred asset is likely to be recovered, it may be appropriate to recognize the related deferred tax asset.

Different jurisdictions have different requirements for determining tax obligations that can range from different forms of taxation to different tax rates based on taxable income. When comparing financial statements of entities that conduct business in different jurisdictions subject to different tax legislation, the analyst should be cautious in reaching conclusions because of the potentially complex tax rules that may apply.

6.1 Recognition of a Valuation Allowance

Deferred tax assets must be assessed at each balance sheet date. If there is any doubt whether the deferral will be recovered, then the carrying amount should be reduced to the expected recoverable amount. Should circumstances subsequently change and suggest the future will lead to recovery of the deferral, the reduction may be reversed.

Under U.S. GAAP, deferred tax assets are reduced by creating a valuation allowance. Establishing a valuation allowance reduces the deferred tax asset and income in the period in which the allowance is established. Should circumstances change to such an extent that a deferred tax asset valuation allowance may be reduced, the reversal will increase the deferred tax asset and operating income. Because of the subjective judgment involved, an analyst should carefully scrutinize any such changes.

6.2 Recognition of Current and Deferred Tax Charged Directly to Equity

In general, IFRS and U.S. GAAP require that the recognition of deferred tax liabilities and current income tax should be treated similarly to the asset or liability that gave rise to the deferred tax liability or income tax based on accounting treatment. Should an item that gives rise to a deferred tax liability be taken directly to equity, the same should hold true for the resulting deferred tax.

The following are examples of such items:

- Revaluation of property, plant, and equipment (revaluations are not permissible under U.S. GAAP);
- Long-term investments at fair value;
- Changes in accounting policies;
- Errors corrected against the opening balance of retained earnings;

- Initial recognition of an equity component related to complex financial instruments; and
- Exchange rate differences arising from the currency translation procedures for foreign operations.

Whenever it is determined that a deferred tax liability will not be reversed, an adjustment should be made to the liability. The deferred tax liability will be reduced and the amount by which it is reduced should be taken directly to equity. Any deferred taxes related to a business combination must also be recognized in equity.

Depending on the items that gave rise to the deferred tax liabilities, an analyst should exercise judgment regarding whether the taxes should be included with deferred tax liabilities or whether it should be taken directly to equity. It may be more appropriate simply to ignore deferred taxes.

EXAMPLE 5

Taxes Charged Directly to Equity

The following information pertains to Anderson Company (a hypothetical company). A building owned by Anderson Company was originally purchased for €1,000,000 on 1 January 2004. For accounting purposes, buildings are depreciated at 5 percent a year on a straight-line basis, and depreciation for tax purposes is 10 percent a year on a straight-line basis. On the first day of 2006, the building is revalued at €1,200,000. It is estimated that the remaining useful life of the building from the date of revaluation is 20 years. *Important*: For tax purposes the revaluation of the building is not recognized.

Based on the information provided, the following illustrates the difference in treatment of the building for accounting and tax purposes.

	Carrying Amount of Building	Tax Base of Building
Balance on 1 January 2004	€1,000,000	€1,000,000
Depreciation 2004	50,000	100,000
Balance on 31 December 2004	€950,000	€900,000
Depreciation 2005	50,000	100,000
Balance on 31 December 2005	€900,000	€800,000
Revaluation on 1 January 2006	300,000	n/a
Balance on 1 January 2006	€1,200,000	€800,000
Depreciation 2006	60,000	100,000
Balance on 31 December 2006	€1,140,000	€700,000
Accumulated depreciation		
Balance on 1 January 2004	€0	€0
Depreciation 2004	50,000	100,000
Balance on 31 December 2004	€50,000	€100,000
Depreciation 2005	50,000	100,000
Balance on 31 December 2005	€100,000	€200,000
Revaluation at 1 January 2006	(100,000)	n/a
Balance on 1 January 2006	€0	€200,000
Depreciation 2006	60,000	100,000
Balance on 30 November 2006	€60,000	€300,000

	Carrying Amount	Tax Base
On 31 December 2004	€950,000	€900,000
On 31 December 2005	€900,000	€800,000
On 31 December 2006	€1,140,000	€700,000

31 December 2004: On 31 December 2004, different treatments for depreciation expense result in a temporary difference that gives rise to a deferred tax liability. The difference in the tax base and carrying amount of the building was a result of different depreciation amounts for tax and accounting purposes. Depreciation appears on the income statement. For this reason the deferred tax liability will also be reflected on the income statement. If we assume that the applicable tax rate in 2004 was 40 percent, then the resulting deferred tax liability will be 40% × (€950,000 − €900,000) = €20,000.

31 December 2005: As of 31 December 2005, the carrying amount of the building remains greater than the tax base. The temporary difference again gives rise to a deferred tax liability. Again, assuming the applicable tax rate to be 40 percent, the deferred tax liability from the building is 40% × (€900,000 − €800,000) = €40,000.

31 December 2006: On 31 December 2006, the carrying amount of the building again exceeds the tax base. This is not the result of disposals or additions, but is a result of the revaluation at the beginning of the 2006 fiscal year and the different rates of depreciation. The deferred tax liability would seem to be 40% × (€1,140,000 − €700,000) = €176,000, *but* the treatment is different than it was for the 2004 and 2005. In 2006, revaluation of the building gave rise to a balance sheet equity account, namely "Revaluation Surplus" in the amount of €300,000, which is not recognized for tax purposes.

The deferred tax liability would usually have been calculated as follows:

	2006	2005	2004
Deferred tax liability (closing balance at end of fiscal year)	€176,000	€40,000	€20,000
(Difference between tax base and carrying amount)			
2004: €(950,000 − 900,000) × 40% = 20,000			
2005: €(900,000 − 800,000) × 40% = 40,000			
2006: €(1,140,000 − 700,000) × 40% = 176,000			

The change in the deferred tax liability in 2004 is €20,000, in 2005: €20,000 (€40,000 − €20,000) and, it would seem, in 2006: €136,000 (€176,000 − €40,000). In 2006, although it would seem that the balance for deferred tax liability should be €176,000, the revaluation is not recognized for tax purposes. Only the portion of the difference between the tax base and carrying amount that is not a result of the revaluation is recognized as giving rise to a deferred tax liability.

The effect of the revaluation surplus and the associated tax effects are accounted for in a direct adjustment to equity. The revaluation surplus is reduced by the tax provision associated with the excess of the fair value over the carry value and it affects retained earnings (€300,000 × 40% = €120,000).

The deferred tax liability that should be reflected on the balance sheet is thus not €176,000 but only €56,000 (€176,000 – €120,000). Given the balance of deferred tax liability at the beginning of the 2006 fiscal year in the amount of €40,000, the change in the deferred tax liability is only €56,000 – €40,000 = €16,000.

In the future, at the end of each year, an amount equal to the depreciation as a result of the revaluation minus the deferred tax effect will be transferred from the revaluation reserve to retained earnings. In 2006 this will amount to a portion of depreciation resulting from the revaluation, €15,000 (€300,000 ÷ 20), minus the deferred tax effect of €6,000 (€15,000 × 40%), thus €9,000.

7 PRESENTATION AND DISCLOSURE

We will discuss the presentation and disclosure of income tax related information by way of example. The Consolidated Statements of Operations (Income Statements) and Consolidated Balance Sheets for Micron Technology (MU) are provided in Exhibits 2 and 3, respectively. Exhibit 4 provides the income tax note disclosures for MU for the 2004, 2005, and 2006 fiscal years.

MU's income tax provision (i.e., income tax expense) for fiscal year 2006 is $18 million (see Exhibit 2). The income tax note disclosure in Exhibit 4 reconciles how the income tax provision was determined beginning with MU's reported income before taxes (shown in Exhibit 2 as $433 million for fiscal year 2006). The note disclosure then denotes the income tax provision for 2006 that is current ($42 million), which is then offset by the deferred tax benefit for foreign taxes ($24 million), for a net income tax provision of $18 million. Exhibit 4 further shows a reconciliation of how the income tax provision was derived from the U.S. federal statutory rate. Many public companies comply with this required disclosure by displaying the information in percentage terms, but MU has elected to provide the disclosure in absolute dollar amounts. From this knowledge, we can see that the dollar amount shown for U.S. federal income tax provision at the statutory rate ($152 million) was determined by multiplying MU's income before taxes by the 35 percent U.S. federal statutory rate ($433 × 0.35 = $152). Furthermore, after considering tax credits and changes in the valuation allowance for deferred tax assets, MU's $18 million tax provision for 2006 is only 4.16 percent of its income before taxes ($18 ÷ $433 = 4.16%).

In addition, the note disclosure in Exhibit 4 provides detailed information about the derivation of the deferred tax assets ($26 million current and $49 million noncurrent) and deferred tax liabilities ($28 million noncurrent) that are shown on MU's consolidated balance sheet for fiscal year 2006 in Exhibit 3.

Exhibit 2	Micron Technology, Inc. Consolidated Statements of Operations (Amounts in Millions except Per Share)		
For the Year Ended	31 Aug. 2006	1 Sept. 2005	2 Sept. 2004
Net sales	$5,272	$4,880	$4,404
Cost of goods sold	4,072	3,734	3,090
Gross margin	1,200	1,146	1,314
Selling, general and administrative	460	348	332

Exhibit 2 (Continued)

For the Year Ended	31 Aug. 2006	1 Sept. 2005	2 Sept. 2004
Research and development	656	604	755
Restructure	—	(1)	(23)
Other operating (income) expense, net	(266)	(22)	—
Operating income	350	217	250
Interest income	101	32	15
Interest expense	(25)	(47)	(36)
Other non-operating income (expense), net	7	(3)	3
Income before taxes	433	199	232
Income tax (provision)	(18)	(11)	(75)
Noncontrolling interests in net income	(7)	—	—
Net income	$408	$188	$157
Earnings per share:			
Basic	$0.59	$0.29	$0.24
Diluted	$0.56	$0.27	$0.24
Number of shares used in per share calculations:			
Basic	692	648	641
Diluted	725	702	646

Exhibit 3 Micron Technology, Inc. Consolidated Balance Sheets (Dollars in Millions)

As of	31 Aug. 2006	1 Sept. 2005
Assets		
Cash and equivalents	$1,431	$524
Short-term investments	1,648	766
Receivables	956	794
Inventories	963	771
Prepaid expenses	77	39
Deferred income taxes	26	32
Total current assets	5,101	2,926
Intangible assets, net	388	260
Property, plant and equipment, net	5,888	4,684
Deferred income taxes	49	30
Goodwill	502	16
Other assets	293	90
Total assets	$12,221	$8,006
Liabilities and shareholders' equity		

(continued)

| Exhibit 3 | (Continued) |

As of	31 Aug. 2006	1 Sept. 2005
Accounts payable and accrued expenses	$1,319	$753
Deferred income	53	30
Equipment purchase contracts	123	49
Current portion of long-term debt	166	147
Total current liabilities	1,661	979
Long-term debt	405	1,020
Deferred income taxes	28	35
Other liabilities	445	125
Total liabilities	2,539	2,159
Commitments and contingencies	—	—
Noncontrolling interests in subsidiaries	1,568	—
Common stock of $0.10 par value, authorized 3 billion shares, issued and outstanding 749.4 million and 616.2 million shares	75	62
Additional capital	6,555	4,707
Retained earnings	1,486	1,078
Accumulated other comprehensive loss	(2)	—
Total shareholders' equity	8,114	5,847
Total liabilities and shareholders' equity	$12,221	$8,006

| Exhibit 4 | Micron Technology, Inc. Income Taxes Note to the Consolidated Financial Statements |

Income (loss) before taxes and the income tax (provision) benefit consisted of the following:

(Millions)	2006	2005	2004
Income (loss) before taxes:			
U.S.	$351	$108	($19)
Foreign	82	91	251
	$433	$199	$232
Income tax (provision) benefit:			
Current:			
U.S. federal	($12)	$—	$—
State	(1)	(3)	—
Foreign	(29)	(18)	(12)
	(42)	(21)	(12)
Deferred:			
U.S. federal	—	—	—
State	—	—	—
Foreign	24	10	(63)

Exhibit 4   (Continued)

(Millions)	2006	2005	2004
	24	10	(63)
Income tax (provision)	($18)	($11)	($75)

The company's income tax (provision) computed using the U.S. federal statutory rate and the company's income tax (provision) benefit is reconciled as follows:

(Millions)	2006	2005	2004
U.S. federal income tax (provision) benefit at statutory rate	$(152)	$(70)	$(81)
State taxes, net of federal benefit	5	6	(9)
Foreign operations	3	9	(44)
Change in valuation allowance	103	(7)	(11)
Tax credits	7	28	7
Export sales benefit	13	16	16
Resolution of tax matters	—	—	37
Other	3	7	10
	$(18)	$(11)	$(75)

State taxes reflect investment tax credits of $23 million, $14 million, and $9 million for 2006, 2005, and 2004, respectively. Deferred income taxes reflect the net tax effects of temporary differences between the bases of assets and liabilities for financial reporting and income tax purposes. The company's deferred tax assets and liabilities consist of the following as of the end of the periods shown below:

($ Millions)	2006	2005
Deferred tax assets:		
Net operating loss and credit carryforwards	$929	$1,202
Basis differences in investments in joint ventures	301	—
Deferred revenue	160	76
Accrued compensation	51	40
Accounts payable	43	25
Inventories	16	33
Accrued product and process technology	11	12
Other	36	87
Gross deferred assets	1,547	1,475
Less valuation allowance	(915)	(1,029)
Deferred tax assets, net of valuation allowance	632	446
Deferred tax liabilities:		
Excess tax over book depreciation	(308)	(315)
Receivables	(91)	—
Intangibles	(68)	—
Unremitted earnings on certain subsidiaries	(58)	(49)

(continued)

Exhibit 4	(Continued)		
($ Millions)		**2006**	**2005**
Product and process technology		(45)	(39)
Other		(15)	(16)
Deferred tax liabilities		(585)	(419)
Net deferred tax assets		$47	$27
Reported as:			
Current deferred tax assets		$26	$32
Noncurrent deferred tax assets		49	30
Noncurrent deferred tax liabilities		(28)	(35)
Net deferred tax assets		$47	$27

The company has a valuation allowance against substantially all of its U.S. net deferred tax assets. As of 31 August 2006, the company had aggregate U.S. tax net operating loss carryforwards of $1.7 billion and unused U.S. tax credit carryforwards of $164 million. The company also has unused state tax net operating loss carryforwards of $1.4 billion and unused state tax credits of $163 million. During 2006, the company utilized approximately $1.1 billion of its U.S. tax net operating loss carryforwards as a result of IMFT, MP Mask, and related transactions.[5] Substantially all of the net operating loss carryforwards expire in 2022 to 2025 and substantially all of the tax credit carryforwards expire in 2013 to 2026.

The changes in valuation allowance of ($114) million and $25 million in 2006 and 2005, respectively, are primarily a result of uncertainties of realizing certain U.S. net operating losses and certain tax credit carryforwards. The change in the valuation allowance in 2006 and 2005 includes $12 million and $2 million, respectively, for stock plan deductions, which will be credited to additional capital if realized.

Provision has been made for deferred taxes on undistributed earnings of non-U.S. subsidiaries to the extent that dividend payments from such companies are expected to result in additional tax liability. Remaining undistributed earnings of $686 million as of 31 August 2006 have been indefinitely reinvested; therefore, no provision has been made for taxes due upon remittance of these earnings. Determination of the amount of unrecognized deferred tax liability on these unremitted earnings is not practicable.

EXAMPLE 6

Financial Analysis Example

Use the financial statement information and disclosures provided by MU in Exhibits 2, 3, and 4 to answer the following questions:

1   MU discloses a valuation allowance of $915 million (see Exhibit 4) against total deferred assets of $1,547 million in 2006. Does the existence of this valuation allowance have any implications concerning MU's future earning prospects?

---

5 Micron Technology entered into profitable joint ventures and acquired profitable companies in 2006. The company was able to apply its net operating tax loss carryforwards (NOLs) toward these profits thereby reducing the income tax payments that would otherwise have been made without the NOLs.

2 How would MU's deferred tax assets and deferred tax liabilities be affected if the federal statutory tax rate was changed to 32 percent? Would a change in the rate to 32 percent be beneficial to MU?

3 How would reported earnings have been affected if MU were not using a valuation allowance?

4 How would MU's $929 million in net operating loss carryforwards in 2006 (see Exhibit 4) affect the valuation that an acquiring company would be willing to offer?

5 Under what circumstances should the analyst consider MU's deferred tax liability as debt or as equity? Under what circumstances should the analyst exclude MU's deferred tax liability from both debt and equity when calculating the debt-to-equity ratio?

Solution to 1:

According to Exhibit 4, MU's deferred tax assets expire gradually until 2026 (2022 to 2025 for the net operating loss carryforwards and 2013 to 2026 for the tax credit carryforwards).

Because the company is relatively young, it is likely that most of these expirations occur toward the end of that period. Because cumulative federal net operating loss carryforwards total $1.7 billion, the valuation allowance could imply that MU is not reasonably expected to earn $1.7 billion over the next 20 years. However, as we can see in Exhibit 2, MU has earned profits for 2006, 2005, and 2004, thereby showing that the allowance could be adjusted downward if the company continues to generate profits in the future, making it more likely than not that the deferred tax asset would be recognized.

Solution to 2:

MU's total deferred tax assets exceed total deferred tax liabilities by $47 million. A change in the federal statutory tax rate to 32 percent from the current rate of 35 percent would make these net deferred assets less valuable. Also, because it is possible that the deferred tax asset valuation allowance could be adjusted downward in the future (see discussion to solution 1), the impact could be far greater in magnitude.

Solution to 3:

The disclosure in Exhibit 4 shows that the reduction in the valuation allowance reduced the income tax provision as reported on the income statement by $103 million in 2006. Additional potential reductions in the valuation allowance could similarly reduce reported income taxes (actual income taxes would not be affected by a valuation allowance established for financial reporting) in future years (see discussion to solution 1).

Solution to 4:

If an acquiring company is profitable, it may be able to use MU's tax loss carryforwards to offset its own tax liabilities. The value to an acquirer would be the present value of the carryforwards, based on the acquirer's tax rate and expected timing of realization. The higher the acquiring company's tax rate, and the more profitable the acquirer, the sooner it would be able to benefit. Therefore, an acquirer with a high current tax rate would theoretically be willing to pay more than an acquirer with a lower tax rate.

Solution to 5:

The analyst should classify the deferred tax liability as debt if the liability is expected to reverse with subsequent tax payment. If the liability is not expected to reverse, there is no expectation of a cash outflow and the liability should be treated as equity. By way of example, future company losses may preclude the payment of any income taxes, or changes in tax laws could result in taxes that are never paid. The deferred tax liability should be excluded from both debt and equity when both the amounts and timing of tax payments resulting from the reversals of temporary differences are uncertain.

8   COMPARISON OF IFRS AND U.S. GAAP

As mentioned earlier, though IFRS and U.S. GAAP follow similar conventions on many tax issues, there are some notable differences (such as revaluation). Exhibit 5 summarizes many of the key similarities and differences between IFRS and U.S. GAAP. Though both frameworks require a provision for deferred taxes, there are differences in the methodologies.

Exhibit 5	Deferred Income Tax Issues IFRS and U.S. GAAP Methodology Similarities and Differences	
Issue	**IFRS**	**U.S. GAAP**
General considerations:		
General approach	Full provision.	Similar to IFRS.
Basis for deferred tax assets and liabilities	Temporary differences—i.e., the difference between carrying amount and tax base of assets and liabilities (see exceptions below).	Similar to IFRS.
Exceptions (i.e., deferred tax is not provided on the temporary difference)	Nondeductible goodwill (that which is not deductible for tax purposes) does not give rise to taxable temporary differences.	Similar to IFRS, except no initial recognition exemption and special requirements apply in computing deferred tax on leveraged leases.
General considerations:		
	Initial recognition of an asset or liability in a transaction that: a) is not a business combination; and b) affects neither accounting profit nor taxable profit at the time of the transaction. Other amounts that do not have a tax consequence (commonly referred to as permanent differences) exist and depend on the tax rules and jurisdiction of the entity.	
Specific applications:		
Revaluation of plant, property, and equipment and intangible assets	Deferred tax recognized in equity.	Not applicable, as revaluation is prohibited.

Exhibit 5	(Continued)

Issue	IFRS	U.S. GAAP
Foreign nonmonetary assets/ liabilities when the tax reporting currency is not the functional currency	Deferred tax is recognized on the difference between the carrying amount, determined using the historical rate of exchange, and the tax base, determined using the balance sheet date exchange rate.	No deferred tax is recognized for differences related to assets and liabilities that are remeasured from local currency into the functional currency resulting from changes in exchange rates or indexing for tax purposes.
Investments in subsidiaries—treatment of undistributed profit	Deferred tax is recognized except when the parent is able to control the distribution of profit and it is probable that the temporary difference will not reverse in the foreseeable future.	Deferred tax is required on temporary differences arising after 1992 that relate to investments in domestic subsidiaries, unless such amounts can be recovered tax-free and the entity expects to use that method. No deferred taxes are recognized on undistributed profits of foreign subsidiaries that meet the indefinite reversal criterion. Deferred tax assets may be recorded only to the extent they will reverse in the foreseeable future.
Investments in joint ventures—treatment of undistributed profit	Deferred tax is recognized except when the venturer can control the sharing of profits and if it is probable that the temporary difference will not reverse in the foreseeable future.	Deferred tax is required on temporary differences arising after 1992 that relate to investment in domestic corporate joint ventures. No deferred taxes are recognized on undistributed profits of foreign corporate joint ventures that meet the indefinite reversal criterion. Deferred tax assets may be recorded only to the extent they will reverse in the foreseeable future.
Investment in associates—treatment of undistributed profit	Deferred tax is recognized except when the investor can control the sharing of profits and it is probable that the temporary difference will not reverse in the foreseeable future.	Deferred tax is recognized on temporary differences relating to investments in investees.
Uncertain tax positions	Reflects the tax consequences that follow from the manner in which the entity expects, at the balance sheet date, to be paid to (recovered from) the taxation authorities.	A tax benefit from an uncertain tax position may be recognized only if it is "more likely than not" that the tax position is sustainable based on its technical merits. The tax position is measured as the largest amount of tax benefit that is greater than 50 percent likely of being realized upon ultimate settlement.
Measurement of deferred tax:		
Tax rates	Tax rates and tax laws that have been enacted or substantively enacted.	Use of substantively enacted rates is not permitted. Tax rate and tax laws used must have been enacted.
Recognition of deferred tax assets	A deferred tax asset is recognized if it is probable (more likely than not) that sufficient taxable profit will be available against which the temporary difference can be utilized.	A deferred tax asset is recognized in full but is then reduced by a valuation allowance if it is more likely than not that some or all of the deferred tax asset will not be realized.
Business combinations—Acquisitions:		
Step-up of acquired assets/liabilities to fair value	Deferred tax is recorded unless the tax base of the asset is also stepped up.	Similar to IFRS.

(continued)

Exhibit 5	(Continued)

Issue	IFRS	U.S. GAAP
Previously unrecognized tax losses of the acquirer	A deferred tax asset is recognized if the recognition criteria for the deferred tax asset are met as a result of the acquisition. Offsetting credit is recorded in income.	Similar to IFRS, except the offsetting credit is recorded against goodwill.
Tax losses of the acquiree (initial recognition)	Similar requirements as for the acquirer except the offsetting credit is recorded against goodwill.	Similar to IFRS.
Subsequent resolution of income tax uncertainties in a business combination	If the resolution is more than one year after the year in which the business combination occurred, the result is recognized on the income statement.	The subsequent resolution of any tax uncertainty relating to a business combination is recorded against goodwill.
Subsequent recognition of deferred tax assets that were not "probable" at the time of the business combination	A deferred tax asset that was not considered probable at the time of the business combination but later becomes probable is recognized. The adjustment is to income tax expense with a corresponding adjustment to goodwill. The income statement shows a debit to goodwill expense and a credit to income tax expense. There is no time limit for recognition of this deferred tax asset.	The subsequent resolution of any tax uncertainty relating to a business combination is recorded first against goodwill, then noncurrent intangibles, and then income tax expense. There is no time limit for recognition of this deferred tax asset.
Presentation of deferred tax:		
Offset of deferred tax assets and liabilities	Permitted only when the entity has a legally enforceable right to offset and the balance relates to tax levied by the same authority.	Similar to IFRS.
Current/noncurrent	Deferred tax assets and liabilities are classified net as noncurrent on the balance sheet, with supplemental note disclosure for 1) the components of the temporary differences, and 2) amounts expected to be recovered within 12 months and more than 12 months from the balance sheet date.	Deferred tax assets and liabilities are either classified as current or noncurrent, based on the classification of the related non-tax asset or liability for financial reporting. Tax assets or liabilities not associated with an underlying asset or liability are classified based on the expected reversal period.
Reconciliation of actual and expected tax expense	Required. Computed by applying the applicable tax rates to accounting profit, disclosing also the basis on which the applicable tax rates are calculated.	Required for public companies only. Calculated by applying the domestic federal statutory tax rates to pre-tax income from continuing operations.

Sources: IFRS: IAS 1, IAS 12, and IFRS 3.
U.S. GAAP: FAS 109 and FIN 48.
"Similarities and Differences—A Comparison of IFRS and U.S. GAAP," PricewaterhouseCoopers, October 2006.

SUMMARY

Income taxes are a significant category of expense for profitable companies. Analyzing income tax expenses is often difficult for the analyst because there are many permanent and temporary timing differences between the accounting that is used for income tax reporting and the accounting that is used for financial reporting on company financial statements. The financial statements and notes to the financial statements of a company provide important information that the analyst needs to assess financial performance and to compare a company's financial performance with other companies. Key concepts in this reading are as follows:

- Differences between the recognition of revenue and expenses for tax and accounting purposes may result in taxable income differing from accounting profit. The discrepancy is a result of different treatments of certain income and expenditure items.

- The tax base of an asset is the amount that will be deductible for tax purposes as an expense in the calculation of taxable income as the company expenses the tax basis of the asset. If the economic benefit will not be taxable, the tax base of the asset will be equal to the carrying amount of the asset.

- The tax base of a liability is the carrying amount of the liability less any amounts that will be deductible for tax purposes in the future. With respect to revenue received in advance, the tax base of such a liability is the carrying amount less any amount of the revenue that will not be taxable in the future.

- Temporary differences arise from recognition of differences in the tax base and carrying amount of assets and liabilities. The creation of a deferred tax asset or liability as a result of a temporary difference will only be allowed if the difference reverses itself at some future date and to the extent that it is expected that the balance sheet item will create future economic benefits for the company.

- Permanent differences result in a difference in tax and financial reporting of revenue (expenses) that will not be reversed at some future date. Because it will not be reversed at a future date, these differences do not constitute temporary differences and do not give rise to a deferred tax asset or liability.

- Current taxes payable or recoverable are based on the applicable tax rates on the balance sheet date of an entity; in contrast, deferred taxes should be measured at the tax rate that is expected to apply when the asset is realized or the liability settled.

- All unrecognized deferred tax assets and liabilities must be reassessed on the appropriate balance sheet date and measured against their probable future economic benefit.

- Deferred tax assets must be assessed for their prospective recoverability. If it is probable that they will not be recovered at all or partly, the carrying amount should be reduced. Under U.S. GAAP, this is done through the use of a valuation allowance.

PRACTICE PROBLEMS

1 Using the straight-line method of depreciation for reporting purposes and accelerated depreciation for tax purposes would *most likely* result in a:

   A valuation allowance.

   B deferred tax asset.

   C temporary difference.

2 In early 2009 Sanborn Company must pay the tax authority €37,000 on the income it earned in 2008. This amount was recorded on the company's 31 December 2008 financial statements as:

   A taxes payable.

   B income tax expense.

   C a deferred tax liability.

3 Income tax expense reported on a company's income statement equals taxes payable, plus the net increase in:

   A deferred tax assets and deferred tax liabilities.

   B deferred tax assets, less the net increase in deferred tax liabilities.

   C deferred tax liabilities, less the net increase in deferred tax assets.

4 Analysts should treat deferred tax liabilities that are expected to reverse as:

   A equity.

   B liabilities.

   C neither liabilities nor equity.

5 Deferred tax liabilities should be treated as equity when:

   A they are not expected to reverse.

   B the timing of tax payments is uncertain.

   C the amount of tax payments is uncertain.

6 When both the timing and amount of tax payments are uncertain, analysts should treat deferred tax liabilities as:

   A equity.

   B liabilities.

   C neither liabilities nor equity.

7 When accounting standards require recognition of an expense that is not permitted under tax laws, the result is a:

   A deferred tax liability.

   B temporary difference.

   C permanent difference.

8 When certain expenditures result in tax credits that directly reduce taxes, the company will *most likely* record:

   A a deferred tax asset.

   B a deferred tax liability.

   C no deferred tax asset or liability.

9 When accounting standards require an asset to be expensed immediately but tax rules require the item to be capitalized and amortized, the company will *most likely* record:

   A a deferred tax asset.

   B a deferred tax liability.

   C no deferred tax asset or liability.

10 A company incurs a capital expenditure that may be amortized over five years for accounting purposes, but over four years for tax purposes. The company will *most likely* record:

   A a deferred tax asset.

   B a deferred tax liability.

   C no deferred tax asset or liability.

11 A company receives advance payments from customers that are immediately taxable but will not be recognized for accounting purposes until the company fulfills its obligation. The company will *most likely* record:

   A a deferred tax asset.

   B a deferred tax liability.

   C no deferred tax asset or liability.

The following information relates to Questions 12–14

Note I
Income Taxes

The components of earnings before income taxes are as follows ($ thousands):

	2007	2006	2005
Earnings before income taxes:			
United States	$ 88,157	$ 75,658	$ 59,973
Foreign	116,704	113,509	94,760
Total	$204,861	$189,167	$154,733

The components of the provision for income taxes are as follows ($ thousands):

	2007	2006	2005
Income taxes			
Current:			
Federal	$30,632	$22,031	$18,959
Foreign	28,140	27,961	22,263
	$58,772	$49,992	$41,222
Deferred:			
Federal	($4,752)	$5,138	$2,336
Foreign	124	1,730	621

(continued)

	2007	2006	2005
	(4,628)	6,868	2,957
Total	$54,144	$56,860	$44,179

12 In 2007, the company's U.S. GAAP income statement recorded a provision for income taxes *closest* to:

A $30,632.

B $54,144.

C $58,772.

13 The company's effective tax rate was *highest* in:

A 2005.

B 2006.

C 2007.

14 Compared to the company's effective tax rate on U.S. income, its effective tax rate on foreign income was:

A lower in each year presented.

B higher in each year presented.

C higher in some periods and lower in others.

15 Zimt AG presents its financial statements in accordance with U.S. GAAP. In 2007, Zimt discloses a valuation allowance of $1,101 against total deferred tax assets of $19,201. In 2006, Zimt disclosed a valuation allowance of $1,325 against total deferred tax assets of $17,325. The change in the valuation allowance *most likely* indicates that Zimt's:

A deferred tax liabilities were reduced in 2007.

B expectations of future earning power has increased.

C expectations of future earning power has decreased.

16 Cinnamon, Inc. recorded a total deferred tax asset in 2007 of $12,301, offset by a $12,301 valuation allowance. Cinnamon *most likely*:

A fully utilized the deferred tax asset in 2007.

B has an equal amount of deferred tax assets and deferred tax liabilities.

C expects not to earn any taxable income before the deferred tax asset expires.

The following information relates to Questions 17–19

The tax effects of temporary differences that give rise to deferred tax assets and liabilities are as follows ($ thousands):

	2007	2006
Deferred tax assets:		
Accrued expenses	$8,613	$7,927

	2007	2006
Tax credit and net operating loss carryforwards	2,288	2,554
LIFO and inventory reserves	5,286	4,327
Other	2,664	2,109
Deferred tax assets	18,851	16,917
Valuation allowance	(1,245)	(1,360)
Net deferred tax assets	$17,606	$15,557
Deferred tax liabilities:		
Depreciation and amortization	$(27,338)	$(29,313)
Compensation and retirement plans	(3,831)	(8,963)
Other	(1,470)	(764)
Deferred tax liabilities	(32,639)	(39,040)
Net deferred tax liability	($15,033)	($23,483)

17 A reduction in the statutory tax rate would *most likely* benefit the company's:

A income statement and balance sheet.

B income statement but not the balance sheet.

C balance sheet but not the income statement.

18 If the valuation allowance had been the same in 2007 as it was in 2006, the company would have reported $115 *higher*:

A net income.

B deferred tax assets.

C income tax expense.

19 Compared to the provision for income taxes in 2007, the company's cash tax payments were:

A lower.

B higher.

C the same.

The following information relates to Questions 20–22

A company's provision for income taxes resulted in effective tax rates attributable to loss from continuing operations before cumulative effect of change in accounting principles that varied from the statutory federal income tax rate of 34 percent, as summarized in the table below.

Year Ended 30 June	2007	2006	2005
Expected federal income tax expense (benefit) from continuing operations at 34 percent	($112,000)	$768,000	$685,000
Expenses not deductible for income tax purposes	357,000	32,000	51,000

(continued)

Year Ended 30 June	2007	2006	2005
State income taxes, net of federal benefit	132,000	22,000	100,000
Change in valuation allowance for deferred tax assets	(150,000)	(766,000)	(754,000)
Income tax expense	$227,000	$56,000	$82,000

20 In 2007, the company's net income (loss) was *closest* to:

   A ($217,000).

   B ($329,000).

   C ($556,000).

21 The $357,000 adjustment in 2007 *most likely* resulted in:

   A an increase in deferred tax assets.

   B an increase in deferred tax liabilities.

   C no change to deferred tax assets and liabilities.

22 Over the three years presented, changes in the valuation allowance for deferred tax assets were *most likely* indicative of:

   A decreased prospect for future profitability.

   B increased prospects for future profitability.

   C assets being carried at a higher value than their tax base.

SOLUTIONS

1 C is correct. Because the differences between tax and financial accounting will correct over time, the resulting deferred tax liability, for which the expense was charged to the income statement but the tax authority has not yet been paid, will be a temporary difference. A valuation allowance would only arise if there was doubt over the company's ability to earn sufficient income in the future to require paying the tax.

2 A is correct. The taxes a company must pay in the immediate future are taxes payable.

3 C is correct. Higher reported tax expense relative to taxes paid will increase the deferred tax liability, whereas lower reported tax expense relative to taxes paid increases the deferred tax asset.

4 B is correct. If the liability is expected to reverse (and thus require a cash tax payment) the deferred tax represents a future liability.

5 A is correct. If the liability will not reverse, there will be no required tax payment in the future and the "liability" should be treated as equity.

6 C is correct. The deferred tax liability should be excluded from both debt and equity when both the amounts and timing of tax payments resulting from the reversals of temporary differences are uncertain.

7 C is correct. Accounting items that are not deductible for tax purposes will not be reversed and thus result in permanent differences.

8 C is correct. Tax credits that directly reduce taxes are a permanent difference, and permanent differences do not give rise to deferred tax.

9 A is correct. The capitalization will result in an asset with a positive tax base and zero carrying value. The amortization means the difference is temporary. Because there is a temporary difference on an asset resulting in a higher tax base than carrying value, a deferred tax asset is created.

10 B is correct. The difference is temporary, and the tax base will be lower (because of more rapid amortization) than the carrying value of the asset. The result will be a deferred tax liability.

11 A is correct. The advances represent a liability for the company. The carrying value of the liability exceeds the tax base (which is now zero). A deferred tax asset arises when the carrying value of a liability exceeds its tax base.

12 B is correct. The income tax provision in 2007 was $54,144, consisting of $58,772 in current income taxes, of which $4,628 were deferred.

13 B is correct. The effective tax rate of 30.1 percent ($56,860/$189,167) was higher than the effective rates in 2005 and 2007.

14 A is correct. In 2007 the effective tax rate on foreign operations was 24.2 percent [($28,140 + $124)/$116,704] and the effective U.S. tax rate was [($30,632 − $4,752)/$88,157] = 29.4 percent. In 2006 the effective tax rate on foreign operations was 26.2 percent and the U.S. rate was 35.9 percent. In 2005 the foreign rate was 24.1 percent and the U.S. rate was 35.5 percent.

15 B is correct. The valuation allowance is taken against deferred tax assets to represent uncertainty that future taxable income will be sufficient to fully utilize the assets. By decreasing the allowance, Zimt is signaling greater likelihood that future earnings will be offset by the deferred tax asset.

16 C is correct. The valuation allowance is taken when the company will "more likely than not" fail to earn sufficient income to offset the deferred tax asset. Because the valuation allowance equals the asset, by extension the company expects *no* taxable income prior to the expiration of the deferred tax assets.

17 A is correct. A lower tax rate would increase net income on the income statement, and because the company has a net deferred tax liability, the net liability position on the balance sheet would also improve (be smaller).

18 C is correct. The reduction in the valuation allowance resulted in a corresponding reduction in the income tax provision.

19 B is correct. The net deferred tax liability was smaller in 2007 than it was in 2006, indicating that in addition to meeting the tax payments provided for in 2007 the company also paid taxes that had been deferred in prior periods.

20 C is correct. The income tax provision at the statutory rate of 34 percent is a benefit of $112,000, suggesting that the pre-tax income was a loss of $112,000/0.34 = ($329,412). The income tax provision was $227,000. ($329,412) − $227,000 = ($556,412).

21 C is correct. Accounting expenses that are not deductible for tax purposes result in a permanent difference, and thus do not give rise to deferred taxes.

22 B is correct. Over the three-year period, changes in the valuation allowance reduced cumulative income taxes by $1,670,000. The reductions to the valuation allowance were a result of the company being "more likely than not" to earn sufficient taxable income to offset the deferred tax assets.

Non-Current (Long-Term) Liabilities

by Elizabeth A. Gordon and Elaine Henry, CFA

LEARNING OUTCOMES

Mastery	The candidate should be able to
☐	**a.** determine the initial recognition, initial measurement and subsequent measurement of bonds;
☐	**b.** describe the effective interest method and calculate interest expense, amortisation of bond discounts/premiums, and interest payments;
☐	**c.** explain the derecognition of debt;
☐	**d.** describe the role of debt covenants in protecting creditors;
☐	**e.** describe the financial statement presentation of and disclosures relating to debt;
☐	**f.** explain the motivations for leasing assets instead of purchasing them;
☐	**g.** distinguish between a finance lease and an operating lease from the perspectives of the lessor and the lessee;
☐	**h.** determine the initial recognition, initial measurement, and subsequent measurement of finance leases;
☐	**i.** compare the disclosures relating to finance and operating leases;
☐	**k.** compare the presentation and disclosure of defined contribution and defined benefit pension plans;
☐	**l.** calculate and interpret leverage and coverage ratios.

Note: New rulings and/or pronouncements issues after the publication of the readings on financial reporting and analysis may cause some of the information in these readings to become dated. Candidates are expected to be familiar with the overall analytical framework contained in the study session readings, as well as the implications of alternative accounting methods for financial analysis and valuation, as provided in the assigned readings. Candidates are not responsible for changes that occur after the material was written.

1 INTRODUCTION

A **non-current** (long-term) **liability** broadly represents a probable sacrifice of economic benefits in periods generally greater than one year in the future. Common types of non-current liabilities reported in a company's financial statements include long-term debt (e.g., bonds payable, long-term notes payable), finance leases, pension liabilities, and deferred tax liabilities. This reading focuses on bonds payable and leases. Pension liabilities are also introduced.

This reading is organised as follows. Section 2 describes and illustrates the accounting for long-term bonds, including the issuance of bonds, the recording of interest expense and interest payments, the amortisation of any discount or premium, the derecognition of debt, and the disclosure of information about debt financings. In discussing the financial statement effects and analyses of these issues, we focus on solvency and coverage ratios. Section 3 discusses leases, including benefits of leasing and accounting for leases by both lessees and lessors. Section 4 provides an introduction to pension accounting and the resulting non-current liabilities. Section 5 discusses the use of leverage and coverage ratios in evaluating solvency. Section 6 concludes and summarises the reading. Practice problems in the CFA Institute format are included after the reading.

2 BONDS PAYABLE

This section discusses accounting for bonds payable—a common form of long-term debt. In some contexts (e.g., some government debt obligations), the word "bond" is used only for a debt security with a maturity of 10 years or longer; "note" refers to a debt security with a maturity between 2 and 10 years; and "bill" refers to a debt security with a maturity of less than 2 years. In this reading, we use the terms bond and note interchangeably because the accounting treatments of bonds payable and long-term notes payable are similar. In the following sections, we discuss bond issuance (initial recognition and measurement); bond amortisation, interest expense, and interest payments; market rates and fair value (subsequent measurement); repayment of bonds, including retirements and redemptions (derecognition); and other issues concerning disclosures related to debt. We also discuss debt covenants.

2.1 Accounting for Bond Issuance

Bonds are contractual promises made by a company (or other borrowing entity) to pay cash in the future to its lenders (i.e., bondholders) in exchange for receiving cash in the present. The terms of a bond contract are contained in a document called an indenture. The cash or sales proceeds received by a company when it issues bonds is based on the value (price) of the bonds at the time of issue; the price at the time of issue is determined as the present value of the future cash payments promised by the company in the bond agreement.

Ordinarily, bonds contain promises of two types of future cash payments: 1) the face value of the bonds, and 2) periodic interest payments. The **face value** of the bonds is the amount of cash payable by the company to the bondholders when the bonds mature. The face value is also referred to as the principal, par value, stated value, or maturity value. The date of maturity of the bonds (the date on which the face value is paid to bondholders) is stated in the bond contract and typically is a number of years in the future. Periodic interest payments are made based on the interest rate promised in the bond contract applied to the bonds' face value. The interest rate promised in the contract, which is the rate used to calculate the periodic interest payments, is referred to as the **coupon rate**, nominal rate, or stated rate. Similarly, the periodic interest payment is referred to as the coupon payment or simply the coupon. For fixed rate bonds (the primary focus of our discussion here), the coupon rate remains unchanged throughout the life of the bonds. The frequency with which interest payments are made is also stated in the bond contract. For example, bonds paying interest semi-annually will make two interest payments per year.[1]

The future cash payments are discounted to the present to arrive at the market value of the bonds. The **market rate of interest** is the rate demanded by purchasers of the bonds given the risks associated with future cash payment obligations of the particular bond issue. The market rate of interest at the time of issue often differs from the coupon rate because of interest rate fluctuations that occur between the time the issuer establishes the coupon rate and the day the bonds are actually available to investors. If the market rate of interest when the bonds are issued equals the coupon rate, the market value (price) of the bonds will equal the face value of the bonds. Thus, ignoring issuance costs, the issuing company will receive sales proceeds (cash) equal to the face value of the bonds. When a bond is issued at a price equal to its face value, the bond is said to have been issued at par.

If the coupon rate when the bonds are issued is higher than the market rate, the market value of the bonds—and thus the amount of cash the company receives—will be higher than the face value of the bonds. In other words, the bonds will sell at a premium to face value because they are offering an attractive coupon rate compared to current market rates. If the coupon rate is lower than the market rate, the market value and thus the sale proceeds from the bonds will be less than the face value of the bonds; the bond will sell at a discount to face value. The market rate at the time of issuance is the **effective interest rate** or borrowing rate that the company incurs on the debt. The effective interest rate is the discount rate that equates the present value of the two types of promised future cash payments to their selling price. For the issuing company, interest expense reported for the bonds in the financial statements is based on the effective interest rate.

On the issuing company's statement of cash flows, the cash received (sales proceeds) from issuing bonds is reported as a financing cash inflow. On the issuing company's balance sheet at the time of issue, bonds payable normally are measured and reported at the sales proceeds. In other words, the bonds payable are initially reported at the face value of the bonds minus any discount, or plus any premium.

Using a three-step approach, the following two examples illustrate accounting for bonds issued at face value and then accounting for bonds issued at a discount to face value. Accounting for bonds issued at a premium involves steps similar to the steps followed in the examples below. For simplicity, these examples assume a flat interest rate yield curve (i.e., that the market rate of interest is the same for each period). More-precise bond valuations use the interest rate applicable to each time period in which a payment of interest or principal occurs.

EXAMPLE 1

Bonds Issued at Face Value

Debond Corp. (a hypothetical company) issues £1,000,000 worth of five-year bonds, dated 1 January 2010, when the market interest rate on bonds of comparable risk and terms is 5 percent per annum. The bonds pay 5 percent interest annually on 31 December. What are the sales proceeds of the bonds when issued, and how is the issuance reflected in the financial statements?

---

1 Interest rates are stated on an annual basis regardless of the frequency of payment.

Solution:

Calculating the value of the bonds at issuance and thus the sales proceeds involves three steps: 1) identifying key features of the bonds and the market interest rate, 2) determining future cash outflows, and 3) discounting the future cash flows to the present.

First, identify key features of the bonds and the market interest rate necessary to determine sales proceeds:

Face value (principal):	£1,000,000	
Time to maturity:	5 years	
Coupon rate:	5%	
Market rate at issuance:	5%	
Frequency of interest payments:	annual	
Interest payment:	£50,000	Each annual interest payment is the face value times the coupon rate (£1,000,000 × 5%). If interest is paid other than annually, adjust the interest rate to match the interest payment period (e.g., divide the annual coupon rate by two for semi-annual interest payments).

Second, determine future cash outflows. Debond will pay bondholders £1,000,000 when the bonds mature in five years. On 31 December of each year until the bonds mature, Debond will make an interest payment of £50,000.

Third, sum the present value[2] of the future payments of interest and principal to obtain the value of the bonds and thus the sales proceeds from issuing the bonds. In this example, the sum is £1,000,000 = (£216,474 + £783,526).

Date	Interest Payment	Present Value at Market Rate (5%)	Face Value Payment	Present Value at Market Rate (5%)	Total Present Value
31 December 2010	£50,000	£47,619			
31 December 2011	50,000	45,352			
31 December 2012	50,000	43,192			
31 December 2013	50,000	41,135			
31 December 2014	50,000	39,176	£1,000,000	£783,526	
Total		£216,474		£783,526	£1,000,000
					Sales Proceeds

The sales proceeds of the bonds when issued are £1,000,000. There is no discount or premium because these bonds are issued at face value. The issuance is reflected on the balance sheet as an increase of cash and an increase in a long-term liability, bonds payable, of £1,000,000. The issuance is reflected in the statement of cash flows as a financing cash inflow of £1,000,000.

The price of bonds is often expressed as a percentage of face value. For example, the price of bonds issued at par, as in Example 1, is 100 (i.e., 100 percent of face value). In Example 2, in which bonds are issued at a discount, the price is 95.79 (i.e., 95.79 percent of face value).

---

2 Alternative ways to calculate the present value include 1) to treat the five annual interest payments as an annuity and use the formula for finding the present value of an annuity and then add the present value of the principal payment, or 2) to use a financial calculator to calculate the total present value.

EXAMPLE 2

Bonds Issued at a Discount

Debond Corp. issues £1,000,000 worth of five-year bonds, dated 1 January 2010, when the market interest rate on bonds of comparable risk and terms is 6 percent. The bonds pay 5 percent interest annually on 31 December. What are the sales proceeds of the bonds when issued, and how is the issuance reflected in the financial statements?

Solution:

The key features of the bonds and the market interest rate are:

Face value (principal):	£1,000,000	
Time to maturity:	5 years	
Coupon rate:	5%	
Market rate at issuance:	6%	
Frequency of interest payments:	annual	
Interest payment:	£50,000	Each annual interest payment is the face value times the coupon rate (£1,000,000 × 5%).

The future cash outflows (interest payments and face value payment), the present value of the future cash outflows, and the total present value are:

Date	Interest Payment	Present Value at Market Rate (6%)	Face Value Payment	Present Value at Market Rate (6%)	Total Present Value
31 December 2010	£50,000	£47,170			
31 December 2011	50,000	44,500			
31 December 2012	50,000	41,981			
31 December 2013	50,000	39,605			
31 December 2014	50,000	37,363	£1,000,000	£747,258	
Total		£210,618		£747,258	£957,876
					Sales Proceeds

The sales proceeds of the bonds when issued are £957,876. The bonds sell at a discount of £42,124 = (£1,000,000 – £957,876) because the market rate when the bonds are issued (6 percent) is greater than the bonds' coupon rate (5 percent). The issuance is reflected on the balance sheet as an increase of cash and an increase in a long-term liability, bonds payable, of £957,876. The bonds payable is composed of the face value of £1,000,000 minus a discount of £42,124. The issuance is reflected in the statement of cash flows as a financing cash inflow of £957,876.

In Example 2, the bonds were issued at a discount to face value because the bonds' coupon rate of 5 percent was less than the market rate. Bonds are issued at a premium to face value when the bonds' coupon rate exceeds the market rate.

Bonds issued with a coupon rate of zero (zero-coupon bonds) are always issued at a discount to face value. The value of zero-coupon bonds is based on the present value of the principal payment only because there are no periodic interest payments.

Such issuance costs as printing, legal fees, commissions, and other types of charges are costs incurred when bonds are issued. Under International Financial Reporting Standards (IFRS), all debt issuance costs are included in the measurement of the liability, bonds payable. Under U.S. generally accepted accounting principles (U.S. GAAP), companies generally show these debt issuance costs as an asset (a deferred charge), which is amortised on a straight-line basis to the relevant expense (e.g., legal fees) over the life of the bonds.[3] Under IFRS and U.S. GAAP, cash outflows related to bond issuance costs are included in the financing section of the statement of cash flows, usually netted against bond proceeds.

2.2 Accounting for Bond Amortisation, Interest Expense, and Interest Payments

In this section, we discuss accounting and reporting for bonds after they are issued. Most companies maintain the historical cost (sales proceeds) of the bonds after issuance, and they amortise any discount or premium over the life of the bond. The amount reported on the balance sheet for bonds is thus the historical cost plus or minus the cumulative amortisation, which is referred to as amortised cost. Companies also have the option to report the bonds at their current fair values.

The rationale for reporting the bonds at amortised historical cost is the company's intention to retain the debt until it matures. Therefore, changes in the underlying economic value of the debt are not relevant from the issuing company's perspective. From an investor's perspective, however, analysis of a company's underlying economic liabilities and solvency is more difficult when debt is reported at amortised historical cost. The rest of this section illustrates accounting and reporting of bonds at amortised historical cost. Section 2.3 discusses the alternative of reporting bonds at fair value.

Companies initially report bonds as a liability on their balance sheet at the amount of the sales proceeds net of issuance costs under IFRS and at the amount of the sales proceeds under U.S. GAAP, ignoring any bond issuance costs. The amount at which bonds are reported on the company's balance sheet is referred to as the carrying amount, carrying value, book value, or net book value. If the bonds are issued at par, the initial carrying amount will be identical to the face value, and usually the carrying amount will not change over the life of the bonds.[4] For bonds issued at face value, the amount of periodic interest *expense* will be the same as the amount of periodic interest *payment* to bondholders.

If, however, the market rate differs from the bonds' coupon rate at issuance such that the bonds are issued at a premium or discount, the premium or discount is amortised systematically over the life of the bonds as a component of interest expense. For bonds issued at a premium to face value, the carrying amount of the bonds is initially greater than the face value. As the premium is amortised, the carrying amount (amortised cost) of the bonds will decrease to the face value. The reported interest expense will be less than the coupon payment. For bonds issued at a discount to face value, the carrying amount of the bonds is initially less than the face value. As the discount is amortised, the carrying amount (amortised cost) of the bonds will increase to the face value. The reported interest expense will be higher than the coupon payment.

The accounting treatment for bonds issued at a discount reflects the fact that the company essentially paid some of its borrowing costs at issuance by selling its bonds at a discount. Rather than there being an actual cash transfer in the future, this "payment" was made in the form of accepting less than the face value for the bonds at the date of issuance. The remaining borrowing cost occurs as a cash interest payment to investors each period. The total interest expense reflects both components of the

---

3 The Financial Accounting Standards Board (FASB), as part of the convergence project with the International Accounting Standards Board (IASB), has proposed that the treatment of issuance costs be amended to that under IFRS.

4 If a company reports debt at fair value, rather than amortised cost, the carrying value may change.

borrowing cost: the periodic interest payments plus the amortisation of the discount. The accounting treatment for bonds issued at a premium reflects the fact that the company essentially received a reduction on its borrowing costs at issuance by selling its bonds at a premium. Rather than there being an actual reduced cash transfer in the future, this "reduction" was made in the form of receiving more than face value for the bonds at the date of issuance. The total interest expense reflects both components of the borrowing cost: the periodic interest payments less the amortisation of the premium. When the bonds mature, the carrying amount will be equal to the face value regardless of whether the bonds were issued at face value, a discount, or a premium.

Two methods for amortising the premium or discount of bonds that were issued at a price other than par are the effective interest rate method and the straight-line method. The effective interest rate method is required under IFRS and preferred under U.S. GAAP because it better reflects the economic substance of the transaction. The effective interest rate method applies the market rate in effect when the bonds were issued (historical market rate or effective interest rate) to the current amortised cost (carrying amount) of the bonds to obtain interest expense for the period. The difference between the interest expense (based on the effective interest rate and amortised cost) and the interest payment (based on the coupon rate and face value) is the **amortisation** of the discount or premium. The straight-line method of amortisation evenly amortises the premium or discount over the life of the bond, similar to straight-line depreciation on long-lived assets. Under either method, as the bond approaches maturity, the amortised cost approaches face value.

Example 3 illustrates both methods of amortisation for bonds issued at a discount. Example 4 shows amortisation for bonds issued at a premium.

EXAMPLE 3

Amortising a Bond Discount

Debond Corp. issues £1,000,000 face value of five-year bonds, dated 1 January 2010, when the market interest rate is 6 percent. The sales proceeds are £957,876. The bonds pay 5 percent interest annually on 31 December.

1 What is the interest *payment* on the bonds each year?

2 What amount of interest *expense* on the bonds would be reported in 2010 and 2011 using the effective interest rate method?

3 Determine the reported value of the bonds (i.e., the carrying amount) at 31 December 2010 and 2011, assuming the effective interest rate method is used to amortise the discount.

4 What amount of interest expense on the bonds would be reported under the straight-line method of amortising the discount?

Solution to 1:

The interest payment equals £50,000 annually (£1,000,000 × 5%).

Solution to 2:

The sales proceeds of £957,876 are less than the face value of £1,000,000; the bonds were issued at a discount of £42,124. The bonds are initially reported as a long-term liability, bonds payable, of £957,876, which comprises the face value of £1,000,000 minus a discount of £42,124. The discount is amortised over time, ultimately, increasing the carrying amount (amortised cost) to face value.

Under the effective interest rate method, interest expense on the bonds is calculated as the bonds' carrying amount times the market rate in effect when the bonds are issued (effective interest rate). For 2010, interest expense is £57,473 =

(£957,876 × 6%). The amount of the discount amortised in 2010 is the difference between the interest expense of £57,473 and the interest payment of £50,000 (i.e., £7,473). The bonds' carrying amount increases by the discount amortisation; at 31 December 2010, the bonds' carrying amount is £965,349 (beginning balance of £957,876 plus £7,473 discount amortisation). At this point, the carrying amount reflects a remaining unamortised discount of £34,651 (£42,124 discount at issuance minus £7,473 amortised).

For 2011, interest expense is £57,921 = (£965,349 × 6%), the carrying amount of the bonds on 1 January 2011 times the effective interest rate. The amount of the discount amortised in 2011 is the difference between the interest expense of £57,921 and the interest payment of £50,000 (i.e., £7,921). At 31 December 2011, the bonds' carrying amount is £973,270 (beginning balance of £965,349 plus £7,921 discount amortisation).

The following table illustrates interest expense, discount amortisation, and carrying amount (amortised cost) over the life of the bonds.

Year	Carrying Amount (beginning of year)	Interest Expense (at effective interest rate of 6%)	Interest Payment (at coupon rate of 5%)	Amortisation of Discount	Carrying Amount (end of year)
	(a)	(b)	(c)	(d)	(e)
2010	£957,876	£57,473	£50,000	£7,473	£965,349
2011	965,349	57,921	50,000	7,921	973,270
2012	973,270	58,396	50,000	8,396	981,666
2013	981,666	58,900	50,000	8,900	990,566
2014	990,566	59,434	50,000	9,434	1,000,000
Total		£292,124	£250,000	£42,124	

Solution to 3:

The carrying amounts of the bonds at 31 December 2010 and 2011 are £965,349 and £973,270, respectively. Observe that the carrying amount of the bonds issued at a discount increases over the life of the bonds. At maturity, 31 December 2014, the carrying amount of the bonds equals the face value of the bonds. The carrying amount of the bonds will be reduced to zero when the principal payment is made.

Solution to 4:

Under the straight-line method, the discount (or premium) is evenly amortised over the life of the bonds. In this example, the £42,124 discount would be amortised by £8,424.80 (£42,124 divided by 5 years) each year under the straight-line method. So, the annual interest expense under the straight-line method would be £58,424.80 (£50,000 plus £8,424.80).

The accounting and reporting for zero-coupon bonds is similar to the example above except that no interest payments are made; thus, the amount of interest expense each year is the same as the amount of the discount amortisation for the year.

EXAMPLE 4

Amortising a Bond Premium

Prembond Corp. issues £1,000,000 face value of five-year bonds, dated 1 January 2010, when the market interest rate is 4 percent. The sales proceeds are £1,044,518. The bonds pay 5 percent interest annually on 31 December.

1 What is the interest *payment* on the bonds each year?

2 What amount of interest *expense* on the bonds would be reported in 2010 and 2011 using the effective interest rate method?

3 Determine the reported value of the bonds (i.e., the carrying amount) at 31 December 2010 and 2011, assuming the effective interest rate method is used to amortise the premium.

4 What amount of interest expense on the bonds would be reported under the straight-line method of amortising the premium?

Solution to 1:

The interest payment equals £50,000 annually (£1,000,000 × 5%).

Solution to 2:

The sales proceeds of £1,044,518 are more than the face value of £1,000,000; the bonds were issued at a premium of £44,518. The bonds are initially reported as a long-term liability, bonds payable, of £1,044,518, which comprises the face value of £1,000,000 plus a premium of £44,518. The premium is amortised over time, ultimately decreasing the carrying amount (amortised cost) to face value.

Under the effective interest rate method, interest expense on the bonds is calculated as the bonds' carrying amount times the market rate in effect when the bonds are issued (effective interest rate). For 2010, interest expense is £41,781 = (£1,044,518 × 4%). The amount of the premium amortised in 2010 is the difference between the interest expense of £41,781 and the interest payment of £50,000 (i.e., £8,219). The bonds' carrying amount decreases by the premium amortisation; at 31 December 2010, the bonds' carrying amount is £1,036,299 (beginning balance of £1,044,518 less £8,219 premium amortisation). At this point, the carrying amount reflects a remaining unamortised premium of £36,299 (£44,158 premium at issuance minus £8,219 amortised).

For 2011, interest expense is £41,452 = (£1,036,299 × 4%). The amount of the premium amortised in 2011 is the difference between the interest expense of £41,452 and the interest payment of £50,000 (i.e., £8,548). At 31 December 2011, the bonds' carrying amount is £1,027,751 (beginning balance of £1,036,299 less £8,548 premium amortisation).

The following table illustrates interest expense, premium amortisation, and carrying amount (amortised cost) over the life of the bonds.

Year	Carrying Amount (beginning of year)	Interest Expense (at effective interest rate of 4%)	Interest Payment (at coupon rate of 5%)	Amortisation of Premium	Carrying Amount (end of year)
	(a)	(b)	(c)	(d)	(e)
2010	£1,044,518	£41,781	£50,000	£8,219	£1,036,299
2011	1,036,299	41,452	50,000	8,548	1,027,751
2012	1,027,751	41,110	50,000	8,890	1,018,861
2013	1,018,861	40,754	50,000	9,246	1,009,615
2014	1,009,615	40,385	50,000	9,615	1,000,000
Total				£44,518	

Solution to 3:

The carrying amounts of the bonds at 31 December 2010 and 2011 are £1,036,299 and £1,027,751, respectively. Observe that the carrying amount of the bonds issued at a premium decreases over the life of the bonds. At maturity, 31 December 2014, the carrying amount of the bonds equals the face value of the bonds. The carrying amount of the bonds will be reduced to zero when the principal payment is made.

> **Solution to 4:**
>
> Under the straight-line method, the premium is evenly amortised over the life of the bonds. In this example, the £44,518 premium would be amortised by £8,903.64 (£44,518 divided by 5 years) each year under the straight-line method. So, the annual interest expense under the straight-line method would be £41,096.36 (£50,000 less £8,903.64).

The reporting of interest payments on the statement of cash flows can differ under IFRS and U.S. GAAP. Under IFRS, interest payments on bonds can be included as an outflow in either the operating section or the financing section of the statement of cash flows. U.S. GAAP requires interest payments on bonds to be included as an operating cash outflow. (Some financial statement users consider the placement of interest payments in the operating section to be inconsistent with the placement of bond issue proceeds in the financing section of the statement of cash flows.) Typically, cash interest paid is not shown directly on the statement of cash flows, but companies are required to disclose interest paid separately.

Amortisation of a discount (premium) is a non-cash item and thus, apart from its effect on taxable income, has no effect on cash flow. In the section of the statement of cash flows that reconciles net income to operating cash flow, amortisation of a discount (premium) is added back to (subtracted from) net income.

2.3 Current Market Rates and Fair Value Reporting Option

Reporting bonds at amortised historical costs (historical cost plus or minus the cumulative amortisation) reflects the market rate at the time the bonds were *issued* (i.e., historical market rate or effective interest rate). As market interest rates change, the bonds' carrying amount diverges from the bonds' fair market value. When market interest rates decline, the fair value of a bond with a fixed coupon rate increases. As a result, a company's economic liabilities may be higher than its reported debt based on amortised historical cost. Conversely, when market interest rates increase, the fair value of a bond with a fixed coupon rate decreases and the company's economic liability may be lower than its reported debt. Using financial statement amounts based on amortised cost may underestimate (or overestimate) a company's debt-to-total-capital ratio and similar leverage ratios.

Companies recently have been given the option to report financial liabilities at fair values. Financial liabilities reported at fair value are designated as financial liabilities at fair value through profit or loss. Even if a company does not opt to report financial liabilities at fair value, the availability of fair value information in the financial statements has increased. IFRS and U.S. GAAP require fair value disclosures in the financial statements unless the carrying amount approximates fair value or the fair value cannot be reliably measured.[5]

A company selecting the fair value option for a liability with a fixed coupon rate will report gains (losses) when market interest rates increase (decrease). When market interest rates increase or other factors cause the fair value of a company's bonds to decline, the company reports a decrease in the fair value of its liability and a corresponding gain. When interest rates decrease or other factors cause the fair value of a company's bonds to increase, the company reports an increase in the fair value of its liability and a corresponding loss. The gains or losses resulting from changes in fair values are recognised in profit or loss.

---

[5] IFRS (IAS 32, IAS 39, and IFRS 7) and U.S. GAAP (FASB ASC 820 and 825).

Few companies have selected the option to report financial liabilities at fair value. Those that have are primarily companies in the financial sector. Reporting standards for financial investments and derivatives already required these companies to report a significant portion of their assets at fair values. Measuring financial liabilities at other than fair value, when financial assets are measured at fair value, results in earnings volatility. This volatility is the result of using different bases of measurement for financial assets and financial liabilities. Goldman Sachs (NYSE:GS) elected to account for some financial liabilities at fair value under the fair value option. In its fiscal year 2008 10-K filing (page 74), Goldman explains this choice:

> The primary reasons for electing the fair value option are to reflect economic events in earnings on a timely basis, to mitigate volatility in earnings from using different measurement attributes and to address simplification and cost-benefit considerations.

Most companies, as required under IFRS and U.S. GAAP, disclose the fair values of financial liabilities. The primary exception to the disclosure occurs when fair value cannot be reliably measured. Example 5 illustrates Sony's fair value disclosures, including the fair values of long-term debt.

EXAMPLE 5

Fair Value Disclosures of Debt and Financial Instruments

The following are excerpts from Notes 2 and 13 of Sony Corporation's (NYSE:SNE) 20-F filing for the fiscal year ended 31 March 2009. These discuss the option for reporting fair values in the balance sheet and illustrate financial statement disclosures of fair values.

Excerpt from **Note 2:** *Summary of significant accounting policies*
... "The Fair Value Option for Financial Assets and Financial Liabilities." ...permits companies to choose to measure, on an instrument-by-instrument basis, various financial instruments and certain other items at fair value that are not currently required to be measured at fair value. The fair value measurement election is irrevocable and subsequent changes in fair value must be recorded in earnings. ... Sony did not elect the fair value option for any assets or liabilities that were not previously carried at fair value.

Excerpt from **Note 13:** *Fair value measurements*
The estimated fair values of Sony's financial instruments are summarised as follows. The following summary excludes cash and cash equivalents, call loans, time deposits, notes and accounts receivable, trade, call money, short-term borrowings, notes and accounts payable, trade and deposits from customers in the banking business because the carrying values of these financial instruments approximated their fair values due to their short-term nature.

	Yen in millions			
	March 31, 2008		March 31, 2009	
	Carrying amount	Estimated fair value	Carrying amount	Estimated fair value
Long-term debt including the current portion	1,020,938	1,024,879	807,687	809,377
Investment contracts included in policyholders' account in the life insurance business	274,779	275,967	286,104	289,905

The fair values of long-term debt including the current portion and investment contracts included in policyholders' account in the life insurance business were estimated based on either the market value or the discounted future cash flows using Sony's current incremental borrowing rates for similar liabilities.

Use the excerpts from the notes to Sony's financial statements to address the following questions:

1 Does Sony report the fair values of its long-term debt on the balance sheet?

2 How does Sony measure the long-term debt reported on the balance sheet?

3 As of 31 March 2008 and 31 March 2009, what is the percent difference in the carrying amount and fair value of Sony's long-term debt?

Solution to 1:

Sony does not report the fair values of its long-term debt on the balance sheet; Sony discloses that it did not elect the fair value option for any assets or liabilities that were not previously carried at fair value in Note 2. In Note 13, we also observe that Sony discloses the estimated fair value of long-term debt separately from its carrying amount.

Solution to 2:

Notes 2 and 13 indicate that Sony did not elect the fair value option. Therefore, the carrying amount of its debt must be its amortised historical cost.

Solution to 3:

In each year, the fair value of Sony's long-term debt is less than 0.5% greater than its carrying amount: 0.4% [= (1,024,879/1,020,938) − 1] on 31 March 2008 and 0.2% [= (809,377/807,687) − 1] on 31 March 2009. Although the estimated fair values are higher, the difference is small and would most likely not materially affect an analysis of the company.

2.4 Derecognition of Debt

Once bonds are issued, a company may leave the bonds outstanding until maturity or redeem the bonds before maturity either by calling the bonds (if the bond issue includes a call provision) or by purchasing the bonds in the open market. If the bonds remain outstanding until the maturity date, the company pays bondholders the face value of the bonds at maturity. The discount or premium on the bonds would be fully amortised at maturity; the carrying amount would equal face value. Upon repayment, bonds payable is reduced by the carrying amount at maturity (face value) of the bonds and cash is reduced by an equal amount. Repayment of the bonds appears in the statement of cash flows as a financing cash outflow.

If a company decides to redeem bonds before maturity and thus extinguish the liability early, bonds payable is reduced by the carrying amount of the redeemed bonds. The difference between the cash required to redeem the bonds and the carrying amount of the bonds is a gain or loss on the extinguishment of debt. Under IFRS, debt issuance costs are included in the measurement of the liability and are thus part of its carrying amount. Under U.S. GAAP, debt issuance costs are accounted for separately from bonds payable and are amortised over the life of the bonds. Any unamortised debt issuance costs must be written off at the time of redemption and included in the gain or loss on debt extinguishment.

For example, a company reporting under IFRS has a £10 million bond issuance with a carrying amount equal to its face value and five years remaining until maturity. The company redeems the bonds at a call price of 103. The redemption cost is £10.3 million (= £10 million × 103%). The company's loss on redemption would be £300 thousand (£10 million carrying amount minus £10.3 million cash paid to redeem the callable bonds).

A gain or loss on the extinguishment of debt is disclosed on the income statement, in a separate line item, when the amount is material. A company typically discloses further detail about the extinguishment in the management discussion and analysis (MD&A) and/or notes to the financial statements.[6] In addition, in a statement of cash flows prepared using the indirect method, net income is adjusted to remove any gain or loss on the extinguishment of debt from operating cash flows and the cash paid to redeem the bonds is classified as cash used for financing activities. (Recall that the indirect method of the statement of cash flows begins with net income and makes necessary adjustments to arrive at cash from operations, including removal of gains or losses from non-operating activities.)

To illustrate the financial statement impact of the extinguishment of debt, consider the notes payable repurchase by B+H Ocean Carriers in Example 6 below.

EXAMPLE 6

Debt Extinguishment Disclosure

The following excerpts are from the 2008 20-F filing of B+H Ocean Carriers (NYSE Alternext: <u>BHO</u>). In its statement of cash flows, the company uses the indirect method to reconcile net income with net cash (used in) provided by operations.

Excerpt from **Consolidated Statements of Income**
For the years ended 31 December 2008, 2007, and 2006

	2008	2007	2006
Revenues:			
⋮	⋮	⋮	⋮
Total revenues	104,908,915	112,416,831	96,879,051
⋮	⋮	⋮	⋮
Total operating expenses	100,279,906	96,140,562	71,018,929

(continued)

---

6 We use the term MD&A generally to refer to any management commentary provided on a company's financial condition, changes in financial condition, and results of operations. In the United States, the Securities and Exchange Commission (SEC) requires a management discussion and analysis for companies listed on U.S. public markets. Reporting requirements for such a commentary as the SEC-required MD&A vary across exchanges, but some are similar to the SEC requirements. Currently, the IASB is developing a standard for a management commentary that would be consistent for all companies reporting under IFRS.

(Continued)

	2008	2007	2006
Income from vessel operations	4,629,009	16,276,269	25,860,122
Other income (expense):			
⋮	⋮	⋮	⋮
Gain on debt extinguishment	2,345,000	—	—
⋮	⋮	⋮	⋮
Total other income (expense), net	11,236,107	(14,257,092)	(7,085,809)
Net income	$15,865,116	$2,019,177	$18,774,313

Excerpt from **Consolidated Statements of Cash Flows**
For the years ended 31 December 2008, 2007, and 2006

	2008	2007	2006
CASH FLOWS FROM OPERATING ACTIVITIES:			
Net Income	$15,865,116	$2,019,177	$18,774,313
Adjustments to reconcile net income to net cash (used in) provided by operating activities:			
⋮	⋮	⋮	⋮
Gain on debt extinguishment	(2,345,000)	—	—
⋮	⋮	⋮	⋮
Total adjustments	(16,635,993)	38,842,386	19,815,773
Net cash (used in) provided by operating activities	(770,877)	40,861,563	38,590,086
⋮	⋮	⋮	⋮
CASH FLOWS FROM FINANCING ACTIVITIES:			
Payments for debt financing costs	(294,999)	(1,526,501)	(1,481,505)
⋮	⋮	⋮	⋮
Purchase of debt securities	(2,155,000)	—	(5,000,000)
⋮	⋮	⋮	⋮
Payments of unsecured debt	—	(31,402,960)	(1,356,092)

Excerpt from **NOTE 2: SUMMARY OF SIGNIFICANT ACCOUNTING POLICIES**

... The carrying amount of the Company's variable rate long-term debt approximates fair value.

Excerpt from **NOTE 8: BONDS PAYABLE**

On December 12, 2006, the Company issued $25 million of unsecured bonds... Interest on the bonds is equal to LIBOR plus 4%, payable quarterly in arrears. ... During the 4th quarter of 2008, the Company repurchased the unsecured bonds with a face value of $4.5 million and realized a $2.3 million gain.

1   The balance in bonds payable was reduced at redemption by:

   A $2,155,000.

   B $2,345,000.

   C $4,500,000.

Solution to 1:

C is correct. The bonds payable is reduced at redemption by the carrying amount of the bonds redeemed. The cash paid to extinguish the bonds plus the gain on redemption equals the carrying amount of the bonds. The carrying amount of the bonds was $4,500,000. In this case, the carrying amount equals the face value. The company recognised a gain of $2,345,000 when it extinguished the debt of $4,500,000 by paying only $2,155,000.

2.5 Debt Covenants

Borrowing agreements (the bond indenture) often include restrictions called covenants that protect creditors by restricting activities of the borrower. Debt covenants benefit borrowers to the extent that they lower the risk to the creditors and thus reduce the cost of borrowing. Affirmative covenants restrict the borrower's activities by requiring certain actions. For instance, covenants may require that the borrower maintain certain ratios above a specified amount or perform regular maintenance on real assets used as collateral. Negative covenants require that the borrower not take certain actions. Covenants may restrict the borrower's ability to invest, pay dividends, or make other operating and strategic decisions that might adversely affect the company's ability to pay interest and principal.

Common covenants include limitations on how borrowed monies can be used, maintenance of collateral pledged as security (if any), restrictions on future borrowings, requirements that limit dividends, and requirements to meet specific working capital requirements. Covenants may also specify minimum acceptable levels of financial ratios, such as debt-to-equity, current, or interest coverage.

When a company violates a debt covenant, it is a breach of contract. Depending on the severity of the breach and the terms of the contract, lenders may choose to waive the covenant, be entitled to a penalty payment or higher interest rate, renegotiate, or call for payment of the debt. Bond contracts typically require that the decision to call for immediate repayment be made, on behalf of all the bondholders, by holders of some minimum percentage of the principal amount of the bond issue.

Example 7 illustrates common disclosures related to debt covenants included in financial statement disclosures (notes to the financial statements).

EXAMPLE 7

Illustration of Debt Covenant Disclosures

The following excerpt is from TORM A/S (NASDAQ:TORM) from the Risk Factors section of Item 3, Key Information, in its fiscal year 2008 20-F filing. The excerpt illustrates debt covenants and their disclosure:

> Certain of our loan agreements contain restrictive covenants, which may limit our liquidity and corporate activities and prevent proper service of debt, which could result in the loss of our vessels.
>
> Some loan agreements impose operating and financial restrictions upon us. These restrictions may limit our ability to:
>
> ▪ change the management of our vessels without the lenders' consent (which they are not entitled to unreasonably withhold); and
>
> ▪ enter into mergers or corporate restructurings, or effect material divestments, if such would be materially adverse to the company.
>
> Our lenders' interests may be different from ours and we cannot guarantee that we will be able to obtain our lenders' permission when needed. This may prevent us from taking actions that are in our best interest.

The following excerpt is an additional excerpt from "Note 8: Bonds Payable" of B+H Ocean Carriers that was referenced in Example 6.

> The bond facility contains certain restrictive covenants which restrict the payment of dividends. The facility requires a minimum value adjusted equity ratio (as defined) of 25%. At December 31, 2008, the Company was in compliance with these covenants and is likely to remain in compliance throughout 2009. However, the bond agreement contains a cross default provision that essentially enables the lender to call the bonds if the Company defaults on a separate loan facility. The Company reclassified its long term debt because of a determination prospectively that certain covenants in certain long term agreements may be breached during 2009. As such, the Company has recorded the entire balance of the bonds as current as of December 31, 2008.

1   Which of the covenants described in the above excerpts is an affirmative covenant?

2   Based on the excerpt from B+H Ocean Carriers, what is the implied consequence of breaching certain covenants?

Solution to 1:

The requirement that "a minimum value adjusted equity ratio (as defined) of 25 percent" be maintained by B+H Ocean Carriers is an example of an affirmative covenant. It requires the issuer to do something. The covenants on TORM A/S require that TORM not take certain actions (e.g., not change management of vessels without lenders' consent and not enter into mergers that would be materially adverse) and are negative covenants.

Solution to 2:

If B+H Ocean Carriers breaches certain covenants, it seems that the entire balance of bonds payable becomes due. The bonds payable have been prospectively moved from non-current to current liabilities.

2.6 Presentation and Disclosure of Long-Term Debt

The non-current (long-term) liabilities section of the balance sheet usually includes a single line item of the total amount of a company's long-term debt due after one year, with the portion of long-term debt due in the next twelve months shown as a current liability. Notes to the financial statements provide more information on the types and nature of a company's debt. These note disclosures can be used to determine the amount and timing of future cash outflows. The notes generally include stated and effective interest rates, maturity dates, restrictions imposed by creditors (covenants), and collateral pledged (if any). The amount of scheduled debt repayments for the next five years also is shown in the notes.

Example 8 contains an excerpt from Johnson & Johnson's 2008 10-K filing that illustrates common long-term debt disclosures.

EXAMPLE 8

Illustration of Long-Term Debt Disclosures

Exhibit 1 is an excerpt from Note 6 of Johnson & Johnson's (NYSE:JNJ) 2008 financial statements that illustrates financial statement disclosure for long-term debt, including type and nature of long-term debt, effective interest rates, and required payments over the next five years. Johnson & Johnson reports its debt at amortised cost.

| Exhibit 1 | Johnson & Johnson |

Excerpt from 6. Borrowings
The components of long-term debt are as follows:

(Dollars in Millions)	2008	Effective Rate %	2007	Effective Rate %
3% Zero Coupon Convertible Subordinated Debentures due 2020	$183	3	178	3
4.95% Debentures due 2033	500	4.95	500	4.95
3.80% Debentures due 2013	500	3.82	500	3.82
6.95% Notes due 2029	294	7.14	294	7.14
6.73% Debentures due 2023	250	6.73	250	6.73
6.625% Notes due 2009	199	6.8	199	6.8
5.55% Debentures due 2017	1,000	5.55	1,000	5.55
5.95% Notes due 2037	995	5.99	995	5.99
5.50% Notes due 2024 (500 GBP1.4759)[b](500 GBP 1.9944)[c]	731	5.71	989	5.71
4.75% Notes due 2019 (1B Euro 1.4000)[b](1B Euro 1.4573)[c]	1,390	5.35	1,447	5.35
5.15% Debentures due 2012	599	5.18	599	5.18
5.86% Debentures due 2038	700	5.86		
5.15% Debentures due 2018	898	5.15		
Other (Includes Industrial Revenue Bonds)	102		132	
	8,341[d]	5.46[a]	7,083[d]	5.47[a]
Less current portion	221		9	—
	$8,120		7,074	

[a] Weighted average effective rate.
[b] Translation rate at December 28, 2008.
[c] Translation rate at December 30, 2007.
[d] The excess of the fair value over the carrying value of debt was $1.4 billion in 2008 and $0.3 billion in 2007.

(continued)

| Exhibit 1 | (Continued) |

The Company has access to substantial sources of funds at numerous banks worldwide. In September 2008, the Company secured a new 364-day and 5-year Credit Facility. Total credit available to the Company approximates $7.7 billion of which $6.3 billion expires September 24, 2009, and $1.4 billion expires September 25, 2013. Interest charged on borrowings under the credit line agreements is based on either bids provided by banks, the prime rate or London Interbank Offered Rates (LIBOR), plus applicable margins. Commitment fees under the agreements are not material.

...

Aggregate maturities of long-term obligations commencing in 2007 are (dollars in millions):

2009	2010	2011	2012	2013	After 2014
$ 221	22	18	620	507	6,953

Use the information in Exhibit 1 to answer the following questions:

1   Why are the effective interest rates unchanged from 2007 and 2008 for the first 11 borrowings listed?

2   Why does the carrying amount of the "4.95% Debentures due 2033" remain the same in 2007 and 2008?

3   Why does the carrying amount of the "4.75% Notes due 2019" decrease from 2007 to 2008?

Solution to 1:

The effective interest rate is the market rate at which the bonds are issued and does not change from year to year.

Solution to 2:

The carrying amount of the "4.95% Debentures due 2033" remains the same because the effective interest rate at which the debentures were issued is the same as the coupon rate. The debentures were issued at par, and the carrying amount does not change.

Solution to 3:

The notes are denominated in euros, with a face value of €1 billion. The dollar/euro translation exchange rate at the end of 2008 was lower than the exchange rate at the end of 2007 (1.4000 versus 1.4573). That decline explains the decrease in carrying value. Note that the face amount of the debt at the translation rate (at the end of 2008, €1 billion times 1.4000 = $1.4 billion) is higher than the carrying amount (at the end of 2008, $1.39 billion). The reason for this difference is that the notes were issued at a discount; the effective interest rate of 5.35 percent is higher than the 4.75 percent coupon rate. The carrying amount of the notes thus reflects the amortisation of the discount at issuance; the amortisation of the discount will increase the carrying amount.

In this reading, we focus on accounting for simple debt contracts. Debt contracts can take on additional features, which lead to more complexity. For instance, convertible debt and debt with warrants are more complex instruments that have both debt and equity features. Convertible debt gives the debt holder the option to exchange the debt for equity. Bonds issued with warrants give holders the right to purchase shares of the issuer's common stock at a specific price, similar to stock options. Issuance of bonds with warrants is more common by non-U.S. companies. Example 9 provides an example of a financial statement disclosure of bonds with warrants issued by a Chinese company.

EXAMPLE 9

Financial Statement Disclosure of Bonds with Warrants

The following excerpt is from the fiscal year 2008 Annual Report of the China Petroleum & Chemical Corporation (NYSE Euronext:SNP).

> **Excerpt from NOTE 29: DEBENTURES PAYABLE**
>
> On 26 February 2008, the Company issued convertible bonds with stock warrants due 2014 with an aggregate principal amount of RMB 30 billion in the PRC (the "Bonds with Warrants"). The Bonds with Warrants with fixed interest rate of 0.8% per annum and interest payable annually, were issued at par value of RMB 100. The Bonds with Warrants were guaranteed by Sinopec Group Company. Each lot of the Bonds with Warrants, comprising ten Bonds with Warrants are entitled to warrants (the "Warrants") to subscribe 50.5 A shares of the Company during the 5 trading days prior to 3 March 2010 at an initial exercise price of RMB 19.68 per share, subject to adjustment for, amongst other things, cash dividends, subdivision or consolidation of shares, bonus issues, rights issues, capital distribution, change of control and other events which have a dilutive effect on the issued share capital of the Company.

If all warrants were exercised, how many shares would be subscribed for?

Solution:

1,515,000,000 shares would be subscribed for [aggregate principal amount divided by par value of a lot times shares subscribed per lot = (RMB 30,000,000,000/RMB 1,000) × 50.5 shares].

In addition to disclosures in the notes to the financial statements, an MD&A commonly provides other information about a company's capital resources, including debt financing and off-balance-sheet financing. In the MD&A, management often provides a qualitative discussion on any material trends, favorable or unfavorable, in capital resources and indicates any expected material changes in their mix and relative cost. Additional quantitative information is typically provided, including schedules summarising a company's contractual obligations (e.g., bond payables) and other commitments (e.g., lines of credit and guarantees) in total and over the next five years.

LEASES

3

A company wishing to obtain the use of an asset can either purchase the asset or lease the asset. Section 3.1 describes some advantages to leasing from the viewpoint of the **lessee** (the party obtaining the use of an asset through a lease). Section 3.2 describes the classification of leases. Section 3.2.1 describes the accounting treatments of different types of leases from the perspective of the lessee, and section 3.2.2 discusses leases from the perspective of the **lessor** (the owner of the asset).

3.1 Advantages of Leasing

A lease is a contract between the owner of an asset—the lessor—and another party seeking use of the asset—the lessee. Through the lease, the lessor grants the right to use the asset to the lessee. The right to use the asset can be for a long period, such as 20 years, or a much shorter period, such as a month. In exchange for the right to use the asset, the lessee makes periodic lease payments to the lessor. A lease, then, is a form of financing to the lessee provided by the lessor that enables the lessee to obtain the *use* of the leased asset.

There are several advantages to leasing an asset compared to purchasing it. Leases can provide less costly financing; they usually require little, if any, down payment and often are at lower fixed interest rates than those incurred if the asset was purchased. This financing advantage is the result of the lessor having advantages over the lessee and/or another lender. The lessor may be in a better position to take advantage of tax benefits of ownership, such as depreciation and interest. The lessor may be better able to value and bear the risks associated with ownership, such as obsolescence, residual value, and disposition of asset. The lessor may enjoy economies of scale for servicing assets. As a result of these advantages, the lessor may offer attractive lease terms and leasing the asset may be less costly for the lessee than owning the asset. Further, the negotiated lease contract may contain less-restrictive provisions than other forms of borrowing.

Companies also use certain types of leases because of perceived financial reporting and tax advantages. Although they provide a form of financing, certain types of leases are not shown as debt on the balance sheet. The items leased under these types of leases also do not appear as assets on the balance sheet. Therefore, no interest expense or depreciation expense is included in the income statement. In addition, in some countries—including the United States—because financial reporting rules differ from tax regulations, a company may own an asset for tax purposes (and thus obtain deductions for depreciation expense for tax purposes) while not reflecting the ownership in its financial statements. A lease that is structured to provide a company with the tax benefits of ownership while not requiring the asset to be reflected on the company's financial statements is known as a synthetic lease.

3.2 Finance (or Capital) Leases versus Operating Leases

There are two main classifications of leases: **finance** (or **capital**) and **operating leases**.[7] The economic substance of a finance (or capital) lease is very different from an operating lease, as are the implications of each for the financial statements for the lessee and lessor. In substance, a finance (capital) lease is equivalent to the purchase of some asset (lease to own) by the buyer (lessee) that is directly financed by the seller (lessor). An operating lease is an agreement allowing the lessee to use some asset for a period of time, essentially a rental.

Under IFRS, the classification of a lease as a finance lease or an operating lease depends on the transfer of the risks and rewards incidental to ownership of the leased asset.[8] If substantially *all* the risks and rewards are transferred to the lessee, the lease is classified as a finance lease and the lessee reports a leased asset and lease obligation on its balance sheet. Otherwise, the lease is reported as an operating lease, in which case the lessee reports neither an asset nor a liability; the lessee reports only the lease expense. Similarly, if the lessor transfers substantially *all* the risks and rewards incidental to legal ownership, the lease is reported as a finance lease and the lessor reports a lease receivable on its balance sheet and removes the leased asset from its

---

7 "Finance lease" is IFRS terminology and "capital lease" is U.S. GAAP terminology.
8 IAS 17 [Leases].

balance sheet. Otherwise, the lease is reported as an operating lease, and the lessor keeps the leased asset on its balance sheet. Examples of situations that would normally lead to a lease being classified as a finance lease include the following:[9]

- The lease transfers ownership of the asset to the lessee by the end of the lease term.

- The lessee has the option to purchase the asset at a price that is expected to be sufficiently lower than the fair value at the date the option becomes exercisable for it to be reasonably certain, at the inception of the lease, that the option will be exercised.

- The lease term is for the major part of the economic life of the asset, even if the title is not transferred.

- At the inception of the lease, the present value of the minimum lease payments amounts to at least substantially all of the fair value of the leased asset.

- The leased assets are of such a specialized nature that only the lessee can use them without major modifications.

Although accounting for leases under U.S. GAAP is guided by a similar principle of the transfer of benefits and risks, U.S. GAAP is more prescriptive in its criteria for classifying capital and operating leases. Four criteria are specified to identify when a lease is a capital lease:[10]

1 Ownership of the leased asset transfers to the lessee at the end of the lease.

2 The lease contains an option for the lessee to purchase the leased asset cheaply (bargain purchase option).

3 The lease term is 75 percent or more of the useful life of the leased asset.

4 The present value of lease payments is 90 percent or more of the fair value of the leased asset.

Only one of these criteria has to be met for the lease to be considered a capital lease by the lessee. On the lessor side, satisfying at least one of these four criteria plus meeting revenue recognition requirements (that is, being reasonably assured of cash collection and having performed substantially under the lease) determine a capital lease. If none of the four criteria are met or if the revenue recognition requirement is not met, the lessor reports the lease as an operating lease.

3.2.1 *Accounting and Reporting by the Lessee*

Because a finance lease is economically similar to borrowing money and buying an asset, a company that enters into a finance lease as the lessee reports an asset (leased asset) and related debt (lease payable) on its balance sheet. The initial value of both the leased asset and lease payable is the lower of the present value of future lease payments and the fair value of the leased asset; in many cases, these will be equal. On the income statement, the company reports interest expense on the debt, and if the asset acquired is depreciable, the company reports depreciation expense. (The lessor, as we illustrate in the next section, reports the sale of an asset and a lease as receivable.)

Because an operating lease is economically similar to renting an asset, a company that enters into an operating lease as the lessee records a lease expense on its income statement during the period it uses the asset. No asset or liability is recorded on its balance sheet. The main accounting differences for a lessee between a finance lease and an operating lease, then, are that reported assets and debt are higher and expenses

---

9 Examples are from IAS 17, paragraph 10, and do not include all indicators that would lead to a lease being classified as a finance lease.
10 FASB ASC Topic 840 [Leases].

are generally higher in the early years under a finance lease. Because of the higher reported debt and expenses under a finance lease, lessees often prefer operating leases to finance leases. (Although classifying a lease as an operating lease can make reported profitability ratios and debt-to-equity ratios appear better, financial analysts are aware of this impact and typically adjust the reported numbers accordingly.)

On the lessee's statement of cash flows, for an operating lease, the full lease payment is shown as an operating cash outflow. For a finance lease, only the portion of the lease payment relating to interest expense reduces operating cash flow; the portion of the lease payment that reduces the lease liability appears as a cash outflow in the financing section.

Example 10 illustrates the accounting of a finance lease by a lessee.

EXAMPLE 10

Determining the Initial Recognition and Measurement and Subsequent Measurement of a Finance Lease for a Lessee

CAPBS Inc. enters into a lease agreement to acquire the use of a piece of machinery for four years beginning on 1 January 2010. The lease requires four annual payments of €28,679 starting on 1 January 2010. The useful life of the machine is four years, and its salvage value is zero. CAPBS accounts for the lease as a finance lease. The fair value of the machine is €100,000. The present value of the lease payments using the company's discount rate of 10 percent is €100,000. (A reminder is relevant for present value calculations: Lease payments are made at the beginning of each period.) The company uses straight-line depreciation.

1 Comment on the appropriateness of CAPBS treating the lease agreement as a finance lease under IFRS and a capital lease under U.S. GAAP.

2 What is the amount reported as a leased asset on the balance sheet on 1 January 2010? What depreciation expense is reported in fiscal year 2010?

3 What is the amount of the machinery reported as a leased asset on the balance sheet on 31 December 2010?

4 What is the amount of the lease liability reported on the balance sheet on 1 January 2010? What interest expense is reported in fiscal year 2010?

5 What is the amount of the lease liability reported on the balance sheet on 31 December 2010? What interest expense is reported in fiscal year 2011?

6 If CAPBS had determined that the above lease was an operating lease, what amount of expenses would be reported on the income statements in fiscal 2010 and 2011? How does this expense compare to the expenses reported under a capital lease?

Solution to 1:

CAPBS should treat this lease as a finance lease under IFRS. The machine is leased for the major part of its useful life (the useful life of the machine and the lease are each four years). Also, the present value of lease payments equals substantially the fair value of the machine (both are €100,000). CAPBS should treat this lease as a capital lease under U.S. GAAP. The machine is leased for more than 75 percent of its useful life, and the present value of the lease payments exceeds 90 percent of the fair value of the leased asset.

Solution to 2:

The amount initially reported as a leased asset on 1 January 2010 is €100,000. Depreciation expense each year is €25,000 [(€100,000 − €0)/4 years].

The table below shows CAPBS's depreciation expense and carrying amount for the leased asset by year.

Year	Initial Recognition Amount	Depreciation Expense	Accumulated Depreciation	Carrying Amount (year-end)
	(a)	(b)	(c)	(d)
2010	€100,000	€25,000	€25,000	€75,000
2011	100,000	25,000	50,000	50,000
2012	100,000	25,000	75,000	25,000
2013	100,000	25,000	100,000	0
		€100,000		

- Column (a) is the lower of the fair value of the machinery and the present value (PV) of lease payments at lease inception. In this example, they are the same.

- Column (b) is the depreciation expense of €25,000 per year [straight-line depreciation = acquisition cost less salvage value divided by useful life = (€100,000 − €0)/4 years].

- Column (c) is the accumulated depreciation on the leased asset calculated as the prior year's accumulated depreciation plus the current year's depreciation expense.

- Column (d) is the carrying amount of the machine (the leased asset), which is the difference between the initial recognition amount and accumulated depreciation.

Solution to 3:

From the table presented in *Solution to 2*, the carrying amount on 31 December 2010 is €75,000.

Solution to 4:

The amount of the lease liability initially recognised on 1 January 2010 is €100,000, which is both the fair value of the leased asset and the present value of lease payments. However, the first lease payment of €28,679, due on 1 January 2010, immediately reduces the lease liability balance to €71,321. Interest expense in 2010 is based on the €71,321 carrying amount. Interest expense reported in fiscal year 2010 is €7,132 (€71,321 × 10%).

The table below shows CAPBS's lease payment, interest expense, and carrying values for its lease liability by year.[11]

---

11 The computations included throughout the example were made using an Excel worksheet; small apparent discrepancies in the calculations are because of rounding.

Year	Lease Liability, 1 January	Annual Lease Payment, 1 January	Interest (at 10%; accrued in previous year)	Reduction of Lease Liability, 1 January	Lease Liability on 31 December after Lease Payment on 1 January Same Year
	(a)	(b)	(c)	(d)	(e)
2010	€100,000	€28,679	€0	€28,679	€71,321
2011	71,321	28,679	7,132	21,547	49,774
2012	49,774	28,679	4,977	23,702	26,072
2013	26,072	28,679	2,607	26,072	0
		€114,717	€14,717	€100,000	

- Column (a) is the lease liability at the beginning of the year.
  - 2010: €100,000
  - Years thereafter: It is the lease liability at the end of the previous year
- Column (b) is the annual lease payment made at the beginning of the year. A portion of the lease payment reduces interest accrued in the previous year, and the remainder of the lease payment reduces the carrying amount of the lease liability.
  - For example, in 2011, the €28,679 paid on 1 January reduces the interest payable of €7,132 that accrued in 2010 (€71,321 × 10%) and then reduces the lease liability by €21,547.
- Column (c) is the interest portion of the 1 January lease payment made on that date. This amount of interest was accrued as interest payable during the *prior* year and is reported as the interest expense of the *prior* year. For example, at 31 December 2010, interest expense and interest payable in the amount of €7,132 was recognised.
- Column (d) is the reduction of the lease liability, which is the difference between the annual lease payment and the interest portion.
- Column (e) is the lease liability on 31 December of a given year just before the lease payment is made on the first day of the next year. It is equal to the lease liability on 1 January of the same year (column a) less the reduction of the lease liability (column d).

Solution to 5:

From the table presented in *Solution to 4*, the interest expense in fiscal year 2011 is €4,977 (€49,744 × 10%).

Solution to 6:

As an operating lease, a rent expense of €28,679 would be reported on the income statement each year. Under a capital lease, the expenses related to the lease are depreciation and interest expense. In 2010, the depreciation expense is €25,000 and the interest expense is €7,132. In 2011, the depreciation expense is €25,000 and the interest expense is €4,977.

A company reporting a lease as an operating lease will typically show higher profits in early years, higher return measures in early years, and a stronger solvency position than an identical company reporting an identical lease as a finance lease. However, the company reporting the lease as a finance lease will show higher operating cash flows because the portion of the lease payment that reduces the carrying amount of the lease liability will be reflected as a financing cash outflow rather than an operating cash outflow. The interest expense portion of the lease payment on the statement of cash flows can be treated as operating or financing cash outflow under IFRS and is treated as an operating cash outflow under U.S. GAAP.

The explicit standards in the United States that determine when a company should report a capital lease versus an operating lease make it easier for a company to structure a lease so that it is reported as an operating lease. The company structures the lease so that none of the four capital lease identifying criteria is met. Similar to debt disclosures, however, lease disclosures show payments under both capital and operating leases for the next five years and afterward. These disclosures can help to estimate the extent of a company's off-balance-sheet lease financing through operating leases. Example 11 illustrates the disclosures of operating and finance leases. Although these disclosures can be used to determine the effect on the financial statements if all operating leases were capitalized, this reading focuses solely on the information that is disclosed.

EXAMPLE 11

Financial Statement Disclosure of Leases by the Lessee

BASF Group (OTC: BASFY) has significant commitments under finance and operating leases. Presented below is selected note disclosure from its fiscal year 2008 financial statements.

27. LEASING

Leased assets

Property, plant and equipment include those assets which are considered to be economically owned through a finance lease. They primarily concern the following items:

Leased assets (million €)	2008		2007	
	Acquisition cost	Net book value	Acquisition cost	Net book value
Land, land rights and buildings	20	13	26	18
Machinery and technical equipment	223	96	226	118
Miscellaneous equipment and fixtures	73	18	71	20
Advance payments and construction in progress	—	—	—	—
	316	127	323	156

Liabilities from finance leases (million €)	2008			2007		
	Minimum lease payments	Interest portion	Leasing liability	Minimum lease payments	Interest portion	Leasing liability
Following year 1	20	5	15	29	6	23
Following year 2	20	5	14	19	5	13
Following year 3	22	5	18	18	5	13
Following year 4	11	2	9	21	5	16
Following year 5	7	2	4	10	3	8
Over 5 years	29	10	20	35	12	23
	108	29	80	132	36	96

In the current business year and in 2007, no additional lease payments arising from contractual obligations were recognized in income above the minimum lease payments.

In 2008, leasing liabilities were not offset by any expected minimum lease payments from sub-leases.

In addition, BASF is a lessee under operating lease contracts. The resulting lease obligations totaling €1,449 million in 2008 and €1,272 in 2007 are due in the following years:

Commitments due to operating lease contracts (million €)		
	Nominal value of the future minimum payments	
	Dec. 31, 2008	Dec. 31, 2007
Less than 1 year	280	292
1–5 years	613	505
Over 5 years	556	475
	1,449	1,272

1   At the end of fiscal year 2008, what is the total amount of finance lease liabilities BASF reports on its balance sheet?

2   Based on finance lease agreements in place at the end of fiscal year 2008, how much will BASF pay out on finance lease commitments in fiscal year 2009?

3   Based on finance lease agreements in place at the end of fiscal year 2008, what is the amount of interest expense that BASF will report in fiscal year 2009?

4   At the end of fiscal 2008, what are BASF's total commitments under operating leases?

5   Based on operating lease agreements in place at the end of fiscal year 2008, what is the minimum amount of rent expense that BASF will report in fiscal year 2009?

6   At the end of fiscal year 2008, what is the amount of leased assets (carrying amount) BASF reports on its balance sheet?

Solution to 1:

€80 million—the total of the 2008 column "Leasing liability" in the "Liabilities from finance leases" table.

Solution to 2:

€20 million—reported in the 2008 column "Minimum lease payments," row "Following year 1," in the "Liabilities from finance leases" table.

Solution to 3:

€5 million—reported in the 2008 column "Interest portion," row "Following year 1," in the "Liabilities from finance leases" table.

Solution to 4:

€1,449 million—the total of the 2008 column "Nominal value of the future minimum payments" in the "Commitments due to operating lease contracts" table.

Solution to 5:

€280 million—reported in the 2008 column "Nominal value of the future minimum payments," row "Less than 1 year," in the "Commitments due to operating lease contracts" table.

Solution to 6:

€127 million—the total of the 2008 column "Net book value" in the "Leased assets" table.

Example 12 contains information from Royal Dutch Shell's (LSE:RDSA) 2008 financial statements. As required by IFRS, the balance sheet presents finance lease obligations in the line items labeled "Debt." Additionally, IFRS require certain disclosures to be made in the notes; the layout of disclosure notes on debt varies across companies. For Royal Dutch, the disclosure note on debt, Note 18[A], first shows a breakdown of total debt reported on the balance sheet into two components: the amount of debt excluding finance lease obligations and the amount of finance lease obligations. Note 18[B] provides disclosures on the component of on-balance-sheet debt, excluding finance lease obligations. Next, Note 18[C] presents information about all the companies' lease obligations—both finance leases (which are a component of the on-balance-sheet total debt) and operating leases (for which no obligation appears on the balance sheet). This disclosure clearly illustrates that although finance leases and operating leases are both contractual obligations, only the finance leases are reported on the balance sheet. As mentioned above, a subsequent reading demonstrates how analysts adjust the total amount of debt as reported on the balance sheet to also include the off-balance-sheet obligations for operating leases. Analysts also should be aware that the International Accounting Standards Board (IASB) and the Financial Accounting Standards Board (FASB) are addressing the lease accounting standards, so these standards may change in the coming years.

EXAMPLE 12

Long-Term Debt and Lease Disclosures

Use the following excerpts taken from Royal Dutch Shell (LSE: RDSA) 2008 consolidated financial statements and notes to the consolidated financial statements to answer the questions below.

Excerpt from CONSOLIDATED BALANCE SHEET

$ million	NOTES	Dec 31, 2008	Dec 31, 2007
LIABILITIES			
Non-current liabilities			
Debt	18	**13,772**	12,363
⋮		⋮	⋮
Current liabilities			
Debt	18	**9,497**	5,736
⋮		⋮	⋮
Total liabilities		**153,535**	143,502
EQUITY			
⋮		⋮	⋮
Total equity		**128,866**	125,968
Total liabilities and equity		**282,401**	269,470

Excerpt from CONSOLIDATED STATEMENT OF CASH FLOWS

	Dec 31, 2008	Dec 31, 2007
Net increase/(decrease) in debt with maturity period within three months	**4,161**	(455)
Other debt: New borrowings	**3,555**	4,565
Repayments	**(2,890)**	(2,796)

Excerpt from **Note 1: Basis of Preparation**

The Consolidated Financial Statements of Royal Dutch Shell plc (the Company) and its subsidiaries (collectively known as "Shell" or the "Shell group") have been **prepared** in accordance with the provisions of the Companies Act 1985, Article 4 of the International Accounting Standards (IAS) Regulation and with International Financial Reporting Standards (IFRS) as adopted by the European Union. As applied to Shell, there are no material differences with IFRS as issued by the International Accounting Standards Board (IASB), therefore the Consolidated Financial Statements have been prepared in accordance with IFRS as issued by the IASB.

Excerpt from **Note 2: Accounting Policies**
Financial liabilities

Debt and accounts payable are recognised initially at fair value based on amounts exchanged and subsequently at amortised cost, except for fixed rate debt subject to fair value hedging, which is re-measured for the hedged risk (see "Derivative contracts").

Interest on debt is accounted for using the effective interest method and, other than interest capitalised, is recognised in income.

Where fair value is not applied subsequent to initial recognition but is required for disclosure purposes, it is based on market prices where available, otherwise it is calculated as the net present value of expected future cash flows.

Excerpt from Note 18: Debt and Lease Arrangements
[A] DEBT ($ million)

	Dec 31, 2008			Dec 31, 2007		
	Debt (excluding finance lease obligations)	Finance lease obligations	Total	Debt (excluding finance lease obligations)	Finance lease obligations	Total
Short-term debt	7,879	—	7,879	3,292	—	3,292
Long-term debt due within one year	1,314	304	1,618	2,290	154	2,444
Current debt	9,193	304	9,497	5,582	154	5,736
Non-current debt	10,061	3,711	13,772	8,533	3,830	12,363
Total	19,254	4,015	23,269	14,115	3,984	18,099

The fair value of debt approximates the carrying amount.

[B] DEBT (EXCLUDING FINANCE LEASE OBLIGATIONS)

The following tables compare contractual cash flows for debt (excluding finance lease obligations) owed by subsidiaries at December 31, by year of maturity, with the carrying amount in the Consolidated Balance Sheet. The carrying amount reflects the effects of discounting, premiums and fair value adjustments where hedging is applied.

2008 — $ million, except where otherwise indicated

	Contractual repayments (excluding interest)								
	2009	2010	2011	2012	2013	2014 and after	Total	Difference from carrying amount	Carrying Amount
Fixed rate dollar	6,821	506	1,001	503	1	3,539	12,371	290	12,661
Average interest rate	2.6%	5.2%	5.6%	5.0%	7.3%	5.4%			
Variable rate dollar debt	521	156	5	—	—	122	804	—	804
Average interest rate	1.8%	3.8%	6.3%	—	—	0.0%			
Fixed rate European debt	568	1,146	285	—	—	2,117	4,116	197	4,313
Average interest rate	2.9%	4.8%	2.0%	—	—	4.6%			
Variable rate European debt	237	—	—	—	—	—	237	—	237
Average interest rate	3.1%	—	—	—	—	—			
Other fixed rate debt	426	—	2	—	1	—	429	—	429
Average interest rate	18.4%	—	11.7%	—	12.4%	—			

(continued)

2008									$ million, except where otherwise indicated
	Contractual repayments (excluding interest)								
	2009	**2010**	**2011**	**2012**	**2013**	**2014 and after**	**Total**	**Difference from carrying amount**	**Carrying Amount**
Other variable rate debt	620	33	143	14	—	—	810	—	810
Average interest rate	9.4%	11.5%	7.8%	4.8%	—	—			
Total	9,193	1,841	1,436	517	2	5,778	18,767	487	19,254

The table above excludes interest estimated to be $827 million in 2009, $480 million in 2010, $389 million in 2011, $316 million in 2012, $290 million in 2013 and $290 million in 2014 and after (assuming interest rates with respect to variable rate debt remain constant and there is no change in aggregate principal amount of debt other than repayment at scheduled maturity as reflected in the table).

The weighted average interest rate on short-term debt excluding the short-term portion of long-term debt at December 31, 2008, was 4% (2007: 7%).

[C] LEASE ARRANGEMENTS

The future minimum lease payments for finance and operating leases and the present value of minimum finance lease payments at December 31, by maturity date are as follows:

2008				$ million
	Total future minimum finance lease payments	**Interest**	**Present value of minimum finance lease payments**	**Total future minimum operating lease payments**
2009	608	304	304	4,648
2010–2013	2,008	1,094	914	9,905
2014 and after	4,076	1,279	2,797	4,712
Total	6,692	2,677	4,015	19,265

Operating lease expenses were as follows ($ million):

	2008	**2007**	**2006**
Minimum lease payments	**3,339**	3,091	2,571
Contingent rentals	**68**	63	59
Sub-lease income	**(161)**	(138)	(132)
Total	**3,246**	3,016	2,498

Use the above information to answer the following questions:

1 How does Royal Dutch Shell initially value its debt on the balance sheet? How is debt subsequently measured on the balance sheet?

2 What method does Shell use to calculate interest expense on its debt?

3 What is the total amount of debt appearing within current liabilities on the balance sheet at 31 December 2008, and what does it include?

4 What is the total amount of debt due after one year appearing on the balance sheet at 31 December 2008, and what does it include?

5 How does the interest rate in 2008 on short-term debt (excluding finance lease obligations and the short-term portion of long-term debt) compare to that in 2007?

6 What is the fair value of Royal Dutch Shell's debt at 31 December 2008?

7 What was Royal Dutch Shell's rent expense in fiscal year 2008 related to operating leases?

8 Comment on the relative magnitude of operating leases compared to finance leases?

9 What are Shell's debt-to-equity ratios for 2008 and 2007? Comment on year-to-year changes.

Solution to 1:

From Note 2, debt is initially reported at fair value based on amounts exchanged. After issuance, debt is reported at amortised cost except for certain fixed rate debt that is subject to fair value hedging. That debt is remeasured to fair value.

Solution to 2:

Note 2 indicates that Shell uses the effective interest rate method to calculate interest expense.

Solution to 3:

The total amount of debt included in current liabilities on the balance sheet is $9,497. Note 18[A] shows that this amount comprises $7,879 short-term debt (excluding finance lease obligations), $1,314 long-term debt due within one year (excluding finance lease obligations), and $304 finance lease obligations. The finance lease obligations are those due within one year.

Solution to 4:

The total amount of debt due after next year (non-current debt) is $13,722. Note 18[A] shows that this amount comprises $10,061 debt (excluding finance lease obligations) and $3,711 finance lease obligations.

Solution to 5:

In Note 18 [B], Shell indicates that the interest rate on short-term debt has declined significantly. The weighted average interest rate at 31 December on short-term debt was 4 percent in 2008 and 7 percent in 2007.

Solution to 6:

From Note 18 [A], Shell reports that the fair value of debt approximates its carrying amount. The carrying amount is $23,269.

Solution to 7:

From Note 18 [C], rent expense on operating leases was $3,246 in 2008.

Solution to 8:

Although operating and finance leases are accounted for differently, we can compare the undiscounted future minimum lease payments under operating leases and finance leases reported in Note 18 [C] to gain an initial understanding of their relative magnitude. The total future minimum lease payments under operating leases of $19,265 are more than two and one-half times the $6,692 under finance leases.

Solution to 9:

Debt-to-equity ratios are calculated as follows ($ million):

	2008	2007
Debt (included in non-current liabilities)	13,772	12,363
Debt (included in current liabilities)	9,497	5,736
Total current and non-current debt	23,269	18,099
Total equity	128,866	125,966
Debt-to-equity	18.06%	14.37%

The debt-to-equity ratio increased to 18.06 percent in 2008 from 14.37 percent in 2007. This increase is primarily attributable to an increase in short-term debt. From Note 18 [A] disclosures, short-term debt increased by $4,587 million (from $3,292 million in 2007 to $7,879 million in 2008), while the current portion of long-term debt decreased by $826 million (from $2,444 million to $1,618 million) and the non-current portion of debt increased by only $1,409 million (from $12,363 million to $13,772 million). The financing section of the statement of cash flows discloses that Shell issued $4,161 million in short-term debt in 2008, compared with repaying short-term debt in 2007.

3.2.2 *Accounting and Reporting by the Lessor*

Similar to accounting and reporting on the lessee side, the lessor also must determine whether a lease is classified as operating or finance. Under IFRS, the determination of a finance lease on the lessor's side mirrors that of the lessee's. That is, in a finance lease the lessor transfers substantially all the risks and rewards incidental to legal ownership.[12] Under U.S. GAAP, the lessor determines whether a lease is a capital or operating lease using the same four identifying criteria as a lessee, plus the additional revenue recognition criteria. That is, the lessor must be reasonably assured of cash collection and has performed substantially under the lease. From the lessor's perspective, U.S. GAAP distinguishes between types of capital leases. There are two main types of capital leases from a lessor's perspective: 1) **direct financing leases**, and 2) **sales-type leases**.[13]

Under IFRS and U.S. GAAP, if a lessor enters into an operating lease, the lessor records any lease revenue when earned. The lessor also continues to report the leased asset on the balance sheet and the asset's associated depreciation expense on the income statement.

Under IFRS, if a lessor enters into a finance lease, the lessor reports a receivable at an amount equal to the net investment in the lease (the present value of the minimum lease payments receivable and any estimated unguaranteed residual value accruing to the lessor).[14] The leased asset is derecognised; assets are reduced by the carrying amount of the leased asset. Initial direct costs incurred by a lessor, other than a manufacturer or dealer lessor, are added to the receivable and reduce the amount of income recognised over the lease term. The lease payment is treated as repayment of

---

12 IAS 17, paragraph 36.
13 A leveraged lease is a third type of capital lease from the lessor's perspective under U.S. GAAP. FASB ASC paragraph 840-3-05-4.
14 Some lease contracts specify minimum lease payments with the potential for additional payments based upon some criteria.

principal (reduces lease receivable) and finance income. The recognition of finance income should reflect a constant periodic rate of return on the lessor's net investment in the lease.

For lessors that are manufacturers or dealers, the initial direct costs are treated as an expense when the selling profit is recognised; typically, selling profit is recognised at the beginning of the lease term. Sales revenue equals the lower of the fair value of the asset or the present value of the minimum lease payments. The cost of sale is the carrying amount of the leased asset less the present value of the estimated unguaranteed residual value.

Under U.S. GAAP, a direct financing lease results when the present value of lease payments (and thus the amount recorded as a lease receivable) equals the carrying value of the leased asset. Because there is no "profit" on the asset itself, the lessor is essentially providing financing to the lessee and the revenues earned by the lessor are financing in nature (i.e., interest revenue). If, however, the present value of lease payments (and thus the amount recorded as a lease receivable) exceeds the carrying amount of the leased asset, the lease is treated as a sales-type lease.

Both types of capital leases have similar effects on the balance sheet: The lessor reports a lease receivable based on the present value of future lease payments and derecognises the leased asset. The carrying value of the leased asset relative to the present value of lease payments distinguishes a direct financing lease from a sales-type lease. A direct financing lease is reported when the present value of lease payment is equal to the value of the leased asset to the lessor. When the present value of lease payments is greater than the value of the leased asset, the lease is a sales-type lease. The income statement effect will thus differ based on the type of lease.

In a direct financing lease, the lessor exchanges a lease receivable for the leased asset, no longer reporting the leased asset on its books. The lessor's revenue is derived from interest on the lease receivable. In a sales-type lease, the lessor "sells" the asset to the lessee and also provides financing on the sale. Therefore, in a sales-type lease, a lessor reports revenue from the sale, cost of goods sold (i.e., the carrying amount of the asset leased), profit on the sale, and interest revenue earned from financing the sale. The lessor will show a profit on the transaction in the year of inception and interest revenue over the life of the lease.

EXAMPLE 13

Determining Initial Recognition and Measurement and Subsequent Measurement of a Finance Lease when the Present Value of Lease Payments Equals the Value of the Leased Asset

DIRFIN Inc. owns a piece of machinery and plans to lease the machine on 1 January 2010. In the lease contract, DIRFIN requires four annual payments of €28,679 starting on 1 January 2010. DIRFIN is confident that the payments will be received. The useful life of the machine is four years, and its salvage value is zero. The present value of the lease payments and the fair value of the machine are each €100,000. The carrying amount for the machine also is €100,000. DIRFIN's discount rate is 10 percent.

1 Comment on the appropriateness of DIRFIN's treating the lease as a finance lease under IFRS and a capital lease under U.S. GAAP.

2 What is the amount of the lease receivable reported on the balance sheet on 1 January 2010? What is interest revenue reported in fiscal year 2010?

3 What is the carrying amount of the machine reported on the balance sheet on 1 January 2010?

4 What is the amount of the lease receivable reported on the balance sheet on 31 December 2010? What is interest income reported in fiscal year 2011?

5 If DIRFIN had determined the above lease was an operating lease, what amount of income would be reported on the income statement in fiscal year 2010?

Solution to 1:

Treating this lease as a finance lease under IFRS and a capital lease under U.S. GAAP is appropriate. Under IFRS, the lease meets at least two of the suggested criteria for a finance lease: 1) The lease term is for the major part of the economic life of the asset, and 2) at inception of the lease, the present value of the minimum lease payments amounts to at least substantially all of the fair value of the leased asset. Under U.S. GAAP, the lease meets more than one of the required criteria for a capital lease: 1) The lease term is 75 percent or more of the useful life of the leased asset (the lease term and useful life are both four years), and 2) the present value is 90 percent or more of the fair value of the leased asset (the present value of lease payments approximately equals the fair value of the machine). The revenue recognition requirement also is met. Under U.S. GAAP, this capital lease is classified as a direct financing lease because the present value of lease payment is equal to the value of the leased asset.

Solution to 2:

DIRFIN removes the leased asset from its records and records a lease receivable. On its income statement, DIRFIN reports interest revenues earned from financing the lease. The table below shows DIRFIN's interest revenue and carrying amounts for the lease receivable.

On 1 January 2010, the lease receivable is initially recorded at €100,000. Immediately after the first lease payment is received on 1 January 2010, the carrying amount of the lease receivable decreases to €71,321 and remains at this amount through 31 December 2010. Interest revenue for 2010 is €7,132 (10 percent interest rate times the loan receivable balance of €71,321 throughout 2010).

Year	Lease Receivable, 1 January	Annual Lease Payment Received, 1 January	Interest (at 10%; accrued in previous year)	Reduction of Lease Receivable, 1 January	Lease Receivable on 31 December after Lease Payment on 1 January of Same Year
	(a)	(b)	(c)	(d)	(e)
2010	€100,000	€28,679	€0	€28,679	€71,321
2011	71,321	28,679	7,132	21,547	49,774
2012	49,774	28,679	4,977	23,702	26,072
2013	26,072	28,679	2,607	26,072	0
		€114,717	€14,717	€100,000	

- Column (a) is the lease receivable at the beginning of the year.
- Column (b) is the annual lease payment received at the beginning of the year, which is allocated to interest and reduction of the lease receivable.
- Column (c) is interest for the year calculated as the lease receivable outstanding for the year multiplied by the interest rate.
- Column (d) is the reduction of the lease receivable, which is the difference between the annual lease payments received and interest. Because the lease payment is due on 1 January, this amount of interest is a receivable at the end of the *prior* year and interest revenue of the *prior* year.
- Column (e) is the lease receivable after the lease payment is received and at the end of the year. It is the lease receivable at 1 January (column a) less the reduction of the lease receivable (column d).

Solution to 3:

DIRFIN effectively sells the machine through the finance lease and so reports no carrying amount for the machine.

Solution to 4:

The lease receivable is €71,321 at 31 December 2010. At 1 January 2011, the lease receivable decreases to €49,774 after the second lease payment is received on 1 January 2011. Interest revenue for 2011 is €4,977 (10 percent interest rate times the loan receivable balance of €49,774 throughout 2011).

Solution to 5:

As an operating lease, rent income of €28,679 would be reported on the income statement.

When a lessor enters into a sales-type lease (a lease agreement where the present value of the future lease payments is greater than the value of the leased asset to the lessor), it will show a profit on the transaction in the year of lease inception and interest revenue over the life of the lease.

EXAMPLE 14

Determining the Financial Statement Impact of a Finance Lease by the Lessor when the Present Value of Lease Payments Is Greater than the Value of the Leased Asset

Assume a (hypothetical) company, Selnow, manufactures machinery and enters into an agreement to lease a machine on 1 January 2010. Under the lease, the company is to receive four annual payments of €28,679 starting on 1 January 2010. Selnow is confident that the payments will be received. The fair value of the machine and present value of the lease payments (using a 10 percent discount rate) are each €100,000, and the carrying amount of the machine is €90,000. The useful life of the machine is four years, and its salvage value is zero.

1 Comment on the appropriateness of Selnow's treatment of the lease agreement as a finance lease under IFRS and a capital lease under U.S. GAAP.

2 Ignoring taxes, what is Selnow's income related to the lease in 2010? In 2011?

Solution to 1:

Treating this lease as a finance lease under IFRS and a capital lease under U.S. GAAP is appropriate.

Under IFRS, the lease meets at least two of the suggested criteria for a finance lease: 1) The lease term is for the major part of the economic life of the asset (the lease term and useful life of the machine are both four years), and 2) at inception of the lease the present value of the minimum lease payments amounts to at least substantially all of the fair value of the leased asset (the present value of lease payments equals the fair value of the machine).

Under U.S. GAAP, the lease meets more than one of the required capital lease criteria, including the following: 1) The lease term is 75 percent or more of the useful life of the leased asset (the lease term and useful life of the machine are both four years), and 2) the present value is 90 percent or more of the fair value of the leased asset. The revenue recognition requirement also is met (Selnow is confident that the payments will be received). Further, under U.S. GAAP this lease is classified as a sales-type lease because the present value of the lease payments is greater than the carrying amount of the leased asset.

There is no difference, however, in accounting between IFRS and U.S. GAAP as a result of this additional classification under U.S. GAAP. The present value of the future lease payments is more than the lessor's carrying amount for the machine, and the difference is the lessor's profit from selling the machine. The lessor will record a profit of €10,000 on the sale of the machine in 2010 (€100,000 present value of lease payments receivable less €90,000 value of the machine).

Solution to 2:

In 2010, Selnow shows income of €17,132 related to the lease. One part of this income is the €10,000 gain on the sale of the machine (sales revenues of €100,000 less costs of goods sold of €90,000). Selnow also shows interest revenue of €7,132 on its financing of the lease (lease receivable of €71,321 after the initial lease payment is received times the 10 percent discount rate). In 2011, Selnow reports only the interest revenue of €4,977 (lease receivable of €49,774 after the 1 January lease payment is received times the 10 percent discount rate). The table below shows lease payments received, interest revenue, and reduction of the lease receivable for Selnow's sales-type lease. Note that this table is the same as DIRFIN's table in Example 13 with the direct financing lease. They are the same because the present value of the lease payments in both cases is the same. It is the carrying amount of the machine that differs between the two examples.

Year	Lease Receivable, 1 January	Annual Lease Payment Received,1 January	Interest (at 10%; accrued in previous year)	Reduction of Lease Receivable, 1 January	Lease Receivable on 31 December after Lease Payment on 1 January of Same Year
	(a)	(b)	(c)	(d)	(e)
2010	€100,000	€28,679	€0	€28,679	€71,321
2011	71,321	28,679	7,132	21,547	49,774
2012	49,774	28,679	4,977	23,702	26,072
2013	26,072	28,679	2,607	26,072	0
		€114,717	€14,717	€100,000	

Exhibit 2 summarises the financial statement impact of operating and financing leases on the lessee and lessor.

Exhibit 2	Summary of Financial Statement Impact of Operating and Financing Leases on the Lessee and Lessor		
	Balance Sheet	**Income Statement**	**Statement of Cash Flows**
Lessee			
Operating Lease	No effect	Reports rent expense	Rent payment is an operating cash outflow
Finance Lease under IFRS (capital lease under U.S. GAAP)	Recognises leased asset and lease liability	Reports depreciation expense on leased asset Reports interest expense on lease liability	Reduction of lease liability is a financing cash outflow Interest portion of lease payment is either an operating or financing cash outflow under IFRS and an operating cash outflow under U.S. GAAP
Lessor			
Operating Lease	Retains asset on balance sheet	Reports rent income Reports depreciation expense on leased asset	Rent payments received are an operating cash inflow
Finance Lease[a]			

Exhibit 2	(Continued)		
	Balance Sheet	**Income Statement**	**Statement of Cash Flows**
When present value of lease payments equals the carrying amount of the leased asset (called a direct financing lease in U.S. GAAP)	Removes asset from balance sheet Recognises lease receivable	Reports interest revenue on lease receivable	Interest portion of lease payment received is either an operating or investing cash inflow under IFRS and an operating cash inflow under U.S. GAAP Receipt of lease principal is an investing cash inflow[b]
When present value of lease payments exceeds the carrying amount of the leased asset (called a sales-type lease in U.S. GAAP)	Removes asset Recognises lease receivable	Reports profit on sale Reports interest revenue on lease receivable	Interest portion of lease payment received is either an operating or investing cash inflow under IFRS and an operating cash inflow under U.S. GAAP Receipt of lease principal is an investing cash inflow[b]

[a] U.S. GAAP distinguishes between a direct financing lease and a sales-type lease, but IFRS does not. The accounting is the same for IFRS and U.S. GAAP despite this additional classification under U.S. GAAP.

[b] If providing leases is part of a company's normal business activity, the cash flows related to the leases are classified as operating cash.

INTRODUCTION TO PENSIONS AND OTHER POST-EMPLOYMENT BENEFITS

4

Pensions and other post-employment benefits give rise to non-current liabilities reported by many companies. Companies may offer various types of benefits to their employees following retirement, such as pension plans, health care plans, medical insurance, and life insurance. Pension plans often are the most significant post-employment benefits provided to retired employees.

The accounting and reporting for pension plans depends on the type of pension plan offered. Two common types of pension plans are **defined-contribution plans** and **defined-benefit plans**. Under a defined-contribution plan, a company contributes an agreed-upon (defined) amount into the plan. The agreed-upon amount is the pension expense. The amount the company contributes to the plan is treated as an operating cash outflow. The only impact on assets and liabilities is a decrease in cash, although if some portion of the agreed-upon amount has not been paid by fiscal year-end, a liability would be recognised on the balance sheet. Because the amount of the contribution is defined and the company has no further obligation once the contribution has been made, accounting for a defined-contribution plan is fairly straightforward.

Accounting for a defined-benefit plan is more complicated. Under a defined-benefit plan, a company makes promises of future benefits to be paid to the employee during retirement. For example, a company could promise an employee annual pension payments equal to 70 percent of his final salary at retirement until death. Estimating the eventual amount of the obligation arising from that promise requires the company to make many assumptions, such as the employee's expected salary at retirement and the number of years the employee is expected to live beyond retirement. The company estimates the future amounts to be paid and discounts the future estimated amounts to a present value (using a rate reflective of a high-quality corporate bond yield) to determine the pension obligation. The discount rate used to determine the pension obligation significantly affects the amount of the pension obligation. The pension obligation is allocated over the employee's employment as part of pension expense.

Most defined-benefit pension plans are funded through a separate legal entity, typically a pension trust fund. A company makes payments into the pension fund, and retirees are paid from the fund. The payments that a company makes into the fund are invested until they are needed to pay the retirees. If the fair value of the fund's assets is higher than the present value of the estimated pension obligation, the plan has a surplus and the company's balance sheet will reflect a net pension asset.[15] Conversely, if the present value of the estimated pension obligation exceeds the fund's assets, the plan has a deficit and the company's balance sheet will reflect a net pension liability.[16] Thus, a company reports either a net pension asset or a net pension liability. Each period, the change in the net pension asset or liability is recognised either in profit or loss or in other comprehensive income.

Under IFRS, the change in the net pension asset or liability each period is viewed as having three general components. Two of the components of this change are recognised as pension expense in profit and loss: (1) employees' service costs and (2) the net interest expense or income accrued on the beginning net pension asset or liability. The service cost during the period for an employee is the present value of the increase in the pension benefit earned by the employee as a result of providing one more year of service. The service cost also includes past service costs, which are changes in the present value of the estimated pension obligation related to employees' service in prior periods, such as might arise from changes in the plan. The net interest expense or income is calculated as the net pension asset or liability multiplied by the discount rate used in estimating the present value of the pension obligation. The third component of the change in the net pension asset or liability during a period—"remeasurements"—is recognised in other comprehensive income. Remeasurements are not amortised into profit or loss over time.

Remeasurements include (a) actuarial gains and losses and (b) the actual return on plan assets less any return included in the net interest expense or income. Actuarial gains and losses can occur when changes are made to the assumptions on which a company bases its estimated pension obligation (e.g., employee turnover, mortality rates, retirement ages, compensation increases). The actual return on plan assets would likely differ from the amount included in the net interest expense or income, which is calculated using a rate reflective of a high-quality corporate bond yield; plan assets are typically allocated across various asset classes, including equity as well as bonds.

Under U.S. GAAP, the change in net pension asset or liability each period is viewed as having five components, some of which are recognised in profit and loss in the period incurred and some of which are recognised in other comprehensive income and amortised into profit and loss over time. The three components recognised in profit and loss in the period incurred are (1) employees' service costs for the period, (2) interest expense accrued on the beginning pension obligation, and (3) expected return on plan assets, which reduces the amount of expense recognised. The other two components are past service costs and actuarial gains and losses. Past service costs are recognised in other comprehensive income in the period in which they arise and then subsequently amortised into pension expense over the future service period of the employees covered by the plan. Actuarial gains and losses are also recognised in

---

15 The amount of any reported net pension asset is capped at the amount of any expected future economic benefits to the company from the plan; this cap is referred to as the asset ceiling.

16 The description of accounting for pensions presented in this reading corresponds to the June 2011 version of IAS 19 *Employee Benefits*, which takes effect on 1 January 2013. Both IFRS and U.S. GAAP require companies to present the amount of net pension liability or asset on the balance sheet.

other comprehensive income in the period in which they occur and then amortised into pension expense over time. In effect, U.S. GAAP allows companies to "smooth" the effects on pension expense over time for these latter two components.

Similar to other forms of employee compensation for a manufacturing company, the pension expense related to production employees is added to inventory and expensed through cost of sales (cost of goods sold). For employees not involved directly in the production process, the pension expense is included with salaries and other administrative expenses. Therefore, pension expense is not directly reported on the income statement. Rather, extensive disclosures are included in the notes to the financial statements.

Example 15 presents excerpts of pension-related disclosures from Novo Nordisk's 2010 Annual Report.

EXAMPLE 15

Pension-Related Disclosures

The following are excerpts of pension-related disclosures from Novo Nordisk's (NYSE:NVO) 2010 Annual Report. NOVO Nordisk reports under IFRS. *These financial statements were issued prior to the updated IFRS for pension accounting, which (effective January 2013) requires companies to show the entire amount of net liability or asset on the balance sheet and to recognise the entire change in that amount each period.*

1 Summary of significant accounting policies
Pensions

The Group operates a number of defined contribution plans throughout the world. In a few countries the group still operates defined benefit plans. The costs for the year for defined benefit plans are determined using the projected unit credit method. This reflects services rendered by employees to the dates of valuation and is based on actuarial assumptions primarily regarding discount rates used in determining the present value of benefits, projected rates of remuneration growth and long-term expected rates of return for plan assets. Discount rates are based on the market yields of high-rated corporate bonds in the country concerned.

21 Retirement Benefit Obligations

DKK million	2010	2009	2008	2007	2006
Retirement obligations	**1,452**	1,063	1,103	885	938
Plan assets	**(766)**	(620)	(649)	(566)	(495)

Use information in the excerpts to answer the following questions:

1 What type(s) of pension plans does Novo Nordisk have?

2 Under the updated standards, what would have been reported on Novo Nordisk's 2009 and 2010 balance sheets with respect to pensions?

3 Under the updated standards, what amount of pension costs would Novo Nordisk have recognised in 2010? Describe how these costs would have been reported.

Solution to 1:

Note 1 "Summary of significant accounting policies" indicates that the company has both defined contribution and defined benefit pension plans. The note indicates that the company continues to operate defined benefit plans in only a few countries.

Solution to 2:

Under the updated standards, Novo Nordisk would have reported a net pension obligation of DKK686 million in 2010 and DKK 443 million in 2009:

(DKK million)	2010	2009
Retirement obligations	1,452	1,063
Plan assets	(766)	(620)
Deficit/(surplus)	686	443

Solution to 3:

Under the updated standards, Novo Nordisk would have reported total pension cost of DKK 243 million in 2010, which is the change in the pension deficit from DKK 443 million in 2009 to DKK 686 million in 2010.

Of the total pension cost, two components would be recognised in profit and loss (service costs and net interest expense on the pension deficit) and one component would be recognised in other comprehensive income (remeasurements).

5 EVALUATING SOLVENCY: LEVERAGE AND COVERAGE RATIOS

Solvency refers to a company's ability to meet its long-term debt obligations, including both principal and interest payments. In evaluating a company's solvency, ratio analyses can provide information about the relative amount of debt in the company's capital structure and the adequacy of earnings and cash flow to cover interest expense and other fixed charges (such as lease or rental payments) as they come due. Ratios are useful to evaluate a company's performance over time compared to the performance of other companies and industry norms. Ratio analysis has the advantage of allowing the comparison of companies regardless of their size and reporting currency.

The two primary types of solvency ratios are leverage ratios and coverage ratios. Leverage ratios focus on the balance sheet and measure the extent to which a company uses liabilities rather than equity to finance its assets. Coverage ratios focus on the income statement and cash flows and measure the ability of a company to cover its debt-related payments.

Exhibit 3 describes the two types of commonly used solvency ratios. The first three leverage ratios use total debt in the numerator.[17] The *debt-to-assets ratio* expresses the percentage of total assets financed with debt. Generally, the higher the ratio, the higher the financial risk and thus the weaker the solvency. The *debt-to-capitalratio* measures the percentage of a company's total capital (debt plus equity) financed through debt. The *debt-to-equity ratio* measures the amount of debt financing relative to equity financing. A *debt-to-equity ratio* of 1.0 indicates equal amounts of debt and equity, which is the same as a debt-to-capital ratio of 50 percent. Interpretations of these ratios are similar. Higher debt-to-capital or debt-to-equity ratios imply weaker solvency. A caveat must be made when comparing debt ratios of companies in different countries. Within certain countries, companies historically have obtained more capital from debt than equity financing, so debt ratios tend to be higher for companies in these countries.

Exhibit 3	Definitions of Commonly Used Solvency Ratios	
Solvency Ratios	**Numerator**	**Denominator**
Leverage ratios		
Debt-to-assets ratio	Total debt[a]	Total assets
Debt-to-capital ratio	Total debt[a]	Total debt[a] + Total shareholders' equity
Debt-to-equity ratio	Total debt[a]	Total shareholders' equity
Financial leverage ratio	Average total assets	Average shareholders' equity
Coverage ratios		
Interest coverage ratio	EBIT[b]	Interest payments
Fixed charge coverage ratio	EBIT[b] + lease payments	Interest payments + lease payments

[a] In this reading, debt is defined as the sum of interest-bearing short-term and long-term debt.
[b] EBIT is earnings before interest and taxes.

The *financial leverage ratio* (also called the 'leverage ratio' or 'equity multiplier') measures the amount of total assets supported by one money unit of equity. For example, a value of 4 for this ratio means that each €1 of equity supports €4 of total assets. The higher the financial leverage ratio, the more leveraged the company in the sense of using debt and other liabilities to finance assets. This ratio often is defined in terms of average total assets and average total equity and plays an important role in the DuPont decomposition of return on equity.[18]

The *interest coverage ratio* measures the number of times a company's EBIT could cover its interest payments. A higher interest coverage ratio indicates stronger solvency, offering greater assurance that the company can service its debt from operating earnings. The *fixed charge coverage ratio* relates fixed financing charges, or

---

17 For calculations in this reading, total debt is the sum of interest-bearing short-term and long-term debt, excluding non-interest-bearing liabilities, such as accrued expenses, accounts payable, and deferred income taxes. This definition of total debt differs from other definitions that are more inclusive (e.g., all liabilities) or more restrictive (e.g., long-term debt only). If the use of different definitions of total debt materially changes conclusions about a company's solvency, the reasons for the discrepancies should be further investigated.
18 The basic DuPont decomposition is: Return on Equity = Net income/Average shareholders' equity = (Sales/Average total assets) × (Net income/Sales) × (Average total assets/Average shareholders' equity).

obligations, to the cash flow generated by the company. It measures the number of times a company's earnings (before interest, taxes, and lease payments) can cover the company's interest and lease payments.

Example 16 demonstrates the use of solvency ratios in evaluating the creditworthiness of a company.

EXAMPLE 16

Evaluating Solvency Ratios

A credit analyst is evaluating and comparing the solvency of two companies—Nokia Corporation (NYSE: NOK) and LM Ericsson Telephone Company (NYSE: ERIC)—at the beginning of 2009. The following data are gathered from the companies' 2008 annual reports and 20-F filings:

	Nokia (€ millions)		Ericsson (SEK millions)	
	2008	2007	2008	2007
Short-term borrowings	3,578	714	1,639	2,831
Current portion of long-term interest bearing debt	13	173	3,903	3,068
Long-term interest bearing debt	861	203	24,939	21,320
Total shareholders' equity	14,208	14,773	140,823	134,112
Total assets	39,582	37,599	285,684	245,117
EBIT	4,966	7,985	16,252	30,646
Interest payments	155	59	1,689	1,513

Use the above information to answer the following questions:

1   A   What are each company's debt-to-assets, debt-to-capital, and debt-to-equity ratios for 2008 and 2007?

    B   Comment on any changes in the calculated leverage ratios from year-to-year for both companies.

    C   Comment on the calculated leverage ratios of Nokia compared to Ericsson.

2   A   What is each company's interest coverage ratio for 2008 and 2007?

    B   Comment on any changes in the interest coverage ratio from year to year for both companies.

    C   Comment on the interest coverage ratio of Nokia compared to Ericsson.

Solution to 1:

A   <u>For Nokia</u>

Debt-to-assets for 2008: 11.2% = (3,578+13+861)/39,582

Debt-to-assets for 2007: 2.9% = (714+173+203)/37,599

Debt-to-capital for 2008: 23.9% = (3,578+13+861)/ (3,578+13+861+14,208)

Debt-to-capital for 2007: 6.9% = (714+173+203)/ (714+173+203+14,773)

Debt-to-equity for 2008: 31.3% = (3,578+13+861)/(14,208)

Debt-to-equity for 2007: 7.4% = (714+173+203)/(14,773)

For Ericsson

Debt-to-assets for 2008: 10.7% = (1,639+3,903+24,939)/(285,684)

Debt-to-assets for 2007: 11.1% = (2,831+3,068+21,320)/(245,117)

Debt-to-capital for 2008: 17.8% = (1,639+3,903+24,939)/
(1,639+3,903+21,320+140,823)

Debt-to-capital for 2007: 16.9% = (2,831+3,068+21,320)/
(2,831+3,068+21,320+134,112)

Debt-to-equity for 2008: 21.6% = (1,639+3,903+24,939)/(140,823)

Debt-to-equity for 2007: 20.3% = (2,831+3,068+21,320)/(134,112)

B Nokia's leverage ratios all increased from 2007 to 2008, suggesting weakening solvency. Comparing debt year to year, we observe that leverage ratios increased because of a significant increase in short-term borrowings and an increase in long-term interest bearing debt without a similar increase in shareholders' equity. In fact, shareholders' equity declined.

On the other hand, Ericsson's leverage ratios appear fairly similar for 2007 and 2008. During 2008, it appears as though Ericsson shifted away from short borrowings to long-term debt.

C In 2007, all three of Nokia's leverage ratios were lower than Ericsson's. In 2008, the opposite was true. Ericsson's capital structure seems fairly constant over the two years, whereas Nokia's capital structure has shifted toward more debt.

Solution to 2:

A For Nokia

Interest coverage ratio for 2008: 32.0 = (4,966/155)

Interest coverage ratio for 2007: 135.3 = (7,985/59)

For Ericsson

Interest coverage ratio for 2008: 9.6 = (16,252/1,689)

Interest coverage ratio for 2007: 20.3 = (30,646/1,513)

B Nokia's interest coverage ratio decreased from 2007 to 2008 because of a decrease in EBIT and an increase in interest payments. Even with the decrease, Nokia appears to have sufficient operating earnings to cover interest payments. Similarly, Ericsson's interest coverage ratio decreased from 2007 to 2008, primarily because of a decrease in EBIT. Ericsson also appears to have sufficient operating earnings to cover interest payments.

C   Nokia's ability to cover interest payments is greater than Ericsson's, although both companies appear to have sufficient operating earnings to cover interest payments.

SUMMARY

Non-current liabilities arise from different sources of financing and different types of creditors. Bonds are a common source of financing from debt markets. Bonds are initially valued at fair value when issued, and then companies have the choice of whether to subsequently measure bonds at fair value or amortised cost.

Leases are related to the use of specific assets. In a finance lease, the lessee assumes substantially all the risks and benefits of ownership of the leased asset so the lessee reports an asset and related obligation. Typically, the lessor will report a lease receivable and derecognise the asset. In an operating lease, the lessee secures the right to use the leased asset but substantially all the risk and rewards of ownership are not transferred. The lessor does not derecognise the asset and reports lease (rent) income, and the lessee reports lease (rent) expense.

Pensions and other post-employment benefits are additional forms of compensation. Employees work currently to earn current salaries and wages and also to earn benefits for retirement or post-employment. Companies with defined contribution plans report the agreed upon contribution paid into a plan as an expense. Defined benefit plans provide for agreed upon future benefits. Understanding the reporting of non-current liabilities when they arise and how they are subsequently valued is important in assessing a company's solvency and potential changes in its solvency.

Key points in accounting and reporting of non-current liabilities include the following:

■   The sales proceeds of a bond issue are determined by discounting future cash payments using the market rate of interest at the time of issuance (effective interest rate). The reported interest expense on bonds is based on the effective interest rate.

■   Future cash payments on bonds usually include periodic interest payments (made at the stated interest rate or coupon rate) and the principal amount at maturity.

■   When the market rate of interest equals the coupon rate for the bonds, the bonds will sell at par (i.e., at a price equal to the face value). When the market rate of interest is higher than the bonds' coupon rate, the bonds will sell at a discount. When the market rate of interest is lower than the bonds' coupon rate, the bonds will sell at a premium.

■   An issuer amortises any issuance discount or premium on bonds over the life of the bonds.

■   If a company redeems bonds before maturity, it reports a gain or loss on debt extinguishment computed as the net carrying amount of the bonds (including bond issuance costs under IFRS) less the amount required to redeem the bonds.

- Debt covenants impose restrictions on borrowers, such as limitations on future borrowing or requirements to maintain a minimum debt-to-equity ratio.

- The carrying amount of bonds is typically amortised historical cost, which can differ from their fair value.

- Companies are required to disclose the fair value of financial liabilities, including debt. Although permitted to do so, few companies opt to report debt at fair values on the balance sheet.

- Accounting standards require leases to be classified as either operating leases or finance (capital) leases. Leases are classified as finance leases when substantially all the risks and rewards of legal ownership are transferred to the lessee.

- When a lessee reports a lease as an operating lease rather than a finance lease, the lessee usually appears more profitable in the early years of the lease and less so later, and it appears more solvent over the whole period.

- When a lessor reports a lease as a finance lease rather than an operating lease, the lessor usually appears more profitable in the early years of the lease.

- In a finance lease where the present value of lease payments equals the carrying amount of the leased asset, a lessor earns only interest revenue. In a finance lease where the present value of lease payments exceeds the carrying amount of the leased asset, a lessor earns both interest revenue and a profit (or loss) on the sale of the leased asset.

- Two types of pension plans are defined contribution plans and defined benefits plans. In a defined contribution plan, the amount of contribution into the plan is specified (i.e., defined) and the amount of pension that is ultimately paid by the plan (received by the retiree) depends on the performance of the plan's assets. In a defined benefit plan, the amount of pension that is ultimately paid by the plan (received by the retiree) is defined, usually according to a benefit formula.

- Under a defined contribution plan, the cash payment made into the plan is recognised as pension expense.

- Under both IFRS and U.S. GAAP, companies must report the difference between the defined benefit pension obligation and the pension assets as an asset or liability on the balance sheet.

- Under IFRS, the change in the defined benefit plan net asset or liability is recognised as a cost of the period, with two components of the change (service cost and net interest expense or income) recognised in profit and loss and one component (remeasurements) of the change recognised in other comprehensive income.

- Under U.S.GAAP, the change in the defined benefit plan net asset or liability is also recognised as a cost of the period with three components of the change (current service costs, interest expense on the beginning pension obligation, and expected return on plan assets) recognised in profit and loss and two components (past service costs and actuarial gains and losses) recognised in other comprehensive income.

- Solvency refers to a company's ability to meet its long-term debt obligations.

- In evaluating solvency, leverage ratios focus on the balance sheet and measure the amount of debt financing relative to equity financing.

- In evaluating solvency, coverage ratios focus on the income statement and cash flows and measure the ability of a company to cover its interest payments.

PRACTICE PROBLEMS

1 A company issues €1 million of bonds at face value. When the bonds are issued, the company will record a:

   A cash inflow from investing activities.

   B cash inflow from financing activities.

   C cash inflow from operating activities.

2 At the time of issue of 4.50% coupon bonds, the effective interest rate was 5.00%. The bonds were *most likely* issued at:

   A par.

   B a discount.

   C a premium.

3 Oil Exploration LLC paid $45,000 in printing, legal fees, commissions, and other costs associated with its recent bond issue. It is *most likely* to record these costs on its financial statements as:

   A an asset under U.S. GAAP and reduction of the carrying value of the debt under IFRS.

   B a liability under U.S. GAAP and reduction of the carrying value of the debt under IFRS.

   C a cash outflow from investing activities under both U.S. GAAP and IFRS.

4 On 1 January 2010, Elegant Fragrances Company issues £1,000,000 face value, five-year bonds with annual interest payments of £55,000 to be paid each 31 December. The market interest rate is 6.0 percent. Using the effective interest rate method of amortisation, Elegant Fragrances is *most likely* to record:

   A an interest expense of £55,000 on its 2010 income statement.

   B a liability of £982,674 on the 31 December 2010 balance sheet.

   C a £58,736 cash outflow from operating activity on the 2010 statement of cash flows.

5 Consolidated Enterprises issues €10 million face value, five-year bonds with a coupon rate of 6.5 percent. At the time of issuance, the market interest rate is 6.0 percent. Using the effective interest rate method of amortisation, the carrying value after one year will be *closest* to:

   A €10.17 million.

   B €10.21 million.

   C €10.28 million.

6 The management of Bank EZ repurchases its own bonds in the open market. They pay €6.5 million for bonds with a face value of €10.0 million and a carrying value of €9.8 million. The bank will *most likely* report:

   A other comprehensive income of €3.3 million.

   B other comprehensive income of €3.5 million.

   C a gain of €3.3 million on the income statement.

7 Innovative Inventions, Inc. needs to raise €10 million. If the company chooses to issue zero-coupon bonds, its debt-to-equity ratio will *most likely*:

   A rise as the maturity date approaches.

B decline as the maturity date approaches.

C remain constant throughout the life of the bond.

8 Fairmont Golf issued fixed rate debt when interest rates were 6 percent. Rates have since risen to 7 percent. Using only the carrying amount (based on historical cost) reported on the balance sheet to analyze the company's financial position would *most likely* cause an analyst to:

A overestimate Fairmont's economic liabilities.

B underestimate Fairmont's economic liabilities.

C underestimate Fairmont's interest coverage ratio.

9 Debt covenants are *least likely* to place restrictions on the issuer's ability to:

A pay dividends.

B issue additional debt.

C issue additional equity.

10 Compared to using a finance lease, a lessee that makes use of an operating lease will *most likely* report higher:

A debt.

B rent expense.

C cash flow from operating activity.

11 Which of the following is *most likely* a lessee's disclosure about operating leases?

A Lease liabilities.

B Future obligations by maturity.

C Net carrying amounts of leased assets.

12 For a lessor, the leased asset appears on the balance sheet and continues to be depreciated when the lease is classified as:

A a sales-type lease.

B an operating lease.

C a financing lease.

13 Under U.S. GAAP, a lessor's reported revenues at lease inception will be *highest* if the lease is classified as:

A a sales-type lease.

B an operating lease.

C a direct financing lease.

14 A lessor will record interest income if a lease is classified as:

A a capital lease.

B an operating lease.

C either a capital or an operating lease.

15 Cavalier Copper Mines has $840 million in total liabilities and $520 million in shareholders' equity. It discloses operating lease commitments over the next five years with a present value of $100 million. If the lease commitments are treated as debt, the debt-to-total-capital ratio is *closest* to:

A 0.58.

B 0.62.

C 0.64.

16 Penben Corporation has a defined benefit pension plan. At 31 December, its pension obligation is €10 million and pension assets are €9 million. Under either IFRS or U.S. GAAP, the reporting on the balance sheet would be *closest* to which of the following?

A €10 million is shown as a liability, and €9 million appears as an asset.

B €1 million is shown as a net pension obligation.

C Pension assets and obligations are not required to be shown on the balance sheet but only disclosed in footnotes.

SOLUTIONS

1 B is correct. The company receives €1 million in cash from investors at the time the bonds are issued, which is recorded as a financing activity.

2 B is correct. The effective interest rate is greater than the coupon rate and the bonds will be issued at a discount.

3 A is correct. Under U.S. GAAP, expenses incurred when issuing bonds are generally recorded as an asset and amortised to the related expense (legal, etc.) over the life of the bonds. Under IFRS, they are included in the measurement of the liability. The related cash flows are financing activities.

4 B is correct. The bonds will be issued at a discount because the market interest rate is higher than the stated rate. Discounting the future payments to their present value indicates that at the time of issue, the company will record £978,938 as both a liability and a cash inflow from financing activities. Interest expense in 2010 is £58,736 (£978,938 times 6.0 percent). During the year, the company will pay cash of £55,000 related to the interest payment, but interest expense on the income statement will also reflect £3,736 related to amortisation of the initial discount (£58,736 interest expense less the £55,000 interest payment). Thus, the value of the liability at 31 December 2010 will reflect the initial value (£978,938) plus the amortised discount (£3,736), for a total of £982,674. The cash outflow of £55,000 may be presented as either an operating or financing activity under IFRS.

5 A is correct. The coupon rate on the bonds is higher than the market rate, which indicates that the bonds will be issued at a premium. Taking the present value of each payment indicates an issue date value of €10,210,618. The interest expense is determined by multiplying the carrying amount at the beginning of the period (€10,210,618) by the market interest rate at the time of issue (6.0 percent) for an interest expense of €612,637. The value after one year will equal the beginning value less the amount of the premium amortised to date, which is the difference between the amount paid (€650,000) and the expense accrued (€612,637) or €37,363. €10,210,618 − €37,363 = €10,173,255 or €10.17 million.

6 C is correct. A gain of €3.3 million (carrying amount less amount paid) will be reported on the income statement.

7 A is correct. The value of the liability for zero-coupon bonds increases as the discount is amortised over time. Furthermore, the amortised interest will reduce earnings at an increasing rate over time as the value of the liability increases. Higher relative debt and lower relative equity (through retained earnings) will cause the debt-to-equity ratio to increase as the zero-coupon bonds approach maturity.

8 A is correct. When interest rates rise, bonds decline in value. Thus, the carrying amount of the bonds being carried on the balance sheet is higher than the market value. The company could repurchase the bonds for less than the carrying amount, so the economic liabilities are overestimated. Because the bonds are issued at a fixed rate, there is no effect on interest coverage.

9 C is correct. Covenants protect debtholders from excessive risk taking, typically by limiting the issuer's ability to use cash or by limiting the overall levels of debt relative to income and equity. Issuing additional equity would increase the company's ability to meet its obligations, so debtholders would not restrict that ability.

10 B is correct. An operating lease is not recorded on the balance sheet (debt is lower), and lease payments are entirely categorised as rent (interest expense is lower.) Because the rent expense is an operating outflow but principal repayments are financing cash flows, the operating lease will result in lower cash flow from operating activity.

11 B is correct. The lessee will disclose the future obligation by maturity of its operating leases. The future obligations by maturity, leased assets, and lease liabilities will all be shown for finance leases.

12 B is correct. When a lease is classified as an operating lease, the underlying asset remains on the lessor's balance sheet. The lessor will record a depreciation expense that reduces the asset's value over time.

13 A is correct. A sales-type lease treats the lease as a sale of the asset, and revenue is recorded at the time of sale equal to the present value of future lease payments. Under a direct financing lease, only interest income is reported as earned. Under an operating lease, revenue from rent is reported when collected.

14 A is correct. A portion of the payments for capital leases, either direct financing or sales-type, is reported as interest income. With an operating lease, all revenue is recorded as rental revenue.

15 C is correct. The current debt-to-total-capital ratio is $840/($840+$520) = 0.62. To adjust for the lease commitments, an analyst should add $100 to both the numerator and denominator: $940/($940+$520) = 0.64.

16 B is correct. The company will report a net pension obligation of €1 million equal to the pension obligation (€10 million) less the plan assets (€9 million).

10

Financial Reporting and Analysis

Evaluating Financial Reporting Quality and Other Applications

This study session covers evaluating financial reporting quality and shows the application of financial statement analysis to debt and equity investments. The most frequently used tools and techniques to evaluate companies include common-size analysis, cross-sectional analysis, trend analysis, and ratio analysis. Beyond mere knowledge of these tools, however, the analyst must recognize the implications of accounting choices on the quality of a company's reported financial results. Then the analyst can apply financial analysis techniques to analytical tasks including the evaluation of past and future financial performance, credit risk, and the screening of potential equity investments. The readings also explain analyst adjustments to reported financials. Such adjustments are often needed to put companies' reported results on a comparable basis.

READING ASSIGNMENTS

Reading 33	Financial Reporting Quality: Red Flags and Accounting Warning Signs *Commercial Lending Review*, by Thomas R. Robinson, CFA, and Paul Munter
Reading 34	Accounting Shenanigans on the Cash Flow Statement *The CPA Journal*, by Marc A. Siegel
Reading 35	Financial Statement Analysis: Applications *International Financial Statement Analysis*, by Thomas R. Robinson, CFA, Elaine Henry, CFA, and Michael A. Broihahn, CFA

Note: New rulings and/or pronouncements issued after the publication of the readings in financial reporting and analysis may cause some of the information in these readings to become dated. Candidates are expected to be familiar with the overall analytical framework contained in the study session readings, as well as the implications of alternative accounting methods for financial analysis and valuation, as provided in the assigned readings. Candidates are not responsible for changes that occur after the material was written.

Financial Reporting Quality: Red Flags and Accounting Warning Signs

by Thomas R. Robinson, CFA, and Paul Munter

LEARNING OUTCOMES

Mastery	*The candidate should be able to:*
☐	**a.** describe incentives that might induce a company's executives to manage reported earnings, financial positions, and cash flows;
☐	**b.** describe activities that will result in a low quality of earnings;
☐	**c.** describe the three conditions that are generally present when fraud occurs, including the risk factors related to these conditions;
☐	**d.** describe common accounting warning signs and methods for detecting each.

Note: New rulings and/or pronouncements issued after the publication of the readings on financial reporting and analysis may cause some of the information in these readings to become dated. Candidates are expected to be familiar with the overall analytical framework contained in the study session readings, as well as the implications of alternative accounting methods for financial analysis and valuation, as provided in the assigned readings. Candidates are not responsible for changes that occur after the material was written.

1   INTRODUCTION

Recent years have seen numerous accounting scandals, some resulting in bankruptcies and even the demise of a major CPA firm. Unfortunately, these scandals are not a new phenomenon. Looking back, we see that scandals such as these have occurred from time to time, in particular when there is a downturn in the economy and managers have felt pressure to meet market earnings expectations or debt covenants or to maintain or increase their personal wealth. By examining recent scandals, we can learn more about warning signs of danger and the techniques used to manipulate reported financial results.

This reading takes a look at red flags and aggressive accounting techniques that have resulted in a reduction of the financial reporting quality of corporate financial statements. Financial reporting quality goes beyond the traditional view of conservatism and earnings quality. Financial reporting quality relates the overall quality of the financial statements and related disclosures to ask how well the reported results fairly present the operations and financial position of a company. In the United States, audits are intended to ensure this fair presentation in accordance with U.S. generally accepted accounting principles (GAAP). Similarly, in the United Kingdom and in the international accounting standards (IAS), there is a desire to achieve a true and fair view of the company. Additionally, CEOs and CFOs of public companies are now required by Section 302 of the Sarbanes-Oxley Act (SOA) to provide quarterly certifications that the information included in Securities and Exchange Commission (SEC) filings represents a fair presentation of operations and financial position.[1]

This reading discusses financial reporting quality and activities that result in low financial reporting quality. We describe some prominent accounting scandals over the years, SEC studies, and related auditing literature to identify nonaccounting red flags that can be used to identify potential problem areas. We also discuss a variety of accounting warning signs, such as aggressive reporting of revenues or off-balance sheet activities. Finally, we show how the red flags can be applied to accounting scandals, using Enron and Sunbeam as examples.

2   FINANCIAL REPORTING QUALITY

The concept of financial reporting quality is not new. The Association for Investment Management and Research (AIMR) has periodically published surveys and other documents on the subject. In a recent survey, AIMR found that a vast majority of portfolio managers and securities analysts surveyed found corporate disclosures and the quality of financial reporting to be very important (43 percent), extremely important (30 percent), or somewhat important (22 percent). Unfortunately, on a 5.0-point scale, these same analysts rated public companies they follow on average 3.4 (C+).[2]

A principal concern of many users of financial statements has been whether or not earnings are overstated. There is a preference by some for the use of conservative accounting practices; those that result in lower earnings in early periods relative to later periods. This is certainly an important consideration, but it is not the only factor that should be used in evaluating financial reporting quality. Companies may be motivated to increase earnings in a particular period to meet analysts' earnings expectations, to

---

[1] *See also* SEC Release No. 33-8124, *Certification of Disclosure in Companies' Quarterly and Annual Reports,* August 29, 2002.
[2] 2003 AIMR Member Survey of Global Corporate Financial Reporting Quality and Corporate Communications and Disclosure Practices, October 2003, www.aimr.org.

meet debt covenants, or to improve incentive compensation. Importantly, management also may have incentives to lower reported earnings in a particular period. For example, management may be motivated to report lower earnings to obtain trade relief, negotiate lower payments to other counterparties from a prior business transaction, or negotiate concessions from unions or others.

In addition to making sure earnings are presented fairly, it also is important that the financial position of the company is presented fairly, particularly from the standpoint of creditors. Just as management might be motivated to overstate earnings, it may have an incentive to overstate assets or understate liabilities to make the company's financial position appear to be more solvent. Conversely, management may want to understate assets to improve certain ratios, such as return on assets. Likewise, it may want to appear less solvent in a quest to negotiate concessions from creditors, vendors, and employees.

The quality of reported cash flow is another factor that needs to be examined. In some recent scandals, companies have been creative in generating operating cash flow from borrowing activities.[3] Financial disclosures or lack thereof also are important.[4] For example, when a company enters into a guarantee to others, this is an obligation that is important to creditors. Some guarantees are required to be measured and reported on the balance sheet as a liability. Other guarantees are not required to be measured and reported, but must be disclosed.[5] Clearly, the adequacy of these disclosures affects financial reporting quality.

Further, a simultaneous examination of all of the financial statements is a useful tool in detecting financial irregularities. For example, a combination of increasing earnings and decreasing operating cash flow may indicate aggressive reporting of earnings. Similarly, fraudulent activities to inflate sales and understate expenses generally lead to a buildup in assets on the balance sheet (often assets, such as receivables and inventory, but, as in the case of WorldCom, it can involve long-lived assets, as well).

We define high financial reporting quality as overall financial reporting, including disclosures, which results in a fair presentation of a company's operations (including both earnings and cash flow) and financial position. Low financial reporting quality, on the other hand, can result from a variety of activities, including the following:

- Following GAAP but selecting alternatives within GAAP that bias or distort reported results to achieve a desired outcome (e.g., selecting a depreciation method that results in higher earnings than the economic depreciation of the assets warrant).

- Using loopholes or bright-lines in accounting principles (e.g., the lessee has a capital lease if the present value of the lease payments is 90 percent or more of the fair value of the property) to structure transactions to achieve a desired outcome that differs from the economic structure of the transaction (e.g., that allows a lessor to structure a lease solely to qualify for immediate sales treatment while still allowing the lessee to treat it as an off-balance sheet arrangement).

---

3 See, e.g., SEC Accounting and Auditing Enforcement Release No. 1631, *In the Matter of Dynegy, Inc.*, September 24, 2002.
4 See, e.g., SEC Accounting and Auditing Enforcement Release No. 1555, *In the Matter of Edison Schools, Inc.*, May 14, 2002, in which the SEC determined that, even though the company's accounting was appropriate, its disclosures were lacking.
5 See SEC Release No. 33-8182, *Disclosure in Management's Discussion and Analysis about Off-Balance Sheet Arrangements and Aggregate Contractual Obligations*, January 27, 2003.

- Using unrealistic or inappropriate estimates and assumptions to achieve a desired outcome (e.g., using extraordinarily long depreciable lives for assets or unrealistically optimistic assumptions about collectibility of receivables and loans).

- Stretching accounting principles to achieve a desired outcome (e.g., using a narrowly defined rule on consolidation of special-purpose entities (SPEs) for a leasing transaction to justify nonconsolidation of SPEs in other types of transactions).

- Engaging in fraudulent financial reporting. Rather than low financial reporting quality, this category actually has no financial reporting quality.

3   RED FLAGS AND ACCOUNTING WARNING SIGNS

The auditing literature can help an analyst, creditor, or investor to begin to identify red flags. In October 2002, the American Institute of Certified Public Accountants (AICPA) published the Statement on Auditing Standards (SAS) No. 99, *Consideration of Fraud in a Financial Statement Audit* (SAS-99). SAS-99 warns practitioners to be alert for the "fraud triangle," or three conditions that are generally present when fraud occurs:

1 *Incentives or pressures* exist that can lead to fraudulent financial reporting, such as pressure to meet debt covenants or analysts' earnings expectations.

2 *Opportunities* to commit fraud exist, such as poor internal control.

3 The individuals themselves are able to *rationalize* their behavior, such as a desire to get the company through a difficult time, after which they plan to undo their accounting games.

Management has a unique ability to perpetrate fraud because it frequently is in a position to directly or indirectly manipulate accounting records and present fraudulent financial information. Fraudulent financial reporting often involves management override of controls that otherwise may appear to be operating effectively. Management can either direct employees to perpetrate fraud or solicit help in carrying it out. In addition, management personnel at a component of the entity may be in a position to manipulate the accounting records of the component in a manner that causes a material misstatement in the consolidated financial statements of the entity. Management override of controls can occur in unpredictable ways.

SAS-99 provides examples of fraud risk factors for each of the conditions of the fraud triangle, as set forth in Exhibits 1, 2, and 3. While these were written with auditors in mind, analysts and others can easily use them as red flags. For example, as shown in Exhibit 3, one risk factor is disputes with auditors. Significant disputes must be reported to the company's audit committee and in SEC filings so that the audit committee and analysts can have access to information for this red flag.

It is important that we learn from previous scandals. In fact, there is much to be learned from reviewing prior accounting scandals. Such postmortem reviews can be very useful in identifying common accounting warning signs that can serve as contemporaneous red flags that help auditors, analysts, and others identify future fraud schemes. In response to the mandate of Section 704 of the SOA, the SEC conducted a study to examine the root causes of recent enforcement actions.[6] In addition, the

---

6 SEC, *Report Pursuant to Section 704 of the Sarbanes-Oxley Act of 2002*, January 2003.

AICPA and others have examined the frequency of financial statement restatements by SEC registrants in recent years. Those studies show a disturbing trend of steadily increasing restatements:

- 157 in 2000;
- 270 in 2001;
- 330 in 2002;
- more than 350 in 2003 (as of September 30).

Exhibit 1	Risk Factors Related to Incentives/Pressures

- Financial stability or profitability is threatened by economic, industry, or entity operating conditions, such as (or as indicated by):
  - high degree of competition or market saturation, accompanied by declining margins
  - high vulnerability to rapid changes, such as changes in technology, product obsolescence, or interest rates
  - significant declines in customer demand and increasing business failures in either the industry or overall economy
  - operating losses making the threat of bankruptcy, foreclosure, or hostile takeover imminent
  - recurring negative cash flows from operations or an inability to generate cash flows from operations while reporting earnings and earnings growth
  - rapid growth or unusual profitability, especially compared to that of other companies in the same industry
  - new accounting, statutory, or regulatory requirements
- Excessive pressure exists for management to meet the requirements or expectations of third parties due to the following:
  - profitability or trend-level expectations of investment analysts, institutional investors, significant creditors, or other external parties (particularly expectations that are unduly aggressive or unrealistic), including expectations created by management in, for example, overly optimistic press releases or annual report messages
  - need to obtain additional debt or equity financing to stay competitive— including financing of major research and development or capital expenditures
  - marginal ability to meet exchange listing requirements or debt repayment or other debt covenant requirements
  - perceived or real adverse effects of reporting poor financial results on significant pending transactions, such as business combinations or contract awards
- Information available indicates that management or the board of directors' personal financial situation is threatened by the entity's financial performance arising from the following:
  - significant financial interests in the entity

(continued)

Exhibit 1	(Continued)

- significant portions of their compensation (e.g., bonuses, stock options, and earn-out arrangements) being contingent upon achieving aggressive targets for stock price, operating results, financial position, or cash flow
- personal guarantees of debts of the entity

■ There is excessive pressure on management or operating personnel to meet financial targets set up by the board of directors or management, including sales or profitability incentive goals.

Source: AICPA, SAS No. 99, Consideration of Fraud in a Financial Statement Audit, October 2002.

Exhibit 2	Risk Factors Related to Opportunities

■ The nature of the industry or the entity's operations provides opportunities to engage in fraudulent financial reporting that can arise from the following:

- significant related-party transactions not in the ordinary course of business or with related entities not audited or audited by another firm
- a strong financial presence or ability to dominate a certain industry sector that allows the entity to dictate terms or conditions to suppliers or customers that may result in inappropriate or non-arm's-length transactions
- assets, liabilities, revenues, or expenses based on significant estimates that involve subjective judgments or uncertainties that are difficult to corroborate
- significant, unusual, or highly complex transactions, especially those close to period end that pose difficult "substance over form" questions
- significant operations located or conducted across international borders in jurisdictions where differing business environments and cultures exist
- significant bank accounts or subsidiary or branch operations in tax-haven jurisdictions for which there appear to be no clear business justification

■ There is ineffective monitoring of management as a result of the following:

- domination of management by a single person or small group (in a non-owner-managed business) without compensating controls
- ineffective board of directors or audit committee oversight over the financial reporting process and internal control

■ There is a complex or unstable organizational structure, as evidenced by the following:

- difficulty in determining the organization or individuals that have controlling interest in the entity
- overly complex organizational structure involving unusual legal entities or managerial lines of authority

Exhibit 2	(Continued)

- high turnover of senior management, counsel, or board members
- Internal control components are deficient as a result of the following:
  - inadequate monitoring of controls, including automated controls and controls over interim financial reporting (when external reporting is required)
  - high turnover rates or employment of ineffective accounting, internal audit, or information technology staff
  - ineffective accounting and information systems, including situations involving reportable conditions

Source: AICPA, SAS No. 99, Consideration of Fraud in a Financial Statement Audit, October 2002.

Exhibit 3	Risk Factors Related to Attitudes/ Rationalizations

Risk factors reflective of attitudes/rationalizations by board members, management, or employees that allow them to engage in and/or justify fraudulent financial reporting may not be susceptible to observation by the auditor. Nevertheless, the auditor who becomes aware of the existence of such information should consider it in identifying the risks of material misstatement arising from fraudulent financial reporting. For example, auditors may become aware of the following information that may indicate a risk factor:

- ineffective communication, implementation, support, or enforcement of the entity's values or ethical standards by management or the communication of inappropriate values or ethical standards
- nonfinancial management's excessive participation in or preoccupation with the selection of accounting principles or the determination of significant estimates
- known history of violations of securities laws or other laws and regulations or claims against the entity, its senior management, or board members alleging fraud or violations of laws and regulations
- excessive interest by management in maintaining or increasing the entity's stock price or earnings trend
- a practice by management of committing to analysts, creditors, and other third parties to achieve aggressive or unrealistic forecasts
- management failing to correct known reportable conditions on a timely basis
- an interest by management in employing inappropriate means to minimize reported earnings for tax-motivated reasons
- recurring attempts by management to justify marginal or inappropriate accounting on the basis of materiality
- the relationship between management and the current or predecessor auditor is strained, as exhibited by the following:
  - frequent disputes with the current or predecessor auditor on accounting, auditing, or reporting matters

(continued)

Exhibit 3	(Continued)

- unreasonable demands on the auditor, such as unreasonable time constraints regarding the completion of the audit or the issuance of the auditor's report

- formal or informal restrictions on the auditor that inappropriately limit access to people or information or the ability to communicate effectively with the board of directors or audit committee

- domineering management behavior in dealing with the auditor, especially involving attempts to influence the scope of the auditor's work or the selection or continuance of personnel assigned to or consulted on the audit engagement

---

Source: AICPA, SAS No. 99, Consideration of Fraud in a Financial Statement Audit, October 2002.

The SEC study, *Report Pursuant to Section 704 of the Sarbanes-Oxley Act of 2002,* reviews 515 enforcement actions between July 31, 1997, and July 30, 2002. The study classified improper accounting practices into four categories:

1 Improper revenue recognition (126 cases), including reporting revenue in advance through techniques, such as holding the accounting period open, billing without shipping (bill and hold), fictitious revenue, and improper valuation of revenue.

2 Improper expense recognition (101 cases), including improper capitalization, overstating inventory, understating bad debts/loan losses, improper use of restructuring reserves, and failure to record asset impairments.

3 Improper accounting in connection with business combinations (23 cases).

4 Other accounting and reporting issues (130 cases), including inadequate disclosures, failure to disclose related party transactions, inappropriate accounting for nonmonetary and round-trip transactions, improper accounting for foreign payments in violation of the Foreign Corrupt Practices Act, improper use of off-balance sheet arrangements, and improper use of non-GAAP financial measures.

Based on these studies and a review of accounting scandals, several common accounting warning signs are apparent:

- **Aggressive revenue recognition.** More than half of the restatements and SEC enforcement cases involve inappropriate revenue recognition practices. Companies are required to disclose in the financial statement footnotes their revenue recognition practices. These disclosures and any other information available about a company's revenue recognition policies should be scrutinized. Aggressive techniques are those that result in the reporting of revenue earlier than may be appropriate (even though they may not technically violate GAAP). These include:
  - Bill-and-hold sales arrangements (invoicing a sale without shipping merchandise);
  - Sales-type leases (lessor reporting leases as a sale, particularly when the lessee is treating the transaction as an operating lease);
  - Recording revenue at the time a contract is signed but before delivery of goods or services;

- Recording revenue prior to fulfilling all of the terms of contracts (e.g., installation or verification that computer equipment/software is functioning according to contract terms); and

- Using swaps or barter arrangements to generate sales.

- **Operating cash flow out of line with reported earnings.** If a company is reporting positive and perhaps growing earnings but operating cash flow is negative or declining, this could indicate accounting irregularities. A cash flow earnings index (operating cash flow divided by net income) is useful in identifying potential problems (a ratio consistently below 1.0 or a ratio that is declining from one period to the next).

- **Growth in revenues out of sync with economy, industry, or peer companies and with growth in receivables.** If a company is reporting high revenue growth that is inconsistent with other companies in its industry or peer group, this could be the result of superior management or products, but also could indicate that the analyst should pay close attention to the quality of these revenues. Particular attention should be paid when receivables are growing faster than revenues or days' receivables are increasing over time. This could indicate nonexistent sales.

- **Growth in inventory out of line with sales growth or days inventory increasing over time.** This could indicate problems with:

  - inventory management;

  - potentially obsolete inventory; or, in some cases

  - inappropriate overstatement of inventory to increase gross and net profits.

- **Classification of nonoperating or nonrecurring income as revenue.** Some companies may attempt to move income items up the income statement to mask deteriorating revenues or show higher revenue growth.

- **Deferral of expenses.** The accounting policies of a company may indicate that current expenditures are being capitalized and deferred to future years through amortization or some other means (e.g., WorldCom). It is important to identify if this is a common industry practice or if the company is boosting current period profits. This often results in an increase in assets with terms, such as "deferred customer acquisition costs," so any assets that appear unusual also can be scrutinized to identify this activity.

- **Excessive use of operating leases by lessees.** While there are legitimate reasons for leasing assets and use of leasing does not violate GAAP, some companies structure equipment acquisitions in the form of operating leases to achieve desirable financial ratios (low debt ratios, higher return on assets). If a company is using these to a greater extent than its peers, this is a potential red flag. It is usually best to adjust the financial statements to see what the ratios would look like if the equipment had been purchased.

- **Classification of expenses or losses as extraordinary or nonrecurring.** While some companies try to move income up the income statement to report certain gains as revenues, the opposite occurs for expenses. If a company has "special" charges year after year, it is usually best to classify them as ordinary operating expenses for evaluation purposes.

- **LIFO liquidations.** For companies using the last-in, first-out (LIFO) method of inventory, they can get an artificial boost to earnings by running the inventory balance low at year-end. Unfortunately, this results in a higher tax bill. This red flag can be identified by reviewing the inventory footnotes for a decline in the LIFO reserve.

- **Gross margins or operating margins out of line with peer companies.** While indicative of good management and cost control, this also can indicate that accounting methods are being selected to improve financial results relative to peers. It is useful to compare the accounting methods in the footnotes to see if they are more or less conservative than peer companies. This also could indicate use of other techniques described previously, such as overstatement of inventory or capitalization of costs.

- **Use of long useful lives for depreciation and amortization.** These should be compared with other peer companies to see if they are reasonable.

- **Use of aggressive pension plan assumptions.** This can result in a misstatement of both earnings and financial leverage. Particularly watch for high discount rates (lowers pension expense and liability) and high expected return on plan assets (lowers pension expense).

- **Common use of fourth-quarter surprises.** Unusually high revenues or low expenses in the final quarter of the year that cannot be attributed to seasonality.

- **Equity method of accounting/frequent use of off-balance sheet SPEs or variable-interest entities.** Use of investments and entities that result in non-consolidation, particularly if the arrangement is not normal in the industry.

- **Other off-balance sheet financing or guarantees.** Recent SEC rules require additional disclosure of these types of activities that should be scrutinized carefully.

The existence of these red flags (the risk factors) and accounting warning signs does not mean that the company is engaged in accounting fraud. The analyst should take care, however, when performing due diligence on companies with multiple red flags. If too many red flags exist, it is certainly appropriate to tread with caution and it may be best to walk away.

4   ACCOUNTING SCANDALS: ENRON

A number of red flags were available in the Enron accounting scandals.[7] We chose Enron to demonstrate warning signs to investors, creditors, and analysts. While Enron engaged in a variety of sophisticated accounting techniques, as documented by the bankruptcy examiner, and these techniques may have been difficult for an outsider to uncover, there were red flags before the collapse of the stock in November 2001. A number of warning signs were available in Enron's calendar year 2000 Form 10K, filed in early April 2001.

In Enron's case, operating cash flow exceeded net income; however, there were items of concern related to cash flow disclosures. Exhibit 4 contains an excerpt from the section on Financial Condition.[8]

Note that investing cash flows exceed operating cash flows by a wide margin in 1998 and 1999, requiring a need for heavy financing. Further, the large increase in operating cash flow for 2000 is in part explained by the "receipt of cash associated with the assumption of a contractual obligation," which sounds more like financing

---

7 A number of excellent books document other accounting scandals. *See, e.g.*, Charles W. Mulford and Eugene E. Comiskey, The Financial Numbers Game: Detecting Creative Accounting Practices (John Wiley & Sons, January 2002), and Howard M. Schilit, Financial Shenanigans, 2nd ed. (McGraw-Hill Trade, March 2002).
8 Enron, Form 10K, Management's Discussion and Analysis, Financial Condition, 2000.

than operating activities. The importance of obtaining financing to support investing cash flows in excess of operating cash flows is apparent in several sections of the 10K, such as:[9]

> Enron is a party to certain financial contracts which contain provisions for early settlement in the event of a significant market price decline in which Enron's common stock falls below certain levels (prices ranging from $28.20 to $55.00 per share) or if the credit ratings for Enron's unsecured, senior long-term debt obligations fall below investment grade. The impact of this early settlement could include the issuance of additional shares of Enron common stock.

Exhibit 4	Enron Disclosures of Cash Flows (Excerpt from the Annual Report Section on Financial Condition, 2000)		
(in Millions)	**2000**	**1999**	**1998**
Cash provided by (used in)			
Operating activities	$4,779	$1,228	$1,640
Investing activities	(4,264)	(3,507)	(3,965)
Financing activities	571	2,456	2,266

Net cash provided by operating activities increased $3,551 million in 2000, primarily reflecting decreases in working capital, positive operating results, and a receipt of cash associated with the assumption of a contractual obligation. Net cash provided by operating activities decreased $412 million in 1999, primarily reflecting increases in working capital and net assets from price risk management activities, partially offset by increased earnings and higher proceeds from sales of merchant assets and investments. The 1998 amount reflects positive operating cash flow from Enron's major business segments, proceeds from sales of interests in energy-related merchant assets, and cash from timing and other changes related to Enron's commodity portfolio, partially offset by new investments in merchant assets and investments.

> Enron's senior unsecured long-term debt is currently rated BBB+ by Standard & Poor's Corporation and Fitch IBCA and Baa1 by Moody's Investor Service. Enron's continued investment grade status is critical to the success of its wholesale businesses as well as its ability to maintain adequate liquidity. Enron's management believes it will be able to maintain its credit rating.

Here we can see that Enron's management was under pressure to support both the stock price and debt rating, providing an incentive for earnings management behavior.

---

9 *Id.*

Enron used a market-value method for reporting revenues. In footnote 1 to the financial statements, Enron reported the use of market value for inventories, which it stated consists primarily of commodities. This is permitted under GAAP, and the amount of inventory on Enron's balance sheet was not large. Enron extended this method, however, to other types of contracts:[10]

> Accounting for Price Risk Management. Enron engages in price risk management activities for both trading and nontrading purposes. Instruments utilized in connection with trading activities are accounted for using the mark-to-market method. Under the mark-to-market method of accounting, forwards, swaps, options, energy transportation contracts utilized for trading activities, and other instruments with third parties are reflected at fair value and are shown as "Assets and Liabilities from Price Risk Management Activities" in the Consolidated Balance Sheet. These activities also include the commodity risk management component embedded in energy outsourcing contracts. Unrealized gains and losses from newly originated contracts, contract restructurings and the impact of price movements are recognized as "Other Revenues." Changes in the assets and liabilities from price risk management activities result primarily from changes in the valuation of the portfolio of contracts, newly originated transactions and the timing of settlement relative to the receipt of cash for certain contracts. The market prices used to value these transactions reflect management's best estimate considering various factors including closing exchange and over-the-counter quotations, time value and volatility factors underlying the commitments.

Exhibit 5	Enron 10K, 2000 (Summary of Footnote 19)	
Quarter	**1999 (Millions)**	**2000 (Millions)**
First	$7,632	$13,145
Second	9,672	16,886
Third	11,835	30,007
Fourth	10,973	40,751
Total	$40,112	$100,789

The use of the mark-to-market method for other types of contracts is somewhat unusual and presents ample opportunities to report revenues and income in any amount that management desires. The bankruptcy examiner's report notes that at least one analyst raised this issue as early as 1999. The analyst pointed out that Enron could recognize revenue from projects before they became operational, and this front-end loading of revenue and profits was limited only by Enron's "financial engineering skills."[11] The mark-to-market gains were reported as other revenue on Enron's income statement as follows:

- 1998: $4,045 million
- 1999: $5,338 million
- 2000: $7,232 million

---

10 *Id.* at n.1.
11 Second Interim Report of Neal Batson, Court Appointed Examiner, US Bankruptcy Court, Southern District of New York, January 21, 2003, p. 26, discussing June 1999 report of JPMorgan.

These amounts exceeded 10 percent of total revenues in 1998 and 1999. Further, without these "other revenues," operating income would have been negative. Enron's risk-management activities were reported as part of its wholesale services business segment, which comprised $94,906 million of revenue out of Enron's total revenue of $100,789 million. Adding to the red flags concerning revenue is the quarterly revenue reported in footnote 19 of Form 10K, as shown in Exhibit 5. In 2000, a disproportionate amount of revenues were reported in the third and fourth quarters, which is out of line with the seasonal trend.

Enron also engaged in securitizations of assets in its so-called price-risk-management business. In some cases, these resulted in sales to SPEs of assets with inflated values, which were really financing-type activities. In one case, Enron reported a gain on the sale of a portion of a joint venture with a major video rental company, when the technology for the venture did not exist.[12] Enron's footnotes indicate that in some cases Enron effectively protected investors in these SPEs from risk:[13]

> Securitizations. From time to time, Enron sells interests in certain of its financial assets. Some of these sales are completed in securitizations, in which Enron concurrently enters into swaps associated with the underlying assets which limits the risks assumed by the purchaser. Such swaps are adjusted to fair value using quoted market prices, if available, or estimated fair value based on management's best estimate of the present value of future cash flow. These swaps are included in Price Risk Management activities above as equity investments. During 2000, gains from sales representing securitizations were $381 million and proceeds were $2,379 million ($545 million of the proceeds related to sales to Whitewing Associates, L.P.).

Assets related to price-risk-management activities when mark-to-market accounting was used increased drastically on the balance sheet during 2000 by $15,872 million. The scope and unusual accounting for these transactions should have been cause for concern.

Enron extended its mark-to-market accounting to equity-method investments. As noted previously, the equity method enables companies to keep assets and liabilities off of the balance sheet. Under the equity method of accounting, Enron should report its percentage share of GAAP income on its income statements. Enron, however, used the market-value method for some equity investees.[14]

> Investments in Unconsolidated Affiliates. Investments in unconsolidated affiliates are accounted for by the equity method, except for certain investments resulting from Enron's merchant investment activities which are included at market value in "Other Investments" in the Consolidated Balance Sheet.

Overall, Enron's disclosures of significant equity-method investment are another red flag, particularly since the income-sharing ratios differ from the voting interests and some entities were valued at fair value, as shown in Exhibit 6.[15]

Enron's net trade receivables on the balance sheet grew from $3,030 million in 1999 to $10,396 million in 2000. The allowance for doubtful accounts grew from $40 million to only $130 million, which calls into question the quality of the receivables and underlying revenues. Other transactions, such as barter of cable capacity, are also recorded, but probably the most disturbing disclosure is that about related-party transactions:

---

12 *Id* at pp. 29–31.
13 Enron, Form 10K, December 31, 2000, n.3.
14 *Id*. at n.1.
15 *Id*. at n.9.

Related Party Transactions

In 2000 and 1999, Enron entered into transactions with limited partnerships (the Related Party) whose general partner's managing member is a senior officer of Enron. The limited partners of the Related Party are unrelated to Enron. Management believes that the terms of the transactions with the Related Party were reasonable compared to those which could have been negotiated with unrelated third parties.

Exhibit 6	Enron Annual Report, 2000 (Unconsolidated Equity Affiliates)

Enron's investment in and advances to unconsolidated affiliates that are accounted for by the equity method is as follows (in millions):

	Net Voting Interest[a]	December 31, 2000	December 31, 1999
Azurix Corp.	34%	$ 325	$ 762
Bridgeline Holdings	40%	229	—
Citrus Corp.	50%	530	480
Dabhol Power Company	50%	693	466
Joint Energy Development Investments L.P. (JEDI)[b]	50%	399	211
Joint Energy Development Investments II L.P. (JEDI II)[b]	50%	220	162
SK—Enron Co. Ltd.	50%	258	269
Transportadora de Gas del Sur S.A.	35%	479	452
Whitewing Associates, L.P.[b]	50%	558	662
Other		1,603	1,572
		$5,294	$5,036

[a]Certain investments have income sharing ratios that differ from Enron's voting interests.
[b]JEDI and JEDI II account for their investments at fair value. Whitewing accounts for certain of its investments at fair value. These affiliates held fair value investments totaling $1,823 million and $1,128 million, respectively, at December 31, 2000, and 1999.

In 2000, Enron entered into transactions with the Related Party to hedge certain merchant investments and other assets. As part of the transactions, Enron i) contributed to newly-formed entities (the Entities) assets valued at approximately $1.2 billion, including $150 million in Enron notes payable, 3.7 million restricted shares of outstanding Enron common stock and the right to receive up to 18.0 million shares of outstanding Enron common stock in March 2003 (subject to certain conditions) and ii) transferred to the Entities assets valued at approximately $309 million, including a $50 million note payable and an investment in an entity that indirectly holds warrants convertible into common stock of an Enron equity method investee. In return, Enron received economic interests in the Entities, $309 million in notes receivable, of which $259 million is recorded at Enron's carryover basis of zero, and a special distribution from the Entities in the form of $1.2 billion in notes receivable, subject to changes in the principal for amounts payable by Enron in connection with the execution of additional derivative instruments. Cash in these Entities of $172.6 million is invested in Enron demand notes. In addition, Enron paid $123 million to purchase share-settled options from the Entities on 21.7 million shares of Enron common stock. The Entities paid Enron $10.7 million to terminate the share-settled options on 14.6 million shares of Enron common stock outstanding. In late 2000, Enron entered into share-settled collar arrangements with the Entities on 15.4 million shares of Enron common stock. Such arrangements will be accounted for as equity transactions when settled.

In 2000, Enron entered into derivative transactions with the Entities with a combined notional amount of approximately $2.1 billion to hedge certain merchant investments and other assets. Enron's notes receivable balance was reduced by $36 million as a result of premiums owed on derivative transactions. Enron recognized revenues of approximately $500 million related to the subsequent change in the market value of these derivatives, which offset market value changes of certain merchant investments and price risk management activities. In addition, Enron recognized $44.5 million and $14.1 million of interest income and interest expense, respectively, on the notes receivable from and payable to the Entities.

It appears that the assets of this related party consisted primarily of receivables from Enron and other Enron securities. Further, Enron engaged in billions of dollars of "derivatives" transactions with the related party. We have only included a portion of the related-party disclosure here. The footnotes go on to describe sales of assets to the related parties on which revenues and income were recognized. This type of self-dealing amounting to billions of dollars is what ultimately led to the collapse of Enron when potential write-downs related to these activities were announced in October 2001.

There were ample red flags outside of SEC filings. In May 2001, Enron's vice chairman resigned; in August 2001, the president resigned. The proxy statement shows that top management pay was largely from bonus and stock awards. The chairman of the board, for example, received more than 90 percent of his compensation from bonus and stock awards and only a small portion from salary.

ACCOUNTING SCANDALS: SUNBEAM

5

As noted previously, the most common improper accounting techniques have involved the recognition of revenue. Sunbeam provides a good case study in accelerating revenue and the accounting warning signs that indicate its presence. In July 1996, Sunbeam's board of directors hired Albert J. Dunlap to turn the company around. According to the SEC, Dunlap and his colleagues engaged in a variety of improper activities to achieve promised sales and earnings targets, as well as to increase the stock price for a sale of the company.[16] The SEC charged that Sunbeam in 1996, 1997, and the first quarter of 1998:

- created "cookie jar" reserves in 1996 to draw on in future years to improve earnings;
- recorded revenue from contingent sales;
- accelerated sales from later periods into the present quarter;
- used improper bill-and-hold transactions.

---

16 SEC Release No. 2001-49, *SEC Sues Former CEO, CFO, Other Top Former Officers of Sunbeam Corporation in Massive Financial Fraud*, May 15, 2001.

Exhibit 7	Sunbeam (Relative Growth in Sales, Receivables, and Inventory)	
	1996	**1997**
Sales	−3.21%	18.69%
Inventory	−22.41%	57.89%
Receivables	−1.28%	38.47%

To uncover accounting warning signs, we examined financial data reported in Sunbeam's Form 10K for 1996 and 1997. As noted previously, increases in sales, receivables, and inventory should generally be in line. Exhibit 7 shows the relative growth in these amounts for Sunbeam for 1996 and 1997.

Note that for 1996, when the new management came in, sales declined slightly, as did receivables. This relationship would be expected. The larger decline in inventory is not usual. It is potentially the result of restructuring charges taken by new management in 1996, as shown in Exhibit 8.[17]

These are the cookie jar reserves referred to by the SEC. By expensing these in 1996, Sunbeam recorded a loss in the current year but set the stage for increasing income in future years. For example, if the cost of sales write-off included some write-offs of inventory, the company would have a higher profit when that inventory was sold in future years. The increase in revenues in 1997 is about 19 percent, but receivables increased by 38 percent, calling into question the quality of both the receivables and sales. Further, the increase in inventory is out of line at 58 percent, which could result from the prior year write-off and subsequent return to more normal levels. It could also indicate an overstatement of inventory to boost profits. The company reported an increase in gross margin in 1997 in spite of the need for a turnaround of the business.

Another indicator of problems with sales and cookie jar reserves is an examination of Sunbeam's cash flow compiled from Form 10K filings, as shown in Exhibit 9. The relationship of net income and operating cash flow in 1994 and 1995 is not unusual. In 1996, net income is a large negative number, yet operating cash flow is positive. The primary reason for this is the large noncash restructuring charges, which reduced 1996 income but not cash flow. In 1997, net income reached record levels for recent years, yet operating cash flow was negative. This was primarily due to the increase in receivables and inventory. The difference would have been greater if not for a sale of receivables that increased operating cash flow by $59 million in 1997.[18]

Exhibit 8	Sunbeam (Restructuring Charges, 1996)
	Pretax Dollar Amount
Restructuring, Impairment, and Other Costs	$154.9
Cost of Sales	92.3
Selling, General, and Administrative	42.5
Estimated Loss from Discontinued Operations	47.9
Total	**$337.6**

17 Sunbeam, Form 10K, 1996, p. 14.
18 Sunbeam, Form 10K, 1997, p. 18.

Exhibit 9	Sunbeam (Cash Flow Compiled from Form 10K Filings)			
Thousands of Dollars	**1994**	**1995**	**1996**	**1997**
Net Income	107,011	50,511	(228,262)	109,415
Operating Cash Flow	80,835	81,516	14,163	(8,249)

An additional warning sign comes in a change in the company's revenue recognition policy footnote from 1996 to 1997:

- 1996: "The Company recognizes revenue from product sales at the time of shipment. Net sales is comprised of gross sales less provisions for expected customer returns, discounts, promotional allowances and cooperative advertising."

- 1997: "The Company recognizes revenues from product sales principally at the time of shipment to customers. In limited circumstances, at the customers' request, the Company may sell seasonal product on a bill and hold basis provided that the goods are completed, packaged and ready for shipment, such goods are segregated and the risks of ownership and legal title have passed to the customer. The amount of such bill and hold sales at December 29, 1997, was approximately 3 percent of consolidated revenues. Net sales is comprised of gross sales less provisions for expected customer returns, discounts, promotional allowances and cooperative advertising."

Further, it appears that the company reduced its bad-debt reserves relative to the increase in receivables. The allowance for doubtful accounts only increased about $1 million from 1996 to 1997, in spite of the large increase in receivables ($82 million). The company's bad-debt expense was about $23.4 million in 1996, but only 8.4 million in 1997.[19]

The company reports in its footnotes that its business is not seasonal, stating:[20]

> On a consolidated basis, Sunbeam sales do not exhibit substantial seasonality. However, sales of outdoor cooking products are strongest in the first half of the year, while sales of appliances and personal care and comfort products are strongest in the second half of the year. In addition, sales of a number of the Company's products, including warming blankets, vaporizers, humidifiers and grills may be impacted by unseasonable weather conditions. During 1997, the Company initiated early buy programs for highly seasonal products such as grills and warming blankets in order to more levelize production and distribution activities.

---

19 *Id.* at p. F-29.
20 *Id.* at p. 6.

Exhibit 10	Sunbeam (Fourth-Quarter Sales Boost Suggests Aggressive Revenue Recognition)		
Percentage of Revenue in Each Quarter		**1996**	**1997**
First Quarter		23.34%	21.70%
Second Quarter		25.80%	24.62%
Third Quarter		23.55%	24.74%
Fourth Quarter		27.31%	28.94%

This provides a hint about the use of aggressive techniques to accelerate revenue into the fourth quarter. Exhibit 10 was compiled from quarterly disclosures in Sunbeam's 1996 and 1997 Form 10K filings. The increase in fourth-quarter revenues in a nonseasonal business is a warning sign.

6   BE ALERT FOR WARNING SIGNS

Studies of prior accounting scandals give us clues to evaluating other companies. While companies may look for more sophisticated methods to manage earnings, many of the recent scandals have involved the same techniques employed in the early years of U.S. capital markets. For example, in the 1930s, McKesson & Robbins created fictitious revenues, overstating receivables and inventory. In the 1980s, Crazy Eddie, Inc., engaged in much the same activities as did Sunbeam in the 1990s. Being alert for red flags that have occurred in past accounting scandals can help to identify potential problems early.

PRACTICE PROBLEMS

1 Management may be under pressure to misstate earnings, and there are many incentives to do so. Which one of the following is *most likely not* an incentive to overreport earnings?

   A To negotiate concessions from unions.

   B To meet analysts' earnings expectations.

   C To improve managements' incentive compensation.

2 Which of the following will *most likely* result in lower financial reporting quality?

   A Engaging in fraudulent financial reporting.

   B A low allowance for uncollectable accounts receivables.

   C Selecting alternatives within accepted accounting principles that distort results to achieve a desired outcome.

3 Accordingly to Statement on Auditing Standards No. 99, *Considerations of Fraud in a Financial Statement Audit*, the three conditions that are generally present when fraud occurs (also known as the "fraud triangle") are incentives that can lead to fraudulent reporting, opportunities to commit fraud, and:

   A poor firm financial performance.

   B rationalizations to justify behavior.

   C ineffective monitoring of management.

4 Accordingly to Statement on Auditing Standards No. 99, *Considerations of Fraud in a Financial Statement Audit*, which of the following statements is *most likely* an indication that excessive pressure exists on management to meet third parties' requirements or expectations?

   A A marginal ability to meet debt repayments or covenants.

   B Significant operations located across international borders.

   C A complex organizational structure with unusual legal entities.

5 Accordingly to Statement on Auditing Standards No. 99, *Considerations of Fraud in a Financial Statement Audit*, which of the following risk factors *most likely* represents an opportunity for management to commit fraud?

   A Revenue estimates that are based on subjective judgments.

   B Excessive interest by management in increasing the stock price.

   C Excessive competition in the industry resulting in declining margins.

6 Accordingly to Statement on Auditing Standards No. 99, *Considerations of Fraud in a Financial Statement Audit*, which of the following *most likely* indicates a risk factor reflective of managements' attitudes that may allow them to rationalize accounting fraud?

   A New regulatory requirements.

   B The dependence of managements' compensation upon meeting aggressive stock price targets.

   C Managements' repeated attempts to justify inappropriate accounting on the basis of materiality.

7 An analyst is *most likely* to detect financial irregularities regarding a company's guarantee to others under an off-balance sheet arrangement through an examination of:

  A the financial disclosures.

  B the cash flow statement.

  C simultaneous examination of all the financial statements.

8 During the period between 31 July 1997 to 30 July 2002, the *most significant* category of enforcement actions by the SEC was improper:

  A revenue recognition.

  B accounting for business combinations.

  C accounting for foreign payments in violation of the Foreign Corrupt Practices Act.

9 Which of the following red flags were present in Enron's 2000 Form 10K?

  A "Cookie jar" reserves.

  B Recognizing revenue on a bill-and-hold basis.

  C Sales to SPEs under its price-risk management business.

10 Which of the following accounting warning signs was present at Sunbeam Corporation over the 1996 to 1997 period?

  A A decrease in gross margins.

  B Increasing revenues and decreasing receivables.

  C Positive operating cash flow that was out of line with its reported earnings.

11 The accounting warning signs of early revenue recognition for Sunbeam included:

  A significant sales to related parties.

  B the use of bill-and-hold transactions.

  C the use of marked-to-market method for contracts.

SOLUTIONS

1 A is correct. Negotiating concessions from unions would likely be an incentive for management to *underreport* rather than *overreport* earnings.

2 C is correct. Selecting alternatives within GAAP that bias or distort reported results to achieve a desired outcome that differs from the economic structure of the transaction can result in lower financial reporting quality.

3 B is correct. In addition to incentives and opportunities for fraud, when it occurs, individuals typically rationalize their behavior, such as a desire to get the company through a difficult time, after which they plan to undo their accounting games.

4 A is correct. A marginal ability to meet debt repayments or covenants, if known, will likely result in some adverse actions by the holder of the debt as he or she tries to secure the investment.

5 A is correct. The need for significant estimates and judgments in the preparation of financial statements provides opportunities to commit fraud.

6 C is correct. Recurring attempts by management to justify marginal or inappropriate accounting on the basis of materiality may indicate a risk factor reflective of attitudes by management that allows it to engage in fraudulent financial reporting.

7 A is correct. While some guarantees may not be reported on the balance sheet as a liability, such guarantees should be disclosed.

8 A is correct. As reported in the SEC study, *Report Pursuant to Section 704 of the Sarbanes-Oxley Act of 2002*, improper revenue recognition accounted for 126 of the 515 enforcement cases.

9 C is correct. The so-called price-risk-management business, in some cases, resulted in sales to SPEs of assets with inflated values which were really financing-type activities.

10 C is correct. There was a positive operating cash flow of $14.2 million compared to a net loss of $228.3 million in 1996. (See Exhibit 9.)

11 B is correct. Sunbeam used bill-and-hold transactions. Enron used the other two methods.

Accounting Shenanigans on the Cash Flow Statement

by Marc A. Siegel

LEARNING OUTCOMES

Mastery	The candidate should be able to:
☐	**a.** describe reasons for investors to assess the quality of cash flow statements;
☐	**b.** analyze and describe the following ways to manage or manipulate the cash flow statement: stretching out payables, financing of payables, securitization of receivables, issuing stock options, and using stock buybacks.

INTRODUCTION

1

CPAs typically focus on uncovering items that would impact the reported earnings or the balance sheet of a company. Knowing that investors use the balance sheet and the income statement to make investment decisions, companies sometimes engage in unusual or aggressive accounting practices in order to flatter their reported figures, especially earnings.

In the wake of recent high-profile scandals, the landscape is beginning to change. The majority of investors are now keenly aware of the concept of quality of earnings. It is now fairly common knowledge in the investment community that corporate management can in various ways manipulate earnings as reflected on the income statement. As a result, certain investors shun reported earnings and instead focus more attention on other metrics to evaluate the operational health of a business. Some metrics are non-GAAP, such as backlog, same-store sales, and bookings. Many analysts have also embraced cash flow measurements. These analysts believe that, notwithstanding the fraud at Parmalat Finanziaria SpA, cash cannot be manipulated.

Marc A. Siegel, CPA, is director of research of the Center for Financial Research & Analysis (www.cfraon-line.com).

"Accounting Shenanigans on the Cash Flow Statement," by Marc A. Siegel, reprinted from *The CPA Journal*, March 2006, copyright © 2006, with permission from the New York State Society of Certified Public Accountants.

Note: New rulings and/or pronouncements issued after the publication of the readings on financial reporting and analysis may cause some of the information in these readings to become dated. Candidates are expected to be familiar with the overall analytical framework contained in the study session readings, as well as the implications of alternative accounting methods for financial analysis and valuation, as provided in the assigned readings. Candidates are not responsible for changes that occur after the material was written.

But this, too, is a misconception. While quality of earnings is now a buzzword, it may be another 10 years before it is as widely understood that the quality of cash flows is just as valid a concern.

Most conceptual definitions of materiality include the concept of factors that affect an investment decision. As Wall Street analysts have lost faith in earnings-based metrics in the wake of Enron, WorldCom, and others, many have gravitated toward the cash flow statement. Companies are regularly evaluated on the basis of free cash flow yield and other measures of cash generation. The focus of audits must change in order to devote more attention to the cash flow statement; the users of financial statements demand it.

2 DISPELLING THE MYTH ABOUT CASH FLOWS

Investors' increased focus on the cash flow statement is beneficial. Analyzing the cash flow statement is integral to understanding a company's financial performance and position because it often provides a check to the quality of the earnings shown in the income statement. Certain accounting shenanigans can, however, either artificially boost reported operating cash flow or present unsustainable cash flows. The increased scrutiny has alerted people to how some companies mask declines in operating cash flow. For example, after WorldCom's reverse-engineering subterfuge, many have learned to look for excessive capitalization of cash expenditures. Others now scrutinize the cash flow statement for nonrecurring sources of cash, such as the receipt of an income tax refund. Certain complex situations can arise that cause reported cash flow from operations to appear higher than it would have otherwise.

As the investment community begins to focus on this metric, auditors should adapt as well. Auditors have little to work with, however; only SFAS 95, Statement of Cash Flows, specifically addresses the cash flow statement, and only 15 paragraphs within SFAS 95 discuss the appropriate categorization of cash expenditures within the cash flow statement. On the other hand, a plethora of authoritative guidance surrounds the calculation and presentation of earnings. The following examples show how companies can employ certain techniques (many of which are within GAAP) to show improved reported cash flows.

3 STRETCHING OUT PAYABLES

The simplest thing that companies can do to improve reported operating cash flow is to slow down the rate of payments to their vendors. Extending out vendors used to be interpreted as a sign that a company was beginning to struggle with its cash generation. Companies now "spin" this as a prudent cash-management strategy. Another consequence of this policy is to boost the reported growth in cash flows from operations. In other words, reported operating cash flows can be improved due solely to a change in policy to slow the payment rate to vendors. If analysts or investors expect the current period improvement to continue, they may be mistaken; vendors will eventually put increasing pressure on the company to pay more timely. Therefore, any benefit may be unsustainable or, at minimum, any year-over-year improvement in operating cash flow may be unsustainable.

Exhibit 1	General Electric: Days Sales Payable, Annual Trend			
Year Ending December 31,	2003	2002	2001	2000
Days Sales Payable (DSP)	53.1	51.5	47.7	40.2

The extension of payables can be identified by monitoring days sales in payables (DSP). This metric is calculated as the end-of-period accounts-payable balance divided by the cost of goods sold and multiplied by the number of days in the period. As DSP grow, operating cash flows are boosted. As Exhibit 1 shows, General Electric Corporation began stretching out its payables in 2001 and therefore received boosts to operating cash flow. The figures show, however, that while the company received a significant benefit to cash flows from operations in 2001, that benefit began to slow in subsequent periods, indicating that GE will probably be unable to continue to fuel growth in operating cash flow using this method. Interestingly, GE modified some executive compensation agreements to include cash flow from operations as a metric on which management is evaluated.

FINANCING OF PAYABLES

4

A more complicated version of stretching out payables is the financing of payables. This occurs when a company uses a third-party financial institution to pay the vendor in the current period, with the company then paying back the bank in a subsequent period. An arrangement between Delphi Corporation and General Electric Capital Corporation shows how seemingly innocuous ventures can affect operating cash flows. The arrangement allowed Delphi to finance its accounts payable through GE Capital. Specifically, GE Capital would pay Delphi's accounts payable each quarter. In return, Delphi would reimburse GE Capital the following quarter and pay a fee for the service.

This agreement provided Delphi with a means to change the timing of its operating cash flows. In the first quarter of the venture, Delphi did not have to expend any cash with respect to accounts payable to vendors. The impact to operating cash flows can be seen in Delphi's accounting for the agreement with GE Capital. After GE Capital paid the amounts due from Delphi to its vendors, Delphi reclassified these items from accounts payable to short-term loans due to GE Capital. Delphi did this in a quarter in which cash flows were seasonally strong and it had access to the accounts-receivable securitization facilities. The reclassification resulted in a decrease to operating cash flow in that quarter, and an increase in financing cash flows. In the subsequent quarter, when Delphi paid GE Capital, the cash outflow was accounted for as a financing activity because it was a repayment of a loan. Normally, cash expenditures for accounts payable are included in operating activities. Therefore, because of the arrangement, Delphi was able to manage the timing of reported operating cash flows each period because the timing and extent of the vendor financing (and offsetting receivables securitizations) was at the discretion of company management.

Another example shows that the accounting profession has been slow to adapt to these types of transactions. During 2004, three companies in the same industry—AutoZone, Pep Boys, and Advance Auto Parts—all financed payments to vendors through a third-party financial institution. In other words, similar to Delphi above, the financial institution paid the vendors on behalf of the respective automotive company. Subsequently, the company paid back the bank, thereby slowing down its rate of payment to the vendors and boosting its operating cash flow. While each of these auto parts companies used a similar process for financing payables, each reflected it differently on its cash flow statement. Interestingly, two of these companies had the same auditor. This disparity in accounting treatment made analysts' comparisons of free cash flow yields for each of these companies irrelevant.

The lesson here is that auditors should ask questions whenever financial intermediaries are inserted in between parties that usually have no financial intermediary.

5　SECURITIZATIONS OF RECEIVABLES

A particularly significant item that could obfuscate both true cash flows and earnings is the securitization of receivables. Securitizations of receivables occur when companies package their receivables, most often those that have a longer term and higher credit quality, and transfer them to a financial institution or a variable interest entity (VIE). If the VIE is bankruptcy-remote (i.e., creditors cannot attach the assets of the VIE if the VIE sponsor files for bankruptcy), then GAAP indicates that the receivables have effectively been sold and the proceeds received should be reflected in the operating section of the cash flow statement.

The issue relates to nonfinancial companies, which are in effect able to boost reported operating cash flow by deciding how much and when to securitize accounts receivable. To the extent that proceeds received from the securitizations increase, any reported improvement in cash flow from operations should be considered unsustainable, because there is a limit to how much a company can securitize.

An interesting corollary to the impact on operating cash flow from securitizations is the impact on earnings. Specifically, in many cases companies can report gains when long-term accounts receivable are securitized. This occurs because the book value of the receivables at the time they are securitized does not include all the future interest income that is to be earned, yet the entity purchasing the receivables will have to pay for that interest. As a result, in this simplified example, because the amount received for the receivables is greater than the book value, a gain is generated. The amount of the gain can be affected as well by a variety of management assumptions, such as the expected default rate of the receivables securitized, the expected prepayment rate, and the discount rate used.

GAAP does not prescribe where on the income statement this gain is to be recorded. While one company may report the gain on sale of the receivables within revenues (the most aggressive approach), another might record it as an offset to selling, general, or administrative expenses. Another company might report the gain "below the line" in other nonoperating income. Marriott Corporation used to record the gain on securitizations of timeshare notes receivables within revenue. Specifically, in 2000, Marriott reported a gain on sale of $20 million within revenue from the securitization of these receivables. In 2001, the company reflected a $40 million gain on sale within revenues, helping to boost both reported revenues growth and pretax earnings growth. In 2002, Marriott's gain on sale was $60 million, again included in revenues, which further fueled reported revenues and earnings growth. In 2003, however, the gain on sale was flat at $60 million. Perhaps coincidentally, Marriott changed its accounting for these gains in 2003 and reported the gains on sale for all years presented as a component of "other" (nonoperating) income.

TAX BENEFITS FROM STOCK OPTIONS

6

Most companies currently follow Accounting Principles Board (APB) Opinion 25, which generally allows companies to avoid recording stock options as an expense when granted. Current IRS rules do not allow a company to take a deduction on its tax return when options are granted. At the time the stock option is exercised, however, the company is permitted to take a deduction on its tax return for that year reflecting the difference between the strike price and the market price of the option. On the external financial statements reported to investors, that deduction reduces (debits) taxes payable on the balance sheet, with the corresponding credit going to increase the equity section (additional paid-in-capital). Exhibit 2 shows the growing benefit that Cisco Corporation's operating cash flow received from this tax benefit.

| Exhibit 2 | Cisco Corporation's Statement of Cash Flows for Three Years Ended July 30, 2004 |

Cisco Corporation Consolidated Statements of Cash Flows			
Years Ended	**July 31, 2004**	**July 28, 2003**	**July 27, 2002**
Cash flows from operating activities:			
Net income	**$ 4,401**	$ 3,578	$ 1,893
Adjustments to reconcile net income to net cash provided by operating activities:			
Cumulative effect of accounting change, net of tax	**567**	—	—
Depreciation and amortization	**1,443**	1,591	1,957
Provision for doubtful accounts	**19**	(59)	91
Provision for inventory	**205**	70	131
Deferred income taxes	**552**	(14)	(573)
Tax benefits from employee stock option plans	**537**	132	61
In-process research and development	**3**	4	53
Net (gains) losses and impairment charges on investments	**(155)**	520	1,127
Change in operating assets and liabilities:			
Accounts receivable	**(488)**	(125)	270
Inventories	**(538)**	(17)	673
Prepaid expenses and other current assets	**(42)**	(61)	(28)
Accounts payable	**54**	35	(174)
Income taxes payable	**260**	(125)	389
Accrued compensation	**(7)**	104	307
Deferred revenue	**688**	(84)	678
Other accrued liabilities	**(378)**	(309)	(268)
Net cash provided by operating activities	**7,121**	5,240	6,587
Cash flows from investing activities:			
Purchases of short-term investments	**(12,206)**	(9,396)	(5,473)
Proceeds from sales and maturities of short-term investments	**13,570**	10,319	5,868
Purchases of investments	**(20,848)**	(18,063)	(15,760)
Proceeds from sales and maturities of investments	**20,757**	12,497	15,317

(continued)

Exhibit 2   (Continued)

Cisco Corporation Consolidated Statements of Cash Flows			
Years Ended	**July 31, 2004**	**July 28, 2003**	**July 27, 2002**
Purchases of restricted investments	—	—	(291)
Proceeds from sales and maturities of restricted investments	—	—	1,471
Acquisition of property and equipment	**(613)**	(717)	(2,641)
Acquisition of businesses, net of cash and cash equivalents	**(104)**	33	16
Change in lease receivables, net	**(159)**	79	380
Change in investments in privately held companies	**(13)**	(223)	(58)
Lease deposits	—	—	320
Purchase of minority interest of Cisco Systems, K.K. (Japan)	**(71)**	(59)	(115)
Other	**153**	94	159
Net cash provided by (used in) investing activities	**466**	(5,436)	(807)
Cash flows from financing activities:			
Issuance of common stock	**1,257**	578	655
Repurchase of common stock	**(9,080)**	(5,984)	(1,854)
Other	**33**	43	30
Net cash used in financing activities	**(7,790)**	(5,363)	(1,169)
Net (decrease) increase in cash and cash equivalents	**(203)**	(5,559)	4,611
Cash and cash equivalents, beginning of fiscal year	**3,925**	9,484	4,873
Cash and cash equivalents, end of fiscal year	**$ 3,722**	$ 3,925	$ 9,484

A question developed over how to classify this tax benefit (reduction of the taxes payable) on the cash flow statement. Some companies had been including it as an addback to net income in the operating section of the cash flow statement; others included it as a financing activity. FASB's Emerging Issues Task Force (EITF) Issue 00-15, released in July 2000, specifically indicated that a reduction in taxes payable should, if significant, be shown as a separate line item on the cash flow statement in the operating section (i.e., as a source of cash). [SFAS 123(R), Share-Based Payment, which requires options to be expensed, also relegates the excess tax benefit to the financing section of the cash flow statement. SFAS 123(R) takes effect for fiscal years beginning after June 15, 2005.] If the company does not disclose the tax benefit in the operating section or in the statement of changes in stockholders equity, then EITF 00-15 provided that the company should disclose any material amounts in the notes to the financial statements. The tax benefit is sometimes disclosed only in the annual statement of stockholders equity, rather than as a separate line item in the operating section of the cash flow statement for investors to analyze.

To the extent that operating cash flow is affected by a growing impact from the tax benefit on stock options, an investor should question whether the reported operating cash flow growth is in fact sustainable and is indicative of improved operations. In fact, the boost to operating cash flow is often greatest in a period when the stock price has increased. In other words, when the stock is performing well, more stock options are exercised, resulting in a higher tax benefit, which is included as a source of operating cash flow, implying improving growth of operating cash flow. Because companies in the technology sector use stock options to a higher degree, these entities may require more-careful scrutiny. (This is an issue, however, only when a company has taxable income and the taxes that it would have paid are avoided by this tax benefit. If a company has a loss, there is no boost to operating cash flow.) Analysts and investors should thoroughly review the cash flow statement, the stockholders equity statement, and the notes to the financial statements to glean the volume of options exercised during the period, and the related tax benefit included as a source of operating cash flow.

STOCK BUYBACKS TO OFFSET DILUTION   7

A second issue related to stock options that affects reported cash flows is the buyback of company stock. A large number of companies have, in recent periods, been buying back their own stock on the open market. In a majority of cases, this activity is due to stock-option activity. Specifically, as stock prices generally increased in 2003, many of those who held stock options exercised those relatively cheap options. If companies did nothing to offset the larger number of outstanding shares that existed as a result of the growing number of in-the-money options, earnings per share would be negatively affected. Management of such companies therefore face a choice: They can allow earnings per share to be diluted by the growing share count or they can buy back company stock to offset that dilution.

From an accounting standpoint, the impact of options on the income statement is usually minimal, as discussed above. On the cash flow statement, the tax benefit of option exercises is a source of operating cash flow, benefiting those companies whose option exercises grow. Cash expended by a company for the buyback of corporate stock, however, is considered a financing activity on the cash flow statement. Consequently, as option exercises grow, so does the boost to operating cash flows for the tax benefit, but the outflows for stock buybacks to offset dilution of earnings are recorded in the financing section of the cash flow statement.

Interestingly, as a company's stock price rises, more options are generally exercised and the company must buy back more stock at the ever-higher market prices. In some cases, the entire amount of cash flow generated by operations in recent periods could be expended to buy back company stock to offset the dilution from in-the-money options. (See Cisco's cash flow statements in Exhibit 2.) Therefore, when analyzing the true earnings power of a company as measured by cash flows, it is important to consider the cash expended to buy back stock to offset dilution. This cash outflow should be subtracted from the operating cash flow in order to calculate the true free cash flow the company generated in the period in question.

OTHER MEANS   8

Many other means exist by which companies can influence the timing or the magnitude of reported free cash flows. Increasing the use of capital lease transactions as a way to acquire fixed assets obfuscates free cash flow because capital expenditures may be understated on a year-over-year basis. The accounting for outstanding checks and financing receivables are additional examples. In fact, General Motors and others have restated prior years' reported cash flow results in order to reflect the SEC's increased scrutiny of finance receivables. The restatement amounted to a downward revision of almost half of the reported operating cash flow.

Some companies have pointed analysts toward different metrics, such as operating cash flows, which are believed to be a more transparent indicator of a company's performance. The quality of a company's cash flows must be assessed, as highly motivated and intelligent management teams have created new ways to obfuscate the true picture of a company's operations. Auditors must be aware of the new focus by users of financial statements on operating cash flows, and adjust their work accordingly in order to provide the most value to the public.

PRACTICE PROBLEMS

1 Which of the following financial statements are commonly misconceived by analysts as the *least* susceptible to manipulation?

    A Balance sheet.

    B Income statement.

    C Cash flow statement.

2 Which of the following will be the *most likely* consequence if a company with constant sales slows down the rate of payments to its vendors?

    A Cost of goods sold will increase.

    B Days sales payable will increase.

    C Accounts payables will decrease.

3 Gill Co. has cost of goods sold of $100 million with an accounts payable balance of $92 million at the end of the first quarter. In the second quarter, the company has cost of goods sold of $100 million with an accounts payable balance of $90 million at the end of the quarter. Assuming that the first and second quarters have 90 and 92 days respectively, which of the following is the *most likely* conclusion from this data? Gill Co. has:

    A slowed its rate of payment to vendors.

    B accelerated its rate of payment to vendors.

    C maintained its rate of payment to vendors.

4 If a firm's annual days sales in payables (DSP) was 60 days, and the annual cost of goods sold is expected to increase by 22% (and the number of days remain constant), which of the following changes in the end-of-period accounts payable balance will *most likely* improve (increase) the operating cash flow?

    A 24% decrease.

    B 20% increase.

    C 24% increase.

5 Analysts should identify instances where payments to vendors are financed through third-party financial institutions because there have been instances where the cash outflow for repayments to these institutions have been classified as a(n):

    A financing activity.

    B investing activity.

    C operating cash flow activity.

6 The ability to improve operating cash flow through securitization activities is *most likely* problematic because:

    A the benefit tends to understate reported earnings.

    B no provisions are made for defaults or prepayments.

    C the benefit is unsustainable on a consistent basis in the future.

7 If accounts receivable are securitized at a value that is more than book value, the *most* aggressive means of reporting the gain on the income statement is within:

    A revenue.

    B nonoperating income.

    C selling, general, and administrative expenses.

8 What is *least likely* to cause a distortion in the true free cash flow of a company assuming that a large stock buyback has taken place to offset the dilutions from options exercised?

    A Stock bought back on the open market.

    B Classifying the cash expended to buy back stock as a financing activity.

    C Classifying the tax benefit of option exercises as an operating cash flow.

9 Which of the following is the *least important* reason why an analyst should review the cash flow statement, the stockholders' equity statement, and the notes to the financial statements for information regarding stock options? To determine:

    A the volume of options exercised in the period.

    B the extent to which cash flows are affected by the tax benefit on stock options.

    C whether the company follows APB No. 25 or SFAS 123(R) to account for stock options.

10 Which of the following is *least likely* to be a reason a company would securitize its accounts receivable? To increase:

    A net income.

    B operating cash flows.

    C financing cash flows.

SOLUTIONS

1 C is correct. Analysts typically focus on the reported earnings (income statement) or the balance sheet of a company believing that "cash cannot be manipulated."

2 B is correct. Days sales payable (DSP) is a metric that measures the extension of payables. The metric is calculated by taking the end-of-period accounts payables divided by the cost of goods sold, multiplied by the number of days in the period. As a company slows down payments, accounts payables increase while costs of goods sold and number of days in the period remain constant. Consequently, DSP will increase.

3 C is correct. The days sales payable (DSP) for both periods is the same at 82.8 days. Quarter 1: ($92 million / $100 million) × 90 days = 82.8 days and Quarter 2: ($90 million / $100 million) × 92 days = 82.8 days. [DSP = (Accounts payable / Costs of goods sold) × (Number of days)]

4 C is correct. If the accounts payable balance increases by 24%, the days sales payable (DSP) becomes 61 days = (60 days) × (1 + 24%) / (1 + 22%). Thus, the DSP has increased from 60 to 61 days, meaning the company has slowed its payments to vendors, increased accounts payable and thereby increased its operating cash flow. [DSP = (Accounts payable / Costs of goods sold) × (Number of days)].

5 A is correct. By classifying these repayments as a financing activity and not part of operating cash flow, management has changed the timing of its operating cash flows.

6 C is correct. The practice is unsustainable due to the limit on the amount of accounts receivable that can be securitized.

7 A is correct. This is the most aggressive approach for recording the gain on the income statement.

8 A is correct. Most stock buy backs occur in the open market and do not result in any distortion of cash flow.

9 C is correct. Since 2005, U.S. GAAP require all companies to follow SFAS 123(R) which requires options to be expensed.

10 C is correct. The securitization of accounts receivable results in an increase in operating cash flows (as receivables decrease), and they are frequently sold at a gain, which increases net income. Financing cash flows are not affected.

Financial Statement Analysis: Applications

by Thomas R. Robinson, CFA, Jan Hendrik van Greuning, CFA,
Elaine Henry, CFA, and Michael A. Broihahn, CFA

LEARNING OUTCOMES

Mastery	The candidate should be able to:
☐	**a.** evaluate a company's past financial performance and explain how a company's strategy is reflected in past financial performance;
☐	**b.** forecast a company's future net income and cash flow;
☐	**c.** describe the role of financial statement analysis in assessing the credit quality of a potential debt investment;
☐	**d.** describe the use of financial statement analysis in screening for potential equity investments;
☐	**e.** explain appropriate analyst adjustments to a company's financial statements to facilitate comparison with another company.

Note: New rulings and/or pronouncements issued after the publication of the readings on financial reporting and analysis may cause some of the information in these readings to become dated. Candidates are expected to be familiar with the overall analytical framework contained in the study session readings, as well as the implications of alternative accounting methods for financial analysis and valuation, as provided in the assigned readings. Candidates are not responsible for changes that occur after the material was written.

International Financial Statement Analysis, by Thomas R. Robinson, CFA, Jan Hendrik van Greuning, CFA, Elaine Henry, CFA, and Michael A. Broihahn, CFA. Copyright © 2007 by CFA Institute.

1

INTRODUCTION

This reading presents several important applications of financial statement analysis. Among the issues we will address are the following:

- What are the key questions to address in evaluating a company's past financial performance?

- How can an analyst approach forecasting a company's future net income and cash flow?

- How can financial statement analysis be used to evaluate the credit quality of a potential fixed-income investment?

- How can financial statement analysis be used to screen for potential equity investments?

- How can differences in accounting methods affect financial ratio comparisons between companies, and what are some adjustments analysts make to reported financials to facilitate comparability among companies.

The reading "Financial Statement Analysis: An Introduction" described a framework for conducting financial statement analysis. Consistent with that framework, prior to undertaking any analysis, an analyst should explore the purpose and context of the analysis. The purpose and context guide further decisions about the approach, the tools, the data sources, and the format in which to report results of the analysis, and also suggest which aspects of the analysis are most important. Having identified the purpose and context, the analyst should then be able to formulate the key questions that the analysis must address. The questions will suggest the data the analyst needs to collect to objectively address the questions. The analyst then processes and analyzes the data to answer these questions. Conclusions and decisions based on the analysis are communicated in a format appropriate to the context, and follow-up is undertaken as required. Although this reading will not formally present applications as a series of steps, the process just described is generally applicable.

Section 2 of this reading describes the use of financial statement analysis to evaluate a company's past financial performance, and Section 3 describes basic approaches to projecting a company's future financial performance. Section 4 presents the use of financial statement analysis in assessing the credit quality of a potential debt investment. Section 5 concludes the survey of applications by describing the use of financial statement analysis in screening for potential equity investments. Analysts often encounter situations in which they must make adjustments to a company's reported financial results to increase their accuracy or comparability with the financials of other companies. Section 6 illustrates several common types of analyst adjustments. Section 7 presents a summary, and practice problems in the CFA Institute multiple-choice format conclude the reading.

APPLICATION: EVALUATING PAST FINANCIAL PERFORMANCE

2

Analysts examine a company's past financial performance for a number of reasons. Cross-sectional analysis of financial performance facilitates understanding of the comparability of companies for a market-based valuation.[1] Analysis of a company's historical performance over time can provide a basis for a forward-looking analysis of the company. Both cross-sectional and trend analysis can provide information for evaluating the quality and performance of a company's management.

An evaluation of a company's past performance addresses not only *what* happened (i.e., how the company performed) but also *why* it happened—the causes behind the performance and how the performance reflects the company's strategy. Evaluative judgments assess whether the performance is better or worse than a relevant benchmark, such as the company's own historical performance, a competitor's performance, or market expectations. Some key analytical questions include the following:

- How and why have corporate measures of profitability, efficiency, liquidity, and solvency changed over the periods being analyzed?

- How do the level and trend in a company's profitability, efficiency, liquidity, and solvency compare with the corresponding results of other companies in the same industry? What factors explain any differences?

- What aspects of performance are critical for a company to successfully compete in its industry, and how did the company perform relative to those critical performance aspects?

- What are the company's business model and strategy, and how did they influence the company's performance as reflected in, for example, its sales growth, efficiency, and profitability?

Data available to answer these questions include the company's (and its competitors') financial statements, materials from the company's investor relations department, corporate press releases, and non-financial-statement regulatory filings, such as proxies. Useful data also include industry information (e.g., from industry surveys, trade publications, and government sources), consumer information (e.g., from consumer satisfaction surveys), and information that is gathered by the analyst firsthand (e.g., through on-site visits). Processing the data typically involves creating common-size financial statements, calculating financial ratios, and reviewing or calculating industry-specific metrics. Example 1 illustrates the effects of strategy on performance and the use of basic economic reasoning in interpreting results.

EXAMPLE 1

A Change in Strategy Reflected in Financial Performance

Apple Inc. (NASDAQ: AAPL) is a company that has evolved and adapted over time. In its 1994 Prospectus (Form 424B5) filed with the U.S. SEC, Apple identified itself as "one of the world's leading personal computer technology companies." At that time, most of its revenue was generated by computer sales. In the prospectus, however, Apple stated, "The Company's strategy is to expand

---

1 Pinto et al. (2010) describe market-based valuation as using price multiples—ratios of a stock's market price to some measure of value per share (e.g., price-to-earnings ratios). Although the valuation method may be used independently of an analysis of a company's past financial performance, such an analysis may provide reasons for differences in companies' price multiples.

its market share in the personal computing industry while developing and expanding into new related business such as Personal Interactive Electronics and Apple Business Systems." Over time, products other than computers became significant generators of revenue and profit. In its 2010 Annual Report (Form 10-K) filed with the SEC, Apple stated in Part I, Item 1, under Business Strategy, "The Company is committed to bringing the best user experience to its customers through its innovative hardware, software, peripherals, services, and Internet offerings. The Company's business strategy leverages its unique ability to design and develop . . . to provide its customers new products and solutions with superior ease-of-use, seamless integration, and innovative industrial design. . . . The Company is therefore uniquely positioned to offer superior and well-integrated digital lifestyle and productivity solutions." Clearly, the company is no longer simply a personal computer technology company.

In analyzing the historical performance of Apple as of the beginning of 2011, an analyst might refer to the information presented in Exhibit 1. Panel A presents selected financial data for the company from 2007 to 2010. Panels B and C present excerpts from the segment footnote. Panel B reports the net sales by product, in millions of dollars, and Panel C reports the unit sales by product, in thousands. [Because Apple manages its business on the basis of geographical segments, the more complete data required in segment reporting (i.e., segment operating income and segment assets) is available only by geographical segment, not by product.]

In 2005, an article in *Barron's* said, "In the last year, the iPod has become Apple's best-selling product, bringing in a third of revenues for the Cupertino, Calif. firm . . . Little noticed by these iPod zealots, however is a looming threat . . . Wireless phone companies are teaming up with the music industry to make most mobile phones into music players" (*Barron's* 27 June 2005, p. 19). The threat noted by *Barron's* was not unnoticed or ignored by Apple.

In June 2007, Apple itself entered the mobile phone market with the launch of the original iPhone, followed in June 2008 by the second-generation iPhone 3G (a handheld device combining the features of a mobile phone, an iPod, and an internet connection device). Soon after, the company launched the iTunes App Store, which allows users to download third-party applications onto their iPhones. As noted in a 2009 *Business Week* article, Apple "is the world's largest music distributor, having passed Wal-Mart Stores in early 2008. Apple sells around 90% of song downloads and 75% of digital music players in the U.S." (*Business Week*, 28 September 2009, p. 34). Product innovations continue as evidenced by the introduction of the iPad in January 2010.

Exhibit 1	Selected Data for Apple Inc. (for the four years ended 25 September 2010)

Panel A: Data for Apple Inc.

(dollars in millions)	Fiscal Year			
	2010	2009	2008	2007
Net sales	$65,225	$42,905	$37,491	$24,578
Gross margin	25,684	17,222	13,197	8,152
Net income	14,013	8,235	6,119	3,495
Cash and marketable securities	51,011	33,992	24,490	15,386
Total current assets	41,678	31,555	30,006	21,956
Total assets	75,183	47,501	36,171	24,878
Total current liabilities	20,722	11,506	11,361	9,280

Panel B: Net Sales by Product

(dollars in millions)	2010	2009	2008	2007
Desktops	$6,201	$4,324	$5,622	$4,023
Portables	11,278	9,535	8,732	6,313
Total Mac net sales	17,479	13,859	14,354	10,336
iPod	8,274	8,091	9,153	8,305
Other music related products and services	4,948	4,036	3,340	2,496
iPhone and related products and services	25,179	13,033	6,742	630
iPad and related products and services	4,958	0	0	0
Peripherals and other hardware	1,814	1,475	1,694	1,303

| Exhibit 1 | (Continued) |

Panel B: Net Sales by Product

(dollars in millions)	2010	2009	2008	2007
Software, service and other sales	2,573	2,411	2,208	1,508
Total net sales	$65,225	$42,905	$37,491	$24,578

Panel C: Unit Sales by Product

(units in thousands)	2010	2009	2008	2007
Desktops	4,627	3,182	3,712	2,714
Portables	9,035	7,214	6,003	4,337
Total Mac unit sales	13,662	10,396	9,715	7,051
Net sales per Mac unit sold	$1,279	$1,333	$1,478	$1,466
iPod unit sales	50,312	54,132	54,828	51,630
Net sales per iPod unit sold	$164	$149	$167	$161
iPhone units sold	39,989	20,731	11,627	1,389
iPad units sold	7,458	0	0	0

Source: Apple Inc. 2008 Form 10-K, 2009 Form 10-K/A, and 2010 Form 10-K.

Using the information provided, address the following:

1 Typically, products that are differentiated either through recognizable brand names, proprietary technology, unique styling, or some combination of these features can be sold at a higher price than commodity products.

   A In general, would the selling prices of differentiated products be more directly reflected in a company's operating profit margin or gross profit margin?

   B Does Apple's financial data (Panel A) reflect a successful differentiation strategy?

2 How liquid is Apple at the end of fiscal 2009 and 2010? In general, what are some of the considerations that a company makes in managing its liquidity?

3 Based on the product segment data for 2007 (Panels B and C), Apple's primary source of revenue was from sales of computers (the $10,336 million in sales of Mac computers represented 42 percent of total net sales) and its secondary source of revenue was from iPods. How has the company's product mix changed since 2007, and what might this change suggest for an analyst examining Apple relative to its competitors?

Solution to 1:

A Sales of differentiated products at premium prices would generally be reflected more directly in the gross profit margin; such sales would have a higher gross profit margin, all else equal. The effect of premium pricing generally would also be reflected in a higher operating margin. Expenditures on advertising and/or research are required to support differentiation, however, which means that the effect of premium pricing on operating profit margins is often weaker than the effect on gross profit margins.

B Based on Apple's financial data in Panel A, the company appears to have successfully implemented a differentiation strategy, with gross margin increasing from 33 percent of sales to 40 percent of sales, as shown in the following table:

	2010		2009		2008		2007	
	$ Millions	Percent of Sales	$ Millions	Percent of Sales	$ Millions	Percent of Sales	$ Millions	Percent of Sales
Net sales	$65,225	100%	$42,905	100%	$37,491	100%	$24,578	100%
Cost of sales	39,541	61%	25,683	60%	24,294	65%	16,426	67%
Gross margin	$25,684	39%	$17,222	40%	$13,197	35%	$8,152	33%

In general, in addition to a successful differentiation strategy, higher gross margins can result from lower input costs and/or a change in sales mix to include more product types with high gross margins.

Solution to 2:

Apple was very liquid at the end of fiscal 2009 and 2010, with current ratios of, respectively, 2.7 ($31,555/$11,506) and 2.0 (= $41,678/$20,722). In addition, the company had 71.6 and 67.8 percent of total assets invested in cash and marketable securities at the end of, respectively, 2009 and 2010. In general, some of the considerations that a company makes in managing its liquidity include the following: (1) maintaining enough cash and other liquid assets to ensure that it can meet near-term operating expenditures and unexpected needs, (2) avoiding excessive amounts of cash because the return on cash assets is almost always less than the company's costs of capital to finance its assets, and (3) accumulating cash that will be used for acquisitions (sometimes referred to as a "war chest," which is illustrated in Exhibit 2). Apple may be accumulating a war chest, but an analyst might, given point 2 above, question the amount of cash and marketable securities on hand.

Solution to 3:

In 2009, the proportion of Apple's total sales from computers declined from 42 percent to 32 percent and the proportion of total sales from iPods declined from 34 percent to 19 percent. The biggest shift in product sales was the increase in iPhone sales from 3 percent in 2007, the year of the product's introduction, to 30 percent in 2009. In 2010, the proportion of Apple's total sales from computers and iPods continued to decline and the proportion from iPhones continued to increase. These proportions in 2010 were, respectively, 27 percent, 13 percent, and 39 percent of total sales. The iPad introduced in fiscal 2010 represented 8 percent of total sales that year. For an analyst examining Apple relative to its competitors, the relevant comparable companies clearly changed from 2007 to 2010. Recently, the company may be more appropriately compared not only with other computer manufacturers but also with mobile phone manufacturers and companies developing competing software and systems for mobile internet devices. Apple's product innovation has reshaped the competitive landscape.

To illustrate the use of a war chest, Exhibit 2 provides descriptions of several companies' cash positions and potential uses of their funds. When a company has accumulated large amounts of cash, an analyst should consider the likely implications for a company's strategic actions (i.e., potential acquisitions) or financing decisions (e.g., share buybacks, dividends, or debt repayment).

Exhibit 2	War Chests

The expression "war chest" is sometimes used to refer to large cash balances that a company accumulates prior to making acquisitions. Some examples are shown here:

Apple Inc.

Exhibit 2   **(Continued)**

Apple (NASDAQ: AAPL) closed 2009 with nearly $40 billion in the bank, in the form of cash, short-term and long-term marketable securities. That "war chest," as one shareholder described it [during Apple's annual shareholder's meeting], has fueled speculation about what the company might do with the funds. Options could include large acquisitions or returning cash to shareholders in the form of a buyback or dividend.

Dan Gallagher, *MarketWatch*, 25 February 2010.

Asahi Breweries

The head of Japan's Asahi Breweries said he expects to have $9.2 billion on tap for acquisitions over the next five years as it looks for new growth drivers outside the shrinking domestic beer market. Asahi President Naoki Izumiya also told Reuters that he wanted to lift its stake in China's Tsingtao Brewery pending regulatory changes, and is eyeing closer ties in South Korea with that country's top soft drinks maker, the Lotte Group.

Taiga Uranaka and Ritsuko Shimizu, *Reuters*, Tuesday, 3 August 2010.

McLeod Russel India Ltd.

McLeod Russel India Ltd., the world's biggest tea grower, plans to use rising prices to build a "war chest" of as much as $250 million to acquire companies. . . . The plantation company, based in Kolkata, may buy tea companies in India and Africa as it targets a 50 percent increase in production to 150 million kilograms in three to four years, said Aditya Khaitan, managing director of McLeod Russel.

Arijit Ghosh and Thomas Kutty Abraham, *Bloomberg*, 14 May 2010.

In calculating and interpreting financial statement ratios, an analyst needs to be aware of the potential impact on the financial statements and related ratios of companies reporting under different accounting standards, such as international financial reporting standards (IFRS), U.S. generally accepted accounting principles (U.S. GAAP), or other home-country GAAP. Furthermore, even within a given set of accounting standards, companies still have discretion to choose among acceptable methods. A company also may make different assumptions and estimates even when applying the same method as another company. Therefore, making selected adjustments to a company's financial statement data may be useful to facilitate comparisons with other companies or with the industry overall. Examples of such analyst adjustments will be discussed in Section 6.

Non-U.S. companies that use any acceptable body of accounting standards (other than IFRS or U.S. GAAP) and file with the U.S. SEC (because their shares or depositary receipts based on their shares trade in the United States) are required to reconcile their net income and shareholders' equity accounts to U.S. GAAP. Note that in 2007, the SEC eliminated the reconciliation requirement for non-U.S. companies using IFRS and filing with the SEC. Example 2 uses reconciliation data from SEC filings to illustrate how differences in accounting standards can affect financial ratio comparisons. The differences in the example are very large.

EXAMPLE 2

The Effect of Differences in Accounting Standards on ROE Comparisons

In the process of comparing the 2009 performance of three telecommunication companies—Teléfonos de México, S.A.B. DE C.V. (NYSE: TMX), Tele Norte Leste Participações S.A. (NYSE: TNE), and Verizon Communications Inc. (NYSE: VZ)—an analyst prepared Exhibit 3 to evaluate whether the differences in accounting standards affect the comparison of the three companies' return on equity (ROE). Panel A presents selected data for TMX for 2008 and 2009 under Mexican GAAP and U.S. GAAP. Panel B presents data for TNE under Brazilian GAAP and U.S. GAAP. Panel C presents data for VZ under U.S. GAAP.

Exhibit 3	Data for TMX, TNE, and VZ for a ROE Calculation (years ended 31 December)

Panel A: Selected Data for Teléfonos de México (TMX)		
(in millions of Mexican pesos)	**2009**	**2008**
Mexican GAAP		
Net income	20,469	20,177
Shareholders' equity	38,321	39,371
U.S. GAAP		
Net income	19,818	19,782
Shareholders' equity	7,465	11,309

Panel B: Selected Data for Tele Norte Leste Participações S.A. (TNE)		
(in millions of Brazilian reais[a])	**2009**	**2008**
Brazilian GAAP		
Net income	(1,056)	1,432
Shareholders' equity	15,352	11,411
U.S. GAAP		
Net income	4,866	1,252
Shareholders' equity	21,967	11,203

Panel C: Selected Data for Verizon Communications Inc.		
(in millions of U.S. dollars)	**2009**	**2008**
U.S. GAAP		
Net income	10,358	12,583
Shareholders' equity	84,367	78,905

[a] "Reais" is the plural of "real."
Sources: TMX's and TME's 2009 Form 20-F; VZ's 2009 10-K.

Based on TMX's reconciliation footnote, the most significant adjustment for TMX between Mexican GAAP and U.S. GAAP was an adjustment to shareholders' equity for "Labor obligations (SFAS 158)." The U.S. accounting standard SFAS 158, *Employers' Accounting for Defined Benefit Pension and Other*

Postretirement Plans, now codified as Accounting Standards Codification (ASC) 715 (i.e., Expenses: Compensation–Retirement Benefits) requires companies to reflect on their balance sheets the funded status of pensions and other post-employment benefits. (Funded status equals plan assets minus plan obligations.) For an underfunded plan—i.e., one in which assets that are held in trust to pay for the obligation are less than the amount of the obligation—the amount of underfunding is shown as a liability and as a reduction to shareholders' equity. [The full reconciliation between shareholders' equity under Mexican FRS and U.S. GAAP (not presented here) shows that the adjustment related to SFAS 158 reduced equity at TMX by 50,028 million pesos and 46,637 million pesos in 2009 and 2008, respectively.]

Based on TNE's reconciliation footnote, the most significant adjustment for TNE between Brazilian GAAP and U.S. GAAP was an increase to net income to recognize a "bargain purchase gain on business combination." A bargain purchase gain under U.S. GAAP results when the purchase price of an acquisition is less than the fair value (as of the acquisition date) of the net identified assets acquired. The adjustment for the bargain purchase gain represented an increase of 6,591 million Brazilian reais to net income as reported under Brazilian GAAP.

Does the difference in accounting standards affect the ROE comparison?

Solution:

When ROE is compared under different standards, both of the non-U.S. companies report significantly higher ROE under U.S. GAAP than under home-country GAAP (Mexican GAAP for TMX and Brazilian GAAP for TNE).

When ROE is compared across companies, TMX's ROE is higher than that of both of the other two companies regardless of whether the comparison is based on home-country amounts or U.S. GAAP amounts. For TNE, however, the company reported a loss and thus a negative ROE under home-country (Brazilian) GAAP but a profit under U.S. GAAP. The ROE for TNE is lower than VZ's ROE when calculations are based on home-country GAAP but higher than VZ's ROE when calculations are based on U.S. GAAP.

Results of the calculations are summarized in the following table, with the calculations based on TMX's Mexican GAAP explained after the table:

Panel A: Teléfonos de México (TMX)

Mexican GAAP

Return on average shareholders' equity	52.69%

U.S. GAAP

Return on average shareholders' equity	211.12%

Panel B: Tele Norte Leste Participações S.A. (TNE)

Brazilian GAAP

Return on average shareholders' equity	−7.89%

U.S. GAAP

Return on average shareholders' equity	29.34%

Panel C: Verizon Communications Inc. (VZ)

U.S. GAAP

Return on average shareholders' equity	12.69%

> For an illustration of the ROE calculation, we have calculated TMX's ROE (with all numbers in thousands of Mexican pesos) as $20,468,983/[(38,320,773 + 39,371,099)/2] = 52.69\%$. Note that TMX's significantly higher ROE under U.S. GAAP is the result of a much lower shareholders' equity under U.S. GAAP than under Mexican GAAP.

In Example 2, the 2009 ROE for both TMX and TNE differed substantially under home-country GAAP and U.S. GAAP. In general, because the reconciliation data are no longer required by the SEC, we cannot determine whether differences in net income, equity, and thus ROE also exist between IFRS and the companies' home-country GAAP (including U.S. GAAP). Historically, research indicates that for most non-U.S. companies filing with the SEC, differences in net income between U.S. GAAP and home-country GAAP average 1–2 percent of market value of equity, but large variations do occur.[2] Additionally, research indicates that for most non-U.S. companies filing with the SEC, ROE was historically higher under IFRS than under U.S. GAAP.[3]

Comparison of the levels and trends in a company's performance provide information about *how* the company performed. The company's management presents its view about causes underlying its performance in the management commentary or management discussion and analysis (MD&A) section of its annual report and during periodic conference calls with analysts and investors. To gain additional understanding of the causes underlying a company's performance, an analyst can review industry information or seek information from additional sources, such as consumer surveys.

The results of an analysis of past performance provide a basis for reaching conclusions and making recommendations. For example, an analysis undertaken as the basis for a forward-looking study might conclude that a company's future performance is or is not likely to reflect continuation of recent historical trends. As another example, an analysis to support a market-based valuation of a company might focus on whether the company's profitability and growth outlook, which is better (worse) than the peer group median, justifies its relatively high (low) valuation. This analysis would consider market multiples, such as price-to-earnings ratio (P/E), price-to-book ratio, and total invested capital to EBITDA (earnings before interest, taxes, depreciation, and amortization).[4] As another example, an analysis undertaken as part of an evaluation of the management of two companies might result in conclusions about whether one company has grown as fast as another company, or as fast as the industry overall, and whether each company has maintained profitability while growing.

---

2 Pownall and Schipper (1999).
3 In a study of European companies' reconciliations in the last year that reconciliations were required by the SEC, Henry, Lin and Yang (2009) found that most of the companies reported IFRS net income higher than U.S. GAAP net income and reported IFRS shareholders' equity lower than U.S. GAAP shareholders' equity. The result was that 28 percent of the sample companies' 2006 ROE under IFRS was more than 5 percentage points higher than under U.S. GAAP whereas fewer than 10 percent of the sample report ROE more than 5 percentage points lower.
4 Total invested capital is the sum of market value of common equity, book value of preferred equity, and face value of debt.

APPLICATION: PROJECTING FUTURE FINANCIAL PERFORMANCE

3

Projections of future financial performance are used in determining the value of a company or its equity component. Projections of future financial performance are also used in credit analysis—particularly in project finance or acquisition finance—to determine whether a company's cash flows will be adequate to pay the interest and principal on its debt and to evaluate whether a company will likely remain in compliance with its financial covenants.

Sources of data for analysts' projections include some or all of the following: the company's projections, the company's previous financial statements, industry structure and outlook, and macroeconomic forecasts.

Evaluating a company's past performance may provide a basis for forward-looking analyses. An evaluation of a company's business and economic environment and its history may persuade the analyst that historical information constitutes a valid basis for such analyses and that the analyst's projections may be based on the continuance of past trends, perhaps with some adjustments. Alternatively, in the case of a major acquisition or divestiture, for a start-up company, or for a company operating in a volatile industry, past performance may be less relevant to future performance.

Projections of a company's near-term performance may be used as an input to market-based valuation or relative valuation (i.e., valuation based on price multiples). Such projections may involve projecting next year's sales and using the common-size income statement to project major expense items or particular margins on sales (e.g., gross profit margin or operating profit margin). These calculations will then lead to the development of an income measure for a valuation calculation, such as net income, earnings per share (EPS) or EBITDA. More complex projections of a company's future performance involve developing a more detailed analysis of the components of performance for multiple periods—for example, projections of sales and gross margin by product line, projection of operating expenses based on historical patterns, and projection of interest expense based on requisite debt funding, interest rates, and applicable taxes. Furthermore, a projection should include sensitivity analyses applied to the major assumptions.

3.1 Projecting Performance: An Input to Market-Based Valuation

One application of financial statement analysis involves projecting a company's near-term performance as an input to market-based valuation. For example, an analyst might project a company's sales and profit margin to estimate EPS and then apply a projected P/E to establish a target price for the company's stock.

Analysts often take a top-down approach to projecting a company's sales.[5] First, industry sales are projected on the basis of their historical relationship with some macroeconomic indicator, such as growth in real gross domestic product (GDP). In researching the automobile industry, for example, the analyst may find that the industry's annual domestic unit car sales (number of cars sold in domestic markets) bears a relationship to annual changes in real GDP. Regression analysis is often used to establish the parameters of such relationships. Other factors in projecting sales may include consumer income or tastes, technological developments, and the availability of substitute products or services. After industry sales are projected, a company's

---

5 The discussion in this paragraph is indebted to Benninga and Sarig (1997).

market share is projected. Company-level market share projections may be based on historical market share and a forward-looking assessment of the company's competitive position. The company's sales are then estimated as its projected market share multiplied by projected total industry sales.

After developing a sales forecast for a company, an analyst can choose among various methods for forecasting income and cash flow. An analyst must decide on the level of detail to consider in developing forecasts. For example, separate forecasts may be made for individual expense items or for more aggregated expense items, such as total operating expenses. Rather than stating a forecast in terms of expenses, the forecast might be stated in terms of a forecasted profit margin (gross, operating, or net). The net profit margin, in contrast to the gross or operating profit margins, is affected by financial leverage and tax rates, which are subject to managerial and legal/regulatory revisions; therefore, historical data may sometimes be more relevant for projecting gross or operating profit margins than for projecting net profit margins. Whatever the margin used, the forecasted amount of profit for a given period is the product of the forecasted amount of sales and the forecast of the selected profit margin.

As Example 3 illustrates, for relatively mature companies operating in non-volatile product markets, historical information on operating profit margins can provide a useful starting point for forecasting future operating profits (at least over short forecasting horizons). Historical operating profit margins are typically less reliable for projecting future margins for a new or relatively volatile business or one with significant fixed costs (which can magnify the volatility of operating margins).

EXAMPLE 3

Using Historical Operating Profit Margins to Forecast Operating Profit

One approach to projecting operating profit is to determine a company's average operating profit margin over the previous several years and apply that margin to a forecast of the company's sales. Use the following information on three companies to answer Questions 1 and 2 below:

■ Johnson & Johnson (JNJ). This U.S. health care conglomerate, founded in 1887, had 2009 sales of around $61.9 billion from its three main businesses: pharmaceuticals, medical devices and diagnostics, and consumer products.

■ BHP Billiton (BHP). This company, with group headquarters in Australia and secondary headquarters in London, is the world's largest natural resources company, reporting revenue of approximately US$50.2 billion for the fiscal year ended June 2009. The company mines, processes, and markets coal, copper, nickel, iron, bauxite, and silver and also has substantial petroleum operations.

■ Baidu. This Chinese company, which was established in 2000 and went public on NASDAQ in 2005, is the leading Chinese language search engine. The company's revenues for 2009 were 4.4 billion renminbi (RMB), an increase of 40 percent from 2008 and more than 14 times greater than revenues in 2005.

   1   For each of the three companies, state and justify whether the suggested forecasting method (applying the average operating profit over the previous several years to a forecast of sales) would be a reasonable starting point for projecting future operating profit.

2 Assume that the 2009 forecast of sales was perfect and, therefore, equal to the realized sales by the company in 2009. Compare the forecast of 2009 operating profit, using an average of the previous four years' operating profit margins, with the actual 2009 operating profit reported by the company given the following additional information:

- JNJ: For the four years prior to 2009, JNJ's average operating profit margin was approximately 25.0 percent. The company's actual operating profit for 2009 was $15.6 billion.

- BHP: For the four years prior to the year ending June 2009, BHP's average operating profit margin was approximately 38.5 percent. The company's actual operating profit for the year ended June 2009 was US$12.2 billion.

- Baidu: Over the four years prior to 2009, Baidu's average operating profit margin was approximately 27.1 percent. The company's actual operating profit for 2009 was RMB1.6 billion.

Using the additional information given, state and justify whether actual results support the usefulness of the stable operating margin assumption.

Solution to 1:

JNJ. Because JNJ is an established company with diversified operations in relatively stable businesses, the suggested approach to projecting the company's operating profit would be a reasonable starting point.

BHP. Because commodity prices tend to be volatile and the mining industry is relatively capital intensive, the suggested approach to projecting BHP's operating profit would probably not be a useful starting point.

Baidu. A relatively new company such as Baidu has limited operating history on which to judge stability of margins. The company appears to have been in a period of rapid growth and is in an industry that has been changing rapidly in recent years. This important aspect about the company suggests that the broad approach to projecting operating profit would not be a useful starting point for Baidu.

Solution to 2:

JNJ. JNJ's actual operating profit margin for 2009 was 25.2 percent ($15.6 billion divided by sales of $61.9 billion), which is very close to the company's three-year average operating profit margin of approximately 25.0 percent. If the average operating profit margin had been applied to perfectly forecasted 2009 sales to obtain forecasted operating profit, the forecasting error would have been minimal.

BHP. BHP's actual operating profit margin for the year ended June 2009 was 24.3 percent ($12.2 billion divided by sales of $50.2 billion). If the company's average profit margin of 38.5 percent had been applied to perfectly forecasted sales, the forecasted operating profit would have been approximately US$19.3 billion, around 58 percent higher than actual operating profit.

Baidu. Baidu's actual operating profit margin for 2009 was 36.4 percent (RMB1.6 billion divided by sales of RMB4.4 billion). If the average profit margin of 27.1 percent had been applied to perfectly forecasted sales, the forecasted operating profit would have been approximately RMB1.2 billion, or around 25 percent below Baidu's actual operating profit.

Although prior years' profit margins can provide a useful starting point in projections for companies with relatively stable business, the underlying data should, nonetheless, be examined to identify items that are not likely to occur again in the following year(s). Such non-recurring (i.e., transitory) items should be removed from computations of any profit amount or profit margin that will be used in projections. Example 4 illustrates this principle.

EXAMPLE 4

Issues in Forecasting

Following are excerpts from the annual reports of two global companies. Indicate the relevance of each disclosure in forecasting the company's future net income. (Business descriptions are from the companies' websites.)

1 Anheuser-Busch InBev SA/NV (Euronext: ABI, NYSE: BUD), the world's largest brewing company by volume, with brands such as Budweiser, Stella Artois, and Beck's, disclosed the following items, which are primarily related to its acquisition of Anheuser-Busch.

  1.1 "The 2009 restructuring charges of (153)m US dollar primarily relate to the Anheuser-Busch integration, organizational alignments and outsourcing activities in the global headquarters, Western Europe and Asia Pacific. These changes aim to eliminate overlap or duplicated processes and activities across functions and zones. These one time expenses as a result of the series of decisions will provide the company with a lower cost base besides a stronger focus on AB InBev's core activities, quicker decision-making and improvements to efficiency, service and quality..."

  1.2 "2009 business and asset disposals resulted in an exceptional income of 1,541m US dollar mainly representing the sale of assets of InBev USA LLC (also doing business under the name Labatt USA) to an affiliate of KPS Capital Partners, L.P. (54m US dollar), the sale of the Korean subsidiary Oriental Brewery to an affiliate of Kohlberg Kravis Roberts & Co. L.P. (428m US dollar) and the sale of the Central European operations to CVC Capital Partners (1,088m US dollar)..."

  Source: 2009 Annual Report, note 8.

2 Nestlé Group (NESN.VX), the largest food and beverages manufacturer in the world, disclosed the following information about the sale of its holding in the eye care company Alcon Inc. (NYSE: ACL).

  2.1 "The most significant divestment was announced on 4 January 2010, with the agreement to sell our remaining holding in Alcon, for about USD 28 billion. The completion of this transaction will bring the total value realised from the three-part disposal of Alcon to over USD 40 billion. Alcon was acquired by Nestlé in 1977 for USD 280 million."

  Source: 2009 Annual Report, Shareholder Letter, p. 4.

  2.2 "On 7 July 2008, the Group sold 24.8% of Alcon outstanding capital to Novartis for a total amount of USD 10.4 billion, resulting in a profit on disposal of CHF 9208 million and in an increase of non-controlling interests of CHF 1537 million. The agreement further included the option for Novartis to acquire Nestlé's remaining shareholding in Alcon at a price of USD 181.– per share from January 2010 until July 2011. During the same period, Nestlé had the option to sell its remaining shareholding in Alcon to Novartis at the lower of either the call price of USD 181.– per share or the average share price during the week preceding the exercise plus a premium of 20.5%. On 4 January 2010, Novartis exercised its call option to acquire the remaining 52% shareholding from Nestlé at a price of USD 181.– per share. The transaction is now pending regulatory approval which can be expected during the course of 2010. As IFRS 5 criteria were met on 31 December 2009, Alcon's related assets and liabilities are classified as a disposal group in Assets held for sale and Liabilities directly associated with assets held for sale. Moreover, Alcon operations are disclosed as discontinued operations in the 2009 Consolidated Financial Statements. The results of Alcon discontinued operations are disclosed separately in the income statement."

Source: 2009 Financial Statements, note 25

2.3 Excerpt from Nestlé's consolidated income statement for the year ended 31 December 2009:

| | (CHF millions) | |
	2009	2008
Sales		
Continuing operations	100,579	103,086
Discontinued operations	7,039	6,822
Total	107,618	109,908
EBIT (earnings before interest, taxes, restructuring and impairments		
Continuing operations	13,222	13,240
Discontinued operations	2,477	2,436
Total	15,699	15,676
Profit for the year		
Continuing operations	9,551	7,656
Discontinued operations	2,242	11,395
Total	11,793	19,051

Source: 2009 Financial Statements.

Discussion of 1.1

This item relates to one-time restructuring charges aimed at eliminating duplication between the pre-acquisition operations of the two companies (InBev and Anheuser-Busch). The restructuring charges themselves are not directly relevant in forecasting the future net income of the company. If the restructuring successfully reduced the company's cost base, however, the combined companies' expenses in the future are likely to be less than the sum of the two individual companies' expenses. Also, if the cost base was successfully reduced, the profit margin for the combined company is likely to be higher than a profit margin calculated as the sum of the individual companies' profits divided by the sum of the individual companies' sales revenues.

Discussion of 1.2

Gains on sales of businesses and assets that result in exceptional income are not a core part of a company's business. This item should typically not be viewed as an ongoing source of earnings and should not, therefore, be a component of forecasts of net income. Additionally, any portion of the company's past income that had been generated by the businesses sold should be excluded from forecasted net income.

Discussion of 2.1

These disclosures pertain to Nestlé's total USD40 billion return on the USD280 million investment in Alcon over 33 years (between 1977 and 2010). The information is not directly relevant to forecasting future net income. Although forecasts of net income must exclude the income from the divested business, information about the amount of that income is disclosed elsewhere.

Discussion of 2.2

Gains on sales of businesses and assets that result in exceptional income are not a core part of a company's business, so neither the CHF9,208 million gain in 2008 nor any further gains on the transaction should be included in ongoing, long-term forecasts. An analyst can, however, use the disclosed information about the sale price and information about the net book value of the investment to estimate the gain that will be reported in 2010 net income. In addition, results of discontinued items should not be included when assessing past performance or when forecasting future net income. As noted, the results of the discontinued items are shown separately on the income statement, as shown in excerpt 2.3.

Discussion of 2.3

Results of discontinued items should not be included when assessing past performance or when forecasting future net income. For example, the company's EBIT margin (EBIT/sales) for continuing operations for 2009 of 13 percent should be included in an analysis (not the 15 percent for the combined continuing and discontinued operations).

In general, when earnings projections are used as a foundation for market-based valuations, an analyst will make appropriate allowance for transitory components of past earnings.

3.2 Projecting Multiple-Period Performance

Projections of future financial performance over multiple periods are needed in valuation models that estimate the value of a company or its equity by discounting future cash flows. The value of a company or its equity developed in this way can then be compared with its current market price as a basis for investment decisions.

Projections of future performance are also used for credit analysis. These projections are important in assessing a borrower's ability to repay interest and principal of debt obligations. Investment recommendations depend on the needs and objectives of the client and on an evaluation of the risk of the investment relative to its expected return—both of which are a function of the terms of the debt obligation itself as well as financial market conditions. Terms of the debt obligation include amount, interest rate, maturity, financial covenants, and collateral.

Example 5 presents an elementary illustration of net income and cash flow forecasting to illustrate a format for analysis and some basic principles. In Example 5, assumptions are shown first; then, the period-by-period abbreviated financial statement resulting from the assumptions is shown.

Depending on the use of the forecast, an analyst may choose to compute further, more specific cash flow metrics. For example, free cash flow to equity, which is used in discounted cash flow approaches to equity valuation, can be estimated as net income adjusted for noncash items, minus investment in net working capital and in net fixed assets, plus net borrowing.[6]

EXAMPLE 5

Basic Example of Financial Forecasting

Assume a company is formed with $100 of equity capital, all of which is immediately invested in working capital. Assumptions are as follows:

Dividends	Non-dividend-paying
First-year sales	$100
Sales growth	10% per year
Cost of goods sold/Sales	20%
Operating expense/Sales	70%
Interest income rate	5%
Tax rate	30%
Working capital as percent of sales	90%

Based on this information, forecast the company's net income and cash flow for five years.

Solution:

Exhibit 4 shows the net income forecasts in Line 7 and cash flow forecasts ("Change in cash") in Line 18.

Exhibit 4	Basic Financial Forecasting					

		Time Period				
	0	1	2	3	4	5
(1) Sales		100.0	110.0	121.0	133.1	146.4
(2) Cost of goods sold		(20.0)	(22.0)	(24.2)	(26.6)	(29.3)
(3) Operating expenses		(70.0)	(77.0)	(84.7)	(93.2)	(102.5)
(4) Interest income		0.0	0.9	0.8	0.8	0.7
(5) Income before tax		10.0	11.9	12.9	14.1	15.3
(6) Taxes		(3.0)	(3.6)	(3.9)	(4.2)	(4.6)
(7) Net income		7.0	8.3	9.0	9.9	10.7

(continued)

---

6 See Pinto, Henry, Robinson, and Stowe (2010) for further information.

| Exhibit 4 | (Continued) |

	Time Period					
	0	1	2	3	4	5
(8) Cash/Borrowing	0.0	17.0	16.3	15.4	14.4	13.1
(9) Working capital (non-cash)	100.0	90.0	99.0	108.9	119.8	131.8
(10) Total assets	100.0	107.0	115.3	124.3	134.2	144.9
(11) Liabilities	0.0	0.0	0.0	0.0	0.0	0.0
(12) Equity	100.0	107.0	115.3	124.3	134.2	144.9
(13) Total liabilities + Equity	100.0	107.0	115.3	124.3	134.2	144.9
(14) Net income		7.0	8.3	9.0	9.9	10.7
(15) Plus: Non-cash items		0.0	0.0	0.0	0.0	0.0
(16) Less: Investment in working capital		−10.0	9.0	9.9	10.9	12.0
(17) Less: Investment in fixed capital		0.0	0.0	0.0	0.0	0.0
(18) Change in cash		17.0	−0.7	−0.9	−1.0	−1.3
(19) Beginning cash		0.0	17.0	16.3	15.4	14.4
(20) Ending cash		17.0	16.3	15.4	14.4	13.1

Exhibit 4 indicates that at time 0, the company is formed with $100 of equity capital (Line 12). All of the company's capital is assumed to be immediately invested in working capital (Line 9). In future periods, because it is assumed that no dividends are paid, book equity increases each year by the amount of net income (Line 14). Future periods' required working capital (Line 9) is assumed to be 90 percent of annual sales (Line 1). Sales are assumed to be $100 in the first period and to grow at a constant rate of 10 percent per year (Line 1). The cost of goods sold is assumed to be constant at 20 percent of sales (Line 2), so the gross profit margin is 80 percent. Operating expenses are assumed to be 70 percent of sales each year (Line 3). Interest income (Line 4) is calculated as 5 percent of the beginning balance of cash/borrowing or the ending balance of the previous period (Line 8) and is an income item when there is a cash balance, as in this example. (If available cash is inadequate to cover required cash outflows, the shortfall is presumed to be covered by borrowing. This borrowing would be shown as a negative balance on Line 8 and an associated interest expense on Line 4. Alternatively, a forecast can be presented with separate lines for cash and borrowing.) Taxes of 30 percent are deducted to obtain net income (Line 7).

To calculate each period's cash flow, begin with net income (Line 7 = Line 14), add back any noncash items, such as depreciation (Line 15), deduct investment in working capital in the period or change in working capital over the period (Line 16), and deduct investment in fixed capital in the period (Line 17).[7] In this simple example, we are assuming that the company does not invest in any fixed capital (long-term assets) but, rather, rents furnished office space. Therefore, there is no depreciation and noncash items are zero. Each period's change in cash (Line 18) is added to the beginning cash balance (Line 19) to obtain the ending cash balance (Line 20 = Line 8).

Example 5 is simplified to demonstrate some principles of forecasting. In practice, each aspect of a forecast presents a range of challenges. Sales forecasts may be very detailed, with separate forecasts for each year of each product line, each geographical, and/or each business segment. Sales forecasts may be based on past results (for

---

7 Working capital represents funds that must be invested in the daily operations of a business to, for example, carry inventory and accounts receivable. The term "investment" in this context means "addition to" or "increase in." The "investment in fixed capital" is also referred to as "capital expenditure" ("capex"). See Pinto et al. (2010), Chapter 4, for further information.

relatively stable businesses), management forecasts, industry studies, and/or macro-economic forecasts. Similarly, gross profit margins may be based on past results or forecasted relationships and may be detailed. Expenses other than cost of goods sold may be broken down into more detailed line items, each of which may be forecasted on the basis of its relationship with sales (if variable) or on the basis of its historical levels. Working capital requirements may be estimated as a proportion of the amount of sales (as in Example 5) or the change in sales or as a compilation of specific forecasts for inventory, receivables, and payables. Most forecasts will involve some investment in fixed assets, in which case, depreciation amounts affect taxable income and net income but not cash flow. Example 5 makes the simplifying assumption that interest is paid on the beginning-of-year cash balance.

Example 5 develops a series of point estimates for future net income and cash flow. In practice, forecasting generally includes an analysis of the risk in forecasts—in this case, an assessment of the impact on income and cash flow if the realized values of variables differ significantly from the assumptions used in the base case or if actual sales are much different from forecasts. Quantifying the risk in forecasts requires an analysis of the economics of the company's businesses and expense structure and the potential impact of events affecting the company, the industry, and the economy in general. When that investigation is completed, the analyst can use scenario anal-ysis or Monte Carlo simulation to assess risk. Scenario analysis involves specifying assumptions that differ from those used as the base-case assumptions. In Example 5, the projections of net income and cash flow could be recast in a more pessimistic scenario, with assumptions changed to reflect slower sales growth and higher costs. A Monte Carlo simulation involves specifying probability distributions of values for variables and random sampling from those distributions. In the analysis in Example 5, the projections would be repeatedly recast with the selected values for the drivers of net income and cash flow, thus permitting the analyst to evaluate a range of possible results and the probability of simulating the possible actual outcomes.

An understanding of financial statements and ratios can enable an analyst to make more detailed projections of income statement, balance sheet, and cash flow statement items. For example, an analyst may collect information on normal inventory and receivables turnover and use this information to forecast accounts receivable, inventory, and cash flows based on sales projections rather than use a composite working capital investment assumption, as in Example 5.

As the analyst makes detailed forecasts, he or she must ensure that the forecasts are consistent with each other. For instance, in Example 6, the analyst's forecast concerning days of sales outstanding (which is an estimate of the average time to collect payment from sales made on credit) should flow from a model of the company that yields a forecast of the change in the average accounts receivable balance. Otherwise, predicted days of sales outstanding and accounts receivable will not be mutually consistent.

EXAMPLE 6

Consistency of Forecasts[8]

Brown Corporation had an average days-of-sales-outstanding (DSO) period of 19 days in 2009. An analyst thinks that Brown's DSO will decline in 2010 (because of expected improvements in the company's collections department) to match the industry average of 15 days. Total sales (all on credit) in 2009 were $300 million,

---

8 Adapted from a past CFA Institute examination question.

and Brown expects total sales (all on credit) to increase to $320 million in 2010. To achieve the lower DSO, the change in the average accounts receivable balance from 2009 to 2010 that must occur is *closest* to:

A   −$3.51 million.

B   −$2.46 million.

C $2.46 million.

D $3.51 million.

Solution:

B is correct. The first step is to calculate accounts receivable turnover from the DSO collection period. Receivable turnover equals 365/19 (DSO) = 19.2 for 2009 and 365/15 = 24.3 in 2010. Next, the analyst uses the fact that the average accounts receivable balance equals sales/receivable turnover to conclude that for 2009, average accounts receivable was $300,000,000/19.2 = $15,625,000 and for 2010, it must equal $320,000,000/24.3 = $13,168,724. The difference is a reduction in receivables of $2,456,276.

The next section illustrates the application of financial statement analysis to credit risk analysis.

4   APPLICATION: ASSESSING CREDIT RISK

Credit risk is the risk of loss caused by a counterparty's or debtor's failure to make a promised payment. For example, credit risk with respect to a bond is the risk that the obligor (the issuer of the bond) will not be able to pay interest and/or principal according to the terms of the bond indenture (contract). **Credit analysis** is the evaluation of credit risk. Credit analysis may relate to the credit risk of an obligor in a particular transaction or to an obligor's overall creditworthiness.

In assessing an obligor's overall creditworthiness, one general approach is credit scoring, a statistical analysis of the determinants of credit default. Credit analysis for specific types of debt (e.g., acquisition financing and other highly leveraged financing) typically involves projections of period-by-period cash flows.

Whatever the techniques adopted, the analytical focus of credit analysis is on debt-paying ability. Unlike payments to equity investors, payments to debt investors are limited by the agreed contractual interest. If a company experiences financial success, its debt becomes less risky but its success does not increase the amount of payments to its debtholders. In contrast, if a company experiences financial distress, it may be unable to pay interest and principal on its debt obligations. Thus, credit analysis has a special concern with the sensitivity of debt-paying ability to adverse events and economic conditions—cases in which the creditor's promised returns may be most at risk. Because those returns are generally paid in cash, credit analysis usually focuses on cash flow rather than accrual income. Typically, credit analysts use return measures related to operating cash flow because it represents cash generated internally, which is available to pay creditors.

These themes are reflected in Example 7, which illustrates the application to an industry group of four groups of quantitative factors in credit analysis: (1) scale and diversification, (2) tolerance for leverage, (3) operational efficiency, and (4) margin stability.

"Scale and diversification" relate to a company's sensitivity to adverse events, adverse economic conditions, and other factors—such as market leadership, purchasing power with suppliers, and access to capital markets—that may affect debt-paying ability.

Financial policies, or "tolerance for leverage," relate to the obligor's ability to service its indebtedness (i.e., make the promised payments on debt). In Example 7, various solvency ratios are used to measure tolerance for leverage. One set of tolerance-for-leverage measures is based on retained cash flow (RCF). RCF is defined by Moody's Investors Service as operating cash flow before working capital changes less dividends. For example, under the assumption of no capital expenditures, a ratio of RCF to total debt of 0.5 indicates that the company may be able to pay off debt from cash flow retained in the business in approximately $1/0.5 = 2$ years (at current levels of RCF and debt); a ratio adjusting for capital expenditures is also used. Other factors include interest coverage ratios based on EBITDA, which are also chosen by Moody's in specifying factors for operational efficiency and margin stability.

"Operational efficiency" as defined by Moody's relates to cost structure: Companies with lower costs are better positioned to deal with financial stress.

"Margin stability" relates to the past volatility of profit margins: Higher stability should be associated with lower credit risk.

EXAMPLE 7

Moody's Evaluation of Quantifiable Rating Factors for a Specific Industry[9]

Moody's considers a number of items when assigning credit ratings for the global aerospace and defense industry, including quantitative measures of three broad factors: size and scale; business profile, revenue sustainability, and efficiency; and financial leverage and flexibility. A company's ratings for each of these factors are weighted and aggregated in determining the overall credit rating assigned. The broad factors, the sub-factors, and weightings are as follows:

Broad Factor	Sub-factors	Sub-factor Weighting (%)	Broad Factor Weighting (%)
Size and scale	Total revenue	10	25
	Operating profit	15	
Business profile, revenue sustainability and efficiency	Expected business profile (e.g., prime contractor versus easily replaced small supplier)	10	25
	Revenue visibility (backlog/revenue)	5	
	Revenue protection (competitive factors; e.g., barriers to entry)	5	
	EBITA/Average assets	5	

(continued)

---

9 "Rating Methodology: Global Aerospace and Defense" (Moody's, 2010), p. 21.

Broad Factor	Sub-factors	Sub-factor Weighting (%)	Broad Factor Weighting (%)
Financial leverage and flexibility	Debt/EBITDA	10	50
	Free cash flow/Net debt	10	
	Retained cash flow/Debt	10	
	Cash and marketable securities/ Debt	10	
	EBIT/Interest	10	
Total		100	100

1   What are some reasons why Moody's may have selected these three broad factors as being important in assigning a credit rating in the aerospace and defense industry?

2   Why might financial leverage and flexibility be weighted so heavily?

Solution to 1:

Size and scale:

- Larger size can strengthen negotiating position with customers and suppliers, leading to better contract terms and potential cost savings.

- Larger scale typically indicates prior success.

- Larger scale can enhance a company's ability to manage and react to variable market conditions.

- Larger scale often indicates greater geographical, product, and customer diversification.

Business profile, revenue sustainability, and efficiency:

- A business profile that provides some protection from competition, a sustainable flow of revenues as indicated by a strong order backlog, and better operating efficiency should contribute to higher and more sustainable cash flows.

Financial leverage and flexibility:

- Strong financial policies should increase the likelihood of cash flows being sufficient to service debt.

Solution to 2:

The level of debt relative to earnings and cash flow is a critical factor in assessing creditworthiness. The higher the current level of debt, the higher the risk of default.

A point to note regarding Example 7 is that the rating factors and the metrics used to represent each can vary by industry group. For example, for heavy manufacturing (manufacturing of the capital assets used in other manufacturing and production processes), Moody's distinguishes order trends and quality as distinctive credit factors affecting future revenues, factory load, and profitability patterns.

Analyses of a company's historical and projected financial statements are an integral part of the credit evaluation process. As noted by Moody's, financial statement information is an important source of information for the rating process:

> Much of the information used in assessing performance for the sub-factors is found in or calculated using the company's financial statements; others are derived from observations or estimates by the analysts. ... Moody's ratings are forward-looking and incorporate our expectations for future financial and operating performance. We use both historical and projected financial results in the rating process. Historical results help us understand patterns and trends for a company's performance as well as for peer comparison.[10]

As noted, Moody computes a variety of ratios in assessing creditworthiness. A comparison of a company's ratios with the ratios of its peers is informative in evaluating relative creditworthiness, as demonstrated in Example 8.

EXAMPLE 8

Peer Comparison of Ratios

A credit analyst is assessing the efficiency and leverage of two aerospace companies on the basis of certain sub-factors identified by Moody's. The analyst collects the information from the companies' annual reports and calculates the following ratios:[11]

	Bombardier Inc.	BAE Systems plc
EBITDA/Average assets	7.5%	10.1%
Debt/EBITDA	3.9	3.1
Retained cash flow to debt	6.1%	13.7%
Free cash flow to net debt	−7.0%	7.7%

Based solely on the data given, which company is more likely to be assigned a higher credit rating, and why?

Solution:

The ratio comparisons are all in favor of BAE Systems plc. BAE has a higher level of EBITDA in relation to average assets, higher retained cash flow relative to debt, and higher free cash flow to net debt. BAE also has a lower level of debt relative to EBITDA. Based on the data given, therefore, BAE is likely to be assigned a higher credit rating.

Before calculating ratios such as those presented in Example 8, rating agencies make certain adjustments to reported financial statements, such as adjusting debt to include off-balance-sheet debt in a company's total debt.[12] We will describe in Section 6 some common adjustments.

---

10 Ibid., p. 7.
11 In calculating financial ratios (values not disclosed in the rating report), Moody's makes various adjustments to the financial data reported by companies in order to better reflect underlying obligations and/or to achieve greater comparability with other companies in the industry. The adjustments made in calculating ratios for this example do not necessarily correspond exactly to those calculated by Moody's.
12 Ibid., p. 6.

Financial statement analysis, especially financial ratio analysis, can also be an important tool in selecting equity investments, as discussed in the next section.

5 APPLICATION: SCREENING FOR POTENTIAL EQUITY INVESTMENTS

Ratios constructed from financial statement data and market data are often used to screen for potential equity investments. **Screening** is the application of a set of criteria to reduce a set of potential investments to a smaller set having certain desired characteristics. Criteria involving financial ratios generally involve comparing one or more ratios with some pre-specified target or cutoff values.

A security selection approach incorporating financial ratios may be applied whether the investor uses top-down analysis or bottom-up analysis. **Top-down analysis** involves identifying attractive geographical segments and/or industry segments, from which the investor chooses the most attractive investments. **Bottom-up analysis** involves selection of specific investments from all companies within a specified investment universe. Regardless of the direction, screening for potential equity investments aims to identify companies that meet specific criteria. An analysis of this type may be used as the basis for directly forming a portfolio, or it may be undertaken as a preliminary part of a more thorough analysis of potential investment targets.

Fundamental to this type of analysis are decisions about which metrics to use as screens, how many metrics to include, what values of those metrics to use as cutoff points, and what weighting to give each metric. Metrics may include not only financial ratios but also characteristics such as market capitalization or membership as a component security in a specified index. Exhibit 5 presents a hypothetical example of a simple stock screen based on the following criteria: a valuation ratio (P/E) less than a specified value, a solvency ratio measuring financial leverage (total debt/assets) not exceeding a specified value, positive net income, and dividend yield (dividends per share divided by price per share) greater than a specified value. Exhibit 5 shows the results of applying the screen in August 2010 to a set of 5,187 U.S. companies with market capitalization greater than $100 million, which compose a hypothetical equity manager's investment universe.

Exhibit 5	Example of a Stock Screen		
		Stocks Meeting Criterion	
Criterion		**Number**	**Percent of Total**
P/E <15		1,471	28.36%
Total debt/Assets ≤ 0.5		880	16.97%
Net income/Sales > 0		2,907	56.04%
Dividend yield > 0.5%		1,571	30.29%
Meeting all four criteria simultaneously		101	1.95%

Source for data: http://google.com/finance/.

Several points about the screen in Exhibit 5 are consistent with many screens used in practice:

- Some criteria serve as checks on the results from applying other criteria. In this hypothetical example, the first criterion selects stocks that appear relatively cheaply valued. The stocks might be cheap for a good reason, however, such as poor profitability or excessive financial leverage. So, the requirement for net income to be positive serves as a check on profitability, and the limitation on financial leverage serves as a check on financial risk. Of course, financial ratios or other statistics cannot generally control for exposure to certain other types of risk (e.g., risk related to regulatory developments or technological innovation).

- If all the criteria were completely independent of each other, the set of stocks meeting all four criteria would be 42, equal to 5,187 times 0.82 percent—the product of the fraction of stocks satisfying the four criteria individually (i.e., $0.2836 \times 0.1697 \times 0.5604 \times 0.3029 = 0.0082$, or 0.82 percent). As the screen illustrates, criteria are often not independent, and the result is that more securities pass the screening than if criteria were independent. In this example, 101 (or 1.95 percent) of the securities pass all four screens simultaneously. For an example of the lack of independence, we note that dividend-paying status is probably positively correlated with the ability to generate positive earnings and the value of the third criterion. If stocks that pass one test tend to also pass another, few are eliminated after the application of the second test.

- The results of screens can sometimes be relatively concentrated in a subset of the sectors represented in the benchmark. The financial leverage criterion in Exhibit 5 would exclude banking stocks, for example. What constitutes a high or low value of a measure of a financial characteristic can be sensitive to the industry in which a company operates.

Screens can be used by both **growth investors** (focused on investing in high-earnings-growth companies), **value investors** (focused on paying a relatively low share price in relation to earnings or assets per share), and **market-oriented investors** (an intermediate grouping of investors whose investment disciplines cannot be clearly categorized as value or growth). Growth screens would typically feature criteria related to earnings growth and/or momentum. Value screens, as a rule, feature criteria setting upper limits for the value of one or more valuation ratios. Market-oriented screens would not strongly emphasize valuation or growth criteria. The use of screens involving financial ratios may be most common among value investors.

Many studies have assessed the most effective items of accounting information for screening equity investments. Some research suggests that certain items of accounting information can help explain (and potentially predict) market returns (e.g., Chan et al. 1991; Lev and Thiagarajan 1993; Lakonishok et al. 1994; Davis 1994; Arbanell and Bushee 1998). Representative of such investigations is Piotroski (2000), whose screen uses nine accounting-based fundamentals that aim to identify financially strong and profitable companies among those with high book value/market value ratios. For example, the profitability measures relate to whether the company reported positive net income, positive cash flow, and an increase in return on assets (ROA).

An analyst may want to evaluate how a portfolio based on a particular screen would have performed historically. For this purpose, the analyst uses a process known as "back-testing." **Back-testing** applies the portfolio selection rules to historical data and calculates what returns would have been earned if a particular strategy had been used. The relevance of back-testing to investment success in practice, however, may be limited. Haugen and Baker (1996) described some of these limitations:

- Survivorship bias: If the database used in back-testing eliminates companies that cease to exist because of a bankruptcy or merger, then the remaining companies collectively will appear to have performed better.

- Look-ahead bias: If a database includes financial data updated for restatements (where companies have restated previously issued financial statements to correct errors or reflect changes in accounting principles),[13] then there is a mismatch between what investors would have actually known at the time of the investment decision and the information used in the back-testing.

- Data-snooping bias: If researchers build a model on the basis of previous researchers' findings, then use the same database to test that model, they are not actually testing the model's predictive ability. When each step is backward looking, the same rules may or may not produce similar results in the future. The predictive ability of the model's rules can validly be tested only by using future data. One academic study has argued that the apparent ability of value strategies to generate excess returns is largely explainable as the result of collective data snooping (Conrad, Cooper, and Kaul, 2003).

EXAMPLE 9

Ratio-Based Screening for Potential Equity Investments

Below are two alternative strategies under consideration by an investment firm:

Strategy A: Invest in stocks that are components of a global equity index, have a ROE above the median ROE of all stocks in the index, and have a P/E less than the median P/E.

Strategy B: Invest in stocks that are components of a broad-based U.S. equity index, have a ratio of price to operating cash flow in the lowest quartile of companies in the index, and have shown increases in sales for at least the past three years.

Both strategies were developed with the use of back-testing.

1 How would you characterize the two strategies?

2 What concerns might you have about using such strategies?

Solution to 1:

Strategy A appears to aim for global diversification and combines a requirement for high relative profitability with a traditional measure of value (low P/E). Strategy B focuses on both large and small companies in a single market and apparently aims to identify companies that are growing and have a lower price multiple based on cash flow from operations.

---

13 In the United States, restatements of previously issued financial statements have increased in recent years. The U.S. Government Accounting Office (2002) reported 919 restatements by 834 public companies from January 1997 to June 2002. The *Wall Street Journal* has reported that the number of restatements increased from 613 in 2004 to 1,195 in 2005 (*Wall Street Journal*, 2006).

Solution to 2:

The use of *any* approach to investment decisions depends on the objectives and risk profile of the investor. With that crucial consideration in mind, we note that ratio-based benchmarks may be an efficient way to screen for potential equity investments. In screening, however, many questions arise.

First, unintentional selections can be made if criteria are not specified carefully. For example, Strategy A might unintentionally select a loss-making company with negative shareholders' equity because negative net income divided by negative shareholders' equity arithmetically results in a positive ROE. Strategy B might unintentionally select a company with negative operating cash flow because price to operating cash flow will be negative and thus very low in the ranking. In both cases, the analyst can add additional screening criteria to avoid unintentional selections; these additional criteria could include requiring positive shareholders' equity in Strategy A and requiring positive operating cash flow in Strategy B.

Second, the inputs to ratio analysis are derived from financial statements, and companies may differ in the financial standards they apply (e.g., IFRS versus U.S. GAAP), the specific accounting method(s) they choose within those allowed by the reporting standards, and/or the estimates made in applying an accounting method.

Third, back-testing may not provide a reliable indication of future performance because of survivorship bias, look-ahead bias, or data-snooping bias. Also, as suggested by finance theory and by common sense, the past is not necessarily indicative of the future.

Fourth, implementation decisions can dramatically affect returns. For example, decisions about frequency and timing of portfolio re-evaluation and changes affect transaction costs and taxes paid out of the portfolio.

ANALYST ADJUSTMENTS TO REPORTED FINANCIALS   6

When comparing companies that use different accounting methods or estimate key accounting inputs in different ways, analysts frequently adjust a company's financials. In this section, we first provide a framework for considering potential analyst adjustments to facilitate such comparisons and then provide examples of such adjustments. In practice, required adjustments vary widely. The examples presented here are not intended to be comprehensive but, rather, to illustrate the use of adjustments to facilitate a meaningful comparison.

6.1 A Framework for Analyst Adjustments

In this discussion of potential analyst adjustments to a company's financial statements, we use a framework focused on the *balance sheet*. Because the financial statements are interrelated, however, adjustments to items reported on one statement may also be reflected in adjustments to items on another financial statement. For example, an analyst adjustment to inventory on the balance sheet affects cost of goods sold on the income statement (and thus also affects net income and, subsequently, the retained earnings account on the balance sheet).

Regardless of the particular order in which an analyst considers the items that may require adjustment for comparability, the following aspects are appropriate:

- *Importance* (*materiality*). Is an adjustment to this item likely to affect the conclusions? In other words, does it matter? For example, in an industry where companies require minimal inventory, does it matter that two companies use different inventory accounting methods?

- *Body of standards.* Is there a difference in the body of standards being used (U.S. GAAP versus IFRS)? If so, in which areas is the difference likely to affect a comparison?

- *Methods.* Is there a difference in accounting methods used by the companies being compared?

- *Estimates.* Is there a difference in important estimates used by the companies being compared?

The following sections illustrate analyst adjustments—first, those relating to the asset side of the balance sheet and then those relating to the liability side.

6.2 Analyst Adjustments Related to Investments

Accounting for investments in the debt and equity securities of other companies (other than investments accounted for under the equity method and investments in consolidated subsidiaries) depends on management's intention (i.e., whether to actively trade the securities, make them available for sale, or in the case of debt securities, hold them to maturity). When securities are classified as "financial assets measured at fair value through profit or loss" (similar to "trading" securities in U.S. GAAP), unrealized gains and losses are reported in the income statement. When securities are classified as "financial assets measured at fair value through other comprehensive income" (similar to "available-for-sale" securities in U.S. GAAP), unrealized gains and losses are not reported in the income statement and, instead, are recognized in equity. If two otherwise comparable companies have significant differences in the classification of investments, analyst adjustments may be useful to facilitate comparison.

6.3 Analyst Adjustments Related to Inventory

With inventory, adjustments may be required for different accounting methods. As described in previous readings, a company's decision about inventory method will affect the value of inventory shown on the balance sheet as well as the value of inventory that is sold (cost of goods sold). If a company not reporting under IFRS[14] uses LIFO (last-in, first-out) and another uses FIFO (first-in, first-out), comparability of the financial results of the two companies will suffer. Companies that use the LIFO method, must also, however, disclose the value of their inventory under the FIFO method. To recast inventory values for a company using LIFO reporting on a FIFO basis, the analyst adds the ending balance of the LIFO reserve to the ending value of inventory under LIFO accounting. To adjust cost of goods sold to a FIFO basis, the analyst subtracts the change in the LIFO reserve from the reported cost of goods sold under LIFO accounting. Example 10 illustrates the use of a disclosure of the value of inventory under the FIFO method to make a more consistent comparison of the current ratios of two companies reporting in different methods.

---

14 IAS No. 2 does not permit the use of LIFO.

EXAMPLE 10

Adjustment for a Company Using LIFO Accounting for Inventories

An analyst is comparing the financial performance of Carpenter Technology Corporation (NYSE: CRS), a U.S. company operating in the specialty metals industry, with the financial performance of a similar company that uses IFRS for reporting. Under IFRS, this company uses the FIFO method of inventory accounting. Therefore, the analyst must convert results to a comparable basis. Exhibit 6 provides balance sheet information on CRS.

Exhibit 6	Data for Carpenter Technology Corporation	

	30 June	
	2010	2009
Total current assets	820.2	749.7
Total current liabilities	218.1	198.5

NOTE 6. INVENTORIES

Inventories consist of the following ($ millions):

	30 June	
	2010	2009
Raw materials	$30.7	$29.5
Work in process	109.1	90.8
Finished goods	63.8	65.1
	$203.6	$185.4

If the first-in, first-out method of inventory had been used instead of the LIFO method, inventories would have been $331.8 and $305.8 million higher as of June 30, 2010 and 2009, respectively.

Source: 10-K for Carpenter Technology Corporation for the year ended 30 June 2010.

1 Based on the information in Exhibit 6, calculate CRS's current ratio under FIFO and LIFO for 2009 and 2010.

2 CRS makes the following disclosure in the risk section of its MD&A. Assuming an effective tax rate of 35 percent, estimate the impact on CRS's tax liability.

> **"We value most of our inventory using the LIFO method, which could be repealed resulting in adverse affects on our cash flows and financial condition.**
>
> The cost of our inventories is primarily determined using the Last-In First-Out ("LIFO") method. Under the LIFO inventory valuation method, changes in the cost of raw materials and production activities are recognized in cost of sales in the current period even though these materials and other costs may have been incurred at significantly different values due to the length of time of our production

cycle. Generally in a period of rising prices, LIFO recognizes higher costs of goods sold, which both reduces current income and assigns a lower value to the year-end inventory. Recent proposals have been initiated aimed at repealing the election to use the LIFO method for income tax purposes. According to these proposals, generally taxpayers that currently use the LIFO method would be required to revalue their LIFO inventory to its first-in, first-out ("FIFO") value. As of June 30, 2010, if the FIFO method of inventory had been used instead of the LIFO method, our inventories would have been about $332 million higher. This increase in inventory would result in a one time increase in taxable income which would be taken into account ratably over the first taxable year and the following several taxable years. The repeal of LIFO could result in a substantial tax liability which could adversely impact our cash flows and financial condition."

Source: 10-K for Carpenter Technology Corporation for the year ended 30 June 2010.

3   CRS reported cash flow from operations of $115.2 million for the year ended 30 June 2010. In comparison with the company's operating cash flow, how significant is the additional potential tax liability?

Solution to 1:

The calculations of CRS's current ratio (current assets divided by current liabilities) are as follows:

	2010	2009
I. Current ratio (unadjusted)		
Total current assets	$820.2	$749.7
Total current liabilities	$218.1	$198.5
Current ratio (unadjusted)	3.8	3.8
II. Current ratio (adjusted)		
Total current assets	$820.2	$749.7
Adjust inventory to FIFO, add:	331.8	305.8
Total current assets (adjusted)	$1,152	$1,056
Total current liabilities	218.1	198.5
Current ratio (adjusted)	5.3	5.3

To adjust the LIFO inventory to FIFO, add the excess amounts of FIFO cost over LIFO cost to LIFO inventory and increase current assets by an equal amount. The effect of adjusting inventory on the current ratio is to increase the current ratio from 3.8 to 5.3 in both 2009 and 2010. CRS has greater liquidity according to the adjusted current ratio.

Solution to 2:

Assuming an effective tax rate of 35 percent, we find the total increase in CRS's tax liability to be $116.1 million (0.35 × $331.8 million).

Solution to 3:

The additional tax liability would be greater than the entire amount of the company's cash flow from operations of $115.2 million; the additional tax liability would be apportioned, however, over several years.

In summary, the information disclosed by companies that use LIFO allows an analyst to calculate the value of the company's inventory as if the company were using the FIFO method. In Example 10, the portion of inventory valued under the LIFO method was a relatively small portion of total inventory; the LIFO reserve (excess of FIFO cost over LIFO) was also relatively small. If the LIFO method is used for a substantial part of a company's inventory and the LIFO reserve is large relative to reported inventory, however, the adjustment to a FIFO basis can be important for comparison of the LIFO-reporting company with a company that uses the FIFO method of inventory valuation. Example 11 illustrates a case in which such an adjustment would have a major impact on an analyst's conclusions.

EXAMPLE 11

Analyst Adjustment to Inventory Value for Comparability in a Current Ratio Comparison

Company A reports under IFRS and uses the FIFO method of inventory accounting. Company B reports under U.S. GAAP and uses the LIFO method. Exhibit 7 gives data pertaining to current assets, LIFO reserves, and current liabilities of these companies.

Exhibit 7	Data for Companies Accounting for Inventory on Different Bases	
	Company A (FIFO)	Company B (LIFO)
Current assets (includes inventory)	$ 300,000	$ 80,000
LIFO reserve	NA	$ 20,000
Current liabilities	$ 150,000	$ 45,000

NA = not applicable.

Based on the data given in Exhibit 7, compare the liquidity of the two companies as measured by the current ratio.

Solution:

Company A's current ratio is 2.0. Based on unadjusted balance sheet data, Company B's current ratio is 1.78. Company A's higher current ratio indicates that Company A appears to be more liquid than Company B; however, the use of unadjusted data for Company B is not appropriate for making comparisons with Company A.

After adjusting Company B's inventory to a comparable basis (i.e., to a FIFO basis), the conclusion changes. The following table summarizes the results when Company B's inventory is left on a LIFO basis and when it is placed on a FIFO basis for comparability with Company A.

	Company A (FIFO)	Company B Unadjusted (LIFO basis)	Company B Adjusted (FIFO basis)
Current assets (includes inventory)	$ 300,000	$ 80,000	$ 100,000
Current liabilities	$ 150,000	$ 45,000	$ 45,000
Current ratio	2.00	1.78	2.22

When both companies' inventories are stated on a FIFO basis, Company B appears to be the more liquid, as indicated by its current ratio of 2.22 versus Company A's ratio of 2.00.

The adjustment to place Company B's inventory on a FIFO basis was significant because Company B was assumed to use LIFO for its entire inventory and its inventory reserve was $20,000/$80,000 = 0.25, or 25 percent of its reported inventory.

As mentioned earlier, an analyst can also adjust the cost of goods sold for a company using LIFO to a FIFO basis by subtracting the change in the amount of the LIFO reserve from cost of goods sold. Such an adjustment would be appropriate for making profitability comparisons with a company reporting on a FIFO basis and is important to make when the impact of the adjustment would be material.

6.4 Analyst Adjustments Related to Property, Plant, and Equipment

Management generally has considerable discretion in determination of depreciation expense. Depreciation expense affects the values of reported net income and reported net fixed assets. Analysts often consider management's choices related to depreciation as a qualitative factor in evaluating the quality of a company's financial reporting, and in some cases, analysts may adjust reported depreciation expense for a specific analytical purpose.

The amount of depreciation expense depends on both the accounting method and the estimates used in the calculations. Companies can use the straight-line method, an accelerated method, or a usage method to depreciate fixed assets (other than land). The straight-line method reports an equal amount of depreciation expense each period, and the expense is computed as the depreciable cost divided by the estimated useful life of the asset (when acquired, an asset's depreciable cost is calculated as its total cost minus its estimated salvage value). Accelerated methods depreciate the asset more quickly; they apportion a greater amount of the depreciable cost to depreciation expense in the earlier periods. Usage-based methods depreciate an asset in proportion to its usage. In addition to selecting a depreciation method, companies must estimate an asset's salvage value and useful life to compute depreciation.

Disclosures required for depreciation often do not facilitate specific adjustments, so comparisons of companies concerning their decisions in depreciating assets are often qualitative and general. The accounts that are associated with depreciation include the balance sheet accounts for gross property, plant, and equipment (PPE) and accumulated depreciation; the income statement amount for depreciation expense; and the statement of cash flows disclosure of capital expenditure (capex) and asset disposals. The relationships among these items can reveal various pieces of information. Note, however, that PPE typically includes a mix of assets with different depreciable lives and salvage values, so the items in the following list reflect general relationships in the total pool of assets.

- Accumulated depreciation divided by gross PPE, from the balance sheet, suggests how much of the useful life of the company's overall asset base has passed.

- Accumulated depreciation divided by depreciation expense suggests how many years' worth of depreciation expense have already been recognized (i.e., the average age of the asset base).

- Net PPE (net of accumulated depreciation) divided by depreciation expense is an approximate indicator of how many years of useful life remain for the company's overall asset base.

- Gross PPE divided by depreciation expense suggests the average life of the assets at installation.

- Capex divided by the sum of gross PPE plus capex can suggest what percentage of the asset base is being renewed through new capital investment.

- Capex in relation to asset disposal provides information on growth of the asset base.

As Example 12 shows, these relationships can be evaluated for companies in an industry to suggest differences in their strategies for asset utilization or areas for further investigation.

EXAMPLE 12

Differences in Depreciation

An analyst is evaluating the financial statements of two companies in the same industry. The companies have similar strategies with respect to the use of equipment in manufacturing their products. The following information is provided (amounts in millions):

	Company A	Company B
Net PPE	$1,200	$750
Depreciation expense	$120	$50

1 Based on the information given, estimate the average remaining useful lives of the asset bases of Company A and Company B.

2 Suppose that, based on a physical inspection of the companies' plants and other industry information, the analyst believes that the actual remaining useful lives of Company A's and Company B's assets are roughly equal at 10 years. Based only on the facts given, what might the analyst conclude about Company B's reported net income?

Solution to 1:

The estimated average remaining useful life of Company A's asset base is 10 years (calculated as net PPE divided by depreciation expense, or $1,200/$120 = 10 years). For Company B, the average remaining useful life of the asset base appears to be far longer, 15 years ($750/$50).

> **Solution to 2:**
>
> If 10 years were used to calculate Company B's depreciation expense, the expense would be $75 million (i.e., $25 million higher than reported) and higher depreciation expense would decrease net income. The analyst might conclude that Company B's reported net income reflects relatively more aggressive accounting estimates than estimates reflected in Company A's reported net income.

6.5 Analyst Adjustments Related to Goodwill

Goodwill arises when one company purchases another for a price that exceeds the fair value of the net identifiable assets acquired. Net identifiable assets include current assets, fixed assets, and certain intangible assets that have value and meet recognition criteria under accounting standards. A broad range of intangible assets might require valuation in the context of a business combination—for example, brands, technology, and customer lists. Goodwill is recorded as an asset and essentially represents the difference between the purchase price and the net identifiable assets. For example, assume ParentCo purchases TargetCo for a purchase price of $400 million and the fair value of TargetCo's identifiable assets is $300 million (which includes the fair values of current assets, fixed assets, and a recognized brand). ParentCo will record total assets of $400 million consisting of $300 million in identifiable assets (including the fair value of the brand) and $100 million of goodwill. The goodwill is tested annually for impairment and if the value of the goodwill is determined to be impaired, ParentCo will then reduce the amount of the asset and report a write-off resulting from impairment.

One of the conceptual difficulties with goodwill arises in comparative financial statement analysis. Consider, for example, two hypothetical U.S. companies, one of which has grown by making an acquisition and the other of which has grown internally. Assume that the economic value of the two companies is identical: Each has an identically valuable branded product, well-trained workforce, and proprietary technology. The company that has grown by acquisition will have recorded the transaction to acquire the target company and its underlying net assets on the basis of the total consideration paid for the acquisition. The company that has grown internally will have done so by incurring expenditures for advertising, staff training, and research, all of which are expensed as incurred under U.S. GAAP. Given the immediate expensing, the value of the internally generated assets is not capitalized onto the balance sheet and is thus not directly reflected on the company's balance sheet (revenues, income, and cash flows should reflect the benefits derived from the investment in the intangible assets). Ratios based on asset values and/or income, including profitability ratios (such as ROA) and market value to book value (MV/BV),[15] will generally differ for the two companies because of differences in the accounting values of assets and income related to acquired intangibles and goodwill, although, by assumption, the economic value of the companies is identical.

EXAMPLE 13

Ratio Comparisons for Goodwill

Miano Marseglia is an analyst who is evaluating the relative valuation of two securities brokerage companies: TD Ameritrade Holding Corporation (NasdaqGS: AMTD) and the Charles Schwab Corporation (NYSE: SCHW). As one part of

15 MV/BV equals the total market value of the stock (the market capitalization) divided by total stockholders' equity. It is also referred to as the price-to-book ratio because it can also be calculated as price per share divided by stockholders' equity per share.

an overall analysis, Marseglia would like to see how the two companies compare with each other and with the industry based on market value to book value. Because both companies are large players in the industry, Marseglia expects them to sell at a higher MV/BV than the industry median of 1.2. He collects the following data on the two companies.

	SCHW	AMTD
Market capitalization on January 2010 (market price per share times the number of shares outstanding)	$21,871	$11,525
Total shareholders' equity as of most recent quarter	$5,073	$3,551
Goodwill	$528	$2,472
Other intangible assets	$23	$1,225

Marseglia computes the MV/BV for the companies as follows:

SCHW $21,871/$5,073 = 4.3

AMTD $11,525/$3,551 = 3.2

As expected, each company appears to be selling at a premium to the industry average MV/BV of 1.2. The companies have similar MV/BVs (i.e., they are somewhat equally valued relative to the book value of shareholders' equity), but based solely on MV/BV, AMTD appears to be a better value. Marseglia is concerned, however, because he notes that AMTD has significant amounts of goodwill and acquired intangible assets. He wonders what the relative value would be if the MV/BV were computed after adjusting book value, first, to remove goodwill and, second, to remove all intangible assets. Book value reduced by all intangible assets (including goodwill) is known as "tangible book value." The median price/tangible book value for the industry is 1.3.

1 Compute the MV/BV adjusted for goodwill and the price/tangible book value for each company.

2 Which company appears to be a better value based *solely* on this data? (Note that the MV/BV is only one part of a broader analysis. Much more evidence related to the valuations and the comparability of the companies would be required to reach a conclusion about whether one company is a better value.)

Solution to 1:

	($ millions)	
	SCHW	AMTD
Total stockholders' equity	$5,073	$3,551
Less: Goodwill	$528	$2,472
Book value, adjusted	$4,545	$1,079
Adjusted MV/BV	**4.8**	**10.7**

	($ millions)	
	SCHW	**AMTD**
Total stockholders' equity	$5,073	$3,551
Less: Goodwill	$528	$2,472
Less: Other intangible assets	$23	$1,225
Tangible book value	$4,522	($146)
MV/tangible book value	**4.8**	**NM**

NM = not meaningful.

Solution to 2:

After adjusting for goodwill, SCHW appears to be selling for a lower price relative to book value than does AMTD (4.8 versus 10.7). Both companies are selling at a premium to the industry, particularly AMTD, after adjusting for goodwill.

SCHW is also selling for a higher multiple than the industry (4.8 versus 1.3) based on price/tangible book value. AMTD has a negative tangible book value and, therefore, its price/tangible book value is not meaningful. Based on this interpretation and based on *solely* on this information, Marseglia would conclude that AMTD is relatively more expensive than SCHW.

6.6 Analyst Adjustments Related to Off-Balance-Sheet Financing

A number of business activities give rise to obligations that, although they are economically liabilities of a company, are not required to be reported on a company's balance sheet. Including such off-balance-sheet obligations in a company's liabilities can affect ratios and conclusions based on such ratios. In this section, we describe adjustments to financial statements related to one type of off-balance-sheet obligation, the operating lease. (Note that revised leasing standards proposed in 2011 eliminate the existing operating lease distinction; if implemented, these standards are likely to change or even eliminate adjustments required for operating leases.)

The rights of a lessee (the party that is leasing some asset) may be similar to the rights of an owner, but if the terms of the lease can be structured so it can be accounted for as an operating lease, the lease is treated like a rental contract and neither the leased asset nor the associated liability is reported on the balance sheet.[16] The lessee simply records the periodic lease payment as a rental expense in its income statement. In contrast, when a company actually owns an asset, the asset is shown on the balance sheet, together with any corresponding liability, such as financing for the asset. Similarly, if a lease is accounted for as a capital lease—essentially equivalent to ownership—the leased asset and associated liability appear on the lessee's balance sheet.

---

16 A lessee classifies a lease as an operating lease if certain guidelines concerning the term of the lease, the present value of the lease payments, and the ownership of the asset at the end of the lease term are satisfied. Under U.S. GAAP, FASB ASC 840-10-25 (Leases: Overall–Recognition)] specifies the criteria for classification.

What is of concern to analysts is when a lease conveys to the lessee most of the benefits and risks of ownership but the lease is accounted for as an operating lease—giving rise to off-balance-sheet financing. International accounting standard setters have stated that the entities should not avoid balance sheet recording of leases through artificial leasing structures.

A 2005 report by the U.S. SEC on off-balance-sheet financing estimates that more than 63 percent of companies in the United States report having an operating lease. The SEC estimate of total future lease payments under operating leases was $1.2 trillion over the remaining terms of the leases.

Because companies are required to disclose in their financial statements the amount and timing of lease payments, an analyst can use this information to answer the question: How would a company's financial position look if operating lease obligations were included in its total liabilities?

Exhibit 8 presents selected items from the balance sheet of AMR Corporation (the parent of American Airlines) and the text of the footnote from the financial statements about the company's leases. We use the information in this exhibit to illustrate analyst adjustments.

Exhibit 8	Lease Arrangements of AMR Corporation (NYSE: AMR) Selected Items from Balance Sheet ($ millions)	

	31 December	
	2009	**2008**
Total Assets	$25,438	$25,175
Current maturities of long-term debt	$1,024	$1,845
Long-term debt, less current maturities	9,984	8,423
Total long-term debt	11,008	10,268
Current obligations under capital leases	90	107
Obligations under capital leases, less current obligations	599	582
Total long-term debt and capital leases	$11,697	$10,957

From Footnote 5. Leases

AMR's subsidiaries lease various types of equipment and property, primarily aircraft and airport facilities. The future minimum lease payments required under capital leases, together with the present value of such payments, and future minimum lease payments required under operating leases that have initial or remaining non-cancelable lease terms in excess of one year as of December 31, 2009, were (in millions):

Year Ending December 31,	Capital Leases	Operating Leases
2010	$181	$1,057
2011	184	1,032
2012	134	848
2013	119	755
2014	98	614

(continued)

Exhibit 8	(Continued)	
Year Ending December 31,	**Capital Leases**	**Operating Leases**
2015 and thereafter	436	5,021
	$1,152	$9,327 [1]
Less amount representing interest	463	
Present value of net minimum lease payments	$689	

(1) As of December 31, 2009, included in Accrued liabilities and Other liabilities and deferred credits on the accompanying consolidated balance sheet is approximately $1.2 billion relating to rent expense being recorded in advance of future operating lease payments.
Source: AMR Corporation's Form 10-K for period ending 31 December 2009.

To evaluate the company's solvency, we can calculate the debt-to-assets ratio, defined as the ratio of total debt to total assets. When we include obligations under capital leases (amounting to $689 million in 2009), the debt-to-assets ratio for 2009 is 46.0 percent (total long-term debt/total assets = $11,697/$25,438). The company's footnote on leases discloses a total of $9.3 billion of future payments for operating leases on an undiscounted basis. The footnote also indicates that of this amount, only $1.2 billion is shown on the balance sheet. To determine the impact of including operating lease obligations in total liabilities, we can calculate the present value of the future operating lease payments. Calculating the present value of these payments requires a discount rate. We can estimate an appropriate discount rate from the information about the present value of the capital lease payments. Using the present value of the capital lease payments and the schedule of future payments, we can calculate the internal rate of return (i.e., the return that results in the discounted future payments equaling the present value). The internal rate of return from the capital lease information can then be used as the discount rate to estimate the present value of the series of operating lease payments.

For AMR, the present value of the capital lease payments is $689 million. Exhibit 9 shows different assumed streams of payments based on the information given in the footnote and illustrates the sensitivity of the analysis to assumptions about the timing of cash flows. Each assumed stream results in a different implied discount rate on the lease or internal rate of return to the lease. Using the stream of payments shown in the footnote and assuming that all of the $436 million payments indicated for 2015 and thereafter are made in the year 2015 results in an internal rate of return of 15.04 percent. Based on the schedule of payments shown, a more reasonable assumption, however, is that the $436 million payments do not all occur in a single year. One approach to estimating the timing of these payments is to assume that the payments in 2015 and subsequent years equal the average annual payments in years 2010–2014 of $143 = ($181 + $184 + $134 + $119 + $98)/5. Using this approach, we assume payments in 2015 and the following three years that total the amount shown in the footnote for 2015and the internal rate of return of the capital lease is 13.90 percent. Given that lease payments have been generally declining over 2010–2015, another approach is to assume that the amount of the lease payment after 2015 remains constant in subsequent years at an amount equal to the payment in 2014 until the total amount shown in the note for 2015 is reached. Using this assumption, we find the internal rate of return of the capital lease payments is 13.24 percent.[17]

Exhibit 9	Present Value of Operating Lease Payments Using a Discount Rate Derived from Present Value of Capital Lease Payments ($ millions)				
	Capital Lease			**Operating Lease**	
	Payments (as given in footnote)	**Payments Including Estimated Annual Payments for 2015 and Thereafter (Through 2018)**	**Payments Including Estimated Annual Payments for 2015 and Thereafter (Through 2019)**	**Payments As Given**	**Payments Including Estimated Annual Payments for 2015 and Thereafter**
Present value, *given*	($689)	($689)	($689)		
2010	$181	$181	$181	$1,065	$1,065
2011	$184	$184	$184	$1,039	$1,039
2012	$134	$134	$134	$973	$973
2013	$119	$119	$119	$872	$872
2014	$98	$98	$98	$815	$815
2015 and thereafter	$436	$143	$98	$7,453	$815
		$143	$98		$815
		$143	$98		$815
		$7	$98		$815
			$44		$815
					$815
					$815
					$815
					$815
					$118
Internal rate of return	15.04%	13.90%	13.24%		
Present value of operating lease payments with 15.04% discount rate					$5,193

(continued)

---

17 If the term structure of the capital and operating leases can be assumed to be similar, an alternative, shortcut, way to estimate the present value of future operating lease payments that do not appear on the balance sheet is to assume that the relationship between the discounted and undiscounted operating lease payments is approximately the same as the relationship between the discounted and undiscounted capital lease payments. The discounted capital lease payments of $689 million as reported on the balance sheet are 64.9 percent of the undiscounted noncurrent capital lease payments of $1,062 million ($1,152 million total minus $90 million current liabilities). Applying the same relationship to operating lease payments, we find that 64.9 percent of the undiscounted noncurrent operating lease payments of $8,127 million ($9,327 million total minus $1,200 million current) equals $5.3 billion, close to the estimate of the present value of future operating lease payments given in Exhibit 9 with a discount rate of 13.90 percent.

| Exhibit 9 | (Continued) |
| | | | | |

	Capital Lease			Operating Lease	
	Payments (as given in footnote)	**Payments Including Estimated Annual Payments for 2015 and Thereafter (Through 2018)**	**Payments Including Estimated Annual Payments for 2015 and Thereafter (Through 2019)**	**Payments As Given**	**Payments Including Estimated Annual Payments for 2015 and Thereafter**
Present value of operating lease payments with 13.90% discount rate					$5,466
Present value of operating lease payments with 13.24% discount rate					$5,632

We developed discount rate estimates of 13.90 percent and 13.24 percent. Using a discount rate of 13.90 percent, the present value of future operating lease payments would be roughly $5.5 billion, and using a discount rate of 13.24 percent, the present value would be around $5.6 billion. Because $1.2 billion of the amounts related to operating leases already appear on the balance sheet (as disclosed in the company's lease footnote), the value of the future operating lease payments that do not appear on the balance sheet are estimated to be in the range of $5,466 million – $1,200 million = $4,266 million to $5,632 million – $1,200 million = $4,432 million. The lower the assumed discount rate, the higher the present value of the lease payments.

We now add the present value of the off-balance-sheet future operating lease payments to the company's total assets and total debt. Making this adjustment increases the debt-to-assets ratio to an amount between ($11,697 + $4,266)/($25,438 + $4,266) = 67.5 percent and ($11,697 + $4,432)/($25,438 + $4,432) = 68.1 percent. The discount rates implied by the company's capital lease structure are significantly higher, however, than yields on investment-grade bonds as of the date of the example; therefore, an analyst might choose to examine the sensitivity of the lease obligation to alternative discount rates.

EXAMPLE 14

Analyst Adjustment to Debt for Operating Lease Payments

An analyst is evaluating the capital structure of two (hypothetical) companies, Koller Semiconductor and MacRae Manufacturing, as of the beginning of 2010. Koller Semiconductor makes somewhat less use of operating leases than MacRae Manufacturing. The analyst has the additional information in Exhibit 10.

Exhibit 10		
	Koller Semiconductor	**MacRae Manufacturing**
Total debt	$1,200	$2,400
Total equity	$2,000	$4,000

Exhibit 10   (Continued)

	Koller Semiconductor	MacRae Manufacturing
Average interest rate on debt	10%	8%
Lease payments on operating leases:		
2010	10	90
2011	18	105
2012	22	115
2013	25	128
2014 and thereafter	75	384

Based on the information given in Exhibit 10 and assuming no adjustment to equity, discuss how adjusting for operating leases affects the companies' solvency on the basis of debt/debt-plus-equity. (Assume payments after 2013 occur at the same rate as for 2013. For example, for Koller Semiconductor, the payments for 2014 through 2016 would be assumed to be $25 each year.)

Solution:

Before the adjustment is made, the companies' debt/debt-plus-equity are identical, both at 37.5 percent. To make the adjustment for operating leases, the first step is to calculate the present value of the operating lease payments. Assuming that payments after 2013 occur at the same rate as for 2013, the analyst finds Koller's payment would be $25 in 2014, 2015, and 2016. The present value of $25 discounted for five years at 10 percent is $15.52. MacRae's payment is assumed to be $128 in each of 2014, 2015, and 2016. The present value of $128 discounted for five years at 8 percent is $87.11. Calculations for 2015 and 2016 are made in the same manner, resulting in the present values shown in Exhibit 11.

Exhibit 11

	Koller Semiconductor	MacRae Manufacturing
2010	$9.09	$83.33
2011	$14.88	$90.02
2012	$16.53	$91.29
2013	$17.08	$94.08
2014	$15.52	$87.11
2015	$14.11	$80.66
2016	$12.83	$74.69
Total present value	$100.04	$601.18

After the present value of capitalized lease obligations is added to total debt, MacRae Manufacturing's debt/debt-plus-equity is significantly higher, at 42.9 percent, than the debt/debt-plus-equity of Koller Semiconductor, as shown in Exhibit 12. The higher ratio reflects the impact of lease obligations on MacRae's solvency, as measured by debt/debt-plus-equity.

Exhibit 12

| | Koller Semiconductor | | MacRae Manufacturing | |
	Before Capitalizing	After Capitalizing	Before Capitalizing	After Capitalizing
Total debt	$1,200	$1,300	$2,400	$3,001
Total equity	$2,000	$2,000	$4,000	$4,000
Debt/(Debt + Equity)	37.5%	39.4%	37.5%	42.9%

The adjustment for operating leases essentially treats the transaction as if the asset subject to the operating lease had been purchased rather than leased. The present value of the capitalized lease obligations is the amount owed and the amount at which the asset is valued. Further adjustments reflect the reduction of rent expenses (if the asset is owned, rent would not be paid), the related interest expense on the amount owed, and a depreciation expense for the asset. The reduction of rent expense can be estimated as the average of two years of rent expense. Interest expense is estimated as the interest rate times the present value of the lease payments. Depreciation is estimated on a straight-line basis for the number of years of future lease payments.

EXAMPLE 15

Effect on Coverage Ratio for Operating Lease Adjustment

The analyst is also evaluating the interest coverage ratio of the companies in the previous example, Koller Semiconductor and MacRae Manufacturing.

	Koller Semiconductor	MacRae Manufacturing
EBIT before adjustment	$850	$1,350
Interest expense before adjustment	$120	$192

The prior-year (2009) rent expense was $11 for Koller Semiconductor and $90 for MacRae Manufacturing.

Using the information in Example 14 and the additional information given here, discuss how adjustment for operating leases affects the companies' solvency as measured by their coverage ratios.

Solution:

Interest coverage is calculated as EBIT divided by interest. For the adjustments, rent expense is the average of two years of rent. For Koller Semiconductor, rent expense is calculated as ($11 + $10)/2. The cost of interest on lease obligations is estimated as the interest rate multiplied by the present value of the lease payments. For Koller Semiconductor, this interest expense is calculated as 10% × $100.04, and for MacRae Manufacturing, it is calculated as 8% × $601.18. Depreciation is estimated on a straight-line basis by dividing the present value of lease payments by the number of years of lease payments (seven years). After the adjustment, both companies show a decline in interest coverage ratio, reflecting the increased obligation associated with the operating leases. Also the apparent difference in the coverage between the two companies is larger than it was in Example 12.

Exhibit 13

	Koller Semiconductor	MacRae Manufacturing
Interest coverage before adjustment	7.1	7.0
EBIT before adjustment	$850.0	$1,350.0
Rent expense (an add-back to EBIT)	10.5	90.0
Depreciation (a deduction from EBIT)	(14.3)	(85.9)
EBIT after adjustment	$846.2	$1354.1
Interest expense before adjustment	$120.0	$192.0
Assumed cost of interest on lease obligation (to add to interest)	10.0	48.1
Interest expense after adjustment	$130.0	$240.1
Interest coverage after adjustment	6.5	5.6

In summary, adjusting a company's financial statements to include amounts of lease payments provides a more complete picture of the company's financial condition and enables the comparison of companies with varying arrangements for financing assets. The analyst may also need to adjust for amounts associated with other off-balance-sheet financing arrangements.

SUMMARY

This reading described selected applications of financial statement analysis, including the evaluation of past financial performance, the projection of future financial performance, the assessment of credit risk, and the screening of potential equity investments. In addition, the reading introduced analyst adjustments to reported financials. In all cases, the analyst needs to have a good understanding of the financial reporting standards under which the financial statements were prepared. Because standards evolve over time, analysts must stay current in order to make good investment decisions.

The main points in the reading are as follows:

■ Evaluating a company's historical performance addresses not only what happened but also the causes behind the company's performance and how the performance reflects the company's strategy.

■ The projection of a company's future net income and cash flow often begins with a top-down sales forecast in which the analyst forecasts industry sales and the company's market share. By projecting profit margins or expenses and the level of investment in working and fixed capital needed to support projected sales, the analyst can forecast net income and cash flow.

■ Projections of future performance are needed for discounted cash flow valuation of equity and are often needed in credit analysis to assess a borrower's ability to repay interest and principal of a debt obligation.

■ Credit analysis uses financial statement analysis to evaluate credit-relevant factors, including tolerance for leverage, operational stability, and margin stability.

■ When ratios constructed from financial statement data and market data are used to screen for potential equity investments, fundamental decisions include which metrics to use as screens, how many metrics to include, what values of those metrics to use as cutoff points, and what weighting to give each metric.

■ Analyst adjustments to a company's reported financial statements are sometimes necessary (e.g., when comparing companies that use different accounting methods or assumptions). Adjustments include those related to investments; inventory; property, plant, and equipment; goodwill; and off-balance-sheet financing.

REFERENCES

Abarbanell, J.S., and B.J. Bushee. 1998. "Abnormal Returns to a Fundamental Analysis Strategy." *Accounting Review*, vol. 73, no. 1:19–46.

Benninga, Simon Z., and Oded H. Sarig. 1997. *Corporate Finance: A Valuation Approach.* New York: McGraw-Hill Publishing.

Chan, L.K.C., Y. Hamao, and J. Lakonishok. 1991. "Fundamentals and Stock Returns in Japan." *Journal of Finance*, vol. 46, no. 5:1739–1764. doi:10.2307/2328571

Conrad, J., M. Cooper, and G. Kaul. 2003. "Value versus Glamour." *Journal of Finance*, vol. 58, no. 5:1969–1996.

Davis, J. L. 1994. "The Cross-Section of Realized Stock Returns: The Pre-COMPUSTAT Evidence." *Journal of Finance*, vol. 49, no. 5:1579–1593.

Haugen, R.A., and N.L. Baker. 1996. "Commonality in the Determinants of Expected Stock Returns." *Journal of Financial Economics*, vol. 41, no. 3:401–439.

Henry, Elaine, Stephen Lin, and Yang Ya-wen. 2009. "The European-U.S. 'GAAP Gap': IFRS to U.S. GAAP Form 20-F Reconciliations." *Accounting Horizons*, vol. 23, no. 2:121–150.

Lakonishok, J., A. Shleifer, and R.W. Vishny. 1994. "Contrarian Investment, Extrapolation and Risk." *Journal of Finance*, vol. 49, no. 5:1541–1578.

Lev, B., and S.R. Thiagarajan. 1993. "Fundamental Information Analysis." *Journal of Accounting Research*, vol. 31, no. 2:190–215.

Pinto, Jerald E., Elaine Henry, Thomas R. Robinson, and John D. Stowe. 2010. *Equity Asset Valuation*, 2nd edition. Hoboken, NJ: John Wiley & Sons.

Piotroski, J.D. 2000. "Value Investing: The Use of Historical Financial Statement Information to Separate Winners from Losers." *Journal of Accounting Research*, vol. 38, Supplement:1–41.

Pownall, G., and K. Schipper. 1999. "Implications of Accounting Research for the SEC's Consideration of International Accounting Standards for U.S. Securities Offerings." *Accounting Horizons*, vol. 13, no. 3:259–280.

PRACTICE PROBLEMS

1 Projecting profit margins into the future on the basis of past results would be *most* reliable when the company:

   A is in the commodities business.

   B operates in a single business segment.

   C is a large, diversified company operating in mature industries.

2 Galambos Corporation had an average receivables collection period of 19 days in 2003. Galambos has stated that it wants to decrease its collection period in 2004 to match the industry average of 15 days. Credit sales in 2003 were $300 million, and analysts expect credit sales to increase to $400 million in 2004. To achieve the company's goal of decreasing the collection period, the change in the average accounts receivable balance from 2003 to 2004 that must occur is *closest* to:

   A −$420,000.

   B $420,000.

   C $836,000.

3 Credit analysts are likely to consider which of the following in making a rating recommendation?

   A Business risk but not financial risk

   B Financial risk but not business risk

   C Both business risk and financial risk

4 When screening for potential equity investments based on return on equity, to control risk, an analyst would be *most likely* to include a criterion that requires:

   A positive net income.

   B negative net income.

   C negative shareholders' equity.

5 One concern when screening for stocks with low price-to-earnings ratios is that companies with low P/Es may be financially weak. What criterion might an analyst include to avoid inadvertently selecting weak companies?

   A Net income less than zero

   B Debt-to-total assets ratio below a certain cutoff point

   C Current-year sales growth lower than prior-year sales growth

6 When a database eliminates companies that cease to exist because of a merger or bankruptcy, this can result in:

   A look-ahead bias.

   B back-testing bias.

   C survivorship bias.

7 In a comprehensive financial analysis, financial statements should be:

   A used as reported without adjustment.

   B adjusted after completing ratio analysis.

   C adjusted for differences in accounting standards, such as international financial reporting standards and U.S. generally accepted accounting principles.

8   When comparing financial statements prepared under IFRS with those pre-
    pared under U.S. GAAP, analysts may need to make adjustments related to:

    A   realized losses.

    B   unrealized gains and losses for trading securities.

    C   unrealized gains and losses for available-for-sale securities.

9   When comparing a U.S. company that uses the last in, first out (LIFO) method
    of inventory with companies that prepare their financial statements under
    international financial reporting standards (IFRS), analysts should be aware that
    according to IFRS, the LIFO method of inventory:

    A   is never acceptable.

    B   is always acceptable.

    C   is acceptable when applied to finished goods inventory only.

10 An analyst is evaluating the balance sheet of a U.S. company that uses last in,
    first out (LIFO) accounting for inventory. The analyst collects the following
    data:

	31 Dec 05	31 Dec 06
Inventory reported on balance sheet	$500,000	$600,000
LIFO reserve	$ 50,000	$70,000
Average tax rate	30%	30%

    After adjusting the amounts to convert to the first in, first out (FIFO) method,
    inventory at 31 December 2006 would be closest to:

    A $600,000.

    B $620,000.

    C $670,000.

11 An analyst gathered the following data for a company ($ millions):

	31 Dec 2000	31 Dec 2001
Gross investment in fixed assets	$2.8	$2.8
Accumulated depreciation	$1.2	$1.6

    The average age and average depreciable life of the company's fixed assets at the
    end of 2001 are *closest* to:

	Average Age	**Average Depreciable Life**
A	1.75 years	7 years
B	1.75 years	14 years
C	4.00 years	7 years

12 To compute tangible book value, an analyst would

    A   add goodwill to stockholders' equity.

    B   add all intangible assets to stockholders' equity.

    C   subtract all intangible assets from stockholders' equity.

13 Which of the following is an off-balance-sheet financing technique? The use of

  A capital leases.

  B operating leases.

  C the last in, first out inventory method.

14 To better evaluate the solvency of a company, an analyst would most likely add to total liabilities

  A the present value of future capital lease payments.

  B the total amount of future operating lease payments.

  C the present value of future operating lease payments.

SOLUTIONS

1 C is correct. For a large, diversified company, margin changes in different business segments may offset each other. Furthermore, margins are most likely to be stable in mature industries.

2 C is correct. Accounts receivable turnover is equal to 365/19 (collection period in days) = 19.2 for 2003 and needs to equal 365/15 = 24.3 in 2004 for Galambos to meet its goal. Sales/turnover equals the accounts receivable balance. For 2003, $300,000,000/19.2 = $15,625,000, and for 2004, $400,000,000/24.3 = $16,460,905. The difference of $835,905 is the increase in receivables needed for Galambos to achieve its goal.

3 C is correct. Credit analysts consider both business risk and financial risk.

4 A is correct. Requiring that net income be positive would eliminate companies that report a positive return on equity only because both net income and shareholders' equity are negative.

5 B is correct. A lower value of debt/total assets indicates greater financial strength. Requiring that a company's debt/total assets be below a certain cutoff point would allow the analyst to screen out highly leveraged and, therefore, potentially financially weak companies.

6 C is correct. Survivorship bias exists when companies that merge or go bankrupt are dropped from the database and only surviving companies remain. Look-ahead bias involves using updated financial information in back-testing that would not have been available at the time the decision was made. Back-testing involves testing models in prior periods and is not, itself, a bias.

7 C is correct. Financial statements should be adjusted for differences in accounting standards (as well as accounting and operating choices). These adjustments should be made prior to common-size and ratio analysis.

8 C is correct. IFRS makes a distinction between unrealized gains and losses on available-for-sale debt securities that arise as a result of exchange rate movements and requires these changes in value to be recognized in the income statement, whereas U.S. GAAP does not make this distinction.

9 A is correct. LIFO is not permitted under IFRS.

10 C is correct. To convert LIFO inventory to FIFO inventory, the entire LIFO reserve must be added back: $600,000 + $70,000 = $670,000.

11 C is correct. The company made no additions to or deletions from the fixed asset account during the year, so depreciation expense is equal to the difference in accumulated depreciation at the beginning of the year and the end of the year, or $0.4 million. Average age is equal to accumulated depreciation/depreciation expense, or $1.6/$0.4 = 4 years. Average depreciable life is equal to ending gross investment/depreciation expense = $2.8/$0.4 = 7 years.

12 C is correct. Tangible book value removes all intangible assets, including goodwill, from the balance sheet.

13 B is correct. Operating leases can be used as an off-balance-sheet financing technique because neither the asset nor liability appears on the balance sheet. Inventory and capital leases are reported on the balance sheet.

14 C is correct. The present value of future operating lease payments would be added to total assets and total liabilities.

Glossary

A priori probability   A probability based on logical analysis rather than on observation or personal judgment.

Abnormal profit   Equal to accounting profit less the implicit opportunity costs not included in total accounting costs; the difference between total revenue (TR) and total cost (TC).

Abnormal return   The amount by which a security's actual return differs from its expected return, given the security's risk and the market's return.

Absolute advantage   A country's ability to produce a good or service at a lower absolute cost than its trading partner.

Absolute dispersion   The amount of variability present without comparison to any reference point or benchmark.

Absolute frequency   The number of observations in a given interval (for grouped data).

Accelerated book build   An offering of securities by an investment bank acting as principal that is accomplished in only one or two days.

Accelerated methods   Depreciation methods that allocate a relatively large proportion of the cost of an asset to the early years of the asset's useful life.

Account   With the accounting systems, a formal record of increases and decreases in a specific asset, liability, component of owners' equity, revenue, or expense.

Accounting (or explicit) costs   Payments to non-owner parties for services or resources they supply to the firm.

Accounting loss   When accounting profit is negative.

Accounting profit   Income as reported on the income statement, in accordance with prevailing accounting standards, before the provisions for income tax expense. Also called *income before taxes* or *pretax income*.

Accounts payable   Amounts that a business owes to its vendors for goods and services that were purchased from them but which have not yet been paid.

Accounts receivable   Amounts customers owe the company for products that have been sold as well as amounts that may be due from suppliers (such as for returns of merchandise). Also called *commercial receivables* or *trade receivables*.

Accounts receivable turnover   Ratio of sales on credit to the average balance in accounts receivable.

Accrued expenses   Liabilities related to expenses that have been incurred but not yet paid as of the end of an accounting period—an example of an accrued expense is rent that has been incurred but not yet paid, resulting in a liability "rent payable." Also called *accrued liabilities*.

Accrued interest   Interest earned but not yet paid.

Accrued revenue   Revenue that has been earned but not yet billed to customers as of the end of an accounting period.

Accumulated depreciation   An offset to property, plant, and equipment (PPE) reflecting the amount of the cost of PPE that has been allocated to current and previous accounting periods.

Acid-test ratio   A stringent measure of liquidity that indicates a company's ability to satisfy current liabilities with its most liquid assets, calculated as (cash + short-term marketable investments + receivables) divided by current liabilities.

Acquisition method   A method of accounting for a business combination where the acquirer is required to measure each identifiable asset and liability at fair value. This method was the result of a joint project of the IASB and FASB aiming at convergence in standards for the accounting of business combinations.

Action lag   Delay from policy decisions to implementation.

Active investment   An approach to investing in which the investor seeks to outperform a given benchmark.

Active return   The return on a portfolio minus the return on the portfolio's benchmark.

Active strategy   In reference to short-term cash management, an investment strategy characterized by monitoring and attempting to capitalize on market conditions to optimize the risk and return relationship of short-term investments.

Activity ratio   The ratio of the labor force to total population of working age. Also called *participation ratio*.

Activity ratios   Ratios that measure how efficiently a company performs day-to-day tasks, such as the collection of receivables and management of inventory. Also called *asset utilization ratios* or *operating efficiency ratios*.

Add-on interest   A procedure for determining the interest on a bond or loan in which the interest is added onto the face value of a contract.

Add-on rates   Bank certificates of deposit, repos, and indices such as Libor and Euribor are quoted on an add-on rate basis (bond equivalent yield basis).

Addition rule for probabilities   A principle stating that the probability that A or B occurs (both occur) equals the probability that A occurs, plus the probability that B occurs, minus the probability that both A and B occur.

Agency bonds   See *quasi-government bond*.

Aggregate demand   The quantity of goods and services that households, businesses, government, and foreign customers want to buy at any given level of prices.

Aggregate demand curve   Inverse relationship between the price level and real output.

Aggregate income   The value of all the payments earned by the suppliers of factors used in the production of goods and services.

Aggregate output   The value of all the goods and services produced in a specified period of time.

Aggregate supply   The quantity of goods and services producers are willing to supply at any given level of price.

Aggregate supply curve   The level of domestic output that companies will produce at each price level.

Aging schedule   A breakdown of accounts into categories of days outstanding.

All-or-nothing (AON) orders   An order that includes the instruction to trade only if the trade fills the entire quantity (size) specified.

Allocationally efficient   Said of a market, a financial system, or an economy that promotes the allocation of resources to their highest value uses.

Allowance for bad debts   An offset to accounts receivable for the amount of accounts receivable that are estimated to be uncollectible.

Alternative investment markets   Market for investments other than traditional securities investments (i.e., traditional common and preferred shares and traditional fixed income instruments). The term usually encompasses direct and indirect investment in real estate (including timberland and farmland) and commodities (including precious metals); hedge funds, private equity, and other investments requiring specialized due diligence.

Alternative trading systems   Trading venues that function like exchanges but that do not exercise regulatory authority over their subscribers except with respect to the conduct of the subscribers' trading in their trading systems. Also called *electronic communications networks* or *multilateral trading facilities*.

American depository receipt   A U.S. dollar-denominated security that trades like a common share on U.S. exchanges.

American depository share   The underlying shares on which American depository receipts are based. They trade in the issuing company's domestic market.

American option   An option that can be exercised at any time until its expiration date.

American-style   Said of an option contract that can be exercised at any time up to the option's expiration date.

Amortisation   The process of allocating the cost of intangible long-term assets having a finite useful life to accounting periods; the allocation of the amount of a bond premium or discount to the periods remaining until bond maturity.

Amortised cost   The historical cost (initially recognised cost) of an asset, adjusted for amortisation and impairment.

Amortizing bond   Bond with a payment schedule that calls for periodic payments of interest and repayments of principal.

Annual percentage rate   The cost of borrowing expressed as a yearly rate.

Annuity   A finite set of level sequential cash flows.

Annuity due   An annuity having a first cash flow that is paid immediately.

Anticipation stock   Excess inventory that is held in anticipation of increased demand, often because of seasonal patterns of demand.

Antidilutive   With reference to a transaction or a security, one that would increase earnings per share (EPS) or result in EPS higher than the company's basic EPS—antidilutive securities are not included in the calculation of diluted EPS.

Arbitrage   1) The simultaneous purchase of an undervalued asset or portfolio and sale of an overvalued but equivalent asset or portfolio, in order to obtain a riskless profit on the price differential. Taking advantage of a market inefficiency in a risk-free manner. 2) The condition in a financial market in which equivalent assets or combinations of assets sell for two different prices, creating an opportunity to profit at no risk with no commitment of money. In a well-functioning financial market, few arbitrage opportunities are possible. 3) A risk-free operation that earns an expected positive net profit but requires no net investment of money.

Arbitrageurs   Traders who engage in arbitrage. See *arbitrage*.

Arc elasticity   An elasticity based on two points, in contrast with (point) elasticity. With reference to price elasticity, the percentage change in quantity demanded divided by the percentage change in price between two points for price.

Arithmetic mean   The sum of the observations divided by the number of observations.

Arms index   A flow of funds indicator applied to a broad stock market index to measure the relative extent to which money is moving into or out of rising and declining stocks.

Ascending price auction   An auction in which an auctioneer calls out prices for a single item and potential buyers bid directly against each other, with each subsequent bid being higher than the previous one.

Asian call option   A European-style option with a value at maturity equal to the difference between the stock price at maturity and the average stock price during the life of the option, or $0, whichever is greater.

Ask   The price at which a dealer or trader is willing to sell an asset, typically qualified by a maximum quantity (ask size). See *offer*.

Ask size   The maximum quantity of an asset that pertains to a specific ask price from a trader. For example, if the ask for a share issue is $30 for a size of 1,000 shares, the trader is offering to sell at $30 up to 1,000 shares.

Asset allocation   The process of determining how investment funds should be distributed among asset classes.

Asset beta   The unlevered beta; reflects the business risk of the assets; the asset's systematic risk.

Asset class   A group of assets that have similar characteristics, attributes, and risk/return relationships.

Asset swap   Converts the periodic fixed coupon of a specific bond to a Libor plus or minus a spread.

Asset utilization ratios   Ratios that measure how efficiently a company performs day-to-day tasks, such as the collection of receivables and management of inventory.

Asset-based loan   A loan that is secured with company assets.

Asset-based valuation models   Valuation based on estimates of the market value of a company's assets.

Assets   Resources controlled by an enterprise as a result of past events and from which future economic benefits to the enterprise are expected to flow.

Assignment of accounts receivable   The use of accounts receivable as collateral for a loan.

At the money   An option in which the underlying's price equals the exercise price.

Auction   A type of bond issuing mechanism often used for sovereign bonds that involves bidding.

Autarkic price   The price of a good or service in an autarkic economy.

Autarky   A state in which a country does not trade with other countries.

Automated Clearing House (ACH)   An electronic payment network available to businesses, individuals, and financial institutions in the United States, U.S. Territories, and Canada.

Automatic stabilizer   A countercyclical factor that automatically comes into play as an economy slows and unemployment rises.

Available-for-sale   Debt and equity securities not classified as either held-to-maturity or held-for-trading securities. The investor is willing to sell but not actively planning to sell. In general, available-for-sale securities are reported at fair value on the balance sheet.

Average fixed cost   Total fixed cost divided by quantity.

Average product   Measures the productivity of inputs on average and is calculated by dividing total product by the total number of units for a given input that is used to generate that output.

Average revenue   Quantity sold divided into total revenue.

Average total cost   Total costs divided by quantity.

Average variable cost   Total variable cost divided by quantity.

Back simulation Another term for the historical method of estimating VAR. This term is somewhat misleading in that the method involves not a *simulation* of the past but rather what *actually happened* in the past, sometimes adjusted to reflect the fact that a different portfolio may have existed in the past than is planned for the future.

Back-testing With reference to portfolio strategies, the application of a strategy's portfolio selection rules to historical data to assess what would have been the strategy's historical performance.

Backup lines of credit A type of credit enhancement provided by a bank to an issuer of commercial paper to ensure that the issuer will have access to sufficient liquidity to repay maturing commercial paper if issuing new paper is not a viable option.

Balance of payments A double-entry bookkeeping system that summarizes a country's economic transactions with the rest of the world for a particular period of time, typically a calendar quarter or year.

Balance of trade deficit When the domestic economy is spending more on foreign goods and services than foreign economies are spending on domestic goods and services.

Balance sheet The financial statement that presents an entity's current financial position by disclosing resources the entity controls (its assets) and the claims on those resources (its liabilities and equity claims), as of a particular point in time (the date of the balance sheet). Also called *statement of financial position* or *statement of financial condition*.

Balance sheet ratios Financial ratios involving balance sheet items only.

Balanced With respect to a government budget, one in which spending and revenues (taxes) are equal.

Balloon payment Large payment required at maturity to retire a bond's outstanding principal amount.

Bank discount basis A quoting convention that annualizes, on a 360-day year, the discount as a percentage of face value.

Bar chart A price chart with four bits of data for each time interval—the high, low, opening, and closing prices. A vertical line connects the high and low. A cross-hatch left indicates the opening price and a cross-hatch right indicates the close.

Barter economy An economy where economic agents as house-holds, corporations, and governments "pay" for goods and services with another good or service.

Base rates The reference rate on which a bank bases lending rates to all other customers.

Basic EPS Net earnings available to common shareholders (i.e., net income minus preferred dividends) divided by the weighted average number of common shares outstanding.

Basis point Used in stating yield spreads, one basis point equals one-hundredth of a percentage point, or 0.01%.

Basket of listed depository receipts An exchange-traded fund (ETF) that represents a portfolio of depository receipts.

Bearer bonds Bonds for which ownership is not recorded; only the clearing system knows who the bond owner is.

Behavioral equations With respect to demand and supply, equations that model the behavior of buyers and sellers.

Behavioral finance A field of finance that examines the psychological variables that affect and often distort the investment decision making of investors, analysts, and portfolio managers.

Behind the market Said of prices specified in orders that are worse than the best current price; e.g., for a limit buy order, a limit price below the best bid.

Benchmark A comparison portfolio; a point of reference or comparison.

Benchmark issue The latest sovereign bond issue for a given maturity. It serves as a benchmark against which to compare bonds that have the same features but that are issued by another type of issuer.

Benchmark rate Typically the yield-to-maturity on a government bond having the same, or close to the same, time-to-maturity.

Benchmark spread The yield spread over a specific benchmark, usually measured in basis points.

Bermuda-style Said of an option contract that can be exercised on specified dates up to the option's expiration date.

Bernoulli random variable A random variable having the outcomes 0 and 1.

Bernoulli trial An experiment that can produce one of two outcomes.

Best bid The highest bid in the market.

Best effort offering An offering of a security using an investment bank in which the investment bank, as agent for the issuer, promises to use its best efforts to sell the offering but does not guarantee that a specific amount will be sold.

Best offer The lowest offer (ask price) in the market.

Beta A measure of systematic risk that is based on the covariance of an asset's or portfolio's return with the return of the overall market.

Bid The price at which a dealer or trader is willing to buy an asset, typically qualified by a maximum quantity.

Bid size The maximum quantity of an asset that pertains to a specific bid price from a trader.

Bid–ask spread The difference between the prices at which dealers will buy from a customer (bid) and sell to a customer (offer or ask). It is often used as an indicator of liquidity.

Bid–offer spread The difference between the prices at which dealers will buy from a customer (bid) and sell to a customer (offer or ask). It is often used as an indicator of liquidity.

Bilateral loan A loan from a single lender to a single borrower.

Binomial model A model for pricing options in which the underlying price can move to only one of two possible new prices.

Binomial random variable The number of successes in n Bernoulli trials for which the probability of success is constant for all trials and the trials are independent.

Binomial tree The graphical representation of a model of asset price dynamics in which, at each period, the asset moves up with probability p or down with probability $(1 - p)$.

Block brokers A broker (agent) that provides brokerage services for large-size trades.

Blue chip Widely held large market capitalization companies that are considered financially sound and are leaders in their respective industry or local stock market.

Bollinger Bands A price-based technical analysis indicator consisting of a moving average plus a higher line representing the moving average plus a set number of standard deviations from average price (for the same number of periods as used to calculate the moving average) and a lower line that is a moving average minus the same number of standard deviations.

Bond Contractual agreement between the issuer and the bondholders.

Bond equivalent yield   A calculation of yield that is annualized using the ratio of 365 to the number of days to maturity. Bond equivalent yield allows for the restatement and comparison of securities with different compounding periods.

Bond indenture   The governing legal credit agreement, typically incorporated by reference in the prospectus.

Bond market vigilantes   Bond market participants who might reduce their demand for long-term bonds, thus pushing up their yields.

Bond option   An option in which the underlying is a bond; primarily traded in over-the-counter markets.

Bond yield plus risk premium approach   An estimate of the cost of common equity that is produced by summing the before-tax cost of debt and a risk premium that captures the additional yield on a company's stock relative to its bonds. The additional yield is often estimated using historical spreads between bond yields and stock yields.

Bonus issue of shares   A type of dividend in which a company distributes additional shares of its common stock to shareholders instead of cash.

Book building   Investment bankers' process of compiling a "book" or list of indications of interest to buy part of an offering.

Book value   The net amount shown for an asset or liability on the balance sheet; book value may also refer to the company's excess of total assets over total liabilities. Also called *carrying value.*

Boom   An expansionary phase characterized by economic growth "testing the limits" of the economy.

Bottom-up analysis   With reference to investment selection processes, an approach that involves selection from all securities within a specified investment universe, i.e., without prior narrowing of the universe on the basis of macroeconomic or overall market considerations.

Break point   In the context of the weighted average cost of capital (WACC), a break point is the amount of capital at which the cost of one or more of the sources of capital changes, leading to a change in the WACC.

Breakeven point   The number of units produced and sold at which the company's net income is zero (revenues = total costs); in the case of perfect competition, the quantity where price, average revenue, and marginal revenue equal average total cost.

Bridge financing   Interim financing that provides funds until permanent financing can be arranged.

Broad money   Encompasses narrow money plus the entire range of liquid assets that can be used to make purchases.

Broker   1) An agent who executes orders to buy or sell securities on behalf of a client in exchange for a commission. 2) See *futures commission merchants.*

Brokered market   A market in which brokers arrange trades among their clients.

Broker–dealer   A financial intermediary (often a company) that may function as a principal (dealer) or as an agent (broker) depending on the type of trade.

Budget constraint   A constraint on spending or investment imposed by wealth or income.

Budget surplus/deficit   The difference between government revenue and expenditure for a stated fixed period of time.

Business risk   The risk associated with operating earnings. Operating earnings are uncertain because total revenues and many of the expenditures contributed to produce those revenues are uncertain.

Buy-side firm   An investment management company or other investor that uses the services of brokers or dealers (i.e., the client of the sell side firms).

Buyback   A transaction in which a company buys back its own shares. Unlike stock dividends and stock splits, share repurchases use corporate cash.

Buyout fund   A fund that buys all the shares of a public company so that, in effect, the company becomes private.

CBOE Volatility Index   A measure of near-term market volatility as conveyed by S&P 500 stock index option prices.

CD equivalent yield   A yield on a basis comparable to the quoted yield on an interest-bearing money market instrument that pays interest on a 360-day basis; the annualized holding period yield, assuming a 360-day year.

Call   An option that gives the holder the right to buy an underlying asset from another party at a fixed price over a specific period of time.

Call market   A market in which trades occur only at a particular time and place (i.e., when the market is called).

Call money rate   The interest rate that buyers pay for their margin loan.

Call option   An option that gives the holder the right to buy an underlying asset from another party at a fixed price over a specific period of time.

Call protection   The time during which the issuer of the bond is not allowed to exercise the call option.

Callable bond   A bond containing an embedded call option that gives the issuer the right to buy the bond back from the investor at specified prices on pre-determined dates.

Callable common shares   Shares that give the issuing company the option (or right), but not the obligation, to buy back the shares from investors at a call price that is specified when the shares are originally issued.

Candlestick chart   A price chart with four bits of data for each time interval. A candle indicates the opening and closing price for the interval. The body of the candle is shaded if the opening price was higher than the closing price, and the body is clear if the opening price was lower than the closing price. Vertical lines known as wicks or shadows extend from the top and bottom of the candle to indicate the high and the low prices for the interval.

Cannibalization   Cannibalization occurs when an investment takes customers and sales away from another part of the company.

Cap   1) A contract on an interest rate, whereby at periodic payment dates, the writer of the cap pays the difference between the market interest rate and a specified cap rate if, and only if, this difference is positive. This is equivalent to a stream of call options on the interest rate. 2) A combination of interest rate call options designed to hedge a borrower against rate increases on a floating-rate loan.

Capacity   The ability of the borrower to make its debt payments on time.

Capital account   A component of the balance of payments account that measures transfers of capital.

Capital allocation line   (CAL) A graph line that describes the combinations of expected return and standard deviation of return available to an investor from combining the optimal portfolio of risky assets with the risk-free asset.

Capital asset pricing model   (CAPM) An equation describing the expected return on any asset (or portfolio) as a linear function of its beta relative to the market portfolio.

Capital budgeting   The allocation of funds to relatively long-range projects or investments.

Capital consumption allowance A measure of the wear and tear (depreciation) of the capital stock that occurs in the production of goods and services.

Capital deepening investment Increases the stock of capital relative to labor.

Capital expenditure Expenditure on physical capital (fixed assets).

Capital market expectations An investor's expectations concerning the risk and return prospects of asset classes.

Capital market line (CML) The line with an intercept point equal to the risk-free rate that is tangent to the efficient frontier of risky assets; represents the efficient frontier when a risk-free asset is available for investment.

Capital market securities Securities with maturities at issuance longer than one year.

Capital markets Financial markets that trade securities of longer duration, such as bonds and equities.

Capital rationing A capital rationing environment assumes that the company has a fixed amount of funds to invest.

Capital restrictions Controls placed on foreigners' ability to own domestic assets and/or domestic residents' ability to own foreign assets.

Capital stock The accumulated amount of buildings, machinery, and equipment used to produce goods and services.

Capital structure The mix of debt and equity that a company uses to finance its business; a company's specific mixture of long-term financing.

Capital-indexed bonds Type of index-linked bond. The coupon rate is fixed but is applied to a principal amount that increases in line with increases in the index during the bond's life.

Caplet Each component call option in a cap.

Captive finance subsidiary A wholly-owned subsidiary of a company that is established to provide financing of the sales of the parent company.

Carrying amount The amount at which an asset or liability is valued according to accounting principles.

Carrying value The net amount shown for an asset or liability on the balance sheet; book value may also refer to the company's excess of total assets over total liabilities. For a bond, the purchase price plus (or minus) the amortized amount of the discount (or premium).

Cartel Participants in collusive agreements that are made openly and formally.

Cash In accounting contexts, cash on hand (e.g., petty cash and cash not yet deposited to the bank) and demand deposits held in banks and similar accounts that can be used in payment of obligations.

Cash conversion cycle A financial metric that measures the length of time required for a company to convert cash invested in its operations to cash received as a result of its operations; equal to days of inventory on hand + days of sales outstanding − number of days of payables. Also called *net operating cycle*.

Cash equivalents Very liquid short-term investments, usually maturing in 90 days or less.

Cash flow additivity principle The principle that dollar amounts indexed at the same point in time are additive.

Cash flow from operating activities The net amount of cash provided from operating activities.

Cash flow from operations The net amount of cash provided from operating activities.

Cash flow yield The internal rate of return on a series of cash flows.

Cash market securities Money market securities settled on a "same day" or "cash settlement" basis.

Cash markets See *spot markets*.

Cash prices See *spot prices*.

Cash settlement A procedure used in certain derivative transactions that specifies that the long and short parties engage in the equivalent cash value of a delivery transaction.

Cash-settled forwards See *non-deliverable forwards*.

Central bank funds market The market in which deposit-taking banks that have an excess reserve with their national central bank can loan money to banks that need funds for maturities ranging from overnight to one year. Called the Federal or Fed funds market in the United States.

Central bank funds rates Interest rates at which central bank funds are bought (borrowed) and sold (lent) for maturities ranging from overnight to one year. Called Federal or Fed funds rates in the United States.

Central banks The dominant bank in a country, usually with official or semi-official governmental status.

Certificate of deposit An instrument that represents a specified amount of funds on deposit with a bank for a specified maturity and interest rate. It is issued in small or large denominations, and can be negotiable or non-negotiable.

Change in polarity principle A tenet of technical analysis that once a support level is breached, it becomes a resistance level. The same holds true for resistance levels; once breached, they become support levels.

Change in quantity supplied A movement along a given supply curve.

Change in supply A shift in the supply curve.

Change of control put A covenant giving bondholders the right to require the issuer to buy back their debt, often at par or at some small premium to par value, in the event that the borrower is acquired.

Character The quality of a debt issuer's management.

Chart of accounts A list of accounts used in an entity's accounting system.

Cheapest-to-deliver bond A bond in which the amount received for delivering the bond is largest compared with the amount paid in the market for the bond.

Classified balance sheet A balance sheet organized so as to group together the various assets and liabilities into subcategories (e.g., current and noncurrent).

Clawback A requirement that the GP return any funds distributed as incentive fees until the LPs have received back their initial investment and a percentage of the total profit.

Clearing The process by which the exchange verifies the execution of a transaction and records the participants' identities.

Clearing instructions Instructions that indicate how to arrange the final settlement ("clearing") of a trade.

Clearinghouse An entity associated with a futures market that acts as middleman between the contracting parties and guarantees to each party the performance of the other.

Closed economy An economy that does not trade with other countries; an *autarkic economy*.

Closed-end fund A mutual fund in which no new investment money is accepted. New investors invest by buying existing shares, and investors in the fund liquidate by selling their shares to other investors.

Coefficient of variation (CV) The ratio of a set of observations' standard deviation to the observations' mean value.

Coincident economic indicators Turning points that are usually close to those of the overall economy; they are believed to have value for identifying the economy's present state.

Collateral   The quality and value of the assets supporting an issuer's indebtedness.

Collateral trust bonds   Bonds secured by securities such as common shares, other bonds, or other financial assets.

Collateralized bond obligations   A structured asset-backed security that is collateralized by a pool of bonds.

Collateralized debt obligations   A securitized pool of fixed-income assets.

Collateralized loan obligations   A structured asset-backed security that is collateralized by a pool of loans.

Collateralized mortgage obligation (CMO)   A structured asset-backed security that is collateralized by a pool of mortgages.

Collaterals   Assets or financial guarantees underlying a debt obligation above and beyond the issuer's promise to pay.

Combination   A listing in which the order of the listed items does not matter.

Commercial paper   A short-term, negotiable, unsecured promissory note that represents a debt obligation of the issuer.

Commercial receivables   Amounts customers owe the company for products that have been sold as well as amounts that may be due from suppliers (such as for returns of merchandise). Also called *trade receivables* or *accounts receivable*.

Committed capital   The amount that the limited partners have agreed to provide to the private equity fund.

Committed lines of credit   A bank commitment to extend credit up to a pre-specified amount; the commitment is considered a short-term liability and is usually in effect for 364 days (one day short of a full year).

Commodity swap   A swap in which the underlying is a commodity such as oil, gold, or an agricultural product.

Common market   Level of economic integration that incorporates all aspects of the customs union and extends it by allowing free movement of factors of production among members.

Common shares   A type of security that represent an ownership interest in a company.

Common stock   See *common shares*.

Common value auction   An auction in which the item being auctioned has the same value to each auction participant, although participants may be uncertain as to what that value is.

Common-size analysis   The restatement of financial statement items using a common denominator or reference item that allows one to identify trends and major differences; an example is an income statement in which all items are expressed as a percent of revenue.

Company analysis   Analysis of an individual company.

Comparable company   A company that has similar business risk; usually in the same industry and preferably with a single line of business.

Comparative advantage   A country's ability to produce a good or service at a lower relative cost, or opportunity cost, than its trading partner.

Competitive strategy   A company's plans for responding to the threats and opportunities presented by the external environment.

Complements   Said of goods which tend to be used together; technically, two goods whose cross-price elasticity of demand is negative.

Complete markets   Informally, markets in which the variety of distinct securities traded is so broad that any desired payoff in a future state-of-the-world is achievable.

Complete preferences   The assumption that a consumer is able to make a comparison between any two possible bundles of goods.

Completed contract   A method of revenue recognition in which the company does not recognize any revenue until the contract is completed; used particularly in long-term construction contracts.

Component cost of capital   The rate of return required by suppliers of capital for an individual source of a company's funding, such as debt or equity.

Compounding   The process of accumulating interest on interest.

Comprehensive income   The change in equity of a business enterprise during a period from nonowner sources; includes all changes in equity during a period except those resulting from investments by owners and distributions to owners; comprehensive income equals net income plus other comprehensive income.

Conditional expected value   The expected value of a stated event given that another event has occurred.

Conditional probability   The probability of an event given (conditioned on) another event.

Conditional variances   The variance of one variable, given the outcome of another.

Consistent   With reference to estimators, describes an estimator for which the probability of estimates close to the value of the population parameter increases as sample size increases.

Conspicuous consumption   Consumption of high status goods, such as a luxury automobile or a very expensive piece of jewelry.

Constant returns to scale   The characteristic of constant per-unit costs in the presence of increased production.

Constant-cost industry   When firms in the industry experience no change in resource costs and output prices over the long run.

Constant-yield price trajectory   A graph that illustrates the change in the price of a fixed-income bond over time assuming no change in yield-to-maturity. The trajectory shows the "pull to par" effect on the price of a bond trading at a premium or a discount to par value.

Constituent securities   With respect to an index, the individual securities within an index.

Consumer choice theory   The theory relating consumer demand curves to consumer preferences.

Consumer surplus   The difference between the value that a consumer places on units purchased and the amount of money that was required to pay for them.

Consumption   The purchase of final goods and services by individuals.

Consumption basket   A specific combination of the goods and services that a consumer wants to consume.

Consumption bundle   A specific combination of the goods and services that a consumer wants to consume.

Contingency provision   Clause in a legal document that allows for some action if a specific event or circumstance occurs.

Contingent claims   Derivatives in which the payoffs occur if a specific event occurs; generally referred to as options.

Contingent convertible bonds   Bonds that automatically convert into equity if a specific event or circumstance occurs, such as the issuer's equity capital falling below the minimum requirement set by the regulators. Also called *CoCos*.

Continuation patterns A type of pattern used in technical analysis to predict the resumption of a market trend that was in place prior to the formation of a pattern.

Continuous random variable A random variable for which the range of possible outcomes is the real line (all real numbers between $-\infty$ and $+\infty$ or some subset of the real line).

Continuous time Time thought of as advancing in extremely small increments.

Continuous trading market A market in which trades can be arranged and executed any time the market is open.

Continuously compounded return The natural logarithm of 1 plus the holding period return, or equivalently, the natural logarithm of the ending price over the beginning price.

Contra account An account that offsets another account.

Contraction The period of a business cycle after the peak and before the trough; often called a *recession* or, if exceptionally severe, called a *depression*.

Contractionary Tending to cause the real economy to contract.

Contractionary fiscal policy A fiscal policy that has the objective to make the real economy contract.

Contracts for differences See *non-deliverable forwards*.

Contribution margin The amount available for fixed costs and profit after paying variable costs; revenue minus variable costs.

Conventional bond See *plain vanilla bond*.

Conventional cash flow A conventional cash flow pattern is one with an initial outflow followed by a series of inflows.

Convergence The tendency for differences in output per capita across countries to diminish over time; in technical analysis, a term that describes the case when an indicator moves in the same manner as the security being analyzed.

Conversion factor An adjustment used to facilitate delivery on bond futures contracts in which any of a number of bonds with different characteristics are eligible for delivery.

Conversion price For a convertible bond, the price per share at which the bond can be converted into shares.

Conversion ratio For a convertible bond, the number of common shares that each bond can be converted into.

Conversion value For a convertible bond, the current share price multiplied by the conversion ratio.

Convertible bond Bond that gives the bondholder the right to exchange the bond for a specified number of common shares in the issuing company.

Convertible preference shares A type of equity security that entitles shareholders to convert their shares into a specified number of common shares.

Convexity adjustment For a bond, one half of the annual or approximate convexity statistic multiplied by the change in the yield-to-maturity squared.

Core inflation The inflation rate calculated based on a price index of goods and services except food and energy.

Correlation A number between -1 and $+1$ that measures the comovement (linear association) between two random variables.

Correlation coefficient A number between -1 and $+1$ that measures the consistency or tendency for two investments to act in a similar way. It is used to determine the effect on portfolio risk when two assets are combined.

Cost averaging The periodic investment of a fixed amount of money.

Cost of capital The rate of return that suppliers of capital require as compensation for their contribution of capital.

Cost of debt The cost of debt financing to a company, such as when it issues a bond or takes out a bank loan.

Cost of goods sold For a given period, equal to beginning inventory minus ending inventory plus the cost of goods acquired or produced during the period.

Cost of preferred stock The cost to a company of issuing preferred stock; the dividend yield that a company must commit to pay preferred stockholders.

Cost recovery method A method of revenue recognition in which the seller does not report any profit until the cash amounts paid by the buyer—including principal and interest on any financing from the seller—are greater than all the seller's costs for the merchandise sold.

Cost structure The mix of a company's variable costs and fixed costs.

Cost-push Type of inflation in which rising costs, usually wages, compel businesses to raise prices generally.

Counterparty risk The risk that the other party to a contract will fail to honor the terms of the contract.

Cournot assumption Assumption in which each firm determines its profit-maximizing production level assuming that the other firms' output will not change.

Covariance A measure of the co-movement (linear association) between two random variables.

Covariance matrix A matrix or square array whose entries are covariances; also known as a variance–covariance matrix.

Covenants The terms and conditions of lending agreements that the issuer must comply with; they specify the actions that an issuer is obligated to perform (affirmative covenant) or prohibited from performing (negative covenant).

Covered bond Debt obligation secured by a segregated pool of assets called the cover pool. The issuer must maintain the value of the cover pool. In the event of default, bondholders have recourse against both the issuer and the cover pool.

Covered call An option strategy involving the holding of an asset and sale of a call on the asset.

Credit With respect to double-entry accounting, a credit records increases in liability, owners' equity, and revenue accounts or decreases in asset accounts; with respect to borrowing, the willingness and ability of the borrower to make promised payments on the borrowing.

Credit analysis The evaluation of credit risk; the evaluation of the creditworthiness of a borrower or counterparty.

Credit curve A curve showing the relationship between time to maturity and yield spread for an issuer with comparable bonds of various maturities outstanding, usually upward sloping.

Credit default swap (CDS) A type of credit derivative in which one party, the credit protection buyer who is seeking credit protection against a third party, makes a series of regularly scheduled payments to the other party, the credit protection seller. The seller makes no payments until a credit event occurs.

Credit derivatives A contract in which one party has the right to claim a payment from another party in the event that a specific credit event occurs over the life of the contract.

Credit enhancements Provisions that may be used to reduce the credit risk of a bond issue.

Credit migration risk The risk that a bond issuer's creditworthiness deteriorates, or migrates lower, leading investors to believe the risk of default is higher. Also called *downgrade risk*.

Credit risk The risk of loss caused by a counterparty's or debtor's failure to make a promised payment. Also called *default risk*.

Credit scoring model A statistical model used to classify borrowers according to creditworthiness.

Credit spread option An option on the yield spread on a bond.

Credit-linked coupon bond Bond for which the coupon changes when the bond's credit rating changes.

Credit-linked note Fixed-income security in which the holder of the security has the right to withhold payment of the full amount due at maturity if a credit event occurs.

Credit-worthiness The perceived ability of the borrower to pay what is owed on the borrowing in a timely manner; it represents the ability of a company to withstand adverse impacts on its cash flows.

Cross-default provisions Provisions whereby events of default such as non-payment of interest on one bond trigger default on all outstanding debt; implies the same default probability for all issues.

Cross-price elasticity of demand The percent change in quantity demanded for a given small change in the price of another good; the responsiveness of the demand for Product A that is associated with the change in price of Product B.

Cross-sectional analysis Analysis that involves comparisons across individuals in a group over a given time period or at a given point in time.

Cross-sectional data Observations over individual units at a point in time, as opposed to time-series data.

Crossing networks Trading systems that match buyers and sellers who are willing to trade at prices obtained from other markets.

Crowding out The thesis that government borrowing may divert private sector investment from taking place.

Cumulative distribution function A function giving the probability that a random variable is less than or equal to a specified value.

Cumulative preference shares Preference shares for which any dividends that are not paid accrue and must be paid in full before dividends on common shares can be paid.

Cumulative relative frequency For data grouped into intervals, the fraction of total observations that are less than the value of the upper limit of a stated interval.

Cumulative voting Voting that allows shareholders to direct their total voting rights to specific candidates, as opposed to having to allocate their voting rights evenly among all candidates.

Currencies Monies issued by national monetary authorities.

Currency option An option that allows the holder to buy (if a call) or sell (if a put) an underlying currency at a fixed exercise rate, expressed as an exchange rate.

Currency option bonds Bonds that give the bondholder the right to choose the currency in which he or she wants to receive interest payments and principal repayments.

Currency swap A swap in which each party makes interest payments to the other in different currencies.

Current account A component of the balance of payments account that measures the flow of goods and services.

Current assets (or liquid assets) Assets that are expected to be consumed or converted into cash in the near future, typically one year or less.

Current cost With reference to assets, the amount of cash or cash equivalents that would have to be paid to buy the same or an equivalent asset today; with reference to liabilities, the undiscounted amount of cash or cash equivalents that would be required to settle the obligation today.

Current government spending With respect to government expenditures, spending on goods and services that are provided on a regular, recurring basis including health, education, and defense.

Current liabilities Short-term obligations, such as accounts payable, wages payable, or accrued liabilities, that are expected to be settled in the near future, typically one year or less.

Current ratio A liquidity ratio calculated as current assets divided by current liabilities.

Current yield The sum of the coupon payments received over the year divided by the flat price; also called the *income* or *interest yield* or *running yield*.

Curve duration The sensitivity of the bond price (or the market value of a financial asset or liability) with respect to a benchmark yield curve.

Customs union Extends the free trade area (FTA) by not only allowing free movement of goods and services among members, but also creating a common trade policy against nonmembers.

Cyclical See *cyclical companies*.

Cyclical companies Companies with sales and profits that regularly expand and contract with the business cycle or state of economy.

Daily settlement See *mark to market* and *marking to market*.

Dark pools Alternative trading systems that do not display the orders that their clients send to them.

Data mining The practice of determining a model by extensive searching through a dataset for statistically significant patterns. Also called *data snooping*.

Data snooping See *data mining*.

Date of book closure The date that a shareholder listed on the corporation's books will be deemed to have ownership of the shares for purposes of receiving an upcoming dividend; two business days after the ex-dividend date.

Date of record The date that a shareholder listed on the corporation's books will be deemed to have ownership of the shares for purposes of receiving an upcoming dividend; two business days after the ex-dividend date.

Day order An order that is good for the day on which it is submitted. If it has not been filled by the close of business, the order expires unfilled.

Day trader A trader holding a position open somewhat longer than a scalper but closing all positions at the end of the day.

Days in receivables Estimate of the average number of days it takes to collect on credit accounts.

Days of inventory on hand (DOH) An activity ratio equal to the number of days in the period divided by inventory turnover over the period.

Day's sales outstanding Estimate of the average number of days it takes to collect on credit accounts.

Dead cross A technical analysis term that describes a situation where a short-term moving average crosses from above a longer-term moving average to below it; this movement is considered bearish.

Deadweight loss A net loss of total (consumer and producer) surplus.

Dealers A financial intermediary that acts as a principal in trades.

Dealing securities Securities held by banks or other financial intermediaries for trading purposes.

Debentures Type of bond that can be secured or unsecured.

Debit   With respect to double-entry accounting, a debit records increases of asset and expense accounts or decreases in liability and owners' equity accounts.

Debt incurrence test   A financial covenant made in conjunction with existing debt that restricts a company's ability to incur additional debt at the same seniority based on one or more financial tests or conditions.

Debt-rating approach   A method for estimating a company's before-tax cost of debt based upon the yield on comparably rated bonds for maturities that closely match that of the company's existing debt.

Debt-to-assets ratio   A solvency ratio calculated as total debt divided by total assets.

Debt-to-capital ratio   A solvency ratio calculated as total debt divided by total debt plus total shareholders' equity.

Debt-to-equity ratio   A solvency ratio calculated as total debt divided by total shareholders' equity.

Declaration date   The day that the corporation issues a statement declaring a specific dividend.

Decreasing returns to scale   Increase in cost per unit resulting from increased production.

Decreasing-cost industry   An industry in which per-unit costs and output prices are lower when industry output is increased in the long run.

Deductible temporary differences   Temporary differences that result in a reduction of or deduction from taxable income in a future period when the balance sheet item is recovered or settled.

Deep-in-the-money   Options that are far in-the-money.

Deep-out-of-the-money   Options that are far out-of-the-money.

Default probability   The probability that a borrower defaults or fails to meet its obligation to make full and timely payments of principal and interest, according to the terms of the debt security. Also called *default risk*.

Default risk   The probability that a borrower defaults or fails to meet its obligation to make full and timely payments of principal and interest, according to the terms of the debt security. Also called *default probability*.

Default risk premium   An extra return that compensates investors for the possibility that the borrower will fail to make a promised payment at the contracted time and in the contracted amount.

Defensive companies   Companies with sales and profits that have little sensitivity to the business cycle or state of the economy.

Defensive interval ratio   A liquidity ratio that estimates the number of days that an entity could meet cash needs from liquid assets; calculated as (cash + short-term marketable investments + receivables) divided by daily cash expenditures.

Deferred coupon bond   Bond that pays no coupons for its first few years but then pays a higher coupon than it otherwise normally would for the remainder of its life. Also called *split coupon bond*.

Deferred income   A liability account for money that has been collected for goods or services that have not yet been delivered; payment received in advance of providing a good or service.

Deferred revenue   A liability account for money that has been collected for goods or services that have not yet been delivered; payment received in advance of providing a good or service.

Deferred tax assets   A balance sheet asset that arises when an excess amount is paid for income taxes relative to accounting profit. The taxable income is higher than accounting profit and income tax payable exceeds tax expense. The company expects to recover the difference during the course of future operations when tax expense exceeds income tax payable.

Deferred tax liabilities   A balance sheet liability that arises when a deficit amount is paid for income taxes relative to accounting profit. The taxable income is less than the accounting profit and income tax payable is less than tax expense. The company expects to eliminate the liability over the course of future operations when income tax payable exceeds tax expense.

Defined benefit pension plans   Plan in which the company promises to pay a certain annual amount (defined benefit) to the employee after retirement. The company bears the investment risk of the plan assets.

Defined contribution pension plans   Individual accounts to which an employee and typically the employer makes contributions, generally on a tax-advantaged basis. The amounts of contributions are defined at the outset, but the future value of the benefit is unknown. The employee bears the investment risk of the plan assets.

Deflation   Negative inflation.

Degree of confidence   The probability that a confidence interval includes the unknown population parameter.

Degree of financial leverage   (DFL) The ratio of the percentage change in net income to the percentage change in operating income; the sensitivity of the cash flows available to owners when operating income changes.

Degree of operating leverage   (DOL) The ratio of the percentage change in operating income to the percentage change in units sold; the sensitivity of operating income to changes in units sold.

Degree of total leverage   The ratio of the percentage change in net income to the percentage change in units sold; the sensitivity of the cash flows to owners to changes in the number of units produced and sold.

Degrees of freedom (df)   The number of independent observations used.

Delivery   A process used in a deliverable forward contract in which the long pays the agreed-upon price to the short, which in turn delivers the underlying asset to the long.

Delivery option   The feature of a futures contract giving the short the right to make decisions about what, when, and where to deliver.

Delta   The relationship between the option price and the underlying price, which reflects the sensitivity of the price of the option to changes in the price of the underlying.

Demand   The willingness and ability of consumers to purchase a given amount of a good or service at a given price.

Demand and supply analysis   The study of how buyers and sellers interact to determine transaction prices and quantities.

Demand curve   Graph of the inverse demand function.

Demand function   A relationship that expresses the quantity demanded of a good or service as a function of own-price and possibly other variables.

Demand shock   A typically unexpected disturbance to demand, such as an unexpected interruption in trade or transportation.

Demand-pull Type of inflation in which increasing demand raises prices generally, which then are reflected in a business's costs as workers demand wage hikes to catch up with the rising cost of living.

Dependent With reference to events, the property that the probability of one event occurring depends on (is related to) the occurrence of another event.

Depository bank A bank that raises funds from depositors and other investors and lends it to borrowers.

Depository institutions Commercial banks, savings and loan banks, credit unions, and similar institutions that raise funds from depositors and other investors and lend it to borrowers.

Depository receipt A security that trades like an ordinary share on a local exchange and represents an economic interest in a foreign company.

Depreciation The process of systematically allocating the cost of long-lived (tangible) assets to the periods during which the assets are expected to provide economic benefits.

Depression See *contraction.*

Derivative pricing rule A pricing rule used by crossing networks in which a price is taken (derived) from the price that is current in the asset's primary market.

Derivatives A financial instrument whose value depends on the value of some underlying asset or factor (e.g., a stock price, an interest rate, or exchange rate).

Descending price auction An auction in which the auctioneer begins at a high price, then lowers the called price in increments until there is a willing buyer for the item being auctioned.

Descriptive statistics The study of how data can be summarized effectively.

Development capital Minority equity investments in more mature companies that are looking for capital to expand or restructure operations, enter new markets, or finance major acquisitions.

Diffuse prior The assumption of equal prior probabilities.

Diffusion index Reflects the proportion of the index's components that are moving in a pattern consistent with the overall index.

Diluted EPS The EPS that would result if all dilutive securities were converted into common shares.

Diluted shares The number of shares that would be outstanding if all potentially dilutive claims on common shares (e.g., convertible debt, convertible preferred stock, and employee stock options) were exercised.

Diminishing balance method An accelerated depreciation method, i.e., one that allocates a relatively large proportion of the cost of an asset to the early years of the asset's useful life.

Diminishing marginal productivity Describes a state in which each additional unit of input produces less output than previously.

Direct debit program An arrangement whereby a customer authorizes a debit to a demand account; typically used by companies to collect routine payments for services.

Direct format With reference to the cash flow statement, a format for the presentation of the statement in which cash flow from operating activities is shown as operating cash receipts less operating cash disbursements. Also called *direct method.*

Direct method See *direct format.*

Direct taxes Taxes levied directly on income, wealth, and corporate profits.

Direct write-off method An approach to recognizing credit losses on customer receivables in which the company waits until such time as a customer has defaulted and only then recognizes the loss.

Disbursement float The amount of time between check issuance and a check's clearing back against the company's account.

Discount To reduce the value of a future payment in allowance for how far away it is in time; to calculate the present value of some future amount. Also, the amount by which an instrument is priced below its face (par) value.

Discount interest A procedure for determining the interest on a loan or bond in which the interest is deducted from the face value in advance.

Discount margin See *required margin.*

Discount rates In general, the interest rate used to calculate a present value. In the money market, however, discount rate is a specific type of quoted rate.

Discounted cash flow models Valuation models that estimate the intrinsic value of a security as the present value of the future benefits expected to be received from the security.

Discouraged worker A person who has stopped looking for a job or has given up seeking employment.

Discrete random variable A random variable that can take on at most a countable number of possible values.

Discriminatory pricing rule A pricing rule used in continuous markets in which the limit price of the order or quote that first arrived determines the trade price.

Diseconomies of scale Increase in cost per unit resulting from increased production.

Dispersion The variability around the central tendency.

Display size The size of an order displayed to public view.

Distressed investing Investing in securities of companies in financial difficulties. Private equity funds typically buy the debt of mature companies in financial difficulties.

Divergence In technical analysis, a term that describes the case when an indicator moves differently from the security being analyzed.

Diversification ratio The ratio of the standard deviation of an equally weighted portfolio to the standard deviation of a randomly selected security.

Dividend A distribution paid to shareholders based on the number of shares owned.

Dividend discount model (DDM) A present value model that estimates the intrinsic value of an equity share based on the present value of its expected future dividends.

Dividend discount model based approach An approach for estimating a country's equity risk premium. The market rate of return is estimated as the sum of the dividend yield and the growth rate in dividends for a market index. Subtracting the risk-free rate of return from the estimated market return produces an estimate for the equity risk premium.

Dividend payout ratio The ratio of cash dividends paid to earnings for a period.

Dividend yield Annual dividends per share divided by share price.

Divisor A number (denominator) used to determine the value of a price return index. It is initially chosen at the inception of an index and subsequently adjusted by the index provider, as necessary, to avoid changes in the index value that are unrelated to changes in the prices of its constituent securities.

Domestic content provisions   Stipulate that some percentage of the value added or components used in production should be of domestic origin.

Double bottoms   In technical analysis, a reversal pattern that is formed when the price reaches a low, rebounds, and then sells off back to the first low level; used to predict a change from a downtrend to an uptrend.

Double coincidence of wants   A prerequisite to barter trades, in particular that both economic agents in the transaction want what the other is selling.

Double declining balance depreciation   An accelerated depreciation method that involves depreciating the asset at double the straight-line rate. This rate is multiplied by the book value of the asset at the beginning of the period (a declining balance) to calculate depreciation expense.

Double top   In technical analysis, a reversal pattern that is formed when an uptrend reverses twice at roughly the same high price level; used to predict a change from an uptrend to a downtrend.

Double-entry accounting   The accounting system of recording transactions in which every recorded transaction affects at least two accounts so as to keep the basic accounting equation (assets = liabilities + owners' equity) in balance.

Down transition probability   The probability that an asset's value moves down in a model of asset price dynamics.

Downgrade risk   The risk that a bond issuer's creditworthiness deteriorates, or migrates lower, leading investors to believe the risk of default is higher. Also called *credit migration risk*.

Drag on liquidity   When receipts lag, creating pressure from the decreased available funds.

Drawdown   A reduction in net asset value (NAV).

DuPont analysis   An approach to decomposing return on investment, e.g., return on equity, as the product of other financial ratios.

Dual-currency bonds   Bonds that make coupon payments in one currency and pay the par value at maturity in another currency.

Duration gap   A bond's Macaulay duration minus the investment horizon.

Dutch Book theorem   A result in probability theory stating that inconsistent probabilities create profit opportunities.

Dutch auction   An auction in which the auctioneer begins at a high price, then lowers the called price in increments until there is a willing buyer for the item being auctioned.

Earnings per share   The amount of income earned during a period per share of common stock.

Earnings surprise   The portion of a company's earnings that is unanticipated by investors and, according to the efficient market hypothesis, merits a price adjustment.

Economic costs   All the remuneration needed to keep a productive resource in its current employment or to acquire the resource for productive use; the sum of total accounting costs and implicit opportunity costs.

Economic indicator   A variable that provides information on the state of the overall economy.

Economic loss   The amount by which accounting profit is less than normal profit.

Economic order quantity–reorder point (EOQ–ROP)   An approach to managing inventory based on expected demand and the predictability of demand; the ordering point for new inventory is determined based on the costs of ordering and carrying inventory, such that the total cost associated with inventory is minimized.

Economic profit   Equal to accounting profit less the implicit opportunity costs not included in total accounting costs; the difference between total revenue (TR) and total cost (TC). Also called *abnormal profit* or *supernormal profit*.

Economic rent   The surplus value that results when a particular resource or good is fixed in supply and market price is higher than what is required to bring the resource or good onto the market and sustain its use.

Economic stabilization   Reduction of the magnitude of economic fluctuations.

Economic union   Incorporates all aspects of a common market and in addition requires common economic institutions and coordination of economic policies among members.

Economics   The study of the production, distribution, and consumption of goods and services; the principles of the allocation of scarce resources among competing uses. Economics is divided into two broad areas of study: macroeconomics and microeconomics.

Economies of scale   Reduction in cost per unit resulting from increased production.

Effective annual rate   The amount by which a unit of currency will grow in a year with interest on interest included.

Effective annual yield (EAY)   An annualized return that accounts for the effect of interest on interest; EAY is computed by compounding 1 plus the holding period yield forward to one year, then subtracting 1.

Effective convexity   A *curve convexity* statistic that measures the secondary effect of a change in a benchmark yield curve on a bond's price.

Effective duration   The sensitivity of a bond's price to a change in a benchmark yield curve.

Efficient market   A market in which asset prices reflect new information quickly and rationally.

Elastic   Said of a good or service when the magnitude of elasticity is greater than one.

Elasticity   The percentage change in one variable for a percentage change in another variable; a measure of how sensitive one variable is to a change in the value of another variable.

Elasticity of supply   A measure of the sensitivity of quantity supplied to a change in price.

Electronic communications networks   See *alternative trading systems*.

Electronic funds transfer (EFT)   The use of computer networks to conduct financial transactions electronically.

Elliott wave theory   A technical analysis theory that claims that the market follows regular, repeated waves or cycles.

Embedded option   Contingency provisions that provide the issuer or the bondholders the right, but not the obligation, to take action. These options are not part of the security and cannot be traded separately.

Empirical probability   The probability of an event estimated as a relative frequency of occurrence.

Employed   The number of people with a job.

Endogenous variables   Variables whose equilibrium values are determined within the model being considered.

Enterprise value   A measure of a company's total market value from which the value of cash and short-term investments have been subtracted.

Equal weighting   An index weighting method in which an equal weight is assigned to each constituent security at inception.

Equilibrium condition   A condition necessary for the forces within a system to be in balance.

Equipment trust certificates   Bonds secured by specific types of equipment or physical assets.

Equity   Assets less liabilities; the residual interest in the assets after subtracting the liabilities.

Equity forward   A contract calling for the purchase of an individual stock, a stock portfolio, or a stock index at a later date at an agreed-upon price.

Equity options   Options on individual stocks; also known as stock options.

Equity risk premium   The expected return on equities minus the risk-free rate; the premium that investors demand for investing in equities.

Equity swap   A swap transaction in which at least one cash flow is tied to the return to an equity portfolio position, often an equity index.

Equity-linked note   Type of index-linked bond for which the final payment is based on the return of an equity index.

Estimate   The particular value calculated from sample observations using an estimator.

Estimation   With reference to statistical inference, the subdivision dealing with estimating the value of a population parameter.

Estimator   An estimation formula; the formula used to compute the sample mean and other sample statistics are examples of estimators.

Eurobonds   Type of bond issued internationally, outside the jurisdiction of the country in whose currency the bond is denominated.

Eurodollar   A dollar deposited outside the United States.

European option   An option that can only be exercised on its expiration date.

European-style   Said of an option contract that can only be exercised on the option's expiration date.

Event   Any outcome or specified set of outcomes of a random variable.

Ex-date   The first date that a share trades without (i.e. "ex") the dividend.

Ex-dividend date   The first date that a share trades without (i.e. "ex") the dividend.

Excess kurtosis   Degree of peakedness (fatness of tails) in excess of the peakedness of the normal distribution.

Excess supply   A condition in which the quantity ready to be supplied is greater than the quantity demanded.

Exchange for physicals (EFP)   A permissible delivery procedure used by futures market participants, in which the long and short arrange a delivery procedure other than the normal procedures stipulated by the futures exchange.

Exchanges   Places where traders can meet to arrange their trades.

Execution instructions   Instructions that indicate how to fill an order.

Exercise   The process of using an option to buy or sell the underlying.

Exercise price   The fixed price at which an option holder can buy or sell the underlying. Also called *strike price, striking price*, or *strike*.

Exercise rate   The fixed rate at which the holder of an interest rate option can buy or sell the underlying.

Exercise value   The value obtained if an option is exercised based on current conditions.

Exercising the option   The process of using an option to buy or sell the underlying.

Exhaustive   Covering or containing all possible outcomes.

Exogenous variables   Variables whose equilibrium values are determined outside of the model being considered.

Expansion   The period of a business cycle after its lowest point and before its highest point.

Expansionary   Tending to cause the real economy to grow.

Expansionary fiscal policy   Fiscal policy aimed at achieving real economic growth.

Expected inflation   The level of inflation that economic agents expect in the future.

Expected loss   Default probability times Loss severity given default.

Expected value   The probability-weighted average of the possible outcomes of a random variable.

Expenses   Outflows of economic resources or increases in liabilities that result in decreases in equity (other than decreases because of distributions to owners); reductions in net assets associated with the creation of revenues.

Experience curve   A curve that shows the direct cost per unit of good or service produced or delivered as a typically declining function of cumulative output.

Export subsidy   Paid by the government to the firm when it exports a unit of a good that is being subsidized.

Exports   Goods and services that an economy sells to other countries.

Externality   An effect of a market transaction that is borne by parties other than those who transacted.

Extra dividend   A dividend paid by a company that does not pay dividends on a regular schedule, or a dividend that supplements regular cash dividends with an extra payment.

FIFO method   The first in, first out, method of accounting for inventory, which matches sales against the costs of items of inventory in the order in which they were placed in inventory.

FX swap   The combination of a spot and a forward FX transaction.

Face value   The amount of cash payable by a company to the bondholders when the bonds mature; the promised payment at maturity separate from any coupon payment.

Factor   A common or underlying element with which several variables are correlated.

Factor markets   Markets for the purchase and sale of factors of production.

Fair value   The amount at which an asset could be exchanged, or a liability settled, between knowledgeable, willing parties in an arm's-length transaction; the price that would be received to sell an asset or paid to transfer a liability in an orderly transaction between market participants.

Fed funds rate   The U.S. interbank lending rate on overnight borrowings of reserves.

Federal funds rate   The U.S. interbank lending rate on overnight borrowings of reserves.

Fiat money   Money that is not convertible into any other commodity.

Fibonacci sequence   A sequence of numbers starting with 0 and 1, and then each subsequent number in the sequence is the sum of the two preceding numbers. In Elliott Wave Theory, it is believed that market waves follow patterns that are the ratios of the numbers in the Fibonacci sequence.

Fiduciary call   A combination of a European call and a risk-free bond that matures on the option expiration day and has a face value equal to the exercise price of the call.

Fill or kill   See *immediate or cancel order*.

Financial account   A component of the balance of payments account that records investment flows.

Financial flexibility   The ability to react and adapt to financial adversities and opportunities.

Financial leverage The extent to which a company can effect, through the use of debt, a proportional change in the return on common equity that is greater than a given proportional change in operating income; also, short for the financial leverage ratio.

Financial leverage ratio A measure of financial leverage calculated as average total assets divided by average total equity.

Financial risk The risk that environmental, social, or governance risk factors will result in significant costs or other losses to a company and its shareholders; the risk arising from a company's obligation to meet required payments under its financing agreements.

Financing activities Activities related to obtaining or repaying capital to be used in the business (e.g., equity and long-term debt).

Firm commitment offering See *underwritten offering*.

First lien debt Debt secured by a pledge of certain assets that could include buildings, but may also include property and equipment, licenses, patents, brands, etc.

First mortgage debt Debt secured by a pledge of a specific property.

First price sealed bid auction An auction in which envelopes containing bids are opened simultaneously and the item is sold to the highest bidder.

First-degree price discrimination Where a monopolist is able to charge each customer the highest price the customer is willing to pay.

Fiscal multiplier The ratio of a change in national income to a change in government spending.

Fiscal policy The use of taxes and government spending to affect the level of aggregate expenditures.

Fisher effect The thesis that the real rate of interest in an economy is stable over time so that changes in nominal interest rates are the result of changes in expected inflation.

Fisher index The geometric mean of the Laspeyres index.

Fixed charge coverage A solvency ratio measuring the number of times interest and lease payments are covered by operating income, calculated as (EBIT + lease payments) divided by (interest payments + lease payments).

Fixed costs Costs that remain at the same level regardless of a company's level of production and sales.

Fixed price tender offer Offer made by a company to repurchase a specific number of shares at a fixed price that is typically at a premium to the current market price.

Fixed rate perpetual preferred stock Nonconvertible, non-callable preferred stock that has a fixed dividend rate and no maturity date.

Fixed-for-floating interest rate swap An interest rate swap in which one party pays a fixed rate and the other pays a floating rate, with both sets of payments in the same currency. Also called *plain vanilla swap* or *vanilla swap*.

Flags A technical analysis continuation pattern formed by parallel trendlines, typically over a short period.

Flat price The full price of a bond minus the accrued interest; also called the *quoted* or *clean* price.

Float In the context of customer receipts, the amount of money that is in transit between payments made by customers and the funds that are usable by the company.

Float factor An estimate of the average number of days it takes deposited checks to clear; average daily float divided by average daily deposit.

Float-adjusted market-capitalization weighting An index weighting method in which the weight assigned to each constituent security is determined by adjusting its market capitalization for its market float.

Floaters See *floating-rate notes*.

Floating-rate notes A note on which interest payments are not fixed, but instead vary from period to period depending on the current level of a reference interest rate.

Floor A series of put options on an interest rate, with each option expiring at the date on which the floating loan rate will be reset, and with each option having the same exercise rate. A floor in general can have an underlying other than the interest rate.

Floor traders Market makers that buy and sell by quoting a bid and an ask price. They are the primary providers of liquidity to the market.

Floorlet Each component put option in a floor.

Flotation cost Fees charged to companies by investment bankers and other costs associated with raising new capital.

Foreign currency reserves Holding by the central bank of non-domestic currency deposits and non-domestic bonds.

Foreign direct investment Direct investment by a firm in one country (the source country) in productive assets in a foreign country (the host country).

Foreign exchange gains (or losses) Gains (or losses) that occur when the exchange rate changes between the investor's currency and the currency that foreign securities are denominated in.

Foreign portfolio investment Shorter-term investment by individuals, firms, and institutional investors (e.g., pension funds) in foreign financial instruments such as foreign stocks and foreign government bonds.

Forward commitments Class of derivatives that provides the ability to lock in a price to transact in the future at a previously agreed-upon price.

Forward contract An agreement between two parties in which one party, the buyer, agrees to buy from the other party, the seller, an underlying asset at a later date for a price established at the start of the contract.

Forward curve A series of forward rates, each having the same timeframe.

Forward market For future delivery, beyond the usual settlement time period in the cash market.

Forward price The fixed price or rate at which the transaction scheduled to occur at the expiration of a forward contract will take place. This price is agreed on at the initiation date of the contract.

Forward rate The interest rate on a bond or money market instrument traded in a forward market. A forward rate can be interpreted as an incremental, or marginal, return for extending the time-to-maturity for an additional time period.

Forward rate agreement (FRA) A forward contract calling for one party to make a fixed interest payment and the other to make an interest payment at a rate to be determined at the contract expiration.

Fractile A value at or below which a stated fraction of the data lies.

Fractional reserve banking Banking in which reserves constitute a fraction of deposits.

Free cash flow The actual cash that would be available to the company's investors after making all investments necessary to maintain the company as an ongoing enterprise (also referred to as free cash flow to the firm); the internally generated funds that can be distributed to the company's investors (e.g., shareholders and bondholders) without impairing the value of the company.

Free cash flow to equity (FCFE)　The cash flow available to a company's common shareholders after all operating expenses, interest, and principal payments have been made, and necessary investments in working and fixed capital have been made.

Free cash flow to the firm (FCFF)　The cash flow available to the company's suppliers of capital after all operating expenses have been paid and necessary investments in working capital and fixed capital have been made.

Free float　The number of shares that are readily and freely tradable in the secondary market.

Free trade　When there are no government restrictions on a country's ability to trade.

Free trade areas　One of the most prevalent forms of regional integration, in which all barriers to the flow of goods and services among members have been eliminated.

Free-cash-flow-to-equity models　Valuation models based on discounting expected future free cash flow to equity.

Frequency distribution　A tabular display of data summarized into a relatively small number of intervals.

Frequency polygon　A graph of a frequency distribution obtained by drawing straight lines joining successive points representing the class frequencies.

Full price　The price of a security with accrued interest; also called the *invoice* or *dirty* price.

Fundamental analysis　The examination of publicly available information and the formulation of forecasts to estimate the intrinsic value of assets.

Fundamental value　The underlying or true value of an asset based on an analysis of its qualitative and quantitative characteristics. Also called *intrinsic value.*

Fundamental weighting　An index weighting method in which the weight assigned to each constituent security is based on its underlying company's size. It attempts to address the disadvantages of market-capitalization weighting by using measures that are independent of the constituent security's price.

Funds of hedge funds　Funds that hold a portfolio of hedge funds.

Future value (FV)　The amount to which a payment or series of payments will grow by a stated future date.

Futures commission merchants (FCMs)　Individuals or companies that execute futures transactions for other parties off the exchange.

Futures contract　A variation of a forward contract that has essentially the same basic definition but with some additional features, such as a clearinghouse guarantee against credit losses, a daily settlement of gains and losses, and an organized electronic or floor trading facility.

Futures price　The agreed-upon price of a futures contract.

G-spread　The yield spread in basis points over an actual or interpolated government bond.

GDP deflator　A gauge of prices and inflation that measures the aggregate changes in prices across the overall economy.

Gains　Asset inflows not directly related to the ordinary activities of the business.

Game theory　The set of tools decision makers use to incorporate responses by rival decision makers into their strategies.

Gamma　A numerical measure of how sensitive an option's delta is to a change in the underlying.

General equilibrium analysis　An analysis that provides for equilibria in multiple markets simultaneously.

General partner　The partner that runs the business and theoretically bears unlimited liability.

Geometric mean　A measure of central tendency computed by taking the *n*th root of the product of *n* non-negative values.

Giffen good　A good that is consumed more as the price of the good rises.

Gilts　Bonds issued by the U.K. government.

Giro system　An electronic payment system used widely in Europe and Japan.

Global depository receipt　A depository receipt that is issued outside of the company's home country and outside of the United States.

Global minimum-variance portfolio　The portfolio on the minimum-variance frontier with the smallest variance of return.

Global registered share　A common share that is traded on different stock exchanges around the world in different currencies.

Gold standard　With respect to a currency, if a currency is on the gold standard a given amount can be converted into a prespecified amount of gold.

Golden cross　A technical analysis term that describes a situation where a short-term moving average crosses from below a longer-term moving average to above it; this movement is considered bullish.

Good-on-close　An execution instruction specifying that an order can only be filled at the close of trading. Also called *market on close.*

Good-on-open　An execution instruction specifying that an order can only be filled at the opening of trading.

Good-till-cancelled order　An order specifying that it is valid until the entity placing the order has cancelled it (or, commonly, until some specified amount of time such as 60 days has elapsed, whichever comes sooner).

Goods markets　Markets for the output of production.

Goodwill　An intangible asset that represents the excess of the purchase price of an acquired company over the value of the net assets acquired.

Government equivalent yield　A yield that restates a yield-to-maturity based on 30/360 day-count to one based on actual/actual.

Greenmail　The purchase of the accumulated shares of a hostile investor by a company that is targeted for takeover by that investor, usually at a substantial premium over market price.

Grey market　The forward market for bonds about to be issued. Also called "when issued" market.

Gross domestic product　The market value of all final goods and services produced within the economy in a given period of time (output definition) or, equivalently, the aggregate income earned by all households, all companies, and the government within the economy in a given period of time (income definition).

Gross margin　Sales minus the cost of sales (i.e., the cost of goods sold for a manufacturing company).

Gross profit　Sales minus the cost of sales (i.e., the cost of goods sold for a manufacturing company).

Gross profit margin　The ratio of gross profit to revenues.

Grouping by function　With reference to the presentation of expenses in an income statement, the grouping together of expenses serving the same function, e.g. all items that are costs of goods sold.

Grouping by nature   With reference to the presentation of expenses in an income statement, the grouping together of expenses by similar nature, e.g., all depreciation expenses.

Growth cyclical   A term sometimes used to describe companies that are growing rapidly on a long-term basis but that still experience above-average fluctuation in their revenues and profits over the course of a business cycle.

Growth investors   With reference to equity investors, investors who seek to invest in high-earnings-growth companies.

Haircut   See *repo margin*.

Harmonic mean   A type of weighted mean computed by averaging the reciprocals of the observations, then taking the reciprocal of that average.

Head and shoulders pattern   In technical analysis, a reversal pattern that is formed in three parts: a left shoulder, head, and right shoulder; used to predict a change from an uptrend to a downtrend.

Headline inflation   The inflation rate calculated based on the price index that includes all goods and services in an economy.

Hedge funds   Private investment vehicles that typically use leverage, derivatives, and long and short investment strategies.

Hedge portfolio   A hypothetical combination of the derivative and its underlying that eliminates risk.

Held for trading   Debt or equity financial assets bought with the intention to sell them in the near term, usually less than three months; securities that a company intends to trade. Also called *trading securities*.

Held-to-maturity   Debt (fixed-income) securities that a company intends to hold to maturity; these are presented at their original cost, updated for any amortization of discounts or premiums.

Herding   Clustered trading that may or may not be based on information.

Hidden order   An order that is exposed not to the public but only to the brokers or exchanges that receive it.

High water marks   The highest value, net of fees, which a fund has reached. It reflects the highest cumulative return used to calculate an incentive fee.

Histogram   A bar chart of data that have been grouped into a frequency distribution.

Historical cost   In reference to assets, the amount paid to purchase an asset, including any costs of acquisition and/ or preparation; with reference to liabilities, the amount of proceeds received in exchange in issuing the liability.

Historical equity risk premium approach   An estimate of a country's equity risk premium that is based upon the historical averages of the risk-free rate and the rate of return on the market portfolio.

Historical simulation   Another term for the historical method of estimating VAR. This term is somewhat misleading in that the method involves not a *simulation* of the past but rather what *actually happened* in the past, sometimes adjusted to reflect the fact that a different portfolio may have existed in the past than is planned for the future.

Holder-of-record date   The date that a shareholder listed on the corporation's books will be deemed to have ownership of the shares for purposes of receiving an upcoming dividend; two business days after the ex-dividend date.

Holding period return   The return that an investor earns during a specified holding period; a synonym for total return.

Holding period yield (HPY)   The return that an investor earns during a specified holding period; holding period return with reference to a fixed-income instrument.

Homogeneity of expectations   The assumption that all investors have the same economic expectations and thus have the same expectations of prices, cash flows, and other investment characteristics.

Horizon yield   The internal rate of return between the total return (the sum of reinvested coupon payments and the sale price or redemption amount) and the purchase price of the bond.

Horizontal analysis   Common-size analysis that involves comparing a specific financial statement with that statement in prior or future time periods; also, cross-sectional analysis of one company with another.

Horizontal demand schedule   Implies that at a given price, the response in the quantity demanded is infinite.

Household   A person or a group of people living in the same residence, taken as a basic unit in economic analysis.

Hurdle rate   The rate of return that must be met for a project to be accepted.

Hypothesis   With reference to statistical inference, a statement about one or more populations.

Hypothesis testing   With reference to statistical inference, the subdivision dealing with the testing of hypotheses about one or more populations.

I-spread   The yield spread of a specific bond over the standard swap rate in that currency of the same tenor.

IRR rule   An investment decision rule that accepts projects or investments for which the IRR is greater than the opportunity cost of capital.

Iceberg order   An order in which the display size is less than the order's full size.

If-converted method   A method for accounting for the effect of convertible securities on earnings per share (EPS) that specifies what EPS would have been if the convertible securities had been converted at the beginning of the period, taking account of the effects of conversion on net income and the weighted average number of shares outstanding.

Immediate or cancel order   An order that is valid only upon receipt by the broker or exchange. If such an order cannot be filled in part or in whole upon receipt, it cancels immediately. Also called *fill or kill*.

Impact lag   The lag associated with the result of actions affecting the economy with delay.

Imperfect competition   A market structure in which an individual firm has enough share of the market (or can control a certain segment of the market) such that it is able to exert some influence over price.

Implicit price deflator for GDP   A gauge of prices and inflation that measures the aggregate changes in prices across the overall economy.

Implied forward rates   Calculated from spot rates, an implied forward rate is a break-even reinvestment rate that links the return on an investment in a shorter-term zero-coupon bond to the return on an investment in a longer-term zero-coupon bond.

Implied volatility   The volatility that option traders use to price an option, implied by the price of the option and a particular option-pricing model.

Import license   Specifies the quantity of a good that can be imported into a country.

Imports   Goods and services that a domestic economy (i.e., house-holds, firms, and government) purchases from other countries.

In the money   Options that, if exercised, would result in the value received being worth more than the payment required to exercise.

Incentive fee (or performance fee)   Funds distributed by the general partner to the limited partner(s) based on realized profits.

Income   Increases in economic benefits in the form of inflows or enhancements of assets, or decreases of liabilities that result in an increase in equity (other than increases resulting from contributions by owners).

Income constraint   The constraint on a consumer to spend, in total, no more than his income.

Income elasticity of demand   A measure of the responsiveness of demand to changes in income, defined as the percentage change in quantity demanded divided by the percentage change in income.

Income statement   A financial statement that provides information about a company's profitability over a stated period of time. Also called *statement of operations* or *profit and loss statement*.

Income tax paid   The actual amount paid for income taxes in the period; not a provision, but the actual cash outflow.

Income tax payable   The income tax owed by the company on the basis of taxable income.

Income trust   A type of equity ownership vehicle established as a trust issuing ownership shares known as units.

Increasing marginal returns   Where the marginal product of a resource increases as additional units of that input are employed.

Increasing returns to scale   Reduction in cost per unit resulting from increased production.

Increasing-cost industry   An industry in which per-unit costs and output prices are higher when industry output is increased in the long run.

Incremental cash flow   The cash flow that is realized because of a decision; the changes or increments to cash flows resulting from a decision or action.

Indenture   Legal contract that describes the form of a bond, the obligations of the issuer, and the rights of the bondholders. Also called the *trust deed*.

Independent   With reference to events, the property that the occurrence of one event does not affect the probability of another event occurring.

Independent projects   Independent projects are projects whose cash flows are independent of each other.

Independently and identically distributed (IID)   With respect to random variables, the property of random variables that are independent of each other but follow the identical probability distribution.

Index of Leading Economic Indicators   A composite of economic variables used by analysts to predict future economic conditions.

Index-linked bond   Bond for which coupon payments and/or principal repayment are linked to a specified index.

Indexing   An investment strategy in which an investor constructs a portfolio to mirror the performance of a specified index.

Indifference curve   A curve representing all the combinations of two goods or attributes such that the consumer is entirely indifferent among them.

Indifference curve map   A group or family of indifference curves, representing a consumer's entire utility function.

Indirect format   With reference to cash flow statements, a format for the presentation of the statement which, in the operating cash flow section, begins with net income then shows additions and subtractions to arrive at operating cash flow. Also called *indirect method*.

Indirect method   See *indirect format*.

Indirect taxes   Taxes such as taxes on spending, as opposed to direct taxes.

Industry   A group of companies offering similar products and/or services.

Industry analysis   The analysis of a specific branch of manufacturing, service, or trade.

Inelastic   Insensitive to price changes.

Inelastic supply   Said of supply that is insensitive to the price of goods sold.

Inferior goods   A good whose consumption decreases as income increases.

Inflation   The percentage increase in the general price level from one period to the next; a sustained rise in the overall level of prices in an economy.

Inflation Reports   A type of economic publication put out by many central banks.

Inflation premium   An extra return that compensates investors for expected inflation.

Inflation rate   The percentage change in a price index—that is, the speed of overall price level movements.

Inflation uncertainty   The degree to which economic agents view future rates of inflation as difficult to forecast.

Inflation-linked bond   Type of index-linked bond that offers investors protection against inflation by linking the bond's coupon payments and/or the principal repayment to an index of consumer prices. Also called *linkers*.

Information cascade   The transmission of information from those participants who act first and whose decisions influence the decisions of others.

Information-motivated traders   Traders that trade to profit from information that they believe allows them to predict future prices.

Informationally efficient market   A market in which asset prices reflect new information quickly and rationally.

Initial margin   The amount that must be deposited in a clearinghouse account when entering into a futures contract.

Initial margin requirement   The margin requirement on the first day of a transaction as well as on any day in which additional margin funds must be deposited.

Initial public offering   (IPO) The first issuance of common shares to the public by a formerly private corporation.

Installment method   With respect to revenue recognition, a method that specifies that the portion of the total profit of the sale that is recognized in each period is determined by the percentage of the total sales price for which the seller has received cash.

Installment sales   With respect to revenue recognition, a method that specifies that the portion of the total profit of the sale that is recognized in each period is determined by the percentage of the total sales price for which the seller has received cash.

Intangible assets   Assets lacking physical substance, such as patents and trademarks.

Interbank market   The market of loans and deposits between banks for maturities ranging from overnight to one year.

Interbank money market The market of loans and deposits between banks for maturities ranging from overnight to one year.

Interest Payment for lending funds.

Interest coverage A solvency ratio calculated as EBIT divided by interest payments.

Interest rate A rate of return that reflects the relationship between differently dated cash flows; a discount rate.

Interest rate call An option in which the holder has the right to make a known interest payment and receive an unknown interest payment.

Interest rate cap A series of call options on an interest rate, with each option expiring at the date on which the floating loan rate will be reset, and with each option having the same exercise rate. A cap in general can have an underlying other than an interest rate.

Interest rate collar A combination of a long cap and a short floor, or a short cap and a long floor. A collar in general can have an underlying other than an interest rate.

Interest rate floor A series of put options on an interest rate, with each option expiring at the date on which the floating loan rate will be reset, and with each option having the same exercise rate. A floor in general can have an underlying other than the interest rate.

Interest rate forward See *forward rate agreement.*

Interest rate option An option in which the underlying is an interest rate.

Interest rate put An option in which the holder has the right to make an unknown interest payment and receive a known interest payment.

Interest rate swap A swap in which the underlying is an interest rate. Can be viewed as a currency swap in which both currencies are the same and can be created as a combination of currency swaps.

Intergenerational data mining A form of data mining that applies information developed by previous researchers using a dataset to guide current research using the same or a related dataset.

Intermarket analysis A field within technical analysis that combines analysis of major categories of securities—namely, equities, bonds, currencies, and commodities—to identify market trends and possible inflections in a trend.

Intermediate goods and services Goods and services purchased for use as inputs to produce other goods and services.

Internal rate of return (IRR) The discount rate that makes net present value equal 0; the discount rate that makes the present value of an investment's costs (outflows) equal to the present value of the investment's benefits (inflows).

Interpolated spread The yield spread of a specific bond over the standard swap rate in that currency of the same tenor.

Interquartile range The difference between the third and first quartiles of a dataset.

Interval With reference to grouped data, a set of values within which an observation falls.

Interval scale A measurement scale that not only ranks data but also gives assurance that the differences between scale values are equal.

Intrinsic value See *fundamental value.*

Inventory The unsold units of product on hand.

Inventory blanket lien The use of inventory as collateral for a loan. Though the lender has claim to some or all of the company's inventory, the company may still sell or use the inventory in the ordinary course of business.

Inventory investment Net change in business inventory.

Inventory turnover An activity ratio calculated as cost of goods sold divided by average inventory.

Inverse demand function A restatement of the demand function in which price is stated as a function of quantity.

Investing activities Activities which are associated with the acquisition and disposal of property, plant, and equipment; intangible assets; other long-term assets; and both long-term and short-term investments in the equity and debt (bonds and loans) issued by other companies.

Investment banks Financial intermediaries that provide advice to their mostly corporate clients and help them arrange transactions such as initial and seasoned securities offerings.

Investment opportunity schedule A graphical depiction of a company's investment opportunities ordered from highest to lowest expected return. A company's optimal capital budget is found where the investment opportunity schedule intersects with the company's marginal cost of capital.

Investment policy statement (IPS) A written planning document that describes a client's investment objectives and risk tolerance over a relevant time horizon, along with constraints that apply to the client's portfolio.

Investment property Property used to earn rental income or capital appreciation (or both).

January effect Calendar anomaly that stock market returns in January are significantly higher compared to the rest of the months of the year, with most of the abnormal returns reported during the first five trading days in January. Also called *turn-of-the-year effect.*

Joint probability The probability of the joint occurrence of stated events.

Joint probability function A function giving the probability of joint occurrences of values of stated random variables.

Just-in-time (JIT) method Method of managing inventory that minimizes in-process inventory stocks.

Keynesians Economists who believe that fiscal policy can have powerful effects on aggregate demand, output, and employment when there is substantial spare capacity in an economy.

Kondratieff wave A 54-year long economic cycle postulated by Nikolai Kondratieff.

Kurtosis The statistical measure that indicates the peakedness of a distribution.

LIFO layer liquidation With respect to the application of the LIFO inventory method, the liquidation of old, relatively low-priced inventory; happens when the volume of sales rises above the volume of recent purchases so that some sales are made from relatively old, low-priced inventory. Also called *LIFO liquidation.*

LIFO method The last in, first out, method of accounting for inventory, which matches sales against the costs of items of inventory in the reverse order the items were placed in inventory (i.e., inventory produced or acquired last are assumed to be sold first).

Labor force The portion of the working age population (over the age of 16) that is employed or is available for work but not working (unemployed).

Labor markets Markets for labor services.

Labor productivity The quantity of goods and services (real GDP) that a worker can produce in one hour of work.

Laddering strategy   A form of active strategy which entails scheduling maturities on a systematic basis within the investment portfolio such that investments are spread out equally over the term of the ladder.

Lagging economic indicators   Turning points that take place later than those of the overall economy; they are believed to have value in identifying the economy's past condition.

Laspeyres index   A price index created by holding the composition of the consumption basket constant.

Law of demand   The principle that as the price of a good rises, buyers will choose to buy less of it, and as its price falls, they will buy more.

Law of diminishing returns   The smallest output that a firm can produce such that its long run average costs are minimized.

Law of one price   The condition in a financial market in which two equivalent financial instruments or combinations of financial instruments can sell for only one price. Equivalent to the principle that no arbitrage opportunities are possible.

Law of supply   The principle that a rise in price usually results in an increase in the quantity supplied.

Lead underwriter   The lead investment bank in a syndicate of investment banks and broker–dealers involved in a securities underwriting.

Leading economic indicators   Turning points that usually precede those of the overall economy; they are believed to have value for predicting the economy's future state, usually near-term.

Legal tender   Something that must be accepted when offered in exchange for goods and services.

Lender of last resort   An entity willing to lend money when no other entity is ready to do so.

Leptokurtic   Describes a distribution that is more peaked than a normal distribution.

Letter of credit   Form of external credit enhancement whereby a financial institution provides the issuer with a credit line to reimburse any cash flow shortfalls from the assets backing the issue.

Level of significance   The probability of a Type I error in testing a hypothesis.

Leverage   In the context of corporate finance, leverage refers to the use of fixed costs within a company's cost structure. Fixed costs that are operating costs (such as depreciation or rent) create operating leverage. Fixed costs that are financial costs (such as interest expense) create financial leverage.

Leveraged buyout   (LBO) A transaction whereby the target company management team converts the target to a privately held company by using heavy borrowing to finance the purchase of the target company's outstanding shares.

Liabilities   Present obligations of an enterprise arising from past events, the settlement of which is expected to result in an outflow of resources embodying economic benefits; creditors' claims on the resources of a company.

Life-cycle stage   The stage of the life cycle: embryonic, growth, shakeout, mature, declining.

Likelihood   The probability of an observation, given a particular set of conditions.

Limit down   A limit move in the futures market in which the price at which a transaction would be made is at or below the lower limit.

Limit move   A condition in the futures markets in which the price at which a transaction would be made is at or beyond the price limits.

Limit order   Instructions to a broker or exchange to obtain the best price immediately available when filling an order, but in no event accept a price higher than a specified (limit) price when buying or accept a price lower than a specified (limit) price when selling.

Limit order book   The book or list of limit orders to buy and sell that pertains to a security.

Limit up   A limit move in the futures market in which the price at which a transaction would be made is at or above the upper limit.

Limitations on liens   Meant to put limits on how much secured debt an issuer can have.

Limited partners   Partners with limited liability. Limited partnerships in hedge and private equity funds are typically restricted to investors who are expected to understand and to be able to assume the risks associated with the investments.

Line chart   In technical analysis, a plot of price data, typically closing prices, with a line connecting the points.

Linear interpolation   The estimation of an unknown value on the basis of two known values that bracket it, using a straight line between the two known values.

Linear scale   A scale in which equal distances correspond to equal absolute amounts. Also called *arithmetic scale*.

Linker   See *inflation-linked bond*.

Liquid market   Said of a market in which traders can buy or sell with low total transaction costs when they want to trade.

Liquidating dividend   A dividend that is a return of capital rather than a distribution from earnings or retained earnings.

Liquidation   To sell the assets of a company, division, or subsidiary piecemeal, typically because of bankruptcy; the form of bankruptcy that allows for the orderly satisfaction of creditors' claims after which the company ceases to exist.

Liquidity   The ability to purchase or sell an asset quickly and easily at a price close to fair market value. The ability to meet short-term obligations using assets that are the most readily converted into cash.

Liquidity premium   An extra return that compensates investors for the risk of loss relative to an investment's fair value if the investment needs to be converted to cash quickly.

Liquidity ratios   Financial ratios measuring the company's ability to meet its short-term obligations.

Liquidity trap   A condition in which the demand for money becomes infinitely elastic (horizontal demand curve) so that injections of money into the economy will not lower interest rates or affect real activity.

Load fund   A mutual fund in which, in addition to the annual fee, a percentage fee is charged to invest in the fund and/or for redemptions from the fund.

Locals   Market makers that buy and sell by quoting a bid and an ask price. They are the primary providers of liquidity to the market.

Lockbox system   A payment system in which customer payments are mailed to a post office box and the banking institution retrieves and deposits these payments several times a day, enabling the company to have use of the fund sooner than in a centralized system in which customer payments are sent to the company.

Locked limit   A condition in the futures markets in which a transaction cannot take place because the price would be beyond the limits.

Lockup period   The minimum period before investors are allowed to make withdrawals or redeem shares from a fund.

Logarithmic scale A scale in which equal distances represent equal proportional changes in the underlying quantity.

London Interbank Offered Rate (Libor or LIBOR) Collective name for multiple rates at which a select set of banks believe they could borrow unsecured funds from other banks in the London interbank market for different currencies and different borrowing periods ranging from overnight to one year.

Long The buyer of a derivative contract. Also refers to the position of owning a derivative.

Long position A position in an asset or contract in which one owns the asset or has an exercisable right under the contract.

Long-lived assets Assets that are expected to provide economic benefits over a future period of time, typically greater than one year. Also called *long-term assets*.

Long-run average total cost curve The curve describing average total costs when no costs are considered fixed.

Long-run industry supply curve A curve describing the relationship between quantity supplied and output prices when no costs are considered fixed.

Long-term contract A contract that spans a number of accounting periods.

Long-term equity anticipatory securities (LEAPS) Options originally created with expirations of several years.

Longitudinal data Observations on characteristic(s) of the same observational unit through time.

Look-ahead bias A bias caused by using information that was unavailable on the test date.

Loss severity Portion of a bond's value (including unpaid interest) an investor loses in the event of default.

Losses Asset outflows not directly related to the ordinary activities of the business.

Lower bound The lowest possible value of an option.

M^2 A measure of what a portfolio would have returned if it had taken on the same total risk as the market index.

Macaulay duration The approximate amount of time a bond would have to be held for the market discount rate at purchase to be realized if there is a single change in interest rate. It indicates the point in time when the coupon reinvestment and price effects of a change in yield-to-maturity offset each other.

Macroeconomics The branch of economics that deals with aggregate economic quantities, such as national output and national income.

Maintenance covenants Covenants in bank loan agreements that require the borrower to satisfy certain financial ratio tests while the loan is outstanding.

Maintenance margin The minimum amount that is required by a futures clearinghouse to maintain a margin account and to protect against default. Participants whose margin balances drop below the required maintenance margin must replenish their accounts.

Maintenance margin requirement The margin requirement on any day other than the first day of a transaction.

Management buy-ins Leveraged buyout in which the current management team is being replaced and the acquiring team will be involved in managing the company.

Management buyout (MBO) An event in which a group of investors consisting primarily of the company's existing management purchase all of its outstanding shares and take the company private.

Management fee A fee based on assets under management or committed capital, as applicable. Also called *base fee*.

Manufacturing resource planning (MRP) The incorporation of production planning into inventory management. A MRP analysis provides both a materials acquisition schedule and a production schedule.

Margin The amount of money that a trader deposits in a margin account. The term is derived from the stock market practice in which an investor borrows a portion of the money required to purchase a certain amount of stock. In futures markets, there is no borrowing so the margin is more of a down payment or performance bond.

Margin bond A cash deposit required by the clearinghouse from the participants to a contract to provide a credit guarantee. Also called a *performance bond*.

Margin call A request for the short to deposit additional funds to bring their balance up to the initial margin.

Margin loan Money borrowed from a broker to purchase securities.

Marginal cost The cost of producing an additional unit of a good.

Marginal probability The probability of an event *not* conditioned on another event.

Marginal product Measures the productivity of each unit of input and is calculated by taking the difference in total product from adding another unit of input (assuming other resource quantities are held constant).

Marginal propensity to consume The proportion of an additional unit of disposable income that is consumed or spent; the change in consumption for a small change in income.

Marginal propensity to save The proportion of an additional unit of disposable income that is saved (not spent).

Marginal rate of substitution The rate at which one is willing to give up one good to obtain more of another.

Marginal revenue The change in total revenue divided by the change in quantity sold; simply, the additional revenue from selling one more unit.

Marginal revenue product The amount of additional revenue received from employing an additional unit of an input.

Marginal value The added value from an additional unit of a good.

Marginal value curve A curve describing the highest price consumers are willing to pay for each additional unit of a good.

Mark to market The revaluation of a financial asset or liability to its current market value or fair value.

Market A means of bringing buyers and sellers together to exchange goods and services.

Market anomaly Change in the price or return of a security that cannot directly be linked to current relevant information known in the market or to the release of new information into the market.

Market bid–ask spread The difference between the best bid and the best offer.

Market discount rate The rate of return required by investors given the risk of the investment in a bond; also called the *required yield* or the *required rate of return*.

Market equilibrium The condition in which the quantity willingly offered for sale by sellers at a given price is just equal to the quantity willingly demanded by buyers at that same price.

Market float The number of shares that are available to the investing public.

Market liquidity risk The risk that the price at which investors can actually transact—buying or selling—may differ from the price indicated in the market.

Market mechanism   The process by which price adjusts until there is neither excess supply nor excess demand.

Market model   A regression equation that specifies a linear relationship between the return on a security (or portfolio) and the return on a broad market index.

Market multiple models   Valuation models based on share price multiples or enterprise value multiples.

Market order   Instructions to a broker or exchange to obtain the best price immediately available when filling an order.

Market structure   The competitive environment (perfect competition, monopolistic competition, oligopoly, and monopoly).

Market value   The price at which an asset or security can currently be bought or sold in an open market.

Market-capitalization weighting   An index weighting method in which the weight assigned to each constituent security is determined by dividing its market capitalization by the total market capitalization (sum of the market capitalization) of all securities in the index. Also called *value weighting*.

Market-on-close   An execution instruction specifying that an order can only be filled at the close of trading.

Market-oriented investors   With reference to equity investors, investors whose investment disciplines cannot be clearly categorized as value or growth.

Marketable limit order   A buy limit order in which the limit price is placed above the best offer, or a sell limit order in which the limit price is placed below the best bid. Such orders generally will partially or completely fill right away.

Marking to market   A procedure used primarily in futures markets in which the parties to a contract settle the amount owed daily. Also known as the *daily settlement*.

Markowitz efficient frontier   The graph of the set of portfolios offering the maximum expected return for their level of risk (standard deviation of return).

Matching principle   The accounting principle that expenses should be recognized when the associated revenue is recognized.

Matching strategy   An active investment strategy that includes intentional matching of the timing of cash outflows with investment maturities.

Matrix pricing   Process of estimating the market discount rate and price of a bond based on the quoted or flat prices of more frequently traded comparable bonds.

Maturity premium   An extra return that compensates investors for the increased sensitivity of the market value of debt to a change in market interest rates as maturity is extended.

Maturity structure   A factor explaining the differences in yields on similar bonds; also called *term structure*.

Mean absolute deviation   With reference to a sample, the mean of the absolute values of deviations from the sample mean.

Mean excess return   The average rate of return in excess of the risk-free rate.

Mean–variance analysis   An approach to portfolio analysis using expected means, variances, and covariances of asset returns.

Measure of central tendency   A quantitative measure that specifies where data are centered.

Measure of value   A standard for measuring value; a function of money.

Measurement scales   A scheme of measuring differences. The four types of measurement scales are nominal, ordinal, interval, and ratio.

Measures of location   A quantitative measure that describes the location or distribution of data; includes not only measures of central tendency but also other measures such as percentiles.

Median   The value of the middle item of a set of items that has been sorted into ascending or descending order; the 50th percentile.

Medium of exchange   Any asset that can be used to purchase goods and services or to repay debts; a function of money.

Medium-term note   A corporate bond offered continuously to investors by an agent of the issuer, designed to fill the funding gap between commercial paper and long-term bonds.

Menu costs   A cost of inflation in which businesses constantly have to incur the costs of changing the advertised prices of their goods and services.

Mesokurtic   Describes a distribution with kurtosis identical to that of the normal distribution.

Mezzanine financing   Debt or preferred shares with a relationship to common equity due to a feature such as attached warrants or conversion options and that is subordinate to both senior and high yield debt. It is referred to as mezzanine because of its location on the balance sheet.

Microeconomics   The branch of economics that deals with markets and decision making of individual economic units, including consumers and businesses.

Minimum efficient scale   The smallest output that a firm can produce such that its long run average cost is minimized.

Minimum-variance portfolio   The portfolio with the minimum variance for each given level of expected return.

Minsky moment   Named for Hyman Minksy: A point in a business cycle when, after individuals become overextended in borrowing to finance speculative investments, people start realizing that something is likely to go wrong and a panic ensues leading to asset sell-offs.

Mismatching strategy   An active investment strategy whereby the timing of cash outflows is not matched with investment maturities.

Modal interval   With reference to grouped data, the most frequently occurring interval.

Mode   The most frequently occurring value in a set of observations.

Modern portfolio theory   (MPT) The analysis of rational portfolio choices based on the efficient use of risk.

Modified duration   A measure of the percentage price change of a bond given a change in its yield-to-maturity.

Momentum oscillators   A graphical representation of market sentiment that is constructed from price data and calculated so that it oscillates either between a high and a low or around some number.

Monetarists   Economists who believe that the rate of growth of the money supply is the primary determinant of the rate of inflation.

Monetary policy   Actions taken by a nation's central bank to affect aggregate output and prices through changes in bank reserves, reserve requirements, or its target interest rate.

Monetary transmission mechanism   The process whereby a central bank's interest rate gets transmitted through the economy and ultimately affects the rate of increase of prices.

Monetary union   An economic union in which the members adopt a common currency.

Money   A generally accepted medium of exchange and unit of account.

Money convexity   For a bond, the annual or approximate convexity multiplied by the full price.

Money creation   The process by which changes in bank reserves translate into changes in the money supply.

Money duration   A measure of the price change in units of the currency in which the bond is denominated given a change in its yield-to-maturity.

Money market   The market for short-term debt instruments (one-year maturity or less).

Money market securities   Fixed-income securities with maturities at issuance of one year or less.

Money market yield   A yield on a basis comparable to the quoted yield on an interest-bearing money market instrument that pays interest on a 360-day basis; the annualized holding period yield, assuming a 360-day year.

Money multiplier   Describes how a change in reserves is expected to affect the money supply; in its simplest form, 1 divided by the reserve requirement.

Money neutrality   The thesis that an increase in the money supply leads in the long-run to an increase in the price level, while leaving real variables like output and employment unaffected.

Money-weighted return   The internal rate of return on a portfolio, taking account of all cash flows.

Moneyness   The relationship between the price of the underlying and an option's exercise price.

Monopolist   Said of an entity that is the only seller in its market.

Monopolistic competition   Highly competitive form of imperfect competition; the competitive characteristic is a notably large number of firms, while the monopoly aspect is the result of product differentiation.

Monopoly   In pure monopoly markets, there are no substitutes for the given product or service. There is a single seller, which exercises considerable power over pricing and output decisions.

Monte Carlo simulation   An approach to estimating a probability distribution of outcomes to examine what might happen if particular risks are faced. This method is widely used in the sciences as well as in business to study a variety of problems.

Mortgage-backed securities   Debt obligations that represent claims to the cash flows from pools of mortgage loans, most commonly on residential property.

Moving average   The average of the closing price of a security over a specified number of periods. With each new period, the average is recalculated.

Moving-average convergence/divergence oscillator   (MACD) A momentum oscillator that is constructed based on the difference between short-term and long-term moving averages of a security's price.

Multi-factor model   A model that explains a variable in terms of the values of a set of factors.

Multi-market indices   Comprised of indices from different countries, designed to represent multiple security markets.

Multi-step format   With respect to the format of the income statement, a format that presents a subtotal for gross profit (revenue minus cost of goods sold).

Multilateral trading facilities   See *alternative trading systems*.

Multinational corporation   A company operating in more than one country or having subsidiary firms in more than one country.

Multiplication rule for probabilities   The rule that the joint probability of events A and B equals the probability of A given B times the probability of B.

Multiplier models   Valuation models based on share price multiples or enterprise value multiples.

Multivariate distribution   A probability distribution that specifies the probabilities for a group of related random variables.

Multivariate normal distribution   A probability distribution for a group of random variables that is completely defined by the means and variances of the variables plus all the correlations between pairs of the variables.

Muni   A type of non-sovereign bond issued by a state or local government in the United States. It very often (but not always) offers income tax exemptions.

Municipal bonds   A type of non-sovereign bond issued by a state or local government in the United States. It very often (but not always) offers income tax exemptions.

Mutual fund   A professionally managed investment pool in which investors in the fund typically each have a pro-rata claim on the income and value of the fund.

Mutually exclusive projects   Mutually exclusive projects compete directly with each other. For example, if Projects A and B are mutually exclusive, you can choose A or B, but you cannot choose both.

n Factorial   For a positive integer n, the product of the first n positive integers; 0 factorial equals 1 by definition. n factorial is written as $n!$.

NDFs   See *non-deliverable forwards*.

NPV rule   An investment decision rule that states that an investment should be undertaken if its NPV is positive but not undertaken if its NPV is negative.

Narrow money   The notes and coins in circulation in an economy, plus other very highly liquid deposits.

Nash equilibrium   When two or more participants in a non-coop-erative game have no incentive to deviate from their respective equilibrium strategies given their opponent's strategies.

National income   The income received by all factors of production used in the generation of final output. National income equals gross domestic product (or, in some countries, gross national product) minus the capital consumption allowance and a statistical discrepancy.

Natural rate of unemployment   Effective unemployment rate, below which pressure emerges in labor markets.

Negative externality   A negative effect (e.g., pollution) of a market transaction that is borne by parties other than those who transacted; a spillover cost.

Neo-Keynesians   A group of dynamic general equilibrium models that assume slow-to-adjust prices and wages.

Net book value   The remaining (undepreciated) balance of an asset's purchase cost. For liabilities, the face value of a bond minus any unamortized discount, or plus any unamortized premium.

Net exports   The difference between the value of a country's exports and the value of its imports (i.e., value of exports minus imports).

Net income   The difference between revenue and expenses; what remains after subtracting all expenses (including depreciation, interest, and taxes) from revenue.

Net operating cycle   An estimate of the average time that elapses between paying suppliers for materials and collecting cash from the subsequent sale of goods produced.

Net present value   (NPV) The present value of an investment's cash inflows (benefits) minus the present value of its cash outflows (costs).

Net profit margin   An indicator of profitability, calculated as net income divided by revenue; indicates how much of each dollar of revenues is left after all costs and expenses. Also called *profit margin* or *return on sales*.

Net realisable value   Estimated selling price in the ordinary course of business less the estimated costs necessary to make the sale.

Net revenue   Revenue after adjustments (e.g., for estimated returns or for amounts unlikely to be collected).

Net tax rate   The tax rate net of transfer payments.

Netting   When parties agree to exchange only the net amount owed from one party to the other.

Neutral rate of interest   The rate of interest that neither spurs on nor slows down the underlying economy.

New Keynesians   A group of dynamic general equilibrium models that assume slow-to-adjust prices and wages.

New classical macroeconomics   An approach to macroeconomics that seeks the macroeconomic conclusions of individuals maximizing utility on the basis of rational expectations and companies maximizing profits.

New-issue DRP   Dividend reinvestment plan in which the company meets the need for additional shares by issuing them instead of purchasing them.

No-load fund   A mutual fund in which there is no fee for investing in the fund or for redeeming fund shares, although there is an annual fee based on a percentage of the fund's net asset value.

Node   Each value on a binomial tree from which successive moves or outcomes branch.

Nominal GDP   The value of goods and services measured at current prices.

Nominal rate   A rate of interest based on the security's face value.

Nominal risk-free interest rate   The sum of the real risk-free interest rate and the inflation premium.

Nominal scale   A measurement scale that categorizes data but does not rank them.

Non-accelerating inflation rate of unemployment   Effective unemployment rate, below which pressure emerges in labor markets.

Non-cumulative preference shares   Preference shares for which dividends that are not paid in the current or subsequent periods are forfeited permanently (instead of being accrued and paid at a later date).

Non-current assets   Assets that are expected to benefit the company over an extended period of time (usually more than one year).

Non-current liabilities   Obligations that broadly represent a probable sacrifice of economic benefits in periods generally greater than one year in the future.

Non-cyclical   A company whose performance is largely independent of the business cycle.

Non-deliverable forwards   Cash-settled forward contracts, used predominately with respect to foreign exchange forwards. Also called *contracts for differences*.

Non-participating preference shares   Preference shares that do not entitle shareholders to share in the profits of the company. Instead, shareholders are only entitled to receive a fixed dividend payment and the par value of the shares in the event of liquidation.

Non-renewable resources   Finite resources that are depleted once they are consumed, such as oil and coal.

Non-satiation   The assumption that the consumer could never have so much of a preferred good that she would refuse any more, even if it were free; sometimes referred to as the "more is better" assumption.

Non-sovereign bonds   A bond issued by a government below the national level, such as a province, region, state, or city.

Non-sovereign government bonds   A bond issued by a government below the national level, such as a province, region, state, or city.

Nonconventional cash flow   In a nonconventional cash flow pattern, the initial outflow is not followed by inflows only, but the cash flows can flip from positive (inflows) to negative (outflows) again (or even change signs several times).

Noncurrent assets   Assets that are expected to benefit the company over an extended period of time (usually more than one year).

Nonparametric test   A test that is not concerned with a parameter, or that makes minimal assumptions about the population from which a sample comes.

Nonsystematic risk   Unique risk that is local or limited to a particular asset or industry that need not affect assets outside of that asset class.

Normal distribution   A continuous, symmetric probability distribution that is completely described by its mean and its variance.

Normal good   A good that is consumed in greater quantities as income increases.

Normal profit   The level of accounting profit needed to just cover the implicit opportunity costs ignored in accounting costs.

Notching   Ratings adjustment methodology where specific issues from the same borrower may be assigned different credit ratings.

Notes payable   Amounts owed by a business to creditors as a result of borrowings that are evidenced by (short-term) loan agreements.

Notice period   The length of time (typically 30 to 90 days) in advance that investors may be required to notify a fund of their intent to redeem.

Notional principal   An imputed principal amount.

Number of days of inventory   An activity ratio equal to the number of days in a period divided by the inventory ratio for the period; an indication of the number of days a company ties up funds in inventory.

Number of days of payables   An activity ratio equal to the number of days in a period divided by the payables turnover ratio for the period; an estimate of the average number of days it takes a company to pay its suppliers.

Number of days of receivables   Estimate of the average number of days it takes to collect on credit accounts.

Objective probabilities   Probabilities that generally do not vary from person to person; includes a priori and objective probabilities.

Off-the-run   Seasoned government bonds are off-the-run securities; they are not the most recently issued or the most actively traded.

Offer   The price at which a dealer or trader is willing to sell an asset, typically qualified by a maximum quantity (ask size).

Official interest rate   An interest rate that a central bank sets and announces publicly; normally the rate at which it is willing to lend money to the commercial banks. Also called *official policy rate* or *policy rate*.

Official policy rate An interest rate that a central bank sets and announces publicly; normally the rate at which it is willing to lend money to the commercial banks.

Offsetting A transaction in exchange-listed derivative markets in which a party re-enters the market to close out a position.

Oligopoly Market structure with a relatively small number of firms supplying the market.

On-the-run The most recently issued and most actively traded sovereign securities.

One-sided hypothesis test A test in which the null hypothesis is rejected only if the evidence indicates that the population parameter is greater than (smaller than) θ_0. The alternative hypothesis also has one side.

One-tailed hypothesis test A test in which the null hypothesis is rejected only if the evidence indicates that the population parameter is greater than (smaller than) θ_0. The alternative hypothesis also has one side.

Open economy An economy that trades with other countries.

Open interest The number of outstanding contracts in a clearinghouse at any given time. The open interest figure changes daily as some parties open up new positions, while other parties offset their old positions.

Open market operations The purchase or sale of bonds by the national central bank to implement monetary policy. The bonds traded are usually sovereign bonds issued by the national government.

Open-end fund A mutual fund that accepts new investment money and issues additional shares at a value equal to the net asset value of the fund at the time of investment.

Open-market DRP Dividend reinvestment plan in which the company purchases shares in the open market to acquire the additional shares credited to plan participants.

Operating activities Activities that are part of the day-to-day business functioning of an entity, such as selling inventory and providing services.

Operating breakeven The number of units produced and sold at which the company's operating profit is zero (revenues = operating costs).

Operating cash flow The net amount of cash provided from operating activities.

Operating cycle A measure of the time needed to convert raw materials into cash from a sale; it consists of the number of days of inventory and the number of days of receivables.

Operating efficiency ratios Ratios that measure how efficiently a company performs day-to-day tasks, such as the collection of receivables and management of inventory.

Operating leverage The use of fixed costs in operations.

Operating profit A company's profits on its usual business activities before deducting taxes. Also called *operating income*.

Operating profit margin A profitability ratio calculated as operating income (i.e., income before interest and taxes) divided by revenue. Also called *operating margin*.

Operating risk The risk attributed to the operating cost structure, in particular the use of fixed costs in operations; the risk arising from the mix of fixed and variable costs; the risk that a company's operations may be severely affected by environmental, social, and governance risk factors.

Operational independence A bank's ability to execute monetary policy and set interest rates in the way it thought would best meet the inflation target.

Operationally efficient Said of a market, a financial system, or an economy that has relatively low transaction costs.

Opportunity cost The value that investors forgo by choosing a particular course of action; the value of something in its best alternative use.

Option A financial instrument that gives one party the right, but not the obligation, to buy or sell an underlying asset from or to another party at a fixed price over a specific period of time. Also referred to as *contingent claim* or *option contract*.

Option contract See *option*.

Option premium The amount of money a buyer pays and seller receives to engage in an option transaction.

Option price The amount of money a buyer pays and seller receives to engage in an option transaction.

Option-adjusted price The value of the embedded option plus the flat price of the bond.

Option-adjusted spread OAS = Z-spread − Option value (in basis points per year).

Option-adjusted yield The required market discount rate whereby the price is adjusted for the value of the embedded option.

Order A specification of what instrument to trade, how much to trade, and whether to buy or sell.

Order precedence hierarchy With respect to the execution of orders to trade, a set of rules that determines which orders execute before other orders.

Order-driven markets A market (generally an auction market) that uses rules to arrange trades based on the orders that traders submit; in their pure form, such markets do not make use of dealers.

Ordinal scale A measurement scale that sorts data into categories that are ordered (ranked) with respect to some characteristic.

Ordinary annuity An annuity with a first cash flow that is paid one period from the present.

Ordinary shares Equity shares that are subordinate to all other types of equity (e.g., preferred equity). Also called *common stock* or *common shares*.

Organized exchange A securities marketplace where buyers and seller can meet to arrange their trades.

Other comprehensive income Items of comprehensive income that are not reported on the income statement; comprehensive income minus net income.

Other receivables Amounts owed to the company from parties other than customers.

Out of the money Options that, if exercised, would require the payment of more money than the value received and therefore would not be currently exercised.

Out-of-sample test A test of a strategy or model using a sample outside the time period on which the strategy or model was developed.

Outcome A possible value of a random variable.

Over-the-counter (OTC) markets A decentralized market where buy and sell orders initiated from various locations are matched through a communications network.

Overbought A market condition in which market sentiment is thought to be unsustainably bullish.

Oversold A market condition in which market sentiment is thought to be unsustainably bearish.

Own-price The price of a good or service itself (as opposed to the price of something else).

Own-price elasticity of demand The percentage change in quantity demanded for a percentage change in own price, holding all other things constant.

Owner-of-record date   The date that a shareholder listed on the corporation's books will be deemed to have ownership of the shares for purposes of receiving an upcoming dividend; two business days after the ex-dividend date.

Owners' equity   The excess of assets over liabilities; the residual interest of shareholders in the assets of an entity after deducting the entity's liabilities. Also called *shareholders' equity*.

Paasche index   An index formula using the current composition of a basket of products.

Paired comparisons test   A statistical test for differences based on paired observations drawn from samples that are dependent on each other.

Paired observations   Observations that are dependent on each other.

Pairs arbitrage trade   A trade in two closely related stocks involving the short sale of one and the purchase of the other.

Panel data   Observations through time on a single characteristic of multiple observational units.

Par curve   A sequence of yields-to-maturity such that each bond is priced at par value. The bonds are assumed to have the same currency, credit risk, liquidity, tax status, and annual yields stated for the same periodicity.

Par value   The amount of principal on a bond.

Parallel shift   A parallel yield curve shift implies that all rates change by the same amount in the same direction.

Parameter   A descriptive measure computed from or used to describe a population of data, conventionally represented by Greek letters.

Parametric test   Any test (or procedure) concerned with parameters or whose validity depends on assumptions concerning the population generating the sample.

Pari passu   On an equal footing.

Partial equilibrium analysis   An equilibrium analysis focused on one market, taking the values of exogenous variables as given.

Participating preference shares   Preference shares that entitle shareholders to receive the standard preferred dividend plus the opportunity to receive an additional dividend if the company's profits exceed a pre-specified level.

Passive investment   A buy and hold approach in which an investor does not make portfolio changes based on short-term expectations of changing market or security performance.

Passive strategy   In reference to short-term cash management, it is an investment strategy characterized by simple decision rules for making daily investments.

Payable date   The day that the company actually mails out (or electronically transfers) a dividend payment.

Payment date   The day that the company actually mails out (or electronically transfers) a dividend payment.

Payments system   The system for the transfer of money.

Payoff   The value of an option at expiration.

Payout   Cash dividends and the value of shares repurchased in any given year.

Payout policy   A company's set of principles guiding payouts.

Peak   The highest point of a business cycle.

Peer group   A group of companies engaged in similar business activities whose economics and valuation are influenced by closely related factors.

Pennants   A technical analysis continuation pattern formed by trendlines that converge to form a triangle, typically over a short period.

Per capita real GDP   Real GDP divided by the size of the population, often used as a measure of the average standard of living in a country.

Per unit contribution margin   The amount that each unit sold contributes to covering fixed costs—that is, the difference between the price per unit and the variable cost per unit.

Percentage-of-completion   A method of revenue recognition in which, in each accounting period, the company estimates what percentage of the contract is complete and then reports that percentage of the total contract revenue in its income statement.

Percentiles   Quantiles that divide a distribution into 100 equal parts.

Perfect competition   A market structure in which the individual firm has virtually no impact on market price, because it is assumed to be a very small seller among a very large number of firms selling essentially identical products.

Perfectly elastic   Said of a good or service that is infinitely sensitive to a change in the value of a specified variable (e.g., price).

Perfectly inelastic   Said of a good or service that is completely insensitive to a change in the value of a specified variable (e.g., price).

Performance appraisal   The evaluation of risk-adjusted performance; the evaluation of investment skill.

Performance bond   See *margin bond*.

Performance evaluation   The measurement and assessment of the outcomes of investment management decisions.

Performance measurement   The calculation of returns in a logical and consistent manner.

Period costs   Costs (e.g., executives' salaries) that cannot be directly matched with the timing of revenues and which are thus expensed immediately.

Periodicity   The assumed number of periods in the year, typically matches the frequency of coupon payments.

Permanent differences   Differences between tax and financial reporting of revenue (expenses) that will not be reversed at some future date. These result in a difference between the company's effective tax rate and statutory tax rate and do not result in a deferred tax item.

Permutation   An ordered listing.

Perpetual bonds   Bonds with no stated maturity date.

Perpetuity   A perpetual annuity, or a set of never-ending level sequential cash flows, with the first cash flow occurring one period from now. A bond that does not mature.

Personal consumption expenditures   All domestic personal consumption; the basis for a price index for such consumption called the PCE price index.

Personal disposable income   Equal to personal income less personal taxes.

Personal income   A broad measure of household income that includes all income received by households, whether earned or unearned; measures the ability of consumers to make purchases.

Plain vanilla bond   Bond that makes periodic, fixed coupon payments during the bond's life and a lump-sum payment of principal at maturity. Also called *conventional bond*.

Plain vanilla swap   An interest rate swap in which one party pays a fixed rate and the other pays a floating rate, with both sets of payments in the same currency.

Planning horizon   A time period in which all factors of production are variable, including technology, physical capital, and plant size.

Platykurtic Describes a distribution that is less peaked than the normal distribution.

Point and figure chart A technical analysis chart that is constructed with columns of X's alternating with columns of O's such that the horizontal axis represents only the number of changes in price without reference to time or volume.

Point estimate A single numerical estimate of an unknown quantity, such as a population parameter.

Point of sale (POS) Systems that capture transaction data at the physical location in which the sale is made.

Policy rate An interest rate that a central bank sets and announces publicly; normally the rate at which it is willing to lend money to the commercial banks.

Population All members of a specified group.

Population mean The arithmetic mean value of a population; the arithmetic mean of all the observations or values in the population.

Population standard deviation A measure of dispersion relating to a population in the same unit of measurement as the observations, calculated as the positive square root of the population variance.

Population variance A measure of dispersion relating to a population, calculated as the mean of the squared deviations around the population mean.

Portfolio company In private equity, the company that is being invested in.

Portfolio demand for money The demand to hold speculative money balances based on the potential opportunities or risks that are inherent in other financial instruments.

Portfolio planning The process of creating a plan for building a portfolio that is expected to satisfy a client's investment objectives.

Position The quantity of an asset that an entity owns or owes.

Position trader A trader who typically holds positions open overnight.

Positive externality A positive effect (e.g., improved literacy) of a market transaction that is borne by parties other than those who transacted; a spillover benefit.

Posterior probability An updated probability that reflects or comes after new information.

Potential GDP The level of real GDP that can be produced at full employment; measures the productive capacity of the economy.

Power of a test The probability of correctly rejecting the null—that is, rejecting the null hypothesis when it is false.

Precautionary money balances Money held to provide a buffer against unforeseen events that might require money.

Precautionary stocks A level of inventory beyond anticipated needs that provides a cushion in the event that it takes longer to replenish inventory than expected or in the case of greater than expected demand.

Preference shares A type of equity interest which ranks above common shares with respect to the payment of dividends and the distribution of the company's net assets upon liquidation. They have characteristics of both debt and equity securities. Also called *preferred stock*.

Preferred stock See *preference shares*.

Premium In the case of bonds, premium refers to the amount by which a bond is priced above its face (par) value. In the case of an option, the amount paid for the option contract.

Prepaid expense A normal operating expense that has been paid in advance of when it is due.

Present value (PV) The present discounted value of future cash flows: For assets, the present discounted value of the future net cash inflows that the asset is expected to generate; for liabilities, the present discounted value of the future net cash outflows that are expected to be required to settle the liabilities.

Present value models Valuation models that estimate the intrinsic value of a security as the present value of the future benefits expected to be received from the security. Also called *discounted cash flow models*.

Pretax margin A profitability ratio calculated as earnings before taxes divided by revenue.

Price The market price as established by the interactions of the market demand and supply factors.

Price elasticity of demand Measures the percentage change in the quantity demanded, given a percentage change in the price of a given product.

Price floor A minimum price for a good or service, typically imposed by government action and typically above the equilibrium price.

Price index Represents the average prices of a basket of goods and services.

Price limits Limits imposed by a futures exchange on the price change that can occur from one day to the next.

Price multiple A ratio that compares the share price with some sort of monetary flow or value to allow evaluation of the relative worth of a company's stock.

Price priority The principle that the highest priced buy orders and the lowest priced sell orders execute first.

Price relative A ratio of an ending price over a beginning price; it is equal to 1 plus the holding period return on the asset.

Price return Measures *only* the price appreciation or percentage change in price of the securities in an index or portfolio.

Price return index An index that reflects *only* the price appreciation or percentage change in price of the constituent securities. Also called *price index*.

Price stability In economics, refers to an inflation rate that is low on average and not subject to wide fluctuation.

Price takers Producers that must accept whatever price the market dictates.

Price to book value A valuation ratio calculated as price per share divided by book value per share.

Price to cash flow A valuation ratio calculated as price per share divided by cash flow per share.

Price to earnings ratio (P/E ratio or P/E) The ratio of share price to earnings per share.

Price to sales A valuation ratio calculated as price per share divided by sales per share.

Price value of a basis point A version of money duration, it is an estimate of the change in the full price of a bond given a 1 basis point change in the yield-to-maturity.

Price weighting An index weighting method in which the weight assigned to each constituent security is determined by dividing its price by the sum of all the prices of the constituent securities.

Priced risk Risk for which investors demand compensation for bearing (e.g. equity risk, company-specific factors, macroeconomic factors).

Primary bond markets Markets in which issuers first sell bonds to investors to raise capital.

Primary capital markets (primary markets) The market where securities are first sold and the issuers receive the proceeds.

Primary dealers Financial institutions that are authorized to deal in new issues of sovereign bonds and that serve primarily as trading counterparties of the office responsible for issuing sovereign bonds.

Primary market The market where securities are first sold and the issuers receive the proceeds.

Prime brokers Brokers that provide services including custody, administration, lending, short borrowing, and trading.

Principal The amount of funds originally invested in a project or instrument; the face value to be paid at maturity.

Principal amount Amount that an issuer agrees to repay the debt holders on the maturity date.

Principal business activity The business activity from which a company derives a majority of its revenues and/or earnings.

Principal value Amount that an issuer agrees to repay the debt holders on the maturity date.

Prior probabilities Probabilities reflecting beliefs prior to the arrival of new information.

Priority of claims Priority of payment, with the most senior or highest ranking debt having the first claim on the cash flows and assets of the issuer.

Private equity securities Securities that are not listed on public exchanges and have no active secondary market. They are issued primarily to institutional investors via non-public offerings, such as private placements.

Private investment in public equity An investment in the equity of a publicly traded firm that is made at a discount to the market value of the firm's shares.

Private placement Typically a non-underwritten, unregistered offering of securities that are sold only to an investor or a small group of investors. It can be accomplished directly between the issuer and the investor(s) or through an investment bank.

Private value auction An auction in which the value of the item being auctioned is unique to each bidder.

Probability A number between 0 and 1 describing the chance that a stated event will occur.

Probability density function A function with non-negative values such that probability can be described by areas under the curve graphing the function.

Probability distribution A distribution that specifies the probabilities of a random variable's possible outcomes.

Probability function A function that specifies the probability that the random variable takes on a specific value.

Producer price index Reflects the price changes experienced by domestic producers in a country.

Producer surplus The difference between the total revenue sellers receive from selling a given amount of a good and the total variable cost of producing that amount.

Production function Provides the quantitative link between the level of output that the economy can produce and the inputs used in the production process.

Production opportunity frontier Curve describing the maximum number of units of one good a company can produce, for any given number of the other good that it chooses to manufacture.

Productivity The amount of output produced by workers in a given period of time—for example, output per hour worked; measures the efficiency of labor.

Profit The return that owners of a company receive for the use of their capital and the assumption of financial risk when making their investments.

Profit and loss (P&L) statement A financial statement that provides information about a company's profitability over a stated period of time.

Profit margin An indicator of profitability, calculated as net income divided by revenue; indicates how much of each dollar of revenues is left after all costs and expenses.

Profitability ratios Ratios that measure a company's ability to generate profitable sales from its resources (assets).

Project sequencing To defer the decision to invest in a future project until the outcome of some or all of a current project is known. Projects are sequenced through time, so that investing in a project creates the option to invest in future projects.

Promissory note A written promise to pay a certain amount of money on demand.

Property, plant, and equipment Tangible assets that are expected to be used for more than one period in either the production or supply of goods or services, or for administrative purposes.

Prospectus The document that describes the terms of a new bond issue and helps investors perform their analysis on the issue.

Protective put An option strategy in which a long position in an asset is combined with a long position in a put.

Pseudo-random numbers Numbers produced by random number generators.

Public offer See *public offering*.

Public offering An offering of securities in which any member of the public may buy the securities. Also called *public offer*.

Pull on liquidity When disbursements are paid too quickly or trade credit availability is limited, requiring companies to expend funds before they receive funds from sales that could cover the liability.

Pure discount bonds See *zero-coupon bonds*.

Pure discount instruments Instruments that pay interest as the difference between the amount borrowed and the amount paid back.

Pure-play method A method for estimating the beta for a company or project; it requires using a comparable company's beta and adjusting it for financial leverage differences.

Put An option that gives the holder the right to sell an underlying asset to another party at a fixed price over a specific period of time.

Put option An option that gives the holder the right to sell an underlying asset to another party at a fixed price over a specific period of time.

Put/call ratio A technical analysis indicator that evaluates market sentiment based upon the volume of put options traded divided by the volume of call options traded for a particular financial instrument.

Putable bonds Bonds that give the bondholder the right to sell the bond back to the issuer at a predetermined price on specified dates.

Putable common shares Common shares that give investors the option (or right) to sell their shares (i.e., "put" them) back to the issuing company at a price that is specified when the shares are originally issued.

Put–call parity An equation expressing the equivalence (parity) of a portfolio of a call and a bond with a portfolio of a put and the underlying, which leads to the relationship between put and call prices.

Quantile A value at or below which a stated fraction of the data lies. Also called *fractile*.

Quantitative easing   An expansionary monetary policy based on aggressive open market purchase operations.

Quantity   The amount of a product that consumers are willing and able to buy at each price level.

Quantity demanded   The amount of a product that consumers are willing and able to buy at each price level.

Quantity equation of exchange   An expression that over a given period, the amount of money used to purchase all goods and services in an economy, $M \times V$, is equal to monetary value of this output, $P \times Y$.

Quantity theory of money   Asserts that total spending (in money terms) is proportional to the quantity of money.

Quartiles   Quantiles that divide a distribution into four equal parts.

Quasi-fixed cost   A cost that stays the same over a range of production but can change to another constant level when production moves outside of that range.

Quasi-government bonds   A bond issued by an entity that is either owned or sponsored by a national government. Also called *agency bond*.

Quick assets   Assets that can be most readily converted to cash (e.g., cash, short-term marketable investments, receivables).

Quick ratio   A stringent measure of liquidity that indicates a company's ability to satisfy current liabilities with its most liquid assets, calculated as (cash + short-term marketable investments + receivables) divided by current liabilities.

Quintiles   Quantiles that divide a distribution into five equal parts.

Quota rents   Profits that foreign producers can earn by raising the price of their goods higher than they would without a quota.

Quotas   Government policies that restrict the quantity of a good that can be imported into a country, generally for a specified period of time.

Quote-driven market   A market in which dealers acting as principals facilitate trading.

Quoted interest rate   A quoted interest rate that does not account for compounding within the year. Also called *stated annual interest rate*.

Quoted margin   The specified yield spread over the reference rate, used to compensate an investor for the difference in the credit risk of the issuer and that implied by the reference rate.

Random number   An observation drawn from a uniform distribution.

Random number generator   An algorithm that produces uniformly distributed random numbers between 0 and 1.

Random variable   A quantity whose future outcomes are uncertain.

Range   The difference between the maximum and minimum values in a dataset.

Ratio scales   A measurement scale that has all the characteristics of interval measurement scales as well as a true zero point as the origin.

Real GDP   The value of goods and services produced, measured at base year prices.

Real income   Income adjusted for the effect of inflation on the purchasing power of money.

Real interest rate   Nominal interest rate minus the expected rate of inflation.

Real risk-free interest rate   The single-period interest rate for a completely risk-free security if no inflation were expected.

Realizable (settlement) value   With reference to assets, the amount of cash or cash equivalents that could currently be obtained by selling the asset in an orderly disposal; with reference to liabilities, the undiscounted amount of cash or cash equivalents expected to be paid to satisfy the liabilities in the normal course of business.

Rebalancing   Adjusting the weights of the constituent securities in an index.

Rebalancing policy   The set of rules that guide the process of restoring a portfolio's asset class weights to those specified in the strategic asset allocation.

Recession   A period during which real GDP decreases (i.e., negative growth) for at least two successive quarters, or a period of significant decline in total output, income, employment, and sales usually lasting from six months to a year.

Recognition lag   The lag in government response to an economic problem resulting from the delay in confirming a change in the state of the economy.

Record date   The date that a shareholder listed on the corporation's books will be deemed to have ownership of the shares for purposes of receiving an upcoming dividend; two business days after the ex-dividend date.

Redemption yield   See *yield to maturity*.

Redemptions   Withdrawals of funds by investors.

Refinancing rate   A type of central bank policy rate.

Registered bonds   Bonds for which ownership is recorded by either name or serial number.

Relative dispersion   The amount of dispersion relative to a reference value or benchmark.

Relative frequency   With reference to an interval of grouped data, the number of observations in the interval divided by the total number of observations in the sample.

Relative price   The price of a specific good or service in comparison with those of other goods and services.

Relative strength analysis   A comparison of the performance of one asset with the performance of another asset or a benchmark based on changes in the ratio of the securities' respective prices over time.

Relative strength index   A technical analysis momentum oscillator that compares a security's gains with its losses over a set period.

Renewable resources   Resources that can be replenished, such as a forest.

Rent   Payment for the use of property.

Reorganization   Agreements made by a company in bankruptcy under which a company's capital structure is altered and/or alternative arrangements are made for debt repayment; U.S. Chapter 11 bankruptcy. The company emerges from bankruptcy as a going concern.

Repo   A form of collateralized loan involving the sale of a security with a simultaneous agreement by the seller to buy the same security back from the purchaser at an agreed-on price and future date. The party who sells the security at the inception of the repurchase agreement and buys it back at maturity is borrowing money from the other party, and the security sold and subsequently repurchased represents the collateral.

Repo margin   The difference between the market value of the security used as collateral and the value of the loan. Also called *haircut*.

Repo rate   The interest rate on a repurchase agreement.

Repurchase agreement   A form of collateralized loan involving the sale of a security with a simultaneous agreement by the seller to buy the same security back from the purchaser at an agreed-on price and future date. The party who sells the security at the inception of the repurchase agreement and buys it back at maturity is borrowing money from the other party, and the security sold and subsequently repurchased represents the collateral.

Repurchase date   The date when the party who sold the security at the inception of a repurchase agreement buys the security back from the cash lending counterparty.

Repurchase price   The price at which the party who sold the security at the inception of the repurchase agreement buys the security back from the cash lending counterparty.

Required margin   The yield spread over, or under, the reference rate such that an FRN is priced at par value on a rate reset date.

Required rate of return   See *market discount rate.*

Required yield   See *market discount rate.*

Required yield spread   The difference between the yield-to-maturity on a new bond and the benchmark rate; additional compensation required by investors for the difference in risk and tax status of a bond relative to a government bond. Sometimes called the *spread over the benchmark.*

Reservation prices   The highest price a buyer is willing to pay for an item or the lowest price at which a seller is willing to sell it.

Reserve requirement   The requirement for banks to hold reserves in proportion to the size of deposits.

Residual claim   The owners' remaining claim on the company's assets after the liabilities are deducted.

Resistance   In technical analysis, a price range in which selling activity is sufficient to stop the rise in the price of a security.

Restricted payments   A bond covenant meant to protect creditors by limiting how much cash can be paid out to shareholders over time.

Retail method   An inventory accounting method in which the sales value of an item is reduced by the gross margin to calculate the item's cost.

Retracement   In technical analysis, a reversal in the movement of a security's price such that it is counter to the prevailing longterm price trend.

Return on assets (ROA)   A profitability ratio calculated as net income divided by average total assets; indicates a company's net profit generated per dollar invested in total assets.

Return on equity (ROE)   A profitability ratio calculated as net income divided by average shareholders' equity.

Return on sales   An indicator of profitability, calculated as net income divided by revenue; indicates how much of each dollar of revenues is left after all costs and expenses.

Return on total capital   A profitability ratio calculated as EBIT divided by the sum of short- and long-term debt and equity.

Return-generating model   A model that can provide an estimate of the expected return of a security given certain parameters and estimates of the values of the independent variables in the model.

Revaluation model   The process of valuing long-lived assets at fair value, rather than at cost less accumulated depreciation. Any resulting profit or loss is either reported on the income statement and/or through equity under revaluation surplus.

Revenue   The amount charged for the delivery of goods or services in the ordinary activities of a business over a stated period; the inflows of economic resources to a company over a stated period.

Reversal patterns   A type of pattern used in technical analysis to predict the end of a trend and a change in direction of the security's price.

Reverse repo   A repurchase agreement viewed from the perspective of the cash lending counterparty.

Reverse repurchase agreement   A repurchase agreement viewed from the perspective of the cash lending counterparty.

Reverse stock split   A reduction in the number of shares outstanding with a corresponding increase in share price, but no change to the company's underlying fundamentals.

Revolving credit agreements   The strongest form of short-term bank borrowing facilities; they are in effect for multiple years (e.g., 3–5 years) and may have optional medium-term loan features.

Rho   The sensitivity of the option price to the risk-free rate.

Ricardian equivalence   An economic theory that implies that it makes no difference whether a government finances a deficit by increasing taxes or issuing debt.

Risk averse   The assumption that an investor will choose the least risky alternative.

Risk aversion   The degree of an investor's inability and unwillingness to take risk.

Risk budgeting   The establishment of objectives for individuals, groups, or divisions of an organization that takes into account the allocation of an acceptable level of risk.

Risk management   The process of identifying the level of risk an entity wants, measuring the level of risk the entity currently has, taking actions that bring the actual level of risk to the desired level of risk, and monitoring the new actual level of risk so that it continues to be aligned with the desired level of risk.

Risk premium   An extra return expected by investors for bearing some specified risk.

Risk tolerance   The amount of risk an investor is willing and able to bear to achieve an investment goal.

Robust   The quality of being relatively unaffected by a violation of assumptions.

Rule of 72   The principle that the approximate number of years necessary for an investment to double is 72 divided by the stated interest rate.

Running yield   See *current yield.*

Safety stock   A level of inventory beyond anticipated needs that provides a cushion in the event that it takes longer to replenish inventory than expected or in the case of greater than expected demand.

Safety-first rules   Rules for portfolio selection that focus on the risk that portfolio value will fall below some minimum acceptable level over some time horizon.

Sales   Generally, a synonym for revenue; "sales" is generally understood to refer to the sale of goods, whereas "revenue" is understood to include the sale of goods or services.

Sales returns and allowances   An offset to revenue reflecting any cash refunds, credits on account, and discounts from sales prices given to customers who purchased defective or unsatisfactory items.

Sales risk   Uncertainty with respect to the quantity of goods and services that a company is able to sell and the price it is able to achieve; the risk related to the uncertainty of revenues.

Salvage value   The amount the company estimates that it can sell the asset for at the end of its useful life. Also called *residual value.*

Sample   A subset of a population.

Sample excess kurtosis A sample measure of the degree of a distribution's peakedness in excess of the normal distribution's peakedness.

Sample kurtosis A sample measure of the degree of a distribution's peakedness.

Sample mean The sum of the sample observations, divided by the sample size.

Sample selection bias Bias introduced by systematically excluding some members of the population according to a particular attribute—for example, the bias introduced when data availability leads to certain observations being excluded from the analysis.

Sample skewness A sample measure of degree of asymmetry of a distribution.

Sample standard deviation The positive square root of the sample variance.

Sample statistic A quantity computed from or used to describe a sample.

Sample variance A sample measure of the degree of dispersion of a distribution, calculated by dividing the sum of the squared deviations from the sample mean by the sample size minus 1.

Sampling The process of obtaining a sample.

Sampling distribution The distribution of all distinct possible values that a statistic can assume when computed from samples of the same size randomly drawn from the same population.

Sampling error The difference between the observed value of a statistic and the quantity it is intended to estimate.

Sampling plan The set of rules used to select a sample.

Saving In economics, income not spent.

Say's law Named for French economist J.B. Say: All that is produced will be sold because supply creates its own demand.

Scalper A trader who offers to buy or sell futures contracts, holding the position for only a brief period of time. Scalpers attempt to profit by buying at the bid price and selling at the higher ask price.

Scenario analysis Analysis that shows the changes in key financial quantities that result from given (economic) events, such as the loss of customers, the loss of a supply source, or a catastrophic event; a risk management technique involving examination of the performance of a portfolio under specified situations. Closely related to stress testing.

Screening The application of a set of criteria to reduce a set of potential investments to a smaller set having certain desired characteristics.

Scrip dividend schemes Dividend reinvestment plan in which the company meets the need for additional shares by issuing them instead of purchasing them.

Sealed bid auction An auction in which bids are elicited from potential buyers, but there is no ability to observe bids by other buyers until the auction has ended.

Search costs Costs incurred in searching; the costs of matching buyers with sellers.

Seasoned offering An offering in which an issuer sells additional units of a previously issued security.

Seats Memberships in a derivatives exchange.

Second lien A secured interest in the pledged assets that ranks below first lien debt in both collateral protection and priority of payment.

Second price sealed bid An auction (also known as a Vickery auction) in which bids are submitted in sealed envelopes and opened simultaneously. The winning buyer is the one who submitted the highest bid, but the price paid is equal to the second highest bid.

Second-degree price discrimination When the monopolist charges different per-unit prices using the quantity purchased as an indicator of how highly the customer values the product.

Secondary bond markets Markets in which existing bonds are traded among investors.

Secondary market The market where securities are traded among investors.

Secondary precedence rules Rules that determine how to rank orders placed at the same time.

Sector A group of related industries.

Sector indices Indices that represent and track different economic sectors—such as consumer goods, energy, finance, health care, and technology—on either a national, regional, or global basis.

Secured bonds Bonds secured by assets or financial guarantees pledged to ensure debt repayment in case of default.

Secured debt Debt in which the debtholder has a direct claim—a pledge from the issuer—on certain assets and their associated cash flows.

Securitized bonds Bonds created from a process that involves moving assets into a special legal entity, which then uses the assets as guarantees to secure a bond issue.

Security characteristic line A plot of the excess return of a security on the excess return of the market.

Security market index A portfolio of securities representing a given security market, market segment, or asset class.

Security market line (SML) The graph of the capital asset pricing model.

Security selection The process of selecting individual securities; typically, security selection has the objective of generating superior risk-adjusted returns relative to a portfolio's benchmark.

Self-investment limits With respect to investment limitations applying to pension plans, restrictions on the percentage of assets that can be invested in securities issued by the pension plan sponsor.

Sell-side firm A broker or dealer that sells securities to and provides independent investment research and recommendations to investment management companies.

Semi-strong-form efficient market A market in which security prices reflect all publicly known and available information.

Semiannual bond basis yield An annual rate having a periodicity of two; also known as a *semiannual bond equivalent yield*.

Semiannual bond equivalent yield See *semiannual bond basis yield*.

Semideviation The positive square root of semivariance (sometimes called *semistandard deviation*).

Semilogarithmic Describes a scale constructed so that equal intervals on the vertical scale represent equal rates of change, and equal intervals on the horizontal scale represent equal amounts of change.

Semivariance The average squared deviation below the mean.

Seniority ranking Priority of payment of various debt obligations.

Sensitivity analysis Analysis that shows the range of possible outcomes as specific assumptions are changed.

Separately managed account (SMA) An investment portfolio managed exclusively for the benefit of an individual or institution.

Serial maturity structure Structure for a bond issue in which the maturity dates are spread out during the bond's life; a stated number of bonds mature and are paid off each year before final maturity.

Settlement The process that occurs after a trade is completed, the securities are passed to the buyer, and payment is received by the seller.

Settlement date Date when the buyer makes cash payment and the seller delivers the security.

Settlement period The time between settlement dates.

Settlement price The official price, designated by the clearinghouse, from which daily gains and losses will be determined and marked to market.

Share repurchase A transaction in which a company buys back its own shares. Unlike stock dividends and stock splits, share repurchases use corporate cash.

Shareholder wealth maximization To maximize the market value of shareholders' equity.

Shareholder-of-record date The date that a shareholder listed on the corporation's books will be deemed to have ownership of the shares for purposes of receiving an upcoming dividend; two business days after the ex-dividend date.

Shareholders' equity Assets less liabilities; the residual interest in the assets after subtracting the liabilities.

Sharpe ratio The average return in excess of the risk-free rate divided by the standard deviation of return; a measure of the average excess return earned per unit of standard deviation of return.

Shelf registration Type of public offering that allows the issuer to file a single, all-encompassing offering circular that covers a series of bond issues.

Short The seller of an asset or derivative contract. Also refers to the position of being short an asset or derivative contract.

Short position A position in an asset or contract in which one has sold an asset one does not own, or in which a right under a contract can be exercised against oneself.

Short selling A transaction in which borrowed securities are sold with the intention to repurchase them at a lower price at a later date and return them to the lender.

Short-run average total cost curve The curve describing average total costs when some costs are considered fixed.

Short-run supply curve The section of the marginal cost curve that lies above the minimum point on the average variable cost curve.

Shortfall risk The risk that portfolio value will fall below some minimum acceptable level over some time horizon.

Shutdown point The point at which average revenue is less than average variable cost.

Simple interest The interest earned each period on the original investment; interest calculated on the principal only.

Simple random sample A subset of a larger population created in such a way that each element of the population has an equal probability of being selected to the subset.

Simple random sampling The procedure of drawing a sample to satisfy the definition of a simple random sample.

Simple yield The sum of the coupon payments plus the straight-line amortized share of the gain or loss, divided by the flat price.

Simulation Computer-generated sensitivity or scenario analysis that is based on probability models for the factors that drive outcomes.

Simulation trial A complete pass through the steps of a simulation.

Single price auction A Dutch auction variation, also involving a single price, is used in selling U.S. Treasury securities.

Single-step format With respect to the format of the income statement, a format that does not subtotal for gross profit (revenue minus cost of goods sold).

Sinking fund arrangement Provision that reduces the credit risk of a bond issue by requiring the issuer to retire a portion of the bond's principal outstanding each year.

Skewed Not symmetrical.

Skewness A quantitative measure of skew (lack of symmetry); a synonym of skew.

Small country A country that is a price taker in the world market for a product and cannot influence the world market price.

Solvency With respect to financial statement analysis, the ability of a company to fulfill its long-term obligations.

Solvency ratios Ratios that measure a company's ability to meet its long-term obligations.

Sovereign bonds A bond issued by a national government.

Sovereign yield spread An estimate of the country spread (country equity premium) for a developing nation that is based on a comparison of bonds yields in country being analyzed and a developed country. The sovereign yield spread is the difference between a government bond yield in the country being analyzed, denominated in the currency of the developed country, and the Treasury bond yield on a similar maturity bond in the developed country.

Sovereigns A bond issued by a national government.

Spearman rank correlation coefficient A measure of correlation applied to ranked data.

Special dividend A dividend paid by a company that does not pay dividends on a regular schedule, or a dividend that supplements regular cash dividends with an extra payment.

Special purpose entity A non-operating entity created to carry out a specified purpose, such as leasing assets or securitizing receivables; can be a corporation, partnership, trust, limited liability, or partnership formed to facilitate a specific type of business activity. Also called *special purpose vehicle* or *variable interest entity*.

Special purpose vehicle See *special purpose entity*.

Specific identification method An inventory accounting method that identifies which specific inventory items were sold and which remained in inventory to be carried over to later periods.

Speculative demand for money The demand to hold speculative money balances based on the potential opportunities or risks that are inherent in other financial instruments. Also called *portfolio demand for money*.

Speculative money balances Monies held in anticipation that other assets will decline in value.

Speculative value The difference between the market price of the option and its intrinsic value, determined by the uncertainty of the underlying over the remaining life of the option.

Split coupon bond See *deferred coupon bond*.

Sponsored A type of depository receipt in which the foreign company whose shares are held by the depository has a direct involvement in the issuance of the receipts.

Spot curve A sequence of yields-to-maturity on zero-coupon bonds. Sometimes called *zero* or *strip curve* because coupon payments are "stripped" off of the bonds.

Spot markets Markets in which assets are traded for immediate delivery.

Spot prices The price of an asset for immediately delivery.

Spot rates A sequence of market discount rates that correspond to the cash flow dates; yields-to-maturity on zero-coupon bonds maturing at the date of each cash flow.

Spread In general, the difference in yield between different fixed income securities. Often used to refer to the difference between the yield-to-maturity and the benchmark.

Spread over the benchmark See *required yield spread*.

Spread risk Bond price risk arising from changes in the yield spread on credit-risky bonds; reflects changes in the market's assessment and/or pricing of credit migration (or downgrade) risk and market liquidity risk.

Stable With reference to an equilibrium, one in which price, when disturbed away from the equilibrium, tends to converge back to it.

Stackelberg model A prominent model of strategic decision-making in which firms are assumed to make their decisions sequentially.

Stagflation When a high inflation rate is combined with a high level of unemployment and a slowdown of the economy.

Standard cost With respect to inventory accounting, the planned or target unit cost of inventory items or services.

Standard deviation The positive square root of the variance; a measure of dispersion in the same units as the original data.

Standard normal distribution The normal density with mean (μ) equal to 0 and standard deviation (σ) equal to 1.

Standardizing A transformation that involves subtracting the mean and dividing the result by the standard deviation.

Standing limit orders A limit order at a price below market and which therefore is waiting to trade.

Stated annual interest rate A quoted interest rate that does not account for compounding within the year. Also called *quoted interest rate*.

Statement of cash flows A financial statement that reconciles beginning-of-period and end-of-period balance sheet values of cash; provides information about an entity's cash inflows and cash outflows as they pertain to operating, investing, and financing activities. Also called *cash flow statement*.

Statement of changes in equity (statement of owners' equity) A financial statement that reconciles the beginning-of-period and end-of-period balance sheet values of shareholders' equity; provides information about all factors affecting shareholders' equity. Also called *statement of owners' equity*.

Statement of financial condition The financial statement that presents an entity's current financial position by disclosing resources the entity controls (its assets) and the claims on those resources (its liabilities and equity claims), as of a particular point in time (the date of the balance sheet).

Statement of financial position The financial statement that presents an entity's current financial position by disclosing resources the entity controls (its assets) and the claims on those resources (its liabilities and equity claims), as of a particular point in time (the date of the balance sheet).

Statement of operations A financial statement that provides information about a company's profitability over a stated period of time.

Statement of owners' equity A financial statement that reconciles the beginning of-period and end-of-period balance sheet values of shareholders' equity; provides information about all factors affecting shareholders' equity. Also called *statement of changes in shareholders' equity*.

Statement of retained earnings A financial statement that reconciles beginning-of-period and end-of-period balance sheet values of retained income; shows the linkage between the balance sheet and income statement.

Statistic A quantity computed from or used to describe a sample of data.

Statistical inference Making forecasts, estimates, or judgments about a larger group from a smaller group actually observed; using a sample statistic to infer the value of an unknown population parameter.

Statistically significant A result indicating that the null hypothesis can be rejected; with reference to an estimated regression coefficient, frequently understood to mean a result indicating that the corresponding population regression coefficient is different from 0.

Statutory voting A common method of voting where each share represents one vote.

Step-up coupon bond Bond for which the coupon, which may be fixed or floating, increases by specified margins at specified dates.

Stock dividend A type of dividend in which a company distributes additional shares of its common stock to shareholders instead of cash.

Stock-out losses Profits lost from not having sufficient inventory on hand to satisfy demand.

Stop order An order in which a trader has specified a stop price condition. Also called *stop-loss order*.

Stop-loss order See *stop order*.

Store of value The quality of tending to preserve value.

Store of wealth Goods that depend on the fact that they do not perish physically over time, and on the belief that others would always value the good.

Straight-line method A depreciation method that allocates evenly the cost of a long-lived asset less its estimated residual value over the estimated useful life of the asset.

Strategic analysis Analysis of the competitive environment with an emphasis on the implications of the environment for corporate strategy.

Strategic asset allocation The set of exposures to IPS-permissible asset classes that is expected to achieve the client's long-term objectives given the client's investment constraints.

Strategic groups Groups sharing distinct business models or catering to specific market segments in an industry.

Street convention Yield measure that neglects weekends and holidays; the internal rate of return on cash flows assuming payments are made on the scheduled dates, even when the scheduled date falls on a weekend or holiday.

Stress testing A set of techniques for estimating losses in extremely unfavorable combinations of events or scenarios.

Strike The fixed price at which an option holder can buy or sell the underlying.

Strike price The fixed price at which an option holder can buy or sell the underlying.

Strike rate The fixed rate at which the holder of an interest rate option can buy or sell the underlying.

Striking price The fixed price at which an option holder can buy or sell the underlying.

Strong-form efficient market   A market in which security prices reflect all public and private information.

Structural (or cyclically adjusted) budget deficit   The deficit that would exist if the economy was at full employment (or full potential output).

Structural subordination   Arises in a holding company structure when the debt of operating subsidiaries is serviced by the cash flow and assets of the subsidiaries before funds can be passed to the holding company to service debt at the parent level.

Subjective probability   A probability drawing on personal or subjective judgment.

Subordinated debt   A class of unsecured debt that ranks below a firm's senior unsecured obligations.

Substitutes   Said of two goods or services such that if the price of one increases the demand for the other tends to increase, holding all other things equal (e.g., butter and margarine).

Sunk cost   A cost that has already been incurred.

Supernormal profit   Equal to accounting profit less the implicit opportunity costs not included in total accounting costs; the difference between total revenue (TR) and total cost (TC).

Supply   The willingness of sellers to offer a given quantity of a good or service for a given price.

Supply curve   The graph of the inverse supply function.

Supply function   The quantity supplied as a function of price and possibly other variables.

Supply shock   A typically unexpected disturbance to supply.

Support   In technical analysis, a price range in which buying activity is sufficient to stop the decline in the price of a security.

Supranational bonds   A bond issued by a supranational agency such as the World Bank.

Surety bond   Form of external credit enhancement whereby a rated and regulated insurance company guarantees to reimburse bondholders for any losses incurred up to a maximum amount if the issuer defaults.

Survey approach   An estimate of the equity risk premium that is based upon estimates provided by a panel of finance experts.

Survivorship bias   The bias resulting from a test design that fails to account for companies that have gone bankrupt, merged, or are otherwise no longer reported in a database.

Sustainable growth rate   The rate of dividend (and earnings) growth that can be sustained over time for a given level of return on equity, keeping the capital structure constant and without issuing additional common stock.

Sustainable rate of economic growth   The rate of increase in the economy's productive capacity or potential GDP.

Swap contract   An agreement between two parties to exchange a series of future cash flows.

Swaption   An option to enter into a swap.

Syndicated loans   Loans from a group of lenders to a single borrower.

Syndicated offering   A bond issue that is underwritten by a group of investment banks.

Synthetic call   The combination of puts, the underlying, and risk-free bonds that replicates a call option.

Synthetic put   The combination of calls, the underlying, and risk-free bonds that replicates a put option.

Systematic risk   Risk that affects the entire market or economy; it cannot be avoided and is inherent in the overall market. Systematic risk is also known as non diversifiable or market risk.

Systematic sampling   A procedure of selecting every kth member until reaching a sample of the desired size. The sample that results from this procedure should be approximately random.

t-Test   A hypothesis test using a statistic (t-statistic) that follows a t-distribution.

TRIN   A flow of funds indicator applied to a broad stock market index to measure the relative extent to which money is moving into or out of rising and declining stocks.

Tactical asset allocation   The decision to deliberately deviate from the strategic asset allocation in an attempt to add value based on forecasts of the near-term relative performance of asset classes.

Target balance   A minimum level of cash to be held available—estimated in advance and adjusted for known funds transfers, seasonality, or other factors.

Target capital structure   A company's chosen proportions of debt and equity.

Target independent   A bank's ability to determine the definition of inflation that they target, the rate of inflation that they target, and the horizon over which the target is to be achieved.

Target semideviation   The positive square root of target semivariance.

Target semivariance   The average squared deviation below a target value.

Tariffs   Taxes that a government levies on imported goods.

Tax base   The amount at which an asset or liability is valued for tax purposes.

Tax expense   An aggregate of an entity's income tax payable (or recoverable in the case of a tax benefit) and any changes in deferred tax assets and liabilities. It is essentially the income tax payable or recoverable if these had been determined based on accounting profit rather than taxable income.

Tax loss carry forward   A taxable loss in the current period that may be used to reduce future taxable income.

Taxable income   The portion of an entity's income that is subject to income taxes under the tax laws of its jurisdiction.

Taxable temporary differences   Temporary differences that result in a taxable amount in a future period when determining the taxable profit as the balance sheet item is recovered or settled.

Technical analysis   A form of security analysis that uses price and volume data, which is often displayed graphically, in decision making.

Technology   The process a company uses to transform inputs into outputs.

Technology of production   The "rules" that govern the transformation of inputs into finished goods and services.

Tenor   The time-to-maturity for a bond or derivative contract. Also called *term to maturity*.

Term maturity structure   Structure for a bond issue in which the bond's notional principal is paid off in a lump sum at maturity.

Term structure   See *maturity structure*.

Term structure of credit spreads   The relationship between the spreads over the "risk-free" (or benchmark) rates and times-to-maturity.

Term structure of yield volatility   The relationship between the volatility of bond yields-to-maturity and times-to-maturity.

Terminal stock value   The expected value of a share at the end of the investment horizon—in effect, the expected selling price. Also called *terminal value*.

Terminal value The expected value of a share at the end of the investment horizon—in effect, the expected selling price.

Termination date The date of the final payment on a swap; also, the swap's expiration date.

Terms of trade The ratio of the price of exports to the price of imports, representing those prices by export and import price indices, respectively.

Theory of the consumer The branch of microeconomics that deals with consumption—the demand for goods and services—by utility-maximizing individuals.

Theory of the firm The branch of microeconomics that deals with the supply of goods and services by profit-maximizing firms.

Theta The rate at which an option's time value decays.

Third-degree price discrimination When the monopolist segregates customers into groups based on demographic or other characteristics and offers different pricing to each group.

Time to expiration The time remaining in the life of a derivative, typically expressed in years.

Time value The difference between the market price of the option and its intrinsic value, determined by the uncertainty of the underlying over the remaining life of the option.

Time value of money The principles governing equivalence relationships between cash flows with different dates.

Time-period bias The possibility that when we use a time-series sample, our statistical conclusion may be sensitive to the starting and ending dates of the sample.

Time-series data Observations of a variable over time.

Time-weighted rate of return The compound rate of growth of one unit of currency invested in a portfolio during a stated measurement period; a measure of investment performance that is not sensitive to the timing and amount of withdrawals or additions to the portfolio.

Top-down analysis With reference to investment selection processes, an approach that starts with macro selection (i.e., identifying attractive geographic segments and/or industry segments) and then addresses selection of the most attractive investments within those segments.

Total comprehensive income The change in equity during a period resulting from transaction and other events, other than those changes resulting from transactions with owners in their capacity as owners.

Total costs The summation of all costs, where costs are classified according to fixed or variable.

Total expenditure The total amount spent over a time period.

Total factor productivity A scale factor that reflects the portion of growth that is not accounted for by explicit factor inputs (e.g. capital and labor).

Total fixed cost The summation of all expenses that do not change when production varies.

Total invested capital The sum of market value of common equity, book value of preferred equity, and face value of debt.

Total probability rule A rule explaining the unconditional probability of an event in terms of probabilities of the event conditional on mutually exclusive and exhaustive scenarios.

Total probability rule for expected value A rule explaining the expected value of a random variable in terms of expected values of the random variable conditional on mutually exclusive and exhaustive scenarios.

Total product The aggregate sum of production for the firm during a time period.

Total return Measures the price appreciation, or percentage change in price of the securities in an index or portfolio, plus any income received over the period.

Total return index An index that reflects the price appreciation or percentage change in price of the constituent securities plus any income received since inception.

Total return swap A swap in which one party agrees to pay the total return on a security. Often used as a credit derivative, in which the underlying is a bond.

Total revenue Price times the quantity of units sold.

Total surplus The difference between total value to buyers and the total variable cost to sellers; made up of the sum of consumer surplus and producer surplus.

Total variable cost The summation of all variable expenses.

Tracking error The standard deviation of the differences between a portfolio's returns and its benchmark's returns; a synonym of active risk.

Tracking risk The standard deviation of the differences between a portfolio's returns and its benchmark's returns; a synonym of active risk. Also called *tracking error*.

Trade creation When regional integration results in the replacement of higher cost domestic production by lower cost imports from other members.

Trade credit A spontaneous form of credit in which a purchaser of the goods or service is financing its purchase by delaying the date on which payment is made.

Trade diversion When regional integration results in lower-cost imports from non-member countries being replaced with higher-cost imports from members.

Trade payables Amounts that a business owes to its vendors for goods and services that were purchased from them but which have not yet been paid.

Trade protection Government policies that impose restrictions on trade, such as tariffs and quotas.

Trade receivables Amounts customers owe the company for products that have been sold as well as amounts that may be due from suppliers (such as for returns of merchandise) Also called *commercial receivables* or *accounts receivable*.

Trade surplus (deficit) When the value of exports is greater (less) than the value of imports.

Trading securities Securities held by a company with the intent to trade them. Also called *held-for-trading securities*.

Traditional investment markets Markets for traditional investments, which include all publicly traded debts and equities and shares in pooled investment vehicles that hold publicly traded debts and/or equities.

Transactions money balances Money balances that are held to finance transactions.

Transactions motive In the context of inventory management, the need for inventory as part of the routine production–sales cycle.

Transfer payments Welfare payments made through the social security system that exist to provide a basic minimum level of income for low-income households.

Transitive preferences The assumption that when comparing any three distinct bundles, A, B, and C, if A is preferred to B and simultaneously B is preferred to C, then it must be true that A is preferred to C.

Transparency Said of something (e.g., a market) in which information is fully disclosed to the public and/or regulators.

Treasury Inflation-Protected Securities A bond issued by the United States Treasury Department that is designed to protect the investor from inflation by adjusting the principal of the bond for changes in inflation.

Treasury shares   Shares that were issued and subsequently repurchased by the company.

Treasury stock   Shares that were issued and subsequently repurchased by the company.

Treasury stock method   A method for accounting for the effect of options (and warrants) on earnings per share (EPS) that specifies what EPS would have been if the options and warrants had been exercised and the company had used the proceeds to repurchase common stock.

Tree diagram   A diagram with branches emanating from nodes representing either mutually exclusive chance events or mutually exclusive decisions.

Trend   A long-term pattern of movement in a particular direction.

Treynor ratio   A measure of risk-adjusted performance that relates a portfolio's excess returns to the portfolio's beta.

Triangle patterns   In technical analysis, a continuation chart pattern that forms as the range between high and low prices narrows, visually forming a triangle.

Trimmed mean   A mean computed after excluding a stated small percentage of the lowest and highest observations.

Triple bottoms   In technical analysis, a reversal pattern that is formed when the price forms three troughs at roughly the same price level; used to predict a change from a downtrend to an uptrend.

Triple tops   In technical analysis, a reversal pattern that is formed when the price forms three peaks at roughly the same price level; used to predict a change from an uptrend to a downtrend.

Trough   The lowest point of a business cycle.

True yield   The internal rate of return on cash flows using the actual calendar including weekends and bank holidays.

Trust deed   See *indenture*.

Trust receipt arrangement   The use of inventory as collateral for a loan. The inventory is segregated and held in trust, and the proceeds of any sale must be remitted to the lender immediately.

Turn-of-the-year effect   Calendar anomaly that stock market returns in January are significantly higher compared to the rest of the months of the year, with most of the abnormal returns reported during the first five trading days in January.

Two-fund separation theorem   The theory that all investors regardless of taste, risk preferences, and initial wealth will hold a combination of two portfolios or funds: a risk-free asset and an optimal portfolio of risky assets.

Two-sided hypothesis test   A test in which the null hypothesis is rejected in favor of the alternative hypothesis if the evidence indicates that the population parameter is either smaller or larger than a hypothesized value.

Two-tailed hypothesis test   A test in which the null hypothesis is rejected in favor of the alternative hypothesis if the evidence indicates that the population parameter is either smaller or larger than a hypothesized value.

Two-week repo rate   The interest rate on a two-week repurchase agreement; may be used as a policy rate by a central bank.

Type I error   The error of rejecting a true null hypothesis.

Type II error   The error of not rejecting a false null hypothesis.

Unanticipated (unexpected) inflation   The component of inflation that is a surprise.

Unbilled revenue   Revenue that has been earned but not yet billed to customers as of the end of an accounting period. Also called *accrued revenue*.

Unclassified balance sheet   A balance sheet that does not show subtotals for current assets and current liabilities.

Unconditional probability   The probability of an event *not* conditioned on another event.

Underemployed   A person who has a job but has the qualifications to work a significantly higher-paying job.

Underlying   An asset that trades in a market in which buyers and sellers meet, decide on a price, and the seller then delivers the asset to the buyer and receives payment. The underlying is the asset or other derivative on which a particular derivative is based. The market for the underlying is also referred to as the *spot market*.

Underwriter   A firm, usually an investment bank, that takes the risk of buying the newly issued securities from the issuer, and then reselling them to investors or to dealers, thus guaranteeing the sale of the securities at the offering price negotiated with the issuer.

Underwritten offering   A type of securities issue mechanism in which the investment bank guarantees the sale of the securities at an offering price that is negotiated with the issuer. Also known as *firm commitment offering*.

Unearned fees   Unearned fees are recognized when a company receives cash payment for fees prior to earning them.

Unearned revenue   A liability account for money that has been collected for goods or services that have not yet been delivered; payment received in advance of providing a good or service. Also called *deferred revenue* or *deferred income*.

Unemployed   People who are actively seeking employment but are currently without a job.

Unemployment rate   The ratio of unemployed to the labor force.

Unexpected inflation   The component of inflation that is a surprise.

Unit elastic   An elasticity with a magnitude of 1.

Unit labor cost   The average labor cost to produce one unit of output.

Unit normal distribution   The normal density with mean (μ) equal to 0 and standard deviation (σ) equal to 1.

Unitary elastic   An elasticity with a magnitude of 1.

Units-of-production method   A depreciation method that allocates the cost of a long-lived asset based on actual usage during the period.

Univariate distribution   A distribution that specifies the probabilities for a single random variable.

Unlimited funds   An unlimited funds environment assumes that the company can raise the funds it wants for all profitable projects simply by paying the required rate of return.

Unsecured debt   Debt which gives the debtholder only a general claim on an issuer's assets and cash flow.

Unsponsored   A type of depository receipt in which the foreign company whose shares are held by the depository has no involvement in the issuance of the receipts.

Unstable   With reference to an equilibrium, one in which price, when disturbed away from the equilibrium, tends not to return to it.

Up transition probability   The probability that an asset's value moves up.

Utility function   A mathematical representation of the satisfaction derived from a consumption basket.

Utils   A unit of utility.

Validity instructions   Instructions which indicate when the order may be filled.

Valuation allowance   A reserve created against deferred tax assets, based on the likelihood of realizing the deferred tax assets in future accounting periods.

Valuation ratios   Ratios that measure the quantity of an asset or flow (e.g., earnings) in relation to the price associated with a specified claim (e.g., a share or ownership of the enterprise).

Value at risk   (VAR) A money measure of the minimum value of losses expected during a specified time period at a given level of probability.

Value investors   With reference to equity investors, investors who are focused on paying a relatively low share price in relation to earnings or assets per share.

Variable costs   Costs that fluctuate with the level of production and sales.

Variable-rate note   Similar to a floating-rate note, except that the spread is variable rather than constant.

Variance   The expected value (the probability-weighted average) of squared deviations from a random variable's expected value.

Variation margin   Additional margin that must be deposited in an amount sufficient to bring the balance up to the initial margin requirement.

Veblen good   A good that increases in desirability with price.

Vega   The relationship between option price and volatility.

Venture capital   Investments that provide "seed" or start-up capital, early-stage financing, or mezzanine financing to companies that are in the early stages of development and require additional capital for expansion.

Venture capital fund   A fund for private equity investors that provides financing for development-stage companies.

Vertical analysis   Common-size analysis using only one reporting period or one base financial statement; for example, an income statement in which all items are stated as percentages of sales.

Vertical demand schedule   Implies that some fixed quantity is demanded, regardless of price.

Volatility   As used in option pricing, the standard deviation of the continuously compounded returns on the underlying asset.

Voluntarily unemployed   A person voluntarily outside the labor force, such as a jobless worker refusing an available vacancy.

Voluntary export restraint   A trade barrier under which the exporting country agrees to limit its exports of the good to its trading partners to a specific number of units.

Vote by proxy   A mechanism that allows a designated party—such as another shareholder, a shareholder representative, or management—to vote on the shareholder's behalf.

Warehouse receipt arrangement   The use of inventory as collateral for a loan; similar to a trust receipt arrangement except there is a third party (i.e., a warehouse company) that supervises the inventory.

Warrant   Attached option that gives its holder the right to buy the underlying stock of the issuing company at a fixed exercise price until the expiration date.

Weak-form efficient market hypothesis   The belief that security prices fully reflect all past market data, which refers to all historical price and volume trading information.

Wealth effect   An increase (decrease) in household wealth increases (decreases) consumer spending out of a given level of current income.

Weighted average cost method   An inventory accounting method that averages the total cost of available inventory items over the total units available for sale.

Weighted average cost of capital   A weighted average of the aftertax required rates of return on a company's common stock, preferred stock, and long-term debt, where the weights are the fraction of each source of financing in the company's target capital structure.

Weighted mean   An average in which each observation is weighted by an index of its relative importance.

Wholesale price index   Reflects the price changes experienced by domestic producers in a country.

Winner's curse   The tendency for the winner in certain competitive bidding situations to overpay, whether because of overestimation of intrinsic value, emotion, or information asymmetries.

Winsorized mean   A mean computed after assigning a stated percent of the lowest values equal to one specified low value, and a stated percent of the highest values equal to one specified high value.

Working capital   The difference between current assets and current liabilities.

Working capital management   The management of a company's short-term assets (such as inventory) and short-term liabilities (such as money owed to suppliers).

World price   The price prevailing in the world market.

Yield   The actual return on a debt security if it is held to maturity.

Yield duration   The sensitivity of the bond price with respect to the bond's own yield-to-maturity.

Yield to maturity   Annual return that an investor earns on a bond if the investor purchases the bond today and holds it until maturity. It is the discount rate that equates the present value of the bond's expected cash flows until maturity with the bond's price. Also called *yield-to-redemption* or *redemption yield*.

Yield to redemption   See *yield to maturity*.

Yield-to-worst   The lowest of the sequence of yields-to-call and the yield-to-maturity.

Zero volatility spread (Z-spread)   Calculates a constant yield spread over a government (or interest rate swap) spot curve.

Zero-cost collar   A transaction in which a position in the underlying is protected by buying a put and selling a call with the premium from the sale of the call offsetting the premium from the purchase of the put. It can also be used to protect a floating-rate borrower against interest rate increases with the premium on a long cap offsetting the premium on a short floor.

Zero-coupon bonds   Bonds that do not pay interest during the bond's life. It is issued at a discount to par value and redeemed at par. Also called *pure discount bonds*.

Index